Biographical Dictionary of the United States Secretaries of the Treasury

1789–1995

Biographical Dictionary of the United States Secretaries of the Treasury

1789–1995

Edited by
BERNARD S. KATZ
and
C. DANIEL VENCILL

Greenwood Press
Westport, Connecticut • London

Library of Congress Cataloging-in-Publication Data

Biographical dictionary of the United States secretaries of the
   Treasury, 1789–1995 / edited by Bernard S. Katz and C. Daniel
   Vencill.
      p. cm.
   Includes bibliographical references (p.) and index.
   ISBN 0–313–28012–6 (alk. paper)
    1. United States. Dept. of Treasury—Officials and employees—
Biography—Dictionaries. 2. Finance ministers—United States—
Biography—Dictionaries. I. Katz, Bernard S., 1932– .
II. Vencill, C. Daniel.
HJ268.B5   1996
353.2'092'2—dc20
  [B]   96–2541

British Library Cataloguing in Publication Data is available.

Library of Congress Catalog Card Number: 96–2541
ISBN: 0–313–28012–6

First published in 1996

Greenwood Press, 88 Post Road West, Westport, CT 06881
An imprint of Greenwood Publishing Group, Inc.

Printed in the United States of America

The paper used in this book complies with the
Permanent Paper Standard issued by the National
Information Standards Organization (Z39.48–1984).

10 9 8 7 6 5 4 3 2 1

Contents

Chronology

Washington Administration

Alexander Hamilton, New York, September 11, 1789–January 31, 1795
Oliver Wolcott, Jr., Connecticut, February 3, 1795–March 3, 1797

J. Adams Administration

Oliver Wolcott, Jr., Connecticut, March 4, 1797–December 31, 1800
Samuel Dexter, Massachusetts, January 1, 1801–March 3, 1801

Jefferson Administration

Samuel Dexter, Massachusetts, March 4, 1801–May 13, 1801
Albert Gallatin, Pennsylvania, May 14, 1801–March 3, 1809

Madison Administration

Albert Gallatin, Pennsylvania, March 4, 1809–February 8, 1814
George W. Campbell, Tennessee, February 9, 1814–October 5, 1814
Alexander J. Dallas, Pennsylvania, October 6, 1814–October 21, 1816
William H. Crawford, Georgia, October 22, 1816–March 3, 1817

Monroe Administration

William H. Crawford, Georgia, March 4, 1817–March 6, 1825

J. Q. Adams Administration

Richard Rush, Pennsylvania, March 7, 1825–March 5, 1829

Jackson Administration

Samuel D. Ingham, Pennsylvania, March 6, 1829–June 20, 1831
Louis McLane, Delaware, August 8, 1831–May 28, 1833
William J. Duane, Pennsylvania, May 29, 1833–September 22, 1833

Roger B. Taney, Maryland, September 23, 1833–June 23, 1834

Levi Woodbury, New Hampshire, July 1, 1834–March 3, 1837

Van Buren Administration

Levi Woodbury, New Hampshire, March 4, 1837–March 3, 1841

W. H. Harrison Administration

Thomas Ewing, Ohio, March 4, 1841–April 4, 1841

Tyler Administration

Thomas Ewing, Ohio, April 5, 1841–September 11, 1841

Walter Forward, Pennsylvania, September 13, 1841–March 1, 1843

John C. Spencer, New York, March 8, 1843–May 2, 1844

George M. Bibb, Kentucky, July 4, 1844–March 4, 1845

Polk Administration

George M. Bibb, Kentucky, March 5, 1845–March 7, 1845

Robert J. Walker, Mississippi, March 8, 1845–March 5, 1849

Taylor Administration

William M. Meredith, Pennsylvania, March 8, 1849–July 9, 1850

Fillmore Administration

William M. Meredith, Pennsylvania, July 10, 1850–July 22, 1850

Thomas Corwin, Ohio, July 23, 1850–March 6, 1853

Pierce Administration

James Guthrie, Kentucky, March 7, 1853–March 6, 1857

Buchanan Administration

Howell Cobb, Georgia, March 7, 1857–December 8, 1860

Philip F. Thomas, Maryland, December 12, 1860–January 14, 1861

John A. Dix, New York, January 15, 1861–March 6, 1861

Lincoln Administration

Salmon P. Chase, Ohio, March 7, 1861–June 30, 1864

William P. Fessenden, Maine, July 5, 1864–March 3, 1865

Hugh McCulloch, Indiana, March 9, 1865–April 15, 1865

A. Johnson Administration

Hugh McCulloch, Indiana, April 16, 1865–March 3, 1869

Grant Administration

George S. Boutwell, Massachusetts, March 12, 1869–March 16, 1873

William A. Richardson, Massachusetts, March 17, 1873–June 3, 1874

Benjamin H. Bristow, Kentucky, June 4, 1874–June 20, 1876

Lot M. Morrill, Maine, July 7, 1876–March 3, 1877

Hayes Administration

Lot M. Morrill, Maine, March 4, 1877–March 8, 1877

John Sherman, Ohio, March 10, 1877–March 3, 1881

Garfield Administration

William Windom, Minnesota, March 8, 1881–September 19, 1881

Arthur Administration

William Windom, Minnesota, September 20, 1881–November 13, 1881

Charles J. Folger, New York, November 14, 1881–September 4, 1884

Walter Q. Gresham, Indiana, September 25, 1884–October 30, 1884

Hugh McCulloch, Indiana, October 31, 1884–March 3, 1885

Cleveland Administration

Hugh McCulloch, Indiana, March 4, 1885–March 7, 1885

Daniel Manning, New York, March 8, 1885–March 31, 1887

Charles S. Fairchild, New York, April 1, 1887–March 6, 1889

B. Harrison Administration

William Windom, Minnesota, March 7, 1889–January 29, 1891

Charles Foster, Ohio, February 25, 1891–March 6, 1893

Cleveland Administration

Charles Foster, Ohio, March 4, 1893–March 6, 1893

John G. Carlisle, Kentucky, March 7, 1893–March 3, 1897

McKinley Administration

John G. Carlisle, Kentucky, March 4, 1897–March 5, 1897

Lyman J. Gage, Illinois, March 6, 1897–September 14, 1901

T. Roosevelt Administration

Lyman J. Gage, Illinois, September 15, 1901–January 31, 1902

Leslie M. Shaw, Iowa, February 1, 1902–March 3, 1907

George B. Cortelyou, New York, March 4, 1907–March 7, 1909

Taft Administration

Franklin MacVeagh, Illinois, March 8, 1909–March 5, 1913

Wilson Administration

William G. McAdoo, New York, March 6, 1913–December 15, 1918

Carter Glass, Virginia, December 16, 1918–February 1, 1920

David F. Houston, Missouri, February 2, 1920–March 3, 1921

Harding Administration

Andrew W. Mellon, Pennsylvania, March 4, 1921–August 2, 1923

Coolidge Administration

Andrew W. Mellon, Pennsylvania, August 3, 1923–March 3, 1929

Hoover Administration

Andrew W. Mellon, Pennsylvania, March 4, 1929–February 12, 1932

Ogden L. Mills, New York, February 13, 1932–March 4, 1933

F. D. Roosevelt Administration

William H. Woodin, New York, March 5, 1933–January 1, 1934

Henry Morgenthau, Jr., New York, January 1, 1934–April 12, 1945

Truman Administration

Henry Morgenthau, Jr., New York, April 12, 1945–July 22, 1945

Frederick M. Vinson, Kentucky, July 23, 1945–June 23, 1946

John W. Snyder, Missouri, June 25, 1946–January 20, 1953

Eisenhower Administration

George M. Humphrey, Ohio, January 21, 1953–July 29, 1957

Robert B. Anderson, Connecticut, July 29, 1957–January 20, 1961

Kennedy Administration

C. Douglas Dillon, New Jersey, January 21, 1961–November 22, 1963

L. B. Johnson Administration

C. Douglas Dillon, New Jersey, November 22, 1963–April 1, 1965

Henry H. Fowler, Virginia, April 1, 1965–December 20, 1968

Joseph W. Barr, Indiana, December 21, 1968–January 20, 1969

Nixon Administration

David M. Kennedy, Utah, January 22, 1969–February 10, 1971

John B. Connally, Texas, February 11, 1971–June 12, 1972

George P. Shultz, Illinois, June 12, 1972–May 8, 1974

William E. Simon, New Jersey, May 8, 1974–August 9, 1974

Ford Administration

William E. Simon, New Jersey, August 9, 1974–January 20, 1977

Carter Administration

W. Michael Blumenthal, Michigan, January 23, 1977–August 6, 1979

G. William Miller, Rhode Island, August 7, 1979–January 20, 1981

Reagan Administration

Donald T. Regan, New Jersey, January 22, 1981–February 1, 1985

James A. Baker III, Texas, February 4, 1985–August 17, 1988

Nicholas F. Brady, New Jersey, September 15, 1988–January 19, 1989

Bush Administration

Nicholas F. Brady, New Jersey, January 20, 1989–January 19, 1993

Clinton Administration

Lloyd M. Bentsen, Texas, January 20, 1993–December 22, 1994

Robert E. Rubin, New York, January 10, 1995–present

Introduction

These biographical profiles of the lives of the men who have held the President's Cabinet position of Secretary of the Treasury are written to provide the reader an understanding of the man, the problems he faced, and the contributions he made during his tenure in office.

While the profiles concentrate on the policy problems and the solutions offered by each of the Secretaries, there are also vignettes of the personality and background of the individual chosen to handle the fiscal affairs of the nation, the Secretary of the Treasury. The men represent backgrounds of money and power as well as simplicity and anonymity. Some came to the office with greater stature than when they left, while others left a significant mark on our nation's financial history.

The biographical entries cover, in varying lengths, the lives, problems, and decisions of the Secretaries of the Treasury, beginning with Alexander Hamilton in 1789 and ending with Secretary Robert E. Rubin, appointed in 1995. The entries begin in 1789, when James Madison rose from his seat in Congress and made the motion to establish a Treasury Department with a Secretary at its head. While seemingly a reasonable proposal, for certainly every nation needs within its government a permanent agency to raise income, pay debts, and generally handle its money affairs, his motion engendered considerable resistance, not for the establishment of the agency but rather for its "single head" leadership form, a significant departure from the Continental and Confederation Treasury commissions of the Revolutionary War period.

In the new American nation, the people and its Congress were always suspicious of granting sweeping powers to a single administrator. It was foreseen that the new Treasury would be the largest receiver and disburser of funds, and these functions would have a significant impact on the emerging money centers in this new and growing land. The potential importance of the Treasury in influencing the destiny of the nation was clearly realized at this early date.

The act of September 2, 1789, established the Treasury Department within the executive branch of government and provided that it should be headed by a Secretary whose duty was to

digest and prepare plans for the improvement and management of the revenue, and for the support of public credit; to prepare and submit report estimates of the public revenue, and the public expenditures; to superintend the collection of the revenue; to decide on the forms of keeping and stating accounts and making returns; . . . to make report, and give information to either branch of the legislature, in person or in writing (as he may be required), respecting all matters referred to him by the Senate or House of Representatives, or which shall pertain to his office; and generally to perform all such services relative to the finances, as he shall be directed to perform.

Today, the Secretary of the Treasury is responsible for formulating and recommending domestic and international financial, economic, and tax policy; participating in the formulation of broad fiscal policies that have general significance for the economy; and managing the public debt. The Secretary oversees the activities of the department in carrying out its major law enforcement responsibilities; in serving as the financial agent for the U.S. government; and in manufacturing coins and currency.

The same law provided for a Comptroller, an Auditor, a Treasurer, and a Register; and it required the Secretary to post a bond of $150,000 and to make reports to each session of Congress. Note that the Treasurer and Secretary of the Treasury are two different officers. The Treasurer of the United States was originally charged with the receipt and custody of government funds, but many of these functions have since been assumed by different bureaus of the Department of the Treasury. By 1981, the Treasurer was assigned responsibility for oversight of the Bureau of Engraving and Printing, the U.S. Mint, and the U.S. Savings Bonds Division.

The Deputy Secretary, Undersecretary, and Assistant Secretaries provide important advice and assistance to the Secretary. There are Assistant Secretaries for Domestic Finance, Economic Policy, Enforcement, Tax Policy, Policy Management, International Affairs, Legislative Affairs, and Public Affairs. The duties, for example, of the Assistant Secretary for Economic Policy include informing the Secretary of current and prospective economic developments. The Assistant Secretary reviews and analyzes domestic and international economic issues and developments in financial markets; participates with the Secretary in the Economic Policy Council and the Troika Forecasting Group, which develops official economic projections and advises the President on choices among alternative courses of economic policy; and works closely with officials of the Office of Management and Budget, the Council of Economic Advisers, and other government agencies on the economic forecasts underlying the yearly budget process and advises the Secretary on the economic effects of tax and budget policy.

While this list covers the Secretary's stated duties, over the decades, Presidents have often relied heavily on their Secretary of the Treasury for Cabinet-level economic policy advice. George Washington leaned on Alexander Hamilton, whose four financial reports provided the President with the framework for much of his domestic programs.

Since the Great Depression of the 1930s, the regulatory functions of the Treasury have been articulated and elaborated. The Secretary, in formulating the Treasury's policy, meets regularly with the Director of the Office of Management and Budget and the Chair of the Council of Economic Advisers; frequently, the Chair of the Federal Reserve Board is included. With current statistical information, these officials seek to analyze the economic outlook and coordinate official policy actions.

The four basic responsibilities of the Treasury have been (1) to frame and recommend financial, tax, and fiscal measures; (2) to serve as financial agent for the U.S. government; (3) to enforce certain laws; and (4) to manufacture coins and currency. The Secretary is the chief financial officer of our government. The Treasury formerly included several agencies that have subsequently become autonomous with the expansion of national government. These include the U.S. Postal Service, the Coast Guard, the Bureau of Narcotics, and the parent agencies of the Departments of the Interior, Commerce, and Labor. On the other hand, several wide and diverse powers and duties have devolved on the Treasury, and this has resulted in a corresponding proliferation of policy decisions and an expansion of administrative officers and staff.

In addition to domestic concerns, including management of the public debt, the Secretary of the Treasury represents the United States in foreign financial organizations, including the International Monetary Fund, the International Bank for Reconstruction and Development, the Inter-American Development Bank, and the Asian Development Bank. More than 80 percent of the Treasury's annual appropriation and 90 percent of the personnel are assigned to revenue collection, primarily individual and corporate income taxes. The Treasurer of the United States receives, holds, and pays out public monies; by 1971, some 640 million checks were issued per year, and this number has continued to increase at a 3 percent annual rate. Other functions include the Customs Bureau; Office of Comptroller of the Currency; the Bureau of Engraving and Printing; the Secret Service; the Bureau of Alcohol, Tobacco, and Firearms; the Bureau of the Debt; and the Office of Thrift Supervision.

The internal structure of the Treasury, to ensure faithful performance by different divisions, is essentially what Hamilton devised at its inception.

It is helpful in our understanding of the problems faced by various Secretaries to review the economic environment and policy issues that concerned the Treasury over the years. Modern economists worry that government discretionary monetary and fiscal policy is plagued by time inconsistency. That is, the government makes a policy, and later the policymaker has a strong incentive to renege; rational agents understand this incentive, and this expectation affects their behavior. It was one of the first problems confronted by the first Secretary of the Treasury, Alexander Hamilton.

Hamilton was faced with the question of how to cope with the debts that the new nation had accumulated as it fought for its independence from Britain. The states and revolutionary government had incurred large debts and promised to honor these when the war was concluded. But after the hostilities ended, many politicians and analysts advocated defaulting on the debt, as repaying the creditors would require taxation, which has always been costly and unpopular.

Hamilton opposed this "time inconsistent" policy of debt repudiation. He wisely reasoned that the nation would likely need to borrow again sometime in the future. In his first report to Congress in 1790, he laid the foundation for sound finance: "States, like individuals, who observe their engagements are respected and trusted, while the reverse is the fate of those who pursue an opposite conduct."

Hamilton advocated that the nation make a strong commitment to the policy rule of always honoring its debts. This policy rule that Hamilton originally proposed has continued for over two centuries. In modern times, unlike in Hamilton's day, when Congress debates spending priorities, or deficit reduction, no one proposes defaulting on the public debt. In the case of the public debt, everyone now agrees that our government should be precommitted to a fixed policy rule. By funding the public indebtedness, Hamilton also tried to provide an adequate supply of a circulating medium of exchange to meet the emerging business needs of the country. This, of course, is not a fiscal but a central banking function. Hamilton proposed that all of the national debt, both principal and interest, be paid in hard currency. Creditors could exercise an option to take payment in the form of western land, or they could demand hard currency.

Hamilton's main contribution, as his profile establishes, was in successfully setting up a debt management system and securing faith in the credit of the government. He also made the Treasury a prime agency for promoting the economic development of the country. In August 1790, Congress enacted the well-known Hamiltonian measures for funding not only the Revolutionary War debts of the Confederation but also those debts of the states. Congress had already provided in 1789 a source of federal revenue by levying duties on imports. In 1791, Congress further yielded to Hamilton's concern that income from these duties might be insufficient for both the needs of current expenditures and the servicing of the government debt. It enacted the first of three excise tax bills to be passed during the 1790s. These measures, together with designed open market purchases of securities by the Secretary of the Treasury, soon elevated the credit standing of the United States.

This restoration of public credit had significant effects on our economic growth. In the first instance, the eroded capital values were restored. Paper claims on government that fell as low as fifteen cents on the dollar in early 1788 rose above par by August 1791. In the second place, foreign capital seeking investment in government funds began to flow into the United States at an increasing volume. Foreign holdings of U.S. public debt were $2.7 million on November 13, 1788, and on August 16, 1790, the sum was $5.5 million. Purchased at par and above, these holdings continued to rise, reaching $20 million by May 1795 and $33 million on September 30, 1801.

It is possible that this resurgence of our public credit, by lowering the interest rate on government debt, led in turn to a reduction in the market rate of interest and thus reduced the capital costs of net private investment. This today would be called the "crowding in" of private investment by the reduction of public borrowing and public debt redemption. The contribution of Hamiltonian measures to the increasing economic growth of our new nation cannot be ignored. In effect, what government had done was to tax one group of people (primarily buyers of imported goods and grain farmers who converted their crops into whiskey) for the immediate benefit of a smaller group of people (the securities holders), in order to achieve a later and larger benefit for the American society as a whole. In today's economic jargon, the government adoption of Hamilton's measures was a program of forced savings as a technique for increasing the supply of capital funds in an underdeveloped country. Although part of the increase was direct and immediate, the much greater stimulus came as an external effect on markets via the restored public and private confidence in markets and the potential of the economy. Combined with the new profit opportunities created by growing markets and expanding population, the improved security framework of investment indeed played an important part in the nation's subsequent ability to lure required funds from abroad. Today's massive inward foreign investment in U.S. financial and real assets, including our national debt, attests to the long-range wisdom of our nation's first Treasury Secretary.

On the other hand, Hamilton was accused by his political enemies of not being particularly concerned with the detailed aspects of Treasury operations. Evidently, it was not possible to obtain a clear statement of the public debt from the accounts he presented to Congress. The mundane details involved in the day-to-day operations of the Treasury Department were sadly neglected during the Federalist era. There are those among us today who might voice a similar complaint about attempts to get a full disclosure of the actual deficit for 1996.

It may be said that the new nation's commitment to a balanced budget is as significant for its history as its rejection of a centralized executive and preference for noncentralized, legislative forms of budgeting. James Madison (1809–1817) followed Thomas Jefferson's lead and wanted his administration "to liberate the public resources by an honorable discharge of the public debt." Certainly, by the administrations of James Monroe (1817–1825) and John Quincy Adams (1825–1829), the mandate was to reduce debt and divert the use of customs revenues for the nation's development. Debt reduction took on moralistic overtones. Debt reduction could mean both less and more spending. By the administration of Andrew Jackson (1829), debt reduction had become a patriotic duty. When he realized that the outstanding debt might be paid off during his watch, Jackson waxed profound: "We shall then exhibit the rare example of a great nation, abounding in all the means of happiness and security, altogether free from debt."

His Secretary of the Treasury Levi Woodbury heralded the extinction of our public debt as an "unprecedented spectacle . . . presented to the world."

Until the Federal Reserve Bank system was established in 1913, the Treasury carried out some quasi–central banking functions, but it did so in a rudimentary way. Even after the Fed was established, the Secretary of the Treasury was directly involved in monetary policy decisions. One reason that the United States had not established a central bank was the traditional fear of concentration of financial power. Oddly enough, the original opposition to the office of Secretary of the Treasury was the fear of vesting control of the Treasury Department in one man. Many people do not know that in 1914 the original Board of Governors of the Federal Reserve included Woodrow Wilson's Secretary of the Treasury, William Gibbs McAdoo. To give the Federal Reserve more political independence from the President, the Federal Reserve Act was amended in 1935 to explicitly exclude the Secretary of the Treasury from being a member of the board. Officials of the Fed do not report to the Secretary of the Treasury.

Central banking functions were carried out by the Treasury during the following periods: the first and second Bank of the United States, the War of 1812, the chaotic years of state banking, and the Panic of 1837. The quasi–central banking functions increased during the period of the Independent Treasury System, the Mexican War, the Crisis of 1856, the National Banking System, and the Civil War. The Treasury also tried to improve business conditions during the Panics of 1873 and 1884, the stringency of 1890, the Crisis of 1893, the Spanish-American War, and the 1907 Panic. World War I also saw substantial policymaking activity in monetary affairs, and the Treasury continued to use its central banking powers to combat the agricultural depression of 1920 and refunding of the war debt. During the 1930s Great Depression, the Treasury's central banking activities were greatly increased by its gold and silver policies and expanded duties to maintain economic stability.

One can use the term *Treasury central banking* to encompass those powers and activities of the U.S. Treasury that influence the reserves of private commercial banks. A central bank has the essential role to coordinate the money and banking system with other economic activities so that economic stability is promoted and financial panics averted. It is clear that the Treasury, being the largest disburser and receiver of public funds, may through its transactions affect the reserves of commercial banks. The historical ways by which the Treasury has increased commercial bank reserves (high-powered money) were issuing of paper currency, the depositing of government cash funds in commercial banks, and the prepaying of the interest and principal on its outstanding obligations from idle Treasury cash balances. The Treasury also had the power to run contractionary monetary policy. The Treasury could withdraw its deposits from commercial banks and hold these idle funds in Treasury vaults.

Secretaries of the Treasury were usually keenly aware of their power over the nation's medium of exchange. In Hamilton's time, by funding the public debt, the Treasury was trying to provide an adequate supply of the circulating medium of exchange for the business needs of the country. For the eight years beginning in 1850, the federal budget was in surplus, with revenues greatly exceeding expenditures. Tariff rates remained high, and the end of the Mexican War created budget savings; thus, revenues were greater than the needs of government. These surplus funds could have been used to pay off outstanding debt accumulated during the previous decade's budget deficits. Unfortunately, none of the debt was maturing and due for payment. Instead, under the Independent Treasury System, the surplus accumulated in the Treasury coffers, thus reducing the amount of hard money available for circulation in the country.

Today's textbooks point out that if the Treasury's currency holdings increase and the public's currency holdings are constant or falling, then the depository institutions must be holding less currency and hence fewer reserves. If the increase in the Treasury's currency holdings comes from a reduction in the public's currency holdings, then a rise in one factor that decreases reserves—Treasury cash holdings—is offset by a fall in another factor that decreases reserves—currency held by the public. The Treasury deposits tax payments and receipts from sales of its securities initially into depository institutions. But since it writes its own checks on its account with the Fed, from time to time it has to transfer funds from its accounts with banks to its account with the Fed. When this happens, the Fed credits the Treasury's account and debits the accounts of banks (they lose reserves).

To inject some of these funds back into circulation, Secretary of the Treasury James Guthrie asked Congress for permission to buy government bonds on the open market—even if he had to pay a price above par value (our nation's first open market operations, which presaged the Fed's main policy instrument that was not to be discovered, by accident, until the 1920s). Guthrie was granted this permission, and during the 1850s, he bought a substantial amount of bonds on the open market. By 1857, the debt had been reduced to $28.7 million. There was still an excess demand for money. Guthrie argued that the Treasury had the potential to exercise a fatal control over the currency whenever revenue greatly exceeded expenditure.

By absorbing currency and bank reserves, the Treasury could cause economic problems, as the policy caused severe tightening of credit markets. In spite of these open market purchases of government bonds by the Treasury, customs collections remained high in 1854–1855. As a result, large amounts of specie continued to pile up in the Treasury vaults. Late in 1856, several New York banks had to suspend specie payments. Treasury Secretary Howell Cobb continued buying bonds to help these banks out, believing that the federal government should employ all of its budget surplus, if required, in order to replenish the liquidity of the private banking system. (Too bad this wise advice did not carry over to the Great Contraction of 1929–1933.) By 1857, the United States was reeling from financial panic and depression. In the early months of that year, the balance of hard currency held by the Treasury reached a high of $15.7 million. This policy of holding on to reserves no doubt reduced the nation's high-powered money base and contributed to the panic. As Secretary Cobb continued to pursue central banking functions and purchase bonds, and as government revenue fell, the budget surplus quickly turned to deficit. The Treasury was forced to begin borrowing again, with the result that by the end of 1860, the eve of its biggest challenge, the Civil War, the federal government was in debt by $64.8 million.

The authors of the entries in this book also point up the disputes that have emerged historically between the Federal Reserve Bank and the Treasury over interest rates.

The responsibility for debt management is vested in the Treasury Department. One function of debt management is to carry out the debt transactions necessitated by a current budget deficit or (rarely) surplus, involving either an increase or a decrease in the nation's total debt. Even if the budget were balanced over the fiscal year, the flow of tax receipts and expenditures is not synchronized on a month-to-month basis, and thus intermediate debt financing is required. An additional function, one much more important in scope and size, is the vast refunding operations of the Treasury. They must be undertaken as maturing debt instruments are replaced by new issues of varying maturities.

This operation is conducted by the Debt Management Division of the Treasury, with the help of the Federal Reserve Bank of New York. The function of debt management is basically an executive branch one and does not involve direct congressional participation. Congress has legislated certain restrictions with which debt managers must comply, including an interest rate ceiling, a ceiling on total debt, and the provision that debt obligations may not be issued at a price below their maturing value.

Debt management involves large annual refunding operations. In conducting these operations, as in financing an increase in total debt, the Treasury Secretary must decide what type of debt to issue. Here, the major problem is the choice of which maturity to issue. Traditionally, it was held that the public debt should be well "funded," by which early Treasury Secretaries meant it should be in long-term maturities. The idea came from Britain, where its debt during the nineteenth century was largely in the form of "consols," or perpetual securities with no fixed maturity date that are retired at the government's option, provided it is willing to pay the currently prevailing market price. The long-term bonds, or "well-funded debt," were seen as a stipulation that would protect government against the contingency that creditors would demand their money back at an inopportune time. The modern view is that this is all wrong, and debt management proceeds on the assumption that maturing issues can always be refunded.

Of course, in its refunding, the Treasury could select the term structure of the debt so as to minimize its interest cost. Since the cost of borrowing tends to differ with the maturity of the debt, those issues should be chosen that investors are willing to absorb at the lowest cost. It might be argued that the Treasury should always borrow from the lowest-cost lender, just as it should buy its pencils from the lowest-cost supplier. However, after World War II, this rule proved too simple and led to conflicts with the Fed over the policy's conflict with required monetary restraint.

The Treasury faced massive operating burdens during World War II. Approximately $211 billion of the estimated $323 billion spent in fighting the war was borrowed, and the Secretary of the Treasury was called upon for total mobilization of our country's financial resources. This capitalization put tremendous pressure on the fiscal agencies of the government.

The goal of the Secretary of the Treasury's debt management plan in wartime was the sale of debt at levels of interest that were as low as possible and as stable as feasible. This goal was a failure in World War I when each successive debt offering carried a higher interest rate. The Treasury viewed this as unsatisfactory for two reasons: First, higher interest rates implied higher expenses for debt service, and it was one aim of debt policy to keep those costs at a minimum. Second, when interest rates were rising, it became harder to sell bonds as purchasers became determined to wait until interest rates peaked before making their purchase of bonds. When investors buy government bonds, and then interest rates continue to rise, they suffer a capital loss, especially on longer-term maturities. To avoid interest rate risk, investors prefer very short-term notes.

One way to keep the price of securities from falling is to enlist the help of the Fed to "monetize" these bonds. Then when the Treasury sells a new issue of securities, the Fed prints money and buys those securities to prop up the price and keep rates from rising. However, the Banking Act of 1935 prohibits the Fed from making direct purchases of securities from the Treasury. But the Fed can enter the public market and buy securities in a well-timed fashion to offset Treasury sales of securities to the public. This required careful coordination and cooperation between the central bank and the Treasury.

During World War II, the Fed cooperated with the Treasury in terms of interest rate management. The interest rate on long-term bonds was set at 2.5 percent for the term of the war to reduce costs and eliminate interest rate risk to holders of government bonds. While presidents of some Fed banks indicated they would have preferred to see 3 percent, they agreed with the Secretary of the Treasury to support lower rates. The wartime debt management plan of the Treasury was a relative success. The deficit caused by the war would have been financed in any event, but the entries in this book indicate that the methods used by the Treasury did help to eliminate some of the inflationary gap caused by large government defense expenditures. Certainly, price controls were instituted, but the Treasury's policies made it an easier fight to hold inflation in check.

The Treasury Department has one potentially major monetary stabilization tool, and it received considerable attention in the post–World War II period: debt management. Our national debt is large, and a significant part of it—close to half of the marketable debt—consists of short-term securities due within one year. Treasury sales and redemption of debt, therefore, amount to a substantial sum each year. As the Treasury borrows, it has to decide whether to issue long-term or short-term securities.

This is the essence of debt management, which refers to changes in the composition of the debt, not to the volume of government debt outstanding. This idea was popular in the postwar period, but later interest in it as a viable policy tool tended to wane. But the theory is that shifting between long-term and short-term securities can affect aggregate demand or total planned spending in our economy. If the public holds short-term securities, the greater liquidity of its portfolio makes it more willing to spend. Short-term government securities thus serve as money substitutes. If the Treasury issues short-term securities in place of long-term securities, money demand falls, and other things being equal, the interest rate declines and this stimulates investment. Or if the Treasury wants to restrain aggregate demand, it could redeem short-term securities and issue long-term securities in their place. This method of influencing aggregate expenditures could supplement or reinforce the Fed's countercyclical tools.

Having a big proportion of debt in short-term securities as countercyclical policy would at times hinder monetary policy. A short-term debt requires frequent Treasury refinancing, and such refinancing interferes with monetary policy. During a refinancing period, the Fed is reluctant to tighten money but tries to help Treasury financing by keeping the bond market on an "even keel." A large short-term debt severely restricts the times during which the Fed can feel free to move in a restrictive direction.

In addition, a policy of lengthening the debt is not popular with Secretaries of the Treasury because it raises, or seems to increase, the interest cost of the debt. Over time, it seems that debt management has come to deal only with the housekeeping task of keeping Treasury costs to a minimum.

One duty that evolved was the expectation that the Secretary would interface with the Chair of the Fed on a regular basis. Treasury-Fed relations seemed somewhat strained during the Korean Conflict. The Fed was to help the Treasury with its finances. The Treasury wanted its financing to be at the lowest possible rates; the Fed in turn wanted rates increased to fight incipient inflation. But if the Fed must buy securities willy-nilly to support low interest rates, it cannot exercise any influence over the amount of money and credit in the economy. This impasse is discussed in various profiles.

The *Biographical Dictionary* surveys Treasury–Federal Reserve Bank fights and the personalities involved. What typically caused these conflicts? For one thing, the absence of formal control of monetary policy by elected officials in the United States has, at times, resulted in conflicts between the Fed and the President, who is usually represented by his Cabinet officer, the Secretary of the Treasury. As noted, during World War II the administration increased its control over the Fed. To assist in the financing of large wartime budget deficits, the Fed agreed to hold interest rates on Treasury securities at artificially low levels. It did so by buying up large amounts of bonds not purchased by the private sector, thereby predetermining interest rates. After the war, the Treasury wanted to continue this policy, but the Fed strongly disagreed. The Fed's worry was inflation, because larger purchases of government securities by the Fed increased the monetary base, which potentially increased the money supply growth rate and hence inflation. Price controls that had somewhat contained inflation during the war were lifted after it ended.

Chair of the Board of Governors, Marriner Eccles, particularly objected to the rate-fixing policy. His opposition to the desires of the Truman administration cost him the Fed Chair in 1948, although he continued to fight for Fed independence during the remainder of his term as Governor at the Fed. On March 4, 1951, the wartime policy of fixing the interest rates on Treasury securities was formally terminated via the famous Treasury-Fed Accord.

But conflicts between the Treasury and the Fed did not end with this accord. Rather, President Ronald Reagan and Fed Chair Paul Volcker argued over who was to be blamed for the deep business recession of the early 1980s. Reagan blamed the Fed's contractionary monetary policy. Volcker countered that the Fed could not expand money growth until the budget deficit was safely reduced.

Early in the Bush administration, the conflict was less severe, even though the Treasury typically argued for a more expansionary monetary policy than preferred by the Fed. During the debate in 1991 over reforms of U.S. banking regulations, the Secretary of the Treasury and the Fed fought over who would have greater responsibility in overseeing the banking system. Finally, in late 1991, the Treasury pressured the Fed to reduce short-term interest rates. Although the Fed did reduce the discount rate, there is no way of knowing whether the Secretary's pressure was a factor. In early 1993, the Clinton Treasury argued that the Fed should not raise short-term interest rates in the face of the administration's budget package. In fact, the Fed asserted its independence and raised interest rates seven times in thirteen months.

As an agency, the Treasury has been shaped by the history of the nation it serves: Though its basic functions as mandated by the Constitution remain constant, it has adapted to the ever-changing realities of the nation's development through periodic innovations and reorganizations. The Civil War, for example, had a great effect upon the activities of the Treasury. The loss of customs revenues from the seceded Southern states resulted in establishment of the Bureau of Internal Revenue, as well as the printing of paper currency and the institution of the National Banking System. The growth of international trade after World War I and the U.S. involvement in World War II demanded an active role by the Department of the Treasury in the Bretton Woods Conference in 1944, the establishment of the World Bank, and the leadership of the United States in worldwide economic development efforts.

The management of the money resources of the United States has always been the primary function of the Department of the Treasury and its Secretaries. Whether it is regulating national banks, determining international economic policy, collecting income taxes or customs duties, reporting the government's daily financial transactions, or manufacturing coins or bills for circulation, the one concern that still ties together the activities of our Treasury is money.

In modern times, many other functions and offices have been grafted on to the Treasury Department, and this has given new responsibilities to the Secretary. Have these functions and other duties diluted some of the impact of the Secretary as primary economic adviser to the President? Does today's Secretary have to wear too many hats? Have technical details overwhelmed the Secretary's office? Or has some power shifted to the Fed or the Secretary of State or the Council of Economic Advisers?

One issue that these profiles repeatedly address is the question of whether the Treasury has any significant influence on the amount of spending and debt that government operations entail or whether Secretaries merely implement the fiscal policies determined jointly by the President and the Congress. Not infrequently, Secretaries of the Treasury have played a substantive role in the implementation of economic policy but a minor role in its establishment. None of the Secretaries under Ronald Reagan or George Bush were idea people. Donald Regan and Nicholas Brady were from Wall Street and often represented the Street's interests. The politically ambitious James Baker attempted to use the office as a stepping stone to higher office. All were serious, if not unfaltering, about tax reform and broader adjustments to fiscal policy throughout the budget process.

Over the recent decade ending with President Bush, the office has been schizophrenic on monetary policy; it moved away from public pleading after Reagan's first midterm and then toward vocal posturing about world monetary policy after the Bush midterm. Regan ceased criticizing the Fed, and Baker also moderated his comments while (perhaps out of his league) attempting bold international strokes. The locus of engagement between the big players with the important ideas was really between the President's ideological cadres and Congress. The administrative minions, outgunned and outnumbered by Congress, were often characterized in the press as "nasty bickerers." Regan is the only one of the group who portrays himself as a supply-sider, though he was a latecomer and clearly not a member of the supply-side intellectual leadership. Supply-siders believe that demand-side policies, especially orthodox monetary policies, are completely ineffective. Next, they are convinced that the incentive effects of reduced taxation are very large, so that lowering taxes will dramatically increase economic activity, perhaps to such an extent that government tax revenues actually rise rather than fall.

For Regan and Baker, the position of Secretary was not the high-water mark of their respective government services. Regan, among all three, seems the most public spirited, according to the profiles in this volume. For Brady, this was a career capper and probably more a reward than a real job. As a close friend of the President, he hastened the Bush administration's downfall by solidifying the non-Bush Republican base.

House Speaker Newt Gingrich banned Treasury lobbyists from his office in 1990. Regan was the only one even remotely in touch with the core of the emerging Republican majority, and even that is a possible stretch. Regan was a smooth salesman and an honest broker: He genuinely believed in the President's policy vision. Baker seemed to be padding his résumé. As a master of Washington ways (grand speeches, dynamic scheduling, press leaking, etc.), Baker created the image of efficacy. Whether he really has articulate beliefs, consistent with the Presidents he has served, may never be known. Was he inarticulate—or merely suspicious of the Big Vision of the Reagan presidency? All three of these modern Secretaries had few pretensions about ideology. From one viewpoint, the Treasury is, in fact, no longer an idea factory; rather, it is very much an administrative office dependent on a skilled administrator. In the case of Regan, one had a smooth salesman with powerful skills and a straightforward, Irish-Catholic sentiment. Baker added political acumen to the core Ronald Reagan agenda, no doubt a realistic sensibility, given that Democrats had the numbers and clout beyond their numbers. It is possible to have grand political ambitions and still do a good job.

These personal biographies include assessments of Secretary Lloyd Bentsen and his replacement in the Clinton administration, Secretary Robert Rubin. Bentsen had an uncommon influence on President Bill Clinton virtually from the start. Clinton looked up to the gray, elegant, street-smart aristocrat from south Texas as he did to none of his other advisers, except perhaps Warren Christopher. Bentsen was seventy-one, and Christopher was sixty-seven; both were wealthy and accomplished, and both of them spoke slowly by virtue of decades of experience. Bentsen became highly influential with the President because he had four things going for him, whereas the rest of Clinton's advisers had only two or three at most. He could give political, economic, and congressional advice; and fourth, he could look Clinton in the eye as a political peer and say, "I know what this means politically." From the outset, when others were in a panic, Bentsen argued that the President's economic program should not be rushed out—it would be the President's program for many years to come, and care should be taken with it. His rationale prevailed.

There are several illustrations of the value of the Treasury Secretary as the key Cabinet official. For instance, President Clinton was faced with his campaign pledge to cut the federal deficit in half in four years. At that time, in June, the estimated deficit four years out was $193 billion, but by late July 1992, the deficit was projected to be about $60 billion higher in four years. By the time Clinton was to take office in January 1993, the deficit had become $125 billion larger over the four years than when he had pledged to cut it by half.

It was Bentsen who, in what may be described as a feat of economic acrobatics, supplied Clinton with a way out of his dilemma: the problem of how to live up to his campaign pledge to cut the deficit in half in four years when he was now facing a far higher deficit ($350 billion in fiscal year 1997) than when he had made the pledge. In Little Rock on January 13, 1993, Bentsen effectively told Clinton that when he said he'd cut the deficit in half, he'd actually promised people $145 billion in cuts, and that that's what his goal should be. In effect, Bentsen sidestepped the question of what the deficit would be in four years and came to Clinton's rescue. Historically, the Secretary has handled what has come to be called "spin control."

New Presidents have always said they intend to rely on the Cabinet for advice. But experience with the Cabinet or Cabinet-size committees in several administrations shows that procedure not to be workable or durable. It involves too many people talking too much about subjects of which they know far too little. President Clinton has proposed downsizing the Cabinet to make it more effective. Bentsen was the first potential Cabinet officer interviewed in Little Rock and the first one offered a job. As Clinton selected Bentsen, he had an economic policy mix in mind. He was, however, determined to have better coordination of economic policy than most of his predecessors had and less infighting. Drawing on an idea that had been discussed in Democratic circles for years, Clinton had decided to establish a new National Economic Council to coordinate economic policymaking, including foreign economic policy. Initially, the new body was called the Economic Security Council, but it was decided that this sounded too nationalistic, and the name was dropped.

Managing this council called for a person with standing in the economic world who dealt well with others, especially others with big egos, and Clinton thought he had his man in Robert Rubin, the cochairman of Goldman Sachs, a major fund-raiser for Clinton and an adviser to his campaign. Rubin, it was thought, would get along well with Bentsen because he had advised Bentsen on his portfolio of investments.

These biographical profiles also point up the desirable qualifications to be sought in a Secretary of the Treasury. Secretaries of the Treasury are usually chosen from the ranks of executives of large, successful financial or business firms. The qualities that attainment of such a position demonstrates are useful for the Treasury Secretary. Yet it is not his only or even his principal function to run a large organization and exercise skill in dealing in the financial markets. At least as important is his role of leading but not dominating a group of diverse thinkers about economic policy, organizing and synthesizing but not settling issues, presenting issues fairly to the President, and representing views persuasively to the Congress and the public. The qualities needed to perform this role may be found in Wall Street, but Wall Street success is not necessarily evidence of them.

We, the editors, hope this book will enliven your understanding of the administrations of these public servants and add some crucial intimate details about the lives of our past Secretaries that will make the history of the office of Secretary of the Treasury both interesting and revealing on a personal level. Can a Washington bureaucrat be knowledgeable, creative, and essential for the preservation and success of a market democracy? Has the office of Secretary evolved or devolved? Hopefully, some of the profiles offered in this volume will contribute to scholars investigating themes of public choice theory, the evolution of debt policy, and the inside story of policymaking in Washington, D.C. These biographies will also shed some light on the question of whether the importance of the office varies substantially with the integrity, competence, and ingenuity of the officeholder.

—Bernard S. Katz
—C. Daniel Vencill

A

ROBERT B. ANDERSON (June 4, 1910–August 14, 1989). Robert Bernard Anderson was a devout and gentle man who worked quietly and effectively to discharge his responsibilities from high school teacher to Secretary of the Navy. From an impoverished childhood, this former Democrat rose to serve as Dwight Eisenhower's second Secretary of the Treasury by impressing people with his efficient and low-key mastery of each task he undertook.

Robert Anderson was born on June 4, 1910, to Robert Lee and Lizzie Ethel (Haskew) Anderson of Burleson, Texas, a small town near Ft. Worth. Robert was stricken with polio at age three; this left him with a slight limp and later exempted him from active military service. When he was seven the family moved to a small cotton and dairy farm. He attended public schools in Godley and thereafter received a teacher's certificate from Weatherford College in 1927. To finance further education, Anderson taught Spanish, history, and mathematics at Burleson High School as well as coaching its football team to an unbeaten season in 1929.

He enrolled at the University of Texas Law School in 1930 and became interested in seeking political office at that same time. In a later interview, Anderson ascribed his interest in politics to the Great Depression: "[T]hese were hard times, times when people were thinking of government, when they were turning to government to get things done" ("Tough Minded Texan," 13). Thus, he ran for office while still attending law school. In one memorable year, 1932, Anderson acquired his law degree with the best scholastic record in the school's history, was admitted to the Texas bar, began practicing law in Ft. Worth, was elected to the Texas state legislature, and was appointed Assistant Attorney General of Texas (*Nomination Hearings*, 1).

In 1934 he ably performed the task of State Tax Commissioner while also serving as a member of the State Racing Commission and the State Tax Board. In the previous year, he had also served as adjunct professor of law at his alma mater, the University of Texas.

Robert B. Anderson married Ollie May Rawlins of Austin in 1935. Meanwhile, he drafted the bill that created Texas's first Social Security Agency. Appointed Chairman and Executive Director of the Texas Unemployment Commission in 1936, Anderson also served as a member of the Texas Economy Commission, a member of the executive committee of the Texas Research Council, and Chairman of the state Board of Education ("Anderson, Robert Bernard," 15).

After achieving these early successes in public life, Anderson turned to the world of business. In 1937 he accepted an appointment as the general attorney of the W. T. Waggoner estate headquartered in Vernon, Texas. At that time the estate constituted one of the largest ranches in Texas, encompassing thousands of acres of farmland as well as oil wells and a small oil refinery. In 1941 he became general manager of this $300 million enterprise ("Heir," 58; "Menace," 30).

In 1953 Anderson made his debut on the national scene, accepting an appointment as Secretary of the Navy. This job apparently arose from a recommendation to Eisenhower by Texas Governor Allan Shivers. Although he admitted never having sailed any craft larger than a small boat, Anderson rapidly mastered this new position. His tenure as Secretary of the Navy was marked by his quiet authority and his unwillingness to be dominated by Navy brass. When the naval promotions board passed over Capt. Hyman G. Rickover for the second time, Anderson intervened to promote him to rear admiral and retain in the Navy a man integral to the development of the first atomic submarine ("New No. 2 Man," 48).

Anderson was also credited with the rapid integration of the Navy. Earlier, Republican Adam Clayton Powell had criticized Anderson and accused him of insubordination for allegedly blocking federal efforts to end segregation. However, Anderson's prompt action and Eisenhower's November 1953 announcement of the complete effectiveness of desegregation plans won an official apology from Powell ("Anderson, Robert," 21).

Anderson was appointed Deputy Secretary of Defense in March 1954. In this post, Anderson again impressed Eisenhower when he made a strong case for defending the Nationalist-held Quemoy and Matsu islands during the Formosa Strait crisis of 1954–1955. He also assisted in the formulation of Eisenhower's "open skies" proposal presented at the 1955 Geneva U.S.-Soviet summit conference.

Anderson briefly left public service in 1955 when he accepted the presidency of Ventures, Ltd., a Canadian mining firm. However, when George Humphrey resigned as Secretary of the Treasury in 1957, he recommended Anderson as his successor. Anderson immediately faced a number of problems including the $260 billion national debt, a significant portion of which had to be redeemed in the next year; a $275 billion debt ceiling that restricted the government's ability to finance its operations by borrowing; and a hostile Democratic Congress unwilling to raise the debt ceiling or grant any other concessions but intent on further budget reductions.

Anderson's first challenge was the recession of 1957–1958. This downturn was characterized by steadily rising prices and high unemployment. The launching of *Sputnik* by the Soviet Union in the fall of 1957 aroused expectations of a greater amount of federal expenditures in order to compete with the Soviet Union and to produce a high rate of economic growth. Anderson was concerned about inflation and skeptical about the long-term budgetary impact of a reduction in taxes and, thus, argued against a tax cut as an antirecession measure.

He testified in early 1958 that although he could conceive of situations in which he would consider a tax cut as a cure for recession, this recession did not require such precipitate action. Opinion was divided within the Cabinet. Although the administration's policy, announced in February, was an acceleration of expenditures, there were some who advocated an immediate tax reduction. Vice President Richard Nixon and Secretary of Labor James Mitchell favored an immediate tax reduction to stimulate the economy, whereas Anderson, supported by Chairman of the Federal Reserve Board William McChesney Martin, Jr., argued against such a measure. Anderson asserted that the fundamental problem facing the economy was inflation, and a reduction in taxes to deal with such a temporary slump would only fuel the inflationary forces. In addition, the country needed a fundamental reform of the tax system to encourage productivity and growth. A reduction of income taxes would thus be the wrong kind of tax measure (Stein, 324–31). Finally, he was doubtful that a tax cut would encourage consumer spending, arguing that a concerned citizenry might well choose to increase saving if government actions were interpreted as an indication that the economy was in serious trouble ("Cut Taxes?" 61).

Eisenhower sided with Anderson. In March, Anderson came to an agreement with House Speaker Sam Rayburn, Senate Majority Leader Lyndon Johnson, and Wilbur Mills, Chairman of the House Ways and Means Committee, whereby neither the administration nor the congressional leadership would publicly advocate a tax reduction without prior consultation. By April, there were signs that the rate of decline of the economy was abating and, in May, President Eisenhower announced that the administration had no "present intention" of seeking a tax cut. Thereafter, Anderson was labeled the "strong man of the cabinet" ("Strong Man of the Cabinet?" 32–33).

Attention turned once again to budget balancing. Eisenhower was anxious to generate a surplus in order to reduce the burden of debt and to promote economic growth, maintain a strong dollar, and combat inflation. Thus, although unemployment remained high, the administration restrained expenditures and realized a surplus in 1960.

Although Anderson appeared more flexible than his predecessor regarding deficit spending, he was a firm advocate of fiscal conservatism and quite successful in his handling of congressional Democrats. In pursuit of such conservatism, and despite the recession, Anderson floated a long-term bond issue during the spring of 1958, maintaining that short-term financing was inflationary. He consistently argued in support of reducing the national debt in prosperous times in order to promote increases in productivity and economic growth. However, this conservatism was balanced by a willingness to accept an expansion in defense spending and a liberal approach to foreign aid. During 1958–1960 the administration attempted to increase the flow of private funds to developing countries and to place the U.S. foreign aid effort within a multilateral context. Thus, Anderson supported the granting of a special tax status to U.S. business corporations if they conducted business with developing countries. In August 1958, he recommended that the United States propose an extension of the quota and capital of the World Bank and the International Monetary Fund (IMF) as well as supporting the establishment of a lending agency to be called the International Development Agency (IDA). The IDA would lend money to developing countries at soft terms (less than market rates of interest) and allow the borrowers to repay at least part of the loan in their domestic currency (Kaufman, 158–62). Anderson testified in favor of legislation to increase U.S. contributions to the IMF and the World Bank ("Administration Supports Legislation," 445–54) as well as that establishing the IDA.

When the international balance of payments shortfall became acute in 1958–1959 and a precipitous decline in the U.S. holdings of gold occurred, Anderson rejected trade restrictions and advocated several policies designed to stimulate the inflow of funds to the United States. Thus, he urged Eisenhower to support a new policy whereby Development Loan Funds were to be tied to American purchases, that is, employed by the loan recipient only to finance the purchase of U.S. goods and services. When the balance of payments situation did not improve despite the adoption of this policy, Anderson proposed cutbacks in U.S. military expenditures abroad. These reductions included a decrease in "the number of military dependents in Europe, the integration of America's logistics system with the logistic systems of its NATO allies, and an increase in the defense contribution of other NATO countries" (Kaufman, 193).

Although both the Defense and the State Departments opposed these proposals, Eisenhower supported Anderson, and the United States reduced the presence of military dependents and moved to increase burden sharing. While a trip to Germany by Anderson and Undersecretary of State C. Douglas Dillon in November 1960 did not succeed in reducing the foreign exchange costs of maintaining U.S. troops in Germany, it did achieve some aid and trade concessions (Saulnier, 140; "Behind the Shock Tactics," 25–26). Additionally, Anderson repeatedly urged members of the General Agreement on Tariffs and Trade (GATT) to reduce their tariffs on U.S. exports and liberalize trade policies. He was successful in obtaining a promise of lower tariff and trade barriers from Britain, France, and Germany ("The Quiet Crusader").

In the area of domestic policy, Anderson's signal failure was his inability to improve the debt situation of the U.S. government. In 1958 he exhorted institutional investors to purchase more long-term Treasury securities through an appeal to their patriotism; he did not succeed ("Off on the Wrong Track," 128). In June 1959 he attempted to gain greater flexibility in debt management and asked Congress to end the ceiling on interest payable on savings bonds and long-term bonds (Anderson, 1959). When the House Ways and Means Committee shelved his request, he argued that he had no alternative but to shift more of the national debt into short-term securities, a move that he considered inflationary ("Anderson Taking World View," 85; "Anderson, Robert," 22). However, when Congress declined to raise this ceiling of 4.25 percent, he refused to support an amendment that would have restricted the independence of the Fed ("A Notable Fiscal Recovery").

Upon leaving public service at the end of the Eisenhower administration, Anderson became partner in the brokerage investment firm Carl M. Loeb, Rhoades, & Co. During the 1960s, he advised Presidents John Kennedy, Lyndon Johnson, and Richard Nixon on fiscal matters as well as handling diplomatic assignments for President Johnson, including one involving the renegotiation of the Panama Canal treaties. He also served as a partner in the Robert B. Anderson Company, a firm of international financial services consultants, as well as Chairman of the American Gas & Chemical Company. Among the companies of which he was a director were Pan American World Airways and Goodyear Tire and Rubber.

In spite of his many years of distinguished service in various state and federal offices, Anderson suffered public disgrace at the end of his life. In 1987, he pleaded guilty to charges of illegally operating a Caribbean bank and evading taxes on over $127,000 of personal income during 1983–1985. This undisclosed income included $79,000 received as a consultant to the Unification Church International led by the Rev. Sun Myung Moon. Anderson was sentenced to a month in jail, five months of house arrest, and five years of probation, suspended from practicing law in New York State, and subsequently disbarred.

He died in New York City on August 14, 1989, of complications arising from surgery on cancer of the esophagus. He had been a prominent layman of the Methodist Church and a member of Phi Delta Phi, Chancellors, Order of the Coif, and the Masonic order (thirty-third degree, Shriner). He was survived by two sons, Gerald Lee and James Richard Anderson.

BIBLIOGRAPHY

"Administration Supports Legislation to Increase U.S. Contributions to International Monetary Fund and World Bank." *Department of State Bulletin*, March 30, 1959, 445–54.

Anderson, Robert B. "Is a Tax Cut at This Time Sound?" *Congressional Digest*, June 1958, 173–77.

———. "Should the Interest Rate Ceiling Be Raised on Long Term U.S. Government Bonds?" *Congressional Digest*, November 1959, 266–74.

———. "The Balance of Payments Problem." *Foreign Affairs*, April 1960, 419–32.

———. "Financial Policies for Sustainable Growth." *Journal of Finance*, May 1960, 127–28.

"Anderson, Robert Bernard." In *The National Cyclopedia of American Biography*. Vol. 1. New York: James T. White and Company, 1960.

"Anderson, Robert B(ernard)." In *Political Profiles: The Eisenhower Years*, edited by Eleonora Schoenebaum. New York: Facts on File, 1977.

"Anderson Taking World View of Finance." *Business Week*, August 29, 1959, 84–88.

"Behind the Shock Tactics in Bonn." *Business Week*, December 3, 1960, 25–26.

"Cut Taxes? How Soon? How Far? Here's Who Will Shape Decisions." *U.S. News and World Report*, April 11, 1958, 60–63.

"Heir to Money Problems." *U.S. News and World Report*, June 7, 1957, 56–58.

Kaufman, Burton. *Trade and Aid: Eisenhower's Foreign Economic Policy 1953–1961*. Baltimore: Johns Hopkins University Press, 1982.

"Menace—and the Man Facing It." *Newsweek*, June 10, 1957, 29–30.

Morgan, Iwan. *Eisenhower versus "The Spenders."* New York: St. Martin's Press, 1990.

"New No. 2 Man in Defense Gets Things Done Quietly." *U.S. News and World Report*, March 19, 1954, 48–50.

Nomination Hearings before the Committee on Finance, United States Senate (85th Congress 1st Session) on Nomination of Robert B. Anderson, Secretary of the Treasury-Designate, June 28, 1957. Washington, D.C.: Government Printing Office, 1957.

"A Notable Fiscal Recovery." *Fortune*, August 1960, 92–95f.

"Off on the Wrong Track." *Business Week*, October 4, 1958, 128.

"The Quiet Crusader." *Time*, November 23, 1959, 21–24.

Saulnier, Raymond. *Constructive Years: The U.S. Economy under Eisenhower*. New York: University Press of America, 1991.

Stein, Herbert. *The Fiscal Revolution in America*. Washington, D.C.: American Enterprise Institute Press, 1990.

"Strong Man of the Cabinet? . . . Quiet Bob Anderson of Texas." *Newsweek*, June 9, 1958, 32–33.

"Tough Minded Texan in the Treasury." *New York Times Magazine*, July 7, 1957, 12–13.

VIBHA KAPURIA-FOREMAN

B

JAMES A. BAKER III (April 28, 1930–). James A. Baker III was born in Houston on April 28, 1930, the son of a prominent attorney and descendant of one of the founding fathers of Houston. His family's legal, banking, and corporate enterprises provided comfortable surroundings. Like his father, he attended Hill School, a college prep school in Pennsylvania. Jim's father was nicknamed "The Warden" and was known to whip the young man. Baker attended Princeton, where he majored in classics. After receiving a B.A in 1952, he spent two years on active duty as a lieutenant in the U.S. Marine Corps. Having learned to shoot in his youth, he became an expert marksman and was a member of the pistol and rifle team at Camp Lejeune, North Carolina. After completing service, he returned home to study law at the University of Texas at Austin.

Immediately after earning his J.D. degree with honors in 1957, he went to work for Andrews, Kurth, Campbell & Jones, a high-powered law firm in Houston. Though his great-grandfather and grandfather were, respectively, founder and developer of Houston's first legal offices, Baker & Botts, Jim was prevented from joining it because of antinepotism rules. Within a decade at Andrews, he was made partner. He worked there until 1975. In his words, he had a heritage to live up to, and this achievement dispelled his doubts about his ability to make it on his own.

In 1953, he married Mary McHenry, and together they had four children. Mary Baker was active in the Republican Party and worked on George Bush's congressional campaigns. She died in 1970, and in 1973, Baker married Susan Garrett. With three children from her first marriage, and a young daughter born in 1977, the Bakers have eight children and eleven grandchildren. In the mid-1980s, Susan Baker was active politically when she and Tipper Gore campaigned for a warning label on record albums with sexually explicit and violent lyrics.

Jim Baker is smooth and affable. He's a slim, athletic six-footer who wears cowboy boots, chews Red Man tobacco, and listens to country music, particularly Tammy Wynette and George Jones. He is compulsively neat, with dancing-school manners. He likes to hunt wild game and to wade fish in the shallow coastal bays of Texas. He speaks with a distinct Texas twang and plays an excellent game of tennis: Jim plays the baseline, George Bush, the net (Dowd and Friedman).

Until 1970, Jim Baker was apolitical, nominally a moderate Texas Democrat. Family tradition ruled that politics was an unsavory, low occupation. He first tasted real politics in the Senate campaign of Texas Congressman George Bush. Though the campaign was unsuccessful, Baker's political capabilities proved formidable. After running fourteen counties for the 1972 Nixon election, he became state Republican Finance Chairman. In 1975, he was offered a post as Undersecretary of Commerce by Gerald Ford. A year later, President Ford asked him to be delegate hunter at the 1976 Republican National Convention. Baker was instrumental in securing the marginal delegate votes that pushed the incumbent over the top and defeated the challenger, Ronald Reagan. His walkie-talkie code name at the convention: Miracle Man.

Within a week of the party nomination, Baker was appointed chairman of the Ford reelection committee, the third in five months. Down by thirty points in the polls to Jimmy Carter, Baker reengineered Ford's strategy by focusing on the projection of "presidential" image. Carter won but by a thin 1 percent of the total vote. Baker's reputation soared. After a short return to law practice in Texas, he ran for state Attorney General in 1978. He received the highest vote total for a Republican running below the first line on a statewide ticket after conducting a formidable campaign. He lost to a conservative Democrat.

In 1979, Baker guided underdog George Bush's campaign for the presidential nomination. Baker was responsible for Bush's stunning political upset in the Iowa caucuses, which gave him momentum going into the New Hampshire primary. The Baker/Bush team went over the top when they arrogantly refused to allow the other candidates to participate in a scheduled televised debate with Reagan. Baker convinced Bush to pull out of the race prior to the California primary, a move that, according to Baker, secured the Vice Presidential spot on the ticket. Reagan supporters' disdain for moderate Bush (for calling supply-side "voodoo economics," among other reasons) was muted by the decision. Baker joined the Reagan presidential campaign in the final weeks, arguing that money be directed for media and pressing for a showdown debate with Jimmy Carter, because "Reagan never loses a debate." He was right. Baker has been widely regarded, until 1992 at least, as Republicans' best election strategist. Without him, Bush might never have attained high office.

Baker's skills caught the attention of key Ronald Reagan aides. Baker launched ahead, surpassing the California crowd, in particular Edwin Meese, to become Chief of Staff. In that managerial job, he played honest broker. Baker was a member, with Meese and Michael Deaver, of one of the most successful triumvirates ever to operate in the White House. Working on policy formulation and legislative strategy pushed him by necessity into the hot core of the policy debate. It was Baker who was instrumental to the passage of the 1981 federal tax cut proposal. As Jack Kemp remarked, "With all due respect to the President and

Secretary Regan, it was Baker who got the budget and tax package passed." By 1984, Baker's authority was unchallenged.

Clearly, James Baker was one of the most effective and important people to pass through the Office of the Treasury. He is world famous and has few critics of his abilities. As George Shultz, who also worked in several administrations, recalled in his memoir, "[Baker] is second to none." For one, he understands the nature of political leverage: that celebrity and effectiveness are inseparable hand-maidens in Washington, D.C. Second, he has extraordinary political instincts. Baker kept a safe distance from all of the major problems and was never caught with blood on his hands. He is deeply respected by the powerful Democrats. He is largely adored by the media and is reputed to be one of the world's great leaders. Though he considers ideology the path of most resistance, he has even attracted admiration by exhibiting wisdom about the concerns of leadership. In particular, Baker seems to have understood earlier than most Ronald Reagan's dilemma in making the hard spending cut choices (Stockman). Baker's colleagues rarely pub-licly questioned his loyalty, though his lack of vision and his motives to seek higher office are openly discussed. He's one of the greatest "can do" figures to cross the political stage. But few profess to know why.

A few of Baker's detractors argue that his strongest loyalties were to his own ambition, not to specific policies (Reagan; Quayle). Many wonder whether his discomfort with the Right, in economic or social policy, is based on belief or poll watching. Evidence suggests that his policy-by-polling was a true reflection of the thinness of his beliefs. Like the policy jobs that followed, Baker's overall goals always lacked clarity. Nowhere was this more apparent to the public than when he left his spot as Secretary of State to run the 1992 reelection campaign. Baker and Bush ran a purely defensive, subsequently disastrous campaign. They were ideologically pummeled by a New Democrat. Peggy Noonan, in her book *What I Saw at the Revolution*, remarks that when she was called in as speech writer that year for a hemorrhaging campaign, the atmosphere was lifeless, the cause was drained. Baker as a celebrity needs a context, and his effectiveness requires goals. Ronald Reagan provided that leverage, but Bush did not. Baker was successful in his means of economic domestic policy because of the ends of Ronald Reagan. Despite the impressiveness of the résumé, Baker was suited for operations (of any Cabinet office) in a narrow sense but wholly unsuited in the broad sense of offering thoughtful economic advice to the President.

Baker and Don Regan switched jobs. Baker left his Chief position because, as widely reported, he was fatigued. Better for someone else to try the hot seat. Baker thought that Reagan's tax pledge would be too hard to keep with the expected deficits. Donald Regan had designs on the power chair in the White House. From there, Regan could push through the Treasury Tax Reform Act produced by his staff largely in secret during the election year 1984. Assuming the Secretary's position on February 4, 1985, Baker had little experience in tax and finance. He stumbled into the Treasury position because other Cabinet posts were not available except National Security Council, a job that Bill Casey of the

CIA (Central Intelligence Agency) and Caspar Weinberger of Defense preferred to fill with the less impervious Bud McFarlane. Baker acclimated to the office quickly, by embarking on a rigorous media campaign of grand speeches at world summits, again wedding effectiveness with celebrity ("Curiously Insubstantial Treasury").

Baker brought with him from the White House Richard Darman. The Baker/ Darman team was complementary, and the office was often referred to as the Baker/Darman Treasury. Baker was diplomat, master of dealing with people and orchestrating compromises, while Darman was also a savvy operator who could grasp the substance of issues. Baker wanted to be liked; Darman was used to being disliked. Many in Washington, D.C., were quick to criticize Darman, but most were reluctant to criticize Baker because of his position of power and gentlemanly demeanor (Birnbaum and Murray). Baker's successes in the office would lead some to call him the "Henry Kissinger of Tax Policy."

The job swap reinvigorated Reagan's tax reform. The Treasury Tax Reform Act, on announcement, had been deluged by complainers, including many Senators. But Reagan wanted it. Don Regan was one of the few people to listen to Ronald Reagan's public speeches and take the goals seriously. His Treasury had come up with a plan that to most insiders, including Jim Baker, was dead on arrival. Conventional wisdom said that monumental tax reform could only suffer death by a thousand cuts. Even Baker worked hard to preserve tax breaks for oil interests. But Baker's job was to sell it. One Baker aide characterized his thinking on the matter. One, Baker wished that tax reform had not come up in the first place. Two, he wished that the Treasury plan had not come out. Three, he needed to make the best of it since it wouldn't go away. And four, the goal is reduced rates, so he can do anything within reason to get that. To Baker, this was purely an operational issue. More important, tax reform was the issue on which his success as Treasury Secretary would be based.

Baker and Darman intended to hammer out a deal with the Democrats in the same way they had dealt with Social Security in 1982 and 1983: in secret, with consensus from the top leadership and a quick push through legislative chambers. Baker assembled a new tax-writing group in the Treasury and reoriented priorities. Where Regan avoided all talk of politics, Baker talked about little else. The initial stratagem was to divide and conquer the business community by exploiting differences between the interest groups. Although the bill gained steam for a complex set of reasons, the Baker/Darman intuition contributed substantively. Reagan's populist vision of tax fairness did not die. As Darman noted, "[Lobbyists] were brought down by the narrowness of their vision." Thus, Baker's success with tax reform was the last high point of the Reagan presidency.

The open question is still: What does James Baker actually believe about taxes? The best guess is that he has absorbed the antitax sentiment as basic party posture: It is popular, it is an expression of the public's attitude toward overall spending, and its consequences on budgets are subordinate consideration. He probably evolved from conceiving the issue as one about responsible budgeting in the early 1980s to a position later that this was one principle that ought to be accommodated in public life *if* he was to have a public life. Baker had the sense to know which pole holds up the party tent, and as adviser, he was still on the right side of the issue in 1990 when George Bush broke the "Read my lips" pledge. What Baker *really* thinks is irrelevant, because he only commits to those goals he is certain of achieving. Thus, the tax question could be extended similarly to fiscal matters, monetary policy, exchange rates, international debt, the dollar—whatever. Who knows what Jim Baker thinks about economics? He hasn't spoken out in fundamental terms, except in the vaguest generalities. None expect him to.

Many supply-siders have not been awed by Baker's machinations. Economist Paul Craig Roberts, Treasury Staff member under Regan, consistently criticized Baker's goals and methods through his regular *Business Week* columns. He argues that in 1981 Baker picked a needless fight with congressional Democrats to give Reagan a personal victory. The bipartisan supply-side consensus (in particular Nunn, Bentsen, and Long in the Senate) broke when Baker cut off the "boll weevil" southern Democrats from the House leadership. This had the effect of denying them any credit for reducing taxes. The Democrats offered a plan, which lost out to Reagan's, and, with no stake in the outcome, embarked on a shrill and relentless campaign of criticism against the supply-side program. They dragged their feet on spending reduction and blamed the deficit on the tax cut. A charitable interpretation is that Baker simply miscalculated Reagan's ability to overcome the class war rhetoric ("trickle-down economics"). Unfortunately for Baker, the marriage of celebrity and effectiveness got a *divorce*.

As head of the Treasury, Baker was also Chairman of the President's Economic Policy Council. However, much of Baker's actions at the Treasury struck at the heart of the supply-side policy. It's likely that Baker was acting more as a chief political officer for a President-in-waiting. Baker wanted to see Bush succeed Reagan in 1988. That year, Bush's main rival would be Jack Kemp, architect of the supply-side plan, chief "voodoo" economist. Prior to 1984, Baker had tended to side with the volatile David Stockman of OMB (Office of Management and Budget), a strange alliance on its face, and Martin Feldstein of CEA (Council of Economic Advisers), who was considered a grandstanding academic, never quite in tune with other members of the CEA or the President. These administration critics of the supply-side plan were given extraordinary cover by Baker. This frustrated Don Regan, obviously, and exacerbated the divisions within the Reagan team. Hence, Regan publicly asserted his primacy in economic matters during the first Reagan term with "comic regularity" and was forced into secrecy to conceive the Treasury Tax Reform Act. Also, during the Baker Treasury, Roberts argues that the Fed was not held accountable for excessive tightening, since effects on the deficit would be directed against the supply-side program. Baker was astute in distancing himself from the policy undercurrent endorsed by the President while ostensibly operating to advance those policies.

Baker, like his predecessor and successor, managed to dodge the bullet of the

S&L (Savings and Loan) crisis and no doubt helped deep-six the issue during the 1988 Bush campaign. The Tax Reform Act of 1986 included a provision that reduced the depreciation benefits from investing in commercial and residential property. This changed, once again, the accounting for the wear and tear of the life of investments. Consequently, the value of the real estate holdings of banks and savings and loans was adversely affected. It is unclear whether Baker had a conception of the unintended consequences of these tax law changes; he most certainly should have been aware of the financial fragility of the savings and loan industry. Other bank problems arose that were put off to be reckoned with another day. The Farm Credit System was eventually bailed out. This type of agency, the government-sponsored enterprise, is part of the federal "stealth budget" and subject to congressional and administrative tinkering. Oversight of these agencies is not the federal government's—including and especially the Baker Treasury's—strong suit. The preferred method of funding private interests (homeowner, farmers, students, etc.) is to create yet more contingent liabilities of the federal government via the implicit backing from the Treasury. The Regan, Baker, and Brady Treasuries were all complicit in the growth of the off-budget activities of the federal government.

The Third World debt problem was inherited by Baker and persisted over the decade to be handed over to his successor. The Baker plan was to throw good money after bad on the promise of debtor nations to adopt free market domestic reform. These foreign policy loans were induced by the implied backing of the federal government and the enthusiastic Chairman of Citicorp, Walter Wriston, who intoned that sovereign nations don't default. Ultimately, banks conceded to the economic reality, eventually suffering massive charge-offs. Baker's efforts to lower the dollar, thereby reducing the pressure on debtor nations, effectively dispersed part of the costs of the bailout to the consuming public. Though this was clearly an intractable problem, the basic error of Baker's ways was to lend Treasury support to international agencies who underwrote statist policies and debased lending standards. Once again, Baker's hands are clean: The public remembers the Brady Plan. The glimmer of political success is the distinct turn to democracy in Latin America by the end of Baker's service at the State Department. Baker also emphasized coordination of the lowering of interest rates by world central banks to relieve debt pressure and stimulate growth. Robert Bartley of the *Wall Street Journal* editorial page has theorized that Baker's comments on a Sunday after a policy stalemate with the German Bundesbank triggered a liquidity crisis that crashed twenty-three stock markets around the world on Black Monday, October 19, 1987. In an anticipated appearance on a Sunday talk show, Baker announced, "We will not sit back in this country and watch surplus countries jack up interest rates and squeeze growth worldwide on the expectation that the United States somehow will follow by raising its interest rates." Thus, in arguing over the strength of the dollar, Baker implied that he would allow the dollar to plunge, thereby constraining liquidity. The market interpreted his statement as a severing of international cooperation (Bartley, 1992).

Baker again served as director for Bush's 1988 campaign, a big part of which was damage control on social conservative issues. After victory, Baker served as Secretary of State and traveled to ninety foreign countries. In 1991, he added to his weighty pile of public service awards when he received the Presidential Medal of Freedom. Most people are at a loss to remember the Baker foreign policy, since his was, at root, ad hoc. His relationship with the President was unique in history. To outsiders, it was difficult to separate the power balance of two individuals who often finished each other's sentences and who communicated instinctively. But Vice President Quayle has written that it was really Bush who had the upper hand, contrary to press reports. Also, Brent Scowcroft actually had a better working relationship with the President and knew how to win foreign policy battles with Baker.

There is no part of the modern Republicanism that elevates pragmatism over principle. The Republican success in the 1980s was driven by ideas, not successful public relations. But a consistent theme among the party faithful is a reverence to the people who get things done. The entrepreneurs and business and corporate leaders who embrace the party expect efficacy. James Baker was frequently wrong about celebrity and effectiveness, but his record for delivering the goods is undisputed. He leveraged the ideas of others. To the extent that he was a true "honest broker," he contributed organizational prowess to the administrations he served. He succeeded politically while achieving mixed-at-best economic results. Dan Quayle, no fan of Baker's, said that "if you tell him to go in and get a good deal, he will." But what's a good deal? If he's working only for Jim Baker, what is he working for? James A. Baker III is a brilliant political mechanic: He made the car drivable, most of the time, but he was not its driver.

BIBLIOGRAPHY

"A Curiously Insubstantial Treasury," *Economist*, September 22, 1990.

Bartley, Robert. "Black Monday Revisited." *Wall Street Journal*, October 19, 1988.

———. *The Seven Fat Years and How to Do It Again*. New York: Free Press, 1992.

Birnbaum, Jeffrey H., and Alan S. Murray. *Showdown at Gucci Gulch*. New York: Random House, 1987.

Current Biography. New York: H. W. Wilson, 1982.

Dowd, Maureen, and Thomas L. Friedman. "Those Fabulous Bush and Baker Boys." *New York Times Magazine*, May 6, 1990.

Friedman, Benjamin M. *Day of Reckoning: The Consequences of American Policy*. New York: Random House, 1988.

Loomis, Carol. "Why Baker's Debt Plan Won't Work." *Fortune*, December 23, 1985.

Noonan, Peggy. *What I Saw at the Revolution*. New York: Ivy Books, 1990.

Quayle, Dan. *Standing Firm: A Vice Presidential Memoir*. New York: HarperCollins Publishers, 1994.

Reagan, Nancy, with William Novak. *My Turn*. New York: Dell, 1989.

Regan, Donald. *For the Record: From Wall Street to Washington*. New York: St. Martin's Press, 1988.

Roberts, Paul Craig. *Business Week*, various columns, 1983–1986.

Shultz, George. *Turmoil and Triumph: My Years as Secretary of State*. New York: Charles Scribner's Sons, 1993.

Stockman, David A. *The Triumph of Politics: How the Reagan Revolution Failed*. New York: Harper and Row, 1986.
Wall Street Journal Index, 1980–1992.

JEFF SCOTT

JOSEPH W. BARR (January 17, 1918–   ). After Henry Fowler's resignation was effective, President Lyndon Johnson announced the recess appointment of Undersecretary Joseph Barr as the fifty-ninth Secretary of the Treasury as well as Governor for the United States on the International Monetary Fund, the International Bank for Reconstruction and Development (and affiliated institutions), the Inter-American Development Bank, and the Asian Development Bank.

When Joseph Walker Barr was born to Oscar Lynn Barr and Stella Florence (Walker) Barr on January 17, 1918, in Vincennes, Indiana, he was in the sixth generation of his family to live in that state. His family had been in America since his ancestor Michael O'Barr emigrated from Ireland in the 1760s. Michael's son, Hugh, fought in the Revolution. Hugh's son Robert Barr (by then the "O" has disappeared) first went to Indiana in 1810. Hugh Barr joined him in 1814. They settled in Davies County where Barr Township is named for the Revolutionary War veteran Hugh Barr. Robert's son born in 1817, also named Hugh, made a fortune first as merchant and trader, then as banker. Banking became, along with farming and Republican Party politics, the family's principal occupations. Joseph Barr's father was the founder of the O. L. Barr Grain Company as well as a bank director.

At DePauw University, the young Joe Barr majored in economics. He was graduated with a B.A. degree and a Phi Beta Kappa key in 1939 and went on to graduate study in economics at Harvard University. He was a student of Sumner H. Slichter and is said to have been one of few Slichter students to reject the thesis that strong inflationary pressures are inevitable as the economy approaches full employment (Moritz, 48). Barr received his M.A. in theoretical economics in 1941.

Joseph Barr married Beth Ann Williston of Indianapolis on September 3, 1939. They had five children. During World War II Barr served in the United States Navy. He was the commander of a submarine chaser in the Mediterranean and won the Bronze Star for his exploits at Anzio. At his discharge in October 1945, he held the rank of lieutenant commander.

He returned to Indiana to help manage his family's businesses, which included, in addition to banking and grain elevators, farm equipment, real estate, and theaters. He was active in many community activities—and became a Democrat. In 1958 he was elected to the U.S. House of Representatives from Indiana's eleventh district, a traditional Republican stronghold. Upon taking his seat on January 3, 1959, he was assigned to the House Banking and Currency Committee. Partly because of his knowledge of economics, Barr was unusually influential for

a freshman Congressman, helping, for example, to write the legislation establishing the Inter-American Development Bank. He impressed Speaker Sam Rayburn and, more importantly as it turned out, John F. Kennedy, a young Senator
from Massachusetts. Barr and Kennedy shared many interests, including the
United Negro College Fund of which Barr was state chairman. Barr supported
and campaigned for Kennedy in 1960. Perhaps he was too diligent in his support;
for when Kennedy was elected President on November 7, 1960, Barr lost his seat
in the House to his Republican challenger.

In 1961, Barr was appointed Assistant to Undersecretary of the Treasury Henry
Fowler. His main job was to handle Treasury's relations with Congress. Barr
proved to be immensely successful in this position, combining a facility in highly
technical matters with an ability to disarm his opponents, who often emerged
both losing to him and liking him.

He spent the next three years at the Treasury. On July 22, 1963, President
Kennedy announced that he intended to nominate Barr for the Chairmanship
of the Federal Deposit Insurance Corporation when the post was vacated in
August. As it turned out, pressures of his tasks at the Treasury kept him there,
and the appointment had not been made at the time of Kennedy's death; thus,
it was Lyndon Johnson who nominated Barr on January 14, 1964, and he took
office later in the month.

He was to serve eighteen months as Chairman. It was a period of considerable
accomplishment. He did much to improve the safety and soundness of banks,
especially in the detection and prevention of bank crimes and the infiltration
into banking of organized crime. He did frequent battle with Comptroller of the
Currency James J. Saxon, whom Barr accused of wanting to return to the days
of "wildcat banking" in the nineteenth century. Saxon, meanwhile, said that
Barr was making "political footballs" out of national bank failures (Moritz, 50).

When Henry Fowler became Secretary of the Treasury, Joe Barr moved back
as Undersecretary at Fowler's specific request. Extensive experience in economics,
business, politics, and banking made him a valuable addition to the team. His
principal responsibility, as before, was for administration and congressional relations. He served well as the administration's spokesperson in winning approval
for a wide range of policies and programs from 1965 until 1968.

Joseph Barr became the Secretary of the Treasury on December 21, 1968. Early
in 1969, Secretary Barr was one of the first to use the term *taxpayer's revolt* to
indicate a sentiment widespread in the land that the tax system was too complicated, too full of inequities. It was the first step toward what was to become
the Tax Reform Act of 1969. Under the terms of the recess appointment, Secretary Barr's term expired on Inauguration Day, January 20, 1969.

When he left the Treasury, Joseph Barr became the President of American
Security and Trust Company of Washington, D.C. Later he became its Chairman. When he stepped down on May 10, 1974, he announced he planned to
spend more time concentrating on the black angus cattle on his 360-acre Virginia
estate. Less than a month later, however, he moved to an even more visible

job in banking by going from AS&T (then the ninetieth largest bank in the country) to be Chairman and CEO (chief executive officer) of New York's troubled Franklin National Bank, the twentieth largest commercial bank in the nation. He became a partner in J & J Company in 1976 and has served on many corporate boards as well as that of the Student Loan Marketing Association and the Board of Regents of Georgetown University.

In spite of having served only 29.5 days as Secretary of the Treasury, Joseph Walker Barr's signature appeared on at least 100 million series 1963 B one-dollar Federal Reserve Notes, thus maintaining, unbroken, a chain started in 1914 when the signature of the Secretary was first required on currency.

BIBLIOGRAPHY

Jones, William H. "Joseph Barr: Back to Bank Business." *Washington Post,* June 21, 1974, A14.

Moritz, Charles, ed. *Current Biography*. New York: H. W. Wilson Co., 1968.

U.S. Congress. Senate. Committee on Banking and Currency. *Nomination of Joseph W. Barr,* 88th Cong., 2nd sess., January 16, 1964. (For Chairman of the Federal Deposit Insurance Corporation)

U.S. Treasury. *Annual Report of the Secretary of the Treasury for the Fiscal Year Ending January 30, 1969.* Washington, D.C.: Government Printing Office, 1969.

U.S. Treasury. "Barr Family History." Prepared for an Exhibit of the Public Papers of the Honorable Joseph W. Barr, n.d.

EARL W. ADAMS

LLOYD M. BENTSEN (February 11, 1921–   ). Lloyd Millard Bentsen was born to Lloyd M. and Edna Ruth (Colbath) Bentsen in Mission, Texas, on February 11, 1921. Lloyd Bentsen, Sr., and his brother Elmer had migrated to the Lower Rio Grande Valley of Texas from South Dakota to build a land empire. This empire was based upon groceries and land clearance. Lloyd Bentsen, Sr., hired Mexican laborers to clear land and paid them the full contract price (instead of half, as was the custom) in scrip that could only be spent in the Bentsen grocery store. The Bentsen family fortune grew rapidly as Lloyd Bentsen, Sr., bought the land he had cleared—by the 1950s he was reputed to be worth as much as $40 million.

Lloyd Bentsen grew up in McAllen, Texas, attending public schools and living in prosperity. He earned an LL.B. from the University of Texas Law School at Austin in 1942 and was admitted to the bar that same year. Upon graduation he enlisted in the U.S. Army as a private and was assigned to the U.S. Army Air Corps, where he rose to command a B-24 squadron. As a bomber pilot in Europe, he flew fifty missions and was shot down twice. On one of those occasions, he piloted a stricken plane from Austria over the Alps to a crash landing in Yugoslavia, an exploit for which he was awarded the Distinguished Flying Cross. He also earned an Air Medal with three oak leaf clusters. His highest rank was major; he served in the Air Force Reserve from 1950 to 1959 and was promoted to the rank of colonel.

In November 1943, Lloyd Bentsen married former model Beryl Ann Longino of Lufkin, Texas. Upon completion of his military service in July 1945, Bentsen returned to McAllen and opened a private law practice. He also became involved in local Democratic politics, being elected to Hidalgo County judge in 1946. He maintained his law practice and worked as judge until 1948 when he successfully ran in a special election to fill the vacancy caused by the death of Milton H. West, becoming the youngest member of the 80th Congress.

He was elected to the 81st, 82nd, and 83rd Congresses but declined to seek reelection in 1954. His tenure in Congress was distinguished by his vote against the poll tax in 1949 and his call for the use of nuclear weapons against North Korea in 1950. He generally supported the interests of his Texas farming constituency, promoting water conservation and reclamation projects, insect control as well as price supports, and the employment of Mexican farm laborers. On social issues he had a mixed record, supporting federally sponsored low-income housing but opposing federal antidiscrimination laws for employers. He was a militant anti-Communist and favored U.S. military involvement in Indochina and opposed alleged Communist domination of U.S. labor unions.

Bentsen quit Congress in 1954, complaining that the $12,500 salary was inadequate for raising three children and that advancement was too slow. With a stake from his father variously estimated to be between $5 million and $7 million, Bentsen moved to Houston and established Lincoln Consolidated, a holding company that owned Lincoln Liberty Life Insurance Co. and controlled stocks worth millions of dollars in mutual funds, oil, agriculture, and other enterprises, including several Texas banks. The Texas economic boom of the 1950s and 1960s allowed him to build a vast corporate empire including directorships in Lockheed Aircraft, Continental Oil, Panhandle Eastern Pipeline, Trunkline Gas, and the Bank of the Southwest in Houston.

Bentsen returned to politics in 1970. With the support of former Texas Governor John B. Connally and other members of the conservative Democratic establishment in Texas, Bentsen ran a well-organized and well-funded campaign against liberal Senator Ralph W. Yarborough. The primary battle was bitter— Bentsen characterized the incumbent as an ultraliberal associated with antiwar demonstrations and ran advertisements showing the riots at the 1968 Democratic Convention in Chicago to establish this link. Yarborough accused the Bentsen family of being land frauds and exploiters. Bentsen presented himself as a moderate in race relations and appealed to the Mexican-American voters through commercials recorded in fluent Spanish. After defeating Yarborough, Bentsen won labor and minority support to defeat Republican candidate George Bush.

He served in the Senate until 1992, making an unsuccessful run for the Democratic presidential nomination in 1976 and serving as Michael Dukakis's running mate in the 1988 presidential campaign. In the Senate, Bentsen favored a limited form of national health insurance, federal funds to promote medical education, scientific research, preventive health care, bilingual education, public works jobs, and prenatal and neonatal care. He voted for the Equal Employment Opportunity Commission and the Equal Rights Amendment. Bentsen favored aid to the Nicaraguan Contras, the MX missile program, and the Strategic Defense Initiative, as well as a constitutional amendment to permit recited prayer in public schools. He supported clean water and clean air legislation, catastrophic health care, housing and community development assistance, and sixty days' notice for factory closings.

He consistently expressed concern about the federal budget deficit and supported a constitutional amendment to require a balanced federal budget. He believed in the use of government power to help business and the use of the tax code to stimulate saving and investment. Thus, he has favored "selective" credit allocations to help the housing industry, advocated cutting the capital gains tax, and supported accelerated depreciation breaks for business. He was a good friend of the oil and gas and real estate industries. He supported the 1981 Reagan tax cuts and voted for the 1986 tax reforms after saving tax breaks for oil and gas and attempting to protect real estate tax shelters. He supported the Caribbean Basin Initiative and argued in favor of the North American Free Trade Agreement (NAFTA) but was also a proponent of tough retaliatory measures against unfair trading partners.

As the powerful Chair of the Senate Finance Committee from 1987 to 1992, he favored cutting the capital gains tax, imposing higher taxes on upper-income brackets, and permitting bigger IRAs (individual retirement accounts) for savings, school, and first-time home buying. He used the budget reconciliation process to increase Medicaid coverage and to influence energy policy. He also served as a member of the Commerce, Science and Transportation Committee, the Joint Committee on Taxation, and the Joint Economic Committee.

Before receiving a call from President-elect Bill Clinton, Bentsen had been planning to leave politics in 1994 at the end of his Senate term. Instead, he accepted the offer to become Treasury Secretary and the chance to work on lagging investment and unbalanced budgets. In announcing his nomination, President-elect Clinton said, "I wanted someone who had the unique capacity to command the respect of Wall Street while showing an unrelenting concern for the Americans who make their living on Main Street" (*Congressional Quarterly*, 1992, 3824).

Without asking a single question, Bentsen's former colleagues on the Senate Finance Committee voted unanimously to confirm his appointment as Secretary of the Treasury on January 20, 1993. Bentsen stressed the primacy of deficit reduction, even ahead of Clinton's campaign promise of a middle-class tax cut. In addition, he spoke favorably of an investment tax credit as a means of stimulating the economy while disparaging calls to devalue the dollar in order to encourage exports.

Within the Group of Seven (G-7: United States, Britain, France, Germany, Japan, Italy, and Canada) Bentsen argued that the United States was finally taking effective action to reduce the deficit as demanded by its allies. He asked for reciprocal actions by Japan and Germany to stimulate world economic growth, pressing Japan to stimulate its economy while encouraging Germany to reduce interest rates.

During the first quarter of 1993, Bentsen continued to publicly defend President Clinton's demand that Congress pass a $16.3 billion stimulus package despite encouraging economic news showing the economy growing out of the recession. However, he privately advised Clinton to accept a compromise that trimmed the stimulus package. Clinton ignored this advice, pushed for the entire package, and watched the measure defeated in the Senate.

Throughout his first two years in office, Bentsen battled reports that he lacked influence in the administration, that important discussions were carried out in the National Economic Council, and that Deputy Treasury Secretary Roger Altman was a frequent source of advice. However, Bentsen was prominent when it was time to line up votes for the administration's projects such as the budget and the NAFTA. "I've never seen a Secretary of the Treasury doing as much lobbying as I do," he said ("This Wasn't in the Job Description").

Bentsen lobbied heavily to assemble support for President Clinton's first budget, which raised taxes and cut the rate of growth in spending. However, he was criticized for not doing enough to ensure a smooth passage of this legislation. He negotiated with Mexican authorities to wrest concessions to ensure passage of the NAFTA. He also lobbied domestically for the NAFTA, arguing that lower tariffs would result in a net increase in U.S. jobs and that the administration had ensured adequate environmental and labor protection in the supplemental agreement. Finally, Bentsen was a strong supporter of the General Agreement on Tariffs and Trade (GATT), rallying American business to urge its passage.

In the area of banking regulation, Bentsen favored passage of the Fair Trade in Financial Services Act as well as pushed for the incorporation of its provisions in the agreement negotiated in the Uruguay round of the General Agreement on Tariffs and Trade. These provisions would limit the access of foreign banks and financial service companies in the United States if the Treasury found that the home countries of these companies were limiting the access of American companies. In addition, Bentsen favored the removal of restrictions on interstate banking in the United States. He argued that the expansion of interstate banking would ease credit nationwide and strengthen banks by unhitching them from the economies of individual states; this proposal was later written into law. Finally, his plan to create a single banking regulatory agency to supervise all banks and saving and loan agencies faced heavy criticism by Alan Greenspan, Chairman of the Federal Reserve Board, and other officials who feared losing Fed control of bank regulation. President Clinton did not support his Secretary, and a majority of the Senate Banking Committee supported the Fed's stance on this issue.

Although a gun owner, Bentsen urged gun control through more extensive regulation and licensing of gun dealers. He argued that the Bureau of Alcohol, Tobacco, and Firearms, which was within the Department of the Treasury, did not have enough inspectors to regulate the 284,000 gun dealers in the country. Thus, he advocated an increase in the licensing fee of gun dealers to bring the fee more in line with the cost to taxpayers of checking these applications ("Remarks of Treasury Secretary").

In the international arena, Bentsen told Russian leaders that the United States would help expedite delivery of Western aid only after credible signs that Russia was restructuring its budget to phase out loss-making industries, to lower inflation, and to assist the unemployed. In addition, he was an unstinting advocate of American business and argued vigorously for increased access to foreign markets for American products. Thus, on a tour of East Asia in January 1994, he prodded Indonesia to make progress on workers' rights if it wanted to retain its trade privileges; in Thailand, he affirmed that countries that limited access to American financial services would either have to enter into good-faith negotiations with the United States to end these barriers or face a limitation of their access to the American market; and in China he demanded that more be done to improve human rights practices. In China, he achieved a relaxation of rules governing the operation of foreign banks as well as an agreement to step up enforcement of copyright laws. His attempt to persuade Japan to make concessions in its trade talks with the United States foundered because Prime Minister Hosokawa's government faced imminent collapse. Continued political instability in Japan imperilled a trade accord.

During the spring, summer, and fall of 1994, Bentsen's biggest concern was the falling value of the dollar. By November, the United States had intervened in foreign exchange markets four times in an attempt to bolster the value of the dollar. There was some perception that Secretary Bentsen had contributed to the slide of the dollar by his statement in February 1993 that the United States preferred a stronger yen. Subsequently, the currency markets appeared convinced that a weak dollar was a goal of U.S. international economic policy. Thus, despite rising U.S. interest rates and economic growth, as well as assurances by Bentsen that the United States wanted a stronger dollar, the dollar remained weak. Bentsen repeatedly avowed the willingness of the United States to intervene and argued that the value of the dollar had declined too far: "This administration sees no advantage in an undervalued currency" (*Wall Street Journal*, May 5, 1994, A1). In June he stated that it was not the administration's strategy to drive down the dollar or to use the dollar as a bargaining chip. "The dollar is not a tool of our trade policy" (*Washington Post*, June 29, 1994, F1). In October he asserted that the administration would prefer a stronger dollar. However, these public statements as well as repeated national and international efforts to raise the value of the U.S. dollar were only successful for brief periods.

Lloyd Bentsen resigned from his position as Secretary of the Treasury effective December 22, 1994. His Deputy, Frank Newman, served as Acting Secretary until Robert E. Rubin was confirmed on January 10, 1995.

Bentsen's resignation was not unexpected, as it was known by the administration that he wanted to return to Texas by the end of his fourth Senate term. His leaving came with the passing of the latest far-reaching world trade agreement, the last item on Bentsen's economic agenda as Secretary of the Treasury. This agreement, under the auspices of GATT, has reduced tariffs and facilitated trade among the world's trading partners.

Bentsen's other recent achievements included a bill allowing more interstate banking, as well as the President's 1993 tax plan and the North American Free Trade Agreement. This effort, championed through Congress by Bentsen, will gradually eliminate trade barriers with Canada and Mexico in the next decade.

The President's loss is less that of an active economic policymaker and more of an old political hand who knew the tone and temper of the politics inside the Washington beltway. The elder statesman served the President as an active political adviser and not only as economic caretaker of the Treasury.

Bentsen, an active seventy-five, said to reporters in his leaving that after a career in public service he wanted to go back to Texas, to his roots, and return to the private sector while he still had a spring in his step. He has two sons, Lloyd Millard and Lan Chase, and a daughter, Tina.

BIBLIOGRAPHY
"The Ayes of Texas." *Newsweek,* July 25, 1988, 20–22.

Bentsen, Lloyd. "Technology Venturing: A Visionary Challenge for Prosperity, Security, and Opportunities." In *Technology Venturing: American Innovation and Risk Taking,* edited by Eugene Konecci and Robert Kuhn, 45–50. New York: Praeger, 1985.

———. "Caring for Those Harmed by Free Trade." *Christian Science Monitor,* August 25, 1992.

———. "Increasing the Flow of Credit: Interstate Banking." *Vital Speeches,* November 15, 1993, 69–71.

———. "Lower Tariffs Mean More Jobs." *New Perspectives Quarterly,* fall 1993, 32–33.

———. Remarks of Treasury Secretary Lloyd Bentsen. Salt Lake City Business Community, April 18, 1994.

"Bentsen, Beltway Insider, Now Fights the Notion That He's Out of the Loop." *New York Times,* December 28, 1993, D18.

"Bentsen, Lloyd." In *Current Biography Yearbook: 1973.* New York: H. W. Wilson Co., 1973.

"Bentsen, Lloyd." In *Political Profiles: The Nixon/Ford Years,* edited by Eleonora Schoenebaum. New York: Facts on File, 1979.

"The Clinton Team." In *Almanac of American Politics,* edited by Michael Barone and Grant Ujifusa, xxxii–xxxviii. Washington, D.C.: National Journal, 1994.

Congressional Quarterly Weekly Report. July 16, 1988, 1961–64.

———. December 12, 1992, 3801–2, 3824.

"This Wasn't in the Job Description." *Business Week,* June 21, 1993, 36.

Time. July 25, 1988, 22–23.

———. June 14, 1993, 30–31.

Wall Street Journal. January 13, 1993, A2.

———. March 2, 1993, A2.

———. April 8, 1993, A6:5.

———. February 26, 1993, A2.

———. May 5, 1994, A1.

Washington Post. June 29, 1994, F1.

———. October 22, 1994, D2.

VIBHA KAPURIA-FOREMAN

GEORGE M. BIBB (October 30, 1776–April 14, 1859). George Mortimer Bibb of Kentucky, like the other three Tyler appointees to the Treasury Secretary post, came into office under circumstances shrouded with mystery and intrigue. Succeeding Secretary John C. Spencer, Bibb shared Tyler's distrust of Jacksonian authoritarianism; he was the fourth and final Secretary of the Treasury during Tyler's troubled administration. Bibb was a rather obscure choice for Secretary. He was regarded as an "old school" Republican of Virginia who added sectional weight to a Cabinet that, by May 1844, was composed almost exclusively of Southerners. It may be significant that Tyler's Cabinet, as reconstituted, contained one Northerner among five Southerners. Tyler had threaded his way through a maze of policy and partisanship and had emerged with a sectional Cabinet dedicated to a major assault intended to bring Texas into the Union.

Tyler had urged Secretary of the Treasury Walter Forward to resign because of his alleged incompetence. For a replacement, Tyler submitted the name of Caleb Cushing to the Senate for confirmation, but the nomination was rejected. The President was undaunted and twice submitted the nomination, but the Senate resolutely declined to confirm him. Finally, John Spencer, the Secretary of War, was transferred to the Treasury Department, with the Senate sanctioning the move. When Spencer resigned in May 1844, in fruitless anticipation of an appointment to the Supreme Court, Tyler turned to George Bibb, a move that surprised everyone, including Bibb.

Tyler's administration was not noted for great efficiency or good management; the government debt went from about $4.8 million to $28.9 million. According to historian Albert Bolles, there were some slight attempts to economize during Tyler's administration; but extravagant and corrupt expenditure practices had become so well ingrained that reform was slow and difficult. For example, there was evidently considerable misbehavior in the military branch. A committee investigated the expenditures of the commander of the Florida squadron, whose corrupt course toward the government was very clearly proved. In closing its report, the committee argued that there was no reason to believe that cases of abuse and squandering of the public money frequently occurred to the extent of the one in question; but needless expenditures existed throughout the whole service owing to the loose and faulty system of accountability. The committee fully expected that the Secretary of the Treasury could institute fiscal and auditing controls to reduce these corrupt spending practices in government.

Barely a year had passed before Spencer resigned in consequence of receiving a request from President Tyler to deposit $100,000 of Secret Service money with a confidential agent in New York to launch a naval expedition against Mexico. This money laundering scheme was of course contrary to the law. He next received a peremptory order to transfer the money. Spencer, seeing the game was up, coolly wrote a second refusal, and with it sent in a note of resignation. He remained in the department just twenty-four hours afterwards.

With three swift changes of Treasury Secretary (President Tyler inherited Thomas Ewing of Ohio from Gen. William Harrison's administration), efficiency in conducting the affairs of the Treasury was nearly impossible. The wonder was that the Treasury Department business was not managed worse. Thus, poor Bibb was thrust into a rather chaotic situation.

During Bibb's administration of the finances, prosperity returned to the country, and a larger revenue flowed into the Treasury as the economy boomed. There was no longer a deficit, but a surplus, which Bibb recommended should be kept for a sinking fund to pay the debt that had been accumulating since 1837.

No longer did the Secretary of the Treasury need recommend the tapping of new sources for taxation. The supply of new public funds was plentiful, and the wheels of the government rolled easily along.

Yet, according to Bolles, there was a marked difference between Bibb's views and those of the House Committee on Ways and Means with respect to paying off the public debt. Bibb favored a slower liquidation and recommended the issue of new stock for a portion of it, payable in ten or fifteen years, and a reduction of taxes; on the other hand, the committee strongly urged a more rapid repayment of the debt, and the maintenance of the current revenue laws. The committee views prevailed.

The new tariff enacted in 1841 did not produce the expected revenue to the government because for up to two years afterward the economy was in a recession and importations were light. The nation had suffered reversal and had not recovered from liquidating the heavy trade deficit, an accumulation of several years of buying in excess of the products of other nations. Many argued that government expenditures should have been reduced since it was peacetime and bad times had reduced revenues. Thus, the budget could have been balanced in 1844. Instead, the Ways and Means Committee complained that due to fiscal policies of the Tyler administration, which had assumed power on March 4, 1841, the debt by December 1843 had "swelled" to the "startling amount of more than twenty-five million." The committee complained that Tyler and the Secretary of the Treasury had permitted deficiencies in revenue to have accumulated to more than nineteen million within three years.

However, as noted above, this situation soon changed. By the time Bibb made his only report to Congress, at the close of 1844, the nation had fully recovered from its downturn, incomes had risen, bank credit expanded, and the level of imports had increased. Customs duties revenue flowed into the Treasury in an amount sufficient to cover current appropriations and leave a budget surplus. Thus, Bibb may have presided over the first instance of what today's economists would call "built-in, automatic fiscal stabilizers." Taxes automatically fall off in a recession, while government spending is constant or increasing. This, in turn, results in deficits and government borrowing, which provide a demand-side stimulus to the economy and help promote recovery.

Bibb was born on October 30, 1776, in Prince Edward County, Virginia; he was the son of Richard and Lucy Booker Bibb. He had seventeen children, from two marriages. He graduated from Hampden-Sidney and William and Mary College in 1792. There are some reports that he attended Princeton College.

He studied law under Richard Venable and was admitted to the bar in 1798. His legal practice was initially in Virginia. At an early age, he moved to Lexington, Kentucky. Bibb was appointed to the bench of the court of appeals in 1808, the highest court in the state, and in 1809 he was elevated to rank of Chief Justice. He resigned in 1810. Later he represented his state in the United States Senate, elected as a "War Hawk" in 1811. At home, he retained substantial political influence as a Southern Democrat who was opposed to the tariff and abolition. Bibb played a large role in advancing the war against Great Britain and in loyally upholding President James Madison in carrying it out. He resigned his Senate seat in 1814 and moved to Frankfort, Kentucky, to resume his legal practice. In 1817 he was elected to the lower house of the Kentucky legislature and was appointed Chief Justice of the court of appeals again in 1828 but resigned the same year to return to the U.S. Senate, where he served a full six-year term.

Bibb was an early follower of President Andrew Jackson, but he parted company over the bank question. From 1835 to 1844, he served as Chancellor of the Louisville Court of Chancery, holding this post until his appointment as Secretary.

Bibb went out of office on March 4, 1845. He remained in Washington and Georgetown for the remainder of his life, practicing law in the district courts and serving as Chief Clerk in the Attorney General's office. He was described in the end as a typical "gentleman of the old school," ever refusing to "abandon knee-breeches in favor of pantaloons."

Bibb died in Georgetown, District of Columbia, on April 14, 1859; he was buried in the State Cemetery, Frankfort, Kentucky.

BIBLIOGRAPHY

Bolles, Albert S. *The Financial History of the United States from 1789 to 1860.* 4th ed. 3 vols. New York: D. Appleton and Company, 1894; reprint of Vol. 2: New York: Augustus M. Kelley Publishers, 1969.

Chitwood, Oliver Perry. *John Tyler: Champion of the Old South.* New York: Russell & Russell, 1964.

Johnson, Allen, ed. *Dictionary of American Biography.* Vol. 2. New York: Charles Scribner's Sons, 1929.

Lambert, Oscar Doane. *Presidential Politics in the United States, 1841–1844.* Durham, NC: Duke University Press, 1936.

Morgan, Robert J. *A Whig Embattled: The Presidency under John Tyler.* Lincoln: University of Nebraska Press, 1954.

Peterson, Norma Lois. *The Presidencies of William Henry Harrison and John Tyler.* Lawrence: University Press of Kansas, 1989.

Sobel, Robert, ed. *Biographical Directory of the United States Executive Branch, 1774–1977.* Westport, CT: Greenwood Press, 1977.

C. DANIEL VENCILL

W. MICHAEL BLUMENTHAL (January 3, 1926–   ). W. Michael Blumenthal was sworn in as the sixty-fourth Secretary of the Treasury on January 23,

1977. He received President-elect Jimmy Carter's nomination while serving as Chairman and chief executive officer of the Bendix Corporation. Blumenthal served as Treasury Secretary until August 6, 1979.

Werner Michael Blumenthal was born on January 3, 1926, to parents Ewald and Rose Valerie (Markt) Blumenthal in Oranienburg, Germany, a suburb of Berlin. The Blumenthals owned and operated a women's clothing store in Berlin. Being of Jewish ancestry, the Blumenthals were subjected to persecution once the Nazis came to power. In 1938 the family business was seized. Ewald Blumenthal was sent to Buchenwald concentration camp. By selling the remaining family possessions, Rose was able to raise enough money to purchase the release of her husband, with enough left over for passports and passage to Shanghai.

The Blumenthals arrived in Shanghai in 1939 and remained there for the duration of World War II. For a time, they resided at 59 Chusan Road in two rooms located in a three-story house. Later the family was forced to live in a Japanese internment camp. Michael had to work hard at odd jobs in order to obtain food for his father, mother, and sister Stephanie. He has since commented about his life in Shanghai, emphasizing that food was very hard to come by in those days. He further recalls one job he worked where he was entrusted to deliver large sausages door to door in Shanghai. The job was particularly challenging, given his constant hunger and the persistent aroma of the sausages. Michael was able to learn the English language during the brief time he attended a private British school. In the streets, he learned to speak some Chinese, Japanese, French, and Portuguese. During this time, his parents divorced, adding even more misery to an already harsh life.

When the U.S. Seventh Fleet arrived in Shanghai in 1945, Michael Blumenthal rented a boat and traveled to the port where the ships were docked. Looking to earn some money and eventually find a way out of China, he quickly capitalized on his linguistic skills. He was hired by the Americans and eventually became a warehouse supervisor for the U.S. Air Transport Command in Shanghai. Blumenthal was finally able to act on his desire to leave China in 1947. He and his sister immigrated to the United States. They arrived in San Francisco with $60 between them.

Blumenthal quickly found a full-time job as a billing clerk with the National Biscuit Company in San Francisco. After only a few weeks, he decided to pursue a college education. After one year at San Francisco Junior College, he transferred to the University of California at Berkeley. At Berkeley, Blumenthal supported himself by working part-time and summer jobs where, among other things, he worked as a busboy, dishwasher, postal worker, truck driver, and worker at a wax factory. In spite of this environment of hard work and long hours, Blumenthal excelled in his coursework. He was elected to Phi Beta Kappa and finished his B.S. degree in international economics at Berkeley in 1951. In that same year, he married Margaret Eileen Polley, whom he had met while attending Berkeley. In 1952 Michael Blumenthal became a naturalized U.S. citizen.

Next, Blumenthal and his wife traveled to New Jersey after he was offered a scholarship in the Woodrow Wilson School of Public and International Affairs at Princeton University. Helping to make ends meet, his wife worked as a teacher. In 1953 Blumenthal completed an M.A. degree in economics and an M.P.A. degree in public affairs. During the next two years he was a fellow of the Social Science Research Council. In 1956 he was awarded a Ph.D. degree in economics from Princeton University. From 1954 to 1957 he did research and taught economics at Princeton. Blumenthal was also a labor arbitrator for the state of New Jersey from 1955 to 1957.

In 1957 Blumenthal accepted an offer to become a board member and Vice President of Crown Cork International Corporation of Jersey City. He had met the President of Crown Cork while playing chess on board a ship when coming home from a visit to England. Needing a greater challenge than cork manufacturing could offer, in 1961 Blumenthal accepted George W. Ball's invitation to become Deputy Assistant Secretary of State for Economic Affairs in the Kennedy administration. His name had been suggested to Undersecretary of State Ball by Ralph A. Dungan, an aide to President Kennedy and former classmate of Blumenthal's at Princeton.

At the State Department's economic bureau, Blumenthal proved himself more than capable in his day-to-day duties. During the next few years, he served with distinction in delegations to various international trade conferences. In 1963 Blumenthal achieved ambassadorial rank when President Lyndon Johnson made him his Deputy Special Representative for trade negotiations. In this position, Blumenthal became Delegation Chairman and Chief U.S. Negotiator to the Kennedy Round of talks on the General Agreement on Tariffs and Trade (GATT) in Geneva from 1963 to 1967. After the talks ended in 1967, Blumenthal left government service. There has been much speculation as to why he left when he did. Some speculation centers around Blumenthal feeling that his accomplishments were not being adequately rewarded in the form of a top diplomatic post, and other speculation focuses on Blumenthal wanting to disassociate himself from the Johnson administration, which was stepping up involvement in Vietnam at the time.

Back in the private sector, it did not take long for Blumenthal to land another position, this time with many more challenges. In June 1967 he was named board member and President of Bendix International located in New York City. Three years later he was promoted to Vice Chairman of the parent Bendix Corporation in Southfield, Michigan. In February 1971 he succeeded A. P. Fontaine as the Chairman and chief executive officer of Bendix Corporation. In the early 1970s Bendix was a huge international conglomerate with automotive, aerospace, electronics, forest products, building materials, machine tools, and mobile home production lines.

Upon assuming the chairmanship, Blumenthal set about correcting what he felt was a loosely managed organization. He undertook modernization in profitable product lines and eliminated unprofitable ones. Building further upon the strengths of a diversified corporation, Blumenthal took steps to make Bendix even more recession-proof. Internal and external reforms brought about more positive worker attitudes and an end to questionable business deals such as arms deals to the Middle East. In short, he was willing to take unpopular stands in order to bring about the success Bendix was capable of. The results were terrific. During Blumenthal's reign, Bendix sales doubled to almost $3 billion. In 1974 Blumenthal received the Management Man of the Year Award. At the end of 1975, *Dun's Review* listed Bendix as one of the nation's five best-managed corporations.

Having made a big splash in the business world and the Democratic Party not having forgotten about his previous service in the Kennedy and Johnson administrations, Blumenthal was invited by President-elect Carter in late 1976 along with some fifteen other economists and businessmen to Plains, Georgia, for a briefing on the current state of the U.S. economy. This meeting was basically a screening with the incoming administration for those being considered for high-level appointments in Washington.

On December 14, 1976, Jimmy Carter nominated W. Michael Blumenthal as Secretary of the Treasury. Blumenthal accepted the nomination and stepped down from Bendix shortly thereafter. Many believe that Carter's choice was mainly influenced by Blumenthal's balanced experience in business and government. It was also felt by Carter during the late 1976 briefing in Plains that he and Blumenthal saw eye-to-eye on most economic matters.

The credentials Blumenthal brought to the Treasury Department secured approval from all sectors of society: business, labor, academia, and Washington. His nomination was unanimously confirmed by the Senate on January 20, 1977. During his first few months in office, Blumenthal established himself as the nation's chief economic policy official. By March 1977 he had become the sole Chairman of the Cabinet-level Economic Policy Group (EPG) (Charles L. Schultze, previously the cochair of the EPG, retained chairmanship of the President's Council of Economic Advisers). Under the auspices of the Economic Policy Group, Blumenthal attacked urban problems, outlined a comprehensive code of business ethics, and explored policy options for fighting stagflation. In May 1977 he served as President Carter's chief adviser at the London economic summit.

As the pressures and responsibilities of Blumenthal's position grew, so did the toll that was being taken out on the Blumenthal family. In June 1977 the Blumenthals announced their separation. Up to that time, the marriage had lasted over twenty-five years and had produced three daughters.

By August 1977, Blumenthal was undertaking jawboning efforts aimed at depreciating the dollar in hopes that the trade deficit would improve. The logic behind these efforts was that imports would fall and exports would rise since a depressed dollar means that more dollars are required in exchange for a given amount of foreign currency (imported goods become more expensive in the United States). At the same time, fewer units of a foreign currency are required in exchange for a given dollar amount (exported goods become less expensive to foreign buyers). During this period, Blumenthal's jawboning was successful in depreciating the dollar, but desired trade effects were not to be had. Many U.S. businessmen, believing that consumers were not curbing their purchases of imported goods, openly criticized Blumenthal's dollar policy. They believed it was serving only to create more inflation in the United States.

Initially, Blumenthal was described by the press as a Keynesian in orientation toward economic policy. After receiving criticism for the declining dollar, it appeared to many that Blumenthal was becoming more concerned with the sole problem of inflation and less sensitive to the Carter administration's recession-averse tendencies. This perceived reorientation and lack of success in fighting inflation eventually resulted in rumors of Blumenthal not being a team player in the administration.

More sources of strife between Blumenthal and the administration were to emerge in the coming months. G. William Miller, Arthur Burns's replacement at the Federal Reserve since 1978, was committed to the belief that inflation and unemployment could be attacked simultaneously. This and Miller's lack of economics training and government experience may have led to frustration in trying to coordinate Fed monetary policy and Treasury inflation-fighting efforts at that time. Also, by April 1978, Carter had installed Robert Strauss on the Economic Policy Group with the intention of having him take over the stalled drive toward reducing inflation. This move particularly enraged Blumenthal, who already viewed many members of the White House staff as being inexperienced and lacking direction. Fighting inflation and trying to keep the economy out of recession may have simply been an overambitious agenda, given the economic situation and the administrative framework in which Blumenthal was trying to work.

One definite success during the Carter administration in which Blumenthal played an important role was the full diplomatic recognition of the Communist government of the People's Republic of China. This recognition took effect on January 1, 1979. Weeks before, the Chinese government invited Blumenthal to visit China in order to discuss improving ties to the United States. Blumenthal's experience in Shanghai as a youth and in trade policy were probably important factors in China's decision to invite him instead of a State Department official. In early March 1979 Blumenthal went to China and was present at the opening of the U.S. Embassy. His trip was a great success. The Chinese were particularly impressed by his speech during the opening banquet in Peking's Great Hall of the People. Blumenthal began and ended the speech in Chinese.

After returning from China, Blumenthal continued to fight a losing battle with inflation. Dissension was growing in the ranks of the White House staff, and battle lines were becoming more defined. Blumenthal, along with some Federal Reserve officials and a few White House aides, advocated stronger measures to fight inflation. Fed Chairman Miller and many members of the Carter administration were reluctant to risk stronger anti-inflation measures at the expense of sending the economy into recession. In mid-July 1979, after much soul-searching, President Carter decided to make major personnel changes in his Cabinet. Michael Blumenthal and three other Cabinet members were fired. G. William Miller resigned as Chairman of the Federal Reserve and was tapped by Carter to be the next Secretary of the Treasury.

Blumenthal went back to the private sector where he had enjoyed so much of his success before. In October 1979 he was elected as a board member of Burroughs Corporation, a large computer concern located in Detroit, Michigan. By 1981 he was Burroughs's Chairman of the Board and chief executive officer (CEO). Under Blumenthal's leadership, Burroughs merged with Sperry Corporation in 1986 to form the computer firm Unisys. The merger was deemed essential by Blumenthal in remaining competitive with the IBM Corporation. In April 1990 Blumenthal stepped down as CEO of Unisys and went to work as a limited partner at Lazard Freres & Company, an investment banking firm located in New York City. His limited role at Lazard Freres has allowed him time to teach economics again at Princeton University.

BIBLIOGRAPHY

Ajemian, Robert. "The Decline of Mike Blumenthal." *Time*, April 24, 1978, 68.

Current Biography. New York: H. W. Wilson, 1977.

"A Face-off on Dollar Strategy." *Businessweek*, August 8, 1977, 20–21.

Flint, Jerry. "Master of the Game." *Forbes*, May 28, 1990, 200–206.

Katz, Bernard S., ed. *Biographical Dictionary of the Board of Governors of the Federal Reserve System*. Westport, CT: Greenwood Press, 1992.

Nickel, H. "Candid Reflections of a Businessman in Washington." *Fortune*, January 29, 1979, 36–40f.

"A 'Tough Street Kid' Steps in at Burroughs." *Businessweek*, October 29, 1979, 50–51.

Who's Who in America. Chicago: A. N. Marquis, 1994.

STEVEN T. PETTY

GEORGE S. BOUTWELL (January 28, 1818–February 27, 1905). George Sewall Boutwell served as Secretary of the Treasury from March 12, 1869, until March 16, 1873, during the presidency of Ulysses S. Grant. In order to understand the role Boutwell played as Secretary, as well as the other three Secretaries of the Treasury under Grant—William Richardson, Benjamin Bristow, and Lot Morrill—one must understand the temper of the times and, most important, the character of President Grant himself.

Much can be said about Grant's presidency, most of it bad. Grant was elected President of the United States in 1869 because he had led the Union to victory during the Civil War. He was seen as the national savior, and he accepted the presidency as a reward for that service. General Ulysses S. Grant may have possessed the military genius to lead an army to victory, but military genius alone does not qualify one to be President. Yet Grant thought of the presidency not as a responsibility but as a prize. It was said of Grant that after eight years as President he hardly knew any more about running the country than before he was awarded the highest office in the land.

Grant's incompetency over his eight-year presidency was compounded by the complexity of the times. The country was in turmoil coming out of the blood bath called the Civil War. The country and its leaders were divided as to how to come together, North and South again. The problems encountered in the aftermath of the war and the Reconstruction era, and how these were resolved, come to us today in arenas like the continuing struggle for civil rights and our concepts of equality under the law. Another pressing problem then, as now, was how to deal with the economic and monetary policies that affect the prosperity and well-being of the country and its citizens.

Yet in spite of the Civil War debt problems, the country was in the midst of an unparalleled business expansion when Grant took office. The country's population was growing, spurred on by thousands of new immigrants. All over America transportation systems were being built and expanded, particularly the railroads. This in turn fueled industries like iron and steel. Even in the defeated South, there was money to be made in the cotton mills. Unfortunately, Grant's era has come to be known not for its prosperity and growth but for its private and public corruption and a notorious spoils system. It was a sad fact that public morality had fallen to an all-time low, and the President didn't understand or care.

According to Hesseltine, when Grant was inaugurated, he said, "This office has come to me unsought: I commence its duties untrammeled" (143). Grant's selection of his first Cabinet officers signaled his view that the presidency was his to do with as he wished. He did not consult Congress about his Cabinet choices, often picking friends or political cronies for Cabinet posts. For his Secretary of the Treasury he picked Alexander T. Stewart, one of the richest men of that time. Stewart, who owned the largest retail store in the world, was reported to be worth $40 million.

One reason Grant may have selected Stewart was Grant's awe of anyone who was so successful in business. Grant had been an unsuccessful businessman who could never adequately provide for his family. In 1861 when the war started, Grant was thirty-seven years old and reduced to living off his father by working in the family leather goods store. When the war intervened, Grant's fortunes changed. He went from failed businessman to military hero and then to President of the United States. It was said of him that as President he could walk with men of money now.

Congressional leaders were furious about not being consulted about Grant's Cabinet choices, but because of Grant's popularity with the people, they unanimously accepted his choice of Stewart and the others. But Stewart, a businessman with no record of public service, was not to serve, and Grant was to get his first lesson in dealing with Congress. Charles Sumner, a powerful Senator from Massachusetts, was informed of a little-known law of 1789 that prohibited any person engaged in trade or commerce from being Secretary of the Treasury. When Grant was informed of this, he tried to ease his way around the 1789 law by simply asking Congress to waive it. Congressional leaders decided this request would have to go into committee, showing their power by using a delaying tactic that would have delayed the naming of the Secretary of the Treasury, a crucial Cabinet post. Grant's friends and political advisers informed him that in the case of the Secretary of the Treasury, at least, it would be better to confer with Congress, and Grant finally agreed. Congressional leaders suggested Representative George S. Boutwell, a close colleague of the powerful Sumner. Boutwell had worked to help get Grant elected, and he was known as an advocate of conservative fiscal reform. Choosing Boutwell was a good compromise between the powerful Republican leadership and the President.

Yet as far as Grant was concerned, even though Stewart's appointment was blocked, Stewart and other wealthy friends were not forgotten. Throughout his presidency, and on fiscal and monetary policies, Grant would continue to be consistent, not on the policies but as to whom he would turn for advice. When there were decisions to be made, Stewart would have access to the President's ear. The question of whether such policies would help or hurt the farmer, the small tradesman, or the populace at large was often not even considered. Such were the times when George S. Boutwell took over the reins of the United States Treasury.

George Sewell Boutwell, an influential Republican politician, was born in Brookline, Massachusetts on January 28, 1818, the son of Sewell and Rebecca (Marshall) Boutwell. Boutwell, a Puritan, came from old Massachusetts stock. He grew up in Lunenburg, Massachusetts, where as a teenager he worked in a small store while attending school during the winter months. When he was seventeen he became a clerk in a store in Groton, Massachusetts. In Groton he began to study on his own in the hopes of becoming a lawyer. He began to write articles and speak on the political matters of the day. In 1841 he married Sarah Adelia Thayer. He became active in the Democratic Party, and in 1842 he was elected to the lower house of the state legislature where he served until 1850.

Boutwell was an ardent abolitionist and forged an alliance with others of like mind. In 1850 he became Governor of Massachusetts, where he served until 1852. After his term expired he went back to his study of the law, and in January 1862, he was admitted to the bar. In addition to his legal studies, Boutwell remained active in public affairs. In 1855 he was appointed Secretary to the State Board of Education, a post he held until 1861. He also continued writing. In 1859 he wrote *Thoughts on Educational Topics and Institutions*. He had been granted an honorary LL.D. from Harvard, and he served as a Harvard overseer from 1850 to 1860. In 1853 he was a member of the Massachusetts constitutional convention.

By 1855 Boutwell was active in national politics, and it was on the national scene that he would make his mark, working with his Massachusetts colleague Charles Sumner, who would go on to become a powerful congressional leader during the presidencies of Abe Lincoln, Andrew Johnson, and Grant. Because Boutwell so fervently believed in the antislavery movement, he, along with Sumner, was one of the first organizers of the Massachusetts Republican Party.

Throughout his political career, Boutwell would work hard on the party's behalf. He supported Abraham Lincoln for President in 1860, and in 1861, he was a member of the Peace Convention in Washington, which tried unsuccessfully to find a means to resolve the issue of slavery without resorting to war. Working alongside him was Lot M. Morrill, who would go on to become Grant's last Secretary of the Treasury in the waning days of Grant's administration.

In July 1862, President Lincoln appointed Boutwell the first Commissioner of the new Internal Revenue Bureau, a post he would hold for eight months. He was credited with efficiently organizing this newly formed branch of the government. In 1863, he published A Manual of the Direct and Excise Tax System of the United States.

In the election of 1862 the Massachusetts voters elected Boutwell to the U.S. House of Representatives. There he would serve during the Civil War and the difficult Reconstruction era that followed. As Congress and President Lincoln's successor Andrew Johnson worked through the complicated problems of bringing the country together again, Boutwell was an outspoken advocate for policies that would help the newly freed slaves.

Boutwell was an influencial member of the Joint Congressional Committee on Reconstruction. This committee had to resolve how to restore order in the Confederate States and ensure the rights of vanquished Southerners and at the same time ensure that the newly freed slaves were protected and given the rights of other citizens. There were warring factions on all sides of these issues, none more rancorous than the conflict between the Republican leaders of Congress and the Democratic President, Andrew Johnson. Boutwell helped frame the Fourteenth Amendment, which gave the freed slaves the right of citizenship. His firm belief that the former slaves should be entitled to the right to vote led him to advocate the Fifteenth, which passed in 1870.

Boutwell's support of Congress's plans for Reconstruction brought him into fanatical opposition to President Johnson, a former slaveowner who resisted Republican efforts to aid the newly freed slaves. Boutwell and the other Republican leaders would pass Reconstruction legislation, only to have Johnson veto it. Congress would override the veto and push to see the legislation enforced. Johnson would by inaction let the legislation languish. The power struggle finally resulted in Congress bringing about a resolution to impeach President Johnson. Boutwell was selected by his colleagues in the House to chair the committee that drew up the articles of impeachment. He also served as one of the House managers conducting the impeachment proceeding, which failed by one vote.

President Johnson may have been saved from impeachment by merely one vote, but the whole impeachment process had been a sorry affair. Both Johnson and Congress itself were looked upon with disdain by the citizens of the country. While all this was happening, Grant, the popular hero of the war, wisely stood above the political fray and seemingly took no sides in the proceedings. When he was elected President in 1869, it was no wonder that he felt that he could pick his Cabinet without input from a discredited Congress.

Boutwell's term as Secretary lasted a full four years. Unlike many others in the administration, he was able to forge and maintain a friendship with President Grant, and Grant in turn was willing to take his advice. One example of Grant's willingness to listen to Boutwell during turbulent times came when the ever-wavering Grant was deciding whether to support the passage of the 1871 Ku Klux Klan Act. Throughout the South the newly freed slaves were being terrorized, beaten, and murdered by Southerners in secret groups like the Ku Klux Klan. The Fourteenth Amendment was on the books but was not enforced, and the full weight of the federal government—its legislation, courts, and army—were needed to protect the black citizens of the South.

There was a lot of debate on whether the Ku Klux Klan Act should pass, and Grant was getting conflicting advice. Boutwell heard that Grant was on his way to the Capitol to speak against the act, and he rode to the Capitol with Grant in order to dissuade him. Grant was against this legislation because he did not want to commit federal troops to the South. When the pair arrived at the Capitol, Boutwell's advice was reinforced by the bill's congressional managers who gave Grant documented evidence of the atrocities committed against the blacks. Grant ultimately agreed to back the bill, and it passed. Armed with this strong new legislation, federal authorities finally were able to bring some protection to Southerners, both white and black, who were trying to bring about peace and justice in those troubled times.

This case is illustrative of Grant's willingness to listen to his friends (unfortunately, many were corrupt and greedy) and heartily agree with them, only to change his mind when talking to a friend of the opposite opinion. As Secretary of the Treasury and as a Cabinet member, Boutwell was often able to bring Grant around to his own point of view. However, in one crucial matter, Black Friday, Boutwell's advice came almost too late.

In his personal life, Grant never learned how to manage his money, and Grant as President did not know how to make monetary policy. During the Civil War, Grant had seen the shortage of money hurt small businessmen and farmers. Yet by his inauguration he was more conservative in his views on government indebtedness. Rather than expand the money supply, he agreed with Boutwell, a fiscal conservative, who was working to reduce the national debt. The cost of running the Civil War had caused Lincoln to expand the money supply by issuing greenbacks, paper money not backed by gold. Gold was to be used for foreign commerce. After the war, President Johnson's Secretary of the Treasury began to retrench the money supply so that it could once again be backed by gold. When he took over at the Treasury, Boutwell continued this practice. The greenbacks were to be turned in at a discount and exchanged for currency, called specie, which would be backed by gold. This policy hurt some—farmers who wanted to sell crops overseas and the rural poor—and helped others, especially the bankers and businessmen who valued a stable currency.

The monetary supply and the gold supply that backed it also interested another group of people, the speculators who hoped to make their riches by buying and trading gold. Many of these were privy to insider information and prior notice of government intent, which meant that these speculators could get even richer, beating others at the money game. All this speculation came to a head on what has been come to be known as Black Friday, September 24, 1869.

As usual the people with the money had General Grant's attention. The wealthy and infamous speculator Jay Gould and his partner, James Fisk, soon eased their way into a friendship with Grant, entertaining him, his family, and his cronies in the best of style. Gould was known to bribe judges and politicians, defraud competitors, and concoct elaborate schemes to make even more money. None of this stopped Grant from enjoying Gould's hospitality and giving him insider information. For while Gould lavishly entertained Grant, he and the others would talk to Grant about the government's monetary policy. They were careful to be sure that Boutwell, to whom Grant had given a free hand in dealing with fiscal matters, was not privy to these conversations. Over several months' time, Gould and his friends questioned Grant about the money supply and the gold that backed it.

Gould and his friends were gambling that the government would hold on to its gold, and they were trying to corner the gold outside government hands. By way of ensuring this "investment," they bought gold for insiders in the Grant administration, including Grant's sister and her husband James Corbin and even, the rumors said, Grant's wife Julia (McFeely, 329).

So there was Gould and many others like him, speculators buying up the gold supply. Boutwell and the people he listened to felt it was best to contract the money supply and return more to a gold standard, thereby keeping more gold in the government supply. Grant, as usual, was wavering. He led the speculators, when he was talking to them, to believe that they had convinced him; the government would not sell gold.

The price of gold began rising. In March 1869, gold went from $130 an ounce to $145 an ounce on Thursday, September 23. By then, Grant was back in Washington and conferring with Secretary Boutwell about the monetary situation. Boutwell advised Grant that gold selling at $145 an ounce would encourage sales of wheat abroad, thereby helping ensure a stable market for the wheat farmer, and that any gold price higher would just encourage more speculation. Boutwell and Grant agreed that if on Friday the price of gold went up, the government would sell gold.

By Friday, people who traded in gold were in a state of panic. Gould and his cronies were trying to corner the gold market, and people were trying to buy gold on credit. Investors and bankers saw the government doing nothing to stop this frenzy of buying, and the price of gold continued to rise.

When the news broke that the government was finally stepping in to sell gold, pandemonium ensued. Those who were trying frantically to buy more gold a second before now rushed just as frantically to sell it, and the price quickly fell to $135 an ounce. People who had borrowed money to buy gold and the bankers who had lent them the money to buy that gold lost thousands of dollars. The frantic money grubbing and the panic that Black Friday produced had shaken to the core the gold-buying community and the financial world that supplied credit for it. All this chaos undermined the nation's economic stability. Scores of Wall Street speculators were ruined, and hundreds of people lost vast sums of money.

There is no doubt about Grant's lack of discretion and culpability in this sorry affair. An unpleasant investigation by Congress followed. Boutwell's role in this is not as clear. There is no doubt that Gould and his associates believed that they could corner the gold market; there is also no doubt that many people realized what they were up to. In fact, on September 13, the *New York Tribune* published an editorial stating that certain people were conspiring to purchase and take out of circulation $30 million in gold. Boutwell knew of this, and he was warned by editors, financiers, bankers, and friends to step in and stop the conspiracy. Yet for ten days Boutwell did nothing—until panic set in and the country's business came to an almost complete stop. Boutwell's inaction may have been due to inexperience. He was a politician first and foremost and a student of economics and finance second. He was close to the business community, and his overriding goal as Secretary was to reduce the national debt. Toward this goal, he collected taxes from citizens with little regard for the equity of the tax system. He pared national expenses to the last penny, no matter how contractionary this was to the economy. Some areas of the country were affected more than others in this constriction of the national currency. The South needed an expansionary monetary policy to rebuild after the war, and out in the West wheat farmers needed to sell their wheat abroad because they had crops but little money. By constricting the money supply, Boutwell was making money more expensive and putting it into the hands of fewer people.

Except for his attention to reducing the national debt and contracting the money supply, Boutwell seemed uninterested in other financial matters of the day—tax structure, tariff reform, and currency reform. Even the widely acknowledged fact that there were greedy people conspiring to corner the gold market did not capture his immediate attention. Boutwell continued to press for reduction of the national debt.

Hamilton Fish, Grant's Secretary of State, described Boutwell as hard working and honest but secretive, ambitious, narrow, and two-faced. Yet given the people President Grant chose to surround himself with, especially in the Cabinet, Boutwell's secrecy concerning Treasury Department confidential business may have been well founded. One glaring example of individual propensity to profit from insider information was Boutwell's second in command, General Daniel Butterfield. Butterfield was appointed Assistant Secretary of the Treasury by Grant, at the behest of Gould and his cronies. Butterfield's qualification for the job seemed to be that whatever transpired at the Treasury would soon be relayed by him to Gould, who had given Butterfield a tidy account. So Butterfield, like many other public officials during the Grant years, had a financial stake in the very agency that he was supposed to be overseeing.

Boutwell was a stalwart and loyal Republican throughout his career, and the

Republican Party ruled the day. Boutwell had been appointed to the Treasury post because of that party loyalty. In 1873, when Grant started his second term, Boutwell was offered a new post by the Republican leadership. When Senator Henry Wilson from Massachusetts became the Vice President under Grant, Boutwell resigned as Secretary in order to fill his seat in the Senate.

One year later, Boutwell's friend and successor at the Treasury Department, William A. Richardson, would be forced to resign because of what was called the Sanborn Contract Scandal. Because of the public furor over this and other scandals, Grant was forced to name a reformer, Benjamin Helm Bristow, to the Treasury post. When he started his investigations, Bristow uncovered scandals and official misdeeds dating back to the presidency of Abraham Lincoln. William A. Richardson was implicated in one scandal, and while rumors existed about Boutwell's involvement, nothing was formally charged or proved. Boutwell probably owed his Senate seat to the influence of those involved in the Sanborn Contract Scandal. Boutwell was evidently personally honest, yet there is no doubt that corruption and criminal activity permeated the Treasury Department during his watch. Boutwell apparently made no effort to investigate or stop this criminal activity, and during his reign at the Treasury, more people in official circles became involved. Boutwell himself may have not been corrupt, but he allowed corrupt people to profit at the expense of the national Treasury. Unlike Benjamin Bristow, his replacement at the Treasury, Boutwell did not seem interested in civil service reform and worked quietly within the pervasive spoils system.

Boutwell served in the Senate for four years but was defeated in the election of 1877. By then, Grant was out, and Rutherford B. Hayes was President. Although Boutwell would no longer serve as an elected official, he was immediately put to work by the Republican President as a Commissioner responsible for codifying and editing the statutes of the United States. When he completed his work as Commissioner in 1878, he was then appointed as Counsel for the U.S. government before the French and American Claims Commission in 1880. He also resumed his legal practice, where he handled many cases of international law. In 1884 he turned down an appointment as Secretary of the Treasury during the administration of Chester Arthur. But he did agree to serve as U.S. Council to Haiti in 1885, to Hawaii in 1886, and to Chile in 1893 and 1894.

In the final years of his life, Boutwell, the lifelong Republican, resigned from the party because he disagreed with the party's policies toward the Philippines. Because of his opposition, he helped found the Anti-Imperialist League in 1895 and would serve as its President until his death in 1905. He also remained busy writing, and his *The Crisis of the Republic* was published in 1900. Two years later, in 1902, his memoirs, *Reminiscences of Sixty Years in Public Affairs*, were published. On February 27, 1905, George Boutwell died in Groton, Massachusetts.

BIBLIOGRAPHY

Boutwell, George Sewall. *Thoughts on Educational Topics and Institutions*. Boston: Phillips Sampson Co., 1859.

———. *A Manual of the Direct and Excise Tax System of the United States*. Boston: Little, Brown, 1863.

———. *The Crisis of the Republic*. Boston: D. Estes, 1900.

———. *Reminiscences of Sixty Years in Public Affairs*. New York: McClure, Philips and Co., 1902.

Hesseltine, William B. *Ulysses S. Grant, Politician*. New York: Frederick Ungar, 1935; reprinted in 1957 by Dodd, Mead and Co.

McFeely, William S. *Grant, a Biography*. New York: W. W. Norton and Co., 1981.

Nevins, Allan. *Hamilton Fish: The Inner History of the Grant Administration*. New York: Dodd, Mead, and Co., 1936.

Oberholtzer, Ellis P. *Jay Cooke, Financier of the Civil War*. 2 vols. Philadelphia: G. W. Jacobs and Co., 1907.

Vexler, Robert I. *The Vice-Presidents and Cabinet Members*. New York: Oceana Publications, 1975.

Woodward, W. E. *Meet General Grant*. New York: Horace Liveright, Inc., 1928.

JULIANNE CICARELLI

NICHOLAS F. BRADY (April 11, 1930–). Nicholas Frederick Brady was born in New York City on April 11, 1930, to James C. Brady and Eliot (Chace) Brady. Nick Brady's great-grandfather, Anthony Brady, left the Irish potato famine in the midnineteenth century. In New York, he accumulated a $100 million fortune by starting several electric companies in partnerships with Thomas Alva Edison. Nicholas's grandfather, James Cox Brady, founded the Maxwell Motor Company, which later merged with Chrysler Corporation. His father founded the Purolator Courier Corporation. The family holdings today are managed by Nicholas's younger brother, James, a former commercial banker.

Nick Brady, Secretary of the Treasury under both Presidents Reagan and Bush over the period September 15, 1988 to January 19, 1993, was raised in luxurious surroundings on the family estate in Far Hills, New Jersey. His father's business partners included the du Ponts and Rockefellers. Brady attended the exclusive St. Marks School in Massachusetts and went on to Yale, where he earned a Bachelor of Arts in 1952. Fellow students remember him as a quiet, attractive-looking, serious student. At Yale he was a superb squash player and captain of the team. That year, Brady married Katherine Douglas, and together they had four children.

Two years after graduation, he earned a master's degree in business administration from Harvard Business School. After graduating, Brady joined Dillon, Read & Company; Clarence Dillon's residence was next to the Brady family estate. Dillon, Read was an old, elite financial advisory firm, and by 1961, Brady was a Vice President, an expert on complex mergers. He managed a restructuring program for General Mills, his first major account. He helped them acquire forty-five companies in eight years, earning him a solid reputation. Later, he managed acquisitions for several large companies, including Purolator. By 1965, he was in charge of hiring at Dillon, and by 1970 was in charge of the newly created municipal and corporate bond trading desk.

Not content to watch the firm's heritage dissipate in the new investment banking climate, Brady initiated changes in the company's strategy from the soft-sell techniques and narrow product lines to an aggressive and expansive outlook. In 1971, he became President and chief executive officer of the firm. Over the next decade, Brady emphasized quality over quantity. He retained the investment-grade quality of the client base as he adroitly snatched business from competitors. He collected Chevron Corporation as a client and advised the activities of Volkswagen, Southland Royalty, and R. J. Reynolds.

Nick Brady served as Secretary of the Treasury from January 20, 1989 to January 19, 1993. As a person he is a lot like his friend George Bush: friendly, unassuming, cautious, and methodical. He plays golf and tennis and for years served as the Chairman of the Jockey Club, the body that oversees horseracing in the state of New York. Brady is not known for intensity or flair. His head-down approach in the Bush administration did not win many accolades, and Brady's public personality clearly pales in comparison to his two predecessors, James A. Baker and Donald Regan. It was expected that his tenure as Secretary of the Treasury would be able but not innovative. As one colleague has said, "People sort of underestimate him because he comes on as such a good guy. . . . He was the best deal guy of his generation because, one, you could trust him; and two, he doesn't shoot his mouth off."

Brady's managerial style is that of a delegator. At Dillon, he was comfortable making broad policy decisions but hated to manage. He delegated considerable authority and continued that tradition at the Treasury. Brady, like Bush, was considered very nonconfrontational in relations. He dislikes collective decision-making and is impatient when sitting at meetings listening to diverse viewpoints. At the Treasury, Brady was not widely regarded as an articulate spokesman for economic policy. He was passive and reactive and reinforced Bush's image as the patrician and the administration as one of caretakers. The economic problems inherited by Brady (S&Ls, international debt, American productivity) were bandaged clumsily. In the run-up to the election, Brady was so weak politically that Secretary of State Baker was anointed the Economics Czar.

Brady has no discernible economic philosophy. Politically, with neither the dynamism of Jim Baker nor the fortitude of Don Regan, he shrunk the Secretary's role considerably. Brady was consistently at odds with the Fed. He was a plain-vanilla demand-side manager with a chronic yearn for interest rate policy changes to stimulate growth. Brady thought the monetarist inflation-fighting mission of the Fed was counterproductive. Of course, this is true only from the political standpoint of Bush's reelection chances in the wake of a double-dipping recession. The *Economist* newspaper considered him weak, an embarrassment. Brady embraced the notion that low inflation must be bought at the expense of economic growth—residual Keynesianism abandoned by all other financial ministries in the world. They dubbed Brady the invisible man of international finance, partly because he could not disguise the office's lack of clout like the skilled James A. Baker III. The office, under Brady, was "curiously insubstantial."

Brady became politically active in 1969 and again in 1977 when he served as Finance Chairman for New Jersey's unsuccessful Republican gubernatorial candidate. In 1980 he worked on George Bush's presidential campaign and in 1981 served on newly elected New Jersey Governor Thomas H. Kean's transition team. In 1982, Kean appointed Brady U.S. Senator to serve the final eight months of the term of a Democrat convicted for bribery in the Abscam scandal. By agreement, Brady could not run for election. As a Senator, he supported the balanced-budget amendment and voted with President Reagan 82 percent of the time on major bills.

Brady served on seven presidential commissions in the 1980s. The most notable was the Brady Commission, formed to investigate the stock market crash of 1987 and offer solutions. Though many of the reforms were sensible, the overall conclusion was misguided and the policy implications were anathema to the Reagan administration. The Brady Commission report had unfairly singled out computerized program trading as the instigator. Several prominent financial economists found this analysis wanting and pointed out, for example, that twenty-three other exchanges collapsed, too, most of them without program trading. They further pointed out that trading halts (via circuit breakers) do not mitigate price declines but exacerbate them. In the absence of a discernible event to explain the alleged bursting of a bubble, the innovative techniques of the Chicago exchanges were mistakenly singled out for deep regulatory review. Brady himself backtracked slightly on the conclusion of the report during his confirmation hearings. He was "not sure that we were 100 percent right." The report's lukewarm response from the Reagan and then Bush administrations was an indication that such an onerous regulatory change was an idea whose time had gone. And with Fed chairman Greenspan against it, it fizzled.

Brady carried with him to the Treasury an abiding interest in the stakes of New York financial institutions. The Brady Commission report recommendations were consistent with the historical rivalry of the New York and Chicago exchanges. The arthritic New York exchanges have been guilty of using political leverage to hamstring the creative Chicago exchanges. Brady also worked as a lobbyist for a short time in the mid-1980s. He was hired by Unocal, along with Howard Baker, to lobby against T. Boone Pickens. The entrenched Unocal management was a target of a junk bond–financed "hostile raid" by Pickens's Mesa Petroleum. Brady's interest here was simply to thwart the market for corporate control that had been made possible by the West Coast office of upstart firm Drexel Burnham Lambert. Brady liked mergers when big companies took small companies—but not when small companies took big companies. Brady also extended as long as possible the fiction that the Third World debt held by New York banks was par value, when the true market values reflected enormous write-downs.

Nick Brady is a country club, corporate Republican who has little in common with emergent Republicanism. He is an ideological soul mate of Bush, more so than Baker. Like his two predecessors, Brady passed over supply-siders for the deputy spots in Treasury. And Brady met with House Republicans only when he wanted something from them. Tension was so high in 1990 that Newt Gingrich, then Minority Whip (by 1995, Speaker), banned Treasury Department lobbyists from his office. The 1990 budget deal was really a final blow for Bradyism, since it alienated the House Republicans and the libertarian and populist swing voters that had strongly supported Reagan.

Upon entering the Treasury, Brady formed a study group to look at the administration's most perplexing issues. Foremost was the savings and loan crisis, the massive failure of hundreds of savings institutions whose problems had been brewing out of public sight for years. Brady had the misfortune to inherit one of the most difficult problems created by government since the Great Depression. While Brady offered tepid support for broad-based bank reform, the bailout bill that finally emerged was a typical creature of Washington. It was sufficient to disperse the costs widely enough, reward the politically favored (housing interests, for example), and punish the unfavored (junk bonds, for example). Though the legislation defined more meaningful capital standards and put some teeth into enforcement authority, in the end, nothing *fundamentally* changed: Deposit insurance went untouched, interstate banking restrictions were still largely in place, merger and takeover regulation was still rigid. Brady's favored methodology, continuing in the Baker tradition, was to exercise the implicit taxpayer guarantee. The bailout was ultimately financed by tax revenues, monies from asset recoveries, and special industry levies. It was remarked that the Savings and Loan crisis was silent and slow-motion, a mess about which there was no focused public opinion. There were no polls that told the Bush administration how to behave properly.

Many individuals in the administration and Congress blew gaskets over budget deficits while exhibiting indifference to the manipulation of credit subsidies. Fiscal responsibility on the balance sheet does not imply prudence in federal problem solving off the balance sheet. The Brady Treasury did not improve the "stealth" budget, but Brady can be credited with attempting to get better disclosure of the contingent liabilities of the government-sponsored enterprises (GSEs). In May 1990, Brady recommended legislation to limit the credit subsidy created by taxpayer loss exposure in GSEs. Each GSE would be required to obtain an independent credit rating without the presumption of federal credit support. This would have the effect of requiring the GSEs to hold more capital and would allow the nationally recognized (private sector) credit rating agencies to act as more vigorous guardians against credit deterioration. Credit subsidies accruing to each GSE were also to be disclosed in the annual budget of the President. The Brady Treasury deserves commendation for originating this plan, which counts as one of the few sober legislative responses to the thrift crisis.

When the story of the ongoing subordination of banks to public policy is told, the Third World debt problem will feature prominently. This policy theme played out in the Brady Debt plan, formerly the Baker Debt plan. Winding down the massive debt of the developing world was both a domestic banking problem and a foreign policy fiasco. In 1989, the debt had mounted to $1.3 trillion, with principal payments at $131 billion a year. Ronald Reagan's policy for the developing world was like any banker monitoring borrower behavior: Attach conditions to loans and then adjust the conditions if necessary as the loans deteriorate. And deteriorate they did. The Brady Treasury, through the World Bank and the International Monetary Fund, lent new money to replace that of the bank commercial loans that could not be serviced. With Western taxpayers on the hook, still punitive interest costs for the Third World, endless negotiations, and rioting in foreign capitals, the Brady plan was as big of a charade as anything a government has ever done. When it became obvious to banks that they were tools of public policy but did not have access to tax dollars, they built loss reserves. Over time, the balance of power shifted from debtors to creditors; banks like J. P. Morgan declared independence by setting aside reserves equal to 100 percent of their troubled loans.

Brady also failed to make headway on capital gains tax reduction, a key Republican mission. The Bush administration could rightly point a finger at the spoiler George Mitchell, Democratic Senate Majority Leader. But the true resistance formed inside the White House, since Bush, Brady, and Darman were morally intimidated by the fairness issue. Brady, suffering from inherited wealth, could sense the bitter sting of "giveaways to the rich" more than the rest. The conceptual issue was whether to offer tax relief in a recession. On this, there were two schools of thought, and neither was partisan. While the administration bickered over the possible effects of tax relief, it lost sight of the broad mandate inherited from the Reagan years for lowering taxes generally as a constraint on government. Then there was the practical issue of whether Republicans had the numbers in Congress to do what they wanted, anyway. What Brady chose to do was to feebly emphasize monetary policy and harangue bankers to lend (the path of least political resistance). Brady considered tax cuts fiscally irresponsible: There's no such thing as "growth-oriented" tax cuts under the circumstances of credit crunch. Whatever the merits of this line of thinking, Bush and Brady did not read the public mood on middle-class tax relief, and they most certainly misjudged the effects of breaking the "Read my lips, no new taxes" pledge. Brady was the adviser who put taxes on the table; it was not, as was widely reported, Dick Darman of the office of Management and Budget (OMB). The Bush administration gave up the trump card at the beginning, got nothing in return, and allowed the Congress to add insult to injury when the budget deal was actually voted down. Thus, George Bush wagered and lost his presidency on the thin reed of Brady economic policy.

The violation of the tax pledge was an amazing political blunder. The Brady Treasury also misstepped when it was late in forecasting the recession. Ambling around the world in the footsteps of James Baker, Brady was universally condemned for suggesting that all countries could coordinate the lowering of interest rates. The *Economist* found no logic in this strategy whatsoever, except as an attempt to hijack G-7 policy for demand management in the United States.

Brady's desperate goal at this time (May 1991) was to pull Bush out of recession to reinvigorate his reelection chances.

Bush, having purged all of the ideologues from the Reagan years in favor of his friends, was left with people with no ideas, including and especially Nick Brady. Bush's token supply-side was Jack Kemp of Housing and Urban Development (HUD), a man brimming with ideas who always argued in Cabinet meetings with Brady. Kemp made no secret of his desire to be Treasury Secretary and, in hindsight, should have filled that post. Brady combined the weakest elements of his predecessors: Baker had an absence of beliefs, Regan had weak political skills, and Brady had no beliefs and no political skills. He did not rise to the occasion. Failing to take charge of the office, it defeated him—and his boss.

BIBLIOGRAPHY

Bartley, Robert. "Black Monday Revisited." *Wall Street Journal*, October 19, 1988.

———. *The Seven Fat Years and How to Do It Again*. New York: Free Press, 1992.

Brookes, Stephen. "Another Plan to Mop Up the Mess." *Insight*, April 10, 1989.

"A Curiously Insubstantial Treasury." *Economist*, September 22, 1990.

Current Biography. New York: H. W. Wilson, 1988.

"The Diminished Fed." *Economist*, May 4, 1991.

England, Robert Stowe. "No Banking on Brady." *National Review*, March 19, 1990.

Ipsen, Eric. "A Kinder, Gentler Treasury Chief." *Institutional Investor*, March 1989.

Jarrell, Gregg A. "Brady Panel Sold Innovation Short." *Wall Street Journal*, October 19, 1988.

Kane, Edward. "The Changing Institutional Structure of Housing Finance." In *Housing Finance: A New Environment*. San Francisco: Federal Home Loan Bank of San Francisco, December 1990.

Mid-America Institute for Public Policy Research. *Black Monday and the Future of Financial Markets*. Homewood, IL: Dow Jones–Irwin, 1988.

Noonan, Peggy. *What I Saw at the Revolution*. New York: Ivy Books, 1990.

Quayle, Dan. *Standing Firm: A Vice Presidential Memoir*. New York: HarperCollins Publishers, 1994.

Yago, Glenn. *Junk Bonds*. Oxford: Oxford University Press, 1991.

JEFF SCOTT

BENJAMIN H. BRISTOW (June 20, 1832–June 22, 1896). In 1874, William A. Richardson, Grant's unpopular Secretary of the Treasury, was implicated in the Sanborn Contract Scandals that rocked the Treasury Department and was forced to resign. Grant had to appoint a new Secretary of the Treasury, and on June 4, 1874 Benjamin Helm Bristow of Kentucky became Secretary.

There were many reasons why Grant selected Bristow as Secretary of the Treasury, but uppermost was Bristow's reputation for honesty. Although Bristow was aware of the corruption and the greed permeating Grant's administration and other leading politicians of the day, he believed that reform was possible and undertook the Treasury post, intent on making the department an efficient and honorable arm of the government.

Bristow's integrity came from his upbringing and the teachings of his parents. He was born on June 20, 1832, in Elkton, Kentucky. His father, Francis Bristow, a lawyer and the son of a fundamentalist Baptist preacher, was strict but affectionate. His mother, Emily Edwards Helm, came from the prominent and aristocratic Helms family. Her aristocratic family background would give her first son an entry into the ranks of the gentry that controlled Kentucky politics. He would be brought up in the stately and elegant Edwards Hall, which had been passed on to the Bristows from his mother's family.

Benjamin's father was a leading Kentucky politician and one of the state's well-known lawyers. In his work as a politician and as a practicing lawyer, Benjamin's father practiced the religious values he had been taught by his Baptist preacher father. His mother imparted in him a sense of aristocratic "noblesse oblige" and a sense that his upbringing brought with it a responsibility as a future leader of the community. His father instilled in him a sense of humility and taught him that every individual was entitled to justice and equity under the law.

When Benjamin was eighteen he was sent off to Jefferson College in Pennsylvania. Because of his excellent private schooling and academic ability, he was admitted to the school as a senior and graduated in 1851 after only a year of study. He then went on to study law with his father, who had an excellent reputation for the training of young lawyers. Benjamin worked hard for three years and was admitted to the bar in 1854. That same year, he married Abigail S. Briscoe, whose family believed in the Southern traditions and the doctrine of state's rights. Her family was at first against the marriage, calling Benjamin Bristow "Yankee-Hearted." Benjamin somehow overcame the family objections, and after the marriage, he and his wife settled into the family home in Elkton.

In 1857 Benjamin accepted an offer of a law partnership in Hopsinsville, Kentucky, a county seat. In 1860 Benjamin visited Washington, D.C., with his father during the presidential elections. In a letter he sent back to his wife Abby, Benjamin said he had seen enough of political life to disgust him, and it made him even more aware of the comforts of Kentucky home life.

When the Civil War broke out, Benjamin Bristow examined his conscience and came down on the Union side. He helped recruit soldiers for the Union side and fought bravely beside them. He was badly wounded at Shiloh. He recovered and rejoined the fight, recruiting and helping command soldiers for the Twenty-fifth Kentucky Cavalry. He was commissioned a lieutenant colonel and by 1863 had been promoted to colonel.

After the war, he was elected to the Kentucky Senate, working to shore up support for the Union. He was instrumental in helping form the Republican Party in Kentucky: a party he would work for on both the state and national levels, often in spite of personal hardship. He worked on behalf of President Abraham Lincoln in the 1864 presidential campaign and supported the President's policy of emancipation of the slaves. Bristow's work in the Kentucky Senate gave him valuable political experience. His support of Lincoln and the newly formed Republican Party in Kentucky gave him national recognition. Despite his stated distaste of "politics," Bristow was becoming ambitious for future political advancement.

In 1866 he was appointed as U.S. Attorney for the Kentucky District, where he worked against Ku Klux Klan activities, helped ease racial difficulties, and helped investigate frauds against the Internal Revenue Service. In 1870 President Grant appointed him to the newly created post of Solicitor General in the U.S. Department of Justice.

Bristow worked hard for the reelection of President Grant in 1872, often going home to Kentucky to build alliances for the President and making speeches on behalf of Grant and the Republican Party. When the Attorney General was out of Washington, Bristow served as the Acting Attorney General and attended Cabinet meetings. His loyalty and work on behalf of the President led many, and Bristow himself, to feel he should have been rewarded by being named Attorney General or nominated for the Supreme Court. This did not happen, but Bristow was used to the unpredictability of Grant's political appointments.

With the reelection of Grant in 1872, Bristow resigned from his national duties and returned to private practice. Here his experience in Washington rewarded him: He was appointed a counsel to the Texas and Pacific Railroad. Although Bristow knew little about the railroad industry, he was not naive; he knew that his connections in Washington were valued, and he saw his new position as a way to earn enough to replenish the family fortune. Bristow would only be out of public life for two years, but he used his public connections to enable him to take advantage of offers that brought him large fees and a prosperous living.

When Grant finally did offer him a high administrative post, that of the Secretary of the Treasury in 1864, it was Bristow's prior service and his reputation for integrity that earned him the post. The Sanford Scandals, which had caused Secretary of the Treasury Richardson to resign, had brought new public disgrace to the Grant administration, and congressional leaders were demanding that the administration do something to clean up its image. Politically, Grant needed a reformer like Bristow, who would work to bring about reform. Bristow would have his work cut out for him. Graft that reached up into Grant's inner circle would have to be dealt with. In addition to corruption, Bristow would have to deal with the persistent problem facing the economy since the Civil War: what to do with the greenbacks issued to raise money during the war. Since taking office, Grant had wavered to and fro, between fiscal conservatives who wished the greenbacks withdrawn from circulation and businessmen and railroad builders and all the debtor classes who wished to see the money supply expand. When Bristow accepted Grant's appointment, he wrote his daughter that he supposed he would be in the thick of it again. At the same time he voiced displeasure at the appointment, Bristow desired the recognition it brought, and he was ambitious enough to see this appointment as a stepping stone to even higher office.

Bristow's prior experience was the law, but he set right into his new job, familiarizing himself with its policies and procedures. Here his law experience left him in good stead. He was a smart enough lawyer not to let things go on without his knowledge and understanding. This was in marked contrast to the two former Secretaries of the Treasury who had served under Grant. Bristow worked for civil service reform, giving jobs not as political patronage but according to ability and experience. Political patronage in the Treasury was so entrenched that he quickly fired 600 employees, which both saved the government money and increased the efficiency of the department.

Three weeks after taking office, Bristow needed to defend an able assistant who, while investigating corruption, was being framed by a notorious Washington insider ring. The investigation reached up into the Treasury's own Secret Service. After disregarding influence peddling from Grant's inner circle, Bristow was able to fire and replace most of the Secret Service force. Next Bristow had to annul a fraudulent contract for a company doing business with the Treasury Department: The fact that a major stockholder was a presidential friend complicated matters. Another problem Bristow faced was the refunding of the public debt without giving privilege and huge profits to insider financial firms, all pressuring the President and his cronies for access to the government business.

Bristow finally got to the ever-present debate about the Civil War greenbacks versus money backed by precious metals—specie-backed money, as it was called. He worked out a long-term and orderly plan for a return to the specie-backed money. He was successful in getting this plan passed because he was knowledgeable about Washington politics and was able to work with Congress and the Grant administration to get the plan accepted by both. Finally, in 1875, he was able to get the Specie Resumption Act passed. This act reduced the nation's money supply by redeeming the Civil War greenbacks for gold.

In the congressional election of 1874, the Republican Party had suffered major defeats. The Republicans blamed Grant and his administration for bringing about these defeats. Grant's influence and power waned. Grant talked about running for a third term, but there was little support for him in the country. The party was split into factions planning for the next presidential election. One faction of Republicans, including Bristow, felt that the party must reform itself. Those who were dishonest or tied to the Grant administration worked to undermine the reformers. There were people within Grant's inner circle who were working to smear Bristow, telling Grant that Bristow was working against him to gain the presidency for himself.

The Treasury Department chores exhausted and discouraged the overworked Bristow. Day-to-day relations with the President, with all the intrigues, contributed to this exhaustion. In 1875 Bristow had slipped and fallen on the Treasury stairs and was in bed for two weeks. His son, Willy, suffered an attack of meningitis, which seriously affected his eyes and would leave him in delicate health for several years. In June, Bristow sent his wife and two children to Europe while he remained at work in the sweltering city. By August he was exhausted to the point of insomnia. He was discouraged by the corruption in the Grant administration and the Republican Party. In the midst of all this he found himself cleaning up one of the greatest scandals of the day, the Whiskey Ring Scandal.

The Whiskey Ring Scandal has gone down in history as one of the most flagrant plunderings of the national Treasury. Tax was to be paid on distilled liquor, yet distributors and distillers usually avoided these taxes by bribing Treasury agents. When Bristow took office, there was ample evidence that these practices had existed since the Lincoln administration. It was estimated that each year since 1870 from 12 to 15 million gallons escaped the whiskey tax. Bristow soon learned that supervisors and agents at the Internal Revenue Service charged with collecting the tax were in collusion with the whiskey dealers. Plans were often put into place to break up the whiskey ring, but those plans were often leaked or disrupted. It became apparent that there were those who were closest to the President who were undermining Bristow's efforts. One was President Grant's private secretary and closest friend, Orville Babcock. Bristow and his investigators found evidence that Babcock was deeply involved in the whiskey scandals, as were many other high officials and powerful politicians.

Fighting against such highly placed and entrenched corrupt officials was overwhelmingly difficult, but Bristow and the honest people he appointed as his investigators finally prevailed. All across the country the widespread Whiskey Ring was broken up, and indictments had been found against 253 persons. There was a recovery of $3,362,295 for the Treasury. With the smashing of the Whiskey Ring and the end of illicit whiskey, Treasury officials estimated that in 1876 there was an increase of $2,000,000 in whiskey taxes going to the government (Webb, 212). Bristow had been in the job for only a short time, yet managed to break up a ring that had operated with the help of public officials over many long years, at least since Lincoln's time.

As the presidential election of 1876 loomed, Grant's popularity had fallen so low that the Republican leadership became divided among factions: Everyone knew Grant was bringing the Republican Party down to defeat, but what to do about it was not so clear. Two key issues were the economic depression following the Panic of 1873 and the corruption in administration. It was clear that the party had to distance itself from the Grant administration. The reformers in the party frequently mentioned Bristow as a potential presidential candidate. This did not help his relationship with Grant. In the meantime, as a Cabinet member, he was often called up before Congress to represent administrative policies. Congressional leaders from both sides were often interested in airing potential scandals, and often Bristow was seen to represent the corrupt Grant administration.

Before 1876, Bristow had given no sign of wanting the presidency. But he was now viewed by many in the Republican Party as a reform candidate. He was increasingly disillusioned with Grant, and as a loyal Republican, he was worried about the party's chances in the coming election. Bristow was ambitious, and now this ambition became linked with his desire to bring integrity back to the Republican Party. Once he decided he would pursue the presidential nomination, he and Grant became tied to one another. Grant needed Bristow, who was known as a reformer, in the Cabinet because so many of the people around Grant were seen as corrupt. Before the Grant administration was out of office, most of Grant's

Cabinet would be accused of corruption, including Bristow, who had been smeared by troublemakers trying to get him out of the Treasury post. Bristow remained in the Grant administration for two reasons: He believed in the need for reform even more, now that his Republican Party was in trouble; and if he was to get the nomination, he needed the national exposure the Treasury post provided.

By the time the National Republican Party Convention convened in Cincinnati, Ohio, Bristow was a leading contender. His supporters used the slogan "Bristow and Reform." In a crowded field of eight candidates and after seven ballots, Rutherford B. Hayes, a three-term Governor of Ohio, was nominated. The fact that Bristow had alienated powerful men in the Republican Party was one reason for his defeat; another was the split nature of the party. The delegates were more willing to vote for Hayes as a compromise candidate than to see Bristow or one of the other candidates carry the party banner.

Once the party convention was over, Bristow was glad to resign from the Grant administration. In June 1876 he submitted his letter of resignation, then went on to work for the election of Hayes, who was untainted by scandal. Bristow's resignation was greeted with profound regret by both the press and the public. He was cited as one of the best Secretaries of the Treasury and was easily one of the ablest officers in the Cabinet. He had shown strength, integrity, and unyielding courage, and it was his misfortune to serve in an administration that had worked against his reforms (Nevins, 824).

Bristow had, and continued to have, a core of loyal supporters called the Bristowites in the Republican Party and around the country. He was seen as a man of political influence, and this he brought to bear on behalf of Hayes. After Hayes was elected, Bristow was considered for top offices in the Hayes administration, including a seat on the Supreme Court. Bristow, who was never a clever politician, said no to some offices and was passed over for others. He retired from public life in 1878 but would remain influential in national politics as an adviser to five Presidents.

When he left public life, Bristow resumed his law practice, moving his family to New York City. He was active in organizing the American Bar Association, with one of its main goals to reform the legal profession, and was named its permanent President. Bristow helped organize the Civil Service Reform Association, which worked to end the notorious spoils system in government, and was named one of its eight Vice Presidents.

Bristow's life after leaving the Treasury Department was a mix of private and public life. He was able to make a great deal of money because of his business connections and legal work with the leading financiers and industrialists of the day. In the spring of 1896, Bristow was not feeling well and declined to get active in the political campaign of that year. He had represented a case before the Supreme Court, and this case had further tired him out. He suffered from influenza and from sharp pains in his side, which his doctor diagnosed as appendicitis. Urged to have an operation, Bristow decided against it. In June 1896, he began suffering from severe pains. He family was told that he would not recover, and four days later, on June 22, 1896, Benjamin Helms Bristow died.

Upon his death, the *New York Times* eulogized that Benjamin Helms Bristow had made a great deal of history. In his positions as U.S. Attorney for Kentucky and as first Solicitor General of the United States, he used the power of the federal government to help further the cause of the newly freed slaves. He had advocated education and equal access to rights for all citizens. However, it may have been his reign as Secretary of the Treasury where he had made his greatest contributions to the national welfare. Here he began his long battle for civil service reform in a time notorious for public and private corruption. He insisted on sound money and worked on proposals to gain that end. His funding proposals forced a major overhaul of the government's fiscal programs. His successful breakup of the Whiskey Ring was just one example of his courage in fighting corruption—even the most powerful people of the day could not deter him.

BIBLIOGRAPHY

Haworth, Paul L. *The Hayes-Tilden Disputed Election*. Cleveland, OH: Burrows Co., 1906.

Hesseltine, William B. *Ulysses S. Grant, Politician*. New York: F. Unger Publishing Co., 1957.

McFeely, William S. *Grant, a Biography*. New York: W. W. Norton & Co., 1981.

Nevins, Allan. *Hamilton Fish: The Inner History of the Grant Administration*. New York: Dodd, Mead, and Co., 1936.

Vexler, Robert I. *The Vice-Presidents and Cabinet Members*. Vol. 1. New York: Oceana Publications, 1975.

Webb, Ross A. *Benjamin Helm Bristow, Border State Politician*. Lexington: University Press of Kentucky, 1969.

Wright, John W., ed. *The Universal Almanac, 1991*. Kansas City: Andrews and McMeel, 1990.

JULIANNE CICARELLI

C

GEORGE W. CAMPBELL (February 8, 1769–February 17, 1848). Known as a fiery orator and loyal Republican supporter of Presidents Thomas Jefferson and James Madison, George Washington Campbell was Secretary of the Treasury for a short but turbulent seven months during 1814. For most of his tenure in Congress during the years 1803–1818, Campbell was a "War Hawk," joining Henry Clay and John C. Calhoun in support of the war against Britain. Though often characterized as inept or even incompetent by the financial community, Campbell's practical attitude and political skills enabled him to arrange loans to finance the war, when other more qualified candidates for the Treasury post were unwilling to accept the challenge. Campbell also served with distinction as the U.S. Minister to Russia and was an extremely successful lawyer and land speculator in Tennessee.

George Campbell was born in the Parish of Tongue, Shire of Sutherland, Scotland, on February 8, 1769. He was the tenth and youngest child of Archibald Campbell, a physician, and Elizabeth Mackay Campbell. The family moved three years later to a farm in Mecklenburg County, North Carolina. Though many neighbors were probably loyalists during the Revolution, the Campbells were committed patriots to the new nation and sent three sons to battle, two of whom were killed. Too young to fight, George added Washington to his name at that time, in honor of General George Washington. Campbell helped run the family farm after his father's death and was educated by his mother and in country schools. He became a schoolteacher in his early twenties. Through rigorous self-study, he entered the College of New Jersey (now Princeton) and graduated in 1794 with high honors and a prize for outstanding oratory.

After graduation, Campbell taught school in Trenton, New Jersey, and then moved back to North Carolina, all the while studying the law. In 1797 he had established a law practice in Knoxville, Tennessee, then a frontier town of only about fifty homes but forecast to grow rapidly as the new state capital. Campbell began his land investments in Knoxville and quickly became one of the major property owners in the area. He was known as scrupulously honest and fair in his business dealings.

Campbell first ran for Congress in a special election in 1801 and lost. With the growth of the Tennessee delegation, he ran again in 1803 and easily won his first public office. Reflecting his upbringing in frontier towns, Campbell consistently supported the Jeffersonian (later Republican) views of fostering westward expansion through the Louisiana Purchase and federal land programs. Yet he was not a strict "party-line" politician. During the 1804 impeachment proceedings against Chief Justice Samuel Chase (a Federalist), Campbell was one of the few Republicans who thought the case ill-conceived and based on political rather than legal issues. This angered many other Republicans but did not stop them from electing Campbell one of the House "managers" (prosecutors) of the case. Campbell's performance as a prosecutor was judged mediocre and probably one of the worst of his career. This may have reflected his underlying distaste for his party's position, as well as his lack of experience in Congress.

Though originally aligned with conservative Republicans who wanted to avoid conflict with Britain, Campbell (along with the Republican leadership) found his views changed with the British attack on the *Chesapeake* in June 1807. While prior to the attack he had no desire to go to war, by 1808 Campbell viewed Britain as a murderous lion, responsible for several layers of "aggravated insults." Campbell became a prominent advocate of a firm policy against Britain, eventually arguing for a significant increase in the military, as well as the trade embargo. As a Republican (and unlike the Federalists who focused on narrower economic issues), Campbell's views emphasized Britain's attacks on the national interest and sovereignty of the United States.

As one of a relatively small "war party" group in Congress, Campbell's views were not universally popular. Many Northern Congressmen were against the embargo, which hurt the trade-dependent North much more than the South or West. Some Northerners, such as Barendt Gardinier of upstate New York, went so far as to accuse Congress and the President of being controlled by Napoleon's France. Gardinier represented a district profiting from the extensive Canadian trade that would be wiped out by expanding the embargo. Incensed by the slight to his, the South's, and the President's patriotism, Campbell challenged Gardinier to a duel on March 2, 1808, and severely wounded the New York Congressman.

The Gardinier duel had one important result: Campbell met his future wife, Harriet Stoddert, a friend of the family who owned the home where Gardinier went to recover. Harriet was the daughter of Benjamin Stoddert, Secretary of the Navy under John Adams. The couple eventually were wed in July 1812 and had six children, only two of whom outlived their parents.

Campbell's loyalty to the party was rewarded by both Jefferson and Madison. Though Campbell had little financial expertise, he was chosen as Chair of the House Ways and Means Committee, replacing the much more qualified John Randolph of Virginia. Treasury Secretary Albert Gallatin complained that this selection "was improper" and would only give Gallatin additional work. Unfairly or not, Campbell was never to lose his reputation as a relatively inept financier.

In 1809, Campbell declared he would not run again for Congress, due to ill health. He returned home to Knoxville to recuperate for several months and then served on the Tennessee Supreme Court of Errors and Appeals until 1811. By then anxious to return to Washington politics, he was sent to Congress as a Senator from Tennessee in 1811, having been selected by the Tennessee General Assembly to fill a vacated seat.

Campbell was well known by then as a War Hawk. The country was disenchanted with the embargo but was terribly divided over alternatives. These alternatives ran from reconciliation and capitulation to British demands to advocacy of an immediate invasion of Canada and all-out war. Campbell still wanted to avoid war, supporting Madison's efforts at diplomacy backed by a credible military threat. As an illustration of his attitude toward war, Campbell, along with only five other Senators, voted in 1811 against appropriations for the U.S. Navy. The small group argued that the amount appropriated would in no way be sufficient to fund a true fighting force (which they felt was necessary) and thus would be wasted expenditure. Campbell also agreed with Secretary of War John Armstrong in advocating a draft for a militia.

In late 1811 and early 1812, Campbell joined other Senators in urging the Senate to support a buildup of the military. They realized, however, that no funds were available, especially since the embargo had halted the government's main revenue source, import duties. Political considerations made them reluctant to fine the primarily Northern and Federalist violators of the 1811 nonintercourse law, which replaced the embargo. Yielding to political pressure, the Republican-dominated Senate remitted any penalties for violation. The result of this vote was to force Gallatin to borrow the funds. Campbell was again one of only five Senators voting against remission and supporting Madison's view that the war effort needed to be properly funded if it were to be successful.

During the ensuing financial crisis, the increasingly unpopular Gallatin was appointed to the U.S. peace commission being sent to Europe, leaving William Jones (Secretary of the Navy) as acting Treasury Secretary for a few days. Jones immediately forwarded to Congress Gallatin's proposal to cover the almost $30 million deficit with nine different taxes. This proposal was quickly rejected by Congress, knowing the country's ambivalence toward the war and antipathy toward taxes. Seeing the difficulties ahead, Jones begged out of the Treasury job. To many observers it was clear that arranging a suitable loan would be difficult, especially as the country was without a national bank. The charter for the First Bank of the United States had recently expired, and insufficient political support existed for a new bank, even though the country was suffering from inflation and a rampant expansion of notes issued under questionable state banking practices.

To replace Jones, Alexander James Dallas and Richard Roth (both of Pennsylvania) were the first and second choices, but they both declined due to the seeming impossibility of the tasks ahead. Campbell, a logical choice as the administration's leader in Congress, was then nominated and easily approved by the Republican-dominated Senate on February 9, 1814. No one seemed to have much faith in his financial expertise, but the country's situation was so desperate that the financial community had little confidence in the Treasury regardless of who was Secretary. The folly of the situation was aptly characterized by Congressman Samuel Taggart (Massachusetts) who quipped that Campbell's initials "GWC" actually stood for "Government Wants Cash." Clearly, Campbell's main qualifications were political: Madison needed a stable, effective Cabinet, solidified in support of his war strategy. Specific abilities were secondary. In particular, Campbell was the only Cabinet member close to Secretary of War Armstrong, upon whom Madison relied heavily but then often ignored.

Campbell spent much of his seven months in office trying to arrange loans to finance the military. Though he claimed to know little about his duties, and was unwell, in April 1814 he put together a $25 million package of loans from a consortium of large and small Northeast banks. This package was created despite threats from John Jacob Astor that Campbell was dealing with suspect financial institutions. Campbell eventually managed to get Astor to relent and subscribe to the loan, though other better-qualified officials, such as Jones, fully expected Campbell would fail.

As Campbell repeatedly pointed out, the money was still not enough to finance an offensive war, even with the end to the embargo that spring. Finances were driving military and political strategy. Campbell was in the majority of the Cabinet that felt taking too strong an ultimatum (demanding an immediate end to impressment) to the ongoing peace talks with Britain would be unrealistic. He argued for a quick peace treaty, to be followed later by negotiations on impressment and commerce issues.

By July, the United States again was out of money. Campbell went to work on another loan package. Madison wanted to publicize the problem widely, to impress both citizens and bankers of the seriousness of the situation. Campbell, however, argued the practical side: Announcing the Treasury's plight would scare bankers away. Campbell prevailed and raised the funds.

Finances were not Campbell's only difficulties as a member of Madison's Cabinet. During August 1814, with the British threatening Washington, D.C., Campbell found himself acting as an intermediary between Armstrong and Madison, who had for good reason lost his faith in his War Secretary. Armstrong, however, was reluctant to act in defense of the Capitol, and it was too late to protect the town from being sacked. Accompanied by Armstrong, Campbell fled to Frederick, Maryland. Shortly after, Armstrong resigned.

The sacking of the Capitol brought the nation's financial affairs to their lowest level. Banks suspended all specie payments, which meant the Treasury's deposits were inaccessible. The government had no cash to pay its bills. Campbell had to borrow short term at high rates just to keep the government running. With the departure of Armstrong, the recurring financial crises, and the apparently intransigent British position, Campbell felt that his situation was untenable and decided he wanted out of the Cabinet. Madison, appealing to Campbell's loyalty, tried to convince him to stay until the State Department seat was filled, Secretary of State James Monroe having taken over Armstrong's duties in the War Department. In addition, Madison was under pressure to invigorate and broaden the Cabinet to include more pro-war and Federalist members. In the face of all this and suffering from what was probably ulcers, Campbell finally submitted his formal resignation on September 11, 1814—leaving office October 5—saying later that he was "completely humbled by the complexity of the finances."

Upon his departure, Campbell submitted a formal financial statement for his successor and Congress. The country was again short about $24 million. Given his experiences with loans, tax proposals, and other revenue sources, it is not surprising that Campbell had no specific recommendation on how to raise the money. He in fact did not believe it could be raised at that time. Anticipating the coming debate over the chartering of a new national bank, Campbell stated that the Treasury could only reach a permanent solution to the nation's financial problems with a more stable national currency, rather than rely on a myriad of state bank notes with uncertain convertability into specie. Campbell knew that a new national bank was still too controversial to pass Congress, especially given Republican constitutional concerns. Alexander Dallas, Campbell's successor, felt Campbell should have been more open with his views, but Campbell saw no immediate hope for reform.

In retrospect, during the time Campbell served at the Treasury, his department probably was the best-run government agency, given the performance of the other Secretaries, who were better qualified. The lack of funds was hardly Campbell's fault, and he did manage to raise enough money to keep the government going, even when others thought the job was impossible. Campbell the patriot was discouraged by the unwillingness of wealthy businessmen to loan funds to support their government. James Madison commented later on Campbell's performance and said that he held the office at a period when the difficulties were scarcely manageable by the ablest hands, and when those hands were least willing.

Campbell returned to Tennessee, having been considered but not chosen for Attorney General in Madison's new Cabinet. Popular and respected at home, the Tennessee General Assembly again sent him to Washington as a Senator in 1815. In spite of his public reputation in money matters, Campbell was immediately chosen Chairman of the Senate Finance Committee. He actively supported the chartering of the Second Bank of the United States, as well as a protective tariff, and strengthening of the military. During the debate over the bank's charter, Campbell once again showed his agreement with Madison on governmental issues. In question was what to do with the $1.5 million fee paid by the bank for its charter. The popular proposal was to spend this "bonus" on an interstate transportation system of roads and canals. Campbell surprised many Republicans by voting against the "bonus bill." Some attributed his opposition to the extensive river network in Tennessee, which reduced the state's need for roads. Madison surprised them even more by taking Campbell's position and vetoing the bill. The feeling of "old Republicans" like Madison and Campbell was that the government was overstepping its constitutional authority, and it was time to limit the influence of the federal government.

On April 11, 1818, President Madison appointed Campbell U.S. Minister to Russia. Campbell had been supported by Madison and Secretary of War James Monroe but opposed by John Quincy Adams, then Secretary of State. Campbell had two important missions in Russia, a nation of strategic international importance at that time. The first mission was to convince Russia not to support Spain in her colonies' struggle for independence in South America. The second was to help negotiate a commercial treaty developing more markets for U.S. goods. Upon his arrival in St. Petersburg, Campbell discovered that the language of the Russian court was French. Not speaking it, Campbell immediately began intensively studying it on his own, quickly becoming fluent. Through this and his own personal characteristics, Campbell gained the respect of the Russian diplomatic corps and royal family.

Campbell successfully guided both diplomatic goals while in Russia, but the family's time there was marked by personal tragedy. During the winter of 1818–1819, three of his children died of typhus fever, and Campbell began petitioning to return home. It was not until July 7, 1820, that he was relieved of his duties, and Campbell moved his family back to Tennessee, amidst much acclaim for his success overseas.

After taking time off from professional activities, Campbell moved and reopened his law practice in Nashville, following again the country's westward expansion. Like many westerners, he continued to acquire and speculate in land, becoming a wealthy landowner in middle Tennessee. Though he did not actively farm, over this time he owned as many as twenty slaves. Campbell, however, took no part on either side of the deepening debate over slavery. Campbell's most well-known land transaction was the sale of his family's home and estate on "The Knob" (also known as "Campbell's Hill") in Nashville in 1843, to be used for the new state capitol.

Campbell remained active in public and private service outside of his legal practice. He served as a trustee of East Tennessee College and of the University of Nashville. He also was appointed first Vice President of the Bank of the State of Tennessee, serving from 1820 to 1831. He was considered a candidate for the Secretary of War in the Monroe administration (being favored by then-Treasury Secretary William Crawford), but John C. Calhoun was eventually chosen for the position. Campbell also served as a judge of the U.S. District Court of Tennessee.

In 1831 Andrew Jackson's Secretary of State, Edward Livingston, appointed Campbell to his last public office: the French Spoilations Claims Commission. The commission's task was to distribute the money given to the United States by France, settling claims stemming from the Napoleonic period. These claims resulted from French naval seizures of neutral American ships. Over the three years the commission worked, Campbell actively helped resolve over 3,000 claims, finishing on December 31, 1835.

Campbell then moved from Washington, D.C., to Nashville for the last time, returning to his highly successful law practice. He died in Nashville on February 17, 1848, at the age of seventy-nine. At the time of his death, George Washington Campbell was probably the wealthiest man in Tennessee and one of the state's most respected elder statesmen.

BIBLIOGRAPHY

Babcock, Kendric S. *The Rise of American Nationality: 1811–1819*. New York: Harper and Brothers, 1906.

Dangerfield, George. *The Era of Good Feelings*. New York: Harcourt, Brace and Co., 1952.

De Gregorio, William A. *The Complete Book of U.S. Presidents*. New York: Dembner Books, 1984.

"George Washington Campbell." In *Bibliographical Directory of the United States Executive Branch, 1774–1989*, edited by Richard Sobel, 58–59. New York: Greenwood Press, 1990.

Hatzenbuehler, Ronald L., and Robert L. Joie. *Congress Declares War*. Kent, OH: Kent State University Press, 1983.

Jordan, Weymouth T. *George Washington Campbell of Tennessee: Western Statesman*. Tallahassee: Florida State University Press, 1955.

Mooney, Chase C. *William H. Crawford, 1772–1834*. Lexington: University of Kentucky Press, 1974.

Risjord, Norman K. *The Old Republicans*. New York: Columbia University Press, 1965.

Rutland, Robert Allen. *The Presidency of James Madison*. Lawrence: University Press of Kansas, 1990.

Sears, Louis M. *Jefferson and the Embargo*. New York: Octagon Books, 1966.

Stagg, J. C. A. *Mr. Madison's War: Politics, Diplomacy and Warfare in the Early American Republic, 1783–1830*. Princeton, NJ: Princeton University Press, 1983.

KRISTINE L. CHASE

JOHN G. CARLISLE (September 5, 1834–July 31, 1910). John Griffin Carlisle was born on Friday, September 5, 1834, on a farm near Covington, Kentucky. He offers as clear a case as perhaps this country has ever exhibited of a man's rise by sheer ability. He was characterized as a kind and generous man, and while it is rare for persons in high political offices to have no enemies, John Carlisle did not.

He was the oldest child in a family of six boys and seven girls and was given very little chance at formal education. Only after the fall crop harvest and spring planting had been completed did he attend school in a one-room log cabin in Campbell County. His father, Lilbon Hardin Carlisle, had inherited part of the hilly Carlisle farm, which barely provided for a family of fifteen. His wife, Mary Reynolds, had come from Rhode Island, while Lilbon's family had originally come from Virginia.

Carlisle was considered indolent as a child and avoided physical activity of any kind throughout his entire life. However, he would work all day on the farm and spend each night reading and studying. He was quiet and studious and eager to learn whenever possible, once receiving French lessons from a wanderer in exchange for English lessons.

At the early age of sixteen, he began teaching in a one-room log cabin much like the one he had attended. Two years later, in 1852, his father died. Knowing that five brothers would still remain to tend the small farm, Carlisle took the chance to follow his ambitions and study law.

In the summer of 1855 he traveled the enormous distance of fifteen miles into Covington. His first position was as an eighth-grade schoolteacher, and as was the custom, Carlisle boarded with a family in town. He moved in with the Major John A. Goodson family, where he was introduced to his daughter, Mary Jane, who initially "laughed at the ugly, awkward boy—and a few years later married him" (Barnes, 7).

They were married on January 15, 1857. Their only children to survive to adulthood, Lilbon Logan and William Kinkead, both became attorneys.

It didn't take long for Carlisle to become tired of the classroom, so he left the profession to study law in the office of John W. Stevenson, who later served Kentucky as Governor and U.S. Senator. He earned a license and was admitted to the bar in 1858 at the age of twenty-three. That same year, he became a partner with Judge W. B. Kinkead. Carlisle's brilliant mind contributed to his instant success, and he quickly acquired a large practice.

His first trial was a difficult one, which even his closest friends felt he would lose. Using simple language and without any sign of nervousness, Carlisle swayed everyone in the courtroom to his side. After witnessing the trial, a Covington lawyer remarked, "You could see that he had mastered every detail. . . . Without telling an anecdote or cracking a joke there was something so winning in his voice and in his manners that the interest never flagged" (Barnes, 7).

Often winning his cases on sheer intellect, Carlisle was a gifted speaker. An associate once wrote, "He saw the weakness of his adversary and the strength of his own side. The latter he made manifest, and the former he took by the throat and throttled" (Barnes, 498).

According to Isaac F. Marcosson, Carlisle had gone to Kentucky in his later years to deliver speeches on sound money. Marcosson was holding the only copy of the speech Carlisle was about to give, and it was filled with facts and figures. Although Carlisle had made no attempt to memorize the speech he had written the previous day, according to Marcosson, "he did not vary one word or a single figure in an address that consumed two hours and a half for delivery. . . . [T]he moment that he put pen to paper the written word was almost photographically fixed in his memory" (Barnes, 516).

It did not appear to be just the written word that Carlisle could memorize but the spoken word as well. It is told that while playing solitaire, a game he loved to play, he would play an error-free game and at the same time dictate as many as fifty important letters. He would have the letters reread, and if one word was wrong anywhere among the letters, he would immediately catch it (Ellis, 278).

Within a year, in 1859, he had been elected to the Kentucky House of Representatives, where he served until 1861. He was a member of the House Committee on Federal Relations, which issued the Kentucky neutrality resolutions of May 16, 1861. He declined the nomination to serve as an elector on the McClellan Democratic ticket.

Although he sympathized with the Confederate cause during the Civil War, he concerned himself with practicing law instead of fighting. He was defeated in an attempt at the state Senate in August 1865 because the military controlled the election in the state. However, during the first session, the legislature declined to accept eleven new members and called for new elections. Carlisle's opponent was one of those not seated, and in a new election in 1866, Carlisle was elected. He was reelected for a second term but chose to resign in June 1871 to take the office of Lieutenant Governor. He remained in that position until September 1875.

He was selected to run for that office because he favored granting a right-of-way through Kentucky to the Cincinnati Southern Railway, a belief that was opposite that of the candidate the Democrats had nominated for Governor. As it turned out, an intense battle over the right-of-way was fought while Carlisle held that office. When the vote in the Senate ended in a tie, Carlisle's vote became the tie-breaker, and the road passed.

He had been exposed to national politics in 1868 when he served as a delegate-at-large from Kentucky to the Democratic National Convention in New York. He was also chosen as an alternate presidential elector at large for the state in 1876. His first attempt at national office was successful when he was elected to the lower house of the 45th Congress in March 1877.

He was recognized immediately for his speaking ability and his intelligence. He was elected Speaker of the House in December 1883, over Samuel Randall, after only six years in Congress. One supporter of Carlisle's strongly reported, "I am for Carlisle against the world, the flesh and the devil" (Morgan, 182). By this time he was looked upon as the leader of the Democratic Party and was reelected as Speaker in 1885 and 1887 and served until 1889. In all, he was reelected to the House six times, serving until May 1890.

Carlisle believed that the Speaker should not be governed by political party favoritism but by parliamentary law and House rules. He became an expert in parliamentary law, and his totally impartial control of the House gave him a place in history as one of the greatest Speakers ever to hold the position.

According to Republican Representative Hiscock of New York, who was a colleague of Carlisle's, "[H]e is one of the strongest of Democrats, and I am one of the strongest of Republicans; yet my imagination is not strong enough to conceive of his making an unfair ruling or doing an unfair thing against the party opposed to him in the House" (Peck, 309).

He served on the Ways and Means Committee while in the House. He was considered an expert in revenue reform and made a positive impact with the "Carlisle Internal Revenue Bill." He was instrumental in tariff reform and is

credited with being the greatest influence in the movement. He was antiprotectionist and felt that the only advantage to tariffs was in raising revenue. Carlisle
believed the current tariff to be terribly unjust. Being of humble beginnings
himself, he felt that the burden of the current tariff fell too heavily on the ones
least able to pay. He believed that trade should "open the channels of commerce
in all parts of the world and invite the producer and consumer to meet on equal
terms in a free market for the exchange of their commodities. . . . Prohibitions
and embargoes . . . are inconsistent . . . with the spirit of the age in which we
live" (Barnes, 53).

Carlisle resigned from the House on May 26, 1890, to fill the vacancy in the
Senate caused by the death of James B. Beck. He was considered a possible
presidential candidate in 1892, but the party chose Cleveland because of his
ability to capture the independent vote. He resigned from the Senate when
President Cleveland appointed him as Secretary of the Treasury on March 4,
1893, taking office March 7, 1893.

Cleveland had first offered the job in jest during a poker game before Cleveland's second term in office. After drawing four cards, Carlisle won the hand
with four kings. Cleveland's response was, "Take the money, Carlisle; take the
money. If ever I am President again you shall be Secretary of the Treasury. But
don't make that four-card draw too often" (Barnes, 205).

At the time of the appointment, Carlisle was considered an authority on finance and one of the most successful Democratic leaders of his time, second only
to President Cleveland. Many thought him to be a better choice than Secretary
Daniel Manning, who was Cleveland's Secretary of the Treasury under his first
administration. The only criticism of Carlisle was that he personally was not
worth more than $25,000 and that he was not acquainted with the ways of big
business.

Cleveland overlooked the criticism since Carlisle and Cleveland were longtime friends and perfect complements to each other. According to Cleveland,
"We are just right for each other; he knows all I ought to know, and I can bear
all we have to bear" (Barnes, 202).

Historians believe that his acceptance of the Secretary's position was the beginning of his political downfall. "No Secretary of the Treasury in time of peace
has ever faced a more difficult task than he" (Barnes, 519). During the years he
served as Speaker, Carlisle had mindfully protected the Treasury's surplus. He
had introduced an amendment in 1881 to guard against drains on the Treasury
in the event that banks believed a lowering of interest rates on bonds would take
place. Despite Carlisle's efforts, the Harrison administration had set the stage for
financial crisis, and upon his ascension as Secretary, the surplus was gone, the
government was essentially broke, and public confidence was strained.

The $100 million gold reserve being all but drained from the Treasury, Carlisle
announced on April 15, 1893, that gold certificates would no longer be issued
and that gold would be exchanged for notes only when "lawfully available." On
January 14, 1894, the New York *Recorder* displayed the headlines: "Carlisle Must

Raise $30,000,000 in 15 Days. Unless Congress Provides Some Other Means of Getting Money the Treasury Will Be Broke" (Barnes, 310). Three days later, the Treasury issued $50 million of 4 percent bonds, using as the authority the Resumption Act of 1875.

An attempt was being made to maintain parity between gold and silver, but the run on gold had not ceased. The vaults were again drained of gold, and it was again necessary to issue more bonds. In February 1895, the government issued $62,315,400 worth of thirty-four-year 4 percent bonds.

Criticisms of unbusinesslike policies came from an arrangement Carlisle made with a group of New York bankers, including such men as J. P. Morgan and N. M. Rothschild, to purchase the entire amount of bonds for 104.5. These bonds were later quoted at 118, leaving many to question the actions of the Treasury and to question Carlisle's honesty. Some believed that Carlisle was selling the bonds to the bankers for their financial gain. However, many bankers were buying out of patriotism and not profit.

Trying to maintain parity and endorse a sound money policy brought additional heavy criticism from his party leaders. "In his famous silver argument, Carlisle stood against the free coinage of either metal, but favored the unlimited coinage of both. He was charged with having deserted his earlier principles. [But] he later stated that he would rather be right than consistent" (Johnson and Malone, 495).

On January 1, 1896, gold reserves had fallen to their lowest point of only $50 million. It was again announced that the Treasury needed additional gold reserves, and another issue of bonds was ordered. When the public learned that Carlisle intended to sell the entire issue to the same group of bankers, publications printed that if the public were given the chance, the bonds could all be sold. The public was indeed given the chance, which in effect raised the market price, causing the group of bankers to pay 110.6877 for the majority of the $100 million bonds. This saved the government $20 million over thirty years.

When the 1896 election drew near, Carlisle was again considered a promising candidate. However, because Cleveland would not decide whether or not he would run again, Carlisle would not commit until it was too late. In the campaign, he supported the Democratic Party candidates and spoke in favor of the gold standard, which angered the silver Democrats in Kentucky. Opinions turned so against him that while speaking in his own hometown of Covington, Kentucky, he was nearly mobbed by the crowds.

Carlisle left office at the end of the Cleveland administration on March 3, 1897. Because of the sentiment still against him in Kentucky, however, he decided to move to New York City and set up his law practice. He did not involve himself in politics after that except to serve as Vice President of the Anti-Imperialist League.

The last years of John Griffin Carlisle's life were not happy ones. Despite being given invitations by friends, he did not return to Kentucky, saying that his work would not allow it. Indeed, he was certainly a prominent New York attorney who often spoke before the Supreme Court, but friends felt that work was only an excuse not to return to his home state that had essentially rejected him.

Not only had he lost his position in politics and many of his onetime friends; he also suffered within months of each other the loss of both of his sons in 1898. Mrs. Carlisle, who was characterized as a charming hostess who gave the best parties in Washington, and who knew everyone in Washington worth knowing, died on August 4, 1905. Carlisle's longtime friend Grover Cleveland died three years later. Carlisle would have been alone if not for his widowed daughter-in-law and two granddaughters who moved in with him following his wife's death.

Carlisle was generous to a fault and died a poor man. He once handed a man $50 when the man explained that he was a Kentuckian and had been robbed and had no money to take his family home. Thirty minutes later the man and some of his friends drove past Carlisle's home in a drunken folly.

Carlisle died on July 31, 1910, while working on his last case in his apartment at the Hotel Wolcott in New York. His estate consisted of only a house in Washington, mortgaged for $10,000, and a medley of gifts that friends had given him.

The funeral was held in the Capitol, and he was buried in Washington because he could not afford the expense of being buried in Kentucky. His body was later moved to Linden Grove Cemetery in Covington to rest next to his wife.

John Griffin Carlisle entered this life in poverty and left it much the same way, except for the difference his life had made to his family, friends, and the government he spent his life serving.

BIBLIOGRAPHY

Barnes, James A. John G. Carlisle, Financial Statesman. New York: Dodd, Mead and Co., 1931.
Ellis, Edward S. Great Leaders and National Issues of 1896. Non-Partisan Bureau of Political Information. Wm. Ellis Scull, 1896.
Hepburn, A. Barton. A History of Currency in the United States. New York: Macmillan Company, 1924.
Johnson, Allen, and Dumas Malone, eds. Dictionary of American Biography. Vol. 2. New York: Charles Scribner's Sons, 1936.
Johnson, Rossiter, ed. The Twentieth Century Biographical Dictionary of Notable Americans. Vol. 2. Boston: The Biographical Society, 1904.
Morgan, H. Wayne. From Hayes to McKinley, National Party Politics, 1877–1896. Syracuse, NY: Syracuse University Press, 1969.
The National Cyclopaedia of American Biography. New York: James T. White and Co., 1898.
Peck, Harry Thurston. Twenty Years of the Republic, 1885–1905. New York: Dodd, Mead and Co., 1913.

PENNY KUGLER

SALMON P. CHASE (January 13, 1808–May 7, 1873). Salmon Portland Chase led an extraordinary life: teacher, lawyer, political organizer, Senator, Governor, Cabinet officer, Supreme Court Justice, and presidential hopeful. Chase was born in Cornish, New York, on January 13, 1808; he was the eighth of eleven children born to Ihmar Chase and Janet Ralston. The family relocated to Keene, New Hampshire, when Chase was young, and he began his schooling there. His father died when Chase was only nine years old, and for the next three years, his mother struggled to allow him to continue his education. She was doubtlessly relieved when his uncle, Philander Chase, the Episcopal bishop of Ohio, offered to care for him. So in 1820 Chase, age twelve, was sent to Worthington, Ohio, to live and study. Philander Chase was a stern and pious man whose ambition was to prepare young men for the ministry; certainly he must have hoped that Chase would follow such a path. In 1822, his uncle became President of Cincinnati College, and Salmon moved to Cincinnati and matriculated at the college. Chase did not find the college's academic program rigorous, and he completed the first two years of the curriculum in one. Philander Chase only remained as President of Cincinnati College for one year; his resignation and decision to go to England ended Salmon's stay in Ohio. Chase returned to his mother's household in New Hampshire in 1823. He was admitted to Dartmouth College in 1824 as a junior. While not an exceptional student, he received a classical education and graduated eighth in his class. Elected to Phi Beta Kappa, he gave one of the commencement addresses. At age eighteen, Chase graduated from college and faced a career decision. His older brother, Alexander, cautioned him against pursuing a career in the ministry and suggested instead that he consider becoming a lawyer.

Chase took his older brother's advice and went to Washington, D.C., with the goal of studying for and being admitted to the bar. In order to support his studies, he attempted to establish a boy's school. When no students answered his ad, Chase was rescued by A. R. Plumley, who asked him to teach the male students in his expanding school. Among the students were the sons of Henry Clay and William Wirt. Wirt was Attorney General under John Quincy Adams and agreed to assist Chase in his legal studies. An excellent rapport developed between Chase and his mentor, and Chase was treated like a member of the Wirt household during the two years he studied for the bar. Chase was admitted to the bar in one fewer than the normal three years of study.

His three years in Washington had prepared him for his life in law and politics. While he did not involve himself with politics at this time, he did help a Quaker prepare a petition calling for Congress to abolish slavery in the District of Columbia. This was likely his first involvement in an antislavery activity. When Andrew Jackson defeated Adams in 1828, Chase was eager to leave Washington and to move to a city that would offer him an opportunity to rise rapidly in his profession. At age twenty-two, he returned to Cincinnati to begin his law practice.

Chase plunged into the social and intellectual life of Cincinnati and was admitted to the Ohio bar in 1830. He struggled financially and formed numerous law partnerships. In 1832 he joined Edward King and Timothy Walker; shortly thereafter, he formed a partnership with Daniel Caswell, solicitor of the Cincinnati branch of the Bank of the United States. When Caswell left Ohio, Chase assumed the solicitor's position and, in 1834, became solicitor for the Lafayette

Bank as well. His work with these banks familiarized him with existing state banking laws and regulations. Between 1835 and 1838, Chase took on Samuel Eels as a partner. Following that, he formed a relationship with Flamen Ball, which continued for the rest of his life; Ball ran the Cincinnati practice as Chase expanded his horizons beyond the state.

Chase married three times and fathered six daughters. He married Catherine Jane Garniss on March 4, 1834. She died less than two years later from complications as a result of childbirth. Their daughter, Catherine Amelia, died at age four from scarlet fever. Chase married Eliza Ann Smith on September 26, 1839. She bore him three daughters; only Catherine (Kate) Jane born in 1840 survived infancy. Eliza died of a lengthy illness in 1845. Chase married Sarah Belle Dunlop Ludlow in 1846. The following year she bore him a daughter, Janet (Nettie) Ralston. A second daughter born two years later died as an infant. Chase's third and last wife developed tuberculosis and died in 1852. Because his personal life was filled with sorrow, Chase concentrated on his public life.

Chase's first involvement with the black community in Cincinnati was as part of the colonization movement that supported the idea of free blacks returning to Africa. His focus shifted, in 1836, when an antiabolitionist group began to harass James G. Birney, editor of the city's abolitionist newspaper the *Philanthropist*. Chase viewed freedom of the press as an important right, and he agreed to represent the owners of the paper, who sued the mob for damages. From those cases, Chase became involved with a series of trials involving fugitive slaves. In 1840, he began arguing a position that he would maintain over the next two decades: The federal government must separate itself from the institution of slavery; Washington, D.C., should abolish slavery; only states can determine slavery questions; and the Fugitive Slave Act of 1793 should be repealed. By the end of 1845, he had established himself as an antislavery and civil rights attorney.

Politically, Chase began by joining the National Republican Party, precursor to the Whig Party, in 1831. With Jackson's reelection, Chase helped to organize an anti-Jackson pro-Bank Party in 1834. In spite of his antislavery activities, he maintained his Whig connections, assuming them to be helpful in future political life. In 1841, he hoped that the Whig Party under Harrison would repudiate slavery. But with Harrison's death, Tyler, a slaveholder, became President. Chase abandoned the Whigs and joined the Liberty Party. This marked the beginning of many years of intense political activity. Chase set his sights on achieving a seat in the U.S. Senate and used his Free-Soil and Democratic connections to have the Ohio legislature elect him on February 22, 1849. Chase hoped to be embraced by the Democratic Party, but Southern party members objected.

Over the six years Chase served in the Senate, he worked as an antislavery advocate, suggesting many amendments to the Fugitive Slave Act; all were rejected. In 1854, Stephen Douglas proposed establishing the Kansas-Nebraska territory under the rule of popular sovereignty, which allowed settlers of the territories to decide questions on the status of slavery for themselves. Rejecting this proposal, Chase argued that the Kansas-Nebraska territory should be organized according to the terms of the Missouri Compromise of 1820, which prohib-ited slavery in that part of the Louisiana Purchase territory north of thirty-six degrees, thirty minutes latitude. Douglas argued, to the contrary, that the 1850 bill superseded the 1820 law. Chase attempted numerous amendments to the bill; all were rejected. The Kansas-Nebraska Act passed Congress in May 1854. Un-fortunately for Chase, the coalition of Free-Soilers and Democrats who elected him to the Senate fell apart. And, in 1854, he was replaced in the Senate.

Chase began trying to organize a new political coalition of Whigs, Democrats, and Know-Nothings, a new faction largely anti-immigrant and anti-Catholic in its rhetoric. The party was initially known as the Anti-Nebraska Party but, fol-lowing a July 1855 convention, became the Republican Party. Chase emerged from the convention as the new party's candidate for Governor of Ohio. Follow-ing a bitter campaign, he was elected in October 1855 by a very narrow margin. Chase intended to use his new political power to promote the Republican Party nationally with the objective of becoming the party's candidate in the 1856 presidential election.

As Governor, Chase was required to enforce the Fugitive Slave Act in spite of his own personal objections. The governor in the state of Ohio had no real role in the legislative process of the state in the 1850s. However, Chase did push, with varying degrees of success, for better schooling and prisons, women's rights, improved mental health care, reform of the militia, tax reduction, and an ex-pansion of the state banking system.

In February 1856, a gathering of Republicans in Pittsburgh indicated to Chase that he would be a strong contender for the party's presidential nomination. However, by the time of the actual convention the following June, John Frémont, a moderate, was chosen. Chase's outspoken antislavery views were considered too radical. The following year, Chase decided to run for a second term as Gov-ernor in hopes of maintaining his political visibility. He won, but again by a very slim margin. His real objective, however, was to seek the presidential nomination in 1860.

Chase campaigned for the Republican 1860 presidential nomination for two years. As part of his strategy, he got himself elected to the Senate in 1860. His views and those of William Seward, another Republican hopeful, on slavery proved still to be too liberal for a national candidate. Chase received very few votes at the 1860 Chicago convention; Lincoln, a moderate, became the party's choice. In spite of his disappointment, Chase campaigned for the Lincoln ticket. In return, once elected and inaugurated, Lincoln appointed Chase Secretary of the Treasury. The choice of Chase for a Cabinet position was not without op-position. Some argued that Chase was too liberal; some argued that he had no qualifications for the position; some recalled that he had supported free trade and were concerned that he would not enforce the new Morrill protective tariff. Lincoln's decision to include Chase in the Cabinet was largely political, as the two men seem to have had little ideologically in common.

Lincoln and his Cabinet took over the reins of government in March 1861.

Chase began service on March 7. Seven states in the South had voted to secede from the Union largely in response to the Republican presidential victory and what they judged would be an attempt by the new administration to reverse the Kansas-Nebraska bill. Lincoln's own position was one of opposition to slavery in new territories but a willingness to compromise on other issues. He did not oppose the rights of slave states to continue slavery, and he was willing to enforce the Fugitive Slave Act. Various compromise proposals were made in an attempt to reunite the Union and avert military conflict. A particularly ambitious but futile effort was a Washington Peace Conference in February 1861, the month before the inauguration. Chase was a reluctant participant at the meeting because he was not in favor of compromise on the issue of slavery.

One of the first issues to face the new administration was whether or not to attempt to resupply Fort Sumter in South Carolina and Fort Pickens in Florida. Both were federal properties located in states that had joined the Confederacy. Chase urged the President not to abandon the forts, and in April, the decision was made to send provisions to Fort Sumter. In response, the leaders of the Confederacy fired on the fort and asked for its surrender. Fort Sumter surrendered on April 13. When Lincoln heard the news, he set in motion numerous war measures. The call to arms resulted in the secession of the rest of the South from the Union.

Meanwhile, Chase was busy assuming his new role as Secretary of the Treasury. The Treasury Department was a vast bureaucracy that performed such diverse activities as controlling customs, collecting tariffs, performing audits on government departments, keeping track of government revenues, serving as treasurer with respect to the government's monies, and serving as solicitor in civil cases brought by the government. Many appointments had to be made to fill all of the positions, and many new positions were created under the Chase tenure. Most were filled via a patronage system, which gave the Secretary considerable clout.

Chase inherited a budget deficit from the previous administration of approximately $75 million. Revenues from tariffs were down, and the government had been forced to offer rates of 10 to 12 percent in order to sell bonds. In the 1850s, the major sources of revenue for the federal government were tariffs and public land sales. No national banking system was in place, so selling debt was extremely difficult. And new taxes were not a popular way of raising money. Add to this the specter of a civil war with the need to raise even more revenue, and the atmosphere at the Treasury Department was certainly one of crisis.

Chase and others believed the war would last for no longer than a year, so his proposals for raising revenues were based on that estimate. He proposed raising 25 percent of the $320 million he estimated would be necessary through taxing, land sales, and tariffs. Income taxes were levied for the first time in 1861, with incomes above $800 being taxed 3 percent. The Morrill tariff passed the Senate just prior to Lincoln's inauguration and restored tariff rates to about 25 percent. Chase suggested that the rest of the funds needed for the war effort be secured through borrowing. Congress authorized selling twenty-year bonds paying 7 percent interest and two types of Treasury notes: one interest bearing and the other called "demand notes," paying no interest but redeemable in specie. Chase met with bankers in New York to arrange the loans but insisted on the banks paying for the loans in gold rather than through a ledger system that would allow the banks to retain their specie. By December 1861, the banks' reserves were so low that they were forced to suspend their gold payments. December was also the month when the Treasury's annual report came out. Many hoped for a comprehensive financial plan for the country, but none was forthcoming. Rather than calling for large tax increases to fund the war, Chase recommended continued borrowing to finance the war effort. By now the war was costing $2 million a day. Chase attempted to borrow abroad, but an incident in which Confederate diplomats had been forced from a British ship (the *Trent* Affair) in combination with higher tariffs and the desire of most European countries to remain neutral made borrowing abroad impossible.

New sources for financing had to be found. A bill was introduced that both would allow for the issuing of $100 million of non-interest-bearing notes to serve as legal tender and would create a banking system that issued a national currency secured by government bonds. The monetary crisis forced the separation of the two notions, with the legal tender issues deemed the more critical. Chase had always been opposed to paper money, but the impending financial collapse of the government forced him to support the bill, which was approved in February 1862. By the end of 1863, $450 million worth of "greenbacks" were issued to meet emergency needs. The notes could be used to pay all debts within the United States except duties on imports and interest on the public debt. Additionally, $500 million worth of bonds paying 6 percent and redeemable in five years, though maturing in twenty, were issued. The Congress also proposed new tariffs on many items and established a new federal agency for collecting internal taxes, a duty formally performed by the states. Chase turned to Jay Cooke, a Philadelphia banker, for help with the bond sales. Cooke was extremely successful and by the middle of 1864 had sold some $510 million worth.

Chase had previously opposed a national banking system, but his work as Secretary convinced him of the usefulness of a national system with a common currency. The country had spawned some 1,600 separate banks with their own notes, and the number of banks made selling bonds very difficult. His 1861 report recommended the creation of the National Banking System. Banks that joined the system would be issued notes for 90 percent of the value of the bonds they purchased. The bonds themselves remained at the Treasury and were convertible into specie. The measure was opposed in the House by many who favored the state banking system, so the administration introduced the bill into the Senate, where it passed in February 1863 by a narrow margin. The House then followed with its approval, and the National Banking Act became law on February 25, 1863. Chase named Hugh McCulloch, an Indiana banker, as Comptroller of the currency, and it became his job to supervise the new banking association. In order to encourage banks to join, Chase argued for a surtax on state bank currencies; the tax was finally enacted in 1865 after Chase had left his position as Secretary. Several amendments were made to the 1863 law, all in an effort to encourage more participation.

As the war dragged on, numerous financial problems developed. The value of legal tender depreciated relative to gold. Because all imports had to be paid for in gold, gold prices soared, forcing Congress to pass a bill forbidding speculation in gold. Initially reluctant to impose taxes, by 1863 Chase began to urge their increase. As Chase was leaving office, Congress finally acted, increasing both personal taxes and tariffs. By 1865, incomes between $600 and $5,000 were taxed at 5 percent, between $5,000 and $10,000 at 7.5 percent, and above $10,000 at 10 percent. A large portion of the tax revenue was not collected until near the end of the war, and the income tax was discontinued in 1872. By 1864, average tariffs reached 47 percent.

Chase's other duties as Secretary involved controlling trade between Union-controlled areas and the Confederacy. The system involved a complex system of permits and authorizations aimed largely at maintaining the loyalty of border states who were dependent on Confederate states. Trade could be sanctioned with seceded states if it served the Union's interest. Naturally, such a system was subject to widespread abuse and fraud.

Certainly Chase was not schooled in public finance. Except for his experience as a bank solicitor, he was a civil rights lawyer and a politician. Those who have criticized Chase's performance as Secretary of the Treasury point to his issuing of great sums of unredeemable paper money and his refusal to insist on higher taxes to generate the necessary revenues to wage the war. However, the Chase record, when compared with that of his World War I and II counterparts, would show that neither the size of Civil War debt nor the interest rate paid on it were excessive.

From the beginning, Chase urged a vigorous prosecution of the Civil War. Simon Cameron, Lincoln's first appointee as Secretary of War, was poorly equipped for the position. This placed responsibility for the war effort on the shoulders of other Cabinet members. Chase was assigned the western border states. When Cameron was replaced by Edwin Stanton, a Democrat, at the end of 1861, Chase found his influence declining. Perhaps his interest in military matters stemmed from the problems he was encountering at the Treasury and his realization that the longer the war persisted, the worse the financial crisis would become. Having supported George McClellan earlier, Chase urged Lincoln to remove the general from his military post for his poor execution of the war. As the Union lost more and more battles, Chase worried that the Republican administration would not be reelected in 1864.

The question of emancipating slaves of persons or states resisting the Union was forced on the administration by the actions of several generals who freed slaves in parts of the Confederacy under Union control. Initially resistant to the idea, in the summer of 1862, Lincoln informed the Cabinet of his decision to emancipate all slaves within states in insurrection as of January 1, 1863. Certainly

Chase was instrumental in pushing Lincoln in this direction. Chase, however, felt that William Seward, as Secretary of State, had more influence over Lincoln. In December 1862, Chase urged Lincoln to remove Seward for his lack of aggressive pursuit of victory in the war. Lincoln realized that he needed both Secretaries to remain at their posts, so he engineered a situation in which Chase was forced to utter supportive public statements about Seward, thereby averting the loss of either man's counsel. In December 1863, Lincoln announced a plan of tentative reconstruction and amnesty. Chase felt the plan did not go far enough. He wanted a constitutional amendment abolishing slavery. The Thirteenth Amendment passed the Senate but was blocked in the House. Lincoln realized that he had to move slowly with reconciliation plans; Chase, never a moderate either with respect to stance or pace, consistently urged extreme positions taken in haste.

Chase continued his interest in the presidential nomination. Early in 1864 Samuel Pomeroy and others formed a campaign committee for his nomination. They produced pamphlets condemning Lincoln; unfortunately for Chase, the propaganda damaged him more than Lincoln. Chase was forced to withdraw from the race in March, largely as a result of congressional attacks alleging corruption in his role as Secretary. His relationship with Jay Cooke was called into question. Chase felt the attacks were made with Lincoln's tacit approval. A final break with Lincoln occurred over Treasury patronage in New York. A vacancy developed at the Assistant Secretary level; Lincoln wanted Chase to appoint someone the New York contingent favored. Chase insisted on his own choice, M. B. Field, and offered his resignation to Lincoln. To Chase's surprise, Lincoln accepted and the Secretary was suddenly unemployed, leaving office June 30, 1864.

Chase did campaign for Lincoln's successful reelection. Lincoln returned the favor by appointing Chase Chief Justice of the Supreme Court on December 6, 1864, following the death of Chief Justice Roger Taney. Lincoln reasoned that Chase was familiar with many of the laws that would be challenged and believed that Chase had an interest in having them upheld. Chase had told many people of his interest in the Chief Justice appointment; he did not, however, find the work of the Court particularly interesting. He found it difficult to stay out of politics and the issues of Reconstruction and black suffrage. Perhaps because of this, the Chase Court was extremely active.

Following Lincoln's assassination, Andrew Johnson became President. He asked Chase to draft a Reconstruction policy. Chase felt he could influence the new leader and formulated a policy calling for universal suffrage. Chase took a trip to the South to investigate conditions but returned to Washington to find that Johnson had decided to do his own Reconstruction plan.

Chase was involved with two significant trials as Chief Justice: the trial of Jefferson Davis and the impeachment trial of Andrew Johnson. Following the war, Jefferson Davis was held in prison for two years and then indicted for treason. In December 1868, a motion to quash the indictment was argued before Justices Chase and Underwood in Richmond. The Justices disagreed, with Chase arguing that the Fourteenth Amendment precluded punishing Davis. The case was pending before the Supreme Court when, on December 25, 1868, President Johnson issued unconditional pardons to all who had participated in the insurrection. Regarding Johnson's impeachment trial in the spring of 1868, the charges against the President of "high crimes and misdemeanors in office" were largely political and a result of his opposition to the Congress's plan for Reconstruction and his removal of Stanton from the War Department. Chase made no secret of his opposition to Johnson's impeachment and his intention to preside over a fair trial. He forced the Congress to convene as a court, so that rules for evidence would apply and due process would occur. A number of factors contributed to Johnson's acquittal: The charges against him were poorly framed; the trial lasted for eleven weeks and participants became weary of the whole affair; Grant had been named the Republican presidential nominee, so Johnson would not be a candidate for reelection; and Johnson's current term was nearly over.

In 1868, Chase once again sought the presidential nomination. The popularity of Ulysses S. Grant and the anger Chase had generated among the Republican leadership for his handling of Johnson's impeachment trial made Chase's becoming the party's candidate an impossibility. So Chase, to whom specific party affiliation was less important than were principles, attempted to become the choice of the Democratic Party. Support, however, dwindled when the time came for delegates to cast their votes, and Chase once again had to concede defeat.

Numerous cases involving various constitutional issues came before the Chase Court. A number of them involved actions of administrations in wartime, and several cases involved the validity of congressional Reconstruction. In *Mississippi v. Johnson* (1867), the state of Mississippi asked the Court to restrain the President from enforcing the first Reconstruction Act. The Court refused to grant an injunction, saying it could not interfere with the President's performance of his political duties. In the *McCardle* case (1867), the Court ruled that the Congress had the right to take jurisdiction of a case away from the Court. Finally, in the Slaughterhouse Cases (1873), involving an application of the Fourteenth Amendment, the Court ruled that states had the right to define laws regulating their citizens. Chase dissented from the Court's opinion. Later this landmark decision was used to deny black citizens federal protection with respect to their civil rights.

Chase suffered his first stroke in 1870, but his desire to become President never waned. Had the Liberal Republicans offered him the nomination in 1872, he would have accepted. However, his health was failing. On May 6, 1873, Salmon Portland Chase suffered a massive stroke and died the following day.

BIBLIOGRAPHY
Blue, Frederick J. *Salmon P. Chase: A Life in Politics.* Kent, OH: Kent State University Press, 1987.
Chase, Salmon P. *Inside Lincoln's Cabinet: The Civil War Diaries of Salmon P. Chase.* Edited by David Donald. New York: Longmans, Green and Co., 1954.

Faulkner, Harold U. *American Economic History*. 7th ed. New York: Harper and Brothers, 1954.

McCulloch, Hugh. *Men and Measures of Half a Century*. New York: Charles Scribner's Sons, 1888.

Morris, Jeffrey Bradson. "Chase and Waite Courts and Eras." In *Encyclopedia of the American Judicial System*, edited by Robert J. Janosik. New York: Charles Scribner's Sons, 1987.

Phelps, Mary Merwin. *Kate Chase, Dominant Daughter*. New York: Thomas Y. Crowell Co., 1935.

Piatt, Donn. *Memories of the Men Who Saved the Union*. New York: Belford, Clarke, 1887.

Ross, Ishbel. *Proud Kate*. New York: Harper and Brothers, 1953.

Rothschild, Alonzo. *Lincoln: Master of Men*. Boston and New York: Houghton, Mifflin and Company, 1906.

Schuckers, J. W. *The Life and Public Services of Salmon Portland Chase*. New York: D. Appleton and Company, 1874.

Studenski, Paul, and Hermann Kroos. *Financial History of the United States*. 2nd ed. New York: McGraw-Hill, 1963.

Urofsky, Melvin I. *A March to Liberty: A Constitutional History of the United States*. New York: Knopf, 1988.

NANCY M. THORNBORROW

HOWELL COBB (September 7, 1815–October 9, 1868). Howell Cobb of Athens, Georgia, served as James Buchanan's first Secretary of the Treasury from March 7, 1857, to December 8, 1860, the chaotic years immediately preceding the American Civil War. Prior to his appointment, Cobb, an experienced career politician, had served in many positions of leadership and responsibility including Governor of Georgia, Congressman, and Speaker of the House for the 31st Congress. After his withdrawal from Buchanan's Cabinet, he entered the service of the Confederate States of America, first as President of the Provisional Confederate Congress and subsequently in the Army of the Confederacy, retiring in 1865 with the rank of major general.

The economic agenda that Cobb brought to the Treasury reflected the traditional Jacksonian Democratic positions that appeared in that party's 1856 platform. Cobb opposed federally sponsored internal improvements, protective tariffs, and a federally chartered central bank. He also believed in "hard money" and supported the Independent Treasury System under which the government served as its own banker.

Early in his career, Cobb established himself as a political moderate and a staunch Unionist. It was this reputation that earned him an important place in Buchanan's Cabinet. From his position as one of Buchanan's closest advisers within the Cabinet, Cobb played a significant role in crafting administration policy over a wide range of issues. During his tenure as Secretary the issues related to states rights and the extension of slavery divided the nation ever more deeply along regional lines. In the end, he was sadly forced to choose between his belief in the Constitution of the United States, on the one hand, and his loyalty to policies advocated by many in his home state of Georgia, on the other. In response to the election of the Republican candidate, Abraham Lincoln, in November 1860, he chose the latter and resigned. Upon leaving office, he warned his fellow Georgians that with Lincoln's assumption of power, equality and safety within the Union would be replaced with sectionalism and hatred. Because of his decision to support secession, he is more often remembered for his abandonment of Buchanan than for his economic philosophy or his earlier Unionist principles.

Although Cobb spent most of his political career in Washington, his roots were planted firmly in the South. He was born on September 7, 1815, at "Cherry Hill," a cotton plantation owned by his family in Jefferson County, Georgia. His parents were John Addison Cobb, an ambitious cotton planter and entrepreneur who served several terms in the state legislature, and Sarah Rootes Cobb of Virginia. Howell was the eldest of seven children. His brother Thomas R. R. Cobb became an active secessionist and joined Howell in the service of the Confederacy.

In 1819, when Cobb was still a young child, his family transferred its residence to Cobbham in Athens, Georgia, then a growing academic and commercial community. He attended school in Athens, and in August 1834, he was graduated with honors from the University of Georgia (then Franklin College), where he would have taken the required course in political economy.

Cobb's political philosophy and economic outlook were formed during this period. He was strongly influenced by his father, a supporter of Andrew Jackson, especially in his opposition to nullification, the principle advocated by John C. Calhoun that defended the authority of a state to overrule federal law.

On May 26, 1835, Cobb married Mary Ann Lamar, the daughter of a wealthy Huguenot family from Milledgeville, Georgia. Howell followed in the family tradition and showed an early interest in public service and Georgia politics. He read law under General Edward Harden and traveled with him around the Georgia circuit court. Cobb was admitted to the bar in 1836 and briefly practiced law in the Athens area. From 1837 to 1841 he served as Solicitor-General of the Western Circuit of Georgia. In 1840 he ran, unsuccessfully, for Congress, opposing the Whigs, who advocated the recharter of the national bank and federally sponsored internal improvements.

In 1842, Cobb was elected as a Representative to the U.S. Congress. He served from March 4, 1843, to March 3, 1851, a period encompassing the administrations of Tyler, Polk, Taylor, and Filmore. During this period the United States went to war against Mexico, and the issue of slavery posed a constant threat to national unity. Cobb was considered a loyal Democrat and moderate. During the Mexican War (1846–1848), he supported the Polk administration. He was a strong champion for the annexation of Texas and advocated a militant position in the dispute between Oregon and Canada—"Fifty-four, forty or fight." At President Polk's request he shepherded the Walker Bill for lower tariffs through the House.

Cobb rapidly established himself as a party leader and in 1849, during his last term of office, at the age of thirty-four, was elected Speaker of the House for the 31st Congress in a heated contest with Robert Winthrop, a Whig from Massachusetts.

In Cobb's home state of Georgia, the Governor called for a state convention to rule on the validity of the Compromise of 1850, which failed to resolve the slavery and states rights issues. In 1851, Cobb returned to Georgia to support the Compromise legislation and subsequently run for Governor. The Democratic Party in Georgia split down the middle and severed its alliance with the national organization. The majority of the Georgian Democratic leadership formed the Southern Rights Party. Cobb and several prominent Georgia Whigs, including both Alexander Stephens and Robert Toombs, formed the Constitutional Union Party.

After the state convention voted to support the Compromise of 1851, Cobb was nominated by the Constitutional Union Party to run for Governor. He was elected in a landslide, soundly defeating his opponent, Charles J. McDonald, who represented the Southern Rights Party. Although victorious, the win proved costly to Cobb in the long run as he made many enemies among Georgia Democrats and lost the unqualified support of the national Democratic Party.

Cobb served only one term as Governor, but it was an active one. At the end of his term as Governor, the party rejected his bid for the U.S. Senate. He was further disappointed when the newly elected President, Franklin Pierce, for whom Cobb had campaigned enthusiastically, failed to give him a Cabinet position. With his political career in limbo and his finances temporarily in a precarious position, Cobb returned to the practice of law.

Cobb returned to Washington, again as a congressional Representative, from March 4, 1855, to March 3, 1857. Now at odds with the Douglas faction of the Democratic Party, he supported James Buchanan in his bid for the presidency in 1856. He campaigned extensively in Pennsylvania and Indiana, two states critical to Buchanan's election.

When Buchanan was elected in 1856, it came as no surprise that Cobb was selected to hold a ranking position within the Cabinet. It was clear that the most important and most difficult challenge of the Buchanan administration would be to hold the Union together. His Cabinet selections would be critical to success. As a Democrat from Pennsylvania with Southern sympathies, Buchanan needed a Cabinet that was geographically balanced, unified in political philosophy, and not associated with either political extreme.

Cobb was an obvious choice. Not only had he supported Buchanan and his platform on the campaign trail, but he was a Southerner with a strong and visible record of support for the Union. In addition, he was considered by his supporters as intelligent, pragmatic, congenial, a strong leader, and a capable negotiator. Early rumors identified Cobb as first choice for Secretary of State, but he was bypassed so the office could be given to the elderly Lewis Cass, a former presidential candidate from Illinois who represented the interests of the Northwest, a region growing in importance and pivotal to the balance of power. Instead, Cobb was offered the second-ranking Cabinet position, and on March 7, 1857, he assumed office as Buchanan's Treasury Secretary.

Evaluations of Cobb's performance as Treasury Secretary are mixed. He is praised by some observers as an intelligent and able administrator who promoted efficiency in Treasury operations and acted promptly and effectively to avoid a rash of New York City bank failures in the wake of the Panic of 1857. Others denounce him as a politically ambitious opportunist who intended to use his position merely as a stepping stone to the Democratic presidential nomination in 1860. These critics blame him for mismanagement of the chronically empty national Treasury and accuse him, along with the other Southern members of the Cabinet, of attempting to dictate administration policy in areas outside the purview of their portfolios. Some nicknamed Buchanan's Cabinet the "Directory," a reference to the dictatorial regime that ruled postrevolutionary France. A review of the events and conditions prevailing at the time lends some measure of truth to all of these claims.

In fairness to Secretary Cobb, economic and political conditions beyond his control determined that his term would be a stormy one for the Treasury and the administration. When Cobb assumed office in March 1857, the Tariff Act of 1857 reduced tariff rates to their lowest level in half a century. During this period, customs revenue provided the chief source of income for the federal government (86 percent in 1856), and this reduction in rates meant, other things being equal, revenue would be lower for any given level of imports. The Panic of 1857 reduced consumption and therefore imports, providing a second negative influence on customs revenue.

By 1858, the Treasury, which had operated in surplus for the previous seven years, was running a $27.3 million deficit. Not only had tariff revenue decreased, but receipts from the sale of public lands declined by over half between 1856 and 1858. Meanwhile, expenditures, especially military expenditures associated with the Mormon War, had increased. In December 1857 and again in June 1858 Cobb was forced to borrow a total of $40 million to cover the government's deficits. Although conditions improved after 1858, the Treasury continued to operate at a deficit for much of the remainder of the Buchanan administration. The public debt increased from $28.7 million in 1858 to $64.8 million in 1860. Although Cobb was much berated for his poor financial management of the Treasury because of this accumulated debt, it is difficult to see how he could have avoided it under these conditions.

Before reviewing Cobb's policy initiatives during this period, it would be helpful to describe briefly the structure of the Independent Treasury System under which the federal government operated. The Independent Treasury was an outgrowth of the strong Democratic aversion to a central bank and its suspicion of the private banking system in general. During the Panic of 1837 the government had been unable to access funds in insolvent private banks and thus was unable to use the power of the purse to revive the economy. Under the Independent Treasury System the government withdrew itself from the private banking system by acting as its own fiscal agent, maintaining its own accounts in specie (coin), at the Treasury, the mints, and various subtreasuries throughout the country. In theory, all payments or disbursements were in specie or Treasury notes. In practice, this was not always the case, especially in remote areas.

Although the Independent Treasury System protected government assets from the vagaries of insolvent private banks, it did not isolate the banking and credit system from the actions of the Treasury. Its existence meant that government budgetary policy influence extended not only to fiscal policy in the traditional Keynesian sense but to monetary policy as well. In terms of its monetary impact, when the government budget was in surplus, the government was, in effect, drawing specie away from the private sector, potentially reducing the reserve basis for bank notes and credit extension; a government deficit produced the opposite effect. It should be noted that in the years immediately preceding the Panic of 1857, the federal government ran a considerable surplus. This situation could be interpreted as a de facto restrictive monetary initiative. After the panic, and indeed throughout most of Cobb's tenure, the government budget was in deficit. Both fiscal and monetary policy could be interpreted as expansive. The overall monetary impact, of course, would have been determined by a matrix of influences of which the impact of the Independent Treasury on specie was only one factor. To the last, Cobb defended the Independent Treasury System as it was established by the Democratic Presidents of the preceding decade. Not only did Cobb operate his Treasury under this system, he was a strong advocate of its extension to the state level as a measure to prevent the overexpansion of the banking system.

The 1850s was a decade of rapid economic growth in the United States. New farms and towns sprang up as the frontier moved rapidly west. During the second half of the decade, railroads expanded at an average rate of 2,000 miles per year. The discovery of gold in California provided a source for credit expansion and financed a growing stream of imports. The number of banks multiplied, and conditions in Europe provided a strong market for American exports. Such periods are often followed by overexpansion of credit, highly leveraged investment in real estate and emerging industries, and rapidly rising commodity prices. Business cycle theory of the day predicted the economy was ripe for an inevitable recession (or, as it was known at that time, a "revulsion" of trade). By 1857 high commodity prices were choking industrial production, and the end of the Crimean War had both reduced exports to Europe and reversed the influx of European capital to American financial markets. On August 24, 1857, financial panic occurred when the Ohio Life Insurance and Trust Company collapsed, sending banks in New York City scurrying for specie and suspending specie payments.

Cobb confidently expected the revulsion would be short-lived. His recovery strategy had several components and focused on restoring order and stability to financial markets and establishing a sound currency. He believed the real side of the economy had an innate capacity for recovery, and the previous high level of activity would be restored within the year. Further, he argued that the government had little or no legitimate role to play in reviving the industrial sector. Cobb's initial move was to inject gold reserves into the New York banking system by purchasing government securities, thereby restoring specie payments. Many observers have judged this a successful maneuver and credit Cobb with restored monetary stability by year's end. Some authors, however, attribute the recovery in the New York City banking system to private sector initiatives.

Like Buchanan, Cobb identified overextension of credit by the banking system as the cause of the panic. In his annual report of *The State of the Finances* in 1857 he offered several suggestions to reform the banking and monetary system. First, he advised Congress to remove the charters of deficient banks. Second, he recommended that neither federal nor state securities be allowed to back bank notes. Third, he wanted the gold ratio behind the notes reduced from one to seven to one to three. Fourth, he recommended no bank notes under $20 be issued and that all wages be paid in coin. Finally, he advised states to adopt the Independent Treasury System.

Although order in financial markets and the banking system were largely restored by year's end, the country's industrial sector was slower to recover, and persistent unemployment haunted major urban areas and factory towns, especially in the North. Customs revenue stabilized near recession levels, and the federal Treasury remained out of balance. In contrast to the large number of policies Cobb suggested to revive and stabilize the monetary/financial sector, Cobb's suggestions to improve the level of economic activity might be described as "benign neglect," to use a modern phrase. Cobb believed that the federal government had no direct role to play in this part of the recovery. This conclusion reflected both his economic outlook and his political philosophy.

In his first report to the legislature issued in December 1857, Cobb outlined his fiscal formula: Reduce unnecessary public expenditures and increase revenues where advisable. He reasoned that employment of this strategy would reduce the need for government borrowing, and as the Treasury withdrew from money markets, more funding would be available for private sector investment and commerce. Cobb believed that the government should maintain the level of spending to meet contracts that it had begun and where resources were already hired but that it should not enter into any new projects that, although authorized, had not been started. As a result, he believed government economic policies should neither overtly eliminate nor add any jobs. In actuality, the ability to practice economy in government expenditures was limited, and total expenditures increased during the next few years, especially expenditures of the War Department.

On the income side, Cobb recommended that Congress consider reclassifying some imported goods to increase tariff revenues. However, no changes were made until the Morrill Tariff Act of 1861, which restored duties to their pre-1857 levels. This legislation did not become effective until after Cobb had left the Treasury.

Cobb's fiscal conservatism also had a political dimension. In keeping with Jeffersonian tradition, he felt that government expenditures should be limited to those specifically authorized by the Constitution. This belief was also implicit in the Democratic Party platform of 1856. Cobb believed that the federal government should refrain from assuming major responsibility for public improvements such as roads and harbors, even during periods of economic prosperity. After 1858, for example, federal expenditures for rivers and harbors declined.

Although industrial depression continued in the Northeast for the remainder of 1857 and the better part of 1858, by 1860 the recession was completely ended. Indeed, when economic statistics for 1850 are compared with 1860, the Panic of 1857 is largely invisible. Because Cobb optimistically believed that tariff revenues would soon be restored to higher levels, he recommended that the deficit be financed through Treasury notes of short duration rather than through longer-term loans. This strategy was to hurt the Treasury in the closing days of the Buchanan administration, as Treasury notes fell due at a time when political conditions made long-term financing difficult. This brief period of financial confusion in the last months of 1860 had political rather than economic origins and was soon overshadowed by the Civil War and its economic manifestations.

It is clear from the annual reports of the Secretary of the Treasury that Cobb, like most Southern Democrats, supported free trade subject to a revenue tariff. It should be noted, however, that since the customs revenue was the chief source of income for the federal government for much of the nineteenth century, the tariff rate was not insubstantial, bottoming out at around 15 percent (24 percent for protected industries) in 1857 during the Buchanan administration (compared with a 3 percent rate, which would be more common today).

Cobb opposed a protective tariff on two grounds: the negative effect on the consumer and the discouragement of exports. On the first point, Cobb reasoned that a revenue tariff meant that although the consumer pays a higher price for an imported product, part of the price is transferred to the public sector and supports the government's activities. If the tariff is raised to the protective level, that eliminates imports. However, the consumer pays a still-higher price, with all the price differential going to the domestic producer, who shares it with no one (i.e., the producer reaps the entire benefit). Compounding the injury to the consumer, the government must tax him in some other form, so the consumer is left with both a higher price and an additional tax. Cobb continues the analysis with the dubious piece of logic that since there are more consumers than producers, the loss to the consumers outweighs the benefit to the producers. During the controversy over tariffs in the 1800s, there were those who maintained that tariff reduction was the cause of midcentury depressions and financial panics. Cobb adamantly rejected this idea; instead, he blamed the excesses of speculators and the banking system.

In 1860, Cobb seriously entertained running for President, but the Georgia delegation to the Charleston Convention would not support his candidacy because of his earlier defection in 1851. With the election of Abraham Lincoln, he resigned his Cabinet position and headed for the secessionist camp.

After leaving the Treasury, Cobb turned his attention to the emerging confederation of Southern states. Along with former Unionists Alexander Stephens and Robert Toombs, he urged his fellow Georgians to opt for secession. The Georgia Ordinance of Secession was adopted on January 19, 1861. Shortly thereafter, a convention of delegates from the secessionist states met in Montgomery, Alabama. At this meeting, Cobb was unanimously elected President of the assembly, which became the Provisional Confederate Congress. On February 18, 1861, Cobb administered the oath of office to the President of the Confederacy, Jefferson Davis. Alexander Stephens was named Vice President.

Declining any permanent political position in the Davis administration, Cobb joined the Confederate Army while at the same time completing his duties with the Provisional Congress. He quickly organized the 16th Georgia Volunteers from his home district and was commissioned its colonel. His two older sons, John and Lamar, transferred to the regiment, and in 1861, it saw service under General J. B. Magruder in the Peninsula Army stationed just outside Richmond. In 1863, he was promoted to the rank of major general and transferred to Georgia, where he organized auxiliary units assigned to protect the home district in case of emergency. He served in Georgia until April 20, 1865, when he surrendered to General Wilson. He was arrested after the war but rapidly pardoned by President Johnson.

After the war, Cobb retired to private life and opened a law office with James Jackson in Macon, Georgia. His career was cut short on October 9, 1868, when he died suddenly at the Fifth Avenue Hotel in New York City at the age of fifty-three. His body was returned to Georgia, and he is buried at the Oconee Cemetery in Athens, Georgia.

Although he never realized his highest political ambitions and is criticized by some historians for his abandonment of his early Unionist principles, he is well remembered by at least one member of Buchanan's Cabinet, Jeremiah Black, who called Cobb honorable, upright, true to his convictions, perfectly faithful to his duties as he understood them, and a man of great intellectual ability.

BIBLIOGRAPHY

Auer, J. Jeffrey, ed. *Antislavery and Disunion, 1858–1861*. New York: Harper & Row, 1963.

Buchanan, James. *Mr. Buchanan's Administration on the Eve of Rebellion*. New York: D. Appleton and Company, 1865.

Dewey, Davis Rich. *Financial History of the United States*. 12th ed. New York: Augustus M. Kelley Publisher, 1968.

Klein, Philip Shriver. *President James Buchanan: A Biography*. University Park: Pennsylvania State University Press, 1962.

Mitchell, C. A *History of the Greenbacks: With Special Reference to the Economic Consequences of Their Issue: 1862–1865*. Chicago: University of Chicago Press, 1903.

Montgomery, Horace. *Howell Cobb's Confederate Career*. Tuscaloosa, AL: Confederate Publishing Company, 1959.

MARIE McKINNEY

JOHN B. CONNALLY (February 27, 1917–June 15, 1993). John Bowden Connally was the second of the three Secretaries of the Treasury during Richard Nixon's first term. While all three were very different in their backgrounds, demeanor, and behavior, John Connally was certainly the livelier. His predecessor, David Kennedy, was a lifelong banker with an extensive career with the Board of Governors of the Federal Reserve System, as well as in private banking in Chicago. Further, Kennedy was viewed as a "gradualist" and a "thoughtful" person known for not raising his voice.

Connally's successor, George Shultz, educated as a professional economist at Massachusetts Institute of Technology (MIT), with extensive experience including service as a senior staff economist on the Council of Economic Advisers and Director of the Federal Office of Management and Budget, likewise was thoughtful and "professorial." Today, Shultz is a senior researcher at the Hoover Institute at Stanford University.

Connally was never a gradualist. Rather, his style was to paint with broad strokes. Where Kennedy and Shultz would follow a carefully thought out game plan steadily leading to the goal line, Connally would go for the "long bomb."

Where Kennedy and Shultz were both educated, trained, and experienced in economics and banking, Connally's résumé was notably absent of such attributes. When questioned about his qualifications for the job, Connally did acknowledge that he "could add." He was above all a man of supreme self-confidence and one who understood that in public life it was "political economy" that was more important than "economy." It was in the arena of politics where Connally was the master. Nixon called upon him when in 1971 he needed a Secretary of the Treasury who as economic quarterback would throw the long bomb (Wicker).

That John Connally was "Texas big" was due to his father, six-foot-five John Bowden Connally, Sr. John, Sr., had worked as a cowboy, barber, and grocer as well as being a dairyman and tenant farmer. His mother was a former schoolteacher who became the farmer's wife, bearing eight children in all. John, Jr., the third son, was born on February 27, 1917, on the Connally farm in Floresville, Texas, south of San Antonio.

Life on a farm in those days was hard work even for the young children. In 1926 the senior Connally gave up farming to move to San Antonio to run a bus service. The family lived in Harlandale, a suburb of San Antonio. John, Jr., was attracted to debate and drama in elementary and high school. In 1932 the family returned to Wilson County, where John Connally, Sr., bought a large spread of ranch land.

In 1936 John Connally, Sr., was elected the County Clerk. The elder Connally was setting a precedent for his son, who had enrolled at the University of Texas in 1933. The younger Connally, born to modest means, had learned the ethos of hard work from the farming, an appreciation for risk and entrepreneurship from his father's bus business and ranching, and finally a taste for politics.

John Connally attended the University of Texas on a National Youth Administration (NYA) stipend, earning seventeen cents per hour working in the university library. The NYA was Franklin Roosevelt's youth employment agency, which in Texas was directed by the young Lyndon Johnson. Connally was drawn to oratory and in his second year at the university became President of the Atheneum Literary Society and won the campus oratorical contest. He started law school in his third year. As an actor and leading man on the campus stage, he met his future wife Idanell (Nellie) Brill, who was also on the campus stage. In 1938 he was elected student body President. It is noteworthy that Robert (Bobbie) Strauss, future head of the Democratic Party, was his campaign manager. He graduated from the University of Texas in 1939 with a combined bachelor's and law degree.

Following graduation, Connally moved to Washington, D.C., to work as a secretary (legislative assistant) to Lyndon Johnson, who was only nine years his senior. Connally had been sought after by top law firms in Austin and by the State Attorney General. But Connally chose the position with Johnson, where he quickly became First Secretary. Johnson was not noted for courteous treatment of his staff assistants. John Connally was the exception, whom Lyndon Johnson treated as an equal.

Lyndon Johnson was a lieutenant commander in the naval reserve and a member of the House Naval Affairs Committee. Connally soon gained a commission as a naval reserve officer. In 1940 he married Nellie Brill, his college sweetheart.

In 1941 Johnson ran for a one-year replacement term to the U.S. Senate and chose the twenty-four-year-old Connally as his campaign manager. Johnson was defeated. Connally and Johnson were inextricably linked for the rest of their careers.

Following the Japanese attack on Pearl Harbor on December 7, 1941, Lyndon Johnson took leave from Congress for active military duty. Within eight months, during which he was awarded a Silver Star for bravery for action out of New Guinea, Johnson was recalled to Washington by President Roosevelt, as were all members of Congress. Connally was increasingly drawn into the military effort, cutting back on his work for Johnson. In 1943 Connally was sent to Algiers as part of the Lend-lease Program efforts.

In June 1944, John Connally was assigned to the aircraft carrier *Essex*. By December he was promoted to chief flight direction officer. In April 1945 in defense of Okinawa the Japanese used kamikazes. For his efforts, Connally was awarded his first Bronze Star. He was then assigned to the carrier *Bennington* and placed in charge of the Combat Information Center for the entire task force, later being awarded his second Bronze Star.

Discharged in February 1946 as a lieutenant commander, John Connally returned home as a naval hero at age twenty-nine. In 1948, Connally managed Lyndon Johnson's campaign for the U.S. Senate. Winning the Democratic primary by a highly questionable eighty-seven votes, Johnson became known as "Landslide Lyndon." Connally returned to practice law with Johnson's political adviser, Alvin Wirtz. Wirtz died in 1951, and Connally went to work for Sid Richardson, one of the Texas "oil millionaires." While working for Richardson, for nine years, Connally became part of Fort Worth society.

In 1956 Lyndon Johnson was the favorite son candidate for President from Texas. John Connally nominated him at the Democratic National Convention. Connally as the Vice Chairman of the Texas delegation supported John F. Kennedy as the vice presidential candidate to run with Adlai Stevenson. Estes Kefauver emerged as the party's vice presidential candidate.

Tragedy struck the Connallys in April 1958, as their oldest daughter died of self-inflicted wounds. Her death was ruled to be an accident, but it remained a mystery as to whether her death was an accident or suicide. Reston reports that in later years John Connally would recall it as the "greatest tragedy of his life, greater than the assassination in Dallas" (186).

John F. Kennedy and Lyndon B. Johnson both ran for the Democratic nomination for President in 1960. Kennedy ran in the primaries, while Johnson's approach was to win by power brokering. Connally established the "unofficial" Johnson headquarters in Washington, D.C. Connally was instrumental in getting Kennedy's medical problems into the press in an effort to scuttle Kennedy's nomination. The disclosure of Kennedy's Addison's disease had minimal impact, and he went on to win the nomination. Kennedy reluctantly acceded to running with Johnson as his vice presidential candidate. Connally ran the Texas campaign, working hard to convince Kennedy not to repeal the oil depletion allowance. This allowance was a "sacred cow" to oil men, who, of course, were the biggest contributors from Texas.

Connally was named Secretary of the Navy by the victorious Kennedy. This was certainly a most convenient position from the perspective of the Texas oil men. The Navy was the largest buyer of oil, and the Secretary supervised the Navy's vast oil reserves.

During Connally's tenure as Navy Secretary, he oversaw the rapid expansion of nuclear submarines. Kennedy considered appointing him Assistant Secretary for Latin America, but Connally decided to return to Texas and run for Governor in 1962.

John Connally became Governor of Texas in January 1963. He was an elegant man—tall, handsome, and regal. Reston wrote that "he symbolized Texas royalty over Texas peasantry" (213). But while Connally was a member of Fort Worth society—rich, powerful, good looking, and famous—Lee Harvey Oswald had only the city in common with him.

Lee Harvey Oswald was an ex-Marine who had defected to the Soviet Union in 1959 at the age of twenty. While there, he married Marina in April 1960. By July 1961 he had become disenchanted with life in the Soviet Union and decided to return to the United States. The one accomplishment of which he was very proud was his service in the United States Marines. While his original discharge had been "honorable," this was later changed to "undesirable." He became fixated with this downgraded discharge. It would, he felt, jeopardize his chances for decent employment.

Oswald wrote to John Connally on January 31, 1962, asking him as Secretary of the Navy to reinstate his honorable discharge. But Connally had resigned his position as Navy Secretary six weeks earlier. Oswald developed a consuming hatred for Connally, blaming him for the failure to upgrade the discharge.

While Oswald was seething over his undesirable discharge from the Marines, the Democrats in Texas were faced with a major embroglio between the conservative faction headed by Connally and the liberals championed by Senator Ralph Yarborough. President Kennedy flew to Texas on November 21 for a four-city engagement of speaking, fund-raising, campaigning, and fence mending.

On November 22, the presidential motorcade was in Dallas; Governor Connally and his wife Nellie were seated in the front of the limousine, while President Kennedy and his wife Jackie sat behind them. President Kennedy was seated directly behind the Governor. Vice President Johnson and Senator Yarborough followed in a car behind.

At Dealey Plaza by the Texas Book Depository, shots rang out, leaving the young President dead and the Governor gravely wounded. Volumes have been written about this American tragedy and whether Oswald was the lone presidential assassin. From his painful and tragic perspective, John Connally was convinced that the Warren Commission's "single bullet" theory was wrong. Further, he suspected that the intended victim had not been the President but rather himself.

Connally was severely wounded in the back, chest, wrist, and thigh. There was fear that his wounds, as the President's, would be fatal. But by mid-December he was able to leave the hospital. While his energy was severely strapped, he was determined to make a mark as Governor. His friend and political mentor Lyndon Johnson was now President.

With a booming oil-based economy, Texas was running a large state surplus. Connally set out to become the "education governor," with a major emphasis on higher education. He viewed education as the most effective antipoverty program and a good "investment." According to Reston, he sought to "restructure the entire system of higher education . . . and over time, to advance faculty salaries ten percent above the national average," with pay raises for public schoolteachers as well (307).

He had remained independent of Kennedy's and Johnson's positions on race by opposing equality in public accommodations. However, he appointed record numbers of blacks and Hispanics to public office. His popularity among Latinos soared. But his patriarchlike handling of a Latino-led labor march on Austin in the summer of 1966 did much to reduce his popularity with the Latinos.

Connally was tiring. His energy level never fully returned after the Dallas assassination. He announced his decision not to run for Governor on November 10, 1967. The following spring, Connally's popularity was at its peak in Texas. He was perhaps the most popular Governor in the state's history.

Mired in the Vietnam War embroglio, President Lyndon Johnson decided not to seek another term as President. John Connally announced that he would accept the Texas nomination for President. While he was not a contender for the presidency at this time, it would increase his bargaining strength at the convention in Chicago.

The year 1968 was a year of tragedy and turmoil in America. The nation was split over the Vietnam War. Martin Luther King, Jr., was assassinated in April, and Robert Kennedy, the Democratic front-runner, was assassinated in June. At the Democratic National Convention, Connally gave a major speech denouncing the Soviet invasion of Czechoslovakia and the "soft" anti–Vietnam War policies of Senator Eugene McCarthy. This was instrumental in gaining support for the Johnson administration's Vietnam plank.

Governor Connally dropped his favorite son candidacy, releasing his delegates to Vice President Hubert Humphrey, with other southern delegations following suit. Humphrey emerged as the party's candidate. Connally was considered for the vice presidential spot. It would have provided a geographic and ideological balance, but Humphrey picked Senator Edward Muskie of Maine as his running mate. A divided Democratic Party emerged from the disastrously fractious convention. Richard Nixon was elected President.

Richard Milhouse Nixon was inaugurated President on January 20, 1969. David Kennedy, who had spent his entire career in banking, first with the Board of Governors of the Federal Reserve System and then as a private banker in Chicago, was named Secretary of the Treasury. Connally, now aged fifty-two, was appointed by Nixon to the "Ash Commission," named after its head, Roy Ash, the chief executive officer of Litton Industries. The commission's task was to study and make recommendations concerning government reorganization. Connally brought to the commission a firm grasp of politics and made a most favorable impression on President Nixon. To keep Connally in his administration, Nixon appointed him to the Foreign Intelligence Advisory Board in November 1970.

All was not going well at the Treasury. The national economy was weak, suffering from moderate unemployment together with rising rates of inflation. Secretary Kennedy's influence was waning, and particularly troubling to Nixon were the Secretary's ill-advised statements. While by today's standards it would seem minimal, the 4 percent rate of unemployment that Kennedy pronounced "acceptable" certainly was not so in late 1969 and 1970. He was castigated as insensitive by Republican and Democratic critics alike.

The 1970 congressional elections startled Nixon. The unemployment rate was now up to 6 percent, and industrial production was falling. With his reelection bid merely two years away, Nixon needed to take action. He still blamed Fed Chairman William McChesney Martin's tight money policy for his election loss to John Kennedy in 1960. The gradualism of David Kennedy was out of favor. What Nixon needed was someone with political savvy who would make bold moves.

Nixon approached Connally in early December 1970 and was truly excited when Connally agreed to take the position of Treasury Secretary. There was general surprise and disappointment in Nixon's choice. After all, what qualifications did Connally possess? Not entirely in jest, Massachusetts Governor Francis Sargent asked, "Can John add?" (Ashman, 186). Connally was later to admit that "he knew virtually nothing about high finance when he accepted the job" (Reston, 394).

In Connally, Nixon got the economic quarterback who would "throw the long bomb." But Nixon got more than someone who would make bold moves. With Connally, a Democratic Treasury Secretary, the effort to stabilize the economy became bipartisan. With Connally he would have some added leverage with the Democratically controlled Congress. If the program was successful, Nixon would look good going into the 1972 elections. If the efforts failed, the Democrats would be at least partly to blame. But there was more. Nixon was able to get a man he truly admired. In Connally, he got a tough, self-confident Cabinet member, someone who had the traits he himself lacked. Nixon liked and admired Connally, who quickly became the administration's top economic adviser and a leading voice in the Cabinet.

The economic setting was deteriorating on both the domestic and international fronts. With unemployment at 5 percent and rising and inflation at 6 percent at the end of 1970, the nation was faced with "stagflation," inflation along with stagnation. The nation was running a chronic deficit in the balance of payments. Given the then-current gold exchange standard, trading partners could demand to exchange their dollar holdings for gold, which was pegged at $35 per ounce. The U.S. gold reserves continued to dwindle.

Into this milieu came John Connally, being confirmed on February 11, 1971. He made an enormous effort to learn about economic matters and the Treasury. His tutor was William McChesney Martin, the former head of the Federal Reserve. Connally made it clear to the other economic advisers, including Herbert Stein and Paul McCracken of the Council of Economic Advisers, Pete Peterson of the Council of International Economic Policy, George Shultz, Director of the Office of Management and Budget, and Arthur Burns of the Fed, that he was now in charge. Paul Volcker was his Undersecretary for monetary affairs.

He was a quick study, which was essential, given the continued deterioration of the national economy and the need to move decisively at the outset. In his first week as Treasury Secretary, the nation's largest defense contractor, Lockheed, was on the brink of bankruptcy. There had been major cuts in military contracts, which together with cost overruns were a major squeeze. But the L-1011 Airbus program was in jeopardy due to the bankruptcy of Rolls-Royce of England, which produced the engines. The orthodox economists opposed a bailout for the bad precedent that would be set. But Connally was not orthodox, nor was he constrained by ideology. He pressed for a bailout in the form of a $250 million loan guarantee to Lockheed. While Undersecretary of Defense David Packard, Fed Chairman Arthur Burns, and economist John Kenneth Galbraith opposed the measure, Connally vigorously defended the bailout before the

Senate Banking Committee. The measure just squeaked through by three votes in Congress and but one vote in the Senate.

The Lockheed problem paled in comparison to other economic difficulties facing the United States in 1971. The dollar was in retreat. The current international monetary system had been developed by the Allied nations at Bretton Woods, New Hampshire, in 1944 in anticipation of the end of World War II. It was here that the International Monetary Fund (IMF) and the World Bank were born. The system was devised to keep international currency exchange rates stable. The concern was that the uncertainties of currency fluctuations would dampen trade and consequently world economic expansion.

The parties to the Bretton Woods accords agreed to exchange their currencies at set rates relative to the U.S. dollar, with only narrow fluctuations permitted without IMF approval. These currencies could be exchanged for dollars at the set rates. Further, foreign dollar holdings could be exchanged on demand for gold at $35 per ounce. By 1971 the U.S. gold reserves were low. With the dollar overvalued relative to most major foreign currencies, the United States was pricing itself out of international markets. Foreign dollar holdings were growing rapidly and on July 30, 1991, reached $36.2 billion. According to Reston, at the $35 per ounce price of gold, the total U.S. gold reserves amounted to but $12 billion, or about one third of the potential foreign claim.

The international system was beginning to weaken and crack. In May, Germany and the Netherlands allowed their currencies to float, and Austria and Switzerland revalued their currencies. In a speech in Munich, Secretary Connally vowed the United States would never devalue the dollar. In June, he declared before the White House press corps that the administration would accept neither a wage and price board nor wage and price controls.

In July, the President ordered Connally to have a plan for him by August 6. Connally's response was certainly bold. The plan called for closing the gold window and imposing a wage and price freeze. That is, Connally proposed that the United States would unilaterally refuse to exchange foreign dollar holdings for gold. Connally argued that this move might not work but that anything less would certainly fail.

Actions by our allies ensured that action needed to be taken quickly. On August 9, France demanded to exchange $191 million in dollar holdings for gold, and on August 11, Great Britain demanded $3 billion. The diminished gold reserves would soon be at risk of being depleted.

On August 13, the President called his economic advisers to Camp David. Present were John Connally, George Shultz, Paul McCracken, Arthur Burns, Herb Stein, Paul Volcker, Pete Peterson, and speech writer William Safire. The key elements of the program were the end to convertibility (closing the gold window), a ninety-day freeze on wages and prices, a 10 percent surcharge on imports, and an investment tax credit. In the discussions over the program, Reston reports, the economists had been divided. Burns favored the incomes policy but opposed closing the gold window. Shultz and Stein favored closing the gold window but opposed wage and price controls. Volcker was for closing the window but argued that the 10 percent surcharge was too protectionist. Whatever the reservations of his advisers, President Nixon had clearly decided on accepting this program and was now merely concerned with its implementation. On August 15, President Nixon announced his program. A Sunday evening was deliberately chosen, as the financial markets were closed.

The program was officially dubbed the New Economic Policy (NEP). The Dow Jones average soared 32.9 points on Monday. Said Connally of this new policy, "We are at the end of an era in our economic policy." A *New York Times* article quoted him as saying, "American business and labor may have to get used to the idea of living within certain parameters" ("Obituary," D25).

Domestically, the program was generally viewed as satisfactory, at least in the near term. The wage and price controls were viewed favorably, and who could really relate to the gold window closing? But the foreign exchange markets were now in flux. What would be the new exchange rates? It took time to develop an orderly replacement. The 10 percent import surcharge was a sticking point with our trading partners. While Connally argued for its retention, Burns and Kissinger felt it could lead to retaliation.

On December 16, the finance ministers of the ten leading trading nations convened at the Smithsonian Institution. Connally negotiated agreements to realign the currencies, raising the price of gold from $35 to $38 per ounce, with the 10 percent import surcharge being dropped. While the "Smithsonian Agreement" was heralded by the President as a monumental achievement, it was merely a transitional stage on the way to floating exchange rates. It was, however, the first devaluation of the U.S. dollar since the 1930s.

The popularity of controls dropped over time as the predicted shortages emerged. After ninety days the economy entered Phase II, which a contemporary economics principles text described as "more of a thaw than a freeze" (Slesinger and Osman). Wage increases were to be monitored by a fifteen-member board and price issues resolved by another seven-member board.

By the spring of 1972 John Connally was becoming impatient with his job. He had been there for the bold moves, but they were behind him now. On June 12, 1972, he left office as Secretary of the Treasury at the height of his influence and popularity. Of his service, said Nixon, "Never has one cabinet member done more for his country in a year and a half" (Reston, 441).

There was much speculation over what national role Connally would now play. Perhaps he might replace William Rogers as Secretary of State in Nixon's second term; or perhaps he might be Nixon's running mate, although at least nominally Connally was still a Democrat. And dumping Spiro Agnew might rile the conservatives in the Republican Party. Nixon clearly admired Connally and wrote of him, "I believed that John Connally was the only man in either party who clearly had the potential to be a great president" (Reston, 443).

In August 1972, John Connally became head of "Democrats for Nixon," so disenchanted was he with the Democratic candidate, Senator George McGovern.

Many top Democrats were furious with this "turncoat." This action ended any role Connally would have as a Democratic Party leader. Two weeks before the presidential election, Connally gave a half-hour nationally televised address for Nixon and against McGovern.

In January 1973, Lyndon Johnson died, and his eulogy was delivered by his protégé, John Connally. In three months, Connally was a Republican. He, now as a Republican, was invited by President Nixon to serve as his part-time counselor. The "Watergate" affair was unraveling. Connally's advice to Nixon was to burn the tapes. After just over two months in Washington, Connally returned to Texas. It was prudent to distance himself from Nixon and Watergate.

On October 10, 1973, Spiro Agnew resigned as Vice President, having been charged with accepting kickbacks. Connally was viewed as a successor, but there was massive opposition from both Democrats and Republicans. Gerald Ford was confirmed as Vice President. Had Connally been named Vice President, he would of course have become president.

The parity price support system is familiar to all economists but rather arcane to most others, except those who stand to benefit from such a program. Briefly, it is a system of farm price supports instituted during the 1930s to insulate farmers from the declining and fluctuating incomes. There is to be a parity between the prices that farmers receive for their commodities and the prices they must pay. It is left to the Secretary of Agriculture to determine the proportion of parity to be maintained for various supported commodities. In 1971, milk was supported at 79 percent of parity. It would be in the interests of milk producers to have this proportion raised.

One of the major milk lobby groups, the Associated Milk Producers, Inc. (AMPI), had promised $2 million for Nixon's campaign. It was pressing for the parity to be raised from 79 percent to 85 percent. This increase in parity would mean hundreds of millions in added revenues to the dairy industry. AMPI threatened to withdraw its commitment to Nixon's campaign and intimated to Connally that further support would be forthcoming. With the administration's economists uniformly opposed to the increase, Connally convinced Nixon to accept the increase to 85 percent of parity.

In February 1974, Jake Jacobsen, Texan and long-term acquaintance of John Connally and lobbyist for AMPI, was indicted. Connally, accused of accepting $10,000 from Jacobsen, was indicted by a federal grand jury on charges of perjury and conspiracy to obstruct justice. Jacobsen testified against Connally at the trial but was "shattered" as a witness. Connally was exonerated by a federal jury in Washington in 1975. His political career was not dealt a fatal blow.

President Gerald Ford named Connally to his Foreign Intelligence Advisory Board in 1976. Many prominent Republicans wanted Connally as the vice presidential candidate under President Ford. In fact, Connally was on the short list of names Ford took to the Republican convention. But Ford settled on Senator Robert Dole as his running mate.

With his immediate political prospects dimmed, John Connally set his sights on accumulating wealth. He became a director on numerous corporate boards, and in 1977 he went into banking with two Arab sheiks. Politically, it was a disaster, as he could no longer claim neutrality in Middle Eastern affairs. He was charged with anti-Semitism. The charge was unfair, but it took its toll on Connally's political prospects.

On January 24, 1979, John Connally announced for the presidency. This was over a year in advance of the first primaries. In 1979 inflation and unemployment were again major issues, which should have given the former Treasury Secretary a major advantage. The Republican nomination was narrowing to Reagan, a former Democrat, and Connally, likewise an ex-Democrat. Connally suffered from "high negatives" with his reputation as a wheeler-dealer.

On October 11, 1979, Connally gave a major speech on the Middle East at the National Press Club in Washington and "committed political suicide" (Reston, 570). The speech was viewed as proArab and was met with a storm of protest from the American Jewish community. By the end of the month the polls reflected the damage caused by his speech. By December, Connally's campaign was running short of money. His run for the presidency faltered in the early primaries. He won one delegate to the convention. His presidential aspirations over, Connally returned to Texas.

In 1981, John Connally had a net worth of some $6 million. He was rich—but not "Texas rich." Together with Ben Barnes, former Lieutenant Governor of Texas, Connally became a developer of apartment complexes, shopping centers, office buildings, and resorts. By 1983 there were sixteen major projects under way worth a total of $231 million. But the Texas economy was buffeted by falling oil prices and the devaluation of the Mexican peso. Banking and real estate were particularly hard hit. Connally's projects were suffering from cost overruns or poor workmanship due to cost-cutting efforts. On July 31, 1987, Connally declared personal bankruptcy with a debt of some $93 million. By Texas law, he could keep his principal residency and $30,000 worth of possessions (Reston, 602). He was left with his ranch house and only 200 acres.

John Connally had reached the heights in both wealth and political power. He had come close to being President on more than one occasion. He died in Houston on June 15, 1993. Robert S. Strauss, former Democratic National Chairman and one of Connally's oldest friends, said that John Connally was "one of the ablest men I ever knew" ("Obituary," D25).

BIBLIOGRAPHY

Ashman, Charles. *Connally: The Adventures of Big Bad John*. New York: William Morrow & Company, 1974.

Crawford, Ann Fears, and Jack Keever. *John B. Connally: Portrait in Power*. Austin, TX: Jenkins Publishing Company, 1973.

Evans, Rowland, Jr., and Robert D. Novak. *Nixon in the White House: The Frustration of Power*. New York: Random House, 1971.

Genovese, Michael A. *The Nixon Presidency: Power and Politics in Turbulent Times*. Westport, CT: Greenwood Press, 1990.

"Obituary: John Bowden Connally." *New York Times*, June 16, 1993, 1, D25.

Reston, James, Jr. *The Lone Star: The Life of John Connally*. New York: Harper and Row, 1989.

Schoenebaum, Eleanora W., ed. *Political Profiles: The Nixon/Ford Years*. New York: Facts on File, 1979.

Shultz, George P. *Turmoil and Triumph: My Years as Secretary of State*. New York: Charles Scribner's Sons, 1993.

Slesinger, Reuben E., and Jack W. Osman. *Basic Economics: Problems, Principles, Policy*. Berkeley: McCutchan Publishing, 1972.

Wicker, Tom. *One of Us: Richard Nixon and the American Dream*. New York: Random House, 1995.

JACK W. OSMAN

GEORGE B. CORTELYOU (July 26, 1862–October 23, 1940). George B. Cortelyou, in many respects a forerunner of the modern, postwar public official, served as Secretary of the Treasury from 1907 to 1909. The biographical profile that follows considers, in turn, his personal background and contribution to the history of the Treasury.

George Bruce Cortelyou was born in New York City, July 26, 1862. Growing up in New York, Cortelyou graduated from the Hempstead Institute, Long Island, in 1879 and the State Normal School of Westfield, Massachusetts, in 1882. On the basis of this training, Cortelyou attained the position of general law and verbatim reporter with the firm of James E. Munson, holding that post from 1883 to 1885. Following his stint as a law reporter, Cortelyou acted as a principal in New York City's preparatory school system for four years. In 1888 he was wed to Lily Morris Hinds. The couple had five children.

The public service of George B. Cortelyou, service that was to take him to the very highest circles of power, began rather humbly. In 1889 he entered the customs service as a stenographer and typist. Two years later the future Secretary of the Treasury was transferred to the Postmaster General's office in Washington. On the recommendation of Postmaster General Bissel, Cortelyou became stenographer to President Grover Cleveland in 1895. During his service in the Postmaster General's office and as stenographer to the President, Cortelyou found time to earn his LL.B. at the law school of Georgetown University and his LL.M. at George Washington University. Upon the recommendation of President Cleveland, he was appointed Assistant Secretary to President McKinley in March 1897. In April 1900 he became Secretary to the President, a position he continued to occupy under McKinley's successor, Theodore Roosevelt. Changing the nature of the Secretary's job, Cortelyou acquired considerably more power for the office, performing duties that would today fall under the province of the White House Chief of Staff and Presidential Press Secretary. For these duties, he received the substantial annual salary of $6,000.

On February 13, 1903, Cortelyou was appointed Secretary of Commerce and Labor by Roosevelt. He served as Secretary until June 30, 1904, when, at Roosevelt's insistence, he was elected Chairman of the Republican National Committee. Cortelyou was accordingly entrusted with managing the 1904 presidential campaign of Theodore Roosevelt.

Cortelyou was, in fact, Roosevelt's fourth choice for the position. The President had initially made unsuccessful overtures to Senator Elihu Root, W. Murray Crane, the popular Governor of Massachusetts, and Cornelius N. Bliss (the latter did agree, however, to serve as National Committee Treasurer). That Roosevelt was able to force his fourth pick on the party evidences his control over the party apparatus.

The 1904 presidential campaign was, for the most part, a bland, unremarkable event. At the beginning of October, however, the contest began to heat up. On October 1, Joseph Pulitzer, owner of the *New York World*, accused Chairman Cortelyou and Treasurer Bliss of eliciting sizable campaign contributions from the trusts. These contributions, it was implicitly suggested, were provided in exchange for protection from government investigation. Cortelyou and Bliss, under no formal legal requirement to release information regarding campaign contributions, made no formal reply.

For three weeks Judge Alton Brooks Parker, Roosevelt's Democratic rival, ignored the issue as well. Then, on October 24, sensing his waning chances, Parker took the offensive. Attacking Roosevelt's reputation as a trust-buster, Parker argued for an end to "Cortelyouism," his label for the practice of soliciting and accepting campaign contributions in exchange for political concessions.

While others championed his cause, the President made no direct response to Parker's charges until November 4—just four days before the election. Flatly denying all charges leveled against himself and Cortelyou, Roosevelt placed the onus on Judge Parker to produce tangible evidence to substantiate his claims. Unable to do so, Parker fell silent. Roosevelt won the contest handily, taking 336 electoral votes to Parker's 140.

In retrospect the weight of the evidence against Cortelyou is substantial. His ability to exert pressure on the trusts was undeniable. As Secretary of Commerce and Labor, he had had access to a vast array of corporate records. Hearings before a Senate Committee in 1912 revealed that contributions from corporations did, in fact, make up 72.5 percent of the total campaign fund. Before this committee, Cortelyou, it can be noted, in a style too reminiscent of events in the late twentieth century to be taken lightly, was vague and unable to recall the exact details of the contribution process.

The presidential contest successfully concluded, Cortelyou was rewarded on March 4, 1905, with the position of Postmaster General by Roosevelt. During his tenure as Postmaster General, which lasted until March 3, 1907, Cortelyou made a number of substantial contributions. He was able to establish tenure for fourth-class postmasters, the rural free delivery system was perfected, regulations limiting mail fraud were enhanced, the postal deficit was reduced, and significant extensions of parcel post agreements were reached with foreign countries.

On March 4, 1907, Cortelyou was appointed Secretary of the Treasury by Theodore Roosevelt. One event outdistanced all others in importance during

Cortelyou's tenure as Secretary: the Panic of 1907. While the crisis developed in earnest only in the autumn of the year, harbingers of later difficulties faced Cortelyou upon his assumption of the office in March.

In late March, in response to the weakening position of the banking system, Cortelyou placed $70 million in customs receipts with depository national banks. At the same time, he announced that the Treasury would not be making its customary withdrawals from New York banks. Calming the surface for a brief period of time, these actions could not reverse the dangerous undercurrents moving the financial sector toward disaster.

The Panic of 1907 arrived, in typical nineteenth-century fashion, during crop-moving season. A number of factors combined to bring the panic to a head. The San Francisco fire of 1906 had caused heavy losses for insurers, which, in turn, had predictable repercussions on their bank creditors. Relatively high crop movements in 1907, in addition, placed additional demands on correspondent banks in reserve and central reserve cities. Finally, pressure was exerted on the financial system at the conclusion of 1906 by the inability to discount American finance bills in the London market. The proximate cause of the collapse, however, was the failure of the Knickerbocker Trust, which occurred on October 22. The Knickerbocker had liabilities of $35 million at the time of its collapse.

Aware of the coming difficulties, Secretary Cortelyou took a number of steps to stave off a crisis. Prepaying interest on government bonds, Cortelyou made weekly national bank deposits between August 28 and October 14 totaling $28 million. Meeting with leading New York financiers, including J. P. Morgan, George F. Baker, and George W. Perkins, on the night of the Knickerbocker collapse, he pledged Treasury support for a broad range of financial institutions.

Dissatisfied with the results of these steps, Cortelyou decided to pursue more drastic measures in mid-November. On the seventeenth of that month, he announced that the Treasury would offer for sale to the public an additional $50 million in Panama Canal bonds (authorized under the Act of June 28, 1902) and $100 million in 3 percent certificates of indebtedness (authorized under the Act of June 27, 1898). Cortelyou hoped that these instruments would be purchased by individuals hoarding money. Unable to ascertain the full effects of this action, Cortelyou made certain that some funds would flow back into the banking system by allowing banks that purchased these securities to hold 90 percent of the purchase price of the Panama bonds and 75 percent of the certificates in the form of deposits.

While Cortelyou must be given a significant degree of credit for containing the extent of the panic—the difficulties were over by mid-December—one must recognize, in addition, the curative role played by the substantial gold inflows that arose at the conclusion of the year, the contribution of J. P. Morgan, and the role played by the clearinghouses.

Cortelyou's success with the 1907 Panic provided him with sufficient exposure to generate discussion regarding his possible nomination for President. At the conclusion of 1907, with Roosevelt's handpicked successor, William Howard

Taft, out of the country, Republican officials began to consider Cortelyou as one alternative. This discussion was to be short-lived, however. Fearful that party divisions would benefit the chances of the newly elected Governor of New York, Charles Evans Hughes, the White House quickly issued a clear statement endorsing Taft. This announcement effectively ended Cortelyou's bid for greater heights.

Heavily engaged with practical administrative matters during the first months of his tenure as Treasury Secretary, Cortelyou was eventually able to find sufficient time to formulate a number of reform proposals. Two remain worthy of note. Aware of the difficulties caused by the inflexible, population-based structure of the National Banking System, Cortelyou, anticipating the later Federal Reserve arrangement, proposed that the banking facilities of the country be divided up along regional lines. A reserve framework would then be established in each individual zone, with the reserves of that area held within the zone (much like the way in which commercial banks today hold their reserves with a district Federal Reserve Bank).

One of the most pressing problems facing the federal government at the turn of the century was the absence of a centralized budget system. Prior to 1921 each individual governmental department submitted estimates of its expenditures directly to Congress. The latter then dealt with each faction separately. As a result, it was impossible to estimate the condition of the budget, or even determine total annual expenditure ex ante. While a number of previous Secretaries had deprecated the lack of a centralized system, Cortelyou was the first to formulate a comprehensive reform proposal addressing the problem. Noting that federal outlays had risen from $135 million to $678 million over the period 1878–1908, Cortelyou suggested a budget with a number of well-reasoned features. Most impressive was his suggestion that, following the standard European practice, a double budget be developed. Within such a budget, expenditures on capital projects, for example, the Panama Canal, would be separated from outlays supporting current operations. Uninterested in such mundane matters, Teddy Roosevelt let the proposal gather dust. Vindicated by history, many of Cortelyou's suggestions were included in the Budget and Accounting Act of 1921.

Cortelyou left the Treasury on March 7, 1909, returning to New York to head up the Consolidated Gas Company. He died in New York City on October 23, 1940.

BIBLIOGRAPHY

Annual Report of the Secretary of the Treasury. Washington, D.C.: U.S. Government Printing Office, various years.

Lossing, Benson John, ed. *Harper's Encyclopedia of U.S. History*. New York: Harper and Brothers, 1905.

Sobel, Robert, ed. *Biographical Directory of the United States Executive Branch, 1774–1977*. Westport, CT: Greenwood Press, 1977.

PAUL J. KUBIK

THOMAS CORWIN (July 29, 1794–December 18, 1865). Thomas Corwin served as Millard Fillmore's Secretary of the Treasury from July 23, 1850 to March

6, 1853. He was better known as a member of Congress in the 1830s and 1840s than as a Cabinet official.

Thomas Corwin was born on July 29, 1794, in Bourbon County, Kentucky, the fifth child of Matthias Corwin and Patricia Halleck. His parents settled in Lebanon, Ohio, in 1798, where they bought a farm. Because of limited funds, the family selected Thomas's older brother to be educated as a lawyer, leaving Thomas to become self-educated by reading his brother's books. At age twenty-one, Thomas was admitted to the Ohio bar.

In 1822, Thomas Corwin married Sarah Ross, daughter of a congressman and whose mother was related to the Randolph family of Virginia. By that time, Corwin had been elected to the Ohio General Assembly, where he became a Whig, supporting the John Quincy Adams–Henry Clay group. After Andrew Jackson won the 1828 presidential election, the Whigs persuaded Corwin to run for Congress in 1830 in a district that Jackson had carried, but Corwin won. He served from 1831 to 1840 in Congress, mostly during a time when Democrats controlled it. He made a few very impressive speeches that brought him some attention, especially his reply to General Isaac Crary on February 15, 1840, when he defended William H. Harrison, whom Crary had attacked.

Corwin was elected Governor of Ohio in 1840 but was defeated for reelection in 1842. In 1844, he chose not to run for Governor but instead devoted his time to campaign for Henry Clay for President. Even though Clay lost to James K. Polk, the Whigs won the Ohio legislature and elected Corwin to the U.S. Senate. It was during the Mexican War when Corwin reached the climax of his career. He was strongly opposed to this war because he felt its aim was solely to gain territory. He was unsuccessful in getting Senators Daniel Webster and John Crittenden to join him in cutting off appropriations. His opposition to the war influenced very few Senators; on February 11, 1847, his impassioned speech denouncing the war caused some Whigs to join Democrats in labeling this speech traitorous. Corwin withstood an attempt to recall him via petitions.

When President Zachary Taylor, who was elected in 1848, died in July 1850, the new President, Millard Fillmore, nominated Thomas Corwin to succeed William Meredith as Secretary of the Treasury. Corwin served in this post until Fillmore left office in March 1853. This three-year period was characterized by continual Treasury surpluses, even though government expenditures had increased somewhat because of the aftermath of the Mexican War and the acquisition of new territory. Receipts had risen because of the gold discovery in California, which made it easier for Americans to import foreign goods, which were subject to a tariff. The federal debt unilaterally increased by $10 billion after 1850 because of the assumption of the Texas debt.

Corwin, as a Whig, was not in favor of the Democrats' Independent Treasury. He preferred some type of national bank similar to the Second United States Bank. Whigs believed that control by such a bank over the currency could improve the workings of the gold standard by avoiding the large swings in prices and business activity. Consequently, Corwin did deposit some government funds in private banks and trust companies, for which he was criticized by his Democratic successor.

Corwin had a mercantilist fear of too many imports draining the nation's gold supply, even though a great deal of gold was being mined in California. During his period of office, specie in the Treasury rose from $6.6 million to $21.9 million. Yet Corwin lamented that the United States exported mainly farm goods with a low price and income elasticity of demand and imported finished goods with higher income and price elasticities. He was concerned that the famine in Europe that helped American exports of food only increased this country's ability to import more.

The chief contributing factor to the dilemma, as Corwin saw it, was the 1846 Democratic tariff, which was an ad valorem, and not a per-unit, tariff. Corwin argued strongly for a per-unit tariff because he believed it would result in a more predictable revenue. In addition, he felt that the ad valorem tariff could lead to fraud because goods could be evaluated differently at various ports, sometimes using foreign values and other times domestic values. Corwin further argued that the ad valorem tariff caused duties to go up when prices were high, adding to consumer burdens at the wrong time, and caused duties to fall when prices were lower, at a time when these duties would be easier to bear. He urged Congress to regulate U.S. imports more closely so they could always be paid for solely with current exports, because the proceeds from the sale of government lands had to be earmarked for debt retirement.

Corwin was a protectionist. He opposed the dumping of foreign iron, arguing that it would hurt American producers. He cited the fact that between 1845 and 1852, imports increased over four times, from 102,723 tons to 435,149 tons, but that duties only increased by less than half, from $1.8 million to $3.2 million. He definitely feared foreign goods entering the country, putting American industries out of work and then leaving American consumers to the mercy of foreign suppliers. He advocated a protective tariff to discriminate against goods that could be manufactured in this country. Even though gold mines were quite productive in California, Corwin feared the loss of gold from excessive importing, which in his view could cause bankruptcies, prevent Americans from buying needed foreign goods, and cause a ruinous depression in Treasury receipts. However, between 1850 and 1853, the wholesale price level rose from 90.3 to 104.3 (1860 = 100), while consumer prices remained steady. Prices rose more steeply after he left office. Because of the increase in the amount of gold that was flowing into the Treasury, Corwin advocated the printing of gold certificates to save on the expense of shipping and storage.

Another problem for the Treasury during Corwin's period of office was the difficulty in keeping silver for fractional coins. Silver was undervalued compared to gold in the United States, where the ratio was fixed at 16 to 1, while it was overvalued in France and England, where the ratios were 15.5 to 1 and 14.28 to 1, respectively. Therefore, silver flowed to Europe and gold to the United States.

Because of this, Corwin advocated minting token coins with a silver content less than their market value. This law was passed in 1853, after he left office.

Because of the lack of full-bodied silver coins, Spanish silver coins were monopolizing U.S. trade. Corwin wanted silver to be legal tender for debts of $10 or less only, and gold for amounts in excess of $10. He also advocated an annual assaying of all coins of any nation we traded with, because tariffs were paid in such coins.

Another problem on Corwin's watch was the 1847 Loan Act, which stated that government bonds to finance the Mexican War could only be sold at par or above but could only be redeemed at par or below. Corwin wanted this law repealed because he had surplus specie in the Treasury, but the bonds had risen above par. Congress did repeal this law in 1853, but after Corwin had left office. His successor, James Guthrie, accused Corwin of making private arrangements for debt repurchases, which Guthrie felt were a misallocation of public funds.

After leaving Fillmore's Cabinet in March 1853, Corwin lost money in a bad investment in railroad stocks. He seemed to have financial problems all his life, because he was not assertive in collecting his fees from his law practice. During the 1850s, as the slavery question intensified, he left the Whig Party and became a Republican. He was elected to the House of Representatives in 1858 as a member of his new party; after Lincoln was elected in 1860, Corwin served as Chairman of the House Committee of thirty-three, which was designed to allay the fears of the South. During the Civil War, he served as Minister to Mexico. In 1865, he returned to Washington, D.C., to open a law practice but died on December 18 of that year.

BIBLIOGRAPHY

Dictionary of American Biography. New York: Scribner, 1928.

Sechrest, Larry J. Free Banking. Westport, CT: Quorum, 1993.

Secretary of the Treasury. Annual Reports. Washington, D.C.: U.S. Government Printing Office, various years.

Timberlake, Richard H. Monetary Policy in the United States. Chicago: University of Chicago Press, 1993.

DONALD R. WELLS

WILLIAM H. CRAWFORD (February 2, 1772–September 15, 1834). William Harris Crawford served his country in the Senate, as Minister to France, and as Secretary of War and of the Treasury for over seventeen years. One of the most powerful and highly respected men in the United States in the early 1800s, Crawford came as close to the presidency as anyone without gaining the office. Friendship, party loyalty, and personal tragedy were to keep the highest office out of reach. Crawford was an imposing man both intellectually and physically, and in only nine years he went from preparatory school graduate to U.S. Senator and successful plantation owner. A lifelong Jeffersonian Republican, he represented the "Old South" but tempered his politics with independence and a practical approach of doing what worked.

Crawford was born February 2, 1772, in Amherst Country, Virginia. He was the sixth child of Joel and Fanny Harris Crawford, poor farmers whose families had come to America in the mid-1600s. Financial problems caused Crawford's father to move the family to South Carolina when William was seven, then later to Kiokee Creek, Georgia. His father was a rebel sympathizer and was imprisoned for a while in 1780 by the British, who were then in control of the area around Augusta, Georgia.

Because of the family finances, Crawford's schooling was in local schools while he worked on the family farm. He eventually taught in the same schools as he reached his late teens. Not until the age of twenty-two was he able to attend a college preparatory school, Waddel's Academy in Appling, Georgia, with a traditional classical curriculum. His outstanding performance there led to appointment as an assistant teacher in his second year, helping pay his tuition. A fellow student was John C. Calhoun, who would later become Crawford's most bitter rival.

Crawford graduated in 1796 and took a position as an English teacher at the Richmond Academy in Augusta, where he met his wife, Susannah Gerardine, who was one of his students. By 1798, Crawford started studying the law and in 1799 left teaching and established a law office in Lexington, Georgia. He already had developed a reputation as a hardworking, exceptionally intelligent, and outspoken individual. He hated hypocrisy and often could be blunt at a time when society expected eloquent, long-winded discourse. This forceful image was strengthened by his physical size: He was six foot three and weighed over 200 pounds, all of which made him an imposing figure, both physically and mentally.

Around 1800 Crawford's political life began with his public opposition to sales of lands around the Yazoo River. This land had been sold by the Georgia legislature to speculators for exceptionally low prices. Crawford's position aligned him with the eastern Georgia Republican Party, which represented the more-settled and economically secure planters and businessmen. Crawford's group was opposed by the Federalists and the western Republicans, who were led by the Clark family, Crawford's other lifelong nemesis. This political alignment would not change substantially for Crawford's entire political career. His position in the Republican group led to a commission to write the first official digest of Georgia laws in 1799, and when another Republican, Peter Early, was elected to Congress in 1802, Early passed his entire law practice to Crawford. This made Crawford one of the most prominent lawyers in Georgia, only three years after first opening his office.

Crawford consistently refused to provide legal counsel to the Clark faction in their land deals, and in 1802, Peter Van Alen, a land speculator, challenged Crawford to a duel. Crawford killed Van Alen, and Crawford's prowess further increased his prestige in Georgia politics. He fought a second duel in 1806 against John Clark over Clark's suspicion that Crawford was accusing Clark of using counterfeit money in land transactions. Clark seriously wounded Crawford, and Crawford withdrew, renouncing duelling forever.

In 1803, Crawford was elected to the Georgia legislature. His politics were closely patterned on Thomas Jefferson's, emphasizing small government and personal freedom. Crawford was, however, known as an independent and until 1807 concentrated on local and state politics. Representing an area of plantation owners, he voted to end the importation of slaves. His belief in the power of education resulted in votes for free public education and for a lottery to raise money for library books for the state college.

Leader of the Georgia Republican Party by 1806, Crawford was elected to the U.S. Senate in 1807 to fill a vacated seat. He immediately established his independence from the party by being the only Republican to vote against a general embargo against Britain. Crawford felt at that time the embargo was too broad and that all-out war was in any case the better alternative. By 1810, his wider exposure to national politics had tempered his strict "old Republicanism," and he voted against the nonintercourse bill, wishing instead to maintain the embargo even though it hurt the nation. This view was not popular, but Crawford's political standing was strong enough to withstand criticism. He also earned the respect of Treasury Secretary Albert Gallatin, who agreed with him and desperately needed the revenue. When the Senate later remitted the penalties for violating the nonintercourse law, Crawford was one of only five Senators who voted against remission.

Crawford's national political reputation was firmly established during the debate over renewal of the charter of the First Bank of the United States. In December 1810, Crawford urged Gallatin to start working on a new charter, and Crawford was the most prominent defender of the Bank in the Senate. Severely criticized by the other strict constructionist Republicans, he used a liberal interpretation of the U.S. Constitution as his defense of the Bank, indicating his willingness to alter his views based on experience. Crawford was particularly upset by the failure of the Bank and by President James Madison's unwillingness to support it vigorously. Crawford joined others in urging Madison, whose administration was falling apart, to try to rally his supporters and present a united and forceful front to the nation.

Crawford was especially critical of the Madison administration's war policy and of War Secretary William Eustis. Crawford wanted to avoid any European entanglements if possible but felt that if war was needed, it should be prosecuted fully. When Eustis resigned in December 1812, James Monroe was offered the War Department but declined. Crawford was then offered the job but declared himself "ill-suited." Madison eventually got John Armstrong to accept. Crawford's political position continued to strengthen, particularly because of his reputation as being above partisan battles. On March 24, 1813, he was named the first President pro tempore of the Senate, replacing Vice President Clinton, who had died.

Crawford held the Senate position until June 18, when he was appointed U.S. Minister to France, replacing Joel Barlow. Crawford had inherited a difficult job. Barlow had died while trying to catch up with Napoleon in Poland on his retreat from Moscow. France had no stable government, and the U.S. government itself was divided on continental policy. Crawford's basic mission was to act as a source of information for the United States. He succeeded in charming the French court with his humor and flamboyant country manners and sent warnings back to Madison that the British were mobilizing to attack. Crawford was correct, but his warnings were ignored.

In April 1815, Crawford was ordered home from France, to be replaced by Gallatin. He was happy to return home, assuming that he would return to the Senate and enjoy his family and plantation, Woodlawn. He had married Susannah in 1804. Their home was known as "Liberty House" because of his belief in personal freedom for both adults and children. Crawford was also a slaveholder, owning at least twenty.

Susannah and he had eight children, all of whom were educated liberally using the Pestalozzian school principles. He had been named a member of the state college Board of Trustees in 1812. His hobby was agricultural experiments, trying out new seeds and plants for use in the Southern states, and he corresponded with others such as Jefferson about the results of his work.

What Crawford did not know was that he had been appointed War Secretary while he was traveling home. He assumed this position upon his return from Europe, August 1, 1815. With the War of 1812 over, Crawford's primary responsibilities included maintenance of the much-smaller armed forces and dealing with Indian issues. He was known for insisting on equitable treatment of Indian claims, and he angered Andrew Jackson by redoing a treaty made by Jackson. In March 1816 Crawford submitted a report on the Indian situation, which recommended integration of Indians into the U.S. society. His view that U.S. policy should favor Indians over immigrants received substantial negative reaction and would haunt him in future political campaigns.

By 1816, Crawford was one of the most powerful politicians in the United States. Along with Monroe and New York Governor Daniel Tompkins, Crawford was one of three contenders for the 1816 presidency. In the one-party political environment, the Republican congressional caucus determined the candidate and, effectively, the winner. Though he did receive support from Federalists hoping to stop Monroe, who was favored by Madison, Crawford said he was not interested. He admired and was friends with Monroe and felt it was Monroe's turn for the presidency. Even after withdrawing, the caucus vote was sixty-five for Monroe to fifty-four for Crawford, and Crawford stepped aside, not wanting to destroy party unity.

Prior to Monroe's election, Treasury Secretary Alexander Dallas submitted his resignation to President Madison. Though he did not seek the job, Crawford was both Dallas's and Gallatin's first choice for the position, and Crawford was confirmed as Treasury Secretary on October 22, 1816, and then again on March 4, 1817, under President Monroe. He inherited a Treasury Department that was large, inefficient, and loaded with political appointments. He immediately began reducing its size and instituting reforms.

Crawford's first major task was to oversee the January 1817 opening of the

Second Bank of the United States, which had just been chartered. The new bank was poorly run at first, expanding too rapidly and violating many charter provisions. In spite of this, Crawford had to ensure the resumption of specie payments by state banks so that government currency would be acceptable and the government could pay its bills. Congress had set a deadline of February 20 for resumption, but state bankers resisted. Crawford made the deadline by threatening the withdrawal of government funds if banks did not comply. Specie payments resumed uneventfully.

Throughout Crawford's tenure as Treasury Secretary, the government avoided serious budget problems, since increasing trade raised tariff revenues and Monroe's policies did not lead to significant spending on internal improvements. The Panic of 1819, however, resulted in lower tax revenues and put pressure on Crawford to propose spending cuts. His proposal was for broad cuts in the War Department, then headed by Calhoun. Crawford also tried to help people hurt by the panic, allowing settlers faced with foreclosure to extend their payments on government land.

Calhoun was incensed by Crawford's proposed cuts and countered by advocating smaller cuts. Calhoun lost to a coalition of conservative Republicans and Crawford's faction called the "Radicals." The name was adopted from the Radical Party in France and was supposedly organized to protect the Constitution. In reality, Crawford's supporters were generally from the moderate part of the Republican Party, along with many Federalists who respected his practical views toward business and finance.

The differences between Calhoun, Jackson, and Crawford reflected the politics during the Monroe administration. Since Monroe was assured reelection in 1820, all three were vying for the 1824 presidential nomination, along with Secretary of State John Quincy Adams. In 1817, Jackson and Crawford had another public difference over Jackson's incursion into Florida after the Seminole Indians. Crawford felt that Jackson should be punished for violating the law, and Crawford gained even more public support from his position. Personal animosities from such episodes ran high.

By 1823, the four men were rivals in a presidential race that was long on personalities but short on substantive issues. Crawford was still the leading candidate. During the campaign that year, he was accused of misappropriating Treasury funds. The accusations appeared in a series of anonymous letters to a Washington paper. Though he eventually was fully exonerated by a nonpartisan congressional committee, Crawford was always bitter over the incident. He was also upset that Monroe seemed to favor Calhoun and his faction in government appointments. Feelings were high when Crawford confronted Monroe about the appointments, bluntly criticizing the President for not making timely decisions. Monroe responded in kind, and Crawford, often quick to anger, raised his cane against the President. Monroe reached for a nearby fireplace tong and ordered Crawford out of the office. Crawford apologized immediately, but his relations with Monroe were never again as close as they had been.

Crawford's life changed forever in late summer 1823. While on vacation, he apparently contracted erysipelas, an infectious disease with a rash and high fever. Though the evidence is not conclusive, Crawford most likely suffered a paralytic stroke brought on by inappropriate drug treatment. Left temporarily blind, and unable to move or speak, Crawford was hidden by his friends at Virginia Senator Joseph Barbour's home. Though close to death for several weeks, he urged his friends to continue the campaign. As soon as he was able, he had himself driven through the streets of Washington, propped in a carriage, and later attended Cabinet meetings while blind. In November he still was sending Monroe messages that he was "indisposed" and would return in a few days. In reality, Crawford never fully recovered from the illness and would not be fully functional on his own for at least two years. He would always have speech and movement problems, which made him difficult to understand. His mental abilities, though, did not appear to be affected significantly.

In spite of his illness, Crawford was chosen the Republican candidate in the 1824 congressional caucus, but the caucus no longer represented the majority of the party. He did have the largest following in Congress but probably was hurt by the caucus nomination, since that process was now viewed as undemocratic. The actual nomination was shifting to the state legislatures. Crawford ran under the Radical banner, representing the state's rights South and those who wanted small, efficient government. He promised a "broad-bottomed" government and had widespread support, from Thomas Jefferson and Madison of the "old Republicans" to New York's Martin Van Buren. Opposition to Crawford came from anti-South, antislavery forces. Though Crawford did not campaign himself, he continued to affect his opponents who never could tell when he might appear to respond to their statements.

Going into the election, the final race was between Jackson, Adams, Henry Clay, and Crawford. Calhoun had withdrawn to run (successfully) for Vice President. Though Crawford had been forecast originally as a possible winner, the electoral votes cast in November 1824 put him a distant third, with three of twenty-two states. Poor political strategy in New York was blamed for his losing that state's crucial electoral votes, one fourth of those required to win. Adams later won in the House, much to Jackson's displeasure, since Jackson had the most electoral votes.

Crawford accepted his loss with equanimity, possibly because he fully expected to return later to the Senate. He turned down Adams's offer to continue as Treasury Secretary and was still so ill that the letter to Adams was composed by his friends. Crawford left Washington in March 1825 and returned to Woodlawn in Georgia. He recuperated there for at least a year, enjoying his hobby of agricultural experimentation. By July 1826, he again was active on the state college board, where he served until resigning in 1830 when the Clark political faction took over the board. Crawford had been granted an honorary LL.D. from the college in 1824.

Crawford was appointed a Superior Court Judge on the Western Circuit in 1827. He successfully ran for reelection in both 1828 and 1831. One of his key decisions as a Judge involved establishing a state's right of jurisdiction over Indians, a decision setting an important precedent in U.S. law.

Never giving up an active interest in national politics, Crawford's hopes of a Senate seat were still alive until 1830, when he was passed over by the Georgia legislature. He argued against any rash Southern actions in the debates over nullification and secession, reflecting the nationalism he had adopted from years of federal service. Crawford was closely involved in the presidential races of 1828 and 1832. His political supporters were gravitating toward Jackson, and the Radicals had received important positions in the Jackson administration. Crawford never publicly supported Jackson, but he did work hard against Calhoun. Consulting with Adams, Crawford sent an influential letter to Jackson, revealing that Calhoun had lied about his support of Jackson in a crucial Cabinet meeting over ten years earlier. This letter was instrumental in diverting support from Calhoun to Jackson in the 1832 election.

Crawford's last public office was as a representative to the Georgia state constitutional convention, which began in 1833. Still hoping for national office, in September 1834 he sent a letter to Jackson, requesting consideration for a Supreme Court appointment. Soon afterward, Crawford complained of feeling unwell, and he died the following day, September 15, 1834, at the home of a friend. The cause of death was given as an "affection of the heart." Crawford was buried at his Woodlawn, whose site is today near Crawford, Georgia.

BIBLIOGRAPHY
Babcock, Kendric Charles. *The Rise of American Nationality: 1811–1819*. New York: Harper & Bros., 1906.

Coit, Margaret L. *John C. Calhoun: An American Portrait*. Boston: Houghton Mifflin Company, 1961.

"Crawford, William H." *The National Cyclopedia of American Biography*. Vol. 5. New York: James T. White and Co., 1907.

Dangerfield, George. *The Awakening of American Nationalism: 1815–1828*. New York: Harper and Row, 1965.

Livermore, Shaw, Jr. *The Twilight of Federalism: The Disintegration of the Federalist Party, 1815–1830*. Princeton: Princeton University Press, 1962.

May, Ernest R. *The Making of the Monroe Doctrine*. Cambridge: Belknap Press of Harvard University Press, 1975.

Mooney, Chase C. *William H. Crawford, 1772–1834*. Lexington: University Press of Kentucky, 1974.

Risjord, Norman K. *The Old Republicans: Southern Conservatism in the Age of Jefferson*. New York: Columbia University Press, 1965.

Southwick, Leslie H., comp. *Presidential Also-Rans and Running Mates, 1788–1980*. Jefferson, NC: McFarland & Co., 1984.

Stagg, J. C. A. *Mr. Madison's War: Politics, Diplomacy and Warfare in the Early American Republic*. Princeton: Princeton University Press, 1983.

"William Harris Crawford." In *Biographical Directory of the United States Executive Branch, 1774–1989*, edited by Robert Sobel, 84–85. Westport, CT: Greenwood Press, 1990.

KRISTINE L. CHASE

D

ALEXANDER J. DALLAS (June 21, 1759–January 16, 1817). Known to his friends as a brilliant thinker and loyal supporter, to his opponents as a stubborn and rude aristocrat, Alexander James Dallas helped guide the United States financially out of the War of 1812 and into economic stability. His background as a foreign-born "outsider," as well as his natural independence, helped him avoid constitutional politics and spearhead the formation of the Second Bank of the United States.

Tall, attractive, and an excellent conversationalist, Dallas was active socially but also devoted to his family. A favorite pastime in the Dallas household was a casual late-evening discussion over supper with his children. One son, George Mifflin Dallas, went on to become Vice President of the United States under Polk, and the family's name graces Dallas, Texas.

Alexander James Dallas was born on June 21, 1759, at Dallas Castle, Kingston, Jamaica. He was the third son of Dr. Robert C. and Sarah (Cormack) Dallas. Dallas's mother died shortly after his birth, and his father, a native Scot, remarried and moved the family back to England. Dallas studied in London and Edinburgh and while in London often was invited to Benjamin Franklin's home, as Franklin's grandson went to the same school. The death of Dallas's father forced Dallas to leave school in 1774. Continuing to study the law, he went to work in a bank, which failed two years later, and he moved to Devonshire to live with his stepmother.

While in Devonshire, Dallas met Arabella Maria Smith (known as Maria), daughter of George Smith, a British Army major stationed in the Caribbean. Though Maria was only sixteen, the couple was determined to wed. Unable to receive her family's approval in England, Dallas sailed to the Caribbean, only to be denied by Maria's father. In response, they eloped on September 4, 1780, and settled in Jamaica, where Dallas practiced law. In 1783, George Smith died, leaving Maria a sufficient inheritance that, combined with a small legacy from Robert Dallas, enabled them to move to Philadelphia and escape the tropical climate that harmed her health. They chose Philadelphia on the advice of an actor wintering in Jamaica. After only two weeks in the United States, they decided to become permanent residents, becoming citizens on June 17, 1783.

With his exceptional native intellect and determination, and Maria's outgoing and charming capabilities as a hostess, Dallas quickly gained respect in Philadelphia and by 1785 had been admitted to the Supreme Court bar in Pennsylvania. He financed his legal studies in America by working as an accountant. The family's income was supplemented with Dallas's writing for local publications. It was during this time that he was introduced to constitutional politics. As a reporter and editor for the *Pennsylvania Evening Herald*, Dallas covered the state convention for ratification of the U.S. Constitution with studied impartiality. His impartiality angered Federalists, resulting in his dismissal from the paper. This experience undoubtedly colored his views on constitutional issues, views that would become important later in the controversy over a national bank.

Over the next decade, Dallas became a very successful lawyer and politician in Pennsylvania, owning both a mansion in Philadelphia and a house in the country. He and Maria were always known as a social and free-spending household. They eventually had nine children, three of whom died in infancy. Dallas filled his free time with his family and with editing of the *Columbia Magazine*, as well as authoring several respected legal publications. Dallas's early support of the theater in Philadelphia helped form many influential friendships with state and civic leaders. Aaron Burr was a family friend, and Burr fled to their home after his duel with Hamilton in 1804. Their closest friends were Albert Gallatin and his wife. The Dallases met Gallatin when they all were young unknowns in Philadelphia in the early 1790s.

Dallas's political activities increased in 1791, when he was appointed Secretary of the Commonwealth (Secretary of State) of Pennsylvania, an office he held until 1801. Starting in 1794, he also served as the Paymaster and aide-de-camp for the new Governor Mifflin during the Whiskey Rebellion. Aggressive in political organizing, Dallas was a founder of the Pennsylvania Democratic Society in 1793, which put him into a formal opposition with the ruling Federalist Party in Philadelphia that would last the rest of his life. Federalist opposition to Dallas deepened with his widely published essay "Features of Mr. Jay's Treaty." This essay argued strongly against the treaty Secretary of State John Jay had negotiated with Britain in 1794.

Supporting Jefferson in the 1800 election earned Dallas an appointment as the U.S. Attorney for eastern Pennsylvania in 1801, a post he would hold until becoming Secretary of the Treasury in 1814. During Dallas's tenure as U.S. Attorney, he represented the federal government in the Olmstead case, involving jurisdiction between state and federal courts. Dallas's role in this case earned him forever the resentment of the traditional Republican leadership in Pennsylvania but the loyalty of President James Madison. Always considered an independent-minded foreigner, he was now an outsider in his own state's party. Ironically,

Dallas had been one of the founders of the Democratic-Republican Party in 1805 and the leader of the party in Pennsylvania in 1808.

Through his extensive legal practice, Dallas became a respected friend of many wealthy and influential businessmen. Prominent among his friends were John Jacob Astor, of New York, and Stephen Girard, of Pennsylvania. The latter was a regular client of Dallas's. By 1813, Dallas had become deeply involved in facilitating financing for the war. Dallas acted as an intermediary in arranging loan agreements between then-Treasury Secretary Gallatin and the financiers, even to the extent of holding government financial meetings at Dallas's home.

Dallas first was offered the Treasury post by President Madison in February 1814, after Gallatin had been reassigned to the U.S. peace commission. Dallas's candidacy also was championed by John Jacob Astor, who wanted a national bank partly to protect the millions he had lent to the shaky government. Dallas, Madison's first choice, turned down the nomination for several reasons. First, he was uncertain of being confirmed, given stiff opposition from several Republican Senators, including those from his home state. In addition, there was no clear administration support for a new national bank, which Dallas made a precondition for acceptance; he did not want to move his family to Washington; and he disliked other members of Madison's Cabinet, particularly Armstrong, the War Secretary.

Dallas, however, did not remove himself from the controversy over a new bank, arguing publicly against those Federalists and conservative Republicans who continued to cite constitutional reasons against a bank. He also lobbied prominent government officials, such as Naval Secretary William Jones (who would later become the first President of the Second Bank of the United States). Dallas felt that constitutional reasons existing in the 1700s no longer applied in 1814, evidencing a flexible interpretation of the Constitution. Dallas never had much sympathy or understanding for Madison's and many Republican's strict views on the Constitution.

After the burning of Washington and the resignation of Treasury Secretary Campbell in October 1814, Madison again looked to Dallas. This time Dallas actively sought the appointment, both from a sense of duty to the government and because many of the earlier obstacles had been cleared. His Senate opponents and Armstrong were gone, and Madison promised support for the bank. The Senate Republicans who had viewed Dallas only as a last resort realized that the time had come to put aside politics and pick the best-qualified candidate. Madison formally appointed Dallas Secretary of the Treasury on October 5, 1814, and he was confirmed by the Senate the next day.

Dallas inherited a Treasury that was close to collapse. Revenues were almost nonexistent and lenders reluctant to provide funds, especially since the Treasury notes (T-notes) in circulation were heavily discounted. T-note issues had financed about one third of the war expenditures and, along with state bank note issues, had caused substantial inflation. The prior Secretary, George Washington Campbell, had gotten little help from Congress, but the new political crisis convinced a majority of Congress that action was finally necessary. The crisis peaked with the sacking of Washington, D.C. By the end of 1814, practically all state banks south of the Hudson River had suspended specie payments, making the paper T-notes nearly worthless and effectively locking up government deposits.

The revenue problem was quickly addressed by several new taxes proposed by Dallas and passed by Congress. For the financial system, Dallas had worked closely with Astor and Girard and, on October 17, 1814, sent to Congress a proposal for a Second Bank of the United States. The proposal was essentially identical to the First Bank, whose charter had lapsed in 1811 amid great political turmoil. Dallas fully expected quick passage of his proposal, but his lack of political astuteness, as well as his impatience with those who did not share his goals, led to a battle over the bank that would take two years.

One reason for Dallas's rush was the appearance of another financial proposal on the House floor, originating with John Eppes of Virginia, son-in-law of Jefferson. Eppes's plan involved additional T-note issues, to be used as currency and paid back in five years with future tax revenues. Dallas deplored any such plan that would continue short-run inflationary finance. He wanted a long-run, permanent change to a stable currency and banking system. He did not sympathize with the opposition's desire for a short-run solution to solve what it regarded as a short-run wartime need.

Led by John C. Calhoun, the majority in Congress did favor a new bank but substantially amended Dallas's proposal. Rather than firmly backing his Treasury Secretary, Madison wavered, caught between his own desire for a strong bank and his attraction to a short-term politically acceptable solution. As passed by the House in late October, the bank would be financed with T-note paper money, rather than the long-term government bonds that Dallas and Astor preferred, and would resemble a state commercial bank more than a central bank. Finance with bonds would have given substantial control to the holders of those bonds: Astor and the other bankers.

So disturbed was Dallas with the House action that he ignored Madison's recommendation to not disparage Congress. Instead, Dallas sent a message to the House, severely criticizing its behavior, claiming that it had acted without "wisdom, patriotism, and fortitude." Not surprisingly, this message only added to Dallas's reputation as an unusual Republican: an aristocratic snob, out of place in his party. In addition, Dallas's close association with Astor and other well-known financiers led to claims that the Second Bank was, like the First, a thinly disguised plot for Northern bankers to gain control of the bank.

The bank bill underwent several revisions in the House and Senate, including Calhoun's addition of a clause prohibiting the suspension of specie payments. Dallas felt this clause would result in a continual specie drain from the bank into New England banks. Unwilling to bend on his demands, Dallas told Madison he wanted to resign the Treasury post by the end of that congressional session. By the time the bill reached Madison's desk on January 30, 1815, Dallas had convinced the President of its flaws, and Madison vetoed it.

Dallas continued negotiations with Congress, but international events over-shadowed any bank bill. In February 1815 a much-improved version of the bill passed the Senate in January, only to bog down again in the House. However, news of the end of the war with Britain reached Washington at that time. This reduced the financial urgency, even though the government was still broke from past expenditures. Dallas had sent a $56 million budget to Congress (including projected military expenditures for 1815), with a $41 million deficit. The war's end meant the deficit would be much smaller, and the resulting euphoria and nationalism enabled Congress to pass much-needed tax legislation to close the budget gap. The bank bill was tabled indefinitely by both houses.

Dallas spent most of 1815 working on other issues. Just prior to the news of peace, Madison had given Dallas an assignment to write an explanation of the U.S. position with respect to the war. It appeared to many that the project partially was designed to keep Dallas occupied while the bank controversy con-tinued. Intended as a piece of propaganda to convince otherwise neutral observers in Europe, Dallas's work was later published in a pamphlet titled "Exposition on the Causes and Character of the Late War." The "Exposition" established the U.S. position on claims to Louisiana and Florida.

Dallas also served concurrently as Secretary of War from March through Oc-tober, and his responsibilities there effectively diverted his attention from Trea-sury issues. William Crawford had been picked for the job, but he was out of the country until that fall. As War Secretary, Dallas was one of the principal critics of Andrew Jackson's use of martial law in New Orleans after the end of the war. Dallas oversaw the politically difficult reduction in the armed forces to a peace-time level. In addition, he championed the reestablishment of an American presence on the western frontier, building forts from the Great Lakes to St. Louis in defense against both Indians and the British.

Dallas knew, however, that the underlying financial system weakness had not disappeared, especially since the country had no nationally accepted currency. Astor and Girard had continued their lobbying, but this time quietly from the sidelines. More important, a dramatic shift had occurred in Republican politics, with the West, as represented by Calhoun, now desiring a more stable currency to facilitate trade and manufacturing. Further, the constitutional issues that had haunted the First Bank, and underlain much Republican opposition, had disap-peared with time.

On December 24, 1815, Dallas sent to Calhoun a new bank proposal, which they jointly revised. Calhoun submitted this to Congress on January 8, 1816. In the revised plan, Dallas got the bond financing and a substantial government ownership (with 20 percent of the capital from the government, as well as five of the twenty-five directors). Calhoun insisted and got a clause that guaranteed specie payments and severely limited government loans the bank could make. Calhoun carefully guided the bill through Congress, eventually gaining wide, bipartisan support. This time, the only real opposition came from New England (the one part of the country with a reasonably sound banking system). The West and South were solidly for the bill, and only one Congressman even raised the constitutional issues. The bill establishing a Second Bank of the United States had passed both houses by April 3, was signed by Madison on April 10, and received its charter on April 13, 1816. Not surprisingly, Astor and Girard were two of the five original government-appointed directors.

With the bank finally established, Dallas turned his attention to increasing revenues. He wrote a detailed report on tariffs, then the principal revenue source for the federal government. Dallas knew a general tariff would bring in needed funds, now that the war was over and manufacturing trade booming. His proposals fit well with the goals of those who wanted to protect the new manufacturing industries, particularly in the West. Based on his proposal, Congress passed a general tariff bill in March 1816, with duties up to 25 percent on imported goods. This law set the pattern for U.S. trade policy, to be known as the "American System." The tariff law was extremely successful: In just the first year, tariff revenues were $36 million, three times Dallas's estimate.

In the spring of 1816, Dallas announced that he wished to resign effective October 1, or earlier if an acceptable successor could be found. Though the family had enjoyed Washington social life, Dallas found government service financially costly and wanted to return to his law practice in Philadelphia. While Madison searched for his replacement, Dallas continued his Treasury duties at a full pace. He changed federal land office procedures, by sending Washington-based inspectors to the field to ensure that the government was receiving the payments due. He also started work on a plan to implement the resumption of specie payments by state banks, which were mandated to begin by early 1817. Dallas left the Treasury post on October 21, 1816, before the plan was complete, and his successor, William Crawford, was the Secretary who actually oversaw the opening of the Second Bank and implementation of the new financial regulations.

In September 1816, Dallas summed up the current state of the Treasury for the President. In his final report, Dallas noted that the Treasury now had a $20 million surplus. Crawford was formally appointed his successor on October 22. Though several groups tried to convince Dallas to run either for President or for Congress, he knew he lacked a solid political base on which to build a campaign.

Dallas returned home to Philadelphia and quickly resumed his law practice. He was not to enjoy his new life for long. During a trial in early January 1817 he was stricken with dizziness and severe stomach pains, the symptoms of an ailment from which he had suffered intermittently all his life. Diagnosed in the past as either "stomach gout" or the result of almost drowning in the Thames River as a child, Dallas did not recover and died on January 16, 1817, at his home. He was only fifty-eight years old and left his wife and six children, two of whom were still at home. Among many other tributes, the U.S. Supreme Court wore black crepe on their robes throughout the month of February to honor the service of Dallas to his country.

BIBLIOGRAPHY
"Alexander James Dallas." In *Biographical Directory of the United States Executive Branch, 1774–1989*, edited by Robert Sobel, 91–92. Westport, CT: Greenwood Press, 1990.
Babcock, Kendric Charles. *The Rise of American Nationality: 1811–1819*. New York: Harper & Bros., 1906.
Belohlavek, John M. *George Mifflin Dallas: Jacksonian Patrician*. University Park: Pennsylvania State University Press, 1977.
Coit, Margaret L. *John C. Calhoun, American Portrait*. Boston: Houghton Mifflin, 1961.
"Dallas, Alexander James." In *The National Cyclopedia of American Biography*. Vol. 5. New York: James T. White and Co., 1907.
Dangerfield, George. *The Awakening of American Nationalism: 1815–1828*. New York: Harper and Row, 1965.
De Gregorio, William A. *The Complete Book of U.S. Presidents*. New York: Dembner Books, 1984.
Faulkner, Harold Underwood. *American Economic History*. New York: Harper & Bros., 1960.
Mooney, Chase C. *William H. Crawford, 1772–1834*. Lexington: University Press of Kentucky, 1974.
Risjord, Norman K. *The Old Republicans: Southern Conservatism in the Age of Jefferson*. New York: Columbia University Press, 1965.
Rutland, Robert Allen. *The Presidency of James Madison*. Lawrence: University Press of Kansas, 1990.
Stagg, J. C. A. *Mr. Madison's War: Politics, Diplomacy and Warfare in the Early American Republic*. Princeton: Princeton University Press, 1983.
Walters, Raymond, Jr. "The Origins of the Second Bank of the U.S." *Journal of Political Economy* 53, no. 2 (June 1945): 115–31.
———. *Alexander James Dallas*. New York: Da Capo Press, 1969 (Reprint of 1943 edition, University of Pennsylvania Press).
                                                      KRISTINE L. CHASE

SAMUEL DEXTER (May 14, 1761–May 3, 1816). Samuel Dexter filled in as temporary Secretary of the Treasury for only a brief time period. He was born on May 14, 1761, in Boston, Massachusetts. He was the son of Samuel Dexter, an erudite student of history, a merchant, and philanthropist, and Hannah (Sigourney) Dexter.

Dexter was married to Catherine Gordon on March 7, 1786, just before his twenty-fifth birthday. His wife was the daughter of William Gordon, a noted legislator, Congressman, and Attorney General of New Haven, Connecticut.

As the youngest child of Samuel and Hannah, Dexter received a fine preparatory education and was admitted to Harvard College in 1777 at age sixteen. He graduated in four years, with highest honors, a member of the class of 1781. After Harvard, Dexter studied law under the tutelage of Levi Lincoln in Worcester, Massachusetts, and was admitted to the bar after a normal period of supervised practice in 1784. His law practice was established in Lunenberg in 1786, and he eventually settled in Boston in 1788.

By this point in his life, Dexter had acquired an interest in politics, perhaps deciding to following in his father's footsteps, and was elected as representative from Charleston to the state House of Representatives (1788–1790). He served in this office for two years and was praised for his convictions, judgment, and persuasive influence over legislative deliberations. Dexter's friends and political colleagues encouraged him to seek higher office. He became a Massachusetts congressional representative in the 1793–1795 term. His successes in these positions allowed him to successfully campaign for the U.S. Senate, and he was eventually elected, serving from March 4, 1799, to May 30, 1800.

The turnover time in which he held high appointive offices began to accelerate due to the political turmoil and changing fortunes faced by his Federalist Party. We do know that President John Adams appointed Dexter interim Secretary of War. To accommodate the new President's wishes during the last sixty days of his administration, Dexter resigned from the U.S. Senate effective May 30, 1800, and entered his duties in Adams's Cabinet on June 12, 1800. He held this office only until December 31, 1800, a scant six months, until he was named ad interim Secretary of the Treasury, a position he filled from January 1, 1801, to March 3, 1801, about the time of the inauguration of President Jefferson.

In an early article, Judge Story reported that Dexter's temperament and intellectual endowment ill suited him for that minute diligence and attention to intricate details that the Treasury Department imposed on incumbents, even though he gave the job his intense application of effort, and his success was undoubted. For a brief period of time, Dexter additionally filled in for the Secretary of State in order to administer the oath of office to the great jurist John Marshall on his appointment as Chief Justice of the U.S. Supreme Court.

President Adams did offer Dexter a foreign embassy position, but he turned it down and remained in office until after the accession of Jefferson, when Gallatin succeeded him. For the next fifteen years, Dexter returned to private life to develop his professional legal career and to provide for his wife and only child, eight-year-old Franklin. His law practice in Roxbury, Massachusetts, blossomed, and it is said that he was a regular fixture in Washington, D.C., arguing important cases before the Supreme Court every winter. Evidently, he was an eloquent and persuasive debater with acute logic, and in his courtroom pleading, he relied more on the strength of his arguments than on grandstanding or flashy appeals to the jury. In 1807 he appeared as leading counsel for the defense of Thomas O. Selfridge, accused of the murder of Charles Austin, a Harvard student. The prominence of the participants made this a highly celebrated case, and it was the media sensation of the day. In his address to the jury, Dexter is said to have combined the closest reasoning with the most finished eloquence.

Although he began his political career as an inveterate Federalist, following in the steps of Hamilton and Wolcott at the Treasury, at some point he parted company with his past and took up with Republican causes. Certainly, by 1812 he was openly supporting President Jefferson's war policies. Dexter was outspoken in his advocating a war with England. He had always shown considerable independence of thought and always approached both political and legal problems in his own fashion. His position on the War of 1812 was completely in character. He argued that the war was a just one, and he declined to follow the Federalist official line. On the other hand, he was adamantly against the embargo and nonintercourse policy and unsuccessfully contested its constitutionality. Yet he never fully became a card-carrying Republican and never considered himself a member of that organization.

In fact, after being nominated as the Republican candidate for Governor of Massachusetts in 1816, just a few weeks before his untimely death, he published a speech to the electors declaring that he had fundamental, irreconcilable differences with the Republican Party. Surprisingly, the party went forward with his name on the ballot, and in spite of his position paper, he was very nearly elected to the governorship. A recount of the votes confirmed the close final outcome: He had received a mere 2,000 votes less than his opponent, with some 47,000 votes cast.

About the same time he was running for state office, President Madison offered him a special embassy position (or mission) to the Court of Spain, but he declined it in 1815.

Due to his brief interim appointment to the office, it is quite difficult to assess Dexter's practical or significant contributions while he was Secretary of the Treasury. His short tenure marked the end of a Federalist era in that office, and most of the permanent achievements were now in place by early 1801. Dexter left office with the country's finances in a sound state, and the Federalists should get some of the credit, which is perhaps too fully granted to Gallatin's administration over the ten years after Dexter. The early Federalist accomplishments that ended with Dexter might include: putting into operation a revenue system that was varied in its scope and embraced customs duties, excise tax, and a direct tax; the formation of a Treasury administration system on lines that have been substantially followed up to the present time; and safely restoring the credit of the government (if the debt had not been reduced as much as the Federalists had hoped, the fault was not so much their responsibility as it was due to unforeseen, exogenous, unfavorable events).

Dexter was duly recognized for his public service. For example, he was awarded an honorary LL.D. degree from Harvard College in 1813. His interests outside of law included his involvement in the temperance movement. He was the first President of the first society formed in Massachusetts for the promotion of temperance.

On May 3, 1816, Dexter died of scarlet fever at the young age of fifty-five while in Athens, New York, to attend the wedding of his son Franklin, who, like his father, also graduated from Harvard College and later received an LL.D. degree in 1857, forty-four years after his father was so honored.

BIBLIOGRAPHY

Malone, Dumas, ed. *Dictionary of American Biography*. New York: Charles Scribner's Sons, 1932.

The National Cyclopaedia of American Biography, Being the History of the United States. New York: James T. White & Co., 1893.

Story, Judge. "Sketch of the Life and Character of the Hon. Samuel Dexter." *Mason* 1 (1857): 523.

Wilson, James Grant, and John Fiske. *Appletons' Cyclopaedia of American Biography*. New York: D. Appleton and Company, 1888.

C. DANIEL VENCILL

C. DOUGLAS DILLON (August 21, 1909–   ). It was literally by accident that C. (Clarence) Douglas Dillon became active in politics. When the Republican Chairman in his New Jersey County, who was a house painter, fell off a roof and broke his leg, Dillon became acting Chairman in 1934.

Douglas Dillon was born in Geneva, Switzerland, on August 21, 1909, while his parents were spending a year abroad. They brought him to the States at the age of three months, and he spent his childhood in New Jersey and New York. He was named for his father, Clarence Dillon, founder of the investment banking firm Dillon, Reed and Company, a fabled financier of the 1920s. Worth a half a billion dollars, he once wrote a personal check, as head of a syndicate, to buy Dodge Motor Company, for $146 million (Heller, 67). His grandfather was Samuel Lapowski, who had emigrated from Poland to start a store in Abilene and had adopted "Dillon," his mother's maiden name.

The middle name, which he always used, Douglas, came from his mother, Anne McEldin Douglas of Milwaukee, Wisconsin. She was descended from the first presiding officer of the House of Burgesses in the colony of Virginia. Douglas was their only son.

He was educated at Groton School, from which he was graduated in 1927, and at Harvard. Manager of the football team and elected Treasurer of his class, which is a permanent post, he was a magna cum laude graduate in 1931 with a major in American history and literature. While at Harvard he was a member of Spee Club—as was John F. Kennedy. On March 10 during his senior year, having finished his thesis, he married Phyllis Chess Ellsworth from Boston, a graduate of Miss Porter's School. During their marriage they had two daughters. After Phyllis Dillon's death, Dillon married Susan S. Sage on January 1, 1983.

After his graduation, he went to work for his father's firm and for $185,000 bought a seat on the New York Stock Exchange, of which he was a member from 1931 until 1936. He was elected Vice President and Director of Dillon, Reed in 1938. In 1940 he went to Washington to work for the U.S. Naval Department and joined the U.S. Naval Reserves in October 1940. At the outbreak of the war the following year, he was called to active duty. He served two years in the Pacific Theater, seeing action at Guam, Saipan, and the Philippines, and was awarded the Air Medal and the Legion of Merit for valorous service. At the time of his discharge in 1945, he had achieved the rank of lieutenant commander.

Returning to the family's firm, he became Chairman of the Board of Dillon, Reed in 1946. He was also a Director of the United States and Foreign Securities Corporation, another family enterprise.

A friend and protégé of John Foster Dulles, Douglas Dillon became more active in politics in the later 1940s. He worked for the election of Dewey in 1948, serving in particular as an adviser in foreign affairs, and was an early supporter of Dwight Eisenhower's candidacy for President. He was instrumental in swinging New Jersey to Eisenhower away from Taft as the 1952 Republican presidential nominee.

After Eisenhower took office in 1953, he named Douglas Dillon U.S. Ambassador extraordinary and plenipotentiary to France. It was a good choice in many ways. Dillon, owner of Château Haut-Brion, was a connoisseur of fine wines who said he could taste a Bordeaux and identify it by vineyard or year but usually not both (Heller, 68). Since 1931 he had been a trustee of the Metropolitan Museum of Art in New York; in Paris he became friendly with the director of the Louvre and did an excellent job of developing cultural relations between the two nations. In spite of his popularity in France, during his tenure as Ambassador, relations between France and the United States were strained on three particular occasions. The Suez crisis, the crisis in Indochina, and the controversial admission of West Germany to NATO (North Atlantic Treaty Organization) all occurred during his watch in Paris. His extraordinary diplomatic and political skills helped to maintain reasonable relations between the two countries while the United States was denouncing France's invasion of Egypt before the United Nations, and France was strenuously opposing Germany's addition to NATO. These abilities did not go unappreciated by then-Secretary of State John Foster Dulles, who named him Deputy Undersecretary of State for Economic Affairs in 1957. In June 1958 he became Undersecretary for Economic Affairs with the particular mission of promoting trade and coordinating mutual assistance among the nations. His creation, the so-called Dillon Plan, led to the formation of the Organization for Economic Cooperation and Development, better known as the OECD. By June 1959, he was Undersecretary of State, the second-highest office in the Department of State.

John F. Kennedy was elected President in November 1960, and he began to put together the Cabinet that would serve with him. The OECD treaty was signed in December, and in the same month, Kennedy approached Dillon about the possibility of his serving as Secretary of the Treasury in the new Cabinet. Dillon is reported to have talked the offer over with President Eisenhower and Vice President Nixon, since his position as a major policy adviser might weaken Republican chances of blaming Democrats for anything that might go wrong in the economy. Eisenhower is reported to have agreed that he should serve. Thus, Douglas Dillon became the Republican among Democrats in the new administration. He was sworn into office as Secretary of the Treasury on January 21, 1961.

Douglas Dillon did not completely leave behind the world of diplomacy when he moved from State to Treasury. As the head of the U.S. delegation to the Punta del Este Conference in August 1961, he played an important role in creating the Alliance for Progress. He also was a central figure in deliberations during the Missile Crisis in Cuba in 1963.

The U.S. economy in early 1961 was in a weak recovery phase from the recession that, some believed, had secured Kennedy's election. Unemployment was high, growth was sluggish, and there was a persistent balance of payments problem accompanied by an outflow of gold. These three issues were to be the foci of the new administration's economic policy.

From the outset, even as early as the confirmation hearings, Dillon made it clear that he would direct his efforts toward solutions using fiscal and monetary means (U.S. Congress, 14). He said he would work closely with Chairman William McChesney Martin, of the Board of Governors of the Federal Reserve System, and with Walter Heller, who became Chairman of the President's Council of Economic Advisers. The frequent meetings of these three principal economic advisers to the President caused them to become known as the "Troika" in the popular press.

In Dillon's view, the balance of payments deficit was the nation's most pressing problem, and he convinced Kennedy that reducing it should be the first priority. Dillon brought Robert Roosa from the New York Federal Reserve Bank to be Undersecretary for Monetary Affairs. The two were the architects of several measures designed to achieve this end. The Interest Equalization Act of 1963 was among them. Meanwhile, the Fed was "doing the twist," simultaneous open market operations buying securities in the long-term market and selling short-term securities in an attempt to lower long-term interest rates to encourage investment and growth, while pushing short-term rates higher to stem the outflow of gold. The Trade Expansion Act of 1962 was another attempt to encourage foreign trade—especially U.S. exports.

President Kennedy had promised "to get the country moving again." Dillon and Assistant Secretary for Tax Policy, Stanley Surrey, along with Heller, directed the formation of the various packages to achieve a more vigorous economy. The Investment Tax Credit and liberalization of depreciation methods for tax purposes were viewed as means of subsidizing investment in new plant and equipment to increase productivity in U.S. production and to improve the competitiveness of the nation in international trade. These policies went into effect in 1962.

Dillon at first was less enthusiastic for a massive cut in corporate and personal income tax rates than his colleagues at the President's Council of Economic Advisers. Some of them saw it as the conservative pull of a Republican among them, resisting fiscal stimulus if it came at the expense of budget balance. On the other hand, as early as in his confirmation hearings, Dillon had pointed out that the appropriate balance to seek for the federal budget was one over a business cycle—not on an annual basis (U.S. Congress, 8).

By late 1962, Dillon had also come to agree that the high marginal rates of the income tax were exerting too great a drag on the economy's demand for output. Although there are many who can justly claim to have played a role in the great "Kennedy Tax Cut," it was, in the end, the Treasury Secretary who had to craft the actual program and sell it to Congress. Although the House passed the tax cut bill in September 1963 (271 to 155), the Senate had not passed it before Kennedy's death. Thus, it was President Lyndon Johnson who signed the tax cuts into law on February 25, 1964. For this watershed in modern economic policy, Secretary Dillon deserves special credit.

Secretary Dillon made it known to President Johnson that he wished to return to private life and resigned his office effective April 1, 1965. He returned to Wall Street as President of the United States and Foreign Securities Corporation, founded by his father in 1924 and tied with the State Street Investment Corporation of Boston as the oldest extant investment company. In 1971 he returned to Dillon, Reed and Company to serve as Chairman of the Board, where he remained until 1981.

Continuing to be active in government, he served on the Senior Advisory Group on Vietnam, which urged deescalation of the war in 1968. He served in the 1970s on the Treasury's Advisory Committee on International Monetary Reform. In 1985 he became honorary Chairman of the Committee for the Preservation of the Treasury and funded the replicated chandeliers in the Cash Room in the Main Treasury Building. He was President of the Board of Overseers of Harvard, President of the Metropolitan Museum of Art from 1970 to 1978, and has chaired the Rockefeller Foundation and the Brookings Institution.

Among the many colleges and universities that have presented Dillon honorary degrees are Harvard, Columbia, New York University, Princeton, Pennsylvania, Lafayette, Williams, and Rutgers. In 1985, President George Bush awarded Douglas Dillon the Medal of Freedom.

At the time he left office it was said that the brilliantly equipped Dillon had earned the reputation of being the best Secretary that the Treasury had in modern times.

BIBLIOGRAPHY

Baker, Russell. "Twelve Men Close to Kennedy." *New York Times Magazine*, January 27, 1961.

Gammons, Ann, ed. *Who's Who in American Politics*. New York: Bowker, 1979.

Heller, Deane F. *The Kennedy Cabinet: American Men of Destiny*. Derby, CT: Monarch Books, 1961.

"President." *The New Yorker*, April 4, 1970, 35–36.

Sleven, Joseph H. "Fowler Is Rebuilding Treasury Image." *Washington Post*, July 17, 1965.

Sobel, Robert, ed. *Biographical Directory of the United States Executive Branch, 1774–1977*. Westport, CT: Greenwood Press, 1977.

Treasury Historical Association. *An Evening with the Secretaries: A Bicentennial Celebration*, May 17, 1990.

U.S. Congress. Senate. Committee on Finance. *Nominations*, 87th Cong., 1st sess., January 11, 13, 1961.

U.S. Treasury Department. *Annual Reports of the Secretary of the Treasury*. Washington, D.C.: Government Printing Office, various years.

EARL W. ADAMS

JOHN A. DIX (July 24, 1798–April 21, 1879). Although John Adams Dix served as Secretary of the Treasury for only six weeks during the final days of James Buchanan's administration, he has received high marks from historians for his performance in office. Dix took charge of the Treasury on January 15, 1861, succeeding Howell Cobb of Georgia and Philip F. Thomas of Maryland, and served until March 6, 1861, when he turned the office over to Salmon P. Chase, Abraham Lincoln's Treasury Secretary.

Dix was chosen to be Treasury Secretary at a critical juncture in the final days of the Buchanan administration. The election of Lincoln in November 1860 triggered a surge of secessionist activity in the South. Convinced that the South could no longer find safety in the Union, Howell Cobb resigned on December 8, 1860, to become a leader in the Georgia secessionist movement. He left behind him in Washington an empty Treasury and incomplete Treasury financing. Many Northern investors were no longer willing to place their trust in Cobb's Treasury. Buchanan then named his Commissioner of Patents, Philip Francis Thomas of Maryland, to serve as Treasury Secretary. Thomas, who was sympathetic to the Southern secessionist movement, failed to gain the confidence of the New York financial community. He, too, encountered difficulties borrowing to meet government obligations. Within a month, Thomas also had resigned.

Acting upon the strong suggestion from a group of New York bankers, Buchanan appointed John Adams Dix to fill the Treasury post. The appointment was part of a major structural and philosophical change in Buchanan's Cabinet. Before the election of Abraham Lincoln in November 1860, the Cabinet had been dominated by Southerners and Southern sympathizers. Dix was not only a Northerner but earlier in his political career had participated in the Barnburner movement, a faction of the Democratic Party that had opposed the extension of slavery into territories where it had not been permitted previously. Thus, Dix's appointment was part of a symbolic demonstration that the Buchanan administration could be relied upon to defend the Union, as well as a pragmatic necessity, given the immediate threat of government insolvency. Dix's experience as a public administrator, military officer, attorney, and scholar, his reputation for honesty, and his strong commitment to the preservation of the Union helped restore confidence in the President and his administration during its last six weeks.

John Adams Dix was born on July 24, 1798, in Boscawen, New Hampshire, a small village in the southern part of the state. In his memoirs, Dix describes the village as containing thirty houses along a single street a mile long. He descended from a long line of New Englanders. His parents were Colonel Timothy Dix and Abigail (Wilkins) Dix of Amherst, Massachusetts, who died while Dix was still a child. Colonel Dix was a merchant, civic leader, and postmaster in the small community. He believed strongly in the value of education and helped establish the first village school. He saw to it that his son John received the best education he could afford with his limited resources.

When the United States declared war against England in 1812, Dix arranged to become a cadet in his father's regiment, the Fourteenth Infantry of New Hampshire, stationed in Baltimore. While training, he attended classes at St. Mary's College. After graduation, he was made an ensign and accompanied his father to Sackett's Harbor on the ill-fated campaign to capture Montreal. On November 14, 1813, Dix's father died of pneumonia at French Mills, leaving the young Dix without financial resources and with responsibility for his stepmother and eight younger brothers and sisters. Dix remained with the army in northern New York and in July 1814 fought in the Battle of Lunday Lane, considered one of the bloodiest battles of the War of 1812.

By the end of the War of 1812 Dix held the rank of Second Lieutenant. He pursued his military career, serving in a variety of locations before being appointed aide-de-camp to General Jacob Brown, Commander of the northern half of the U. S. Army. While in the military, Dix was also given the opportunity to study law under Attorney General Wirt and was admitted to the Washington bar in 1826. The same year he married Catherine Morgan, daughter of a wealthy New York landowner. He traveled with his new bride to Denmark, where he served as a military attaché. This post allowed the young Dixes to become acquainted with Europe. After returning from Denmark, he resigned from the army on July 28, 1828, with the rank of captain and moved to Cooperstown, New York, where he practiced law and managed some of his father-in-law's property.

Dix became active in Otsego County politics and in 1830 was appointed Adjutant-General for the State of New York. With this appointment, he became a member of the Albany Regency directed by the powerful Martin Van Buren. In 1831 he was appointed Regent of the University of New York and served in this capacity until 1846. In 1833 when State Comptroller Silas Wright was appointed to the U.S. Senate and A. C. Flagg, Secretary of State, became Comptroller, Dix replaced Flagg as Secretary of State and served in this position until 1839.

The Panic of 1837 weakened the hold of Van Buren's political machine in Albany, and with the election of Republican William Seward as Governor in 1838, Dix was retired from his position as Secretary of State. He then founded and edited Northern Light, a journal devoted to "practical business matters" intended to stimulate discussions in the area of political economy. The journal was intended to be "free from all political discussion." Except for a brief period abroad in Europe (due to his wife's illness), he continued to be active in New York politics. In 1841, he served as a member of the New York State Assembly.

In 1844 Van Buren persuaded the popular Silas Wright to run for Governor of New York and lend support to the candidacy of Democrat James K. Polk in his bid for the presidency. When Wright resigned his senatorship, Dix was appointed by the New York legislature to complete his unexpired term, and from December 1, 1844, to March 4, 1849, he served in the United States Senate. He supported Polk in the annexation of Texas, the Oregon bill, and the Mexican War.

Still, Dix's position was not strong enough for the Southern (and dominant) wing of the Democratic Party. As a protégé of Van Buren, Dix became linked with the Barnburner movement, the faction of the New York State Democratic

Party that opposed the extension of slavery into the territories. The Barnburners, led by a retired Van Buren, were opposed by the Hunkers, more conservative New York Democrats who allied themselves more with the Southern Democrats. The two factions were not able to compromise at the 1848 party convention in Baltimore, and after the nomination of Lewis Cass for the presidency, the Barnburners walked out of the convention. Although conservative Barnburners, such as Dix and to a large extent Van Buren, opposed the formation of a third party with its own candidates, when the third-party Free Soil movement was organized with Martin Van Buren as its presidential candidate, a reluctant John Dix was persuaded to run for Governor of New York under the Free Soil label. The divided Democratic Party lost the national election to Zachary Taylor and Millard Fillmore, and in New York, Dix was defeated for Governor by Hamilton Fish, the Whig candidate.

In 1853, Dix was offered the post of interim Assistant Treasurer at New York but declined the position. Dix instead retired from political life, practiced law in New York City, and served as President of both the Mississippi and Missouri Railroad and the Chicago and Rock Island Railroad. He continued to participate in politics as a private citizen and actively supported Buchanan in 1856.

In May 1860, when New York Postmaster Isaac Fowler was dismissed for mismanagement and corrupt practices, Dix was recalled to public service. As Postmaster, Dix not only demonstrated his management talents but also ended questionable political practices such as forcing postal employees to "donate" a portion of their salaries to the treasury of the reigning political party. His service in the New York Post Office renewed his reputation as an able and honest administrator.

In January 1861, Buchanan summoned Dix to Washington to discuss the possibility of his serving in the Cabinet. It is believed that Buchanan's original intention was to offer Dix the War Department, where he would replace John Floyd of Virginia. The immediate reason behind the invitation was the impasse the Treasury had reached with the New York financial community. The meeting with Dix came at the request of a group of New York bankers who no longer trusted the Buchanan administration and was a precondition for the extension of further credit to the federal government. They were no longer willing to lend the government the funds needed to meet its obligations unless they were given a clear signal that the Buchanan administration stood with the Union. Dix's presence in the Cabinet would serve as this signal.

In the end, Dix chose to accept the Treasury portfolio. He described the next six weeks as the most exciting of his life. During the period until Lincoln's inauguration, Dix performed three vital functions for the administration and for the nation: He completed the necessary Treasury financings and thereby secured sufficient credit to keep the nation solvent through the end of the Buchanan administration; he moved forcefully and dramatically to protect Treasury property and revenue in the Southern states that had seceded from the Union; and he acted as an adviser and confidant to Buchanan, providing the President's regime with the leadership and stability required to maintain confidence in the government.

Upon assuming office, the pending Treasury auction for $5 million in notes begun by Thomas was completed. By month's end, Dix had reevaluated the Treasury's position and estimated that at least another $20 million to $25 million would be needed to tide the government over until July 1, the beginning of the next fiscal year. In early February the Congress authorized an additional $25 million in long-term loans. Dix advertised for bids for $8 million of the authorization in February. The subscription was completed promptly at an average interest rate of 6.63 percent. Dix was able to hand the Treasury over to his successor, Salmon Chase, with a positive balance of $6 million.

The second major task that Dix performed was protection of customs revenue and federal property in the seceding states. In truth, protection of this property was almost impossible, but the symbolism in Dix's intentions should not be underrated. The most famous incident occurred on January 29, 1861, when Dix received word from New Orleans that the Captain of the Treasury revenue cutter *McCelland* refused to surrender his vessel to federal officials so it could be returned to New York. Dix, after consulting with General Winfield Scott and Attorney General Stanton (but not the President), sent a telegram ordering that the captain be arrested and the cutter seized. He added that if anyone attempted to haul down the Union flag, the officers were to shoot them on the spot. This response rang a sympathetic chord in the North and earned Dix his reputation as a defender of the Union. In actuality, according to some accounts, the ship was surrendered and the flag disappeared (reportedly to be returned to Dix later in his life as a gesture of esteem).

Dix also acted as a very visible adviser to the President. While serving as Secretary, Dix lived at the White House and consulted with the President on most evenings from ten to eleven o'clock. By this time, all remaining secessionists had left the Cabinet, and Buchanan was firmly resolved to do all he could to hold the country together, short of provoking war. Dix's presence in the White House lent a large measure of credibility to the administration.

In his brief tenure as Secretary, Dix's work was confined to accomplishment of short-term imperatives. His economic ideas, though strongly held, were therefore not reflected in any long-term policy initiatives. From earlier writings, it is clear that in economic matters Dix was a moderate New York Democrat, especially on issues related to money and the banking system. He was strongly conservative regarding federal and state support of internal improvements, such as railroads and inland waterways, especially when public sector borrowing was required as part of the financing. Although a strong believer in the benefits of free trade, subject to a revenue tariff, he was not unsympathetic to the appeals of certain protectionists.

With the inauguration of Lincoln, Dix left the Treasury and rejoined the military as a volunteer, accepting a commission as major general. He was rated one of the more able volunteer generals. During the Civil War he was stationed first in Maryland at Fort Monroe, where he participated in the Virginia campaign, and later in New York City after the draft riots. He was loyal to the Union and in the 1864 presidential election backed Lincoln.

After the war, Dix returned to private life and from 1863 to 1868 served as the first President of the Union Pacific Railroad. He also served as acting President of the Erie Railroad when it was in trouble in 1872. In 1872, at the age of seventy-four, he was elected Governor of New York as a Republican and served an uneventful two-year term but was defeated in his bid for reelection in 1874. He served in several honorary posts including Controller of the Trinity Church Corporation. His son Morgan Dix was Rector of Trinity Church in New York City for many years. John Adams Dix died on April 21, 1879, in New York City and is buried in Trinity Cemetery.

BIBLIOGRAPHY

Auchampaugh, Philip Gerald. *James Buchanan and His Cabinet on the Eve of Secession.* Boston: J. S. Canner and Company, 1926.

Baker, Jean H. *The Politics of Continuity: Maryland Political Parties from 1858 to 1870.* Baltimore: Johns Hopkins University Press, 1973.

Buchanan, James. *Mr. Buchanan's Administration on the Eve of Rebellion.* New York: D. Appleton and Company, 1865.

Dewey, Davis Rich. *Financial History of the United States.* 12th ed. New York: Augustus M. Kelley Publisher, 1968.

Dix, John Adams. *Speeches and Occasional Addresses.* New York: D. Appleton and Company, 1864.

Dix, Morgan. *Memoirs of John Adams Dix.* Compiled by his son. New York: Harper & Brothers, 1883.

Johnson, Rossiter, ed. *The Twentieth Century Biographical Dictionary of Notable Americans.* Boston: Biographical Society, 1904.

Nevins, Allan. *Ordeal of the Union.* New York: Charles Scribner's Sons, 1947.

Niven, John. *Martin Van Buren: The Romantic Age of American Politics.* New York: Oxford University Press, 1983.

Sobel, Robert, ed. *Biographical Directory of the United States Executive Branch, 1774–1977.* Westport, CT: Greenwood Press, 1977.

Studenski, Paul, and Herman E. Krooss. *Financial History of the United States.* New York: McGraw-Hill Book Company, 1963.

MARIE McKINNEY

WILLIAM J. DUANE (May 9, 1780–September 27, 1865). William J. Duane's term of office as Secretary of the Treasury only lasted from May 29 to September 22, 1833. Given the events of history, Duane's contribution to the Jacksonian administration was, ironically, to expand the powers of the presidency and not that of the economy.

While Secretary of the Treasury, Duane, appointed by President Andrew Jackson, refused to carry out Jackson's directive to remove government deposits from the Second Bank of the United States. This refusal led to Duane's firing as Secretary of the Treasury, which in turn led to confrontation with the Senate who had confirmed Duane. The Senate argued that only they could dismiss Duane as it was they who approved his appointment. Jackson held and argued his position successfully. Duane was gone, and presidential power expanded.

William John Duane was born on May 9, 1780, in Clonwell, Tipperary County, Ireland, the son of William and Catherine (Corcoran). Duane was educated through the tutoring efforts of his mother and some fifteen months in a private school. The family lived in Ireland and London before immigrating to the United States in 1796.

After arriving in the United States, Duane worked in the composing room of his father's paper, the *True Believer*. His father assumed the editorship in 1798 of the *Aurora* in Philadelphia, Pennsylvania, after the death of its founder, John Bache. The *Aurora* was an influential voice of the Jeffersonian Democrats against the Federalists under both its founder and Duane senior. In the 1820s the paper was a staunch supporter of Andrew Jackson and was critical of John Quincy Adams and Henry Clay.

William J. Duane left journalism in 1806 to become a partner in a paper business with William Levis. He soon became involved in local politics and was elected to the Pennsylvania House of Representatives in 1809, where he served as Chairman of the Committee on Roads and Inland Navigation. His writings and political efforts showed him to be a strong proponent for government support on these issues.

Throughout the early 1800s, Duane attempted to foster his political career, but with mixed results, losing bids for the U.S. House of Representatives in 1816 and the Pennsylvania House in 1817, but his tenacity paid off, and he was finally reelected to the Pennsylvania position in 1819.

While his political fortune was careening from failure to success, his professional career continued to advance. Having left his paper business in 1812 to study law, he was admitted to the Pennsylvania bar on June 13, 1815, and soon established a profitable law practice. In 1820 he was appointed prosecuting attorney for the mayor's court of Philadelphia and held that position for three years. It was observed that his only "failure" during his term of office was leniency for the financially bankrupt.

In 1824, Duane refused a nomination for Congress but did become a member of the Philadelphia Committee of Correspondence and was shortly elected to membership on the Philadelphia Select Council. In 1831, as a reward for both his and his father's service to the Democratic Party, President Jackson appointed Duane as a Commissioner under the 1930 treaty with Denmark. As a Commissioner, Duane heard claims by U.S. citizens against the Danish government resulting from Danish seizure of American property.

Duane's next move within the government, that of being appointed to the high position of Secretary of the Treasury by President Andrew Jackson, had little to do with his skills or talents but was predicated more on the family's loyalty to the Democratic Party and having resided in the politically correct city Philadelphia. But this is rushing the story.

Upon his election, President Jackson declared war on the Second Bank of the United States (Bank). It wasn't that Jackson was antibank or antibusiness; he simply distrusted monopolistic bankers and large business. He also did not like paper money nor those that served to further the interests of the wealthy and privileged class, as he believed the Bank served. He was also certain that the powerful, centralized Bank threatened republican government and liberty and that it was his personal mandate to rid the country of this creation.

The Bank had been chartered by the federal government in 1816 for a limited period of time, and its charter required that it be renewed periodically. The Bank, by the 1830s, was big business, and its main branch was in Philadelphia, with twenty-nine others located in various cities. When Jackson assumed the presidency, monies deposited in the Bank amounted to about $13 million, with half of the total being government deposits. It also held about 50 percent of U.S. specie reserves.

While the government's ownership of the Bank was only about 20 percent of the outstanding stock, the Bank provided important services to the economy in its function as a lending institution and also as the fiscal arm of the government, both collecting and disbursing revenue. These latter services were provided at no charge to the government, and in exchange the government placed all its deposits with the Bank. These deposits were a major source of income to the Bank, the proceeds of which went to the stockholders, primarily private and foreign holders. Nevertheless, the Bank's power and influence had to be curtailed or the Bank had to go.

The Bank was to be rechartered in 1836, and Jackson was disposed for the recharter if certain changes and safeguards were imposed. The pro-Bank forces did not want to see any populist changes to their source of loans and income and antagonized Jackson by sponsoring an early attempt at recharter in 1832. Nicholas Biddle, President of the Bank, and prime instigator of the early recharter movement, calculated that Jackson would not interfere with congressional approval of the Bank in an election year.

The recharter bill passed Congress in the summer of 1832, but Jackson was adamant: He issued a searing veto and killed it. Along with the veto was issued one of the strongest and most important messages issued by a President to his Congress—Jackson developed the concept that the President was not restricted to vetoes on constitutional grounds alone but could veto a bill when he believed it was harmful to the country and its citizens.

After surviving an override attempt to his veto, and interpreting his victory over Henry Clay in the 1832 election as a mandate to continue his war on the Bank, Jackson was determined to effectively slay the "hydraheaded monster."

Honing in on concerns about the safety of public monies, Jackson decided to remove federal funds from the Bank and deposit them in state banks run by men who were known and more disposed to Jacksonian policies. However, by law, only the Secretary of the Treasury could remove the funds from the Bank. Jackson's Secretary at that time, Louis McLane, was not of the same mind as Jackson, as he believed that such an action would destabilize the financial system. Jackson was determined to let McLane go and find a Secretary who would carry out his instructions.

McLane was easily disposed of with a "promotion" replacing Edward Livingston as Secretary of State. In the Cabinet shakeup, Livingston became Minister to France. McLane's replacement at the Treasury, however, was another problem. There was considerable sentiment among Jackson's political advisers to have the new Secretary come from Pennsylvania. As the Bank was headquartered in Philadelphia, they felt it would be good politics to have someone from the state as head of the Treasury. Jackson agreed and selected William J. Duane as McLane's replacement. The basis of Jackson's selection still remains somewhat of a mystery. In fact, one observer has maintained that Duane was an unknown at that time and that even today his personality and character remain dim, if at all visible, on the pages of history.

Duane has been variously described as a distinguished lawyer and as the bottom of the Philadelphia bar. It has also been said that he was managing the General Bank in Philadelphia as well as a successfully practicing lawyer. Commentary on his personal qualities run between "possessing a well-disciplined mind" and being a "small-minded, inconsequential bureaucrat."

While history states that Jackson told his Vice President, Van Buren, that Duane's name "flashed into my mind" quite suddenly, it is also suggested that Van Buren mentioned Duane to McLane, who suggested it to the President. The highest order of probability suggests that William Duane, the son of Colonel Duane, an old friend of Jackson and editor of the far-famed journal *Aurora,* was chosen primarily because Jackson remembered him as "a chip off the old block."

Duane was indeed from Pennsylvania and had worked for the Girard banking interests in Philadelphia. He had chaired the committee on banks in the Pennsylvania House and was known to be anti-Bank. Also, as the son of the editor William Duane, his appointment would unite the Jeffersonian and Jacksonian parties. The reasoning for the appointment was sound, but someone failed to obtain Duane's attitude toward the question of withdrawing government funds from the Bank.

On June 2, 1833, shortly after he was sworn in as Secretary, Duane was visited by Amos Kendall, the Jacksonian adviser who was the most adamant in proposing the removal of the funds. Kendall told Duane that the decision to remove the funds had been finalized and that he would soon be directed by the President to transfer the money to the state banks. When Duane complained to Jackson about the visit, the President assured him that the final decision had not been made and would not be decided until Jackson returned from a tour to New England. However, on June 26, while visiting Boston, Jackson sent Duane two communications on the Bank. In the first, Jackson announced that he had decided that the withdrawals should be concluded as soon as possible, enabling a new banking system to be in place when Congress reconvened. He also suggested that an agent, Amos Kendall, should be appointed to find banks in Baltimore, Philadelphia,

New York, and Boston. In the second communication, Jackson detailed his reasons for reaching his conclusions about the Bank.

Duane believed that only the Secretary of the Treasury was empowered to withdraw funds and could only do so at the consent of Congress. Duane based his argument on the belief that the law creating the Treasury Department never called it an "executive" department and that the Secretary was required to make his reports to Congress, not the President.

On Jackson's return to Washington in July, Duane further explained his position in a letter to Jackson where he argued that although he did not approve of renewing the Bank's charter, he believed the Bank's removal to be but an act of vengeance. He also argued that replacing the Bank with substitute state banks, without the direction of Congress, would be unwise and improper.

In subsequent meetings with Jackson, Duane refused to bend to the President's will and stood by his position. His obstinacy further isolated him from the discussions on the subject within the administration, although both McLane and Van Buren believed there was strong merit in Duane's position.

By September 1833, Jackson was ready to move on the Bank. In a Cabinet meeting on September 10, Jackson announced his decision to withdraw funds from the Bank. With this blatant override of his Secretary's position, Jackson anticipated a resignation by Duane in due course. Duane, however, said nothing. The President then offered Duane the position of Minister to Russia. Duane refused the sobriquet.

On September 18, 1933, Jackson laid out his arguments to his Cabinet, detailing his complaints against the Bank, and declared his power to take action. Duane then asked if he was being directed to remove the deposits. Jackson answered that he was and that he was to do so on the President's authority, that the responsibility was Jackson's alone. On the nineteenth, Jackson asked for Duane's decision. Duane then asked for two additional days to respond. However, when a notice of Jackson's decision was published in a Jacksonian Washington newspaper, the *Globe*, on September 20, Duane decided not to obey the President and not to resign. He informed Jackson of his decision personally, and on September 22, Jackson informed Duane that his services were no longer required.

Duane's dismissal marked the first time a member of the executive branch whose appointment had been confirmed by the Senate had been dismissed from office. Jackson believed that all executive appointees fell under his authority. Having previously established his right to remove lower-level executive appointees, Jackson was certain of his authority to remove Cabinet-level officials and proceeded accordingly. While Congress argued and fumed, Jackson immediately appointed Roger Taney as the new Secretary of the Treasury and moved ahead with his plan against the Bank.

Upon his dismissal Duane left politics forever and returned to his law practice in Philadelphia. Determined to defend his reputation, Duane wrote a pamphlet in 1834 entitled "Narrative and Correspondence Concerning the Removal of the Deposits and Occurrences Connected Therewith."

Little was heard from Duane after his return to Philadelphia, and he died quietly in the City of Brotherly Love on September 27, 1865.

BIBLIOGRAPHY

The Biographical Encyclopedia of Pennsylvania of the Nineteenth Century. Philadelphia: Galaxy, 1874.

Duane, William. *Biographical Memoir of William J. Duane*. Philadelphia: Claxton, Remsen, and Haffelinger, 1868.

Scharf, Thomas J., and Thompson Westcott. *History of Philadelphia, 1609–1884*. Philadelphia: L. H. Everts and Co., 1884.

Sumner, William G. *Andrew Jackson*. New York: Haskell House, 1968.

Temin, Peter. *The Jacksonian Economy*. New York: Norton, 1969.

RONALD ROBBINS AND BERNARD S. KATZ

E

THOMAS EWING (December 28, 1789–October 26, 1871). Thomas Ewing served as Secretary of the Treasury from March 4, 1841, to September 11, 1841. He was appointed to the office by newly inaugurated President William Henry Harrison, who died one month later on April 4, 1841. Ewing and the other members of the Cabinet were continued in office by John Tyler, Harrison's successor. Ewing and all other Cabinet members except Secretary of State Daniel Webster resigned on September 11, 1841, just two days after Tyler vetoed a bank bill that had been drafted by Ewing.

Thomas Ewing was the second son of George and Rachel (Harris) Ewing. He was born in West Liberty, Ohio County, West Virginia, which was then part of Virginia. Although Ewing stated he attached little importance to remote ancestry, his biographers trace his lineage to an officer in the Army of William of Orange. The son of this ancestor came to New Jersey about 1718. George Ewing, descendant of this immigrant, served in the American Revolution and then migrated to West Ohio County, now part of West Virginia, where his son Thomas was born. The family moved to Ames Township, Athens County, Ohio, in 1798, and it is there, on the edge of civilization, that Thomas Ewing spent his boyhood.

His elder sister taught him to read, and his parents encouraged him to read everything he could lay his hands on. A circulating library that opened in Ames Township stimulated him and enabled him to satisfy his craving for knowledge. By virtue of being an avid reader, he acquired an adequate elementary education.

To secure funds for college, Ewing worked for several years in the Kanawha salt works. He enrolled in Ohio University at Athens but soon ran out of money and returned to Kanawha (literally back to the salt mines), where he saved enough to return to Ohio University. In 1815, he was one of two persons to receive the first B.A. degrees granted by that institution.

Ewing next studied law in the office of Philemon Beecher of Lancaster, Ohio, and was admitted to the bar in 1816. He was regarded by his peers as a very able and successful lawyer at this time and in his later years. For several years he served as prosecuting attorney for Fairfield County and, in that capacity, freed the district of counterfeiters. This was his first involvement with the monetary system and banking problems.

Ewing tried for a seat in the Ohio legislature in 1823 but was defeated. In 1830, however, he was elected to the U.S. Senate and took office as a Whig in 1831. In the Senate he supported the Whig protective tariff policy. Also, he was strong in his criticism of the Democratic administration of President Jackson— of Jackson's "Specie Circular," a directive to government agents to accept payment for land in specie only, and of Jackson's removal of government deposits from the United States Bank. Ewing advocated rechartering the Second Bank of the United States, whose corporate charter was to expire in 1836, and supported legislation to develop the West by revising the land laws and lowering postal rates. Ewing lost his bid for reelection in 1836 and returned to Lancaster, Ohio, to practice law.

Ewing returned to public office in 1841. The Whig Party gained control of Congress in 1840 and elected William H. Harrison President and John Tyler— of "and Tyler too" fame—Vice President. President Harrison appointed Ewing Secretary of the Treasury upon his inauguration on March 4, 1841. Harrison died just one month later on April 4, 1841, and President Tyler retained Ewing and all other Harrison Cabinet appointees in office. No issues of significance to the Treasury Department had arisen during Harrison's brief presidency, but Ewing became involved in the national bank issue soon after Tyler took office.

The question of a national bank had been controversial since George Washington's first administration, and some knowledge of its history is necessary if one is to understand the problem facing Ewing. The first national bank in the United States, that is, a bank that received its corporate charter from the federal government rather than a state government, was organized in 1791. This bank, the First Bank of the United States, received a twenty-year charter from Congress, 1791–1811, upon the recommendation of Alexander Hamilton and over the objection of Thomas Jefferson. A limited life charter, in this case twenty years, was common for corporations in that era. The bank was jointly owned by the government and private investors, again a common practice in that era of banking.

The bank operated for profit but also performed many functions of a modern central bank. It acted as the government's fiscal agent by helping it borrow money, by facilitating the collection of revenue, and by holding its deposits. Also acting as a bank, it discounted promissory notes and issued bank notes. The notes of state banks received by the U.S. Bank were promptly presented for redemption, which limited the state banks' ability to issue notes and thus limited the supply of circulating currency.

Despite the performance of these useful functions, the bank was not rechartered in 1811. There were several reasons for this decision:

1. The Federalists had created the bank, and there were charges that the bank's lending policies favored Federalists. By 1811 the Federalists had lost control of Congress.

2. Some of the private investors were foreign. These stockholders could not vote and, therefore, did not control the bank, but they did receive dividends that were labeled "tribute" by the bank's critics.

3. The anti-Federalists, basing their arguments on the absence of specific provisions for bank charters in the Constitution, claimed the bank was unconstitutional. The Constitution granted Congress the exclusive right to coin money and to regulate its value, but there was some question whether this power applied to paper money.

4. A sizable portion of the population disapproved of paper money whether issued by the government or by banks. This was the argument of the "hard money" faction.

5. State banks resented the limitations placed on their ability to issue bank notes. This group constituted what would today be called a powerful "easy money" lobby.

Despite this formidable array of opposition, the bill to recharter the bank in 1811 lost only after Vice President George Clinton broke a seventeen–seventeen tie in the Senate.

There was no national bank in existence from 1811 to 1816. As a result, there was no fiscal agent of the government and there was difficulty financing the War of 1812. Also, state bank note issue was excessive and unregulated. Congress recognized the need to regulate the notes issued by state banks but believed it lacked the constitutional authority to do so directly. Therefore, it voted to charter the Second Bank of the United States for the period 1816–1836. This bank, because of its size, would dominate the nation's banking system and control the issuance of bank notes.

The Second Bank of the United States experienced some difficulties but, on the whole, accomplished its mission. Nevertheless, it aroused strong opposition. As noted above, some persons objected to all forms of paper money, while others objected to the bank's practice of restricting the issuance of state bank notes. Finally, there was the constitutional issue. This was first raised by Thomas Jefferson in 1791 and was cited by President Jackson when, in 1832, he vetoed a bill that would have extended the term of the bank's charter.

Senator Ewing's condemnation of Jackson's action has been noted. The rechartering of the bank was an issue in the 1832 election in which Jackson defeated Senator Henry Clay and was reelected President. The bank's charter expired in 1836, and for a few years, the question of a national bank appeared to be settled. The issue arose again when the Whigs won the election of 1840.

As noted, President Harrison was inaugurated on March 4, 1841, with John Tyler as Vice President. Senator Henry Clay of Kentucky, the leader of the Whig Party and a candidate for President in three elections, promptly presented an agenda for congressional action that included the reestablishment of a national bank. Vice President John Tyler, who had become President upon the death of Harrison, indicated he did not agree with the creation of the proposed bank. He based his opposition on "States Rights." He did not believe the Constitution granted the federal government the right to impose a bank on the states.

Secretary of the Treasury Ewing, assisted by other Whigs and after conferring with Tyler, proposed a compromise plan. Under the terms of the Ewing bill, Congress would not impose a national bank on the states. Rather, Congress, acting as the legislative body for the District of Columbia, but not as the legislative body for the whole nation, would authorize a Washington, D.C., bank just like the states authorized a Virginia or a Pennsylvania bank. The bank created by Congress would act as the government's fiscal agent. Also, it could discount promissory notes and issue bank notes like other commercial banks. It was to be jointly owned by the government and private investors and could establish branches in the states where permission was granted. It was to be assumed permission was granted if a state did not take negative action within one year of the granting of the new bank's charter. In brief, it was to be a national bank by a different name (the bill presented to Congress used the term "Fiscal Corporation") and with legal authority that Ewing and others thought was acceptable to Tyler.

Tyler vetoed the bill, citing the bank's authority to discount promissory notes by state branches, which, he argued, meant the bank would operate like a commercial bank not only in the District of Columbia but in the states.

Ewing, assisted by other Whig leaders, again conferred with the President and prepared a second compromise bill. This bank would not have the power to discount promissory notes in the states, but it would have the right to deal in bills of exchange. Secretary Ewing and many Congressmen believed Tyler would sign the bill, but, on September 9, 1841, the President sent Congress a veto message. Again the veto was based on "States Rights" and the claim that dealing in bills of exchange was a function of commercial banks.

Ewing, acting in his capacity as Secretary of the Treasury, had now drafted two bank bills for the President, had seen them passed by Congress, and then vetoed by Tyler. On September 11, 1841, Ewing and all other members of the Cabinet except Daniel Webster, the Secretary of State, resigned amid a firestorm of protest by the Whigs against Tyler and applause from many Democrats.

Ewing went back to Lancaster, Ohio, where he earned a reputation as an outstanding lawyer and logician. He returned to national public office in 1849. Zachary Taylor, a Whig, was elected President in 1848, and he appointed Ewing Secretary of the newly created Department of the Interior. Ewing organized the department. He maintained his belief that government should assist in the development of the western lands and recommended a mint be established in Denver, near the gold fields, and that a railroad be built to the Pacific Ocean.

President Taylor died on July 9, 1850, and was succeeded by Vice President Fillmore. A rift developed in the Whig Party, and William Meredith resigned as Secretary of the Treasury. Thomas Corwin, a Senator from Ohio, became the new Treasury Secretary. Ewing resigned as Secretary of the Interior so that he could be named to complete Corwin's unexpired term in the Senate.

In this term as a Senator, Ewing differed with the Whig leader Henry Clay. He opposed the passage of the Fugitive Slave Law and favored admission of California to the Union without restrictions. Both items were part of what is now known as the Compromise of 1850. Also, Ewing disagreed with Clay on certain issues dealing with the results of the Mexican war.

When his term expired in 1851, Ewing left public office but maintained a keen interest in public affairs. President Lincoln named him to the short-lived "Peace Convention" of 1861, and he acted as a voluntary and unofficial adviser to Lincoln during the Civil War.

After the war, Ewing sided with the Democrats in opposing the Reconstruction policy of the Republicans. He was an adviser to President Andrew Johnson, who, in 1868, recommended Ewing's appointment as Secretary of War. This was near the end of Johnson's term of office, and Congress did not act on the recommendation.

Ewing died on October 26, 1871, in Lancaster, Ohio.

BIBLIOGRAPHY

Chitwood, Oliver Perry. *John Tyler, Champion of the Old South*. New York: D. Appleton Century Company, 1939.

Cleanes, Freeman. *Old Tippecanoe*. New York: Charles Scribner's Sons, 1939.

Sause, George G. *Money, Banking and Economic Activity*. Boston: D. C. Heath, 1966, chap. 8.

Seager, Robert, II. *And Tyler Too*. New York: McGraw-Hill Book Company, 1963.

Whitney, David C. *The American Presidents*. New York: Doubleday & Company, 1967.

Wise, Henry A. *Seven Decades of the Union*. Philadelphia: J. B. Lippincott & Co., 1871.

GEORGE G. SAUSE

F

CHARLES S. FAIRCHILD (April 30, 1842–November 24, 1924). Charles Stebbins Fairchild had been ably serving as Assistant Secretary of the Treasury since his appointment. In 1886, when Daniel Manning, the then–Treasury Secretary, became ill, President Cleveland asked Manning to take a leave of absence and temporarily promoted Fairchild to the position of Secretary of the Treasury. Manning's resignation became official in February 1887, and Fairchild's appointment as Treasury Secretary was made permanent on April 1, 1887. He served in this capacity until the end of President Cleveland's first term, leaving office on March 6, 1889.

Charles Stebbins Fairchild was born on April 30, 1842, to Sidney and Helen Fairchild in Cazenovia, New York. Both his parents were descendants of English families who had resided in New England since about 1660.

In 1863 he graduated from Harvard College and two years later received his law degree from the Harvard Law School. Upon becoming an attorney, he joined his father in private practice in Albany, New York. This was the main business center of the New York Central Railroad. He married Helen Lincklaen in 1871. It was one of her family members who had founded Cazenovia in 1793.

Charles, like his father who was an "aggressive Democrat," also became active in politics. His first speech "was a eulogy upon that great Democrat, William L. Marcy" (Johnson and Malone, 252). He got his education and training in politics from Democratic stalwarts such as Samuel Tilden and Horatio Seymour. He also considered Manning among his close friends while growing up in that era.

Tilden, who was elected the Governor of New York in 1875, had become aware of the good work that Fairchild, as Deputy Attorney General, had performed in obtaining the convictions of the New York Police Commissioners. Under Tilden's guidance, Fairchild also directed the prosecution's case in the Canal Ring frauds, and in 1875, Governor Tilden supported Fairchild's nomination for the Attorney General at the Democratic Party's convention in Syracuse. He was elected in November of the same year.

Two years later Tilden was no longer the Governor, and Tammany Hall was now in control of the party. So when Fairchild tried to get renominated, he failed and returned to private practice in 1877. He remained so until President Cleveland selected him for Assistant Secretary of the Treasury in 1885.

Cleveland's strength as a political candidate lay in his unquestioned honesty and integrity. In his political career as Mayor of Buffalo and Governor of New York, he undertook an effective attack on corruption and kept defying the political bosses. This brought Cleveland great statewide support. It was, therefore, no surprise that a critical element of his campaign for the presidency was to root out corruption and establish honesty and efficiency in the administration of federal government.

His choice of people for the Cabinet was widely acclaimed, and in the selection of Manning and Fairchild as Secretary and Assistant Secretary of the Treasury, respectively, the President would find two very useful allies in his desire to have the government bureaucracy run more professionally.

Not only his Cabinet but many of the Assistant Secretaries and bureau heads were also caught up in this reform fever. Notable among the Assistant Secretaries was the service performed by Fairchild in cleaning up the government. Manning was quite aware of Fairchild's work as Attorney General of New York, and so three weeks after assuming office, Fairchild was appointed by Manning to head a commission with the assigned task of overhauling the entire Treasury Department and suggesting ways of running it more like a business. From this effort came several measures, such as an agreement that at least 500 of the 2,300 clerical workers could be laid off; basic changes in some of the methods used for Treasury bookkeeping; and changes in the monthly balance sheets. Drastic cuts were also made in the expense of running the U.S. Custom Houses. These had become a way of keeping party hacks on the government payroll. While nothing in the nature of a major fraud was exposed, Manning and Fairchild managed to bring about some efficiency in operations. Under Cleveland, this success was also repeated in other departments.

Compared to the task of cleaning up the Treasury, which Fairchild managed quite competently, trouble of a much greater magnitude was looming for him in 1887, when he was just barely ready to take over the position of Secretary of the Treasury on a permanent basis. Fairchild had essentially assumed all the duties of the office of Secretary of the Treasury since the early months of 1886 due to the illness that befell Manning.

The great troubling issue had to do with a huge national surplus. Over a period of time the government's revenues were increasing far in excess of its expenditures. Large sums of currency were being withdrawn from general circulation. To avoid a direct contraction, the Treasury had increased its purchases of outstanding bonds. In fiscal year 1886, it bought bonds worth $50 million, and next year the bond repurchase was increased to $125 million. This, however, seemed but a temporary measure.

The Treasury report for fiscal year 1886 indicated that the government surplus would be about $94 million. Even if the growing government accumulation of gold were to be used to purchase bonds that could be called at par, it would retire that class of federal debt within a year. The alternative seemed to be to let the Treasury keep removing enormous sums from general circulation in a manner certain to interfere with normal business activity and, at the same time, entice Congress to engage in extravagant spending.

The Treasury report formally offered two ways of dealing with this surplus revenue. Since tariff on imports accounted for a major share of the revenue, Congress should attack the tariff and find a way of lowering it. Failing to do this, it could use the surplus to retire the whole volume of greenbacks, which amounted to about $346 million. The Treasury plan would not involve a currency contraction, for it would pay out a new gold or silver dollar in exchange for every greenback dollar canceled. Using the surplus at the rate of $100 million a year, the Treasury could retire all the greenbacks in three and a half years.

However, these proposals and other alternatives of dealing with the Treasury surplus were summarily rejected by the Congress, and the enormity of the impending crisis loomed clearly.

All over the country the discussion was focusing more and more on the need to lower the tariff. Cleveland had until now taken a cautious approach to the tariff issue. But by the summer of 1886, he was convinced that he had overlooked the importance of the tariff question. Fairchild provided two reasons that helped Cleveland decide that something must be done about the tariffs. First, Fairchild urged that measures such as the lowering of the luxury tax or the internal tax on whiskey and tobacco, and a refunding measure, would not sufficiently reduce the Treasury surplus. Second, Fairchild had impressed upon the President that all the 3 percent bonds had been canceled, and the sinking-fund requirements of the current fiscal year (1886–1887) had already been met. This meant that by December 1887 the Treasury surplus would be about $55 million, which by the end of the fiscal year would reach $140 million.

Faced with these irrefutable facts, Cleveland resolved to attack tariffs and concluded that a decisive blow must be struck to reduce it. President Cleveland articulated his view on it by stating that "when more of the people's sustenance is exacted through the form of taxation than is necessary . . . such exaction becomes ruthless extortion." The tariff, according to him, was a tax "as certainly as if it was paid at fixed periods into the hands of the tax-gatherers" (Barnes, 440).

To get things started, the President called a meeting of key congressional leaders at Oak View. There Cleveland along with Fairchild met with these leaders, including Speaker John Carlisle; Representative William Scott, Representative Samuel J. Randall's rival in Pennsylvania; and Texas Democrat Roger Mills. Randall, who was well known as a powerful protectionist, was deliberately excluded from these meetings because Cleveland wanted to send a strong signal of his intentions of attacking the tariff by introducing a bill in Congress during its next session.

In his annual message to Congress on December 6, 1887, which was devoted entirely to the issue of tariff reform, the President linked the Treasury surplus to the exorbitantly high taxes on necessities such as sugar, coffee, and clothing. The tariff, he argued, was a scheme that offered selected domestic manufacturers protection and favor from the government, enabling them to regulate supply and prices. The scheme, thus, ended up victimizing the poor.

John Carlisle and Texas Democrat Roger Mills began work on the bill to be submitted to Congress, and Fairchild was to advise them on the financial impact of such a proposal. In April 1887, the administration introduced its bill in Congress. It was moderate in nature, calling for an average reduction in duties of 7 percent. It called for a major downward revision in duties on raw materials. Raw wool was placed on the free list, and tariffs on finished wool products were also lowered substantially. In a decided tilt for the South, the bill called for moderate reductions of duties on cotton goods, sugar, and iron ore, while calling for significant cutbacks of duties on finished iron and steel, glass, and wood products, thus striking at the northern interest.

The Republican members in Congress engaged in considerable lambasting of the Mills bill. Their efforts, however, were not persuasive enough and failed to generate the necessary support among Randall Democrats to kill the measure. The bill, thus, passed in the House on July 21, with the voting almost strictly along party lines.

The tariff issue would not die down with the passage of this bill. In fact, it became the dominant theme of Cleveland's bid for a second term as President. While it occupied center stage, another pressing problem that Fairchild and the Treasury had to deal with was the silver problem. The precise nature of the silver problem was the continued fall in the value of the silver dollar.

Since the passage of the act of February 28, 1878, government had by law been purchasing silver bullion and coining it as silver dollars. By November 30, 1888, according to the Treasury report, the government had already coined more than 312 million silver dollars, about 61 million were in circulation, and approximately 237 million were in certificates. The problem all along was that while the act of 1878 forced the government to ensure that the value of the silver dollar be maintained at par with gold as a monetary unit, almost by common agreement the other leading commercial nations had excluded silver from coinage as full legal tender.

This put a tremendous pressure on the value of silver bullion, which in fact kept falling during the entire period the act had been in force. In 1878, the price of fine silver, in London, was $1.20 per ounce. By 1888, this value had declined to $0.96 per ounce. The recommendation by Fairchild, as Treasury Secretary, was to suspend the further coinage of silver dollars. President Cleveland concurred with this recommendation.

The silver camp in the Democratic Party was strong and not willing to give up the coinage and use of the silver dollar as legal currency. Fairchild would not get the opportunity to bring a satisfactory end to this problem because Cleveland lost the 1888 presidential election. When Cleveland regained the presidency four years later, Fairchild was his first choice for the Treasury position, but Fairchild refused. Therefore, Cleveland selected John G. Carlisle for the position.

After leaving the Treasury in 1889, Fairchild returned to New York City to become a banker and a philanthropist. In 1892 he once again emerged from private life to enter into political life. It was Fairchild, with his urbane personality and mastery in political preparation, who provided the quiet impetus to the movement for Cleveland's nomination as the Democratic Party candidate in 1892.

Fairchild and others of the conservative wing in the party were successful in getting Cleveland reelected as President. Trouble was nonetheless brewing in the Democratic Party. Cleveland agreed with the conservative leaders such as Fairchild and Carlisle, among others, about the importance of maintaining a strong gold standard. He had so far managed to keep the party true to the gold standard. This he was able to do only by exerting great pressure upon a hostile majority of silver supporters in the Democratic Party.

In 1892 the eastern leaders of the party—Carlisle and Fairchild, among others—who thought that the silver question was settled with the repeal of the silver purchase law, saw their support for the gold standard come under increased attack from the silver supporters. This and other misfortunes during Cleveland's second administration considerably weakened the conservative element of the Democratic Party. It was, therefore, natural for Fairchild to oppose the candidacy of William Bryan as the nominee for the Democratic ticket in 1896.

He was permanent Chairman of the Syracuse convention that chose a gold Democratic delegation to go to Indianapolis, and he was also a member of the monetary commission. He continued to remain somewhat active in party politics in his old age. At the age of eighty-two, on November 24, 1924, Fairchild died at "Lorenzo," the old family home at Cazenovia.

BIBLIOGRAPHY

Barnes, J. A. *Wealth of the American People: A History of Their Economic Life*. New York: Prentice-Hall, Inc., 1949.

Friedman, M., and Anna Schwartz. *A Monetary History of the United States 1867–1960*. Princeton: Princeton University Press, 1963.

Hacker, L. M. *Major Documents in American Economic History*. Princeton: D. Van Nostrand Company, Inc., 1961.

Johnson, A., and Dumas Malone, eds. *Dictionary of American Biography*. New York: Charles Scribner's Sons, 1931.

Kroos, H. E., ed. *Documentary History of Banking and Currency in the United States*. New York: Chelsea House Publishers, 1977.

McGrane, R. C. *The Economic Development of the American Nation*. Boston: Ginn and Company, 1942.

Nevins, A. *Grover Cleveland: A Study in Courage*. New York: Dodd, Mead & Company, 1933.

Richardson, J. D., ed. *A Compilation of the Messages and Papers of the Presidents*. Washington, D.C.: Bureau of National Literature, 1911.

Schlesinger, A. M., ed. *History of American Presidential Elections*. New York: Chelsea House Publishers, 1971.

Shannon, F. A. *Economic History of the People of the United States*. New York: Macmillan Company, 1934.

Tugwell, R. *Grover Cleveland*. New York: Macmillan Company, 1968.

Vexler, R. I., ed. *Grover Cleveland: Chronology—Documents—Bibliographical Aids*. New York: Oceana Publishers, 1968.

NAYYER HUSSAIN

WILLIAM P. FESSENDEN (October 16, 1806–September 8, 1869). William Pitt Fessenden—lawyer, orator, Maine politician, Representative, Senator, and Secretary of the Treasury—was born on October 16, 1806, in Boscawen, New Hampshire. He was the son of Samuel Fessenden and Ruth Greene, who never married. His father took Fessenden to Fryeburg, Maine, when he was only a few days old; he never saw his natural mother again. He was raised by his paternal grandmother until age seven. In 1813, his father married Deborah Chandler and moved Fessenden to New Gloucester, Maine, where he ultimately became the oldest son in a family of nine boys and one girl. Fessenden attended North Yarmouth Academy, but his father's tutoring provided much of his early education. Just prior to his thirteenth birthday, he was admitted to Bowdoin College. Because he was so young, he formally entered in the winter of 1821 as a sophomore, having completed his freshman studies while boarding nearby. Fessenden was considered a good student; however, his "disrespectful" behavior got him in considerable trouble with the administration. In 1823, when he should have received his diploma, his name was not listed with the graduates. He had been sent home for violating various school rules and for being considered a bad influence on other students. His degree was conferred the following year in absentia.

Fessenden's father, Samuel, became quite powerful in Maine politics. He was elected the major general of the Maine militia and moved to Portland in 1822. So, after leaving Bowdoin, Fessenden rejoined his family in Portland and began to study law. An age of twenty-one was required for admission to the Maine bar; in 1822, Fessenden was only sixteen. For two years he apprenticed with Charles Davies; following that, he spent a scant four months working with his Uncle Thomas in New York City. He was admitted to the Maine bar just short of his twenty-first birthday.

Along with the practice of law, Fessenden began his career of public speaking and oration. In a July 4, 1827, speech, he declared himself committed to a set of objectives that he maintained throughout his life: sound banking, public schools, antislavery causes, and protective tariffs. In that same year he moved to Bridgeton and opened a law office. In 1829, he became engaged to Elizabeth Longfellow, Henry Wadsworth Longfellow's sister. They never married, as she died six months after the engagement. Fessenden returned to Portland and opened his own law office, but business was poor and he was forced to rejoin his father's firm, Fessenden and Deblois, in October 1830. The following year he became engaged to Ellen Maria Deering, the daughter of a wealthy Portland merchant. They married on April 23, 1832.

In 1831, the capital of Maine moved to Augusta. Fessenden, a member of the National Republican Party (precursor to the Whig Party), became the legislative representative from the Portland district. The Main legislature was composed largely of Jacksonian Democrats at that time. Fessenden was not reelected to his legislative seat in 1832, so he returned to his father's law office. His first son had been born, and he needed to think of his family responsibilities. Fessenden and his father began to develop divergent political views, with Samuel becoming the leader of the abolitionist movement in Maine, while William held to the more moderate stance of the Missouri Compromise of 1820: no extension of slavery to any new territories in the Louisiana Purchase north of thirty-six degrees, thirty minutes latitude.

Fessenden left Portland again in 1833. This time he attempted to establish a law practice in Bangor, Maine. The area was expanding due to land and timber speculation, but the number of other lawyers also attracted to the region made for stiff competition. He returned to Portland eighteen months later. He established a partnership with William Willis, which continued for the next twenty years. The success of the partnership seems to have been due to the two partners' complementary skills: Fessenden's courtroom expertise and Willis's research skills. Within a few years, theirs was one of the most prominent firms in Portland.

Between 1837 and 1839, Fessenden worked on his law practice and politics. His family was growing, and he was the father of three sons. In 1837, Fessenden took time away from his other endeavors to make his only trip "west," visiting Ohio, Kentucky, and Illinois. He accompanied Daniel Webster, his godfather, whose eye was on the Whig presidential nomination in 1840. Upon his return, he managed Edward Kent's successful 1837 campaign for the Maine governorship. The economic times were tough, and the Whigs managed to capture not only the governorship but also the lower house of the state legislature.

In January 1840, Fessenden returned to the state legislature after an eight-year absence. He became chair of a committee to revise Maine's statutes. At the end of the year he was nominated by the Whigs to go to Congress. He took to the stump to make his case to the voters of Maine. The Whigs won the governorship, the state legislature, and half of the congressional seats. Fessenden became the first Whig Congressman ever elected from Portland. He was thirty-four years old.

In 1841, Fessenden took his seat in the 27th Congress. The Whig Party was made up of men whose major bond was their opposition to Jacksonian democracy rather than their support of any single program. Therefore, on issues like slavery, the party had no consensus. Fessenden was appointed to the House Committee on Naval Affairs, chaired by Virginian Henry Wise. Through this association, Fessenden developed a stereotypical view of Southerners as selfish, inconsistent, and unreasonable people. He appears to have maintained this perspective throughout the remainder of his life.

Fessenden endorsed Clay's program with its major components: a new national banking system and more tariff protection. He spoke for the Loan Bill to raise money for defense because the United States and Great Britain were still sparring over the Northeast boundary question. He surprised his Maine constituents by voting against an amendment to the Fortification Bill that would have provided money for repairs to the Portland Harbor, saying the monies were not requested and, therefore, must not be needed. He voted against the Sub-Treasury Act, a hard currency measure that would remove specie from circulation, because he felt it would stifle the economic recovery. He argued in favor of the Bankruptcy Bill because he felt that unsound monetary policy had created the economic hard times, and therefore, the government was obliged to help people. Tyler vetoed the Whig's bank legislation, thereby thwarting their chance to make major changes in the banking system. During his two-year term, Fessenden lost considerable respect for Congress. Time and again he observed Southerners using the "gag" rule to block anything connected with issues of slavery.

He returned to Portland in early 1843, and between then and 1854, his law firm and family prospered. His family grew to four sons and one daughter, who died of scarlet fever as a child. In 1843, Fessenden was appointed to the Board of Trustees of Bowdoin College, a position he maintained until his death. All four of his sons attended the college.

The issue in Maine in 1852 was temperance; Fessenden ran as a temperance Whig and reclaimed his seat in the Augusta legislature. The Governor's job went to a moderate Whig, William Crosby. Fessenden had become one of the most powerful Whigs in the state. His name was mentioned as a possible replacement for the retiring Democratic Senator, but there were not enough votes in the lower house to elect a minority member. The legislature could not decide between Fessenden and Democrat John Dana, so the session ended with only one Maine Senator. The issue was resolved in January 1854 with the selection of Fessenden, whose views on both slavery extension and temperance matched the majority of Maine's citizens. Some believe, however, that he was selected as part of a deal worked out with Morrill Democrats in which Fessenden would support Anson Morrill for Governor and, in return, Morrill would support Fessenden for Senator. (The Governor's election had ended with none of the three candidates getting a majority, as was required by Maine law, so the legislature had to select the new Governor.) No matter how his selection was achieved, Fessenden ended up in Washington just in time for the Kansas-Nebraska Bill debate.

Fessenden believed that the Missouri Compromise of 1820, prohibiting slavery in that part of the Louisiana Purchase territory north of thirty-six degrees, thirty minutes latitude, had settled the question of slavery in the territories. Douglas was sponsoring a bill repealing the Missouri Compromise and establishing the Kansas-Nebraska territory as slave or free in accordance with desires of the settlers themselves, that is, "popular sovereignty." Fessenden argued eloquently against the bill; however, it passed the Senate with a large majority. Upon returning to Maine, Fessenden discovered that the Senate's passage of the bill enraged many people. Whigs, Free-Soilers, and Democrats were all angry, including Fessenden's father and Anson Morrill. The Kansas-Nebraska Bill passed the House in May 1854, and President Franklin Pierce signed it into law.

Fessenden returned to Washington for the opening of the 34th Congress in December 1855. In 1856 he returned to Washington in December in time to hear outgoing President Pierce chide the Republicans and the Northern members of Congress for encouraging sectionalistic bickering, for urging violation of the Fugitive Slave Act, and for encouraging violence in Kansas. Fessenden responded on the floor of the Senate to the President's accusations. He expressed his belief that all new territories should be free and that the Kansas-Nebraska Bill only aided slaveholders and certainly not even all Southerners were slaveowners.

When Fessenden returned to the Senate in December 1857, he was appointed to the Senate Finance Committee. That, along with the regular Senate business, kept him extremely busy. His wife had died in the summer, and he was doubtless grateful to have his thoughts occupied.

In the summer of 1858 Fessenden worked tirelessly for the election of Republicans to the state legislature. His senatorial term was about to expire, and he sought to be reappointed. Republicans won handily in Maine, and in January 1859, Fessenden received word that he had indeed been unanimously reelected. His health constantly a factor, Fessenden looked forward to the 1860 presidential election. The Democrats, unable to select a candidate satisfactory to Northern and Southern factions, ran both John Breckinridge and Stephen Douglas. The Republicans had a number of possible candidates, among whom the name of Fessenden was mentioned. Fessenden had made it clear that he had no interest in the presidency. The convention selected Abraham Lincoln, a moderate, whose election in November thrilled Fessenden.

Lincoln's election triggered the secession of the Deep South states. When the 36th Congress assembled in the winter of 1860–1861, many compromise measures were suggested to keep the Union together.

The fall of Fort Sumter to Confederate forces occurred when Congress was not in session, so Lincoln took charge of making war preparations without their consent. He called up state militias, blockaded Southern ports, and suspended the writ of habeas corpus in some areas. While some in Congress objected, Fessenden was not among them. Fessenden was appointed Chair of the Senate Finance Committee, which gave him responsibility for raising funds for the war effort. All appropriations measures came to the Finance Committee. Fessenden proposed a bill removing duties from arms and war materials, and he proposed an increase in the Morrill Tariff to increase revenues. Tariffs became one of the only ways the country had of receiving specie during the war years. Fessenden also approved of an income tax that initially was set at 3 percent for incomes in excess of $800; the rate was raised in 1862 and in 1865 before being rescinded in 1872. While Fessenden preferred to tax citizens to pay for the war, the majority in Congress preferred to borrow and let future generations share the cost. Secretary Chase asked to borrow $250 million by issuing various types of bonds and Treasury notes. Fessenden shepherded the request through the Congress.

The financial outlook was, however, bleak. The Treasury was forced to suspend specie payments as of January 1, 1862. The dire financial conditions sent Secretary Chase back to Congress with a request for the issuance of more bonds and notes, with $500 million of them paying 6 percent interest and redeemable in not less than five years or more than twenty years. The act also called for the creation of $150 million worth of legal tender, irredeemable in specie but legal for all transactions and government debts. Fessenden was opposed to the idea of "greenbacks," particularly if they were allowed to pay custom duties, the source of most of the government's specie. Fessenden urged that interest payments and duties be paid in specie, and the bill was so amended.

In February 1863, Secretary Chase was once again in need of funds to run the government. This time the Senate approved issuing $900 million in long-term government bonds paying 6 percent and $500 million in short-term Treasury notes. Chase requested that an additional $300 million of legal tender be issued, but the Finance Committee only allowed half the request, raising the total number of greenbacks issued to $450 million. Fessenden's committee also considered the formation of a national banking association, originally requested by Secretary Chase in 1861. The banking system in the country in 1860 consisted of nearly 1,600 separate banks, each with its own notes. The lack of a national banking system with a common currency made financing the war an even more difficult task. The National Currency Act, establishing a Bureau of Currency overseen by a Comptroller, passed in February 1863. Fessenden had grave concerns about destroying the state banking system and only supported the bill and the subsequent National Banking Act because both Secretary Chase and President Lincoln said they were essential.

In June 1864, Fessenden was looking forward to returning home to Maine; however, Salmon Chase's resignation and Lincoln's appointment of Fessenden to take his place as Secretary of the Treasury curtailed those plans. Fessenden attempted to decline the appointment, saying that his health really did not permit. He urged Lincoln to appoint Hugh McCulloch, the Comptroller of the Currency. Lincoln insisted that Fessenden take the position; his colleagues in the Senate unanimously approved his appointment; Chase encouraged him; and Fessenden reluctantly accepted, taking office on July 5, 1864.

The first problem confronting Fessenden was how to raise the necessary $800 million for the coming year and how to pay $100 million of current bills. Not much revenue was expected, and Fessenden was on record as opposed to legal tender notes. Fessenden traveled to New York and attempted to borrow $50 million for the most pressing current needs, but the bankers turned him down. So, once again, the decision was made to issue bonds: three-year "seven-thirties" paying 7.3 percent interest, payable in paper. He enlisted Jay Cooke's help for planning strategy for selling the bonds. Cooke, a Philadelphia financier used by Secretary Chase, suggested using either the national banking system or Jay Cooke and Company to handle the distribution. Fearing that he would suffer the same criticism as had befallen Chase for paying fees to Jay Cooke, Fessenden decided to use the national banking system for the sale. Initially, sales went well, but it soon became clear that they were lagging and that another source of funds would have to be found. Fessenden considered sending Chase to Europe in search of foreign loans, but public opposition curtailed that option. Instead, Fessenden issued $40 million worth of long-term gold bearing "five-twenties" government securities; these, too, sold poorly. Too much uncertainty was in the air, and people were absorbed with the upcoming election.

Four months into Fessenden's management, things were very grim at the Treasury. The debt had climbed to over $2 billion, an increase of $300 million. And the Secretary had unpaid requisitions of $130 million. Fortunately, a number of events transpired that turned the financial picture around: Lincoln was reelected in early November, settling the political uncertainty; Jay Cook agreed to buy $3 million worth of the "five-twenties" bonds and to take an option on $7 million more; and the Union appeared to be triumphing over the Confederacy. Fessenden had received the boost he needed to sell the remainder of the long-term bonds. The "seven-thirty" sales, however, lagged. So after giving the national banks a final chance, he turned the distribution over to Jay Cooke in January 1865. He agreed to pay Cooke a fee of three fourths of 1 percent on the first $50 million, five eighths of 1 percent on the second $50 million, and the rest at a fixed rate. Congress also approved issuing $100 million more of the "seven-thirty" notes. Within a few weeks, Cooke had sold nearly a third as many notes as Fessenden had sold through the national banks in five months. On March 3, 1865, Fessenden got Congress to approve an additional $600 million of "seven-thirty" notes. On the same day, he resigned as Secretary of the Treasury to resume his duties in the Senate, having been reelected to his seat by the Maine legislature. In the eight months he served, Fessenden met the financial crises of the war, oversaw Confederate properties seized in the war, and coordinated purchases of cotton coming from the South. In addition, he improved the operations and personnel of the Treasury Department whose size had grown enormously through the Chase years.

Following his resignation, Fessenden returned to Maine to rest. He had not even taken time from his secretarial duties to campaign for the Senate seat he wished to reclaim. By the time the 39th Congress reconvened in December 1866, the political landscape had undergone significant changes: Southern states had refused to ratify the Fourteenth Amendment, and the fall elections had produced a group of new members of Congress more radical in their approach to Reconstruction. Fessenden and other moderates thus saw their roles in decision making reduced. On March 2, 1867, both houses passed the Reconstruction Bill, requiring black suffrage as a condition of Reconstruction, and then overrode the President's veto to make it the law. Fessenden, believing ratification of the Fourteenth Amendment to be the appropriate readmission test, voted reluctantly with the majority. When the congressional session adjourned in March, Fessenden resigned from the Senate Finance Committee.

In the spring and summer of 1867, Johnson's disagreements with Congress over Reconstruction encouraged the House Judiciary Committee to investigate the possibility of the President's impeachment. On May 11, 1868, Fessenden made public his opposition to the trial and to Johnson's impeachment. He had not approved of the Tenure of Office Act and felt Johnson not to be guilty of impeachable crimes. On May 16, 1868, he voted against most of his Republican colleagues and for Johnson's acquittal. Those in favor of Johnson's impeachment fell one vote short of the two thirds necessary.

Fessenden was attacked on many fronts for his vote against impeachment. In Maine, his choices for legislative seats were beaten. However, Fessenden did support the Republicans' presidential candidate, Ulysses S. Grant, and campaigned for him in Maine. By the time he returned to Washington in December 1868, some of the animosity of his colleagues had subsided. One of the last issues he championed on the floor of the Senate was a bill to instruct the government to repay its "five-twenty" loans in coin rather than paper.

In April 1869, Fessenden left Washington to return to Maine for the last time. A movement was growing to oust him from the Senate in 1871; however, Fessenden did not live to suffer that indignity. He died on the night of September 8, 1869.

BIBLIOGRAPHY

Belz, Herman. *Reconstructing the Union Theory and Policy during the Civil War*. Ithaca, NY: Cornell University Press, 1969.

Faulkner, Harold U. *American Economic History*. 7th ed. New York: Harper and Brothers Publishers, 1954.

Fessenden, Francis. *Life and Public Services of William Pitt Fessenden*. Boston and New York: Houghton, Mifflin and Company, 1907.

Hepburn, A. Barton. *A History of Currency in the United States*. New York: Macmillian Company, 1924.

Jellison, Charles A. *Fessenden of Maine Civil War Senator*. Syracuse, NY: Syracuse University Press, 1962.

Myers, Margaret G. *A Financial History of the United States*. New York: Columbia University Press, 1970.

Studenski, Paul, and Hermann Krooss. *Financial History of the United States*. 2nd ed. New York: McGraw-Hill, 1963.

NANCY M. THORNBORROW

CHARLES J. FOLGER (April 16, 1818–September 4, 1884). The accession of Chester Arthur to the presidency due to the death of President James Garfield led to a number of Garfield's Cabinet appointees resigning from their positions. So after Arthur was sworn in as the President on September 22, 1881, he set about the task of selecting candidates for these Cabinet vacancies. For the position of Secretary of the Treasury, President Arthur nominated Edwin Morgan of New York to replace William Windom of Minnesota. However, Morgan declined the position due to ill health, and it was offered to Charles James Folger, who accepted it and was immediately confirmed by the Senate on November 14, 1881.

Charles James Folger was born on April 16, 1818, on the island of Nantucket. His family later moved to settle in Geneva, New York. He traced his family origin to John Folger, who came from England in 1635. His ancestors were for generations New England whalers.

Folger did not follow in the whalers' footsteps and chose instead the legal profession to earn his livelihood. He attended Hobart College and graduated with the highest honors in 1836. Folger then took up the study of law and three years later was admitted to the bar in Albany. In 1840 he returned to Geneva, where he maintained a home for the rest of his life. At the age of twenty-six, he married Susan Rebecca Worth on June 17, 1844.

His first appointment to public office was in 1844 as a judge of the court of common pleas in Ontario County. While originally a Democrat, he switched over to the Republican Party in 1854. Folger was elected to the state Senate in 1861 and served until 1869. For four of these years he was President pro tempore, and for the entire period he served as the Chairman of the Judiciary Committee. In this capacity he became known as a "keen critic of unsound legislation" and for taking a conservative course in legal issues (Johnson and Malone, 486).

Folger resigned from the Senate in 1869 to accept President Grant's offer of appointment as United States Assistant Treasurer in New York City. He served in this capacity for a year and in 1870 was elected as an associate judge of the state court of appeals. In 1880, on the death of Chief Justice Church (New York Supreme Court), Folger was designated by Governor Cornell to complete the unexpired term of that office.

At this time President Garfield offered Folger the position of Attorney General, which he declined. He accepted, however, the Treasury portfolio offered by President Arthur. Folger's term in the Treasury Department was marked with the distinction of the department achieving the largest to date reduction in public debt. He worked toward maintaining a high standard of personnel, and during his administration, the offices in the Treasury Department were put in the classified service under Civil Service Rules.

Before we move on to discussing Folger's work as Treasury Secretary, his running for the office of the Governor of New York merits mention as an important element of his political career. In the spring of 1882, the nomination of Folger as the Republican candidate for the Governor of New York had been under discussion. Initially, Secretary Folger showed little interest in the nomination, and one of his associates—James Butler of the Treasury—reported that "Secretary Folger does not seek or desire the nomination for Governor" (Howe, 199). However, by August of that year, Folger had decided to seek the nomination, this despite little or no support from President Arthur.

Charles Folger beat Governor Cornell to win the Republican nomination, but his candidacy was tinged with controversy, and he always seemed on the defensive. This opportunity was not lost on his opponent Grover Cleveland, and the elections ended with a resounding victory for Cleveland by a margin of over 200,000 votes. President Arthur, for his lack of support of Folger's candidacy, received a great deal of blame for the Republican's defeat. And in fact this may have been one of the important reasons for Arthur's subsequent inability to become the Republican Party nominee for the presidential elections of 1884.

Let us now return to the discussion of Folger's work as Treasury Secretary. A historical study of U.S. governments, both in past years and today, shows that few have had the opportunity to "complain of an embarrassing excess of funds. Yet this was the rather happy perplexity which faced" (Howe, 227) the administration of President Arthur. A surplus of a few million dollars would have created little or no problem, but in 1881, according to the Treasury Department estimates, the revenues for the year would exceed expenditures by $130 million. In fact, during the fiscal years 1882–1884, the surplus would remain well over $100 million. The fiscal year ending June 30, 1885, saw the first drop of the Treasury surplus to below the $100 million mark. Thus, this surplus that averaged over $100 million a year during his entire term caused President Arthur great concern.

The Treasury surpluses quite naturally became the focus of activity for Secretary Charles Folger and later his successor Hugh McCulloch. The problem of returning the money to circulation was a major one, but no matter how it was solved, by depositing it in the various national banks or by the Treasury using it to buy government bonds in times of money stringency and selling them to reduce an excess of currency in circulation, it would not rid the government of the surplus.

The solution to reducing or eliminating this surplus would be to spend it by lavish appropriations, distribute it among the states, as was done in 1836, use it to pay off the public debt, or lower taxes. During his tenure as head of the Treasury, Folger recommended that the surplus be used to pay off the debt and lower the taxes. President Arthur proclaimed full support for both these recommendations in his annual messages.

Let us get into this in more detail. In 1881, knowing that the Treasury surplus would exceed $100 million, Secretary Folger developed a set of recommendations so that the President could then decide as to what would be the best way to tackle this problem of growing government surpluses.

One of the things that Folger felt should be done was to make provisions enabling the early retirement of silver certificates. He also argued that the act that required the government to issue these certificates should be repealed. Under the act, the government was required to maintain "silver at or near the gold standard" (Richardson, 4633). So far, a total of 66 million of these silver certificates were outstanding, which Folger felt were unnecessarily adding to the paper currency.

The Secretary was also in favor of repealing the provision of the act of February 28, 1878, that required the government to coin a fixed amount of silver dollars each month. So far, to comply with the act, the Treasury Department had already coined 102 million silver dollars, while only about 34 million of these coins were in circulation. Folger wanted to replace the above provision with one that would give the Treasury the flexibility to decide how many silver dollars needed to be coined in order to meet the demand. Furthermore, he advised the President against resumption of issuing gold certificates and felt that the national banks could retire currency only if they had given sufficient advance notice regarding their intentions to do so.

As stated earlier, the Secretary wanted to use part of the surplus to retire public debt. To achieve this objective the Treasury took the position that unless outstanding bonds issued earlier at 5 and 6 percent could be funded at a much lower rate, no legislation should be forthcoming to refinance them and the government should continue to use the surplus to retire these bonds.

The Treasury Secretary's report shows that in the fiscal year ending June 30, 1882, the government applied about $166 million toward redemption of various bonds. The following year the Secretary's report shows that about $134 million were applied to redeeming old bonds. This means that between the years of 1881 and 1883 President Arthur's administration was able to retire somewhat more than $400 million of public debt. No previous administration had been able to retire such a large amount of public debt.

It bears mentioning here that in the congressional elections of 1882, the Republican Party was soundly trounced, and the House reverted to Democratic control. Thus, President Arthur would not find any support for his plans to spend on building the Navy, but at the same time, it meant strong support for his suggestions of putting restraints on expenditures.

In addition, Secretary Folger, by emphasizing the grave contrast between conditions in 1836 and in 1883, was able to stifle any attempts to have this surplus distributed among the states. The major difference between the two periods was that as of 1883 the total public debt outstanding was $1.25 billion, which carried an annual interest charge of more than $50 million (Howe, 228).

These two reasons greatly helped in preventing any extravagant expenditures from the government surplus. This state of affairs turned President Arthur's and Secretary Folger's attention to reducing the tax burden of the people. It was felt that if the revenue laws remained unchanged, then the surplus would continue to grow; and even if the "annual receipts and expenditures should continue as at present the entire debt could be paid in ten years" (Richardson, 4635).

This meant that the only meaningful way to reduce and perhaps eliminate the surplus would be to bring about reforms on the revenue side. To effect lowering of the taxes, Folger recommended that all internal revenue taxes should be abolished except those on tobacco, distilled spirits and fermented liquors, and taxes on the manufacturers and dealers of these articles. President Arthur urged Congress for this tax relief in 1881 and again the following year. This proposal for lowering taxes had broad support among the public.

The President also wanted to revise the tariff laws in order to bring about a reduction in tariffs. However, he wanted to move with caution in this regard. Secretary Folger recommended appointing a commission to deliberate carefully on the question of tariff reduction. To this effect the President appointed a nine-man Tariff Commission on May 15, 1882. The commission completed its deliberations and submitted its report to the President on December 4, 1882. Its final report recommended substantial tariff reductions. President Arthur endorsed the findings of this commission. The following year, in January, both the Senate and the House began debate on the tariff reform. This resulted in the so-called "Mongrel Tariff" of 1883, which the President signed on March 3, 1883. He signed it with serious misgivings, having desired much greater reductions in duties than the 5 percent that the bill proposed.

The Treasury estimated that this lowering of duties as proposed under the bill would reduce government revenue by about $50 to $60 million. In actuality, however, the increased revenues from liquor taxes brought about much less of a reduction on revenues. Therefore, paying off the public debt seemed to be the only meaningful way of disposing of the surplus revenues.

This limited success achieved by Secretary Folger and President Arthur in bringing about meaningful tariff reductions would leave the subsequent administration of Cleveland grappling with the same problem.

About three weeks after President Arthur signed the Mongrel Tariff bill, his Cabinet suffered its first casualty. Postmaster General Timothy Howe died on March 25, 1883. He was, however, not the only Cabinet casualty. Around the same time, the pressures of the office had finally begun to take its toll on Folger's physical well-being. His health deteriorated to such an extent that he was obliged to abandon his desk at the Treasury and return home to Geneva for complete rest.

This illness would end the chapter on Folger's long and distinguished career in public service. Folger was a gentle and modest man. His correspondence "discloses the saving grace of a rich sense of humor" (Johnson and Malone, 487). While Folger did suffer a resounding defeat in his bid to become the Governor of New York, nonetheless his tenure as Treasury Secretary would be remembered for successfully managing to reduce the public debt by over $400 million. This was the largest such debt reduction effected by any administration until that time.

By the middle of 1884, the chances of Folger recovering from his illness appeared to be very slim. The newspapers were now carrying daily reports on his health, and rumors began circulating that he would be forced to resign and Richard Crowley would be appointed in his place. President Arthur put a stop to these rumors, and Folger retained his Treasury position. Folger, however, never recovered from his illness, and on September 4, 1884, a few months after his sixty-sixth birthday, he died at his home in Geneva, New York.

BIBLIOGRAPHY

Barnes, J. A. *Wealth of the American People: A History of Their Economic Life*. New York: Prentice-Hall, Inc., 1949.

Doenecke, J. D. *The Presidencies of James A. Garfield & Chester A. Arthur*. Lawrence: Regents Press of Kansas, 1981.

Furer, H. B. *James A. Garfield 1831–1881 and Chester A. Arthur 1830–1886: Chronology— Documents—Bibliographical Aids*. New York: Oceana Publishing Company, 1970.

Howe, G. F. *Chester A. Arthur: A Quarter Century of Machine Politics*. New York: Frederick Ungar Publishing Company, 1957.

Johnson, A., and Dumas Malone, eds. *Dictionary of American Biography*. New York: Charles Scribner's Sons, 1931.

Kroos, H. E., ed. *Documentary History of Banking and Currency in the United States*. New York: Chelsea House, 1977.

Nevins, A. *Grover Cleveland: A Study in Courage*. New York: Dodd, Mead & Company, 1933.

Richardson, J. D., ed. *A Compilation of the Messages and Papers of the Presidents*. Washington, D.C.: Bureau of National Literature, 1911.

NAYYER HUSSAIN

WALTER FORWARD (January 24, 1786–November 24, 1852). Walter Forward was born on January 24, 1786, in Old Granby (now East Granby), Hartford County, Connecticut. The son of Samuel and Susannah (Holcombe) Forward, he attended public schools. When he was fourteen, the family moved to Aurora, Ohio, where he worked on his father's farm. After three years of farming, at only seventeen years of age, he left home without a penny in his pockets and somehow worked his way to Pittsburgh, a bustling metropolis with a population of 5,000. There by pure chance he obtained a job together with the opportunity to study law in the office of Henry Baldwin, one of the best-known attorneys in Pennsylvania and subsequently Associate Justice of the United States Supreme Court. Forward quickly learned both law and politics from his mentor in this ideal environment and was admitted to the bar in 1806. From 1806 to 1822, he gained fame as a prominent Pittsburgh attorney. Along the way, he became the editor of Baldwin's Democratic newspaper, *Tree of Liberty*, but later in life grew disillusioned with this political position and as a result helped form the Whig Party in 1834.

Forward married Henrietta Barclay of Greensburg, Pennsylvania, on January 31, 1808. The couple had no children. He was a Methodist and a staunch supporter of temperance, active in intellectual debate, and founded the Pittsburgh Philosophical and Philological Society. Forward was also a lifelong champion of "internal improvements," or what today would be called investment in the social infrastructure.

He was the U.S. Representative from 1822 to 1825 and the Pennsylvania state constitutional convention delegate in 1837–1838. Among his accomplishments, he advocated suitable funding for the education of the poor at public expense. As a member of the 17th Congress, he was the logical choice to fill the vacant seat of Henry Baldwin; he was elected to the 18th Congress and served from October 8, 1822, to March 3, 1825. Both in his service on the committee on manufactures and on the floor of the House, Forward argued for the enactment of a high protective tariff, a policy that he vigorously upheld during the remainder of his political life. Later he was an unsuccessful candidate for reelection to Congress in 1824.

In 1824 he was a member of the congressional caucus—the last of its kind ever held—which nominated William H. Crawford for the presidency; but as a protest against his method of nominating Presidents, he threw his support behind Andrew Jackson in the campaign. Four years later he was definitely allied with the National Republicans.

Forward declined the presidential nomination in 1824. He became a delegate to the general convention of National Republicans at Baltimore in 1830. He declined an appointment of district attorney for the western district of New York. Later, as a reward for his service in the 1840 campaign, President Harrison appointed him district attorney for the western district of Pennsylvania. Upon declining this position, he was named by Harrison the first Comptroller of the Currency, from April 6, 1841, to September 13, 1841. He remained in office long enough to report twice annually concerning the administration of the Treasury Department. Forward replaced Ewing, who resigned when Tyler began to manifest a disinclination to remain in harmony with the party that had elected him.

President Tyler appointed Forward Secretary of the Treasury in the reorganized Cabinet on September 13, 1841. Although embarrassed in many ways by the defection of the Whig leaders from Tyler and by his own repeated disagreement with the policies of the President, he continued in office until March 1, 1843.

Forward served as Secretary of the Treasury under the nation's first one-term President, John Tyler. Tyler's administration was chaotic; he lost the confidence of the people and had no prayer for reelection. Twice Tyler vetoed bills to establish a Third Bank of the United States, prompting the resignation of his entire Cabinet except for the Secretary of State, Daniel Webster. The grounds for the vetoes were that the bills did not specify that state approval for branch banks would be required for the banks to be established. The Whig leadership was enraged; they believed he had betrayed them by reneging on a promise to sign the legislation into law if it were approved by Congress. Apparently, he also lost the backing of his party when he carried out a program that favored a Southern state's rights party dedicated to the annexation of Texas. Tyler did sign Texas into the Union just prior to the expiration of his term of office. He was a strict constitutionalist and backed the concept of secession.

Forward made the most of his one-and-a-half year tenure as Secretary. Just a few months after taking office, Forward submitted his first *Annual Treasury Report on the Finances* to Congress on December 20, 1841; it projected the 1842 budget deficit at $14,218,570.68. He recommended that Congress extend the term of a loan already authorized and roll over the Treasury notes previously issued. He proposed a specific new revenue source to avert the 1842 deficit crisis. One source that appealed to him was "imposts upon such foreign articles imported as may be selected, with due regard to a rigid restriction, in amount, to the actual wants of the government, and a proper economy in its administration." Forward also thought it prudent that the Treasury maintain a surplus cash reserve of about $2 million to meet extraordinary emergencies faced by the public sector.

Forward had taken office during a period of great financial upheaval as well as turmoil within the administration. The serious decrease in federal government revenue was triggered by the Panic of 1837, and the subsequent federal deficit provided a favorable opportunity for the mercantilists and protectionists. Now it could be argued not only that the tariff dues were set too low to afford adequate protection to American businesses but that they were also inadequate to produce enough revenue to support a Treasury so embarrassed that it was compelled to borrow continually by selling Treasury notes in the capital market.

Treasury Secretary Ewing's short tenure had been able to accomplish no improvement in fiscal matters. Forward thus inherited in Treasury finances a deficit of more than $500,000. A recent $3.5 million loan was a partial failure owing to the legal restriction on the Treasury of not being able to market the Treasury notes at rates below par, as well as the attempt to negotiate a loan in Europe. The state debts competing with the federal government provided a serious stumbling block to borrowing abroad on behalf of the United States. For example, potential British bondholders were unable or unwilling to distinguish between federal and state-level governments and their securities. Recourse was to issue short-term Treasury notes to supply the immediate revenue shortfall of the government. Forward found that the outstanding Treasury notes on December 18, 1841, amounted to about $7.4 million.

Whatever difference of opinion existed with regard to the necessity of additional protection to manufacturers, some expedient, it was universally conceded, was necessary to increase the public revenue. As no one favored direct taxation, a revision of the tariff was the only popular mode of enriching the Treasury. Whether he was moved by popular sentiment or not, Forward concluded that the only legitimate mode of raising revenues, and preserving the nation's credit rating, was in a revision of the tariff; and in order to obtain a full understanding of the subject, he ordered the first series of "comparative tariffs" to be prepared in the fall of 1841. The compiler of this special study was selected for the task, and he set to work.

The resulting report detailed a comparative, synoptical tariff of fourteen nations—the first attempt of the kind completed either in America or Europe. Forward's report on the tariff in 1842 proved to be an able and persuasive document and was largely responsible for the new tariff act passed by Congress on August 30, 1842. Forward's annual report at the close of 1841 discussed tariffs, not only with reference to increasing the duties because the government needed a larger revenue but also with reference to various important changes in the mode of collecting customs duties. If the law of 1832 should be extended: "It is fully acknowledged," he said, "that all the duties should be laid with primary reference to revenue; and it is admitted, without hesitation or reserve, that no more money should be raised, under any pretense whatever, than such an amount as is necessary for an economical administration of the government." But within those limits, and incidental to the raising of such revenue, he believed there might be "such a discrimination in imposing duties, that, while no part of the country should suffer a loss or inconvenience, a most beneficial degree of protection could be extended to the labor and industry of large masses of the people."

The Tariff Act of 1842 was highly protective; duties were increased, but not uniformly, back to the level of the tariff of 1832. According to historian Davis Dewey, the average rate on dutiable articles was 23.1 percent in 1842, 35.7 percent in 1843, 35.1 percent in 1844, and 32.5 percent in 1845. Specific duties were levied whenever practicable, and special consideration was given to iron. On some individual commodities, the rates were extremely high. Based on the then-prevailing prices, the ad valorem incidence of the import taxes was cotton bagging, 53 percent; railroad iron, $25 per ton, or 77 percent; pig iron, 72 percent; rolled iron, 51 percent; nails, 43 percent; window glass, 62 to 165 percent; refined sugar, 100 percent; salt, eight cents per bushel, or 61 percent; and so forth. The 1842 tariff ultimately framed from the facts of Forward's report was regarded at the time as immensely successful in producing a vast surplus of revenue. More than $10 million of surplus revenue resulted from Forward's sagacity; this amounted to more than one third of the amount of the national indebtedness by 1844.

Forward believed that in peacetime, structural deficits were to be avoided at all costs. His first *Annual Report to Congress* declared: "The creation of debt, by loans and other resorts, for revenue to supply deficiencies of regular income, cannot but be regarded, in a time of peace, as injudicious and objectionable. The general credit of the government, always good, has been greatly raised, both at home and abroad, by the fact that it has full paid off and discharged the debt created by the Revolution, and by a subsequent war with England and wars with the Indian tribes." A high credit rating was needed to enable immediate and large borrowing, should an unforeseen war suddenly break out.

Dissatisfied with his performance for some unknown reason, Tyler encouraged his resignation. Forward complied and resigned his Treasury post in order to return to the practice of law. At the time, it was reported that "ill health and some undercurrent of official intrigue induced him to resign." He was succeeded by John C. Spencer of New York on March 8, 1843.

After several successful years in private practice, Forward was named by Taylor chargé d'affaires to Denmark on November 8, 1849, and he served in Copenhagen for two years until late 1851. He resigned in order to accept the position of "President Judge" of the Allegheny County District Court, to which he had been promoted by popular election.

Forward fell ill while on the bench and died three days later, of bilious cholic, at age sixty-six in Pittsburgh, Pennsylvania, on November 24, 1852. He was buried in Allegheny Cemetery.

BIBLIOGRAPHY

Chidsey, Donald Barr. *And Tyler Too*. New York: Thomas, Nelson, 1978.

Dewey, Davis R. *Financial History of the United States*. 12th ed. New York: Longmans Green & Company, 1934; New York: Augustus M. Kelley Publishers, 1968.

Elliot, Jonathan. "Mr. Forward: Annual Treasury Report on the Finances, 1841, 1842" [Extracts] and "Expenses of the Loan of 1841 and 1842." In *The Funding System* of the United States and of Great Britain. Washington, D.C.: Blair and Rives, 1845; New York: Augustus M. Kelley Publishers, 1968.

Ewing, Robert M. "Hon. Walter Forward." *Western Pennsylvania Historical Magazine*, April 1925.

Johnson, Allen, and Dumas Malone, eds. *Dictionary of American Biography*. Vol. 6. New York: Charles Scribner's Sons, 1931.

Morgan, Robert J. *A Whig Embattled: The Presidency under John Tyler*. Lincoln: University of Nebraska Press, 1954.

Morris, Dan, and Inez Morris. *Who Was Who in American Politics*. New York: Hawthorn Books, 1974.

The National Cyclopaedia of American Biography. Vol. 6. New York: James T. White & Co., 1892 and 1929.

"Obituary: The Late Walter Forward." *New York Times*, December 4, 1852, 2.

Seager, Robert, II. *And Tyler Too: A Biography of John and Julia Gardiner Tyler*. New York: McGraw-Hill, 1963.

Sobel, Robert, ed. *Biographical Directory of the United States Executive Branch, 1774–1977*. Westport, CT: Greenwood Press, 1977.

C. DANIEL VENCILL

CHARLES FOSTER (April 12, 1828–January 9, 1904). Following the sudden death of Secretary William Windom, President Harrison once again found himself faced with the selection of a Secretary of the Treasury. The man he chose was Charles Foster, a businessman and former Ohio Governor.

Charles Foster's family tree was rooted in England, but in 1632, the first of his ancestors arrived on American soil at Oldham, Massachusetts. Almost 200 years later, in 1826, Laura Crocker of New York was followed to Ohio by Charles W. Foster, and they were married the same year. Their son Charles was born in Seneca County, Ohio, on April 12, 1828. In 1832 Charles's father built a double log house that housed not only the family but also the family dry-goods store.

Charles began public school at the age of four and at the age of twelve entered an academy at Norwalk. Two years later he left the school because of illness in the family to help his father with the store. By the age of eighteen he had become his father's partner in the store, and by age nineteen he was in complete charge of the running of the store. Six years later in 1853, Foster married Ann M. Olmsted, the daughter of a judge, and the couple had two daughters.

The Foster store was the center of commerce and credit in the Black Swamp region of Ohio, and the impact the store had was acknowledged in 1854 when the towns of Rome and Risdon united and formed the new town of Fostoria.

Although he was considered to be primarily a merchant, Foster's business interests included banking as well as gas and oil. During the Civil War, Foster was an active recruiter for and financial supporter of the Union. Although he expected to be commissioned colonel in the 101st Ohio regiment of the Union Army, Foster agreed to remain at home in the store at the insistence of his parents, as he was their only surviving child. Foster did serve the war effort by allowing families of soldiers to buy from his store on credit and became well known for his generosity.

Foster had become a prominent resident in his district for his financial and business success and for his contribution to the war effort. Friends urged the conservative Republican to run for Congress in 1870, arguing that the party had no other candidate who could carry the heavily Democratic district. Foster not only was victorious in the 1870 election but also successfully ran in the 1872, 1874, and 1876 elections, from March 4, 1871, to March 3, 1879.

Foster was first appointed to serve on the Committee on Claims, where he gained considerable respect among the members for his diligence and hard work. Foster served on the Ways and Means Committee and was appointed to the Subcommittee on Internal Revenue Affairs. He was acclaimed for his fight to expose the frauds that existed in the Treasury Department. One such conflict dealt with what became known as the Sanborn Contracts. Under these contracts, J. D. Sanborn, who was considered to be the right-hand man of the infamous Massachusetts Congressman Ben Butler, was given the right to collect unpaid taxes and to receive a 50 percent commission on what he collected. Publicly debating such a corrupt character increased Foster's popularity with the people as well as caused the repeal of the law.

Foster was concerned with the radical fringe of the Republican Party and worked to restrain the influence the group had on Southern Reconstruction after the war. Serving as a Chairman of a subcommittee investigating the 1874 contested election in Louisiana, he publicly denounced the Radical wing in the state.

Two years later, he was once again involved in Southern politics. Foster was a strong supporter of Rutherford B. Hayes, who was a friend and from the same congressional district. It became Foster's task to assure Southern voters that if Hayes were elected President, he would withdraw federal troops from the South. Only a week before inauguration was to take place, an article in the *Ohio State Journal* suggested that the "bayonet rule" should be enforced in the South. Wrongly attributing the article to Hayes, Southern supporters became nervous. Foster informed Hayes that "the Southern people who had agreed to stand by us were seized with a fright, if not a panic" (Barnard, 382). Foster attempted to calm fears and prevent a filibuster (designed to postpone the electoral vote count) by speaking to Congress on Hayes's behalf. "The flag will float over States, not provinces; over free men, and not subjects," Foster promised (Barnard, 382). Further assurance was necessary, however, to convince some that Foster was indeed speaking on Hayes's behalf. Foster signed a statement assuring South Carolina and Louisiana that Hayes would allow them to conduct their state affairs as they wished. Although this was not enough to prevent the filibuster from taking place, once the votes were counted, Hayes would win the election by one electoral vote.

This was not the first time that Foster had assisted Hayes in an election. In the 1875 Ohio Governor's election, Hayes, with heavy party support, was reluctantly opposing Judge Alphonso Taft. Judge Taft had been involved in a controversial lawsuit five years earlier. The Board of Education in Cincinnati had bowed to pressure by the Catholic Church to ban the use of the King James version of the Bible in Cincinnati public schools. A lawsuit resulted in a loss for the Catholics; however, Taft issued a statement agreeing with the Catholics and supporting the school's right to ban the Bible.

This issue was brought to light in the gubernatorial election. Taft wrote a letter to Foster hoping to quiet the issue, but the letter backfired when Foster read it to the convention. It was later suspicioned that Foster, who had asked for the letter from Taft, had had such a result in mind, thus assuring that the party nomination would go to Hayes. Whatever the plan, Hayes became the next Governor of Ohio.

Foster failed to be reelected to Congress in 1878 because of redistricting of the state that was prompted by the democratically controlled Ohio legislature. Although he was given the opportunity to run in the Toledo district, he chose to run in his newly formed and heavily Democratic district, knowing that he would probably face defeat. His public life did not end with the defeat as the Republican Party nominated Foster over Judge Taft in 1879 for Governor of Ohio. He ran as a sound-money candidate opposing Thomas Ewing, the Greenback candidate. Foster was a supporter of allowing paper currency to be redeemed for gold, as he had demonstrated during his congressional days.

This was a campaign of "firsts" as Foster introduced the idea of forecasting election results using preelection polls. In districts where election polls were not promising, he would send in campaign workers to improve his standing. For the first time in an Ohio campaign, large sums of money were used in an attempt to win the election, which Foster did by more than 17,000 votes. He again ran for Governor in 1881 and won the election by an even wider margin.

It was during this campaign that his failure to serve his country in the military was used against him in his political career. Democratic papers referred to him as "a man who knew no higher occupation during the war than measuring calico" (Johnson, 544). He was nicknamed "Calico Charlie" by the opposition, but supporters cleverly converted the title originally intended to discredit him into one of credit for his valuable contributions during the war. In an effort to promote their candidate, Foster supporters wore clothing of calico, decorated towns with it, and even printed newspapers on it.

Foster was a businessman first, and this was evident in his political affairs as well. Foster established bipartisan boards to effectively manage public institutions, strongly promoted mine inspections, proposed forest protection, and revised the tax system. He served as a delegate-at-large at the Republican National Convention in 1880 with instructions that his support would go to John Sherman. It was believed that Foster planned and successfully orchestrated the swinging of the vote from the Garfield-nominated John Sherman to Garfield himself, thus putting Garfield, a longtime friend of Foster's, on the road to the Republican nomination for President. Foster's hope was for a chance at the vice presidency if Bland were nominated or Garfield's vacated Senate seat if Garfield was given the nomination. Sherman's feelings of betrayal were not healed until Foster withdrew from the senatorial contest. Although Foster was considered for a Cabinet position under Garfield, he remained in the Governor's office for the remainder of his term.

During his time as Governor of Ohio, Foster was probably most criticized for his handling of the controversial liquor issue, which most politicians chose to avoid, because of its volatility. He not only supported a high tax on liquor but also sponsored the Pond Law, which taxed saloons as well. During the 1883 election, he supported the voters' right to choose between prohibition or a license system. These measures along with the entire Republican ticket were defeated, causing considerable damage to Foster's role as a Republican Party leader. He did manage to stay in the inner circle of the party and retain a portion of his party influence because of his political savvy. His ability to accurately analyze voting records and predict election results won him the title of "Old Figgers, Jr." (Downes, 114).

Foster regained his former status as a leader in the Republican Party in 1889 when President Benjamin Harrison appointed him to chair a commission that successfully negotiated a treaty with the Sioux Indians, something that the government had been attempting for years.

Even with such success, Foster was again defeated for Congress in 1890, but on February 21, 1891, Harrison named him to the Cabinet position of Secretary of the Treasury. He assumed office February 25, 1891.

Foster was always the sound-money supporter. He promoted international bimetallism but rejected the idea of federal free coinage of silver because of the possible inflationary pressure put on the economy. While in Congress, he voted to override President Hayes's veto of the Bland-Allison Act, which limited the coinage of silver and favored larger allocations of silver only on an international level. He supported the Sherman Silver Purchase of 1890 and believed that the parity of gold and silver should be maintained.

In the last month of his term as Secretary of the Treasury, Foster averted a crisis for the Cleveland administration. From November 1892 to February 1893, gold reserves were being drained from the Treasury partly because government expenditures were $5 million more than revenue. This shortage of currency caused the Treasury to redeem any greenbacks or Treasury notes for gold. This along with increased exporting of gold caused the $100 million minimum reserve held by the Treasury to be put in jeopardy. The administration was considering the sale of bonds to purchase gold to replenish the loss. The plates with which to print the bonds had already been ordered by Foster with the hope that they would not be needed. To avert the crisis of a possible financial crash in his term of office, Foster sought an alternative solution. He petitioned several New York bankers to exchange $8 million of their gold for legal tender to temporarily avoid the issuing of bonds by the Republicans. The plan worked, and on March 4, the problem was forced onto Cleveland's new administration.

Foster saved the outgoing Republican administration further embarrassment by including a $54 million trust fund as part of the Treasury's assets. The bank note redemption fund had always been treated as a separate fund and not included as assets. By including the fund, the Treasury was able to declare a nominal surplus for 1892–1893 instead of the actual $48 million deficit that would have been reported. Although he was harshly criticized for this action, the practice was continued by future Secretaries.

Foster also successfully converted over half of the $50 million in bonds that were to mature on September 1, 1891, that were paying 4.5 percent interest to 2 percent bonds, which was the lowest rate ever negotiated by a financial officer.

Foster retired from public service on March 6, 1893, following the start of Cleveland's administration and returned home to Fostoria. He had continued his business pursuits while in office, investing in railroads, oil, and mining, but lost much of his fortune in the 1893 crash. He served for fifteen years as the Board of Trustees President for the Toledo State Hospital for the Insane, which was regarded as one of the most progressive and finest-run hospitals in the world. Foster was instrumental in initiating such changes as eliminating the use of restraints on patients and building hospitals using the cottage plan.

Charles Foster died in Springfield, Ohio, on January 9, 1904, and was buried in Fountain Cemetery, Fostoria. "He was a man of medium height, compact figure, genial face, and affable manners. Growing up in the 'woods' with the 'people,' he was always 'Charlie' to everybody, even when governor" (Johnson and Malone, 545).

BIBLIOGRAPHY

Barnard, Harry. Rutherford B. Hayes and His America. New York: Russell & Russell (reissued), 1967.

Barnes, James A. John G. Carlisle, Financial Statesman. New York: Dodd, Mead & Company, 1931.

Clancy, Herbert J. The Presidential Election of 1880. Chicago: Loyola University Press, 1958.

Downes, Randolph C. The Governors of Ohio. Columbus: Ohio Historical Society, 1954.

Johnson, Allen, and Dumas Malone, eds. Dictionary of American Biography. Vol. 3. New York: Charles Scribner's Sons, 1936.

Johnson, Rossiter, ed. The Twentieth Century Biographical Dictionary of Notable Americans. Vol. 4. Boston: The Biographical Society, 1904.

The National Cyclopaedia of American Biography. Vol. 1. New York: James T. White & Company, 1898.

PENNY KUGLER

HENRY H. FOWLER (September 5, 1908–). After Douglas Dillon announced publicly that he planned to resign as Secretary of the Treasury, the rumor mill churned up names of many possible successors. David Rockefeller, President of Chase Manhattan, and Budget Director Kermit Gordon were objects of most frequent speculation. President Lyndon Johnson, however, offered the job to his friend Donald C. Cook, head of American Electric Power Company. Cook declined the bid reportedly because he did not wish to lose valuable retirement rights with his company. "Informed sources," only hours before President Johnson sent the nomination of Henry H. Fowler to the Senate on March 18, 1965, assured the press that the job would go to David M. Kennedy, then Chairman of the Continental Illinois National Bank and Trust Company of Chicago.

It is surprising that Fowler was never once mentioned publicly as a likely choice to serve as Secretary of the Treasury. Although, as was pointed out at the time, he was not a banker, nor an economist, nor a businessman, he possessed a wealth of experience in Treasury administration and a genuine sophistication in Washington politics when he was sworn into office on April 1, 1965. Perhaps the press had overlooked him because, just one year earlier, he had resigned as Undersecretary of the Treasury after three years of distinguished service. Of course, those years of experience gave him unique and, at that time, unprecedented qualifications for his new post.

Henry H. Fowler, usually known as Joe Fowler, was born in Roanoke, Virginia, on September 5, 1908. He was the son of Mack Johnson and Bertha Browning Fowler. After receiving a diploma from Roanoke's Jefferson High School in 1925, he went to nearby Salem to study at Roanoke College, from which he was graduated with a B.A. degree in 1929. A good alumnus of his college, he has served as a member of its Board of Trustees, which he chaired from 1974 to 1981; a grateful alma mater has named him Distinguished Alumnus and awarded him an Honorary LL.D. in 1962.

In 1929 Fowler left Virginia for Connecticut to study at Yale University Law School—LL.B., 1932, and J.S.D., 1933—but he returned to his old southern neighborhood when he completed his education. Taking up private practice of the law, he joined a Washington, D.C., law firm, Covington, Burling and Rublee, in 1933. Another member of the firm was Dean Acheson, who was later to become Secretary of State.

Joe Fowler's "government service" began in 1934 when he joined the legal staff of the Tennessee Valley Authority (TVA). For the next four years, he assisted in the preparation and conduct of the litigation that finally established the constitutionality of the Authority. From this beginning until he became Secretary of the Treasury, he was to spend about equal parts of his career in government and in private law practice.

On October 19, 1938, he married the former Trudye Pamela Hathcote of Knoxville, Tennessee. The Fowlers had three children: two daughters, Mary Anne and Susan Maria, and a son, Henry Hamill (now deceased).

By 1939, Joe Fowler had progressed to Assistant General Counsel of the TVA. In the same year, he was appointed as Chief Counsel for a subcommittee of the U.S. Senate's Committee on Education and Labor (Special Assistant to the Attorney General). In 1941 he was chosen to be Special Counsel to the Federal Trade Commission.

As the United States entered World War II, Fowler's public service shifted toward mobilization problems in a series of important posts associated with the war effort. In 1941 he became Assistant General Counsel of the Office of Production Management. From 1942 to 1944 he was a member of the War Production Board. He served as Economic Adviser to the U.S. Mission for Economic Affairs in London in 1944 and in 1945 became Special Assistant to the Administrator of the Foreign Economic Administration—serving in part in Germany.

After the war, Fowler returned to the private practice of law as a founding senior member of the law firm of Fowler, Leva, Hawes and Symington in Washington. However, at the outbreak of hostilities in Korea, he was called back to government service first as Deputy Administrator of the National Production Authority and then as its Administrator in 1952. From 1952 to 1953 he was Administrator of the Defense Production Administration. During these years, he also served as Director of the Office of Defense Mobilization and on President Harry Truman's National Security Council.

From early in 1953 until the winter of 1961, he worked with his law firm. Never completely out of the public's eye, he was active on two of the task forces of the Commission on Money and Credit concerned especially with policies on economic growth and inflation control. He served on Brookings Institution's National Committee on Government Finance and was a delegate to the Democratic National Convention in 1956 as well as being on the Democratic Advisory Council of the Democratic National Committee from 1958 to 1960.

Even though Henry Fowler was a member of the Commission on Money and Credit, he never signed its final report. He had resigned from the commission before the report came out since President John Kennedy had named him Undersecretary of the Treasury on February 3, 1961, to serve along with Douglas Dillon.

Those years at Treasury were productive ones for Fowler. He made many important contributions, in particular in promoting Kennedy's economic policies. Especially instrumental in improving the rapport of the Kennedy administration with businesspeople, he played important roles in bringing about the investment tax credit, accelerated depreciation allowances, and the interest equalization tax and in 1963 devoted himself to winning approval of the proposed $11 billion tax cut. He also headed a Presidential Task Force investigating solutions to the nation's balance of payments difficulties. For all these contributions Henry Fowler was awarded the Alexander Hamilton Award in 1964. It is the highest honor that the Treasury can bestow. On April 10, 1964, he left the Treasury to return to his substantial corporate law practice.

After serving on the National Independent Committee for President Johnson and Senator Humphrey, which functioned as a campaign group during the presidential election, and briefly helping to run President Johnson's inauguration, Fowler was settling back into his law firm when President Johnson called him to the White House without informing him what he had in mind. He was reportedly offered the Treasury position face-to-face on March 18—and accepted it (Freeburg, 28).

Few of Johnson's Cabinet nominations were met with such wide acclaim. The

Senate Finance Committee held a one-and-one-half-hour hearing with Fowler and then approved him in a sixteen to zero vote. Senator Al Gore of Tennessee abstained, voting "present." Gore declined to comment on his abstention. The full Senate unanimously confirmed Fowler on March 25, and he took the oath of office at the White House as Secretary of the Treasury on April 1, 1965.

Douglas Dillon described Fowler as "a strong man, courageous, highly principled, with a great knowledge of problems that he will face." He took comfort in "knowing that I am going to turn the responsibilities of the Treasury over to a man with the capacity, the understanding, and the wisdom of Henry Fowler" (Freeburg, 47).

At the time of his confirmation, Fowler said he saw his main task as Secretary to advise on the proper mix of monetary and fiscal policies to attain an interrelated complex of goals that included defense of the dollar, adequate economic growth, full employment, avoidance of inflation, and maintenance of fiscal responsibility (Freeburg, 47).

As Undersecretary, Fowler had played a role in achieving a major tax reduction. As Secretary, he had to do the opposite. High rates of inflation had resulted from what was called, at the time, a "guns *and* butter" policy, which the Johnson administration had been pursuing. As the war in Vietnam heated up just when the expansionary effects of the Kennedy tax cuts were hitting the economy, President Johnson at first resisted a tax increase, which would have reduced private consumption, and was reluctant to reduce nondefense government spending on Great Society programs; as a result, more than 100 percent of a full employment output was being demanded. Inflation was inevitable.

Secretary Fowler represented the administration as it changed its economic policy. First he sought a temporary suspension of the investment tax credit in October of 1966. In 1967 and 1968 he won approval for the temporary 10 percent tax surcharge. Henry Fowler was known for his political sensitivity and skill on conciliation. Again and again he demonstrated these skills.

These abilities also served him well in the international arena where he continued to deal with balance of payments deficits. He played a major role in creating the two-tier gold price in March of 1968 and in the establishment of Special Drawing Rights (SDRs) working as a Governor of the International Monetary Fund, in the Group of Ten, and with the heads of the major central banks.

Many reference books cite Fowler's most important contribution as Secretary as the reduction of the silver content in U.S. coins. He said that those that gave him the greatest satisfaction were, first, the handling of federal finances during a war without using economic controls, such as on wages, prices, and credit, but instead via fiscal and monetary policy; second, the demonstration that activist policy in economics must work both ways, that is, expansionary during stagnation and restrictive during more buoyant periods, exemplified by the passage of the Revenue and Expenditure Control Act in June 1968; and third, tackling the balance of payments problems, culminating in the New Action Program announced by President Johnson on January 1, 1968, and the reforms in the international monetary system, especially the establishment of SDRs to provide additional liquidity for expanding world trade ("Fowler Valedictory," 21).

On March 31, 1968, President Johnson announced to the nation that he would not seek reelection. On November 5, Richard Nixon was elected as the new President. On November 8, Henry Fowler sent a letter to the President submitting his resignation effective December 20. He had discussed with the President a year and a half earlier that he wished to return to private life but had been convinced to stay on because of unsolved policy problems. In his letter to Fowler, President Johnson said:

For three and one-half years you have sat at my side at the Cabinet table while we met the tests of our time. I really know that the great adventure we have shared is drawing to a close when I accept your letter of resignation. You leave behind you a legacy to all the American people that few men could claim. When the gold crisis threatened to destroy the world's monetary system, your firm leadership helped to avert disaster and assure the strength of the dollar. You were the grand architect of the most significant reforms in the international monetary system since Bretton Woods. You were the man at the bridge who steered through Congress the anti-inflation tax so essential to our prosperity. And that prosperity—without parallel in the history of nations—will forever bear your mark. Men who know your reputation, and children who have never heard your name, inherit that gift which you have labored so hard to fashion. I know, Joe, at what personal cost you have served the people of America—well beyond the period of your initial commitment. You are one of the American great, who will be long remembered as the Secretary who thought of financial values in the broader context of human values. (Office of the White House Press Secretary)

Still a vigorous sixty-year-old, after leaving the Treasury, Fowler joined Goldman, Sachs and Company as a general partner. He did not go back to the law because he believed he had been away from it too long and felt himself better suited to dealing with economic and financial issues, which had been the predominant features of his public life of the preceding eight years. In 1981 he became a limited partner at Goldman, Sachs but continued to chair Goldman, Sachs International Corporation until 1984.

He served on many corporate boards and remained active in public service. From 1973 until 1985 he was Chairman of the U.S. Treasury Department Advisory Committee on International Monetary Reform. A founder of the Bretton Woods Committee, he served as cochair until 1989. He has been a trustee of the Lyndon Johnson Foundation, a trustee of the Sloan Foundation, and Director of the Carnegie Endowment for Peace. Having chaired the Atlantic Council of the United States, he remains active in this organization and in the Citizen's Network on Foreign Affairs and as honorary Counsellor of the Conference Board.

The only sustained criticism of Henry Fowler's years as Secretary of the Treasury came from a handful of Democratic members of Congress and Senators who believed interest rates should have been lower and that Fowler was too prone to accept the views of William McChesney Martin, the Chairman of the Federal Reserve System.

Most everyone else agreed with Lyndon Johnson's appraisal (Treasury Historical Association): "Mr. Fowler [is] one of the ablest and most dedicated men I know. His years of experience . . . have demonstrated both his competence and his diligence. He is in a long line of distinguished patriotic men who have held this post as Secretary of the Treasury."

BIBLIOGRAPHY

"Fowler Valedictory." *Finance* 87, no. 1 (January 1969).

Freeburg, Russell. "Fowler: A Surprise Choice for the Post." *Finance* 83, no. 4 (April 1965).

Gammons, Ann, ed. *Who's Who in American Politics*. New York: Bowker, 1979.

Office of the White House Press Secretary. "Text of the Letter from the President to Secretary of the Treasury Henry H. Fowler." Press Release, November 8, 1968.

Sobel, Robert, ed. *Biographical Directory of the United States Executive Branch, 1774–1977.* Westport, CT: Greenwood Press, 1977.

Treasury Historical Association. *An Evening with the Secretaries: A Bicentennial Celebration.* May 17, 1990.

U.S. Congress. Senate. Committee on Finance. *Nominations*, 87th Cong., 1st sess., January 25, 1961. (Confirmation of Henry H. Fowler as Undersecretary)

U.S. Treasury. *Annual Report of the Secretary of the Treasury.* Washington, D.C.: Government Printing Office; various years.

EARL W. ADAMS

G

LYMAN J. GAGE (June 28, 1836–January 26, 1927). A period of relative calm in the financial arena, the years 1897–1902 were witness to one of the long-anticipated events in Treasury history: the reestablishment of a formal gold standard. Lyman J. Gage, who held the position of Secretary of the Treasury during those years, was chosen, in part, for his solid support of that system. The biographical profile that follows begins with a brief treatment of the Secretary's personal background, followed by a more detailed discussion of Gage's contribution to the history of the U.S. Treasury.

Scion of one of America's oldest families, Lyman Judson Gage was born in De Ruyter, New York, on June 28, 1836. A descendant of Thomas Gage, who landed at Cape Cod, Massachusetts, in 1640, Lyman was the son of Mary (Judson) and Eli A. Gage. He was to marry three times. In 1864 Gage was wed in a traditional Methodist ceremony to Sarah Etheridge. The marriage lasted ten years, ending only with Sarah's death in 1874. Gage was to marry twice more: in 1887 to his brother's widow, Mrs. Cornelia (Washburn) Gage, and in 1909 to Mrs. Francis Ada Ballou.

The employment history of the future Secretary of the Treasury began in 1850 when he took a position as a mail agent on the Rome and Watertown Railroad. Three years later Gage became a junior clerk at the Oneida Central Bank of Rome, New York. In 1855 Gage moved to Chicago, working for a time as a clerk in a local lumber yard. In 1858 he was hired as a bookkeeper by the Merchants' Savings, Loan and Trust Company. In 1868 he became cashier of the First National Bank of Chicago. Climbing the rungs of power within the bank, Gage reached the President's office in 1892. In that same year, he was offered the Secretary of the Treasury position by President Grover Cleveland. Anxious to remain in his new position at First National, Gage refused.

Instrumental in the 1882 reorganization of the First National Bank, it was during Gage's tenure at that institution that his stature in banking circles increased dramatically. First President of the Chicago Banker's Club, he was elected Vice President of the prestigious American Banker's Association in 1882. In the following year he became President of that organization, going on to serve three consecutive terms in that capacity.

It should not be imagined, however, that Gage's interests were confined by the boundaries of the banking industry. Active in Chicago's public affairs, Gage served as President of the Board of Directors of the World's Columbian Exposition during 1890–1891. He acted as Director and Treasurer of the Art Institute of Chicago and served two terms as President of the Civic Federation of Chicago.

In January 1897 Gage's commitment to public service ascended to new heights when he accepted an offer, extended by President-elect William McKinley, to head the Treasury Department. The position had initially been offered to Nelson Dingley, a Congressman from Maine. Sponsor of the 1897 Tariff Act, Dingley had, in fact, initially accepted the position but, at the insistence of his family and on the advice of his doctor, later removed himself from consideration. In an interesting historical pas de deux, the protectionist Dingley Tariff aided in the creation of a Treasury surplus after 1900, which Gage, in turn, was able to utilize in extending his authority at the Treasury.

Gage, given his experience as President of the First National Bank of Chicago and as an outspoken advocate of the gold standard, was tailor-made for a position in McKinley's Cabinet. Resigning from First National on February 15, 1897, Gage was appointed by McKinley on March 4 and summarily confirmed by the Senate on the following day, taking office on March 6. He replaced John G. Carlisle.

Three features of Gage's term as Secretary of the Treasury merit continuing interest: the nature of the relationship between the Treasury and the financial sector established during his term in office; his handling of the financing of the Spanish-American War; and the adoption of a formal gold standard.

As Secretary of the Treasury Gage continued in the tradition, established by his predecessors, of using the tools at his disposal to promote financial sector stability. In the absence of a domestic central bank, the necessary functions of the latter devolved to the Treasury Department. Previous Treasury Secretaries, including Charles Fairfield (1887–1889) and William Windom (1889–1891), had used a number of devices, including the prepayment of interest on Treasury instruments and manipulation of government deposit accounts (which by July 1901 had surpassed $93 million), to support financial institutions, albeit primarily depository national banks.

In the fall of 1901, wary of the effect of the McKinley assassination on the financial markets, Gage increased government deposits in depository national banks by $5 million, prepaid interest on government instruments due October 1, and purchased $7.7 million in Treasury bonds at a premium of $2.1 million. In prepaying interest payments on government debt, Gage and his fellow Secretaries provided the financial sector, particularly the national banks, with usable funds and, consequently, a degree of flexibility in an otherwise inflexible system. Since the banks were only required to pay bondholders upon the maturity of the bonds they held, the prepayment of interest on government instruments provided usable funds to recipient institutions during the window between the prepayment and the redemption dates.

Gage was keenly aware that the periodic difficulties faced by institutions in the U.S. financial sector were due, in large measure, to the structure of the National Banking System. The National Banking System, established in the course of the Civil War, was home to a number of endemic problems. Gage perceived this clearly when he noted in his 1901 *Annual Report:*

Admirable in many respects, experience shows that our banking system is devised for fair weather, not for storms. This can be clearly shown. The individual banks stand isolated and apart, separated units, with no tie of mutuality between them. There is no obligation of duty from the strong to the weak or exposed, nor any method of legal association for common protection or defense in periods of adversity and depression.

A strong and influential advocate for financial reform, Gage was unable to induce the administration to commit to significant structural change. That development would not materialize until the passage of the Aldrich Act in 1908 and the Federal Reserve Act in 1913.

The Treasury, Gage recognized, was limited, in comparison with a central bank, in its ability to respond to a financial crisis situation. Treasury intervention in the financial sector in any given year was dependent on the existence of a budget surplus. Only this condition provided the Treasury the means of responding to perceived problems in the financial sector. A surplus was, however, a double-edged sword. A Treasury surplus, it was believed, withdrew monies from circulation. As a consequence, bank deposits and reserves decreased, leading, in turn, to a contraction in the volume of lending and business activity. A surplus, then, took on the role of both demon and savior.

Among the successes of Gage's tenure as Secretary, the artful financing of the Spanish-American War ranks highly. Declaring war on Spain on April 25, 1898, Congress quickly provided for the Treasury to issue $400 million in long-term instruments to support expenditures during this short-lived conflict. Half of the issue was to be offered to the public at par, providing a 3 percent return, the remainder at whatever the market would bear.

Unsure of the public's response to this financing arrangement, Gage negotiated with a New York underwriting syndicate to take up the balance of any unsold bonds. This group, led by J. P. Morgan, included the National City Bank, Vermilye and Company, and the Central Trust Company. The prestige lent by this group to the war bond issue guaranteed the success of the venture. The entire issue of $400 million was sold to the public, without intervention by the syndicate. As Gage noted in his 1898 *Annual Report,* the syndicate arrangement he had negotiated "put spirit into the loan from the first moment." Patriotism and the desire of national banks to acquire Treasury bonds did the rest.

The success of Gage's scheme can be viewed against the difficulties faced in previous conflicts. In contrast with the War of 1812 and the Civil War, payments continued to be made on a specie basis throughout the admittedly shorter Spanish-American War. The Treasury was, as a result, able to refrain from the emergency measures adopted in previous conflicts, including the issue of additional new monies.

During Gage's tenure at the Treasury, an event for which he had long campaigned came to pass—the establishment of a formal gold standard. A consistent advocate of the gold standard, in the 1870s Gage had helped organize the Honest Money League of the Northwest, which took a strong stand against irredeemable paper money. He had defended, in addition, the gold standard during the turbulent election of 1896. His stance in this election, as it would for a number of other future Treasury Secretaries—for example, Leslie Shaw (1902–1907) and Franklin MacVeagh (1909–1913)—paved the road to public office.

As Secretary of the Treasury, Gage's power was enhanced by the adoption of a formal gold standard. The United States had been on a de facto gold standard since 1879. The passage of the Gold Standard Act of 1900 merely formalized the international monetary system. Under this legislation, passed March 14 of that fateful year, all forms of money were to be maintained at parity with gold. To ensure the preservation of this standard, a gold reserve of $150 million was to be maintained (succeeding the informal reserve of $100 million created by Secretary Shaw). Congress empowered the Secretary of the Treasury to issue bonds to replenish the gold reserve in the event that it fell below $100 million. The Treasury, already the issuer of its own notes and gold and silver certificates, became, in addition, holder of the nation's specie reserve against currency. These functions, entailing substantial costs, are normally delegated to a central bank. In the absence of the latter the Treasury was forced to assume these responsibilities.

The initial years of the system were trouble free, making this the "golden age" of the gold standard. The success of the system was assured, in large part, by contemporaneous technical improvements in gold mining coupled with substantial discoveries in Alaska, Colorado, and South Africa. Indeed, between 1900 and 1914 the world gold stock doubled.

Despite the successes achieved by Gage during his tenure as Treasury Secretary, a degree of personal animosity developed, as it would in other instances, between Theodore Roosevelt, McKinley's Vice President, and Gage. In the wake of McKinley's assassination in September 1901, the new President, worried over the potential reaction of the financial markets, chose to reappoint Gage on September 15, 1901. His days in office, however, were clearly numbered. Gage served as Secretary of the Treasury until January 31, 1902, when he was replaced by Governor Leslie M. Shaw of Iowa.

After leaving the Treasury, Gage served as President of the United States Trust Company from 1902 to 1906. In 1907, at the age of seventy-one, Gage retired, moving to Point Loma, California. He died, without an heir, in San Diego, on January 26, 1927.

BIBLIOGRAPHY
Annual Report of the Secretary of the Treasury. Washington, D.C.: U.S. Government Printing Office, various years.
Johnson, Rossiter. *The Twentieth Century Biographical Directory of Notable Americans*. Boston: The Biographical Society, 1904.
Lossing, Benson John. *Harper's Encyclopedia of U.S. History*. New York: Harper and Bros., 1905.
Sobel, Robert, ed. *Biographical Directory of the United States Executive Branch, 1774–1977*. Westport, CT: Greenwood Press, 1977.

PAUL J. KUBIK

ALBERT GALLATIN (January 29, 1761–August 13, 1849). Albert Gallatin was Secretary of the Treasury under Presidents Thomas Jefferson (May 14, 1801–March 3, 1809) and James Madison (March 4, 1809–February 8, 1814). He was born on January 29, 1761, to aristocratic parents Jean and Sophie Albertine Gallatin in Geneva, Switzerland. His admirers say his great mistake was being born abroad: That unfortunate fact probably excluded him from higher office, perhaps even the presidency.

Gallatin's parents were married in 1753, and his father died in 1765 when he was four. His sister Susanne died in 1777, but she had been institutionalized for years with a nervous disorder. His mother sent him to live with her dearest friend and distant relative of her husband, Jean, in order to attend to her watch dealer business. Sophie died a few years later in April 1770.

Gallatin studied the philosophical writings of Rousseau and, with other radical student friends, longed for adventure and a romantic return to the state of nature. On the eve of his nineteenth birthday, Gallatin surprised his legal guardian and friends by booking passage with a school chum, Henri Serre, to sail from Nantes, France, to America.

In the period 1780–1781, Gallatin roamed the Maine frontier with his friend Serre, trying his hand at trading with the Native American Indians and other adventures. Finally, he returned to Boston, and Harvard college voted on July 2, 1782, to grant him free use of the library, a room, and meals at the commons at a rate paid by tutors if he desired. He and Serre agreed to teach an extension course in French, and Gallatin took on a class of twenty students. This was satisfying, and as an avid reader of classics and history, he must have enjoyed the opportunity. But he was impatient for adventure and thus left Boston on July 11, 1783, and his travels landed him in Philadelphia. By 1784 he had acquired an interest in land and established headquarters of his holdings at Clare's farm on the Monongahela River in Pennsylvania.

In 1788 he was traveling in Maine and encountered William Bentley, a colleague at Harvard. Bentley had read newspaper reports that he had been scalped during the frontier Indian depredations in 1785. His guardian back in Geneva had heard similar reports and had made official inquires through diplomatic channels as to Gallatin's whereabouts. There were romantic adventures in his life at this time, and he fell in love with the landlady's attractive daughter. Her mother disapproved and perceived Gallatin as a never-do-well who was a hopeless dreamer. Gallatin was not to be denied, and they eloped to be married on May 16, 1789. The end was a sad story. He brought Sophia Allegre, his bride of a few months, from Richmond to "Friendship Hill," the property overlooking the Monongahela River. His happiness was brief; Sophia fell ill and died later that year.

It took him several years to recover from her loss. In fact, he entertained serious thoughts of packing up and returning to Geneva. But romance returned to his life, and on November 1, 1793, he married his second wife, Hannah, the daughter of well-connected Commodore James Nicholson of New York. She was affluent and highly educated and much different than Sophia. Her relatives and friends were socially influential, and many were in Congress or in federal government positions.

Gallatin vividly recounted this story to friends and family to the end of his life: In the summer of 1784 he was conducting business about his 300-acre farm near Georges Creek, Pennsylvania, and heard that General George Washington was traveling through western Virginia and Pennsylvania to locate lands deeded to him and was to stay the night on September 24 in the office of a land agent where he planned to seek advice from local settlers and hunters about the best route for a road across the Alleghenies. Gallatin's curiosity got the better of him. Along with sundry wide-eyed locals, he found himself in the agent's tiny one-room cabin. He negotiated to get close to the pine table where the action was. There Washington sat before spread-out maps and documents, carefully questioning the locals in turn and taking notes. Hours passed as Washington heard detailed testimony, and Gallatin grew more and more impatient at the apparent indecision of the general. Finally, unable to contain himself any longer, he blurted out what had evidently become obvious through his independent investigations: "Oh, it is plain enough, [Gallatin named a spot already mentioned by one of the settlers] *that* route is the most practicable!" This brash impetuousness by the young stranger astonished all present, including the general, who put down his pen and stared in cold silence at the offending eavesdropper—the most withering look, Gallatin recalled years later, that he had received in all his life. Then the general resumed his interrogations. Finally, after a few minutes, he again put down his pen and stared at Gallatin, concluding that he was right. When the locals departed, Gallatin remained, sleeping on the floor beside the agent and his nephew, while the great Revolutionary War hero slept in the only bed. According to family legend, in the morning Washington offered Gallatin a job as his business agent. Gallatin politely refused; he had other fish to fry and his own dream of developments along the western frontier.

Gallatin got his political start in western Pennsylvania. There he came in contact with Alexander J. Dallas, who was to succeed him much later as Secretary of the Treasury. Dallas had mobilized Pennsylvania troops to put down the Republican interior's rebellion against Hamilton's whiskey tax. He met and befriended Gallatin and rescued him from what would have certainly been an ill-fated association with the whiskey rebels. The idealistic and moral Gallatin had brought to the western frontier a Rousseauvian enthusiasm for the virtuous and democratic farmer of the American interior, together with an educational background that soon found him a representative for the farmer in the Pennsylvania legislature. He had arrived with a substantial patrimony (received January 1786), which he invested in thousands of western acres and a series of business enterprises such as a town promotion, a glass works, and a gun factory that employed nearly 100 men.

Very soon Gallatin became known as an ally of Dallas, and both men worked to defeat the Federalists and align Republicanism with booming enterprise. Yet his early accomplishments were pure Hamiltonian exercises. He persuaded lawmakers to retire Pennsylvania's paper currency and pay the state's creditors higher interest than they received under Hamilton's federal assumption of state debts. Next, he led the passage of an act to charter a Republican-controlled Bank of Pennsylvania, which established a relationship with the state government analogous to Hamilton's national bank ties with the federal government. Finally, Gallatin took Hamilton's developmental vision to the extreme and helped author Pennsylvania's policy of chartering and subsidizing corporations to build canals, roads, and turnpikes.

Gallatin's foray into national politics got off to a rocky start. He was elected by the Federalist legislature of Pennsylvania to the U.S. Senate on February 28, 1793. But his eligibility was challenged. He had not been a citizen for the required nine years or more. He was denied his seat by a final vote of fourteen to twelve on February 28, 1794. Undaunted, Gallatin was elected to the U.S. House of Representatives in the autumn of 1794. This was the 4th Congress, and he served for three terms. It is conceded that these six years encompassed one of the stormiest periods in our political history. Gallatin showed an unrivaled grasp of constitutional and international law, great power of argument, and a calmness of temper unruffled by the personal attacks of the New England Federalists, who sneered at his foreign birth.

The Federalists opposed the appointment of Gallatin to the Treasury post because of his role in the Whiskey Rebellion. They regarded him as a prominent leader of the opposition to the excise tax law and therefore responsible for the ensuing troubles. His appointment was further opposed because of his success in forcing the creation of the Ways and Means Committee, which was to be a watchdog over public expenditures. This committee was expected to limit the powers of the executive branch of government, and it immediately set about to investigate what had already been done by the Treasury during Hamilton's and Wolcott's administrations.

The conservative Gallatin had high qualifications for financial office. He possessed a passion for organization and was an excellent, thorough administrator. He differed from Hamilton in that he was more scientific and less politically oriented. Unlike Hamilton, Gallatin feared the extension in the power of central government. He equated strong government with potential corruption and be-

lieved that the new Constitution had gone too far in making the central government powerful. He once said that power is ever apt to corrupt those who are
in possession of it. His ideal of government would have been a republican form
based on frequent elections combined with universal suffrage. Neither a President
nor a Senate would have been included in his ideal form of government because
they were too similar to kings and lords to win his approval. He would have
reduced the power of our government to a single legislature, one confined to its
narrowest possible size. Such a downsized government would possess only the
requisite power for self-defense, with the minimum navy and supporting taxes to
meet that end. Unable to realize this ideal form of government, Gallatin resorted
to preventing an undue and unwarranted interference by government in the
affairs of the citizens.

Gallatin took office and insisted on disclosure and accountability of the Treasury to Congress. He was the father of the Standing Committee on Finance,
which evolved into the now-famous House Ways and Means Committee, to
receive and advise on the reports of the Secretary on revenues, debts, loans,
expenditures, and projections. Gallatin recommended that no monies be spent
except for the specific purposes for which they had been appropriated—a revolutionary idea at the time.

The first thing Gallatin did after taking his seat in Congress, even while the
investigation into his credentials proceeded, was to launch his own investigation
into Hamilton's management of the Treasury. This made him an overnight wun-
derkind among the Secretary's friends and foes alike. The existence of a federal
debt was the center of his criticism of Hamiltonian finance. He regarded debt as
the most potent source of all political evil and the most active center of every
social corruption.

With the Ways and Means Committee he had overturned the Hamiltonian
procedure that the Treasury should formulate tax laws and hand them down to
the House, which was after all constitutionally entrusted with that duty. Also,
he could not reconcile himself to the notion that money appropriated for one
purpose could in fact be used for another. Throughout his legislative career,
Gallatin relentlessly criticized the Hamiltonian policy of granting the Treasury
Secretary arbitrary powers in constructing any appropriation laws as suited the
Treasury's purposes.

On May 14, 1801, Jefferson chose Gallatin for the Treasury. He had already
outlined the condition of the nation's finances and his general policy approach
in a memo to Jefferson on March 14, 1801. Gallatin had already proved himself
in the Pennsylvania assembly to be a wizard of finance, a branch of statesmanship
in which Jefferson was woefully deficient. Gallatin agreed with Jefferson in wishing to pay the national debt as soon as possible. Gallatin would even have retained the excise on whiskey, which his constituents had resisted. Nevertheless,
the President insisted on removing that detested relic of federalism, and this
made his name forever immortal among the mountain men. Although so-called
executive influence over Congress had been a party complaint of the Republicans

when in opposition, Gallatin worked as cozily with the Republican majorities in Congress as Hamilton had with the Federalists. He was able to reduce the national debt from $80 million to $45 million in ten years. He stood for fiscal responsibility, tax relief, and the application of the potential budgetary surpluses to public investment in the social infrastructure, such as roads, canals, and education. His contribution to the administrations of Jefferson and Madison went far beyond finance, budgets, and economics. He advocated minute Treasury reports on a regular, annual basis, as opposed to Hamilton's practice of providing reports to Congress when it suited him.

Few, if any, Secretaries of the Treasury have been more obsessed with economy and debt reduction than Gallatin. Scholars have debated whether this was a flaw or a desirable trait. Gallatin was a safe custodian of the public purse when it came to frugality. Yet did our young nation benefit from his policies of extreme husbandry? Perhaps a bolder and more expansionary fiscal program would have been more suited to our economic development needs. Gallatin did cut the outstanding public debt in half, but the program downsizing, together with a lack of a steady, diverse revenue base, left the country totally unprepared financially for war that came in 1812. Gallatin's pressure for economy had blocked the development of an effective military, and there was no permanent and stable internal revenue to meet the exigencies of the War of 1812.

The Gallatinian fiscal system can be broken down into three eras: 1801 to 1808, the Golden Age of Republican Finance; 1808 to 1812, the Age of Indecision; and 1812 to 1815, the War Years. The last two phases were perhaps financial failures due to inadequate planning and readiness for the enormous demands of wartime emergency finance. Fiscally, Gallatin's fiscal system embraced several components of "sound finance": a reduction in government spending, a balanced budget, alleviation of tax burdens, and a decrease in the outstanding public debt.

Gallatin believed that government expenditures, particularly when based on borrowing, constituted a destruction of national capital. Public expenditures in his view are made for only three purposes: (1) war, which is totally destructive; (2) civil expenditure, an unproductive use of funds; and (3) internal improvements—productive spending on the infrastructure, such as roads and canals. Like Adam Smith, Gallatin believed that the availability of government borrowing to finance current operating expenditures made them more profligate and more likely to embark on foreign wars. To the degree that spending was financed out of current tax revenue, there was a sobering effect. It tended to minimize the scale of government spending and discourage wasteful public ventures. Gallatin feared that the ease with which government could ordinarily borrow would incite rather than curtail extravagant expenditures. Thus, to defray public spending by public debt was the act of the spendthrift. Certainly, he did not see the provision of government services as productive. "Productive" to Gallatin was anything that enhanced the creation of material goods. He reached a rather extreme position that once government began to borrow, it would behave rather like a drug addict:

It would lose all incentive to tax for any purpose and become totally dependent on debt, even issuing new debt to pay interest on the old, accumulating debt. Of course, Gallatin would have accepted, as he did at the time, that certain events such as the Louisiana Purchase make government borrowing not only necessary but socially desirable.

One of Gallatin's early decisions was to articulate guidelines to establish objective hiring criteria in the Secretary's office and put an end to crass political patronage. Under his administration, talent and integrity became the basis for appointing collectors and subordinate officers, not political debts or party loyalties. (Of course, he could not control patronage of presidential appointments.) Treasury officeholders were not to participate actively in campaigns or party politics. One of Gallatin's predictions rings true today. His view was, once a government department, agency, or service becomes established, there is a tendency to perpetuate the bureaucracy and expand it long after the original need has passed. He may have pressed his conjecture to the extreme by opposing any expenditures on the grounds that they automatically breed more and more.

Early in the Jefferson administration, Gallatin proposed that Cabinet meetings be held regularly—once a week or more often. He met with the President virtually every day when they were in the Capitol. Gallatin saw his duty as watchdog—to observe closely the operations of the other executive departments, making certain that sound financial practices were observed. Today, many of these functions are now carried out by the Office of Management and Budget.

Gallatin's ideological identification was with the interests of the landholding class, as opposed to the mercantile capitalists, and this may have acted to hinder sound policies needed for economic development at that time. He was strongly opposed to government debt. He had no desire to see government encourage commercial or industrial development and saw no reason to spend government money for that purpose, especially if the national debt were to go up as a consequence. It was the purpose to which the borrowings were put, not just the large size of the debt, that bothered Gallatin. He believed in the principle that public indebtedness would cause revolution, corruption, and other evils. He was therefore confused about the direction of causality. Usually a revolutionary, dissolute, and corrupt regime would turn to large deficits to finance spending, rather than the other way around. Gallatin had a priority list—those projects to cut out or reduce until the public debt had been paid off entirely. The policy of expenditure cuts was the single instrument to accomplish his fiscal objectives. He did not relate the size of the government expenditures to the growth of our gross domestic product and provided no suggestions on how cost savings could be achieved, short of cutting out an entire government service.

Gallatin thought that the expenditure of borrowed funds constituted a destruction of national capital. Because most government expenditure is akin to consumption, it is wasteful and unproductive, not adding much to the infrastructure. Government borrowing encouraged more unproductive expenditures than would be undertaken by government operating on a pay-as-you-go basis out of current tax or land sale revenue. As today, Gallatin thought it easier to borrow than tax, so a government became more prone to pass new appropriations legislation and spend capriciously. Borrowed money was analogous to a large windfall of wealth that could be squandered by politicians anxious to please the constituents. Government borrowing, Gallatin thought, came from private savings that would have otherwise been wisely invested in private sector enterprises rather than spent on current consumption. Today, one would say that government borrowing "crowds out" private investment by driving up market interest rates. In his Treasury job, Gallatin was right at home because the commitment of the Jefferson administration was debt reduction. Gallatin had some clear ideas as to how this could be accomplished, including the curtailment of the runaway military budget. He insisted on reducing appropriations for the naval and military establishment, the only major expenditure area sufficiently large, if cut, to enable the repeal of the inefficient and unpopular internal duties. To Gallatin, budget balancing and debt reduction always involved spending reduction, not revenue increases.

Gallatin at times seemed inconsistent and ignored the fact that government expenditures on capital goods could properly be financed out of borrowed funds rather than current income. He was the apostle of the balanced budget, and he even opposed short-term tax anticipatory loans. He took an extreme position in his debt management policy. Gallatin also proposed that all foreign-held debt be retired within the period of obligation. Gallatin's forecast was that the tax and expenditure pattern would produce a $2 million budget surplus in 1801, and this should be applied to reducing the externally held public debt. Gallatin promised no new internal taxes and set about to avoid new taxes by forcing economies on the military and naval establishments. Unfortunately, because of the war with Tripoli, any plans of budget savings in the Navy had to be abandoned.

Gallatin had a habit of submitting notes or drafts of messages to Jefferson for comment and to keep the President apprised of fiscal problems. Gallatin usually provided solid economic analysis, as opposed to descriptive narratives. Gallatin and other Republicans had a notion of tax equity that required the avoidance of putting the burden of taxes on the small landowner, farmer, or mechanic. An ideal tax would be raised from the idle rich or wealthy merchants, while taxing foreign mercantile trade. Gallatin's revenue policy was straightforward. He thought the so-called internal tax, such as excises or sales taxes, fell on manufacturing capital. As Hamilton recognized, the new nation badly needed a broad-based, diversified, stable, and permanent system for raising revenue to support the necessary, legitimate activities of government. Gallatin ignored that an infant economy needs an increase in government activity if only in the area of police powers and contract enforcement and other public goods. The internal tax collecting machinery was disassembled in 1801 and not reinstituted until 1813.

The problem with sole reliance on import duties was that war interrupted the flow of international trade, and government revenue to fight said war was then reduced drastically. These "impost" revenues varied with the volume of foreign trade. The internal tax laws needed to be in place, so that tax rates would merely have to be raised to meet war emergency finance. Borrowing may be expensive and difficult, and money printing clearly inflationary. However, Gallatin wanted to increase revenue sources only to retire debt, not to have a ready source available to finance new government spending.

Gallatin was a proponent of a modern view that a direct tax should only be placed on real property. He advocated that the federal government levy its direct tax on items already similarly taxed by the states, because the states were in a position to know what items were best suited for direct taxation in their own jurisdictions. Gallatin was also preoccupied with the notion that there was a limit on taxable capacity. He defined a *direct tax* as one that falls on income-yielding property and an *indirect tax* as one that is levied on expenditures. He recommended a direct tax on all real property, not just land and slaves, in order to avoid penalizing the western and southern states. In defending an earlier proposal for a tax on land, houses, and slaves, Gallatin argued that direct taxes are easier to collect, more equal, and less expensive than excise taxes. However, he viewed these taxes as a pragmatic necessity, arising out of misguided Hamiltonian fiscal policies that always permitted expenditures to outstrip revenues. He specifically stated that direct taxation should be a *temporary* measure. In general, Republicans in that period regarded internal taxes to be odious, inquisitorial, immoral, and inconsistent with democracy. These taxes led to patronage and government corruption. Gallatin also believed that revenue should be raised almost exclusively by imposts and that the use of internal taxes be reserved for emergency periods. Internal taxes at the time included retailers licenses, stamp duties, auction taxes, carriage taxes, taxes on snuff, and so on. Taxes were proposed on sales of horses, manufacture of leather goods, and hats. These did not consider any ability-to-pay arguments; whereas, in the case of imposts, the duties fell mainly on the rich or at least on those who were adding foreign luxuries to their domestic comforts. Gallatin came to the final decision that such internal taxes were unproductive, oppressive, expensive to collect, unequal, and too easy to evade. People preferred an external tax on a necessity as great as salt to any of the existing internal taxes.

Gallatin was concerned that interest on the federal debt was consuming a full two thirds of the entire government budget expenditures. Gallatin conducted his own internal audit of the Treasury's books and discovered a disturbing accounting error in the reports of his predecessor, Secretary Wolcott. In his report to the Sinking Fund Commissioners, Wolcott had placed the Treasury balance at a surplus of $500,718.55. In fact, Gallatin established that there was an accumulated Treasury operating *deficit* of $930,128.64 from its inception until the end year 1799. Gallatin offered the possibility that former reports may have suffered from accidental omissions or a lack of generally accepted accounting practices.

By October 25, 1803, Gallatin provided a report to Congress that showed that public debt reduction under his management had proceeded smoothly, and $12.7 million had been paid off. The only issue was the technical procedures for funding the $15 million required for payment to France to carry out the Louisiana Purchase. Most of the funding was to be made in U.S. stock bearing 6 percent interest. This required legislation necessary to raise $700,000 in tariff duties to pay the interest on the new debt. The Louisiana Purchase, which delighted Gallatin, and the admirable management of its financing proved to be important elements in Jefferson's reelection, which assured Gallatin of four more years to implement his debt redemption plan. Jefferson, Madison, Monroe, and Gallatin had pulled off a mammoth deal: expanding the U.S. territory by 140 percent for a trifling $15 million, with considerably more than a fourth of the price paid on the barrel in cash, without resorting to increases in domestic taxes. This was an extraordinary episode in the history of fiscal packaging. To this day, it remains a mystery why Napoleon on April 30, 1803, ceded not only New Orleans and part of Florida but the whole vast territory of Louisiana to the United States for such a pittance.

Gallatin expanded the role of the Secretary of the Treasury beyond the technicalities of financing government operations. He set a precedent for advising the executive on budget management and resource allocation to promote economic growth and stability of the emerging nation. By this time, the whole assignment of managing the disposition of public lands in the West and elsewhere fell on the desk of the Secretary.

At the outset, he was modest about the role of the Treasury in deciding whether excess revenues should be applied to enhanced national security or military buildup for an inevitable war with England, or spent on public works and infrastructure. He believed these were normative issues, not within the purview or province of the Treasury Department. Nevertheless, he considered the merit of an accumulation of surplus revenue in the Treasury and recognized that internal improvements would increase and spread the national wealth.

Between 1791 and 1808 the debt had fallen from $75.2 million to $57.0 million. Initially, it increased by $7 million and later decreased by more than $20 million, even though the Louisiana Purchase had been completed. By 1805, federal revenues had expanded to the extent that Jefferson promised financing for rivers, canals, roads, arts, manufactures, and education, but only after, Jefferson cleverly insisted, passage of a politically impossible constitutional amendment.

Gallatin tested Jefferson's patience in the Hamiltonian use of central government to promote economic development. Gallatin did not share Jefferson's conviction that a constitutional amendment was prerequisite to a program of national improvements. Gallatin had made his dream public as early as 1802 when he inserted into the law governing the sale of public lands in Ohio a provision for the construction of a highway from the eastern seaboard across the width of the entire state. He made no secret of the reason: to cement the bonds of the Union.

In 1808 Gallatin proposed to Congress a $20 million, ten-year expenditure program for constructing a series of "great canals" to provide safe inland navigation along the coast from Massachusetts to North Carolina, and a great turnpike road from Maine to Georgia. Other infrastructure investments recommended were improved navigation and parallel canals along four of the great rivers flowing into the Atlantic, and roads crossing the mountains from each of these rivers to the Mississippi Valley. He wanted new and improved roads to Detroit, St. Louis, and New Orleans and a series of smaller projects such as canals around the falls of the Ohio and the Niagara. He believed that an equitable apportionment of funds could be obtained by debates among conflicting regional interests on the floor of Congress. Thus, he supported government expenditures on internal improvements to the extent permitted by the revenue constraint—this was the only productive, noncapital-destroying form of government spending.

An ongoing program of public investments could be financed through a permanent rotating fund established by the Treasury via the sale of a "special" U.S. note issued directly to individual citizens. Congress failed to adopt Gallatin's sound proposal; it would have provided crucial linkages for the next two decades prior to the introduction of the steam railroad. On a benefit-cost basis, the plan's basic principles remain valid today.

Gallatin had one of his few sharp disagreements with Jefferson and the Republicans over the rechartering of Hamilton's national bank. He always valued the bank, and therefore, before the 1811 expiration of the twenty-year charter, he supported the extension movement. He prudently waited until Jefferson was leaving office, and encouraged by the tacit support of incoming President Madison, he campaigned in Congress for a recharter of the bank at $30 million—three times the original capital base. Unfortunately for its proponents, the bill was killed, not only from opposition from Jeffersonians and antidevelopmentalists but also by politically powerful stockholders, borrowers, and potential borrowers linked to the growing Republican-chartered state banks.

Gallatin was definitely one of the premier money and banking experts of the time. He had studied David Hume, Adam Smith, and French economist J. B. Say in depth and was familiar with the quantity theory of money. He believed that a sound currency would enable the United States to avoid many woes. The question was, What does the term "sound" mean? He was a fervent bimetallist and inveighed against speculative, inflationary booms created by excessive bank note creation. He had worked out his own homespun notions of modern central banking, and he was convinced that the position of Secretary of the Treasury demanded a rigorous understanding of banking.

The War of 1812 and its aftermath proved too much for Gallatin's fiscal vision, and the financial situation of the country became precarious. In 1812, Gallatin explained to Congress that internal taxes (direct and excise) would be needed to raise $5 million. He wanted all extraordinary expenses of the war to be financed by bond issues, while "ordinary costs," including all debt service charges, should be totally covered by current tax revenue. He then left the matter to Congress and did not press for new internal taxes in his Treasury report of 1812. By the time war arrived, Gallatin had experienced diminished power within the party and Congress and was on his way out as Treasury Secretary. Gallatin's unfortunate solution to the wartime reduction in impost revenues was to down-size the government. Gallatin projected that the war would drastically reduce customs revenues, the import duties that in peacetime amounted to more than 90 percent of government operating revenue. When the War of 1812 had become a reality, Congress relied on Gallatin's earlier optimistic suggestion that loans by themselves could meet all the war's additional expenditures without any new tax legislation. Gallatin finally changed his mind and realized that the country needed new internal taxes. Congress eventually acted and doubled customs du-ties, and tonnage rates on foreign-owned ships were increased. By early 1813, a twenty-cents-a-bushel duty on salt was reimposed. But no move was made on Gallatin's proposal that internal taxes be reinstituted. The first war loan author-ized by Congress was for $11 million on March 14, 1812. A cautious Gallatin proposed that if the loan were not fully subscribed, Treasury notes could be issued to cover the shortfall. The bond issue faced low public confidence; the problem was that no future security of new taxes was pledged by Congress. The debt servicing was to be covered only from existing revenue sources. Thus, the bonds were hard to market. This was to mark the beginning of several years of difficult financial problems confronting the nation. Gallatin had planned to borrow $20 million from the Bank of the United States in the event of war. But in 1811, the Bank of the United States was not rechartered.

In the final analysis, Gallatin is best remembered for his expertise in the area of fiscal administration. In this field, his main contribution was to ensure con-tinued legislative rather than executive control over the nation's finances. His innovation of the Ways and Means Committee, his struggles on behalf of specific appropriations, and his insistence on concise annual Treasury reports all worked to guarantee that spending matters remained in the hands of Congress, where they were placed by the Constitution. He will also be remembered as a critic and check on the Hamiltonian spending excesses. Among Republicans, Gallatin probably knew more about finance than anyone else at the time. However, his appointment as Secretary involved much more than a selection of a financial technician. He did not merely acquiesce in the fiscal views of a political party of which he was a member. Rather, he trained his party in the financial ideals that underlay the Republican creed.

It is clear that Gallatin will always be remembered as an individual with purity of motive and honesty and, above all else, as a man characterized by great tem-perateness. However, we may question whether this moderation, temperateness, and honesty were a sufficient compensation for boldness of action, decisiveness, and breadth in vision in a time that marked the birth of our nation.

Gallatin died in his daughter Frances's arms at Astoria, Long Island, on August 13, 1849, at age eighty-eight years, six months. His wife and lifelong friend, Hannah Nicholson, had died three months earlier on May 14. He had made preparations to divide his estate among his three children, Frances, James, and Albert Rolaz.

In 1813, even before his career had ended, Gallatin, as a concerned father, counseled his son and passed down his deeply held sense of personal honor and values: never to forget the duties of his noble birth; never to dishonor a name that for centuries had never borne a stain; always to be civil, particularly to those who were not equal; to guard against the terrible corruption that could engulf a young country as rich in resources as the United States.

BIBLIOGRAPHY

Adams, Henry. *The Life of Albert Gallatin*. New York: J. B. Lippincott & Co., 1879; reprint: New York: Peter Smith, 1943.

Balinky, Alexander. *Albert Gallatin: Fiscal Theories and Policies*. New Brunswick, NJ: Rutgers University Press, 1958.

Burrows, Edwin G. *Albert Gallatin and the Political Economy of Republicanism, 1761–1800*. New York: Garland Publishing, Inc., 1986.

Gallatin, Albert. *Writings*. Edited by Henry Adams. Philadelphia: Antiquarian Press, 1879.

Gallatin, James. *Diary of James Gallatin*. New York: C. Scribner's Sons, 1916.

Walters, Raymond, Jr. *Albert Gallatin, Jeffersonian Financier and Diplomat*. New York: Macmillan Company, 1957.

C. DANIEL VENCILL

CARTER GLASS (January 4, 1858–May 28, 1946). Carter Glass enjoyed success as a journalist, politician, and government administrator. Largely self-educated, he considered himself to be a "Jeffersonian Democrat." He represented Virginia in the U.S. House of Representatives from 1902 to 1918 and in the U.S. Senate from 1920 until his death in 1946. Widely recognized as a financial expert—indeed, many considered him to be the "father" of the Federal Reserve System—Glass served as Secretary of the Treasury from December 16, 1918, to February 1, 1920. He declined an offer to return to this position during Franklin Roosevelt's administration because he vigorously disliked Roosevelt's deficit spending and expansion of federal programs.

Glass was born on January 4, 1858, in Lynchburg, Virginia, to Robert Henry Glass and Augusta (Christian) Glass. He had three older brothers and one older sister. His mother died in 1860. His father promptly remarried; he and his second wife had seven children. His father was a newspaper editor, who served as a major in the Confederate Army.

His family's financial difficulties forced Glass to leave school at age fourteen, and he became a printer's apprentice on his father's paper. From 1877 to 1880, he worked as a clerk for the auditor of the Atlantic, Mississippi and Ohio Railroad. He then became first a reporter (1880), and then an editor (1887), for the *Lynchburg Daily News*.

His improving financial fortunes allowed him to substantially change his life. He married Aurelia McDearman Caldwell on January 12, 1886; they had four children—Powell, Mary, Carter, Jr., and Augusta. He purchased the *Lynchburg Daily News* in 1888 and acquired two more papers by 1896.

His combative and provocative editorials accurately reflected his pugnacious personality. Short (five feet four inches) with red hair, Glass often worked so intensely that he became ill. His fearlessness and quick temper constantly embroiled him in disputes. As a youth, he once used a bat to chase from a baseball field an umpire and an opposing team that he believed was cheating. As an adult, he often offered to settle disputes with fisticuffs. Yet it was his caustic wit and biting prose that won him many verbal and written debates.

He used the substantial influence of his newspapers to support vigorously the Democratic Party. He was elected to the Virginia Senate in 1898 and reelected in 1900. As an editor and as a state legislator, he vigorously advocated reforms to eliminate monopolies, enact pure drug and food laws, regulate railroad rates, reform labor laws, and increase funding for public education. He developed a reputation as a ferocious debater. Once during a debate, a supporter encouraged Glass, "Give them hell, Carter!" Glass retorted, "Why use dynamite when insect powder will do the work?" (Smith and Beasley, 122).

His actions as a delegate to the Virginia Constitutional Convention of 1901 propelled Glass into a prominent role within Virginia's Democratic Party. Glass wanted to replace the Reconstruction constitution because he thought it had resulted in a corrupt "mobocracy" rather than a democracy. His bombastic and stirring rhetoric persuaded the convention to adopt a grandfather clause, a poll tax, and a literacy test as methods to disenfranchise the poor and illiterate whites and blacks; after the new constitution was implemented, the number of eligible voters fell by over 50 percent.

The Virginia Governor appointed Glass to a vacant seat in the U.S. House of Representatives in 1902; later in that year, he won election to the seat, holding it until 1918. He apparently had little impact during his first decade in Congress; indeed, he did not make a major speech in Congress until 1913 when he promoted banking reform. He regularly supported "progressive" economic reforms such as pure food and drug legislation, stronger antitrust laws, and lower tariffs. He did not support progressive social reforms such as women's suffrage. His most important committee assignment was to the Committee on Banking and Currency. He diligently studied financial economics, and soon his peers recognized him as a congressional expert in the field of financial economics.

In the election of 1912, voters elected Woodrow Wilson as President and a Democratic majority in both the U.S. Senate and House. Glass, as newly appointed Chair of the House Committee on Banking and Currency, assumed major responsibility for monetary reform. He worked closely with his assistant— University of Chicago trained economist H. Parker Willis—and with the Wilson administration, particularly with Treasury Secretary William McAdoo. Glass's original bill created a regional reserve banking system under private control. He considered the regional aspect of his proposal to be essential in preventing Wall Street control. He was hesitant about placing the new system under public control because he, a faithful Jeffersonian Democrat, distrusted too much governmental centralization.

Critics attacked his plan from all sides. New York City bankers, fearing loss of business and influence, denounced the plan's excessive regionalization. The Wilson administration, particularly Treasury Secretary William McAdoo, desired public rather than private control over the system.

After a long and tortuous process, Glass incorporated several of these criticisms into the final compromised legislation—the Federal Reserve Act (Glass-Owen Act). Glass reduced the number of reserve districts. He replaced the privately controlled board with one that had two ex officio members from the government (Secretary of the Treasury and Comptroller of the Currency) and five members appointed by the President and confirmed by the Senate for ten-year terms with staggered appointments. Glass agreed with the provision that no more than one member of the board was to be from any given reserve district in order to guarantee representation from the South and West and to prevent the possibility of Wall Street domination.

Glass did not compromise his insistence that Federal Reserve policy should be guided by the real bills doctrine. In his view, Reserve Banks should only discount "real bills"—short-term commercial paper used to finance self-liquidating business transactions. Glass argued that banks should only finance "productive" commercial, agricultural, and industrial loans and should not finance loans for "speculative" purposes. By discounting only real bills, Reserve Banks would not create too much money and thus would not cause inflation.

Later, many people attempted to claim credit for the Federal Reserve System. Glass probably had the best credentials to be called the "father" of the Federal Reserve System, particularly for his political skill displayed in bringing a legislative proposal to successful fruition.

Glass, who developed great admiration for Woodrow Wilson, worked closely with the Wilson administration on a number of issues. He was particularly involved with formulating the Federal Farm Loan Act (1916). Glass vigorously supported Wilson's wartime policies. When Treasury Secretary McAdoo resigned in 1918, he recommended Glass and Bernard Baruch as possible successors. Wilson thought highly of both men but knew that Baruch wanted to finish his responsibilities as Director of the War Industries Board. Although Glass was reluctant to leave the U.S. House of Representatives, he accepted Wilson's appointment and became Secretary of the U.S. Treasury on December 16, 1918.

Glass promised to continue the fiscal and monetary policies of his predecessor. Most important, he insisted that the Federal Reserve continue to follow the low-interest policy that the Treasury Department had forced it to adopt. He advocated the Treasury's policy not because he wanted the Fed to be subordinate to the Treasury—indeed, he consistently battled throughout his congressional career to maintain the integrity of the Federal Reserve System. Instead, he did not believe in allocating credit by increasing interest rates because that might reduce borrowing for "productive" or "essential" uses by legitimate businesses. He believed that increasing interest rates would not reduce borrowing for speculative purposes.

Glass preferred a policy of "moral suasion," or "direct action," as it was then termed. He wanted to ration credit through discriminatory credit controls where banks would refuse only loans for unproductive or nonessential (speculative) uses; Glass included loans to speculate on Wall Street to fall into this category. Of course, Glass's view represents just another side of his adherence to the real bills doctrine.

Glass's vigorous advocacy during the January 1919 debates convinced the Fed to postpone an increase in the discount rate. With this issue settled for several months, Glass concentrated on supervising the next Treasury bond drive—"Victory Liberty Loan." Glass raised $4.5 billion. He continued McAdoo's practice of using below-market interest rates combined with tax exemptions in issuing the bonds.

Glass's battle with the Federal Reserve Board resumed in October of 1919 when he once again opposed a request for a discount rate increase that Benjamin Strong, President of the New York Reserve Bank, was proposing. Strong believed that "moral suasion" was not effective in checking "speculation" that led to inflation. Moreover, Strong was appalled by the apparent Treasury domination of the Federal Reserve System. Observers later reported that these two headstrong and combative individuals—Glass and Strong—engaged in several heated exchanges concerning monetary policy. Ironically, Glass approved a rate increase in January 1920; he later wrote that he regretted this action.

Glass resigned from the Treasury on February 1, 1920, when Virginia Governor Westmoreland Davis, a political independent, appointed Glass to a seat in the U.S. Senate—a vacancy created by the death of Thomas S. Martin (D-Va.). Glass, who previously had been an opponent of the Democratic machine in Virginia, ultimately made peace with the organization. He soon acquired a reputation for voting his "convictions" as he established his own ideas independently of his constituents. Glass, running unopposed, was elected to the Senate in the November 1924 election. He was reelected in 1930, 1936, and 1942.

In the Senate, he continued to be respected—particularly for his knowledge of monetary affairs—if not always well liked. If anything, he became even more caustic in debate. During the 1920s, most observers continued to consider Glass as an economic progressive in attacking the power of large corporations. He, however, left the progressive ranks when he resisted attempts to enlarge the scope of federal governmental power at the cost of infringing on smaller private enterprises or on the rights of states.

Although he continued his racist rhetoric and beliefs, he was more progressive concerning religious issues. In 1928, he was one of the few southern Democrats who supported the presidential campaign of Alfred E. Smith—a Catholic and a foe of Prohibition. In numerous speeches throughout the South, Glass—a Methodist and a "Dry"—denounced religious intolerance. Several times, he boldly confronted the Ku Klux Klan as he proclaimed his support of religious tolerance.

Between 1928 and 1932, Glass vehemently denounced Herbert Hoover's administration. Glass particularly disliked Hoover's Reconstruction Finance Corporation. At the 1932 Democratic National Convention, Glass successfully urged the delegates to adopt a "sound money" plank of adherence to the gold standard.

Glass had been a friend of Franklin Roosevelt for many years, and he anxiously awaited Roosevelt's administration to carry out the economic policies that Glass had long advocated. Immediately prior to the 1932 election, Glass delivered a radio speech that blistered President Hoover's economic policies. Glass said that "at the expense of the taxpayers, President Hoover has converted the Treasury at Washington into a national pawn-shop and infected the central government with the fatal germ of financial socialism. All semblance of state initiative and community pride has been extinguished, and the minions of Federal bureaucracy are given full sway to distribute huge sums of money picked from the pockets of the American People" (Glass, in Smith and Beasley, 472). Glass's vituperative speech helped Roosevelt's candidacy.

Glass, however, soon developed doubts about Roosevelt's ideas for economic recovery. He sensed that he and Roosevelt fundamentally disagreed on economic issues. When Roosevelt offered the seventy-five-year-old Glass the position of Secretary of the Treasury, Glass declined by stating that he could do the country more good by staying in the Senate. Although he remained personally friendly with Roosevelt, Glass was bitterly disappointed with Roosevelt's policies—particularly with deficit spending, abandonment of the gold standard, and the National Industrial Recovery Act. Indeed, between 1933 and 1939, Glass voted against major New Deal legislation more often than any other Democrat.

Glass remained intensely interested in the nation's financial system. He possessed an acute sense of proprietorship toward the Federal Reserve System. He wrote his only book, *An Adventure in Constructive Finance* (1927), to set the record straight concerning the origins and objectives of the Fed. He vigorously criticized the Fed whenever he perceived it to be moving away from the principles of decentralized money management and adherence to the real bills doctrine.

Glass's reputation as a financial expert—at least by congressional standards—placed him at the center of financial reforms during the 1930s. The 1933 Banking Act contained a part—often referred to as the Glass-Steagall Act—that separated commercial banking from investment banking. Commercial banks were prohibited from underwriting and trading in private domestic securities for their own account; they were limited to accepting deposits and making loans. Glass strongly believed that banks' involvement with securities was responsible for stock market speculation that significantly contributed to the weakening of the banking system and the economy.

Glass also supported the Securities and Exchange Act (1934). Although he often disliked federal agencies because he believed that they trampled states' rights, he viewed the regulation of securities as a federal responsibility. Moreover, this legislation gave the Federal Reserve power over margin requirements for stock purchases. Glass had long favored this type of selective credit control to regulate borrowing for "nonproductive" uses.

Glass bitterly fought the administration's efforts to reform the Federal Reserve System. Roosevelt had angered Glass when he had nominated Marriner Eccles to chair the Federal Reserve Board without consulting Glass. Glass was the only

Senator to vote against Eccles. Moreover, Eccles submitted the bank reform bill to Congress without discussing it with Glass, as he had promised. Eccles tried to apologize to Glass for this action by saying that an interdepartmental committee had just finished rewriting the legislation minutes before it was submitted. Indeed, Eccles had not seen the formal draft until it had gone to Congress. Eccles's attempted apology did not shake Glass's conviction that Eccles was lying to him.

Glass was determined to battle Roosevelt's proposed banking reform. Glass feared that a stronger board would lead to centralized control of credit to replace the decentralized system that he had advocated since 1913. He believed that a strong board, closely tied to the presidency, would result in inflation as it attempted to guarantee an economic recovery. He wanted a larger board than did Eccles so that it would be more likely that western and southern interests would be represented. He was willing to remove the ex officio members, particularly the Treasury Secretary, to reduce the influence of the executive branch.

Glass was less satisfied with the struggle over the composition of the Federal Open Market Committee (FOMC). The 1933 Banking Bill had provided for a Federal Open Market Committee composed of one member from each reserve district with the member designated by the Federal Reserve Bank Board of Directors. Roosevelt and Eccles thought that this arrangement gave private interests too much control over monetary policy. They preferred to place all responsibility for open market operations under the control of the Board of Governors. Glass again objected to the concentration of power. He forced a compromise that the FOMC include representatives from five Federal Reserve Banks (according to a schedule of rotation) as well as the Board of Governors.

Glass suffered his most significant defeat with regard to discount policy. The bill expanded the power of Federal Reserve Banks to make discount loans to member banks by discounting all "satisfactory paper" and not just on "eligible paper." This moved discounting policy further away from Glass's preferred real bills doctrine.

After the Banking Act of 1935 was enacted, Glass found other issues with which to disagree with Roosevelt's administration. Glass led the Senate fight against Roosevelt's court-packing proposal in 1937. He termed the plan to be a "constitutional immorality." Glass stated: "With private property seized at will; the courts openly reviled; rebellion rampant against good order and peace of communities; with governments pleading with mobocracy instead of mastering it. . . . This, with other dangerous evils, contrived or connived at, by governments, is the real crisis which faces the nation and cannot be cured by degrading the Supreme Court of the United States" (Glass, in Smith and Beasley, 502). Glass's opposition contributed to the defeat of Roosevelt's plan.

Roosevelt and Glass continued to battle. Glass, however, strongly supported Roosevelt's foreign policy. Glass had agreed with Woodrow Wilson's vision of the League of Nations. In 1920, Glass had drafted the Democratic platform that strongly endorsed the League.

His colleagues elected him President pro tempore of the Senate in 1941. His poor health forced him to be absent from the Senate after June 1942. He retained his seat until his death on May 28, 1946, at age eighty-eight.

Glass and his wife did not enjoy the Washington social scene. They spent as much time as possible at their Virginia farm where Glass particularly enjoyed raising his pedigreed Jersey cattle. In Washington, he attended Washington Senators' games when they played his favorite professional baseball team, the Philadelphia Athletics. He voraciously read literature. He intensely followed the debate concerning the authorship of Shakespeare's plays; he favored the Baconian side. His wife Aurelia died on June 5, 1937. On June 22, 1940, he married Mary Scott Meade, a widow who was thirty years younger than Glass.

Franklin Roosevelt once referred to Glass as the "Unreconstructed Rebel"; Glass proudly accepted this title. Glass was a southern Democrat who never strayed from his party. Glass was a social reactionary, particularly with regard to issues involving women and blacks. Glass attempted to follow the economic principles, as he understood them, of his political heroes: Thomas Jefferson and Woodrow Wilson. He favored governmental intervention to prevent the excesses of large corporations and to provide a level playing field for small businesses and farmers. He did not support governmental programs that basically just redistributed income—hence, his dislike of many New Deal programs. He left a lasting impact on Virginia politics and on the nation's financial system.

BIBLIOGRAPHY

Benston, George J. *The Separation of Commercial and Investment Banking: The Glass-Steagall Act Revisited and Reconsidered.* New York: Oxford University Press, 1990.

Eccles, Marriner S. *Beckoning Frontiers: Public and Personal Recollections.* New York: Alfred A. Knopf, 1951.

Glass, Carter. *An Adventure in Constructive Finance.* Garden City, NY: Doubleday, Page and Company, 1927; reprint: New York: Arno Press, 1975.

———. "The Facts about the Fiscal Policy of Our Government during the Past Few Years." Radio speech delivered on November 1, 1932. Printed in Smith, Rixey, and Norman Beasley. *Carter Glass: A Biography.* New York: Longmans, Green and Co., 1939, 471–95.

———. "Constitutional Immorality." Radio address delivered on March 29, 1937. Printed in Smith, Rixey, and Norman Beasley. *Carter Glass: A Biography.* New York: Longmans, Green and Co., 1939, 496–510.

Heinemann, Ronald L. *Depression and the New Deal in Virginia: The Enduring Dominion.* Charlottesville: University Press of Virginia, 1983.

Koeniger, A. C. "Carter Glass and the National Recovery Administration." *South Atlantic Quarterly* 74 (Summer 1975): 349–64.

———. "The Politics of Independence: Carter Glass and the Elections of 1936." *South Atlantic Quarterly* 80 (1981): 95–106.

Palmer, James E., Jr. *Carter Glass: Unreconstructed Rebel.* Roanoke: Institute of American Biography, 1938.

Smith, Rixey, and Norman Beasley. *Carter Glass: A Biography.* New York: Longmans, Green and Co., 1939.

Syrett, J. "Jim Farley and Carter Glass: Allies against a Third Term." *Prologue* 15 (Summer 1938): 88–102.

ROBERT STANLEY HERREN

WALTER Q. GRESHAM (March 17, 1832–May 28, 1895). Walter Quintin Gresham may have the dubious distinction of holding the position of Treasury Secretary for the shortest duration. He was already serving in the Cabinet of President Arthur as Postmaster General when Charles Folger, then Secretary of the Treasury, passed away in September 1884, after a prolonged illness, and the President asked Gresham to accept a stopgap appointment.

After taking office on September 25, he held this position until October 30, 1884, when he was appointed Circuit Judge of the Seventh Judicial District to succeed Judge Thomas Drummond, who had previously retired.

Since Gresham was the Treasury Secretary for such a short duration, he obviously did not have the time for any accomplishments relating to the affairs of the Treasury. However, both before and after his extremely short stint at the Treasury, Gresham had to his credit made notable accomplishments in various public offices. In fact, he enjoyed the distinction of serving in the Cabinets of President Arthur, then Grover Cleveland when he became the President for the second time in 1892. That in itself may not be particularly remarkable except for the fact that President Arthur was a Republican and President Cleveland was a Democrat.

Walter Gresham was born on March 17, 1832, to William and Sarah Gresham on the family homestead near Lanesville, Indiana. He attended the log schoolhouse in Gresham Woods. During the next few years, he worked at various jobs and studied at the seminary and also at the State University in Bloomington. In 1852, he took up the study of law and was admitted to the bar in 1854. Soon after that, he formed a successful law partnership with Thomas Slaughter.

Gresham took an early interest in politics and, among other activities, managed the campaign of his law partner who was running for the House seat from the second Indiana district. After being debarred from the old Whig Party, he took an active interest in the organization of the Republican Party. In 1860 he won his first and only political victory by winning a seat in the Indiana legislature.

During the Civil War, he joined General Grant's forces in Tennessee, and this association turned into a lasting friendship. After the war ended, in which Gresham served admirably, he returned to his interest in politics. President Grant appointed Gresham U.S. District Judge for the District of Indiana. Meanwhile, his position was rising rapidly in Republican Party politics, and he was even being mentioned as a presidential possibility.

In April 1883, President Arthur appointed Walter Gresham Postmaster General, with the possibility of having an Arthur-Gresham presidential ticket for the 1884 elections. Gresham's name was on the ballot for the Republican Party ticket in 1888, but the party delegates eventually nominated Benjamin Harrison. When Harrison was elected, Gresham was considered as a possibility to fill a vacancy on the Supreme Court, but he declined.

By this time Gresham's opposition to a protective tariff was becoming particularly pronounced, and with the passage of the McKinley Law of 1890, to which he announced his opposition, Gresham's split from the Republican Party became imminent. Walter Gresham switched over to the Democrats in 1892 and voted for Grover Cleveland. Upon winning the election, President Cleveland offered Gresham the position of Secretary of State, which he accepted.

Gresham's performance of his duties at the State Department showed independent thinking and firm leadership "uninfluenced by jingoist opposition" (Johnson and Malone, 609). He did not, however, leave an enduring stamp on American foreign policy. On May 28, 1895, while still holding office, Gresham died in Washington and was later buried in the Arlington National Cemetery.

BIBLIOGRAPHY

Barnes, J. A. *Wealth of the American People: A History of Their Economic Life*. New York: Prentice-Hall, Inc., 1949.

Doenecke, J. D. *The Presidencies of James A. Garfield & Chester A. Arthur*. Lawrence: Regents Press of Kansas, 1981.

Friedman, M., and Anna Schwartz. *A Monetary History of the United States 1867–1960*. Princeton: Princeton University Press, 1963.

Furer, H. B. *James A. Garfield 1831–1881 and Chester A. Arthur 1830–1886: Chronology—Documents—Bibliographical Aids*. New York: Oceana Publishing Company, Inc., 1970.

Hacker, L. M. *Major Documents in American Economic History*. Princeton: D. Van Nostrand Company, Inc., 1961.

Howe, G. F. *Chester A. Arthur: A Quarter Century of Machine Politics*. New York: Frederick Ungar Publishing Company, 1957.

Johnson, A., and Dumas Malone, eds. *Dictionary of American Biography*. New York: Charles Scribner's Sons, 1931.

Kroos, H. E., ed. *Documentary History of Banking and Currency in the United States*. New York: Chelsea House Publishers, 1977.

McGrane, R. C. *The Economic Development of the American Nation*. Boston: Ginn and Company, 1942.

Nevins, A. *Grover Cleveland: A Study in Courage*. New York: Dodd, Mead & Company, 1933.

Richardson, J. D., ed. *A Compilation of the Messages and Papers of the Presidents*. Washington, D.C.: Bureau of National Literature, 1911.

Schlesinger, A. M., ed. *History of American Presidential Elections*. New York: Chelsea House Publishers, 1971.

Shannon, F. A. *Economic History of the People of the United States*. New York: Macmillan Company, 1934.

PENNY KUGLER

JAMES GUTHRIE (December 5, 1792–March 13, 1869). James Guthrie served as Secretary of the Treasury from March 7, 1853, to March 6, 1857, during the presidency of Franklin Pierce. Guthrie was born on December 5, 1792, in Bardstown, Kentucky, son of Adam Guthrie and Hannah (Polk) Guthrie.

Because of his father's service in the Kentucky militia, James was sent to McAllister's Military Academy, after which he studied law under John Rowan, who was a jurist on the Kentucky Court of Appeals. He practiced law in Bardstown until 1820, when he was appointed the Commonwealth of Kentucky's Attorney and moved to Louisville, where he resided for the rest of his life.

Guthrie married Elizabeth C. Prather of Louisville on May 3, 1821. They had three daughters before she died in 1836.

In 1827, Guthrie was elected to the lower house of the Kentucky legislature and, in 1831, to the Kentucky Senate, where he served until 1841. He was twice chosen Speaker pro tempore of the Senate. In 1835, the Democratic Party nominated him for the U.S. Senate, but he lost the election.

His service on the Internal Improvements Committee led to his promoting Macadam roads, canal building, and the construction of a railroad between Louisville and Lexington. He became wealthy from investing in Louisville real estate and in various banks, in addition to his promotion of roads and canals. In 1849, he was the guiding force as he presided over the third Constitutional Convention of Kentucky. He also served on the Louisville City Council and helped organize that city's public school system. He was a founder of the University of Louisville and served as President of that institution. By 1850, his railroad promotions brought him into contact with leading Southern industrialists who enhanced his position as an important member of the Democratic Party. After Pierce won the 1852 election, Guthrie was selected to head the Treasury Department.

During Guthrie's period of office, 1853 to 1857, the Treasury experienced surpluses because of the large amount of gold mined in California, which financed an increased amount of imports. With specie accumulating in the Treasury, Guthrie was anxious to use these funds to retire some of the federal debt.

The 1847 Loan Act specified that government bonds could be sold only at par or above and redeemed at par or below. This proved to be quite a hindrance to Guthrie's predecessor, Thomas Corwin, who wanted the law repealed, because these bonds were selling above par during the 1850s. This law was repealed in 1853, giving Guthrie the opportunity to announce that $5 million of bonds would be redeemed at a premium of 21 percent on July 1, 1853. Throughout 1853 and 1854, the Treasury purchased $20.1 million of its debt at an average premium of 15 percent. The total debt reduced during Guthrie's four-year term was $38 million of the $63 million outstanding in 1853. With banks holding a great deal of the government debt, the refunding replaced bank earning assets with high-powered specie, permitting an expansion in loans.

Guthrie, in his first annual report, criticized Millard Fillmore's Secretary of the Treasury, Thomas Corwin, for making private arrangements for debt repurchases, calling this a misuse of government funds. In addition, he accused Corwin of ordering certain goods to be imported at a duty that was declared 10 percent below what was actually paid on them and allowing the Collector of Revenue at the Port of New York to deposit the difference in a trust company. Guthrie had this collector removed from office, receiving national attention from this controversy.

Guthrie, as a Democrat, was a hard money man, a believer in the Independent

Treasury, and was opposed not only to a national bank of issue but also to the many chartered and free banks issuing their distinctive small denomination bank notes. He considered bank notes and deposits an inferior money to silver and gold, lamenting the big increase in the number of banks during this period, from 750 in 1853 to 1,416 in 1857. He was about ten years ahead of his time in being the first government official to advocate a tax on private bank notes, hoping to substitute silver and gold coin for denominations under $5. He did advocate a uniform currency, not issued by banks, to be convertible into gold on demand.

Small bank notes circulated in part because of the shortage of silver in the United States in this period. An 1834 law had set the ratio of 16 silver to 1 gold in the United States, but France set the ratio at 15.5 to 1 and Britain at 14.28 to 1. Therefore, silver was undervalued in the United States, causing it to flow to Europe, and gold to America. Congress followed the urging of Thomas Corwin and authorized the minting of token silver coins in 1853. Because of this law, Guthrie was able to use some of the Treasury surplus to advance funds to the mint, so it could pay promptly for newly mined silver. Guthrie wanted these token silver coins to replace small denomination bank notes.

Guthrie, unlike the Whigs who believed in a national bank, felt that the Independent Treasury could have a balancing effect on the economy. Just as the last Democratic Secretary of the Treasury, Robert J. Walker under President Polk, Guthrie used debt retirement as a sort of open market operation. New specie could be injected into the economy in exchange for bonds to offset deflationary shocks. In 1854, banks in Ohio, Indiana, and Illinois suspended specie payments because the railroad bonds, which backed their notes, had fallen in value. The New York money market was experiencing very high rates. Total deposits, bank notes and bank-held specie, declined 5 percent during that year. By an aggressive debt repurchase program, Guthrie was able to inject from $5 to $7 million of new specie into the economy so that by December 1855 the stock of money was restored.

Guthrie also believed that the Independent Treasury could exercise restraint on an overheated economy by allowing specie to accumulate in the Treasury, rather than serve as high-powered money in the banks. But he feared too much specie accumulation would result in a "fatal control" over the economy, necessitating injecting some of it back into the economy either through debt retirement or through loans, which were the forerunner of repurchase agreements. The wholesale price level rose from 104.3 in 1853 to 119.4 in 1857 (1860 = 100), but consumer prices jumped from 92.6 in 1853, where they had been for six years, up to 100 in 1854. After that, they moved very little during Guthrie's term of office, reaching 103.7 in 1857.

Guthrie, unlike the Whig Thomas Corwin, was not a protectionist. He wanted a tariff for revenue only and not for protecting domestic industries. He wanted this tariff to be on manufactured goods only, and not on raw materials, allowing domestic firms to produce goods at lower cost. He advocated reciprocal trade agreements to reduce duties gradually, pointing out that the agreement with

Canada in 1854 produced a tripling of exports and imports in one year, from $7 million to over $21 million.

But Guthrie did agree with Thomas Corwin on one aspect of the tariff: that the ad valorem Act of 1846 should be replaced with a per-unit tariff. He noted the difficulty of assessment with the ad valorem tariff, which needed appraisers in addition to weighers, gaugers, and measurers. He also felt there would be controversy over whether to use the foreign or domestic valuation, which could lead to fraud.

Guthrie received the most attention while heading the Treasury when he removed the New York Collector and the next-most when he created a controversy over his advocacy of taxing small bank notes out of existence; a final thing of note was his use of the Independent Treasury as a primitive vehicle for open market operations. He was called a ruthless reformer, although his policies did not differ much from the previous Democratic administration of Polk, but they did differ from those of the Whigs of Zachary Taylor and Millard Fillmore.

After leaving the Treasury, he successfully revived the languishing Louisville and Nashville Railroad, becoming its President in 1861, the year the Civil War started. He decided to be a Union man during that war and placed his railroad at the disposal of the U.S. government. This proved to be a crucial troop and supply support for the Southwestern campaigns.

In January 1865, the Kentucky Senate elected him to the U.S. Senate, and he bitterly opposed the Republican plan of Reconstruction. His bad health led to his resignation in February 1868, and he died on March 13, 1869.

BIBLIOGRAPHY

Annual Report of the Secretary of the Treasury. Washington, D.C.: U.S. Government Printing Office, various years.

Dictionary of American Bibliography. New York. Scribner, 1928.

Sechrest, Larry J. *Free Banking.* Westport, CT: Quorum, 1993.

Timberlake, Richard H. *Monetary Policy in the United States.* Chicago: University of Chicago Press, 1993.

DONALD R. WELLS

H

ALEXANDER HAMILTON (January 11, 1757–July 12, 1804). Alexander Hamilton, the first and most influential of all Secretaries of the Treasury, was born in the British colony of Nevis, West Indies, on January 11, 1757, and was mortally wounded at the age of forty-seven, on the banks of the Hudson River, in a duel with Aaron Burr on the morning of July 11, 1804.

He was the fourth son of Alexander Hamilton of Grange in Ayrshire, and his mother was Rachel Fawcett. He wrote that his father's affairs had soon "went to wreck," and his mother was living apart from him and dependent on relatives in St. Croix when she died in 1768. Alexander Hamilton was a virtual orphan by age eleven, even though his father lived until 1799.

His early education was brief and mainly due to the Reverend Hugh Knox, a Presbyterian clergyman of Nevis who took a keen interest in the boy and encouraged his progress. Before he was thirteen, it was necessary for him to earn a living, and he secured a job in the general store of Nicholas Cruger, a West Indian merchant. He attracted early attention with a provocative letter to a local newspaper describing a hurricane that swept St. Croix in 1772. His aunts were generous and reacted to his intense interest in a college education, and he was sent to New York in the fall of 1772, where he received preliminary instruction at Francis Barber's grammar school in Elizabethtown, New Jersey. Thereafter, he enrolled in King's College (now Columbia University) in the autumn of 1773. The initial phases of the American Revolution interrupted Hamilton's studies at King's College, and it was not until after the war that he resumed his studies, by then focused on law, and entered the bar as a professional career.

During the war, he was on General Washington's staff and distinguished himself mainly with his pen but also on the battlefield. At one point, Washington sent him to Albany to meet with General Horatio Gates and obtain troops after the Burgoyne campaign where he met Elizabeth Schuyler, the second daughter of General Philip Schuyler, whom he married on December 14, 1780. He later proclaimed the marriage to be a perfect match, and thereby he became connected with a very rich and powerful New York family; this was to prove beneficial in fostering his rise to prominence in government. "It is impossible to be happier than I am in a wife," he wrote in 1797, and he died tenderly devoted to her. He proved to be a dedicated family man, and with Elizabeth, he fathered eight children, one of whom was James Alexander Hamilton; the first child, Philip, was born on January 22, 1782. In fact, he eventually resigned from government because he was unable to adequately support his large family on the relatively meager civil service pay.

In July 1781 he commanded a battalion of light infantry, and on July 2, 1782, he was appointed Continental Receiver of Taxes; he was admitted to the New York City bar in the same year. On July 22, 1782, the New York legislature appointed him a delegate to the Continental Congress, where he was a member from 1782 to 1783. From 1783 to 1787 he practiced law in New York City; in 1784 he assisted in starting the Bank of New York, and in the following year, he assisted in founding the New York Society for Promoting the Manumission of Slaves. From January 12 to April 21, 1787, he was a member of the New York State Assembly and attended the federal Constitutional Convention in Philadelphia.

Hamilton had some leisure time during the war, and he studied finance and government. His letters to Robert Morris demonstrated how to amend the confederation and how to set up a national bank. His letters on the bank so impressed Morris that when Hamilton left the army and was independently studying law, Morris offered him a job as Continental Receiver of Taxes for New York. Collecting taxes in the existing regime was no fun at all and served to convince Hamilton of the defects of the confederation. He was saved from this tedious job by his election to Congress, taking his seat in November 1782.

His reputation as an acute and trustworthy financial adviser had been firmly established by the time the new government was set up, and President Washington naturally turned to him to help guide the financial policies of the fledgling nation through the tough road that lay ahead for the debt-ridden nation. Hamilton took the oath of office as the first Secretary of the Treasury on September 11, 1789.

His economic agenda for the nation was straightforward: indispensable to it was a strong centralized government in which resided powers over commerce and currency adequate to provide checks and balances over the particularism of local interests. Above all, the nation required a sound currency and a stable banking system to promote rapid economic growth and rising per capita real income, and these objectives required the sympathetic encouragement of the propertied classes.

Hamilton was brilliant as a political theorist. Together with Jay and Madison, Hamilton wrote The Federalist Papers; indeed, he contributed the lion's share to this widely read collection. These papers were designed to clarify the need for energetic central government and to influence New York voters in favor of the Constitution. It is thought that these classic sixty-three papers are possibly the most distinguished American contribution to the science of government. Hamilton believed that man's capacity for reason and justice makes free government possible, and his capacity for passion and injustice makes it necessary. *The Federalist* is perhaps the third-most sacred among all writings in American political history; the first two are the Declaration of Independence and the Constitution itself.

To fully understand Hamilton's contributions as Secretary of the Treasury, one must closely study and appreciate his five major policy papers presented to Congress: "Report on the National Bank (2nd. Report), December 13, 1790"; "Report on Mint and Coinage, January 28, 1791"; "First and Second Reports on the Public Credit, January 9, 1790, and January 15, 1795"; and "Report on the Subject of Manufactures, December 5, 1791." Hamilton's policies were both successful and lasting. Yet a perennial issue is whether he merely copied the British system, with its strong central bank and its sinking fund for the reduction and management of the public debt under the auspices of Mr. Pitt, Chancellor of the Exchequer. And did he borrow his major economic ideas from David Hume and Adam Smith?

In his "Report on the Subject of Manufactures," Hamilton has a remarkably modern analysis of the defects inherent in free trader logic. He embraced the argument of David Hume to counter the free trade thesis. Establishment of new industry is risky in untried enterprises; there are intrinsic difficulties in start-up, and other governments use artificial inducements and subsidies for their domestic producers to give them incentives and a competitive edge in world trade. If foreign exporters are subsidized, how could American firms, lacking equivalent government support, compete on a level playing field?

As Lodge observes, Hamilton argued for protecting young industries in order to remove the obstacles to business start-up, dismissing as overstated the concern that protection tends to create monopolies and benefit one class at the expense of the rest of the community. An important service to business is increasing access to capital.

He subordinated his political theory to his pragmatic economic analysis and had no sympathy for the widespread influence of the Physiocratic School with its agrarian and sociological bias. Instead, he aligned with development economics of the English Classical School that emerged from the Industrial Revolution. He was impressed by capitalism, capitalist credit systems with their banks, liquidity, debt funding, and money manipulation. Scholars have argued that Hamilton was determined to replicate in America a British system of finance, and the English system of industrialism appeared to him as the optimal way to achieve his vision for America. With the proven institutions of capitalism, such as the Bank of England and a strong central government, economic progress was assured. A centralized American capitalist system would be more efficient than a system based upon the centralizing agrarianism of Jefferson, and the power of the new federal state would be augmented with the increase of liquid wealth. His philosophy leans to David Hume, and he admired Hobbes and shared his belief that in the absolute state of nature life was "nasty, brutish, and short."

The Swanson thesis denies that Hamilton copied or imported English or French principles of finance. Swanson attacks the conventional wisdom about Hamilton's fiscal policy, arguing that his use of orthodox models and jargon would serve to instill public confidence in the maverick system he had devised. For instance, the copycat view (summarized by Otenasek) states that Hamilton's fiscal policies were "almost slavishly imitative" of the English system.

Against the English imitation thesis, Swanson posits that Hamilton in fact realized that to "market" his complicated scheme for spreading out the repayment of the public debt by long-term funding and using a flexible sinking fund, he would have to make it appear to be a very standard, tried and proven, English model. Jefferson, of course, saw through this ruse and accused Hamilton of using smoke and mirrors to obfuscate the issue and make an end run around the government's moral obligation to avoid straddling future generations with the old generation's debts.

For Jefferson, a sinking fund meant that the old debt would be fully retired with accumulated interest in arrears paid off within a few years. Jefferson's obsession for rapid repayment of the old debt made him especially critical of Hamilton's sinking fund. However, Hamilton's sharp calculations revealed that debt provision would require an annual interest payment of $4,587,445 on a total public debt of $79,124,465. In addition to this interest bill, one must add the then-annual cost of the operations of federal government. Thus, funding via the traditional English model would have required a vast increase in tax revenues. Hamilton was convinced that, as a practical matter, this would be totally infeasible.

Hamilton's accomplishments were bold and innovative; yet his originality may have been exaggerated. He was often criticized as being devoid of any sentiment or idealism. In particular, he was at times arrogant and fixated on his federalism, and on improving the system of credit and finance, with a cool indifference to the social consequences of his policies. He was not the open-minded scholar of history and politics as was, say, Jefferson. He is also characterized as believing the Republic could survive and prosper in its infancy only by enlisting the support of the wealthy merchants, capitalists, and investors and harnessing their interests to those of the central government. He supposedly thought it folly for the young Republic to challenge British economic and military supremacy, whatever the provocation. He believed that pure democracy would lead to mob rule. He looked to the mixed government of the British constitution, at least in theory a perfect balance of democratic (House of Commons), aristocratic (House of Lords), and monarchical (king or queen) elements, for useful models.

The main political problems in 1789 were economic and pitted the farmer against business groups for control of government. As a strong proponent of economic nationalism, Hamilton used all his energies to support and speak for the business, entrepreneurial sector of the economy. He adhered to the principle of class domination; and as an aristocrat married into one of New York's wealthiest families, he deliberately allied himself with the wealthy and landed elites.

He had little faith in the virtues and capacities of the common people. "I am not much attached to the majesty of the multitude," he said during the debate over the Constitution. His incredible comment, characteristically frank and widely deplored by Democrats, was: "The people!—the people is a great beast!" Yet this view is not always seen as a liability; in fact, he has remained one of America's most influential statesmen, and he left an indelible mark on our government's financial institutions, including the development of tools to meet our vast and evolving federal credit and revenue requirements in the past 200 years.

Hamilton inherited a titanic financial problem in September 1789, six months after the new government was formed. The public debt occasioned by the war and Confederation period included certificates, notes, bills of credit, and state debt. Hamilton reckoned the foreign debt, owed mainly to Holland and France, was $12 million, while the domestic debt, state and national, was $65 million. This $77 million was about $19 per farmer in America at that time. Proper funding would stabilize the value of the debt.

The keystone of the debt policy report was the unqualified maintenance of the national credit; the creditors had to have faith in the government. Granted, like all statesmen before or since, he believed that the economy could eventually "grow out of" its debt as national income and product expanded and revenue exceeded government expenditures in the long run. Optimism is eternal, and so is government's need for short- and long-term credit. The new federal government inaugurated its existence with a start-up loan. During September, October, and December 1789, the Bank of New York and the Bank of North America extended $170,000 to cover the paychecks of the President, Vice President, and Congress and other vital costs. In December of 1791, Hamilton's proposed Bank of the United States opened and promptly extended its first loan to the government for $400,000 by May 1792. By the end of that year, the government owed the new bank and the two older banks some $2.5 million. By 1795, the total of short-term borrowing from the Bank of the United States was $4.5 million; by 1796 it was $6.2 million.

Hamilton's plan to fund the war debt was hotly debated. Before anyone ever heard about Hamilton or the U.S. Treasury, many farmers, former soldiers, and artisans sold certificates of indebtedness for one-seventh face value, heavily discounted in the open market for securities. The plan was judged especially unfair by Revolutionary War veterans, who had been forced to sell paper money or certificates the Congress had issued (often their pay) at large discounts. Naturally, the old scrip holders felt Hamilton's funding at par would be a huge windfall profit to current holders, that is, speculators who had purchased these evidences of debt at bargain basement prices, due to the market's perceived risk of default on principal, due to their illiquidity owing to the uncertainties of the postwar union of states and factional divisions, and due to insiders trading on information asymmetries and the ignorance of original certificate holders. Hamilton's plan would confirm a "swindle" and add insult to injury by imposing a tax on old holders to make transfer payments of interest to refund certificates at 100 cents on the dollar to speculators who had guessed correctly. In fact, the value of government certificates was bid up in the market the moment news of Hamilton and his report became known to traders.

The Funding Act of 1790 provided for the issue of federal bonds sufficient to cover all exchanges of the old Continental and Confederation domestic debt. Hamilton also got his way over the assumption of state debts, but only by some horse trading: He negotiated a trade with representatives of the southern states. In exchange for their votes on this part of the funding proposal, the national capital would be moved from Philadelphia and located in a federal district in territory set aside by Virginia and Maryland (Washington, D.C.). Assumption of states' debts was part of Hamilton's goal of consolidating the interests of all the states in order to foster political unity. Left to their own devices, individual states would be forced to secure their own local revenue by adopting different policies of taxation, which would introduce confusion and inhibit industrial develop-ment. States would be strapped for cash because the federal government, in its revenue measures, would be preempting normal import duties revenues that states had depended upon. Of course, the southern states opposed assumption because their debts relative to population were much less than those of the North, and there would be frictional burdens of taxing the South more than proportionally to pay off the northern states' debts.

Hamilton's public debt program had two components, funding and a sinking fund. Funding was to pay the national debt interest; the sinking fund was to pay off the principal. The real secret of good public credit was to provide a foolproof method of extinguishing the debt at the time of its creation. A sinking fund was to be established from Post Office revenue, not to exceed $1 million, which would be earmarked to reduce principal of the debt as redeemed or to buy up govern-ment debt in the open market and retire it early. It is unclear why anyone, let alone Hamilton, could believe that the Post Office would make a profit. By mimicking the then-prevailing British experience, the sinking fund proposed proved to be a mechanism of little practical value. It had no permanent appro-priation out of the government's general revenues to serve as a basis for accu-mulative powers of a sum expanding by compound interest. Congress ended up giving the sinking fund only limited sources of income, the surplus revenues of 1790 plus the proceeds of foreign loans not to exceed $2 million.

Hamilton did not see the Revolutionary War debt (as it was being repaid) as a dead-weight burden on the new nation that ought to be repudiated, as most of the members of Congress believed. Rather, it represented a unique opportunity to revitalize the financial life of the country, increase liquidity and the supply of near money, enhance the country's credit rating, and lower domestic interest rates, which would stimulate investment, raise real estate prices, and benefit all lines of industry and commerce. Hamilton also persuaded Congress to assume payment of the debts of the several states on the ground that such indebtedness had been incurred chiefly during the Revolution by colonies fighting in a com-mon cause. While those states that had paid back most of their debt, such as

Virginia, objected, Hamilton emphasized that his proposal would establish the supremacy of the national government in finance and further strengthen the new nation's credibility.

Even when the revenue system expanded much faster than Hamilton's expectations, the federal government could not consistently balance its annual budget in its first decade. By January 1, 1801, the national debt was $7.5 million greater than it had been ten years earlier. Hamilton's funding and assumption plan had not solved the public debt problem but instead substituted a new problem for an old one. Deficits continued to plague the administrations of Washington and Adams.

The influential Madison was not able to block Hamilton's debt proposals. The assumption and funding measures passed the House of Representatives in July and August 1790, only after extensive debate and much legislative maneuvering.

The second major Hamilton report was on a national bank (December 13, 1790), and it was based on a ten-year study of European banking systems. Hamilton viewed a national bank as "the indispensable engine" driving the nation's finance. This report provided several solid reasons for establishing such a bank. The first was to increase the banking facilities of the country. The bank carried on the activities of any commercial bank—issuing notes (which served as paper money), holding deposits, and making loans. It also acted as a fiscal agent for the federal government, and because of its branches, it also could make interregional transfers of funds, help in tax collections, and provide depository services for government funds.

During the Revolutionary period, metallic money remained in the confusion of the earlier colonial period. Because of the constitutional prohibition on state bills of credit, the only paper currency was the bank notes of the three banks chartered in Boston, New York, and Philadelphia. The supply of money was partially determined by the issue of bank notes by the state banks. Furthermore, the national government had to rely on state banks for the deposit of Treasury funds and to act as fiscal agents to transfer funds. This situation was obviously unsatisfactory to the new Secretary of the Treasury. On December 14, 1790, Hamilton sent his proposal for a national bank to the House of Representatives.

There were at that time only three commercial banks in operation—The Bank of North America (Philadelphia, chartered 1781), the Bank of New York (1784), and the Bank of Massachusetts (Boston, 1784). Hamilton cogently argued that increasing the supply of bank credit would contribute to "the augmentation of the active or productive capital" of the economy and would aid economic growth. Hamilton presaged that as the American population shifted from relatively self-sufficient farm life with exchange and payment in kind to the interdependence of manufacturing and trade, money would be increasingly required as a medium of exchange.

A second motive for Hamilton's bank proposal was to aid his ambitious program to provide for the public debt. Under the Funding Act of 1790, the government had agreed to issue new high-grade securities to holders of the diverse public debts created to finance the Revolutionary War. Hamilton proposed that these new securities be accepted in payment for stock in the Bank of the United States. The securities would be a good asset for the bank, and the prospective profitability of bank stock would make investors eager to acquire the securities (available at prices below par) as a means of buying bank stock cheaply. Both bank and funding programs were part of Hamilton's broader goal of basing the newly formed government on the political support of the well-to-do.

A third purpose was that the new bank could aid the Treasury in managing its revenue collections and disbursements. In addition, the government would need temporary loans. The charter (to last for twenty years) was passed by Congress in February 1791, and the bank opened for business that December. Its capitalization of $10 million was the largest of any American corporation operating during its lifetime. The government "purchased" one fifth of the stock with funds borrowed from the bank. The charter imposed various restrictions on the bank's operations: It was not permitted to deal in commodities or real estate, or to charge more than 6 percent interest on loans, and its bank notes were to be redeemed in specie (gold and silver coin or the equivalent). But the charter did not state any specific or economic objectives to be pursued by the bank. Although Hamilton had not favored branch operations, the bank charter authorized them, and the bank operated branches in Boston, New York, Baltimore, Washington, Norfolk, Charleston, Savannah, and New Orleans, in addition to the head office in Philadelphia. It acted as fiscal agent for the government and, although forbidden to buy government securities in the open market, made "temporary loans" to the Treasury on several occasions.

Under Hamilton's proposal to Congress, the first function of the bank would be to operate as a commercial bank with partial reserves of specie and, through loans, augment the productive capital of the country. With lucidity, Hamilton delineated the functions of a bank as a financial intermediary and as a creator of funds needed for economic expansion so that interest rates would remain low. Following the pattern established by the Bank of England, the national bank would also assist public finance with loans to the national government. Other side benefits were to include the facilitation of tax payments by loans and discounts for persons in business who did not have liquid capital when national taxes fell due, and it would add to the quantity of paper money acceptable for payment of taxes. And although Hamilton at first did not anticipate a number of national bank branch offices, a bank with many branches would lower transactions costs of collecting and transporting coins paid as national taxes. His efficiency argument persuaded Congress even though James Madison argued that the monetary and fiscal powers of Article I, Section 8 of the Constitution gave Congress no express power to create a bank, and he dismissed the necessary-and-proper clause as a mere ruse. The final vote was thirty-nine in favor, twenty against.

Washington, prior to signing the bill, referred it to the Secretary of State, Thomas Jefferson, and to the Attorney General, Edmund Randolph, for their comments and opinions. Both quickly replied with written reports indicating that the bank bill was unconstitutional. Hamilton was provided an appropriate chance for a rebuttal; his logic in defense of the bill prevailed, and Washington signed the bill, granting a twenty-year charter to the first national bank.

The bank evolved to perform an expanded central banking function that its sponsors had not foreseen. This was a monetary stabilization function that prevented overissue of state bank notes with inflationary consequences. The state banks, unregulated by state governments, had convenient attitudes regarding the reserves that should be maintained in specie to meet demands. The Bank of the United States and its branches, by promptly returning bank notes and checks to the issuing state banks, pressured them to maintain adequate reserves in specie. This prevented them from otherwise unregulated overissue. Of course, not all of the serendipitous results can be attributed to Hamilton's banking genius.

On December 5, 1791, Hamilton, after several preliminary and painstaking draft efforts, submitted his most important and widely cited "Report on the Subject of Manufactures." He foresaw an American future that revolved around industry rather than agriculture. Even though Smith's *Wealth of Nations* had been available for ten or more years, its arguments extolling the benefits of free trade had not become widespread or politically significant by 1787 or 1790. It is possible to label the economic issues of the Constitutional Convention as a debate between mercantilists. Hamilton's *Report on the Subject of Manufactures* seems to fall into this methodological camp. However, even though some of Hamilton's measures superficially resemble the doctrines of mercantilists, there is an important distinction; namely, Hamilton believed in the broad development of the economy and the prospects of economic improvement for all sectors of the economy. He departed from the classical economists in that he foresaw economic opposition between manufacturer and landowner. He preached the doctrine of class harmony in the context of an expanding industrial economy. In this document, probably coauthored by Tench Coxe, Hamilton recommended barriers to international trade, such as duties set high enough to exclude imports of foreign articles that competed with domestic production, prohibitions on the export of materials of manufacture, bounties, premiums, statutory encouragement of new inventions, and various laws facilitating transportation. The leading policy of a young nation should be to preserve the balance of trade in its favor. David Hume was his authority (Ortenasek, 79).

Much of Hamilton's argument was pro bounties rather than tariffs, which on equity grounds were seen as more fair, since the entire community, rather than the customers of a specific industry, share the burden of protectionist policy. Hamilton argued that the greater prosperity of industry would serve to promote the welfare of other groups as well.

The report was partly a declaration of economic independence from the Old World to be achieved by a "well-balanced" economy attained via government-protected and -encouraged industry. The well-balanced economy concept recognized the interdependence of various sectors, that the output of one sector is the input of another, and certainly did not downplay or exclude the agricultural sector, as the anti-Federalists alleged. As Cantor states:

In the five years that ensued after his appointment as Secretary, Hamilton completed the work which lies at the foundation of our system of administration, gave life and meaning to the Constitution, and by his policy developed two great political parties. Because he had a hand in every phase of public policy in our early government, he was more than a mere Secretary of Treasury; he was, de facto, Washington's prime minister. (76)

In a letter to Washington of August 18, 1792, Hamilton presented his case for an excise tax system as a new key to reducing the debt, and the need for deficits was to be met by the levying of new excise taxes. Hamilton's "Report on the Subject of Manufactures" had boldly urged the adoption of a high, protective tariff, well above the level required to raise revenues. Such a policy was designed to aid fledgling American industries by hindering foreign competitors and thereby stimulating development of new domestic industries. This was designed to create a balanced economy that would make the nation stronger and free it from dependency on foreign suppliers of finished goods. However, collections of import duties under the Tariff Act of 1790 were not doing the job; they were insufficient to fund the state debts. The House, again led by Madison, who feared a concentration of power in the national government, rejected this third and most controversial of Hamilton's reports. The Revenue Act of 1792 included merely a slight escalation of tariff rates.

By his systematic refunding and payment of the country's debt, Hamilton was able to reduce annual interest charges, and this resulted in savings for the government. To secure the income needed to meet expenses, he presented detailed proposals for customs duties on imports, excise taxes on domestic goods, especially distilled liquor, and procedures for the rapid sales of lands in the national domain.

The new "whiskey tax" had brought about unexpected difficulties; it forced Congress reluctantly, by the act of March 3, 1791, to tax domestic spirits on a sliding scale ranging from nine to twenty-five cents a gallon. The tax on whiskey fell directly on a not-very-numerous group of self-sufficient frontiersmen; it hardly touched the rich landed gentry; it probably fell hardest on small farmers and merchants. The frontiersmen of the four western counties of Pennsylvania particularly were distressed by the excise tax on liquor distilled in the United States. When the war interrupted the importation of rum, many farmers began to distill their own corn whiskey. They subsequently found they could sell their product at a profit. Raising marketable corn had special disadvantages: Transportation of corn to market was difficult and expensive and often involved net losses. Whiskey, on the other hand, had high value per volume and could be used as money in barter trade for other commodities. Hamilton felt sorry for these small farmers and realized that all taxes involve some distortions and equity problems. He did not want collecting agents to have indiscriminate power or jurisdiction to search the homes and buildings of liquor producers; and he favored tax exemptions to owners of small stills with a capacity under fifty gallons.

Hamilton turned his attention to money. He was convinced that the nation was suffering from specie anemia: a shortage of specie, inadequate to support either commerce or Treasury revenue. He proposed a tax "in kind"—paid in goods—to economize on scarce real cash balances; this would presumably free transactions balances to be used for private commerce. Under a system of specie payments, it was required by law or custom that fiat money, usually in the form of bank notes or government paper money issues, be redeemed at par and upon request of the issuing bank or the Treasury in metallic coin. Because our Founding Fathers remembered with disdain the hyperinflation episode caused by excess printing of paper money during the Revolution, and the excess of some states during the Confederation, the decision was made to adopt a specie standard of value. This was implicit in the constitutional grant of power to Congress "to coin money" and "regulate the value thereof" and in the prohibition that the states refrain from the emission of bills of credit or from making anything but gold or silver a legal tender.

The maintenance of specie payments in the United States was difficult from the very beginning. Hamilton recommended in 1791, and Congress adopted in 1792, a bimetallic standard of value, under which the dollar was defined in terms of both silver and gold. The main problem with maintaining specie payments during most of the nineteenth century was America's typically unfavorable trade balance. The tendency for specie to be either hoarded or exported in payment for foreign goods and services was continually exacerbated in times of war and economic crisis. The problems continued far beyond Hamilton's tenure at the Treasury.

It is not widely understood that over the first decade the finances of our new government were far from secure. When in 1790 Hamilton provided his "Report on the Public Credit," he estimated that out of a total annual expenditure of $2,839,200, some 80 percent would be required to service the public debt. For the first ten years, interest charges took 41 percent of all federal revenue, a figure never approached in any subsequent period. As of the February 1996 *Economic Report of the President*, the figure is 17 percent (p. 369, B-76). The revenue came almost solely from customs, and hence upon foreign trade. If a war were to break out, this would have disrupted collections and forced borrowing in a thin domestic market. A system of internal revenue was desperately needed, and in that first critical decade, excises provided about 8 percent of government income. But the collection costs were high, and opposition was intense, resulting, for example, in the Whiskey Rebellion in western Pennsylvania.

On January 28, 1791, Hamilton presented Congress with his Report on Mint and Coinage. Hamilton opted for a bimetallic currency. This means both gold and silver coins, fixed in relative value by law, would be minted and used as money. Here an argument was made for a unit of account and medium of exchange expressed in both gold and silver: a bimetallic standard. While gold was to be preferred to silver for certain reasons, he held that it was not safe to reduce the amount of the medium of exchange by eliminating the monetary value of silver. Hamilton recommended that the mint ratio between gold and silver be one to fifteen—a proportion corresponding to the bullion values at that time—and proposed that the monetary unit consist of 23.75 grains of pure gold or 371.25 grains of pure silver, the amount of silver corresponding as nearly as could be ascertained with that of the Spanish dollar in actual circulation, "each answering to a dollar" in its own currency. This implied the coinage of $10 and $1 gold pieces, $1.10 silver pieces, and one cent and one-half cent copper pieces. Hamilton hoped that the use of both precious metals would increase the total money supply. And with both gold and silver money circulating, he reasoned, the commerce otherwise hampered by a lack of the medium of exchange would now prosper.

The Mint Act of April 2, 1792, basically adopted all of Hamilton's proposals except for the provision of coining a gold dollar. More of the debate was over the cost of the mint and where it was to be located than over the choice of metals to be used. Also, there was a furious debate over whether the coins should be stamped with the picture of the current President or the likeness of the Goddess of Liberty, a more politically neutral statement. The mint was set up in Philadelphia, initially under the control of the Secretary of State. Later, under the advice of Hamilton, it was transferred to the Treasury Department. Complaints that the mint was inefficient and too small were accompanied by arguments that it was too expensive, and very early in its history, attempts were made to privatize the entire operation.

Modern economists find Hamilton's specie logic a bit naive. Bimetallism does require the government to fix the relative value of gold and silver and then freely exchange gold and silver coins at that fixed exchange rate. The problem is, since the supply and demand for gold and silver are not fixed—both metals were continuously mined and both were used in ornamentation and jewelry—there was no reason to believe that the market value of the two metals would remain constant over time. And here lies the difficulty: if the relative price of the two diverged from the U.S. mint price by just a slight percentage, only one of the two metals would remain in circulation as money. The mechanism is simple. If the government offers to swap silver for gold, or vice versa, at a ratio of 15 to 1, and the rest of the world values gold more highly, requiring fully 16 times the weight in silver to relinquish a given amount of gold, Americans can then collect 15 pounds of silver coins and buy 1 pound of gold coins with the silver obtained from the mint. They then ship the pound of gold to London, where world prices prevail, and exchange it for 16 pounds of silver coins. After bringing the silver back to the United States, the trader can once again visit the government mint, this time walking away with 1.067 pounds of gold (16 pounds of silver = 16/15ths pound of gold = 1.067 pounds of gold). This process of arbitrage continues until it is no longer possible to make a risk-free profit or until the government mint runs out of gold. In this example, only the metal that is overvalued at the mint—silver, in this case—remains in circulation as money. If a merchant were lucky enough to be paid gold coins for goods, he would hoard them or sell them in London. The notion that bad money drives out good money is known as "Gresham's Law."

At the end of the Federalist era of domination, the federal government was devoting over 55 percent of its expenditures to the Army and Navy. Another 30 percent went to interest on the national debt. When Hamilton took office, the proportion of interest payments in the government budget was higher than any time in history, namely, 45 percent. Historians conclude that the Federalists had saddled the government with a huge military and interest budget that threatened to topple the entire structure of federal finance. In 1800, the outgoing Adams administration had to resort to the expedient of incurring long-term loans to defray current budget deficits. This is a practice that is very much alive and well today, even in peacetime.

There was a significant net reduction in the domestic and assumed components of the funded debt during Hamilton's administration, as the sinking fund managed to purchase $2,265,023 worth of debt. This came from sinking fund income, namely, from surplus revenue, from foreign loans, and from interest accumulated on the debt purchased.

That the funding system was not used by the Treasury and Congress as a system of domestic borrowing does not imply that no new borrowing of any kind took place in Hamilton's tenure as Secretary. On several occasions, he found revenues inadequate to cover rising government expenditures. The Indian wars, the problems with England, the Algerine troubles, and the western insurrection all produced extraordinary expenses. To cover these government expenses, duties on imports were increased in both 1792 and 1794. New duties were levied on carriages, retail wine and foreign liquor sales, snuff, sugar, and property sold at auction. In this connection, Hamilton pioneered Tax Anticipation Bonds. Because the purposes for which these duties were levied were urgent, and there were lags in collection, the new revenues had to be anticipated to meet the unexpected new expenses.

Thus, during Hamilton's administration, temporary loans in anticipation of revenue were secured from the Bank of New York, the Bank of North America, and the Bank of the United States. By January 1, 1795, the temporary debt to state and the national bank was $2.9 million. Hamilton did not contemplate reproducing the English practice of building up a large floating debt, funding it, and then replicating the process over and over again. These temporary bank loans were based on genuine anticipations of taxes in the sense that the new revenues when collected were adequate to liquidate their respective loans.

As we have seen, Hamilton believed in maintaining a sound credit, in keeping the public debt within bounds, and today would be considered an advocate of a managed currency. He recognized that private enterprise, unregulated, was subject to abuse. He criticized bank abuses as "pernicious" and insisted that "public utility" was "more truly the object of public banks than private profit." He advocated that the federal government improve the infrastructure and cement politicoeconomic interdependence via publicly built highways, canals, and communications systems. Regarding immigration, he was for an open economy, arguing that American government should invigorate our system "by opening an asylum" to the poor and oppressed of other lands.

As an advocate of the supremacy of the Union, his views were to be upheld by Jackson and vindicated by President Abraham Lincoln. Hamilton also anticipated the later assumption by the Supreme Court of powers for the federal government on the basis of three clauses of the Constitution: the necessary and proper clause, the general welfare clause, and the commerce clause. These three important clauses, as Hamilton interpreted them, have together provided the constitutional foundation for much of the activity of our modern federal government in such economic areas as finance, business regulation, taxation, social welfare, and other activities. To Hamilton, the steady expansion of presidential powers by the end of the twentieth century would have been a vindication of his striving for central administrative power, energy, leadership, and efficiency. A leader does not merely react to the masses or public opinion; he or she sets goals and educates the public to the need to attain those goals to achieve social welfare.

Hamilton continually saw political power behind financial power. The funding of the debt, for instance, he believed was necessary not only to establish strong credit but to induce the rentier class receiving interest on the debt to support the new government's aims. From the outset of his term as Secretary of the Treasury, Hamilton tried to convince Congress that Americans had to learn "to distinguish between oppression and the necessary exercise of lawful authority." Hamilton's interest in levying taxes other than tariffs, and in enforcing the federal government's power to levy an excise tax on whiskey, had as much to do with his desire to strengthen government as it did with the need to raise money. Throughout his career, Hamilton remained consistently the extreme centralizer. Politics aside, he continues to be revered as the greatest of all the Secretaries of the Treasury.

It can be agreed that the success of Hamilton's fiscal policies also depended greatly on the quality of their administration, which was always carried out by a small army of subordinates who required and received constant guidance, advice, and supervision from Hamilton. Collectors of the customs in every major seaport were provided detailed instructions for enforcing the revenue laws and reported directly to the Secretary. Hamilton guided the activities of the Coast Guard, personally negotiated contracts for the construction and repair of lighthouses, maintained a close control over the operation of the excise laws, and was the most active of the commissioners of the sinking fund established in 1790 to superintend purchases of the public debt. He might be compared to a prime minister as opposed to a Cabinet member. Offices did not make this man. Hamilton's fiscal activities spilled over into other government departments, and his passion for accuracy and efficiency, as well as his well-documented ambition, opened him up to charges of interdepartmental meddling.

Hamilton was a mere forty-seven years old when Burr's bullet ended his life on July 12, 1804. The Hamilton-Burr feud is interesting. The only mystery is why the duel did not take place years earlier. In 1782, Burr practiced law in New York City, where he and Hamilton became bitter rivals. Burr was elected to the New York State Assembly and appointed State Attorney General in 1789. He was elected to the U.S. Senate in 1790 in a battle against Hamilton's father-in-law. In 1800, Aaron Burr was nominated for Vice President. Confusion arose in the voting for President and Vice President in the electoral college, and this resulted in a tie between Burr and Jefferson. The decision went to the House of Representatives, where after several days and thirty-five ballots the tie was unbroken.

Using a letter-writing campaign, Hamilton, whose contempt for Burr outweighed his strong political opposition of Jefferson, was able to swing his fellow Federalists to switch their support to Jefferson. Thus, as a result of the thirty-sixth ballot, much to his disappointment, Burr lost the presidency and became Vice President (1801–1805). This was not the end of the saga: he was nominated for Governor of New York in 1804, and again Hamilton worked strenuously behind the scenes to ensure his defeat. The long-standing rivalry between Burr and Hamilton had erupted again during the election campaign, and this was the last straw, resulting in Burr's challenging Hamilton to a duel. Burr was a ruined politician by the age of forty-eight but far from finished. He had broken with the Republicans and failed the Federalists. Hamilton was responsible. This was obviously not the first time that Hamilton had crossed his path, but it was to be the last time. In June 1804, barely six weeks after the New York gubernatorial election, Burr wrote to his arch enemy, demanding a retraction of a slur on his character by Hamilton and reported widely in the press. Hamilton refused to retract, Burr challenged him to the infamous duel, and Hamilton accepted. It was sheer folly for Hamilton to accept. First, he was totally opposed to dueling, partly because his son had been killed in a duel. Second, he certainly did not need to establish his courage, which was acknowledged by all.

Hamilton's mysterious life has been the subject of hundreds of biographies. He was first Secretary of the Treasury at age thirty-two and was one of the "little band of patriots" who had helped Washington to unite the states into a permanent Union at the Constitutional Convention of 1787. Hamilton agitated to free the slaves, to establish judicial supremacy, to found a national bank, and to create a triple-A credit rating for U.S. borrowing abroad. He was the founder of the first New York bank, the first conglomerate corporation, and the oldest continuously published newspaper in the United States (the New York *Post*); and in *The Federalist Papers*, he explicated the meaning of the Constitution for all American generations to come. His brief in *People v. Croswell* remains one of the most eloquent defenses of freedom of the press.

In Trinity Churchyard in Lower Manhattan is the sarcophagus where he and his wife Elizabeth Schuyler Hamilton are interred, a short block west of 57 Wall Street, the address of their first New York City home. Their last home was Hamilton Grange, at 287 Convent Avenue in Harlem, a modest two-story house set back from the sidewalk. In the front yard amid a weed patch on a granite pedestal beside a small flagpole is a grimy bronze statue of Hamilton in greatcoat and knee pants. Of the several inscriptions is one by Daniel Webster that reads, "He smote the rock of the national resources and abundant streams of revenue gushed forth; he touched the dead corpse of public credit and it sprang to its feet."

BIBLIOGRAPHY

Cantor, Milton, ed. *Hamilton: Great Lives Observed*. Englewood Cliffs, NJ: Prentice-Hall, Inc., 1971.

Dorfman, Joseph. *The Economic Mind in American Civilization, 1806–1865*. Vol. 1. New York: Viking Press, 1946.

Dunbar, Charles F. "Some Precedents Followed by Alexander Hamilton." *Quarterly Journal of Economics* 3 (1889). Harvard University, George H. Ellis of Boston. New York: Kraus Reprint Corporation, 1961, 32–59.

Hamilton, Alexander, James Madison, and John Jay. *The Federalist Papers*. With Introduction by Clinton Rossiter. New York: A Mentor Book published by the New American Library, 1961.

Hendrickson, Robert A. *The Rise and Fall of Alexander Hamilton*. New York: Dodd, Mead and Company, 1981.

Lodge, Henry Cabot. *Alexander Hamilton*. Boston: Houghton Mifflin, 1882.

Mitchell, Broadus. *Alexander Hamilton*. 2 vols. New York: Macmillan, 1957–1962.

Otenasek, Mildred Busek. *Alexander Hamilton's Financial Policies*. Dissertations in American Economic History, 1939. Reprint: New York: Arno Press, 1977.

Swanson, Donald F. *The Origins of Hamilton's Fiscal Policies*. University of Florida Monographs, Social Sciences, No. 17. Gainesville: University of Florida Press, 1963.

C. DANIEL VENCILL

DAVID F. HOUSTON (February 17, 1866–September 2, 1940). David Franklin Houston enjoyed success as an educator, governmental administrator, and business executive. After a distinguished career in higher education, Houston joined Woodrow Wilson's administration in 1913 as Secretary of Agriculture. On February 2, 1920, he replaced Carter Glass as Treasury Secretary. After the Wilson presidency ended in 1921, Houston entered private business.

Houston spent his youth in humble conditions. He was born in Monroe, North Carolina, on February 17, 1866, to William Henry Houston and Cornelia Anne (Stevens) Houston; he had one older brother and one older sister. His father tried farming, running a country store, and trading horses and mules.

Following graduation from the College of South Carolina in 1887, he embarked on a career in education. He served as a school superintendent in Spartanburg, South Carolina, from 1888 to 1891. From 1891 to 1894, he studied economics and political science in graduate school at Harvard University, where he earned an M.A. degree (1892). Houston next went to the University of Texas at Austin, where he taught political science from 1894 to 1902.

At the University of Texas, his life changed in numerous ways. He married Helen Beall on December 11, 1895; they had five children. He published his most distinguished scholarly work: *A Critical Study of Nullification in South Carolina* (1896). Houston successfully placed the nullification dispute into the larger economic and social context rather than the traditional exclusive focus on personalities. He began his administrative career by serving as the Dean of the faculty from 1899 to 1902.

Houston's administrative career blossomed for several reasons. His integrity and high academic standards won support from his faculty colleagues. A former professor, Charles W. Eliot—President of Harvard University—also strongly endorsed Houston. Within a decade, Houston served as President of the Agricultural and Mechanical College of Texas (1902–1905), as President of the University of Texas at Austin (1905–1908), and as Chancellor of Washington University in St. Louis (1908–1912).

Although his future as a university administrator appeared to be bright, he left Washington University to join the Wilson administration in 1913. Houston had first met Wilson at the College of South Carolina where Wilson's uncle (Dr. James Woodrow) taught political science. While at Washington University, Houston twice talked with Wilson when Wilson had speaking engagements in St. Louis. In 1911, Edward M. House—Houston's good friend from Austin and an intimate member of Wilson's inner circle—arranged for Houston to talk with Wilson about tariff and currency issues. Houston later wrote papers concerning tariff and currency issues for Wilson's campaign. Having received a classical economic training at Harvard, Houston vigorously defended free trade—a position that Wilson shared. In 1913, Wilson accepted the House's recommendation that he appoint Houston as Secretary of the Department of Agriculture. Houston generally favored less governmental intervention into the economy than did most other members of the Wilson administration. He, however, was willing to accept Wilson's decisions to intervene. Although Houston and President Wilson never became close socially, they apparently respected each other.

Houston's interest in agricultural issues began while growing up on a farm. He became involved in promoting attempts to improve rural life during his tenure at Texas A&M, with his emphasis being efforts to improve rural education and transportation. Thus, he was no stranger to the problems of agriculture prior to accepting Wilson's nomination.

In 1926, Houston wrote that he believed the Department of Agriculture's role was "to promote more efficient production, to improve the processes of marketing, to create better credit facilities for the farmer, to make rural life more profitable and attractive, and to make more of the benefits of modern science accrue to the rural population" (15). To accomplish his objectives, Houston reorganized the Agriculture Department. He placed more emphasis on education of farmers and on distribution and marketing of agricultural output than did his predecessors. During his tenure, the department established an Office of Information, an Office of Markets, and a Cooperative Extension Service through passage of the

Smith-Lever Agricultural Extension Act (1914). He also was instrumental in promoting the Federal Aid Road Act (1916) and the Smith-Hughes Vocational Educational Act (1917).

Houston played a role in developing several economic policies during Wilson's administration. He and Treasury Secretary William McAdoo toured the country to collect information concerning the organization of the Federal Reserve System. The Federal Reserve Act had provided for "not less than eight nor more than twelve" districts. Houston realized that from an economic standpoint there should be less than eight districts. He understood, however, that political expediency required the maximum twelve districts with a disportionate number (relative to financial resources) in the South and West. Many critics claimed that several districts were seriously undercapitalized, but Houston countered that although the system was decentralized, it was a national system. Each district bank could draw on resources from the other districts.

Houston supported the Underwood tariff that significantly but gradually lowered tariff rates. He characteristically opposed efforts of farmers who lobbied him for protection; his most heated disputes were with the sugar industry. Houston wanted to promote agriculture that could be sustained without governmental help, and he thought the U.S. sugar industry was not competitive in world markets. He urged Louisiana agriculture to diversify away from cane sugar, and he argued that beet sugar was only sustainable in certain mountainous regions.

Houston was skeptical about establishing a rural credit system that would supply credit to farmers at preferential rates. He convinced the Wilson administration to initially oppose this legislation. However, the political momentum was too strong; and Congress finally passed the Federal Farm Loan Act in 1916. Houston then established the best system of rural credit that he could.

Houston strongly supported the U.S. entry into World War I. He urged U.S. farmers to increase production during 1917 and 1918. By late 1918 with victory imminent, he urged farmers to reduce production as he realized that after the war farmers would face a difficult transition back to a peacetime economy.

Houston was content with staying in the Department of Agriculture. Wilson, however, wanted him to replace Carter Glass, who was leaving the Treasury Department to enter the Senate. Houston reluctantly accepted his new post and became Secretary of the Treasury on February 2, 1920.

Because the war had ended and government outlays were rapidly falling, Houston's tenure at the Treasury was not concerned with new large-scale borrowing. Although there was no new borrowing, Houston's Treasury had to refinance maturing debt and begin plans to retire the debt. Houston differed from his predecessors—McAdoo and Glass—by floating the debt at market rates rather than at preferential rates. To retire the debt, Houston wanted to restrain government spending—he convinced Wilson to oppose the Soldier's Bonus plan— and to keep tax revenues high. He supported some tax reform: ending the excess profits tax, the tax surcharge, and several excise taxes.

Houston's most controversial actions occurred in his role of exofficio member and Chair of the Federal Reserve System. He possessed very classical monetary ideas similar to those of his Harvard mentor, Professor Charles Dunbar. Houston believed that the Federal Reserve needed to adopt policies that would reduce "speculative" spending. He opposed holding the discount rate below market rates because that policy, he believed, would add to inflationary pressures. The Fed belatedly had begun raising the discount rate in late 1919. During 1920, Houston supported subsequent increases in the discount rate. The tighter monetary policy contributed to the sharp deflation and mild recession that occurred during 1920 and 1921. The economy quickly recovered and entered a period of expansion that essentially continued until 1929.

Houston realized that the economy was in the process of making a dramatic, and traumatic, shift from a war- to a peacetime economy. He believed that government could do little to relieve the suffering imposed by a transition that could be harsh, particularly for farmers. Houston considered the recession to be necessary for a realignment of relative prices. He realized, moreover, that as European agricultural production recovered from wartime difficulties, agricultural prices would fall relative to other prices. He believed that prosperity for U.S. farmers resided in free trade policies that opened up foreign markets to U.S. exports. He also advocated educational policies that taught farmers how to improve marketing techniques and to diversify production. To support his ideas, Houston wrote Wilson's veto messages concerning extension of War Finance Corporation credits for agriculture and concerning protectionist legislation aimed at agricultural markets.

Farmers vilified Houston and the Fed's credit policies. They convinced Congress to investigate the Fed's policies during 1920. Farmers were looking for someone to blame for the decline in farm prices, and Houston became the unfortunate "villain."

Houston left office at the end of the Wilson administration on March 3, 1921. He embarked on a career in private business. He served as President of Bell Telephone Securities Company (1921–1925), as Financial Vice President of American Telephone and Telegraph Company (1925–1927), and as President of the Mutual Life Insurance Company of New York (1927–1940). Between 1921 and 1926, he frequently contributed articles concerning public policy issues to periodicals. In 1926, he published a two-volume memoir of his governmental service. Because he opposed the Ku Klux Klan, he attracted some support as a potential compromise candidate who might break the deadlock at the 1924 Democratic National Convention that was held in New York City. After 1926, he essentially disappeared from the U.S. public policy scene. Houston died from a heart attack on September 2, 1940; his wife had died the previous January.

Houston was a successful administrator in his academic, business, and governmental positions. He was not an extrovert who flamboyantly promoted his programs. Instead, he earned people's respect with his cautious, well-reasoned approach to issues and decisions. His contemporaries, including President Wilson, valued his advice and discretion. The New York Times editorial praised

Houston: "Several men who have served in the Cabinet have afterward come to New York. It is doubtful if any of them ever disclosed higher qualities of vigor and integrity than has ex-Secretary David F. Houston" ("D. F. Houston Dies," 17).

Houston possessed a lifelong interest in economic and political issues, particularly those relating to agriculture. He sincerely wanted to improve the quality of rural life and believed his tenure as Agricultural Secretary succeeded in this objective. His experience as Treasury Secretary was more controversial. Although he genuinely grieved for the farmers, he considered the postwar deflation to be part of a necessary adjustment process.

BIBLIOGRAPHY

"D. F. Houston Dies; Served in Cabinet." New York Times, September 3, 1940, 17.

Houston, David Franklin. A Critical Study of Nullification in South Carolina. New York: Longmans, Green and Co., 1896; reprint: New York: Russell and Russell, 1967.

————. "Money and Prices—Discussion." American Economic Review, supp. 1 (April 1911): 46–52.

————. "What You Need to Know About Federal Taxation." World's Work 42 (October 1921): 586–89.

————. "Taxes—Which and Why." World's Work 43 (November 1921): 103–7.

————. Eight Years with Wilson's Cabinet, 1913–1920; With a Personal Estimate of the President. 2 vols. Garden City, NY: Doubleday, Page & Company, 1926.

————, comp. Ordinances of Secession and Other Documents, 1860–1861. New York: A. Lovell & Company, 1893.

Link, Arthur S. "David Franklin Houston." In Dictionary of American Biography, edited by Robert Livingston Schuyler, 321–22. Supp. 2. New York: Charles Scribner's Sons, 1958.

Page, Arthur W. "Houston, of Agriculture." World's Work 27 (December 1913): 149–59.

Payne, John W., Jr. "David F. Houston: A Biography." Ph.D. dissertation, University of Texas, 1953.

ROBERT STANLEY HERREN

GEORGE M. HUMPHREY (March 8, 1890–January 20, 1970). George Magoffin Humphrey was imbued from early childhood with a peculiarly American conservatism. Possessed of the righteousness and self-confidence that comes from being pampered and provided for, he led the life of high accomplishment to which he was bred. His eventual attainment of the office of Secretary of the Treasury—a position he held from January 21, 1953, to July 29, 1957—was not the zenith of his life; it served merely as an epilogue to an extraordinarily successful career.

He was born on March 8, 1890, in Cheboygan, Michigan, to Watts Sherman Humphrey, an attorney, and Caroline (Magoffin) Humphrey, a former schoolteacher. In the year following his birth the family moved to Saginaw, where the Humphreys soon became one of the leading families. The eldest of four children, George enjoyed a comfortable and secure childhood. He was given his first pony at the age of eight and acquired a lifelong love of horses. He played halfback for his high school in Saginaw when they won the state title in 1908, and he served as president of his class for two years.

Upon graduation Humphrey enrolled at the University of Michigan to study engineering. However, after three semesters he changed his mind and transferred to Michigan Law School. He obtained a law degree in 1912 after serving as editor of the *Michigan Law Review* and being elected to the Order of the Coif, the national honor society for students of law. He was admitted to the Michigan bar that same year.

He joined his father's law firm, which then became Humphrey, Grant, & Humphrey, and married Pamela Stark, his childhood sweetheart, in 1913. Over the succeeding four years Humphrey led the life of a small-town lawyer. Most of his work consisted of defending the Michigan Central and Grand Trunk railroad companies against damage and personal injury claims. Over the same period, he operated a lumber business and, in 1917, was considering an opportunity to become Executive Vice President of the largest bank in Saginaw (Coughlan, 102). It was at this time that his life changed abruptly and irreversibly.

Richard Grant, a partner in the Humphrey law firm, was appointed general counsel for the M. A. Hanna Company of Cleveland, Ohio; he asked George Humphrey to join him as an assistant. Although Humphrey had previously refused to go to Detroit to join the legal staff of Michigan Central and knew only a few people in Cleveland, he decided to accept Grant's invitation. "Why in God's name I went to Cleveland, I'll never know. . . . But these things have just happened in my life like fate. A certain combination of circumstances—I don't know what" (Coughlan, 102).

The M. A. Hanna Company had been founded in 1886 by Marcus A. Hanna, who later served as Senator from Ohio as well as becoming the preeminent political figure in the Midwest. Beginning as a provider of groceries and supplies to miners and trappers in the Great Lakes area, the firm had grown into the predominant coal, iron ore, and shipping conglomerate of the region. Humphrey's first task was to untangle the tax affairs of the company. His managerial skills soon became apparent, and his subsequent rise in Hanna was impressively rapid; within a year he had succeeded Grant as general counsel. At that time Hanna was operated as a partnership, and upon the death of one of the principals in 1920, Humphrey was elected a partner and given authority over Hanna's iron ore operations.

The partnership agreement was dissolved in 1922 when Hanna became incorporated. Humphrey was appointed a Vice President of the new corporation and helped guide it from the financial doldrums that ensued during the postwar recession of 1921. Humphrey became Executive Vice President of Hanna in 1926 and promptly set about reorganizing and streamlining its diverse operations. Obsolete and unprofitable properties and business ventures were eliminated, while the profitable and productive operations were consolidated. Under his direction Hanna became a highly successful and constantly expanding industrial enterprise, and Humphrey was duly appointed President in 1929.

During the succeeding two decades Humphrey involved Hanna in a series of lucrative industries and consortia. Among these were the National Steel Corporation, the Pittsburgh Consolidation Coal Company, Phelps Dodge (a copper manufacturer), the Industrial Rayon Corporation, Durez Plastics and Chemicals, and two Cleveland banks. In the 1940s Humphrey foresaw the eventual exhaustion of the Mesabi iron ore lode in Minnesota and organized the Iron Ore Company of Canada in a $200 million venture to develop the rich ore deposits in Labrador. In May 1952 Humphrey became Chairman of the Board of the M. A. Hanna Company; November brought an invitation from President-elect Eisenhower to become Secretary of the Treasury for the new Republican administration.

Humphrey had become Chairman of the Business Advisory Council of the Department of Commerce in 1946. There he came in contact with Paul Hoffman, head of the Economic Cooperation Administration. In 1948, Hoffman asked Humphrey to lead the Industrial Advisory Committee, a delegation of businessmen formed to advise the Allied powers regarding the dismantling of German industrial plants. Humphrey argued against eliminating a large number of plants, maintaining that they would be more useful to European recovery if left in operation (Gafton, 64). His tactful and diplomatic handling of this delicate endeavor favorably impressed General Lucius D. Clay, administrator of the American zone of occupation. It was General Clay who recommended George Humphrey to President-elect Eisenhower and subsequently approached Humphrey about becoming Treasury Secretary (Adams, 53).

Humphrey openly admitted to mixed feelings. He had planned the Labrador deal as the crowning achievement of his career, intending to enter into a retirement devoted to horses, hunting, and grandchildren. But as a lifelong Republican and a businessman who had roundly criticized the New Deal and the Fair Deal for ruining the country, he felt compelled to accept the challenge of being a member of the first GOP administration in twenty years (Coughlan, 106). Eisenhower promptly initiated a meeting and thereafter developed a warm, personal relationship with Humphrey. He later commented, "In cabinet meetings I always wait for George Humphrey to speak. I sit back and listen to others talk while he doesn't say anything. I know that when he speaks up he will say just what I am thinking" ("Secretary of the Treasury," 63).

At the Senate confirmation hearings in January 1953 Humphrey was questioned extensively about his finances. While he had resigned all official positions and directorships, he had chosen to retain his stock in Hanna and its principal affiliates. He defended this choice by arguing that the liquidation of his stock would not resolve potential problems of conflict of interest. "For instance, suppose I sold everything I had. . . . How would you account for what you received for it? Would you leave it in cash in the bank? If so, would you then be under the compulsion of favoring in some way the bank because, of course, the Secretary deals with the bank in some way or another? Would you put it in government bonds? If so, there is nothing that the Secretary of the Treasury could so influence by his conduct as government bonds" (Humphrey, 14).

As Secretary of the Treasury, Humphrey set himself the following tasks: balancing the budget by cutting waste and defense spending, cutting taxes and revising the tax structure, allowing interest rates to be market determined, shifting more of government debt into long-term rather than short-term obligations, and reducing the debt.

His first challenge arose even before Eisenhower took office. On January 3, 1953, Representative Daniel Reed, Chairman of the Ways and Means Committee, introduced "House Bill No. 1" to reduce income taxes by 11 percent on July 1, 1953, concomitant with the expiration of the excess profits tax on June 30. Reed argued that cutting taxes would force reductions in expenditures and facilitate the balancing of the budget. Humphrey was sympathetic to this position but much more interested in putting a brake on inflation and, thus, argued against the tax cut. Over the next few months a large amount of congressional maneuvering was required to prevent the Reed bill from emerging from the Republican Congress as law.

The new Cabinet's first actions on the economic front involved a debate on ending the wage and price controls imposed at the onset of the Korean War. Humphrey and Secretary of Defense Charles E. Wilson favored an immediate lifting of controls in order to stimulate the economy. Upon the advice of Director of the Office of Defense Mobilization Arthur Flemming, Eisenhower approved a rapid but progressive loosening of controls instead of the total and immediate end advocated by Humphrey (Adams, 158–59).

In April 1953 Humphrey put into practice two of his proposals. The Treasury sold $1 billion in new thirty-year government bonds at 3.25 percent, the highest interest rate in nineteen years. This had the effect of absorbing purchasing power and dampening inflationary trends as well as transferring existing debt into long-term bonds.

In preparing his first budget, Humphrey found it surprisingly difficult to cut spending.

In this matter of cutting expenses, I just want to bring to your attention this thing that I had not appreciated as fully when I was here, just engrossed in business . . . about two-thirds of the budget is for security, military preparedness or economic aid. On top of that you have about 20 per cent of the budget . . . that is in fixed items. . . . So when you get right down to it, somewhere from 80 to 90 per cent of the budget has nothing to do with just firing employees, or reducing what you may think are wasteful expenditures, but has to do with our security. (Humphrey, 41)

When the budget outlook was reported to Congress in May, Eisenhower revealed an anticipated deficit of $6.6 billion and requested the continuation of the excess profits tax until January 1954, along with the postponement of certain other tax reductions. The only satisfaction he could offer Republicans was a reduction of individual income taxes on schedule in January 1954.

Meanwhile, Eisenhower and Humphrey campaigned against Reed's proposal for an immediate decrease in taxes. H.R. 1 was immobilized by the Rules Committee, while a majority of the Ways and Means Committee overrode their Chairman and sent the tax extension bill to the floor for a vote (Stein, 291). It was quickly approved; Humphrey could look forward to a reduction of the deficit to $5.6 billion.

By autumn of 1953 the U.S. economy was in recession. "The public finger was pointed at George Humphrey's attempt to tighten credit in April of 1953. . . . Humphrey admitted himself that he had tightened credit too much" (Adams, 162). The major culprit, however, was the rapid decline in military spending resulting from the end of the Korean War. The Federal Reserve moved to increase the money supply and lower interest rates. While maintaining a calm public posture, the administration privately considered numerous countercyclical policies including public works programs (Stein, 302–3).

Thus, in an interview in January 1954, Secretary Humphrey spoke of expecting a "continued high level of activity" and described the contemporary economic trends as "healthy readjustments" (Humphrey, 143). In an address to the nation in March, President Eisenhower rejected a call for further decreasing taxes to combat the recession. Within the Cabinet, some suggested expediting government purchases but "Humphrey thought confidence rested on the belief that the government would follow sound fiscal policies and not act prematurely" (Stein, 304). Humphrey agreed to an acceleration of certain government-financed construction projects shortly thereafter. However, the recession ended with the summer.

Humphrey made some progress toward revising the tax structure, presenting a tax reform bill in January 1954. He was, however, less successful at balancing the budget or reducing the national debt. "Humphrey had come into the cabinet strongly determined to cut both government spending and taxes and to balance the budget, and he had been ready at first to swing his axe at anything that stood in his way. But after listening to [Secretary of State] Dulles talk about the international situation and the importance of Mutual Security and foreign aid, he had not been so sure of the sanctity of his clear-cut convictions" (Adams, 164–65). This change is reflected in the title of a speech given by Secretary Humphrey in April: "Jobs Are More Important Than Tax Cuts."

This change in attitude also explains Humphrey's inability to make much progress toward reducing the debt during the prosperous years from 1955 to 1957. In Cabinet meetings, Humphrey repeatedly argued for further tax reductions, contending that the resulting expansion of the economy would facilitate the achievement of a balanced budget. "Eisenhower was skeptical about the chances of keeping expenditures under such tight control and remarked rather tartly that Humphrey was too quick to recommend tax reductions on the basis of anticipated savings in expenditures that might not necessarily materialize" (Adams, 170). In this, Eisenhower was correct. Although the expansion of the economy in 1955–1957 yielded increased revenues, the rise in expenditures was also large. For the President, tax reduction had a lower priority than budget balancing and, after January 1956, maintaining a surplus. The federal budget showed small surpluses in fiscal years 1956 and 1957, and the debt decreased by $1.7 billion and $.4 billion in those years.

Meanwhile, Humphrey was a tireless campaigner against deficit-financed tax cuts, believing they would fuel inflationary forces. In testimony before the Senate Finance Committee in February 1955, he stated his support for tax cuts in 1956 only if they could be accomplished without increased borrowing ("Cut Taxes in '56?" 106). Thus, he lobbied against the House-approved tax reduction of $20 for every taxpayer and dependent. This bill was subsequently defeated in April; at the same time, Congress acceded to Eisenhower's request for an extension of certain corporation and excise taxes scheduled to expire in April 1956. Similarly, Humphrey urged Congress to curb accelerated tax write-offs of business investment and argued against further expansions in foreign aid ("Incentives to Industry?" 57; Kaufman, 103).

Any appearance of consensus within the Cabinet regarding Eisenhower's budgetary policies abruptly splintered on January 15, 1957. Humphrey gave a press conference criticizing the proposed budget for fiscal year (FY) 1958. In response to questions, he emphasized that the continuation of such large and expanding budget expenditures by the government would result in a depression that would "curl your hair." The budget for FY 1958 contained expenditures of almost $72 billion and was, at that point, the largest peacetime budget in U.S. history. It was based upon minor tax concessions to small businesses, the deferment for yet another year of reductions in corporate income taxes and excise taxes scheduled for April 1, 1956, and a projected surplus of $1.8 billion. This surplus was considered too small to permit a tax decrease.

Humphrey's criticism of the steady rise in government expenditures led to the public perception of a rift within the administration. Eisenhower responded by revealing that he had been aware of Humphrey's intention to release this press statement. "I not only went over every word of it, I edited it, and it expressed my convictions very thoroughly" (Adams, 361). Further, although Humphrey had meant that a continued increase in government spending and in the burden of taxes would eventually lead to a depression, his statement was interpreted as a prediction that a depression was imminent. Finally, his critique provoked both Congress and the White House into attempting to reduce the budget. The succeeding month saw a precipitous cut in Defense Department commitments and probably accelerated the onset of the recession of 1957–1958 (Saulnier, 102–6).

Humphrey believed that the large proposed increase in defense spending was unproductive, absorbing funds that would otherwise provide capital and create jobs. Similarly, he demanded that the considerable social welfare expenditures be prioritized and that the government only spend on those programs it could afford. Thus, he argued for the same fiscal conservatism from government that was expected of households and businesses.

On May 30, 1957, Humphrey resigned, citing a business necessity arising from the illness and subsequent retirement of one of his former partners. Before he left office on July 29, 1957, he presented fourteen days and over 1,500 pages of testimony in June and July before the Senate Finance Committee, which was investigating the financial condition of the United States. Although admitting he had not made enough progress toward converting short-term government debt into long-term obligations, Humphrey defended the Eisenhower administration's economic record. His argument highlighted the healthy rate of growth of the economy, the strength of the dollar, the control of inflation, a $7.5 billion tax cut, and the budget surpluses of 1956 and 1957 (Humphrey, 298–352).

While acting as Secretary of the Treasury, Humphrey also exercised influence in other policy areas. He sat on the National Security Council and advised the President on unifying the armed forces, bringing military spending under control, and the "New Look" in national defense—curtailment of conventional weapons and increased reliance on nuclear arms.

After leaving public service Humphrey became Chairman of the Board of the National Steel Corporation. He also served as the Honorary Chairman of the Board of the M. A. Hanna Company. He resigned from National in 1962 and thereafter devoted himself to horse breeding.

In August 1962 Humphrey found himself testifying before the Senate once again. He faced a subcommittee investigating charges that the M. A. Hanna Company and both Humphrey and his son made excessive and unconscionable profits from a government nickel contract signed a mere four days before he was sworn in. Humphrey adamantly denied all wrongdoing; the allegations quickly faded from public view when no legal action was undertaken.

Humphrey died in Cleveland on January 20, 1970. He was survived by his wife, a son, Gilbert Watts Humphrey, and two daughters, Mrs. Pamela Firman and Mrs. Caroline Butler.

BIBLIOGRAPHY

Adams, Sherman. *Firsthand Report: The Story of the Eisenhower Administration*. New York: Popular Library, 1961.

Coughlan, Robert. "Top Managers in 'Business Cabinet.' " *Life*, January 19, 1953, 100–106f.

"Cut Taxes in '56?" Excerpts from testimony to Senate Finance Committee. *U.S. News and World Report*, March 16, 1953, 106–9.

Gafton, Samuel. "Ike Counts on 'Mr. Hum.' " *Collier's*, May 2, 1953, 60–64.

Humphrey, George. *The Basic Papers of George M. Humphrey*. Edited by Nathaniel Howard. Cleveland, OH: Western Reserve Historical Society, 1965.

"Incentives to Industry? No and Yes." *Newsweek*, August 1, 1955, 57–58.

Kaufman, Burton. *Trade and Aid: Eisenhower's Foreign Economic Policy 1953–1961*. Baltimore: Johns Hopkins University Press, 1982.

Morgan, Iwan. *Eisenhower versus "The Spenders."* New York: St. Martin's Press, 1990.

Saulnier, Raymond. *Constructive Years: The U.S. Economy under Eisenhower*. New York: University Press of America, 1991.

"Secretary of the Treasury: George M. Humphrey." *Life*, March 16, 1953, 63–64.

Sloan, John. "Eisenhower, Humphrey and Neustadt: A Note on the Battle of the Budget for FY 1958." *Western Political Quarterly* 42 (1989): 691–99.

Stein, Herbert. *The Fiscal Revolution in America*. Washington, D.C.: American Enterprise Institute Press, 1990.

VIBHA KAPURIA-FOREMAN

I

SAMUEL D. INGHAM (September 16, 1779–June 5, 1860). Samuel Delucenna Ingham was a prominent politician and successful entrepreneur from the state of Pennsylvania. His youngest son, William A. Ingham, described Samuel as a man of medium height, with broad shoulders and light blue eyes. His disposition was sober and distant, even toward his children (W. Ingham, 1917, 30).

Samuel Delucenna Ingham was born in the village of Great Springs near the town of New Hope in Bucks County, Pennsylvania, on September 16, 1779. He was the only son and the oldest of four children born into the family of Dr. Jonathan and Ann (Welding) Ingham, which had resided in Bucks County for four generations. Although the Inghams were Quakers, Jonathan had early on broken his ties with the "broad brim" sect. Jonathan was devoted to classical studies and presided over Samuel's early education, tutoring him in the classical tradition. The doctor, however, was a very busy man, and at the age of ten, Samuel was sent to a private school that taught in the classical tradition.

Before Samuel reached his fourteenth birthday, his father died from yellow fever, ending Samuel's formal education. Due to ensuing financial difficulty, his mother indentured Samuel to a paper maker on Pennypacker Creek, fifteen miles from Philadelphia. He remained in the service of the paper maker for five years. After fulfilling his contractual obligations, he returned home to aid his mother in running the family farm.

In 1798 Samuel accepted the manager's position at a paper mill located near Bloomfield in eastern New Jersey. During his employment at the mill Samuel met his future wife, Rebecca Dodd, whom he married in 1800 after attaining his twenty-first birthday. The couple returned home, and Samuel built a paper mill on the family property and settled down to raising a family and running the mill and family farm.

Samuel became involved in local politics and was elected to the Pennsylvania House of Representatives in 1806. He declined reelection in 1808 due to pressing business affairs. In the same year, Governor Thomas McKean appointed Samuel as Justice of the Peace in Bucks County. In 1812, he was elected to the U.S.

House of Representatives as a Jeffersonian Democrat. During his tenure in the House he was a member of the Ways and Means Committee and Chairman of the committee overseeing the U.S. Post Office. He served in the House until July 6, 1818, resigning due to his wife's deteriorating health. Upon his return home, he was appointed to the office of Prothonotary of the Court of Common Pleas of Bucks County. In 1819, Samuel was appointed Secretary of the Commonwealth by Governor Findlay. Rebecca died in 1819, leaving Samuel to raise their five children. He spent the next two years at home, raising his children and tending to his business interests.

In 1822, Samuel married Deborah Kay Hall of Salem, New Jersey; they had three children. In October he was elected to the 17th U.S. Congress. He was reappointed to the House Ways and Means Committee and to the chairmanship of the Post Office Committee. Ingham remained in the House until March 4, 1829, resigning to join the Cabinet of President Andrew Jackson.

During his tenure in the House, Ingham was a strong supporter of John C. Calhoun and Andrew Jackson. There is speculation that Ingham played a role in the scandal that arose after the 1824 presidential election. The "bargain and corruption cry" scandal arose over the selection of John Q. Adams as President by the House, even though Andrew Jackson received a majority of the popular vote. Henry Clay, the new Secretary of State, accused Ingham of being the author behind fellow Pennsylvania Congressman George Kremer's letter accusing Adams and Clay of conspiring to and succeeding in stealing the presidency from Andrew Jackson. Adding fuel to the fire, Ingham wrote an election pamphlet attacking Adams's character and accusing him of being a monarchist. Adams never forgave Ingham for those personal attacks.

In 1828 Andrew Jackson won the presidential election, and Ingham, a staunch supporter of Jackson and Vice President–elect Calhoun, was offered the portfolio of the U.S. Treasury. Ingham served as Secretary of the Treasury for two years, from March 6, 1829, to June 20, 1831. During his tenure as Secretary, Ingham addressed three major economic issues: the Second U.S. Bank; elimination of the federal debt; and U.S. commercial policy.

Andrew Jackson had made a campaign pledge to eliminate the public debt. Ingham, with the cooperation of Nicholas Biddle, president of the Second U.S. Bank, orchestrated a large payment toward the debt in the early summer of 1829 as a first step in fulfillment of Jackson's pledge. The transaction was handled by the Bank and earned the praise of Ingham in a letter to Biddle dated June 19: "I cannot close this communication without expressing the satisfaction of the department at the arrangements which the bank has made for effecting these payments in a manner so accommodating to the Treasury, and so little embarrassing to the community" (Parton, 260).

The relationship, however, soured over the Portsmouth affair. In October, after several communications between Biddle and Ingham concerning the actions of the President of the bank's Portsmouth branch, Ingham referred to Biddle as being "altogether too touchy" and stated that the administration had the power to withdraw public funds if the administration deemed it necessary (Parton, 266–67). This implied threat was not carried out during Ingham's watch, but the relationship between the Treasury and the bank remained strained. The public debt issue would also remain unresolved at the end of Ingham's tenure as Secretary.

During this period in history, administration of U.S. commercial policy was the responsibility of the Treasury. During his tenure as Secretary, Ingham advocated in his annual reports to Congress for a reduction in import tariffs and in taxes, in general. He viewed all taxes as a necessary evil to pay off a greater economic evil, the public debt. He believed that the public debt and high taxes needed to pay off that debt led to a misallocation of resources and lessened American manufacturers' ability to compete with foreign producers. Ingham was also concerned with smuggling and recommended changes in custom house regulations and duty application procedures. He pointed to the amount of smuggling occurring under the present system as proof of the system's inefficiency and need for reform.

Ingham's son, William, wrote that his father was an ardent protectionist and had made numerous public statements in favor of tariffs (W. Ingham, 1917, 29). There is no written evidence of Ingham expounding this view during his tenure as Secretary. To the contrary, Ingham argued for reductions in the tariff as Secretary of the Treasury: "Whatever the objects may, in the wisdom of the Government, be found, for the application of surplus revenue, after the public debt be paid, there will probably remain a considerable amount, which may be dispensed with, by a reduction of the import duties, without prejudice to any branch of domestic industry" (S. Ingham, "1829," 17). It is clear from his official statement to Congress that Ingham believed U.S tariff rates were excessive.

Ingham's favored place in the Jackson Cabinet was abruptly terminated by his actions toward John Eaton and the role of Ingham's wife Deborah in what has become known as the Margaret Eaton scandal. Margaret Eaton was the wife of John Eaton, Jackson's Secretary of War, fellow Tennessean, and lifelong friend. Jackson was also a friend of Mrs. Eaton's family. It was the second marriage for both parties. Washington's social elite, which included Cabinet family members, refused to recognize Mrs. Eaton socially. The snubbing of Mrs. Eaton infuriated President Jackson. It reminded Jackson of the pain and humiliation false rumors had inflicted upon his own dearly loved departed wife, Elizabeth, during his term in Congress. Jackson went so far as to have his personal aide, Major William Lewis, investigate all of the rumors. Major Lewis found no proof to verify any of the scandalous gossip (Parton, 184–205). Jackson then demanded that his Cabinet members and their families welcome Mrs. Eaton into their social circle. The Cabinet members refused, except Secretary of State Martin Van Buren.

Jackson came to believe that the ringleaders of the social boycott of Mrs. Eaton were Mrs. Ingham and Mrs. Calhoun. Jackson concluded that their husbands' refusal to put an end to snubbing was motivated by a political scheme, with the sole purpose of driving Major Eaton from the Cabinet (Munroe, 295). Events surrounding the scandal left the Cabinet paralyzed, forcing Jackson to dissolve the Cabinet in the Spring of 1831. Ingham left office on June 20, 1831. The correspondence between Jackson and Ingham reveals that they parted on good terms. However, Ingham refuted Jackson's version of the Cabinet dissolution publicly in May and hinted that it was due solely to his family's refusal to accept Mrs. Eaton socially. In June, a story appeared in the *United States Telegraph*, blaming the dissolution of the Cabinet on Mrs. Eaton and Jackson's desire to regulate the private lives of his Cabinet officers (McCrary, 232–34). These events enraged Major Eaton and drove the final nail in Ingham's political coffin. Eaton challenged Ingham to a duel over the article; Ingham refused. Ingham packed up his family and left Washington for Baltimore on June 22, 1831, thus ending his political career (Parton, 364–68).

The Ingham family returned to New Hope, Pennsylvania, and Ingham rede-voted himself to business. He helped develop the anthracite coal fields in Pennsylvania and was one of the founding members and for a time President of the Beaver Meadow Railroad Company. Later, he helped organize the Hazelton Coal Co. and through his coal interests became involved in the political issues surrounding the construction of the Lehigh Navigation and Delaware Division canals.

As a private citizen, Ingham spent considerable energy lobbying the state legislature for improvement of Pennsylvania's inland waterways to benefit Pennsylvania's coal industry. In 1849 Samuel Ingham moved the family to Trenton, New Jersey, and became involved in the Trenton Mechanics Bank. On June 5, 1860, Ingham died at his home in Trenton. He was buried in the cemetery of the Thompson Memorial Church located at Great Springs, Pennsylvania. He was survived by his wife Deborah and five of his eight children.

Samuel D. Ingham lived during a turbulent period in American history. His contributions to the new nation and the state of Pennsylvania were significant. Yet because he lived in the age of Monroe, Jackson, and Adams, Ingham's shadow pales. His involvement in scandalous events adds no luster to his legacy. Concerned with his reputation, Ingham burned his entire collection of correspondence in 1849 in the fear that those letters would tarnish his reputation if published after his death (W. Ingham, 1917, 29). The destruction of Ingham's confidential correspondence is regrettable from a historical point of view and leaves several questions about his character unanswered.

BIBLIOGRAPHY

Catterall, R. C. *The Second Bank of the United States*. Chicago: Chicago University Press, 1903.

Hammond, B. *Banks and Politics in America*. Princeton: Princeton University Press, 1957.

Ingham, S. D. "Report on Finances. December, 1829." In *Reports of the Secretary of the Treasury of the United States*. Washington, D.C.: Blair & Rives Publisher, 1837a.

———. "Report on Finances. December, 1830." In *Reports of the Secretary of the Treasury of the United States*. Washington, D.C.: Blair & Rives Publisher, 1837b.

"Samuel D. Ingham." In *Appleton's Cyclopedia of American Biography*. Vol. 3. New York: D. Appleton and Co., 1888.

Ingham, W. A. "Samuel D. Ingham, Secretary of the United States Treasury." In *The Bucks County Historical Society*. Doylestown, PA: Published by the Society, 1917.

McCrary, R. C. " 'The Long Agony Is Nearly Over': Samuel D. Ingham Reports on the Dissolution of Andrew Jackson's First Cabinet." *Pennsylvania Magazine of History and Biography* 100, no. 2 (1976): 231–42.

McGrane, R. C. *The Correspondence of Nicholas Biddle Dealing with National Affairs 1807–1844*. Boston: Houghton Mifflin Publishing Co., 1919.

Munroe, J. *Louis McLane: Federalist and Jacksonian*. New Brunswick, NJ: Rutgers University Press, 1973.

Parton, J. *Life of Andrew Jackson*. Vol. 3. New York: Mason Brothers, 1861.

SCOTT W. FAUSTI

K

DAVID M. KENNEDY (July 21, 1905–   ). David Matthew Kennedy was born on July 21, 1905, and grew up on a ranch near Randolph, Utah. He was the son of strict Mormon parents, George and Katherine Johnson Kennedy. Kennedy, also a devout Mormon, neither drank nor smoked. Indeed, an old friend recalls one time when Kennedy scraped a brandy-flavored topping off a dish of ice cream before eating it. At age ten he was scrambling for nickel tips as a bellboy in a Riverdale, Utah, hotel. "Daddy never had much of a childhood," said the youngest of his four daughters, Mrs. Lewis Cambell. "He never had the time to play and enjoy life like most kids today." As a young man, he answered the call of his church and served two years as a missionary in England. His brand-new wife, Lenora Bingham, whom he had married on November 4, 1925, stayed in Utah, supporting herself by working in a dime store and sending her husband what money she could spare. They had four daughters, Marilyn Ann, Barbara Ann, Carol Joyce, and Patricia Lenore. Kennedy attended public schools and received his bachelor's degree from Weber College in Ogden, Utah, in 1928 prior to his missionary service.

If Kennedy appeared to be characteristically careful with a dollar, that was simply because, out of lifelong habit and conviction, he was. His son-in-law, Jack Whittle, reported, "He still gets sore with us when we pass up a sale in the stores."

At the time of his appointment, associates described him as one of the nicest people, who never raised his voice, in anger or otherwise. His ranching boyhood gave him a taste for horseback riding, fishing, and hunting. He was labeled a "monetary conservative" but not a doctrinaire one. His appointment won praise not only from bankers but from the liberal camp as well. In fact, Lyndon Johnson once considered making Kennedy his Treasury Secretary.

The Treasury under LBJ had been accused of many shortcomings. In suggesting that LBJ's Secretary Henry Fowler resign early in 1968, *Fortune* magazine named, among others, Kennedy as a man who could restore the banking and financial community's confidence in the Treasury. Kennedy served fourteen months in the Eisenhower administration's Treasury as top debt manager; then he headed a

Johnson administration commission that improved federal budgeting. That commission set a record in having its major recommendations adopted within nine months of its creation. The commission's major accomplishment was producing a unified budget. Kennedy also endorsed Secretary Fowler's "paper gold" plan for special drawing rights to expand international reserves. Kennedy found the Johnson administration's direct controls on American capital investment abroad "disruptive," but he proclaimed that these controls were "necessary and justified" as temporary measures.

As President Richard Nixon's first Secretary of the Treasury, Kennedy was appointed on December 11, 1968, and took the oath of office on January 22, 1969. Few incoming Treasury Secretaries have ever had such a witch's brew of problems to deal with: the domestic economy was overheated, and fiscal restraint was not working; the international monetary system was in tatters, with vociferous disagreement over how to mend it. Kennedy believed that the recent price inflation stemmed largely from the inflationary monetary and fiscal policies the United States had been following. His important economic contribution was advocating both a tight budget and restrictive money policy, together with high interest rates to curb inflation. He advocated fighting inflation with high interest rates while retaining the official U.S. price of gold at par. In short, he viewed the problems of the economy primarily in terms of money flow and sought solutions to inflation, unemployment, and balance of payments deficits in those terms. Above all, he portrayed himself as a "gradualist." Like Nixon, his credo was "flexibility." Originally in his term as Secretary, Kennedy was perceived as a strong leader. How that image faded is a fascinating story.

Kennedy, as Treasury Secretary, was a member of the economic "quadriad"—which included, in addition to himself, Federal Reserve Board Chair William McChesney Martin, Budget Director Robert Mayo, and Paul McCracken, Chair of the Council of Economic Advisers. In this economic fraternity of four equals, Kennedy quickly emerged as more equal than the others. Most Washington insiders pegged him as the key strategist in the fight then being waged against inflation. Kennedy had gone a long way toward establishing himself as a champion of fiscal and economic soundness in this administration.

At age twenty-five, Kennedy began a sixteen-year career as staff member of the Board of Governors of the Federal Reserve Bank, although he managed to combine work and study to complete his master's degree at George Washington University in 1935 and his LL.B. in 1937. In 1939 he completed his university education with a degree from the Rutger's Stonier Graduate School of Banking. At the Fed from 1930 to 1946, Kennedy advanced through a series of increasingly responsible positions: technical assistant in the division of bank operations, economist in the division of research and statistics, and finally special assistant to the Chair of the Fed, Marriner S. Eccles.

In 1946, Kennedy, age forty-one, moved to the private sector and began a distinguished career with Continental Illinois National Bank and Trust Company in Chicago, even though he had offers with much larger salaries from several

New York banks. He rose quickly to Second Vice President in 1948 and then to Vice President in 1951. As a Chicago banker, Kennedy's hallmark was equal parts hard work, honesty, and piety. "He has an intense dislike of wasting time," according to John Edmunds, a Chicago lawyer and longtime family friend. "He makes every minute count." As a banker, he was a no-compromise battler. Kennedy was called again for government service and resigned from Continental to serve as special assistant to Secretary of the Treasury George M. Humphrey from October 1953 to December 1954.

In late 1954, Kennedy returned to Continental and was named Vice President. In 1956 he was elected Director and President and in 1959 was elected Chair of the Board of Directors and chief executive officer. By the time he left Continental in 1969, Kennedy had established Continental's community leadership role and pioneered in the area of corporate social responsibility. Kennedy was long active in trying to respond to the urban crisis of that time. His bank was in the midst of efforts to employ and train blacks, finance black business, and provide construction money for inner-city housing. "The men who run American industry today," according to his press quotations of the time, "can no longer shrug their shoulders and say that the poor are always with us, and there is little we can do about it."

He accumulated substantial knowledge of international finance prior to his appointment to the Treasury by virtue of the activities of Continental Bank. Under his initiative, the bank became the first midwestern bank to establish a bank in London and later acquired three Japanese banks. Kennedy, as a result, had traveled abroad frequently and developed numerous contacts with the international banking community.

By 1969, Kennedy's achievements had drawn the attention of the Republican Party. In December 1969, he was named to a team that drafted the preliminary economic policy stance that the Nixon administration was to pursue for the first two years of his administration until Kennedy left office. The draft policy consisted of a number of deflationary measures, including the cooperation of the Federal Reserve to raise interest rates and slow the growth rate of the money supply, and a plan for a balanced budget at high levels of employment. At his confirmation hearings, Kennedy further endorsed his commitment to disinflation and a balanced budget.

When Kennedy took over as Secretary, he inherited a Johnson administration legacy of distortion perhaps not seen since the Civil War. Interest rates once again had risen to very high levels, and Wall Street was convinced that high rates were there to stay. Institutional investors, faced with a 4.5 percent rise in consumer prices in 1968, had become disenchanted with fixed-income securities and had shifted more and more to investments in common stocks. Triple A utility bonds were priced to yield 7 percent, the highest level in American financial history to that time.

In April 1969, Kennedy was confident that both corporate and personal spending would decline within the next few months, due mainly to the proposal to extend the surtax and to the government's determination to cut the budget. Kennedy felt strongly that a budget cut would still be the administration's most effective weapon in curbing inflation. It did not occur to him and other orthodox economists at that time that both monetary and fiscal policy worked with long and highly variable lags. There was still considerable faith in "fine-tuning," with highly coordinated monetary and fiscal policy instruments, to attain the desired point on the Phillips curve trade-off of inflation versus unemployment. Milton Friedman's seminal work showing that it was impossible for monetary policy to peg either real interest rates or a rate of unemployment below the "natural rate," except in the very short run, appeared in 1968, but it had not been absorbed by many government economists.

His nomination as Secretary of the Treasury encountered some immediate resistance as Senator Albert Gore, Democrat from Tennessee, accused Kennedy of conflict of interest because of his stock holdings in Continental Illinois. To finesse this objection, Kennedy agreed to place all his stock in a blind trust. This did not assuage Wright Patman, the powerful Chair of the House Banking Committee. Patman complained to his committee on April 30, 1969, that Kennedy had not done enough to resolve potential conflicts of interest. Patman insisted that Kennedy take two steps: First, give up a "separation allowance" of $200,000 voted him by the bank's directors. This was to be paid in five annual installments after Kennedy left the Treasury post. And second, "renounce" a bank pension of $4,800 per month he had been getting since January, along with premium payments on his life insurance policy.

Less than a year after his appointment, Kennedy's stint as Secretary of the Treasury was immersed in controversy and bad press. He had become an increasing source of embarrassment to the Nixon administration. His chronic foot-in-mouth habits, which were costly in terms of both dollars and prestige, began to appear almost the moment he was appointed. Kennedy was attacked in Congress by the antibanking, low-interest-rate advocates on several occasions. At one point, Kennedy testified on a proposed bill that restricted bank-owned holding companies to banking activities alone, warning that, absent such restraint, within a few years the economy would be dominated by some 50 to 75 centers of economic and financial power. Wright Patman (D–Tex.) ignored the criticism and asserted that the legislation was not tough enough. In July 1969, Patman was incensed after another in a series of prime interest rate hikes by banks. Patman seemed to hold Kennedy personally responsible for failing to prevent the increase.

On December 13, 1968, Kennedy asserted that he believed in balanced federal budgets but added there was such a thing as an "acceptable deficit." Kennedy defined an acceptable deficit as one that can be handled financially without damaging currency or credit or putting pressure on the economy from the budget. This was a very fuzzy definition. He had not yet become familiar with the notion of "full employment budget deficit," a notion sold to Nixon by George Shultz. Robert P. Mayo, the new Budget Bureau Director, said he expected during his administration of the bureau to present Nixon with a balanced budget. Kennedy retorted that he expected that some of Mayo's ideas would conflict with his own, just as some of his Treasury Department aides might disagree with him.

Also in December 1968, Kennedy created an uproar in his very first news conference after his nomination as Secretary. In December 1968, he implied that a rise in the official price of gold from $35 might be an option he would like to leave open to help stabilize the U.S. currency. This remark, which he considered neutral, triggered a speculative run on the dollar, with private traders dumping the dollar in the world market, driving the free market price of gold through the $44 level on the London market. Later, in one of his first statements after assuming office, he reaffirmed his commitment to the long-standing Treasury policy of pegging the price of gold in terms of the dollar. The market price of gold in Europe immediately took a sharp fall. But in June and again in July 1969, he said that the administration might be forced to consider putting controls on wages and prices. President Nixon issued firm denials, but Kennedy's remarks shook business and caused sharp drops in the stock market.

In early September 1969, Kennedy seemed to be back on track as the administration's effective point man on Capitol Hill. He was the opening witness as the Senate Finance Committee began hearings on the most sweeping tax reform measure in U.S. history, one already passed by the House. Kennedy presented a detailed administration blueprint to make the legislation more palatable to complaining private interest groups and a bit less "revolutionary" all around. In submitting his version of tax reform, Kennedy made it clear that Nixon was not reneging on his oft-repeated pledge to support a major reform. The Tax Reform Act of 1969, according to Kennedy, was a milestone in tax legislation. The Administration strongly urged its enactment at the earliest feasible date. At that point, he presented his argument that the House version of the bill had three fundamental defects. His package of more than a dozen highly complicated proposals purportedly corrected the serious defects.

For one thing, he noted that the bill provided for a tax reduction of $2.4 billion annually. This, he argued, was too large a cut in federal revenues in view of existing defense, welfare, and other commitments. He proposed to pare the tax relief provided by the bill almost in half—to $1.3 billion. Next, he noted that the bill provided too large a tax break for individuals and placed too heavy an additional burden on corporations. His counterproposal was to cut the tax break for individuals to $4.8 billion and reduce the additional bite on corporations to $3.5 billion.

Kennedy's final and most serious objection to the tax reform was that it went too far in radically altering the tax treatment of such things as municipal bonds and nonprofit organizations, while not going far enough in its reform of industries such as oil.

In October 1969, he committed yet another faux pas. During questioning by friendly Republican members of Congress on the Joint Economic Committee, he was asked whether the current 4 percent unemployment rate was "acceptable or unacceptable." He ignored a carefully prepared statement hastily handed to him by a Treasury staff aide and replied with more candor than tact that under the circumstances, it was acceptable. To compound matters, he went on to broach anew the notion that if present anti-inflation policies do not work, the administration would have to consider "moving into the field of controls of some kind." Of course, Kennedy was absolutely correct and was presaging the wage-price controls initiated by Nixon two years later on August 15, 1971.

Immediately after his Joint Economic Committee remarks, critics from both parties castigated him as totally insensitive in his portrayal of 4 percent unemployment as "acceptable." This seems rather humorous in view of today's general view that the "natural rate" of unemployment lies in the range of 5.5 to 6 percent. Nevertheless, the stock market dropped again after Kennedy's statement about controls. Once more, Nixon issued public disclaimers disassociating his administration's policy from this stance, and a day later, Kennedy also retracted his statement.

Inexplicably, he was never able to learn how to dodge potentially explosive questions. Thus, by the end of 1969 his fate in Nixon's Cabinet was probably sealed. While even his critics applauded Kennedy's innate midwestern decency and amiability, his continued gaffes had deprived him and his office of political clout in the Cabinet and before Congress. And this was a time the United States desperately needed a Treasury Secretary who exhibited unequivocal power and leadership.

Kennedy had many good points and was a decent economist. From the outset, Kennedy helped the administration educate the American public to the need for tighter money after eight years of liberal Keynesian expansionary policies under Presidents John F. Kennedy and Lyndon Johnson. In February 1969 he called for "fiscal restraint" but also warned against too-rapid deflationary policies, with their tendency to raise unemployment to unacceptable levels. He wanted to avoid a repetition of the abrupt shift in Federal Reserve policy in which the Fed had reverted to easy money even before its 1965–1966 tight-money policies had seen results. He saw the harm to the economy caused by the Fed's stop-and-go monetary policies.

Kennedy fought to reverse the trend toward restrictions on world markets for both goods and capital. He hoped controls were a temporary expedient. The Bretton Woods system (which lasted from 1945 until 1971) was set up to achieve a more liberal international trading system. Kennedy said that he had worked most of his life trying to break down trade barriers and get to convertible currencies. Yet, he noted that in the past few years the United States had moved from one restriction to another. Among the myriad restrictions that were imposed at that time were U.S. mandatory capital controls, British import taxes, French restrictions on capital movements, and the whole system of Continental border taxes.

By early 1970, the economy had cooled down due to the administration's tightening measures. Kennedy continued to serve as the spokesperson for these austerity measures. He cautioned against the removal of the income tax surcharge, imposed during President Johnson's administration, and raised the pos-

sibility of wage and price controls. A short time later he advocated waiting for
signs of recession before shifting to expansionary policies. He was miffed that the
general public did not comprehend the need for monetary and fiscal restraint.

The 1970 congressional elections made a frightening impression on Nixon.
By then, the administration's tight-money policies had begun to work. Unemployment was up from 4 percent to 6 percent, the stock market was down 300
points, and industrial production was falling. Observers concluded that this had
caused the Democrats to make uncharacteristic gains in an off-year election. The
White House did not deny that a Cabinet shakeup was in the offing. Nixon was
already paranoid about his reelection. Recall that he had blamed his 1960 election defeat by John F. Kennedy on the Fed Chair, William McChesney Martin,
who had pursued tight-money and high unemployment policies and soured the
economy prior to the election. Nixon, after that, was always less concerned about
inflation than about recession and unemployment. His advisers were telling him
that he needed some appointments that would solidify his political power in
strategic states. He began to look for candidates with political clout.

In mid-December 1970, Nixon surprised everyone and informed Congress that
former Texas Governor John Connally, a Democrat and crony of Lyndon Johnson, would succeed Kennedy as Treasury Secretary. Nixon argued that this would
give his economic policy a "bipartisan" quality. By making the Treasury post
bipartisan, Nixon hoped to blunt Democratic attacks on his overall antirecession
policies. It was officially announced that the "soft-spoken" Kennedy, a description in diametric contrast to the style of his named successor, had at the time of
his appointment only agreed to serve the administration for two years, a term
now expired. However, Treasury officials confirmed rumors that Kennedy had
only offered to resign as a "scapegoat" after the combination of disappointing
midterm election returns and the continuing economic problems of inflation and
unemployment.

Nixon gently nudged aside his Secretary of the Treasury. He installed a top
Democrat, Connally, where he might absorb some of the blame, should the economy still be sickly during the 1972 election season. The Connally appointment
was entirely Nixon's idea. And no one was terribly surprised to see Kennedy step
down: he had proved an able adviser but a perceived wimp in his advocacy for
the administration's economic policies.

After he left the office of Secretary of the Treasury, Kennedy became Ambassador, a post in which he sought to cope with the hazardous international financial problems of the day. In his new position, at age sixty-five, he had primary
responsibility for keeping tabs on economic developments in the European Economic Community and was assigned to follow progress of multilateral aid where
various countries join in assisting developing countries.

He continued to advise the President and Secretary of State on world monetary
problems. Kennedy was certainly a man of stubborn honesty, someone who was
at his best in quiet negotiation with his peers of the financial community. In his
new ambassadorship, he was primarily engaged in the negotiation and signing of

various trade agreements with major exporters to U.S. markets. The recession had kindled protectionist sentiment in the United States. In 1971, Kennedy found a middle ground between overt protectionism and new tariff barriers, and completely free trade. He negotiated a series of "voluntary export restraint" agreements with Japan, Taiwan, and Italy. These affected such things as shoe and textile shipments to the United States.

In 1972, he was replaced in that post by Donald Rumsfeld, and in early 1973 he retired to private life in Illinois. It was unfortunate that he lacked the ability to win policy battles within the administration or to articulate his views effectively to a broader public. Although he was not the "rainmaker" or the economic Henry Kissinger that Nixon craved, Kennedy was a kind, pious, and candid public servant, with keen knowledge of tax policy and monetary affairs. This is the kind of individual many citizens long for in government service today.

BIBLIOGRAPHY

"Chicago Banker at Treasury." *Business Week*, December 14, 1968, 35.

"The High Cost of David Kennedy." *Time*, October 17, 1969, 98.

"Kennedy Sizes up U.S. Money Problems." *Business Week*, December 28, 1968, 72–73.

Schoenebaum, Eleanora W., ed. *Political Profiles: The Nixon/Ford Years*. New York: Facts on File, Inc., 1979.

"Secretary of Treasury: David Matthew Kennedy." *New York Times*, December 12, 1968, 36.

Sobel, Robert, ed. *Biographical Directory of the United States Executive Branch, 1774–1977*. Westport, CT: Greenwood Press, 1977.

Stein, Herbert. *Presidential Economics: The Making of Economic Policy from Roosevelt to Reagan and Beyond*. New York: Simon & Schuster, Inc., 1985.

"Treasury's Kennedy." *Fortune*, January 1969, 33.

Wicker, Tom. *One of Us: Richard Nixon and the American Dream*. New York: Random House, 1995.

C. DANIEL VENCILL

M

WILLIAM G. MCADOO (October 31, 1863–February 1, 1941). William Gibbs McAdoo was a lawyer, entrepreneur, financier, politician, and government administrator. In the private sector, he succeeded in becoming wealthy in large part because he guided and partially owned the firm that first constructed (four) tunnels under the Hudson River. In the public sector, he served as Secretary of the Treasury from 1913 to 1918 and as U.S. Senator from California from 1932 to 1938, and twice (1920, 1924), he almost obtained the Democratic Party's nomination for President.

Although he obtained wealth and power as an adult, McAdoo spent his youth in more humble conditions. He was born near Marietta, Georgia, on October 31, 1863, to William Gibbs McAdoo and Mary Faith (Floyd) McAdoo; he had two brothers (one older) and four sisters (two older). His father was a lawyer and educator; his mother authored several short stories and novels. The Union Army during the Civil War destroyed their farm. Their economic conditions were consequently strained for many years. From 1879 to 1882, McAdoo was able to attend the University of Tennessee tuition free because his father had obtained an adjunct professorship in English and history there in 1877.

McAdoo left the University of Tennessee in 1882 without graduating. He moved to Chattanooga to become a deputy clerk of the Sixth Federal Circuit Court of Appeals. After studying law at night, he was admitted to the bar in 1885. In addition to beginning his law practice, he also began his family, as he married Sarah Houston Fleming on November 18, 1885. They had six children: Harriet, Francis, Nona, William, Robert, and Sally.

McAdoo stayed in Chattanooga until 1892. His investment in an unsuccessful attempt to electrify a streetcar line in Knoxville forced him into bankruptcy. He was determined that this failure would be only a temporary setback in his drive for success. He moved his family to the bright lights and limitless opportunities of New York City in 1892.

While waiting for his law practice to grow, he sold securities. After several years, he joined William McAdoo (no relation) to form the law firm of McAdoo and McAdoo. Amid much skepticism, he organized the financing and engineering necessary for completing, on March 8, 1904, the first tunnel under the Hudson River. His company, the Hudson and Manhattan Railroad Company, built four such tunnels by 1909. McAdoo's success in this project not only made him wealthy, but it also demonstrated his organizational abilities, his boundless energy, and his characteristic optimism that saw opportunities for improvement where more timid souls saw failures.

McAdoo possessed a lifetime interest in public service. His motto for his railroad company was "The Public Be Pleased," as he stressed service to its consumers; he considered his company "to be a corporation with a soul" (McAdoo, 1931, 104). His financial success and favorable press made him an attractive candidate for public office.

Although he considered himself to be a Jeffersonian Democrat, McAdoo summarized his essential ideology like this: "I like movement and change; I like to make things better, to reshape old forces and worn-out ideals into new and dynamic forms" (McAdoo, 1931, 528). He approved of an activist government that was willing to adopt new programs and to change existing ones, particularly those that supported smaller businesses and farmers. He was intensely partisan as he wrote: "The essential difference between the Democratic and Republican parties is that the vital idea of the Democratic Party is 'people' and the vital ideal of the Republican Party is 'property' " (113). He claimed that the Republican Party had "never exhibited much constructive ability," while "the Democratic Party is humanistic and progressive" (114).

He quickly supported a fellow southerner, Woodrow Wilson, in Wilson's successful 1910 race for Governor of New Jersey. In 1911, he joined a small group, headed by William F. McCombs, that promoted Wilson's presidential candidacy. During Wilson's 1912 presidential race, McAdoo served as an assistant to McCombs, who was Wilson's campaign manager. Despite his grief over his wife's death (February 1912), McAdoo made numerous visits to southern and western states to promote Wilson's candidacy. When McCombs became seriously ill in August, McAdoo assumed his responsibilities (but not his title) as campaign manager—a job for which his enormous capacity for work and his ideological flexibility were ideally suited.

Wilson viewed McAdoo as an obvious choice for Secretary of the Treasury, as McAdoo had demonstrated enormous financial success in private business, a willingness to support substantial economic reform, and political loyalty. Only later did Wilson discover that he had also obtained a son-in-law, as widower McAdoo married Eleanor Randolph Wilson, daughter of President Wilson, in a White House wedding on May 7, 1914. They had two daughters—Ellen and Mary.

Assuming his Cabinet position on March 6, 1913, McAdoo, the consummate promoter, characteristically began to expand the activities of the Treasury Department—most notably in the area of monetary reform. President Wilson gave McAdoo primary responsibility of representing the White House in negotiations with Congress concerning monetary reform legislation. McAdoo believed that the proposals of Senator Nelson Aldrich (R–R.I.) and of Senator Carter Glass (D–Va.) left too much power in the private banking system and did not provide for enough governmental control. McAdoo floated a "National Reserve" plan that placed control of the banking system and monetary policy in the Treasury Department. Although Congress rejected McAdoo's specific proposal, his efforts did support the movement toward more governmental control.

The Federal Reserve Act of 1913 represented a compromise between those who wanted a central bank modeled on European experience and those who contended that regional differences in the United States necessitated a more decentralized structure. Similar to many compromises, the Federal Reserve Act had created a general framework but had left many details to be completed later by others.

As an ex officio member of the Board of Governors, Chair of the Board at meetings that he attended, and Chair of its Organization Committee, McAdoo vigorously strove to implement his ideas. The Federal Reserve Act had provided for "not less than eight nor more than twelve" districts. McAdoo's Organization Committee (McAdoo and Agriculture Secretary David F. Houston) quickly established twelve districts with a disproportionate number (relative to financial resources) in the South and West; his critics on the board claimed that several districts were seriously undercapitalized.

McAdoo further antagonized Federal Reserve Board members because he considered the board to be subservient to the Treasury Department, and he constantly attempted to reduce the status of board members. He particularly upset appointive members—Frederick Delano, W. P. G. Harding, Adolph C. Miller, and Paul Warburg. These men considered themselves to be nonpartisan neutral experts who had responsibility for running the monetary system for the public good and not necessarily for the needs of specific bankers, the Treasury Department, or the executive branch. Although today McAdoo's disputes with board members over location of meetings and over social status of board members may appear petty, the board members wanted to become more independent from the Treasury; both they and McAdoo believed that the higher their status, the more independent they could be.

Another source of friction between McAdoo and the board arose because the Federal Reserve Act had not made the Federal Reserve Banks the only federal regulators of banks nor the chief fiscal agents for the Treasury. The Federal Reserve Act left substantial control for examination and supervision of national banks with the Comptroller of the Currency in the Treasury Department. Moreover, McAdoo deliberately bypassed the reserve banks by moving Treasury funds from its own sub-Treasury branches (the Independent Treasury System) according to his own preferences for allocating funds; he particularly favored southern and western banks that were heavily involved with agricultural loans. Although the Treasury would not formally end the sub-Treasury system until 1921, Mc-

Adoo essentially made the Reserve Banks the effective fiscal agents for the federal government during the war.

In addition, McAdoo and Congress attempted to redirect credit to agricultural areas through the Federal Farm Loan Act (1916). The bureau was administered by a board with the Treasury Secretary as chair ex officio and four appointive members; McAdoo selected the original board members subject to Wilson's approval. The system had twelve district Federal Land Banks that issued bonds against mortgage loans. Obviously, the Federal Land Bank system was modeled after that of the Federal Reserve; its development was necessary to keep farm mortgages out of the Federal Reserve System.

The U.S. entry into World War I intensified the dispute over monetary policy between McAdoo and the board. The financing of government expenditures during the war represented McAdoo's greatest challenge. Although he preferred to use taxes to pay for at least one half of the war effort, he realized that this was not practical. McAdoo successfully promoted his idea that the war should be paid by "one part taxes and two part loans." Although he typically lived for the present and was not much concerned with the longer-run consequences of his economic policies, McAdoo was aware that inflation could result from this method of war financing. Indeed, McAdoo studied the Union government's financing of the Civil War to obtain insights concerning the difficulties of financing a major war effort. He concluded that Treasury Secretary Chase had blundered by not appealing directly to the public for financial support of the war. McAdoo later wrote: "Any great war must necessarily be a popular movement. It is a kind of crusade; and, like all crusades, it sweeps along on a powerful stream of romanticism. Chase did not attempt to capitalize the emotion of the people, yet it was there and he might have put it to work" (McAdoo, 1931, 374). In essence, his vigorous leadership of the Liberty Loan Program that sold bonds to individuals was an effort to reduce inflationary pressures by increasing saving and reducing consumption through appeals to a patriotic crusade. Of course, McAdoo wanted to sell these bonds at as low an interest rate as possible to reduce the interest payments for later generations. McAdoo wanted the Fed to lower its discount rate to encourage banks to borrow funds to buy these securities. Although the Federal Reserve Board considered McAdoo's plan to be highly inflationary, it ultimately accepted his requests. Indeed, the Fed provided a preferential discount rate when the loans were backed by federal securities.

McAdoo's wartime financing program was often contradictory. Although he wanted to reduce consumption demand, he urged banks to borrow, thereby leading to increased reserves and hence money creation. Moreover, he urged the general public to obtain bank loans to purchase bonds that served as the collateral for the loan. His insistence that the interest on the bonds be exempt from federal income taxes thereby reduced the progressivity of the tax system.

Although McAdoo had not been involved in the political controversy concerning the adoption of a federal income tax, he clearly recognized its potential for raising revenue. Critics, however, claimed that his revenue proposals were not progressive enough; and thus McAdoo had abandoned the progressive faith in favor of his millionaire friends. In retrospect, McAdoo had made a typically pragmatic decision, as he had decided that too-high tax rates would weaken support for the war. On the other hand, McAdoo's revenue proposals did shift federal funding from reliance on excise and customs taxes (74 percent of federal revenue in 1916) to more emphasis on income tax (59 percent of federal revenue in 1919). Moreover, McAdoo's proposal for the War Revenue Acts of 1917 and 1918 strongly supported an extremely progressive "excess-profits" tax.

McAdoo's consistent support of low tariffs was more to the liking of progressives. McAdoo viewed low tariff rates and the consequent increase in foreign competition as important ingredients in a battle against market concentration by a small number of firms. He actively worked with Congress in framing the 1914 tariff legislation that lowered tariffs gradually, as McAdoo realized that businesses would need some time to adjust to increased foreign competition.

Moreover, McAdoo was concerned with the expansion of U.S. trade and exports, particularly with Latin American countries. By 1914, he was convinced that a lack of U.S. shipping hindered trade expansion. When the European war reduced the availability of foreign shipping to U.S. exporters, McAdoo concluded that drastic action was necessary. He contended that private capital could and would not quickly enough flow into the shipping industry to provide enough tonnage; thus, governmental action was necessary. For the next two years, he promoted legislation that provided for federal government (majority) ownership of a shipping corporation. He obtained substantial support from southern and western producers of agricultural exports, particularly cotton growers. Congress passed the Shipping Act of 1916 on August 30, 1916. It created a five-person Shipping Board to which Congress allocated $50 million for the purchase and construction of merchant ships to be leased or sold to the private sector. Congress, unlike McAdoo, intended the government to operate these vessels only as a last resort. The board's authority would terminate five years after the war ended; McAdoo preferred a permanent agency. Moreover, Congress did not place Cabinet members on the board; McAdoo, of course, wanted the Secretary of the Treasury to chair the board. McAdoo's disappointment with the final legislation was lessened somewhat because Wilson allowed him to choose the members of the first Shipping Board.

McAdoo also became involved with another "crisis" in the transportation industry—this time involving railroads. To prevent a railroad strike, the Wilson administration had supported the Adamson Act (1916) that established the eight-hour day for most railroad workers. During the mobilization for war of 1917, railroads experienced difficulties in moving goods, particularly to the East Coast. McAdoo vigorously urged Wilson to use the authority granted by the Army Appropriations Act of 1916 by having the federal government assume control and operation of the nation's railroad industry. McAdoo believed a unified system would result in so many efficiencies that the savings thereby generated would pay for new capital improvement, eliminate the need for further rate increases, and provide for wage increases for railroad workers. McAdoo envisioned a scientifically managed, unified system being one of harmony rather than of continual strife. Wilson finally accepted McAdoo's arguments, and he ordered a federal takeover of the nation's railroads on December 26, 1917.

Wilson appointed McAdoo as the first Director-General of the United States Railroad Administration. McAdoo immediately called for patriotic cooperation on the part of all citizens. McAdoo severely curtailed passenger service to facilitate freight service. In May 1918, he ordered a substantial increase in wages—retroactive to January 1, 1918—with larger pay raises for lower-paid employees. In his *Reminiscences*, McAdoo wrote: "I have never done anything in my life that gave me so much satisfaction as raising the pay of the railroad employees" (490). Clearly, McAdoo used his power to implement his vision of proper working conditions.

By 1918 McAdoo was Secretary of the Treasury, Ex Officio Chair of the Federal Reserve Board, Ex Officio Chair of the Federal Farm Loan Board, Director-General of the U.S. Railroad Administration, Chief Sales Manager for the Liberty Loans, Ex Officio Chair of the War Finance Corporation, and Administrator of the Soldiers and Sailors Insurance Company. Clearly, the war years were "crowded years." He successfully handled these stressful and important jobs by using enormous energy and dedication and masterly delegating authority. He usually laid out general guidelines and objectives and then selected people who could achieve those objectives; apparently, he was a good judge of talent. Nevertheless, the multitude of responsibilities took its toll on his health.

Because of poor health and a stated desire to earn a higher income, McAdoo resigned from Wilson's Cabinet on December 15, 1918. He remained actively involved in politics after his resignation. For example, he vigorously—but unsuccessfully—campaigned for permanent federal government control over the railroads.

Many considered McAdoo to be a favorite for the 1920 Democratic presidential nomination. McAdoo ardently supported the League of Nations, women's suffrage, and prohibition. Ironically, while he had lived in New York City for almost three decades, his support was mostly in the South and West. In part, the eastern urban antipathy toward McAdoo resulted from him being a "dry" candidate. Moreover, McAdoo cultivated a Populist image, as his rhetoric overflowed with denunciations of the dangers of urban, northern life. Wilson did not publicly support McAdoo mostly because Wilson hoped that the convention would nominate him for a third term. Several critics of McAdoo later claimed that Wilson did not consider McAdoo to be "reflective" enough for the presidency. Because Wilson would not officially drop out of the race, his loyal son-in-law, McAdoo, refused to officially announce his own candidacy. Even so, McAdoo was a leader on the first thirty-eight ballots before realizing that he could not win the nomination. He then released his supporters, and the convention on the thirty-ninth ballot chose James Cox as the Democratic candidate for President.

In 1924, most political analysts had McAdoo leading the Democratic "horse race" until he became ensnared in the Teapot Dome scandal. McAdoo had provided $150,000 of legal services to Edward Doheny, the principal figure in this sordid affair. Although McAdoo apparently committed no illegal acts, the perception of impropriety damaged his chances, particularly with progressives. Further damaging to McAdoo's progressive support was his reluctance to disavow Ku Klux Klan support. Nevertheless, with strong backing from southern and western delegates, McAdoo battled the eastern "wet" candidate, Al Smith, through 102 ballots. Finally, both men realized that neither could secure the nomination, so they released their supporters; on the next ballot, delegates selected John W. Davis as their nominee for President.

McAdoo's disappointment in failing to become President did not prevent him from participating actively in California politics; he had moved his law practice to Los Angeles in 1922. He surprised many by resurrecting his political career in 1932. During the 1932 Democratic Convention, he led the California delegation in supporting Franklin D. Roosevelt. California voters elected him in 1932 to the U.S. Senate, where he loyally supported the New Deal's "emergency" economic legislation.

McAdoo returned to private life in 1939. In addition to his law practice, he also was Chair of the Board of the government-owned American President Steamship Lines. He had divorced Eleanor Wilson in 1934 and married his third wife, Doris I. Cross, on September 14, 1935. His son, Robert, died in 1937. William Gibbs McAdoo died of a heart attack in Washington, D.C., on February 1, 1941, at age seventy-seven. He was buried in the Arlington National Cemetery.

McAdoo enjoyed considerable success in private business, as an activist Secretary of the Treasury, and in politics. Most contemporaries considered him to be one of the most capable people of his day. Many historians have agreed with this positive assessment. John Broesamle concludes that "McAdoo was a great Secretary of the Treasury" (xi), and Otis L. Graham, Jr., agrees: "McAdoo was one of the most talented men to enter public life in the twentieth century" (482).

McAdoo was not primarily a philosophical person. He possessed "a passion for change." He considered himself to be a "Jeffersonian Democrat" who wanted only the minimal amount of governmental intervention necessary to allow small businesses and farms to flourish. McAdoo's stated economic beliefs were inconsistent with his actions. His ideological flexibility, which critics considered to be ideological "shiftiness," allowed him to rationalize substantial federal intervention to counteract the influence of big business, to provide capital to sectors that private financial institutions refused, and to provide goods that he believed would benefit all of society and that the private sector would not provide. He readily used the premise of "national emergency" to justify unprecedented direct federal government entry and intervention into the private economy. McAdoo apparently was neither aware of nor concerned with his lack of a consistent ideology.

Ultimately, McAdoo's reputation as Secretary of the Treasury depends on how one views his economic policies. He promoted substantial governmental intervention that forever changed the institutional structure of the U.S. economy.

BIBLIOGRAPHY

Broesamle, John J. *William Gibbs McAdoo: A Passion for Change, 1863–1917.* Port Washington, NY: Kennikat, 1973.

Brownlee, W. Elliot. "Wilson and Financing the Modern State: The Revenue Act of 1916." *Proceedings of the American Philosophical Society* 129 (March 1985): 173–210.

Gilbert, Charles. *American Financing of World War I.* Westport, CT: Greenwood Press, 1970.

Graham, Otis L., Jr. "William Gibbs McAdoo." In *Dictionary of American Biography.* Supp. 3, 479–82. New York: Charles Scribner's Sons, 1973.

Kerr, K. Austin. *American Railroad Politics, 1914–1920: Rates, Wages, and Efficiency.* Pittsburgh: University of Pittsburgh Press, 1968.

McAdoo, William Gibbs. *The Challenge: Liquor and Lawlessness versus Constitutional Government.* New York: Century Co., 1928.

———. *Crowded Years: The Reminiscences of William G. McAdoo.* Boston: Houghton Mifflin Co., 1931; reprint: Port Washington, NY: Kennikat Press, 1971.

Shook, Dale N. *William G. McAdoo and the Development of National Economic Policy, 1913–1918.* New York: Garland Publishing, 1985.

Stratton, David H. "Splattered with Oil: William G. McAdoo and the 1924 Democratic Presidential Nomination." *Southwestern Social Science Quarterly* 44 (June 1963): 62–75.

Vance, Joseph C. "The William Gibbs McAdoo Papers." *Library of Congress Journal of Acquisitions* 15 (May 1958): 168–76.

ROBERT STANLEY HERREN

HUGH MCCULLOCH (December 7, 1808–May 24, 1895). In October 1884, when President Arthur asked Hugh McCulloch to join his Cabinet as Treasury Secretary, the Republican Party had already nominated James Blaine as its candidate for the presidential election of 1884. Therefore, President Arthur's administration was in the process of winding down. Thus, McCulloch would essentially be serving in the role of a caretaker for the affairs of the Treasury Department.

While officially he served in Arthur's Cabinet for a period of only five months—from October 31, 1884, until March 3, 1885—he was by far the most qualified of the three individuals who headed the Treasury in Chester Arthur's administration. He had not only served in high positions in banking and in government, but, most important, he had earlier completed a tour of duty as a Treasury Secretary during Lincoln's second term (March 9, 1865, to April 15, 1865) and Andrew Johnson's administration (April 16, 1865, to March 3, 1869).

Hugh McCulloch was born to Hugh and Abigail McCulloch on December 7, 1808, at Kennebunk, Maine. McCulloch entered Bowdoin College but left during the second year of his studies. Many years later, McCulloch was awarded an honorary degree of A.M. by Bowdoin College. After leaving Bowdoin, he studied law in Boston and was admitted to the bar in 1832. The next year McCulloch moved to Fort Wayne, Indiana, started his law practice, and in 1838 married Susan Mann.

In 1835 McCulloch got his first experience in banking when he accepted a position as cashier and manager of the Fort Wayne branch of the State Bank of Indiana. Thus would begin for McCulloch a distinguished career in banking and later in the federal government. McCulloch eventually became President of the bank, a position he held until 1863.

That year would mark McCulloch's entry into government service. In the early part of 1862, McCulloch came to Washington, D.C., on behalf of the old state banks, to voice opposition to the national banking legislation being debated. However, in March 1863, when the national banking legislation became law, Salmon Chase, then Secretary of the Treasury, asked McCulloch to accept appointment as the Comptroller of the Currency in order to establish the new National Banking System. McCulloch performed this task quite successfully, heading the National Banking System until 1865, when he was given the opportunity of heading the Treasury Department.

McCulloch's first challenge dealt with the problem arising immediately after the ending of the Civil War. It was the question of what to do with government's wartime issue of paper money, of which $450 million were in existence at the war's end. They could not be redeemed in gold. McCulloch's recommendation to Congress was to retire these United States notes and return to the gold standard as expeditiously as possible. His position was that only during wartimes did the government have the authority to issue these greenbacks and make them usable as legal tender. Therefore, upon the cessation of hostilities, these powers ought not to remain in force one day more than was necessary for people to return to the constitutional currency. McCulloch knew that contraction of the greenbacks would start a decline in prices and create problems for the economy, but he argued that "the longer contraction is deferred, the greater must the fall eventually be and the more serious its consequences" (Johnson and Malone, 6).

All of this McCulloch cogently laid down in his Treasury report of 1865 to the Congress, and it won him a pledge of cooperation from the House. However, the bill to authorize the issue of bonds to retire the greenbacks failed to win a majority. In 1866, Congress authorized the retirement of only $14 million of greenbacks, but even these powers were revoked two years later.

Twenty years later, during President Cleveland's first term, Treasury Secretary Daniel Manning would be faced with a similar problem of what to do with greenbacks. His proposal was somewhat similar to McCulloch's in that he also felt the greenbacks should be retired. However, where Manning differed from McCulloch's proposal was that in order to avoid a contraction in the currency, he proposed the use of government surplus to retire all the greenbacks. Thus, in exchange for every greenback dollar canceled the Treasury would pay out a new gold or silver dollar. His proposal was also rejected by the Congress.

Since McCulloch failed to get congressional support for his greenback proposal, he directed his energies to tackling other monetary issues. One of them was the policy of "regular and large-scale" retirement of the public debt. But it would be Charles Folger as the head of the Treasury in President Arthur's administration who managed the retirement of almost $400 million of public debt. This would stand out as the largest volume of public debt retired by any administration in American history.

After McCulloch's tenure as head of the Treasury ended in 1869, he became a partner for several years in the London banking house of Jay Cooke, McCulloch and Company. He was seventy-six when called by President Arthur to lead the Treasury during the final months of his administration.

Although the time in office was too short to undertake any actions of a long-term nature, some of the steps he took deserve mention. The most important perhaps was his recommendation in the 1884 Treasury report that the government should immediately suspend the coinage of silver dollars. To comply with the coinage act of February 1878, the government had already coined 27 million silver dollars. This brought total silver dollars outstanding to about $185 million. Of this amount, less than 22 percent was in actual circulation. The President, in his Fourth Annual Message to the Congress, stated that this in itself was sufficient reason for suspending the statute without any further delay. Arthur's position was that unless this step was taken, silver would take over as the sole metallic standard. McCulloch, of course, completely concurred with this conclusion.

McCulloch predicted that continued coinage of silver dollars might, in the event of a panic or other adversity, force the Treasury to use in ordinary payments the gold it held for redemption of U.S. notes. Second, the Treasury might be forced to use silver or silver certificates to meet its gold obligations. All of this would cause grave commercial disturbances and also immensely impair the national credit.

The first of his predictions did come true a few years later, in 1894, and the second was barely prevented.

A second concern that Secretary McCulloch was able to bring to the forefront was related to the nation's shipping interests. He recommended, and President Arthur agreed, that the government should "lend its active assistance to individual enterprise" to direct the flow of American capital in expanding the participation of American steamships in foreign trade. He felt that this course was needed to prevent our foreign carrying trade from remaining almost exclusively in the hands of foreigners.

The "Mongrel tariff" bill of 1883, which President Arthur signed, did not achieve the extent of tariff reductions he desired. Secretary McCulloch was in favor of getting further reductions in tariffs, and upon taking office at the Treasury, McCulloch continued to voice his support for the President's tariff reform policies. After he left the Treasury upon expiration of Arthur's presidency, McCulloch joined other politicians such as Jacob Cox, Montgomery Blair, and Lyman Trumbull in giving enthusiastic aid to President Cleveland's pursuit of tariff reform.

In perhaps his final act as Treasury Secretary on February 26, 1885, he brought to the attention of Congress, with the President's approval, that the Treasury Department would continue to enforce the law, relating to the unorganized territory of Alaska, that prohibited the sale of intoxicating liquors in the district for any purpose but with certain exceptions.

After his retirement from the Treasury for the second time, McCulloch continued to reside near the Washington, D.C., area. In 1888, he published *Men and Measures of Half a Century*, in which he reminisced about his career and his views on the central issues of that period. On May 24, 1895, McCulloch died at "Holy Hill" in Maryland.

BIBLIOGRAPHY

Barnes, J. A. *Wealth of the American People: A History of Their Economic Life*. New York: Prentice-Hall, 1949.

Doenecke, J. D. *The Presidencies of James A. Garfield & Chester A. Arthur*. Lawrence: Regents Press of Kansas, 1981.

Friedman M., and Anna Schwartz. *A Monetary History of the United States 1867–1960*. Princeton: Princeton University Press, 1963.

Furer, H. B. *James A. Garfield 1831–1881 and Chester A. Arthur 1830–1886: Chronology—Documents—Bibliographical Aids*. New York: Oceana Publishing Company, 1970.

Hacker, L. M. *Major Documents in American Economic History*. Princeton: D. Van Nostrand Company, 1961.

Howe, G. F. *Chester A. Arthur: A Quarter Century of Machine Politics*. New York: Frederick Ungar Publishing Company, 1957.

Johnson, A., and Dumas Malone, eds. *Dictionary of American Biography*. New York: Charles Scribner's Sons, 1933.

Kroos, H. E., ed. *Documentary History of Banking and Currency in the United States*. New York: Chelsea House Publishers, 1977.

McGrane, R. C. *The Economic Development of the American Nation*. Boston: Ginn and Company, 1942.

Magill, F. N., ed. *Great Lives from History: American Series*. New Jersey: Salem Press, 1987.

Nevins, A. *Grover Cleveland: A Study in Courage*. New York: Dodd, Mead & Company, 1933.

Richardson, J. D., ed. *A Compilation of the Messages and Papers of the Presidents*. Washington, D.C.: Bureau of National Literature, 1911.

Schlesinger, A. M., ed. *History of American Presidential Elections*. New York: Chelsea House Publishers, 1971.

Shannon, F. A. *Economic History of the People of the United States*. New York: Macmillan Company, 1934.

NAYYER HUSSAIN

LOUIS MCLANE (May 28, 1784–October 7, 1857). Louis McLane was a lawyer, statesman, diplomat, and businessman and was considered by his peers to be first among men in each of these pursuits. His career was multifaceted and shaped by his politics; a staunch Federalist from Delaware, he remained true to his Federalist principles long after his party collapsed. His hot temper and pride, along with his inability to let go of a grudge, may very well have cost him his chance to ascend to the U.S. presidency or the U.S. Supreme Court, two positions he coveted. During his tenure in the Jackson Cabinet, he became estranged from Martin Van Buren, who was once a close friend. This falling out played a leading role in ending his chances of reaching his political goals.

Louis McLane was born on May 28, 1784, in the town of Duck Creek Cross Roads, New Jersey (renamed Smyrna in 1806), the son of a Revolutionary War hero, Allen McLane, and his wife Rebecca (Wells) McLane. Louis's birth date is often given incorrectly in reference sources, and this error may be due to being the second son to bear that name (Munroe, 22). His parents endured great hardship; of fourteen children, only three, Louis, Rebecca, and Allen, survived to adulthood. On February 27, 1797, President Washington appointed Allen McLane Collector of Customs in Wilmington, Delaware, and the family moved to Wilmington that spring.

Louis McLane's father was of Scottish descent. Allen McLane was born in Philadelphia on August 8, 1746. He was an ardent Federalist and a prominent member of the party in Delaware. As a partisan captain in General Washington's army, he became a war hero. Allen had great influence on Louis, instilling a fighting spirit and physical resilience into the boy, which prepared him for the rigors of private and political life in Jacksonian America. His parents were Methodist, and his mother's strong religious beliefs did little to temper Allen's influence on his son. The combination of federalism, Methodism, and a war-hero father provided the catalyst to propel Louis into the forefront of Delaware politics and lifted him to national prominence.

Louis's early education in Smyrna is unclear. His father enrolled him in the Friends school in Wilmington in 1797. On May 3, 1799, at the age of fifteen, he was given a midshipman appointment on the frigate *Philadelphia*, under the command of Stephen Decatur, father of a future American war hero of the same name. The *Philadelphia* was posted to the Guadeloupe station in the Lesser Antilles to protect American shipping during the war scare generated over the French (XYZ) affair. The *Philadelphia* returned home in April 1801 after a successful tour. McLane was then furloughed because of ill health. His furlough was extended, and he resigned on January 16, 1802.

After leaving the Navy, Louis entered Newark Academy (now the University of Delaware) in 1802. He left the academy in 1804 to become a clerk in the law office of a close friend of his father, James A. Bayard. Louis remained with Bayard until after he was admitted to the New Castle bar in December 1807.

Louis spent the next ten years as a young lawyer in Wilmington. He had a natural gift as a public speaker and gained a reputation as a very competent lawyer. These qualities would allow Louis to reach an eminent rank at the bar in his native state.

On December 29, 1812, Louis married Catherine Mary Milligan, the eldest daughter of Robert and Sally (Jones) Milligan. Catherine was a prize; her family was politically and socially connected, she was well educated, and her family was wealthy. She proved to be an effective advocate of her husband in Washington society and a confidante that could temper Louis's emotional responses to events outside his control. Louis and his wife were extremely close. Of thirteen children, only one died in infancy.

In the congressional elections of 1816, young McLane was elected to the U.S. House of Representatives and served ten years. His first years in Washington were clouded by financial difficulties due to investments in Delaware that went bad. Financial pressures precluded Louis from bringing his family to Washington immediately, and the distance from his family had a negative effect on his disposition. In fact, Catherine would spend the winter in Wilmington for seven of the twelve years McLane served in Congress.

Louis McLane was a strong supporter of the Second Bank of the United States during his years in the House. In 1818, he played a pivotal role in the rejection of a House resolution to investigate the daily operations of the bank, successfully arguing before the House that the Congress possessed no power to interfere with the daily operations of the bank.

In 1820, McLane, on the issue of allowing Missouri to enter the Union, voted for entry, against instructions from the Delaware legislature. He based his decision on Federalist principles, that he was an officer of the Union and not the agent of the state. In 1822, McLane was elected Chairman of the powerful Ways and Means Committee. He continued as Chairman until he was elected to the U.S. Senate by the Delaware legislature in the fall of 1826.

McLane's tenure in the House made him a politician of national reputation. He was a champion of the bank, and he believed in tariff protection for American industry. He was an advocate for investing in America's infrastructure. His pet project during his tenure was the Chesapeake and Delaware Canal. He was a staunch supporter of William Crawford and Andrew Jackson, supporting both men for the U.S. presidency.

Upon Andrew Jackson's election to the presidency in 1828, McLane was selected to fill the post of Minister of the United States to the Court of St. James (England). McLane spent two years in England and won the praise of Jackson and the American public by negotiating the West Indies Trade Treaty, which had long been a source of conflict between the two nations. When Jackson's first Cabinet dissolved over the Mrs. Eaton scandal, Jackson recalled McLane to fill the Secretary of the Treasury post vacated by Samuel D. Ingham. McLane took control of the Treasury portfolio on August 8, 1831.

McLane saw his new position as an avenue to further his Federalist beliefs and to ascend in the political hierarchy. His agenda included the bank's rechartering and a new tariff bill to protect domestic industry. He merged his agenda with the President's top economic goals: the selling of public lands to the states and the elimination of all government debt by the end of 1832. The elimination of government debt was of the highest priority for Jackson.

McLane released his Treasury report on December 6, 1831, generating a great stir in Washington. He presented a plan to use the bank and the government's stock holdings in the bank to eliminate the debt by March 3, 1833. The plan would allow Jackson to keep his 1828 campaign pledge and would also put the bank in a very favorable political position. The debt elimination plan was controversial; however, it allowed McLane to make a case for the rechartering of the bank.

Behind the scene, McLane convinced Jackson that, with modification, renewing the bank's charter after the 1832 election was in the best interest of the country. Jackson confirmed this in a letter to James A. Hamilton dated December 12, 1831: "Mr. McLane and myself understand each other, and have not the slightest disagreement about principles, which will be a *sine qua non* in my assent to a bill rechartering the Bank" (Hamilton, 234). McLane also discussed the issue with Nicholas Biddle, President of the bank, during a meeting in Philadelphia on October 19, 1831. McLane warned Biddle that renewal of the bank's charter must come after the election or Jackson would consider the move as a political attack and veto the bill.

Biddle's recollection of this meeting clearly shows this: "If therefore while he is so confident of reelection, this question is put on him as one affecting his reelection, he might be disposed to put his veto on it" (McGrane, 128–31). Nevertheless, in December, Biddle was leaning to recharter immediately, as recommended by Henry Clay and other enemies of Jackson. McLane again warned Biddle through a mutual friend, Thomas Cadwalader: "If you apply now, you assuredly will fail—if you wait, you will as certainly succeed" (McGrane, 150–51). Biddle failed to heed McLane's advice and pressed for renewal in January 1832, and the rest is history.

On the tariff issue, McLane joined forces with his old nemesis John Q. Adams. Adams was Chairman of the House Committee on Manufactures. The House, on January 16, 1832, passed Adams's resolution to empower McLane to do two things: (1) collect information on the condition of American manufacturing and (2) construct a new tariff bill (Munroe, 342). The tariff bill was presented by McLane to Congress in May and was based on information drawn from his *Report on Manufactures*. McLane drafted a bill acceptable to the South. Congress revised the bill, making it offensive to the South, and then passed it in June. The passage of the Adams tariff bill spawned the nullification crisis.

McLane's most important contribution to the field of economics is his *Report on Manufactures*, one of the most valuable sources of information on early American industry. The report is a collection of individual returns from manufactures. It contains unique and extensive information on the microeconomic life of industry during that period.

In May 1833, Jackson again reorganized his Cabinet. Edward Livingston, Secretary of State, was made Minister to France to settle the French Spoilage question. McLane was given the post of Secretary of State, and William J. Duane joined the Cabinet as the new Secretary of the Treasury after McLane left office on May 28.

On June 26, 1833, Jackson sent Duane instructions on how he planned to have federal deposits removed from the bank. Duane resisted Jackson's plan, and Jackson asked Duane to resign on September 22, 1833. McLane argued during that period against Jackson's plan; when Duane resigned, McLane and Lewis Cass, the Secretary of War, both offered their resignations.

Martin Van Buren, Vice President, interceded to stop the second dissolution of the President's Cabinet. Rebecca McLane is credited by Van Buren for being the "voice of reason" persuading Louis to remain in the Cabinet.

With the Cabinet crisis resolved, and the bank issue a lost cause, McLane focused his attention on the French Spoilage issue and his plan for the restructuring of the State Department; this restructuring was his most important contribution as Secretary of State.

When McLane assumed the duties of Secretary, the department had no formal structure. McLane submitted a formal memorandum to President Jackson on August 29, 1833, containing a proposed set of guidelines for daily operations in the State Department. Jackson approved and the regulations were made effective.

The French Spoilage issue was the last straw for McLane. The French refused to honor the indemnity treaty negotiated by William C. Rives in July 1831. McLane argued for strong action against the French, Letters of Marque, which would allow American raids upon French commercial shipping. Jackson was at first in favor but changed his mind after hearing the arguments in favor of prudence by Van Buren. McLane's pride could not bear being overruled on matters of state, and he resigned on June 18, 1834.

Seventeen years of public life ended when McLane loaded his family and possessions on a Potomac steamboat for the trip to Baltimore and then home to Wilmington. McLane settled into private life, trying to decide what direction his life should go. In May 1835 he accepted the presidency of the Morris Canal and Banking Company. The company had a history of poor management and was scandal ridden. McLane brought respectability to the company, and his management skills honed by his years in government service allowed the company to expand its operations and to pay its first dividend on July 14, 1836, after ten years of existence.

McLane's success in turning around the Morris Canal and Banking Company brought an offer to become President of the Baltimore and Ohio Railroad in December 1836. The Board of Directors of the Morris Canal and Banking Company tried to persuade McLane to stay, but on June 15, 1837, they accepted his resignation and gave McLane a large bonus in compensation for his outstanding leadership. The bonus was more than twice his annual salary.

In July 1837, McLane and his family arrived in Baltimore. McLane called the Baltimore and Ohio "a wreck." McLane's first report as President in October 1837 showed a large corporate loss. By the next year the railroad showed a substantial profit. The feat was accomplished by cutting expenses. The railroad doubled the length of its roadbed, reaching Cumberland, Virginia, by the time McLane retired on September 13, 1848. During his tenure as President of the railroad, he was commissioned by U.S. President Polk in June 1845 to undertake a diplomatic mission to England to settle the Oregon boundary dispute. In April

1846, the treaty was signed, setting the forty-ninth parallel as the permanent border between the United States and England.

After McLane retired, he and his family remained in Baltimore. His wife died on July 31, 1849. He eventually recovered and again became active in Maryland politics. He attended the Maryland Constitutional Convention in 1850–1851 as a delegate from Baltimore. His health deteriorated after the convention, and he died in Baltimore on October 7, 1857, with seven of his children at his side.

BIBLIOGRAPHY

"Article on Louis McLane." *Daily National Intelligencer* (Washington, D.C.), July 22, 1834.
Catterall, R. C. *The Second Bank of the United States.* Chicago: Chicago University Press, 1903.
Hamilton, James A. *Reminiscences of James A. Hamilton.* New York: C. Scribner and Company, 1869.
Hungerford, E. *The Story of the Baltimore & Ohio Railroad 1827–1927.* New York: G. P. Putnam's Sons, 1928.
"Louis McLane." In *Appleton's Cyclopedia of American Biography.* Vol. 4. New York: D. Appleton and Co., 1888.
"Louis McLane." In *National Cyclopedia of American Biography.* Vol 6. Ann Arbor, MI: University Microfilms, 1967.
McCormac, E. I. "Louis McLane: Secretary of State." In *The American Secretaries of State and Their Diplomacy,* edited by Samuel F. Bemis. New York: A. A. Knopf, 1928.
McGrane, R. C. *The Correspondence of Nicholas Biddle Dealing with National Affairs 1807–1844.* Boston: Houghton Mifflin Publishing Co., 1919.
McLane, Louis. "Report on Finances. December, 1831." In *Reports of the Secretary of the Treasury of the United States.* Washington, D.C.: Blair and Rives, 1837.
———. *McLane Report on Manufactures. Documents Relative to Manufactures in the United States.* House Document No. 308, 22nd Cong., 1st sess. 2 vols. Washington, D.C., 1833.
Munroe, J. *Louis McLane: Federalist and Jacksonian.* New Brunswick, NJ: Rutgers University Press, 1973.
Parton, J. *Life of Andrew Jackson.* Vols. 1–3. New York: Mason Brothers, 1861.

SCOTT W. FAUSTI

FRANKLIN MACVEAGH (November 22, 1837–July 6, 1934). Franklin MacVeagh held the post of Treasury Secretary from 1909 to 1913. His term in office, the last before the establishment of the Federal Reserve System, signaled the end of an era: an era in which the U.S. Treasury was forced to accept many of the functions performed in other industrial market economies by their respective central banks. The biographical profile that follows addresses, in turn, MacVeagh's personal background and contribution to a Treasury Department about to undergo a radical transformation.

Franklin MacVeagh, the son of Margaret (Lincoln) and Major John MacVeagh, was born on November 22, 1837, in Chester County, Pennsylvania. He died on July 6, 1934. The younger brother of Wayne MacVeagh, Attorney General under President Garfield, Franklin was raised in the Methodist faith. In 1868 he married Emily Eames. The couple had five children.

Educated early in life by private tutors, the future Secretary of the Treasury attended Freeland Seminary (Ursinus College) in Collegeville, Pennsylvania. He graduated from Yale University in 1862 and, two years later, from Columbia Law School. In the latter year MacVeagh was admitted to the bar and began to practice law in Philadelphia. Due to ill health, MacVeagh was forced to give up his legal career. Moving his young family to Chicago, MacVeagh tried his hand at a number of business ventures. In 1817 MacVeagh established himself in the wholesale grocery business with the organization of F. MacVeagh and Company in Chicago.

It was in Chicago that MacVeagh's interest in politics took substantive form. In 1874 he founded and eventually became President of the Citizen's Committee against Graft, an organization that fought corruption in city government. A member of the executive committee of the National Civic Federation, MacVeagh became Vice President of the American Civic Association in 1905. Supporting Republican interests in municipal affairs, MacVeagh was a staunch supporter of Grover Cleveland in his 1884, 1888, and 1892 bids for the presidency. In 1894 MacVeagh became the Democratic candidate for the U.S. Senate seat being vacated by Shelby M. Cullom. The closeness of the election pushed the contest into the legislature, where MacVeagh lost to his Republican opponent.

After his senatorial defeat, while continuing to take an active interest in politics, MacVeagh returned to Chicago to pursue his private business interests for the next fifteen years. It was during this period that MacVeagh broke with the Democratic Party over the silver issue, allying himself with the Republican Party in the pivotal election of 1896. This action was to pay substantial dividends years later.

In 1909 MacVeagh, recommended by his long-standing Republican monetary positions, was picked by William Howard Taft to head the U.S. Treasury. In accepting the Treasury post, MacVeagh became one of the few nonlawyers appointed to the Taft Cabinet. MacVeagh shared this distinction with the Secretary of the Navy and Secretary of Agriculture. An important force in the formation of the Taft Cabinet, the Secretary of State, Philander Chase Knox, negotiated MacVeagh's appointment.

During his tenure as Secretary of the Treasury, which began on March 8, 1909, Franklin MacVeagh, recognizing the shortcomings of the existing National Banking System (NBS), followed in the tradition laid down by his predecessors of aiding the financial sector with the tools at his disposal. MacVeagh's term, while not as innovative as Secretary Leslie Shaw's (1902–1907) or as difficult as that of his immediate predecessor Secretary George Cortelyou (1907–1909), reveals nonetheless his understanding of the problems of the domestic financial sector.

The problems of the U.S. financial system at this time derived largely from those inherent in the existing banking system. The NBS, established by the Banking Acts of 1863 and 1864, had, in fact, plagued Treasury Secretaries since the inception of the system. Created in response to the needs of the national government during the Civil War, the NBS contributed significantly to two of the long-standing problems of the postbellum financial sector: (1) the maldistribution of banking facilities and (2) the recurring autumnal difficulties on the stock market—problems to which the Treasury, in the absence of a domestic central bank, was forced to respond.

The maldistribution of banking facilities resulted from the minimum capital requirements existing under the NBS. Country banks, organized in areas with a population of less than 6,000 people, faced a $50,000 minimum capital requirement. Reserve city banks, set up in towns with a population of between 6,000 and 50,000, had a minimum capital requirement of $100,000, and central reserve city banks, located in cities with populations exceeding 50,000, faced a $200,000 requirement.

These requirements, particularly at the country bank level, were relatively severe. As a result, with state banks being driven out of business by the tax on state bank notes included in NBS legislation, limited banking facilities were found in rural areas—areas with limited population. Banking facilities and, consequently, funds for investment and working capital needs were not evenly distributed within the NBS. While the system drew the ire of individuals from the relatively deprived areas, this framework provided a significant unintended benefit: The system concentrated funds in the cities of the Northeast, providing ample money capital to support the process of industrialization.

The structure of the NBS played a significant role, in addition, in the stock market panics of the nineteenth century. Under the NBS, banks at each level were required to hold reserves against deposits: fifteen, twenty-five, and twenty-five, respectively, at the country, reserve city, and central reserve city bank levels. Only at the central reserve city bank level, however, were banks required to maintain the necessary funds within their own vaults. Country banks needed to keep only two fifths of the reserve on hand. The remainder could be deposited with other national banks. Banks located in reserve cities needed to keep only one half on hand. This system contributed to the practice of placing all surplus funds with correspondent national banks at the next-highest level. Through this process, then, funds tended to accumulate at the central reserve city level—primarily in New York. Central reserve city banks, anxious to generate revenue with these funds, typically placed them in the call loan market.

Unfortunately, the NBS was, in addition, a relatively inflexible system with respect to note issue. As a result, banks in need of funds at one level in the system were required to draw down on their deposits with correspondent institutions. During crop-moving season, in the fall of every year, the country banks required additional funds. Unable to acquire them profitably elsewhere, country bankers were forced to draw down on their funds with reserve city banks. The latter, in turn, were required to draw down on their funds with central reserve city banks. New York city banks, having placed these funds in the call loan market, commonly reacquired them from the same source. The resulting sell-off of equities not infrequently caused difficulties on the stock market. In the absence of a central bank, responsibility for a wide range of financial duties fell to the Treasury.

Secretary MacVeagh faithfully accepted this responsibility. As he acknowledged in his *Annual Report* of 1913: "It has been, and will continue to be, the policy of the Secretary to exercise all the powers of the Department for the protection of the public and the legitimate business interests of the country." In that same year, true to his words, MacVeagh aided a group of Ohio banks by providing them with $2 million in government deposits after a devastating flood reduced confidence in the viability of the local banking system. These funds were secured by state and municipal bonds deemed acceptable to the Secretary.

In contrast with the post–World War II focus on the difficulties associated with deficit spending, the Treasury was faced during MacVeagh's tenure with the problems arising out of a surplus situation. A surplus, it was reasoned at the time, withdrew money from circulation. This, in turn, reduced bank deposits and placed downward pressure on reserves. The latter typically led to a contraction in lending and hence a reduction in the volume of business activity. It was to this process that MacVeagh directed the following comment in his 1912 *Annual Report:* "Taking large sums of actual money out of ordinary financial uses and locking them up as a dead mass in the vaults of the Treasury is a proceeding as unscientific and unreasoned as any other part of our unscientific and unreasoned banking and currency system."

A number of contributions can be attributed to MacVeagh. New auditing procedures were introduced and a significant number of superfluous positions eliminated. Presiding over the Treasury during a period of relative calm, however, MacVeagh's term as Secretary may be remembered more for his public miscues than for his contributions. One observer of the period noted that nothing memorable was accomplished by the Democrat, Franklin MacVeagh, at the Treasury. In April 1910, Senator Albert J. Beveridge of Indiana began his bid for reelection in earnest. President Taft, in response to Beveridge's voting record on legislation sponsored by the President, declined to support the Senator. After a number of weeks, MacVeagh imprudently promised the support of the President to Beveridge—Taft, furious with his Treasury Secretary, again refused to support Beveridge.

In May 1911 MacVeagh committed a more serious blunder. Throughout the early years of the century, a number of pension bills had been submitted for congressional consideration. Discussion focused, in part, on the eligibility provisions of the veteran bills. In the course of this debate, MacVeagh pointed out that a comprehensive pension list had never been compiled. This is not surprising, given the absence of a systematized budget. That eventuality did not arise until 1921. MacVeagh noted, in addition, the increasing cost of veteran's doles in the budget.

These statements generated outraged protests from various veterans groups. More than a few called for his resignation. Thankfully for the Secretary, the discussion moved on quickly to debate more strident positions. These miscues, recalling echoes of late-twentieth-century missteps, explain why, during President Taft's renomination bid, the brother of the President took a clear position regarding the Secretary, suggesting that while MacVeagh meant well, he should have been given a bottle of milk and allowed to crawl on the lap of Mrs. MacVeagh to sleep.

MacVeagh served as Secretary until March 5, 1913. The end of MacVeagh's term as Treasury Secretary marks the end of an era. His replacement, William G. McAdoo, served as Treasury Secretary and Chairman of the Federal Reserve Board (forerunner of the Board of Governors of the Federal Reserve System).

After leaving Washington, MacVeagh again became president of the wholesale grocery firm of Franklin MacVeagh & Co. The firm was dissolved in 1932 as a result of the depression that existed in 1931. His business affairs occupied his time until his last illness.

BIBLIOGRAPHY

Annual Report of the Secretary of the Treasury. Washington, D.C.: U.S. Government Printing Office, various years.

Coletta, Paolo E. *The Presidency of William Howard Taft.* Lawrence: University of Kansas Press, 1973.

Sobel, Robert, ed. *Biographical Directory of the United States Executive Branch, 1774–1977.* Westport, CT: Greenwood Press, 1977.

PAUL J. KUBIK

DANIEL MANNING (May 16, 1831–December 24, 1887). The selection of Cabinet members is a delicate task for any President. It was particularly so with President Cleveland because the professionals among the Democrats wanted the party organization well represented so that it could be kept together for the future. While Cleveland was more interested in ensuring support for his intended reforms, he knew that some of the party leaders would have to be given positions even though it meant offending the reformers who had helped him in his campaign. He deliberated for a few days, but for the three most important positions— Secretaries of the State, Treasury, and Navy—he had already determined his candidates and without consulting anyone made his choices public.

Daniel Manning was his choice for the Treasury post. While it created some surprise and generated criticism, the nomination of Manning was much more meritorious than perceived. In addition to establishing himself as the boss of the Albany Democratic Party, he also had substantial experience in business and finance.

Manning was born on May 16, 1831, in Albany, New York. He was the second son of John and Eleanor Manning. At the age of six he lost his father, and he left school at eleven to seek work to support his family. He was appointed a page in the state Assembly in 1841 and kept that position for two seasons. He learned the printer's trade while working as a route carrier for the *Albany Atlas.* To further better himself he also learned stenography and French. He tried his hand at journalism, and when the *Atlas* and *Argus* merged, he was assigned a reporter's desk in the city department. Manning continued his career as a journalist, moving up to become the legislative correspondent of the *Brooklyn Eagle* newspaper. In 1865 he became part owner and business manager of the *Argus* company and in 1873 became the President of the firm.

Manning's considerable experience in journalism proved invaluable for his career in Democratic Party politics. He was a good friend of Tilden's and in 1877 virtually succeeded Tilden to the chairmanship of the Democratic Party organization in New York State. Manning worked very hard for the candidacy of Tilden and Cleveland as a delegate to the Democratic Party Convention in 1876, 1880, and 1884. Thus, Cleveland was indebted to Manning, particularly for his nominations as Governor of New York and subsequently for the presidency.

When Cleveland selected him for the post of Treasury Secretary, Manning was already well known for his active role in Albany politics. This political acumen of Manning was an invaluable asset for the President because in addition to serving Cleveland very ably as the head of the Treasury, he also proved to be a sound political adviser who diverted the President from making costly errors in his political decisions and leadership policies.

Manning's tenure at the helm of the Treasury Department was short-lived, from March 8, 1885, to March 31, 1887. However, the two years were anything but uneventful. The struggle over presidential appointments was quickly overshadowed "by stubborn battles [that] had broken forth upon the silver question and the reduction of duties" (Nevins, 266). The silver question put Cleveland and Manning in direct confrontation with the majority of their own party in the House of Representatives. Manning and Cleveland representing the eastern banking circles were pitted against a "congressional bloc" that represented silver miners, small farmers of the West, and the debtors group. Manning and Cleveland both agreed that the Bland-Allison Act, under which the westerners were able to obtain unlimited coinage of silver, should be repealed immediately. Both were strong supporters of the gold standard and felt sure that financial disaster would ensue if the gold standard was put in jeopardy.

Under the compulsory provisions of the Bland-Allison Act, which became effective in 1878, the government had purchased silver bullion and coined it at a rate of $2 million a month. Thus, by 1885 the government had already stamped more than 215 million silver dollars, far more than the economy could absorb. Despite the attempts by three administrations, only about 50 million of the silver dollars had found their way into circulation, and the government was left with 165 million silver dollars in its possession. Every month the Treasury was paying out $2 million in gold for 2 million or more in silver dollars to be added to what had already been accumulated. Cleveland feared that this trend would result in the substitution of silver for all the gold the government owned. He called for the repeal of the Bland-Allison Act in his 1885 State of the Union message.

Since the time was approaching when the government would be forced to offer silver to pay its obligations, the desire to hoard gold would be very strong. In

March 1885, Manning took strong measures to avert this threat to the gold reserve. Arthur's policy of bond redemption had been abandoned, allowing the federal revenues to accumulate in the vaults. Also, wherever possible, the Treasury used greenbacks for disbursement instead of gold or silver coins. Manning had also arranged with the New York Clearing House to keep intact or augment, if possible, the stock of gold in the Treasury. This measure was successful beyond Cleveland's expectations, and in the first year of his presidency, the Treasury managed to build gold reserves from $125 million to $151 million.

This peril was soon forgotten by the public, as if it had never occurred. There was no doubt, however, that the country had come close to a financial disaster. Abram Hewitt pointed this out in Congress, referring to the fact that the hoarding of gold had begun with the masters of finance. Three of the large New York banks had already secretly accumulated in reserves $25 million in gold in anticipation of the imminent change. The change, according to Hewitt, did not come because of the superb management of the Secretary of the Treasury.

The success of this new Treasury policy was received angrily by the "free-coinage men" who would have liked nothing better than to see the country forced to a silver standard. The most vocal attack on the President came from Scotchman James Beck of Kentucky, denouncing the policy for "locking up so much money in the Treasury." He was joined by Bland, Warner, and Weaver who accused Cleveland and Manning of open subserviency to Wall and Lombard Streets. Secretary Manning was asked to provide a detailed explanation of the arrangement he had made with the New York Clearing House and other related matters through a resolution pushed through the Coinage Committee.

Manning replied through a detailed report, emphatically defending the administration's policy because the gold reserve of the Treasury had fallen to a dangerously low level of about $114 million in June 1885. To avoid the impending crisis, he had arranged with the New York banks to exchange subsidiary silver, silver certificates for gold and greenbacks. He also demonstrated that this was fully within the law and then went on to present his reasons for calling an end to the Bland-Allison purchases.

According to Manning, true bimetallism could not be achieved without an international agreement. Europe would not have cooperated with the United States to establish bimetallism for two reasons: (1) the preference for an exchange ratio of fifteen and one half to one instead of sixteen to one between silver and gold and (2) the hope that the United States would abandon its gold standard, enabling Europe to flood the United States with silver.

The Cleveland administration was seeking an international agreement on establishing a uniform exchange rate between gold and silver. He sent Manton Marble as a special emissary to Europe to inquire about this issue. Some months following his arrival, there seemed a possibility of reaching an agreement. However, this was laid to rest when in 1888 the British Commission made its report.

At home the proponents of silver coinage were not content and therefore launched a second attack on the administration's policy. This was the Bland bill calling for free and unlimited coinage of silver. While this bill was defeated in Congress, there was no hope of halting the limited coinage that Cleveland and Manning had sought.

Congressional opponents of the administration attacked it in the form of the Morrison surplus resolution. As Treasury Secretary, Manning had stopped buying bonds, and the surplus had grown to become an embarrassment. Proponents of silver coinage were of the view that this surplus could be used to cancel bonds and thereby expand money supply while reducing government's interest payments. Their report stated that the surplus had accumulated to $180 million in excess of all other liabilities. The report went on to urge that all surplus above $100 million be used to retire government bonds.

Manning was opposed to Morrison's proposal on the grounds that it would reduce government's gold reserves to dangerously low levels. His position was that government should have a reasonable level of reserves. Hewitt agreed and argued that prudent business practice dictated that a business should keep on hand reserves equal to one month's disbursements. Based on this practice, he determined that the Treasury should keep a reserve of $168 million.

This Treasury surplus was also putting increased pressure on Cleveland to reduce the tariff, an issue to which Cleveland had paid little attention. The Democratic Party from the days of Polk was known for supporting lower tariffs, and the advocates in the party were pressuring Cleveland to lower them. However, a protectionist wing had developed in the party, and the President did not particularly want to alienate this wing. This, and his fear that such a step would damage established industries, explains somewhat his hesitancy in moving on the question of tariff reduction. His cautious approach was in stark contrast to Manning's, whose annual Treasury report strongly urged the revision of tariffs because many of the rates were actually hurting those it was intended to benefit. Manning through his investigation had concluded that the tariff laws "were a chaos rather than a system" (Nevins, 285). Manning's followers were active and set to work to get Congress to have the tariffs reduced. They advocated total elimination of tariffs on raw materials. All the Democratic candidates supported tariff revision on that principle. And they also managed to get a Republican converted to their position.

This continuous and often acrimonious struggle with the proponents of free silver coinage took its toll on Manning's health, which took a turn for the worse when he suffered a "nervous breakdown." His repeated offers to resign were turned down by Cleveland, who told Manning how ably he had organized and run the Treasury Department, and that he should temporarily hand over the charge of the Treasury to Charles Fairchild and go away for a rest until October. Manning went to Hot Springs to rest, and Cleveland kept him regularly informed of the events and the work of the Cabinet.

Meanwhile, the Democrat-controlled House was bent on creating mischief for the President, and it did so by passing the Morrison resolution. However, the Republican Senate came to Cleveland's rescue by amending the resolution to remove some of its sting. It gave the Treasury a $110 million minimum and a $130 million maximum reserve. The Secretary was also authorized to suspend the resolution in the case of an emergency. The silver supporters managed to reduce the maximum reserve to $120 million. Cleveland was distinctly displeased with this congressional action and gave it a pocket veto.

Manning, while not actively involved in the affairs of the Treasury, nonetheless closely followed the situation and wrote to the President outlining his views. He felt that the House had not succeeded in politically damaging the President and that the Senate had in fact relieved the President of many embarrassments.

It became clear that Manning's deteriorating health would prevent his return to the Treasury. Fairchild was appointed in his place. Manning's absence was a considerable loss to Cleveland's administration, particularly in the later stages of its struggle with the silver supporters in Congress.

It is said that while Manning's illness was the major reason for his departure, his close relationship with Tilden is also cited as contributing to his withdrawal, since Cleveland resented Tilden's desire to be "the power behind the throne" (Johnson and Dumas, 249). Other historians, however, dismiss as unfounded the idea that Manning's relationship with the President was unhappy.

Manning was not a speech maker and was more comfortable working behind the scenes on other candidates' behalf rather than seeking office for himself. It was Manning's keen sense of judgment of men and events, his political sagacity, that stood out clearly in his career and in his short stewardship of the Treasury Department. He managed the affairs of the department very ably, and his Treasury reports were insightful in discussing the important fiscal and monetary issues facing the country at that time.

Nevins is of the view that Manning was not only among the ablest men in Washington at that time; more important, his influence on President Cleveland "has never been rightfully appreciated" (132).

For Cleveland, having Manning in the Cabinet proved to be a great boon. He made sure that the President did not make costly political mistakes by angering the party loyalists. Another important feature of their relationship was the congruity of their views on questions pertaining to sound money doctrine, the tariffs, and opposition to the Bland-Allison Act, among other issues.

Manning regularly used the editorial page of the *Argus* to argue his position on the soundness of the gold standard and to highlight the need to lower tariffs. He warned that if our currency went to a silver basis, it would lead immediately to prices going up and wages going down by 15 to 20 percent to compensate for the difference between the nominal and the real value of the metal in the silver dollar. Whatever position Manning held, he held with great conviction, leaving no doubt as to his views. According to observers, Manning was a perfect example of the superiority of candor over cunning.

History records that when first selected to head the Treasury, Manning was not too keen on going to Washington because of his age, his frail health, and his close circle of friends in Albany. He did, however, go out of loyalty to President Cleveland. And while they did have their share of differences of opinion, Manning was one of the hardest-working members of the Cabinet, regularly burning the proverbial midnight oil in his office—struggling with the issues of the day. He served Cleveland loyally and capably as the Treasury Secretary.

After leaving the Treasury, he returned to New York to assume the presidency of Western National Bank. But in the end, the struggle with the "silver blizzard of 1886" had taken so severe a toll on his already delicate health that he never quite recovered and died on December 24, 1887.

BIBLIOGRAPHY

Barnes, J. A. *Wealth of the American People: A History of Their Economic Life*. New York: Prentice-Hall, 1949.

Friedman M., and Anna Schwartz. *A Monetary History of the United States 1867–1960*. Princeton: Princeton University Press, 1963.

Hacker, L. M. *Major Documents in American Economic History*. Princeton: D. Van Nostrand Company, 1961.

Johnson, A., and Dumas Malone, eds. *Dictionary of American Biography*. New York: Charles Scribner's Sons, 1931.

Kroos, H. E., ed. *Documentary History of Banking and Currency in the United States*. New York: Chelsea House Publishers, 1977.

McGrane, R. C. *The Economic Development of the American Nation*. Boston: Ginn and Company, 1942.

Nevins, A. *Grover Cleveland: A Study in Courage*. New York: Dodd, Mead & Company, 1933.

Richardson, J. D., ed. *A Compilation of the Messages and Papers of the Presidents*. Washington, D.C.: Bureau of National Literature, 1911.

Schlesinger, A. M., ed. *History of American Presidential Elections*. New York: Chelsea House Publishers, 1971.

Shannon, F. A. *Economic History of the People of the United States*. New York: Macmillan Company, 1934.

Tugwell, R. *Grover Cleveland*. New York: Macmillan Company, 1968.

Vexler, R. I., ed. *Grover Cleveland: Chronology—Documents—Bibliographical Aids*. New York: Oceana Publishers, 1968.

NAYYER HUSSAIN

ANDREW W. MELLON (March 24, 1855–August 26, 1937). The greatest Secretary of the Treasury since Alexander Hamilton, and the longest serving, took office on March 4, 1921. Andrew W. Mellon would serve under three Presidents until he was "promoted" to Ambassador in London in 1932. He was the wealthiest man to serve in government and the most esteemed until the depression. Then his policies and service were criticized and condemned, probably with some justification.

Andrew W. Mellon was born in Pittsburgh, Pennsylvania, on March 24, 1855. His father, Thomas Mellon, born in Ireland in 1813, came to the United States in 1818 with his family and settled in the western part of the state on a pioneer farm. Thomas earned an education at Western University and became a successful lawyer and then a Republican judge for ten years. In 1869 he opened T.

Mellon and Sons as a private bank; he had been lending money and dealing in real estate and other enterprises, many successfully. Now he would concentrate on creating a family dynasty with his five sons.

A great believer in education, work, and discipline, he had been much impressed by Ben Franklin's autobiography, which he read as a boy. He married into a local landowning family that had recovered from financial reversals after the death of the father, Jacob Negley. His courtship of Sarah Jane Negley led to a long and happy marriage with eight children. The family was well off, living on a large farm and home in East Liberty. Sarah and Thomas had a close and affectionate relationship, and the children clustered around the homestead as adults. He wrote an interesting biography in his old age after retiring and spent his final years in personal endeavors, dying in 1908. His greatest disappointments were the deaths of three of his young children.

The most successful of his sons became the leader of the many family enterprises but especially the bank. During his years in family and local schools and Western University, Andrew was treated as an equal by his father and spent his youth watching, learning, and acting as an agent for the older man. In 1882 Thomas turned over the bank and supervision of his properties to the young man. The older boys had been established in successful businesses and were doing well. In 1888 A. W. took in his younger brother Richard B. as a partner and in 1890 was made trust executive for the $4 million family fund. His older brothers were less dedicated to business and less successful with their enterprises. Andrew never received a salary from the bank but had access to its earnings.

A. W. and R. B. were a most effective pair. Andrew was cautious, precise, and proper; Richard was outgoing, optimistic, and aggressive. Andrew's friendship with his father's client and borrower, Henry Clay Frick, led to his early involvement as the financier and silent controller of numerous enterprises in western Pennsylvania. Frick also introduced him to Europe and the collecting of art. Later, Andrew's nephew, William Larimer Mellon, would be financed and trained in expanding the oil and other industries and given responsibilities for Gulf Oil and other Mellon enterprises. But A. W. always had the final (and often initial) word. Perhaps the greatest single success was financing, investing in, and advising Pittsburgh Reduction Company, which became Aluminum Corp of America. A near monopoly, it was only somewhat limited by an antitrust case in 1912 and expanded rapidly.

In 1902 T. Mellon and Sons became the Mellon National Bank and the complementary Union Trust. The Mellons controlled the dominant financial institutions in western Pennsylvania, and they continued to expand. They also became the financiers and participants in many new industries springing up around dynamic Pittsburgh. These included Carborundum, Koppers, coal mining, and utilities, along with many less-well-known enterprises.

A. W.'s technique was simple—sound products, good managers, and effective controls, combined with a philosophy of "Let them grow." He was not a Robber Brown or a captain of industry or a Wall Street financier like J. P. Morgan. A slender, handsome man, Andrew was shy and quiet but dedicated and very industrious. His early responsibilities and training made him mature and readily established his influence. His careful personal habits did not preclude smoking little black cigars, drinking (the family owned Overholt Distilling), excellent poker playing, and a taste for art. After his fiancée died in 1883, a mature Mellon continued to live in the family homestead. His passion was business and the family enterprises. In photographs, he appears dapper, assured and standing near the center of a group. He lived well, traveled and associated with the elite of Pittsburgh, but was always reserved, aloof, and an excellent judge of men.

On a transatlantic crossing, he met Nora McMullen of the Guinness Stout family, which held estates in Ireland. A lively, pretty, and enthusiastic young lady of twenty-one, she was impressed with the debonair and courtly older man. After a series of visits, they were married in 1900 and established a home in Pittsburgh. It was a warm relationship, and in 1901 their daughter Ailsa was born. But the forty-five-year-old father returned to his hardworking habits, and Nora grew tired of a dirty industrial city and a limited social life. A new city mansion and family estates in Rolling Rock and elsewhere with only limited visits to the English country life she had known were not enough for her. In 1907 a son Paul was born, but a year later, Nora sought a divorce, which was granted in 1912 after a rather messy court process. Andrew was generous in the financial settlement, and the couple was later friendly, although still remote. She remarried several times, divorcing repeatedly. Nora died in 1973 and was buried next to Andrew by her son Paul.

Although Andrew loved the children and never lost his affection for Nora, he found it difficult to be truly intimate. He was generous and indulgent with them and, despite the disparity in their ages, attempted to be a warm and loving father. But his devotion to business and the family's burgeoning empire was too demanding. An impressive home on secluded Woodland Avenue with swimming pool, bowling alley, and beautiful landscaping provided a fine setting for the young people and their friends. Andrew enjoyed both it and them, albeit somewhat awkwardly. Vacations, at rural estates, trips abroad, and the best schools were provided and enjoyed by both the children and the doting father.

Inevitably the politics of the time and area required some attention from the concerned businessman. The Mellon family remained aloof from obvious political activity but were sources of financial support and influence in local and state politics. The brothers were accustomed to dealing with important people and knew the political leaders. Senators, mayors, and others were aware of, and often obligated to, industrial leaders and protected their interests. The rising role of government in the Progressive era increased the need for such cooperation and protection.

In 1914 the Mellons created the Mellon Institute for Industrial Research as a memorial to their father. It became a prime research facility and provided productive results to Mellon and other companies. Andrew's alma mater became the University of Pittsburgh with his support and assistance. The family had always supported local and worthy philanthropy, and as their wealth grew, so did their support. Typically, it was carefully and quietly done, efficient and unobtrusive; much greater philanthropy would come toward the end of his life.

By the end of World War I, A. W. Mellon was approaching sixty-five and, after restructuring his expanding holdings and companies to peacetime enterprises, ready for a change. The financial and legal situation in the postwar era was bothersome, and he felt the need for a return to normalcy. The approaching election of 1920 provided the opportunity. Pennsylvania was a key state, and its industrialists and politicians were primed to play a major role. The Mellons would help finance the Republican drive to a conservative and nationalistic government and society.

In 1920 Andrew Mellon was a delegate to the National Republican Convention and led local fund-raising. The country was ready for change, and Warren Harding and Calvin Coolidge were elected. Mellon's Senate supporters and other party leaders would push for his appointment to the new Cabinet.

Warren Harding, although from neighboring Ohio and a former newspaper man, had never heard of A. W. Mellon but invited him to Marion to meet him. Typically, the financier and industrial mogul went reluctantly and quietly, was not met at the train station, and walked to Harding's house. After some delay, while he quietly sat in a waiting room, he was recognized and ushered in to the President-elect. The meeting was cordial, though neither man seemed impressed but accepted each other's status. Harding wanted the dynamic and esteemed Herbert Hoover in his Cabinet, but party leaders were reluctant about such a "liberal" international figure. To get Hoover's acceptance, Harding must appoint Mellon as Secretary of the Treasury, although he preferred Charles Dawes.

Mellon was also reluctant. Years earlier he had been quoted, "It is always a mistake for a good businessman to take public office." Besides, he was too rich, too powerful, too involved in giant companies, too old at sixty-five, and a very private person. Moreover, he felt ill equipped for the job—he had no government experience, no national economic policy, and was appalled at the notion of having to replace almost the entire Treasury staff due to the drastic change in administration. It was unbusinesslike! He had always avoided publicity and the press, so the glass bowl of Washington would be an additional burden.

Andrew W. Mellon was almost unknown outside of Pennsylvania. His name had never appeared in the *New York Times*. In 1917, eminent business publisher B. G. Forbes had listed the fifty Foremost Business Leaders in the United States; Mellon was not included, although twelve of them were bankers. Perhaps being unknown was an advantage; he could create his own national image. As *Forbes* magazine concluded, "Harding sought not rubber stamps but strong-willed, independent, assertive figures" such as Hughes, Mellon, and Hoover for his Cabinet. He would be Harding's most successful appointment.

The country was ready for a return to normalcy, and Andrew Mellon would facilitate it. The wartime inflation and the end of a war-geared economy resulted in a sharp decline of prices and business activity. There was a large war debt, but war emergency taxes and reduced government spending combined to create federal budget surpluses. Reducing debt and government activity were necessary as quickly as possible. Naturally, this appealed to the conservative and businesslike new Secretary. He had already been through these changes in his many enterprises and had them performed quickly and efficiently. As he explained to Harding and the Cabinet, in one case they had "just scrapped" an obsolete $12 million plant. The resulting unemployment and reduced spending were just a normal part of the postwar economic conversion.

But President Harding and his advisers were more politically concerned and perhaps more socially responsible. The new President was inclined to appoint cronies and supporters to public office—a rueful mistake. Mellon attempted, successfully, to keep efficient career personnel and appoint qualified people in his department. When Harding insisted on particular appointments, Mellon would stall and eventually force them out. But getting the President to approve more drastic changes was difficult since delay and compromise by a disinterested White House would prevail. But Mellon labored on. His capable appointments, his public pronouncements, his obvious financial competence and experience, and his customary diligence would carry the day with Congress and ultimately the country. He easily won over the press with his candor and availability.

First would come "rigid economy" in government expenditures, already under way. Next would come lowering of taxes, hardly a controversial issue. The real issues would be what taxes and how much to cut. Able Treasury accountants and advisers such as E. Parker Gilbert, a carryover in Treasury, and David Blair of Internal Revenue Service (IRS) provided excellent data. To the House Ways and Means Committee and the Senate Finance Committee, the Secretary testified effectively and made strong recommendations: repeal the excess profits tax, cut income taxes sharply above the $66,000 level, and increase some harmless excise taxes. Trade unions, farmers, and the Progressives were up in arms—this was class legislation. Mellon stuck to his guns, and the business leaders and press applauded. It was not class warfare but the welfare of the economy that was at stake. Congress and Harding retreated from such sweeping changes in the Revenue Bill of 1921 but did cut taxes along his lines.

President Harding was soon in awe of his now-dominant Secretary with his acumen and financial connections. The rising public stature of the distinguished financier coupled with the Cabinet and other scandals of his administration gave the President pause and made him unhappy and insecure. The two men were never close, and Harding's casual attitude toward administration and his associates was no match for the diligence and capable staff of the Secretary. Mellon's ties to the power structure and the enthusiastic acceptance of his program contrasted with Harding's declining public status. The sudden death of President Harding in 1923 gave Mellon the unqualified support of his successor. Calvin Coolidge not only agreed with Mellon; the two men liked and respected each other.

The national debt had reached the unprecedented level of $26.9 billion in

1919. The military cutbacks and high wartime taxes created surpluses that started to reduce the debt. In 1919 the Wilson administration had reduced the income tax from 6 percent to 4 percent and the corporate tax from 12 to 10 percent. By 1922 federal government revenues had declined sharply as a result of the tax cuts and the postwar depression. Mellon urged further tax cuts—especially the war-time surtaxes—to stimulate the economy. President Coolidge supported him in his December 1923 message to Congress. Congress limited the upper-income tax cut proposals, and Coolidge reluctantly signed the bill in June 1924.

The spectacular victory of Coolidge and Dawes and the Republican Party in the November election would ensure the expansion of the "Return to Normalcy." Interestingly, the largest majority of victory was in Mellon's home state, Penn-sylvania. In October 1925 Mellon revealed his new program, and it was enthu-siastically received by the new Congress. The Revenue Act of February 1926 was a Mellon triumph. Inheritance taxes were reduced from 40 to 20 percent, and the capital stock and gift taxes were repealed. Income taxes were reduced 25 percent, and most important, the surtax went from 50 to 25 percent. The justi-fication was simple and direct: High tax rates would be avoided by the rich, while lower rates would increase private investment and public revenues. Mellon's recommendation for an amendment to end tax-exempt securities was ignored, but his elimination of excise taxes on autos and other items was accepted.

The Mellon Plan was almost in place. His objectives had been to reduce the burdensome national debt, cut taxes on upper incomes to increase industrial and economic growth and wealth, and reduce government activity. The first was being achieved, the second was now in place, and limiting government regulation and participation in the economy was continuing. The last objective was less within Treasury's power to control and was a very political issue. Mellon was less successful, *but* he did prevent a veteran's bonus, limited Federal Trade Commis-sion and other antitrust actions, and hampered Mussel Shoal development along with other government projects.

Liberal opposition to huge tax cuts for the wealthy was responded to forcefully by Mellon. Now very comfortable with the press and respected for his candor and availability to them, Mellon was able to present his message effectively. Acceptable tax rates would result in the rich paying their share and thus much more in taxes as a result of energetic investment and business growth. The cre-ation of "productive wealth" would increase jobs, production, and the standard of living (which would also rise with the lower prices from all the tax cuts). Federal surpluses would reduce the national debt and thus interest payments, leaving even more funds for useful private investment. Since interest on the debt was 28 percent of budget expenditures despite short-term debt reduction by a third, this could be significant. And as a clinching argument, Wilson's Treasurers Glass and Houston had recommended similar measures. As Coolidge summarized the program in a speech, it was not only to relieve the wealthy, but to relieve the country as well.

The Mellon Plan was stated at length and justified with tables and statistics, admittedly somewhat generalized, in *Taxation: The People's Business*, published in April 1924. In collected and expanded views and earlier testimony given by Secretary Mellon, he quite candidly stated his philosophy, objectives, and policies. Government finance must provide sufficient revenues, lessen the tax burden, not retard business, and plan for a long period. Since the government is just a business, lower taxes (prices) mean larger revenues. Adam Smith was quoted favorably on the need to not hamper but encourage business. High taxes cause high prices and "are borne ultimately by the consumer." Alexander Hamilton is quoted on reducing the national debt, while Henry Ford, David Guggenheim, and an anonymous woman dressmaker provided anecdotal examples of the negative impact of taxes. The success of his policies to date was showing in the growing prosperity, and it could be continued.

Even more interesting are some unfortunately never-achieved and forgotten recommendations. Mellon was never happy about rentiers—passive investors who merely collect interest. Above all, he objected to the rich not paying their share of taxes by owning tax-exempt bonds. There were over $12 billion of these in existence, enabling wealthy people to avoid any taxes. Moreover, these bonds financed wasteful expenditures and distorted economic decision making. Capital should be used for risk-taking investment in productive enterprises, preferably in new and growing firms.

That had been the secret of the Mellon family fortune. Moreover, there were other loopholes for wealthy taxpayers that deserved closing, but these were not specified. He did argue that interest on the federal debt should not be paid from general revenues because not all people owned bonds, but they all paid taxes. There was no suggestion as to how to pay the interest. Mellon quotes Professor Thomas Adams of Yale approvingly as an authority on tax reduction and tax effects on the economy. However, capital gains should not be taxed as income; they were seen as rewards for entrepreneurial risk taking and business achievement. Mellon had concluded that estate taxes forced sales of property and thus destroyed capital. Communist Russia and landowners in England had seen their capital "evaporate" because of excessive taxation. Anyway, there would be no real debt retirement since one just did not borrow again as bonds mature.

There is a fascinating speech by "Silent Cal" (at the National Republican Club) in 1924 lauding his Secretary of the Treasury and justifying his plan. He makes his own allegiance clear by indicating that after a conference with Secretary Mellon the Treasury would study tax reduction. Thereafter, it would be in Mellon's hands, as were all financial matters including the Federal Reserve Board on which he sat ex officio. The rest of the speech could have been written by Andrew or his people. The Democratic effort to make tax reduction more equitable and aimed at relieving average-consuming taxpayers was dismissed out of hand by the President, saying that the Garner plan was political and impossible in practice. The business of America would be increased by investment by wealthy businessmen through the Mellon Plan, considered economically, socially and morally sound.

Prosperity continued in the United States and even expanded. Tax reductions were made again in 1928 but were more limited. Mellon's philosophy that everyone should pay some support for government and the need to run surpluses to continue national debt reduction were paramount considerations. His belief in limiting the role of government and avoiding interfering in the economy made him oppose measures to solve emerging sectoral problems in agriculture, the South, and specific industries. The war debts problem in Europe involved travel abroad, and he gave his support to the Owen and Dawes plans for their solution. It was necessary to keep Europe functioning, especially as a customer for U.S. industries, and to prevent financial crises. Bank lending abroad was also encouraged for the same reasons.

There were personal problems, too. Some raised questions and investigated his tax returns and business dealings. Mellon had separated himself from the family enterprises when he became Secretary; nevertheless, many of the transactions were designed to retain control. Although he rarely acted directly anymore, his influence and senior status remained and his thinking and opinions were valued and sought by the family. There were accusations that several government actions occurred that benefited his former financial and commercial holdings. While it was unlikely that these interventions were direct or even known by him, they did occur. A notation "This is a Mellon company" on a corporate tax return may have been just a bureaucratic notation, but it did look odd. His reluctance to vigorously enforce prohibition was also noted and criticized. While no actions were taken or deemed necessary while he was "the most respected man in the country," they would prove troublesome when he was not.

The decline of the Mellon image and influence began after Coolidge announced in 1927 that he would not seek another term in office. It was a shock to markets and the nation. Mellon and Republican officials were unable to change the President's mind and reluctantly sought a successor. There was a brief boomlet for Mellon, but his age, wealth, and reluctance made it unrealistic. Secretary of Commerce Hoover had international status from World War I relief activities and had been an effective and visible Secretary of Commerce. He actively sought and received the nomination and went on to a spectacular victory in 1928. The seven years of Coolidge-Mellon prosperity were a major factor in the election.

Hoover and Mellon had never been close despite their long Cabinet service. Their philosophies and policies were different, with Hoover more social minded and less opposed to government. Their backgrounds and training were poles apart—the western engineer-administrator versus the eastern financier-plutocrat from totally different family situations. They were really from different generations and worlds. Hoover was probably hesitant about continuing his elderly colleague as Treasurer but unwilling to disturb a successful program. He reappointed the Secretary despite their differences.

Mellon disliked and often resisted Hoover's ideas, which he found grandiose and unsound. As he was quoted, "I never put an engineer in charge"; he nevertheless supported his election and continued as Secretary. The large majority in Pennsylvania helped show the Mellon influence again. Andrew had grown fond of Washington, together with the power and prestige of public office. Above all he wanted to see his policies continue and the nation's prosperity increase. He had little desire to return to Pittsburgh and the daily grind of business and finance.

The increasing speculation in the stock market concerned both the new President and his Treasury Secretary, but they did not want to disturb prosperity. Mellon did not expect the crash, but he had never been in the speculative New York stock market. His banking experiences in the recessions of 1873, 1893, 1907, and 1921 had shown that the froth and gamblers were liquidated and purged, but sound enterprises survived and grew. He was essentially optimistic about laissez-faire. Hoover was more realistic and far more concerned and cautiously issued warnings. He urged Mellon to do likewise, and the Secretary in public statements mildly suggested that stocks were very high and bonds were a good investment. Both continued to see prosperity and the future of the United States as bright and basically sound. The attitude was "Don't rock the boat" or take direct action even through the Federal Reserve Board. But time was running out, and the world economy was facing serious problems.

The stock market crash of 1929 was shocking, but official assurances continued to be optimistic. It was not business conditions but only speculation. In 1930 Mellon's New Year's message was, "the Nation will make steady progress . . . government finances are sound." By June he was less certain that prosperity was just around the corner, but it was necessary "to curtail output to clear the market." His companies and others were doing just that—laying off people and reducing production. This infuriated Hoover, and he protested to Mellon, but it was just sound business to the old man. Cutting wages and reducing investment were unavoidable as sales and prices fell while profits turned to losses. The Great Depression had begun.

Congress aggravated the situation by passing the Hawley-Smoot Tariff, which raised tariff rates drastically. Despite the objections of over a thousand economists, Hoover reluctantly signed the bill. Mellon persuaded Hoover with not much enthusiasm to veto legislation to support agriculture and other programs to stabilize prices and the economy during the early years of the depression. Efforts to balance the budget by raising taxes were harmful actions.

The depression would isolate and reduce the influence of the aged Secretary. His philosophy of government not intervening in the economy and sound finance provided no answers and precluded action. He would have liked to reduce taxes, but then there would be a bigger deficit. Letting the disturbance work itself out was proving disastrous. Reducing interest rates found few borrowers and no investment. President Hoover, probably correctly, believed his Secretary was out of date and ineffective as well as uncooperative. He became distant, relations were strained, and Undersecretary of the Treasury Odgen Mills became his adviser. As ex officio Chairman of the Federal Reserve Board, Mellon attended meetings but refused to discuss what transpired or what policies would result. As banks failed, he refused or was unable to take any actions.

Criticism and even abuse of the "greatest Treasury Secretary" were now common and growing. Mellon's public image and status declined rapidly, and he became more withdrawn and less available to the press. Public opinion was becoming totally negative as he refused to take any action and seemingly opposed any public efforts to relieve suffering and dismay. Along with most financial and business leaders, he had nothing to offer a bewildered and disillusioned society. It was the end of an era.

Political attacks and investigations had been limited and nonproductive during his tenure. Senate and other attempts to look into his personal finances and actions that might have benefited his "former" holdings were resisted by his strong congressional supporters and proved inconclusive. But the new economic environment and new, aggressive Democratic members of Congress would be more successful. The IRS in the Mellon years had been very easy on business, granting tax rebates and accepting practices that reduced taxes. Several government actions on tariffs, regulations, and policies had proved beneficial to Mellon companies as well as other concerns. Antitrust enforcement had been reduced because the Progressive era was over. That these were Mellon's direct actions or recommendations is doubtful, but he did not object to them. Koskoff concluded that A. W. Mellon was careless about keeping his public and private roles apart; while he was interested, he preferred not to know the details. The attacks would prove more successful after he left the Treasury and Democrats won the election in 1932.

It was obvious that the "most abused" Secretary would have to go with a critical election coming up. He refused to resign—that would be uncharacteristic and admission of failure. An appointment to a respectable post would be necessary: Ambassador to Great Britain was the solution after Charles Dawes resigned voluntarily. Mellon liked and was well known in England, and the war debt problems still threatened the financial recovery. Moreover, in September 1931, Great Britain had suspended gold payments and closed the stock exchange. As other nations took actions to defend their currencies and economies, the international economy faltered. A respected and experienced financier might help get it back on track in the critical post in London and also protect U.S. interests. It would be a serious and responsible opportunity for the aging (seventy-six-year-old) plutocrat. He accepted, mumbling that it was "not a marriage but a divorce," and departed for his new post on February 12, 1932. By then, Ogden Mills had in all respects succeeded him as Secretary, with Mellon's approval.

It was to be a brief diplomatic career for the wealthy patrician. He had British tastes and manners and wore English-style formal attire. The "American mogul" seemed a most typical British aristocrat. His daughter Ailsa joined him as official hostess, and David Finley came along as personal assistant at a dollar-a-year cost to the government. Mellon moved in the best circles and quickly captivated the British. He was an active working Ambassador, according to Secretary of State

Stimson, and very useful to him. As usual, he left the details and operations to capable staff. On several occasions, notably the Kuwait oil concessions, he played a role that was beneficial to the U.S. oil industry and Gulf Oil Corporation. In this instance, Secretary Stimson suggested more restraint by the Ambassador was desirable. But, in total, Mellon left his post with the change of administration in March 1933 after a job well done. However, his contribution to the war debts problem was not significant and was at times misleading. He did defend his country effectively and was bid a fond farewell by a distinguished crowd on his departure for home.

He returned to Pittsburgh and his office at Mellon Bank but now spent more time at the Woodland Avenue home. His apartment residence in Washington provided a base for his frequent returns to defend himself against the increasing attacks from Capitol Hill and several civil cases. Under New Deal Attorney General Homer Cummings, there were several suits for back taxes and several other charges. A grand jury refused to indict him. Congressman Wright Patman expanded his charges and investigations of previous years. Task forces and hearings would expose the details of Mellon's financial manipulations, vast income, holdings, and business activities. The size and scope of these were shocking to a nation trapped in a brutal depression. In the tax case, government prosecutor Robert Jackson was gritty, persevering, and well prepared. Andrew, his able lawyers, subordinates, and associates defended the Mellon camp effectively. The family empire had provided ample opportunity for tax avoidance and asset shifting, while generous gifts to family were permissible and so was philanthropy. The complicated case dragged on for three years, but the Board of Tax Appeals concluded there was no fraud, but there were overdue taxes. Since Mellon had died by then, his estate owed $668,000. There was a general feeling of relief that the whole mess was over. The estate added up to $34 million, and the residuary estate of $23 million went to the A. W. Mellon Education and Charitable Trust.

The Patman efforts were even more drastic. In January 1932 Patman attempted to have the House impeach Secretary Mellon. In hearings, he hauled out earlier charges by other Senators. Meanwhile, Senator Hiram Johnson also held hearings on various international oil dealings by Gulf Oil, presumably helped by the Secretary of the Treasury. Mellon in hearings generally seemed unaware of these activities, and proof of his participation seemed impossible. Patman tried to use these investigations, but his efforts produced much publicity and little else. At his hearings, much testimony and information were collected, but the material was too vast and complicated to exploit. Mellon himself was vague and remote in participation, and his age and frail condition created public sympathy. After Mellon's resignation as Secretary, Patman concluded that there was no point in further investigation as nothing could be done. Thirty years later, still in the House, Patman would pass legislation that limited Mellon tax-free dollars to finance exotic personal interests.

Andrew W. Mellon had one last duty to perform for the nation. In his years as Secretary he had attempted to embellish the national capital with more appropriate capital structures. Now he wanted to create the one thing he felt it lacked. His interest in, and collection of, art had developed over four decades. It would be dedicated to the nation and housed in an edifice appropriate for the national gallery of a rich and powerful country. Earlier he had persuaded President Hoover to set aside an appropriate location for the imposing structure. Mellon provided the funds, selected the architect, and supervised the construction. Naturally, he assigned trusted associate David Finley to handle the details. He stipulated that the building should not bear his name—that might prevent future donations of important works by others. Instead, it was called the National Gallery of Art. Mellon provided over $25 million for construction and set up a foundation to maintain it. It was a national treasure when it opened in 1941. The collection he donated was valued then at over $35 million; today it is priceless.

His illustrious career was ending. A major disappointment for the old man was that his son Paul would not continue the Mellon tradition in finance and business into the third generation. But Paul and his sister and cousins would continue the philanthropy and importance of the family in Pittsburgh and the nation.

Mellon went to his daughter's Long Island estate in the summer of 1937. Old, feeble, and ailing, he passed away quietly on August 26, 1937.

Despite his great wealth and business leadership, Mellon had received little national recognition or attention until his Cabinet appointment. In *The Robber Barons*, Matthew Josephson referred to Mellon only in association with Frick and other tycoons. He may not have been a robber baron, but he was a major capitalist banker. Gustavus Myers's *History of the Great American Fortunes* listed him as paying the fourth-largest income tax in 1925—the only year returns were published—after J. D. Rockefeller, Jr., and the Fords. Later he had two pages on the Mellon banks and briefly described the Mellon brothers' involvement in several corporations. He also briefly described their tax problem during the New Deal. In *The Rich and the Super-Rich*, Ferdinand Lundberg noted the immense wealth given and inherited by Mellon's children and nephews. His analysis of the Temporary National Economic Committee data described the holdings of the powerful family and the creation of their huge charitable foundations. He argues that prior to the depression and New Deal, anything J. P. Morgan, J. D. Rockefeller, and A. W. Mellon agreed on would happen. The biggest thing they agreed on was "not to meddle in each other's domain."

Hoover was critical of Mellon and his reluctance to support Hoover's attempts to counter the economic decline. He was particularly upset by the Secretary's public optimism, cautious statements on speculation, and belief in "liquidation" of troubled weak spots. The man had outlived his times. Most of Mellon's biographers have been favorably impressed with his service and accomplishments despite the inadequacies of his last two years as Secretary.

The fiftieth anniversary of the opening of the National Gallery of Art in 1991 brought articles reviewing its creation and Mellon's crucial role in its establishment and high quality. Also in 1991 financial reporter John Crudele would contrast the Hoover administration antidepression efforts with modern fiscal policies, emphasizing the restraints on government in 1929 and lack of automatic programs imposed on the Treasury and its administration.

Andrew Mellon served almost eleven years under three Presidents. His policies reduced the high national debt from $26 billion to $16 billion. He reduced government expenditures by half, cut taxes sharply, especially for the wealthy, and promoted a seven-year period of general economic prosperity. He left office with the largest deficit to that time in U.S. history, with the nation mired in a deep depression and his fiscal philosophy intact. It is possible that that was all he could do under the circumstances of international depression and economic collapse.

BIBLIOGRAPHY

Barck, Oscar T., Jr., and Nelson M. Blake. *Since 1900*. New York: Macmillan, 1949.

Forbes, B. C. *America's 50 Foremost Business Leaders*. New York: B. C. Forbes Co., 1917. (Reissued 1948)

Great Stories of American Businessmen. New York: American Heritage, 1972.

Groner, Alex. *History of American Business and Industry*. New York: American Heritage, 1972.

Hersh, Burton. *The Mellon Family*. New York: William Morrow, 1978.

Josephson, Matthew. *The Robber Barons*. New York: Harcourt Brace & World, 1934.

Koskoff, David E. *The Mellons*. New York: Thomas Y. Crowell, 1978.

Lundberg, Ferdinand. *The Rich and the Super-Rich*. New York: Lyle Stuart, 1968.

Mellon, Andrew W. *Taxation: The People's Business*. New York: Macmillan, 1924.

Myers, Gustavus. *History of the Great American Fortunes*. New York: Modern Library, 1936.

O'Connor, Harvey. *Mellon's Millions*. New York: Blue Ribbon Books, 1933. (Most of the data in this profile are based on this classic study.)

Seligman, Ben B. *The Potentates*. New York: Dial, 1971.

ALFRED E. PIERCE

WILLIAM M. MEREDITH (June 8, 1799–August 17, 1873). This profile explores the life and work of William Morris Meredith, who served as U.S. Secretary of the Treasury during the brief presidency of Zachary Taylor (1849–1850).

Jonathan Meredith, grandfather of William Morris Meredith, was born in 1740 in Great Britain and was of Welsh ancestry. Around 1755 he migrated to the New World and established himself as a highly successful leather merchant in Philadelphia. His wife, Elizabeth Tucker, bore him seven children. Two daughters and three sons survived to adulthood. These included Elizabeth Ogden, Mary Hawthorn, David, William Tucker, and Jonathan. Sons John Small and Thomas died in early youth. The oldest son, David, inherited the bulk of his father's estate when the latter died in 1811. William Tucker Meredith, the second son of Jonathan and Elizabeth, was born in Philadelphia in 1772, graduated from the University of Pennsylvania in 1790, and received a master's degree three years later. He was admitted to the bar in 1795 and became Solicitor for the City of Philadelphia, a post at which he served during the period 1811–1814. In 1814, William Tucker Meredith became President of Schuylkill Bank, and his career centered more on finance than on law from that point. William Tucker Meredith and his wife Gertrude (Ogden) had eleven children, which included five daughters and six sons.

William Morris Meredith was born in Philadelphia on June 8, 1799. Extremely bright, William Morris graduated from the University of Pennsylvania in 1812 and was valedictorian of his class. He earned a master's degree four years later. By the time he was eighteen years of age, William Morris was admitted to the Philadelphia bar. Not surprisingly, given his extreme youth, it took him several years before he established himself as a successful lawyer with a lucrative practice.

He was elected to represent the (old) city of Philadelphia in the state legislature from 1824 to 1828. Although among the youngest legislators, William Meredith showed great leadership skills that would soon place him among the leading Whigs in Pennsylvania.

In 1825, at the outset of his public career, William Morris turned his attention to welfare reform in Pennsylvania with special reference to the city of Philadelphia. The aftermath of the Panic of 1819, epidemics of typhus and yellow fever in 1818 and 1820, and a severe winter in 1821 helped swell the rolls of Philadelphia's poor relief. By 1825, tax levies for the relief effort were higher than at any point in the previous quarter century. In his 1825 report, Meredith argued that the existence of poor relief provided a powerful disincentive to work. He suggested several reform measures. Among these were that the levy for poor relief should not be increased and that the Guardians of the Poor, appointed officials who administered welfare to the poor, be discontinued. Their task of caring for the impoverished was to be handled by elected representatives who were expected to limit welfare expenditures or face the wrath of voters. Meredith's study sparked other investigations, and these eventually resulted in the state legislature's passing a law in 1828 that both reduced the tax levy each citizen paid on poor relief and set in motion plans to construct a new almshouse in Philadelphia. Once the new almshouse was constructed, cash grants to the poor ended. Nearly 90 percent of the beneficiaries of the latter had been women and children during this period. Lacking a political lobby in the state legislature, they were unable to defend their interests against the Poor Law of 1828.

In 1834 William Morris Meredith married Catharine Keppele, the daughter of a former Philadelphia mayor. The marriage lasted for nearly twenty years, ending in 1853 when Catharine died. The couple had five children: William Meredith (1835–1903), Elizabeth Caldwell (1837–1883), Gertrude Gouverneur (born 1839), Catharine Keppele, and Euphemia Ogden (1842–1891). Although the son, William Meredith, was admitted to the Philadelphia bar in 1860, he never developed an impressive practice.

In 1837 William Morris Meredith was chosen to be a member of the American Philosophical Association. Five years later he was called to the Board of Trustees of the University of Pennsylvania, a post he retained for seventeen years. Interested in transportation and communications, he had been an enthusiastic supporter of the building of the Pennsylvania Railroad, and in 1845 he called for a westward extension of a railroad link from Harrisburg to Pittsburgh. Six years later he, along with future President James Buchanan, was one of the keynote speakers at a celebration on the arrival of the steamship *City of Glasgow* when it inaugurated a new steamship line between Philadelphia and Great Britain.

From 1834 to 1849, Meredith served as a member of the Select Council of Philadelphia. In that same year, he was chosen to be a member of the State Constitutional Convention of Pennsylvania. Among the important issues discussed was the question of suffrage and franchise. Meredith sided with those who wished to limit suffrage to include only "white" freemen; this stipulation was supported by the majority and made its way into the new state constitution, which went into effect in 1839. He opposed term limits for judges, but these were approved by the majority of delegates.

By 1840, Meredith was a first-class lawyer—even by Philadelphia's standards. He took part in several celebrated legal battles, including the famous Girard Will case. Meredith was a clear, effective speaker, with a keen, analytical mind, and could move his audience by both the logic of his argument and the appeal to his audience's emotions (Wainwright, 103). He also combined sharp wit with a droll sense of humor. For example, he was invited to speak before the Mercantile Library Company during the fall of 1839 on the topic of "Intemperance." He made clear to his listeners, however, that the type of intemperance that was the subject of his delivery included intemperance of action, opinion, and speaking— especially speaking too long. He delivered his address in only a third of the time he was allotted, to the surprise and amusement of his audience. The portrait of Meredith offered by Fisher was of a man so dedicated to his career that he had little time for other activities, including society and exercise (Wainwright, 89–90). Apparently, he was relatively careless in his appearance and was in the habit of chewing tobacco and spitting while speaking, which apparently was not uncommon during that period.

A major step in Meredith's political career occurred shortly after William Harrison's 1840 election on the Whig ticket. Meredith was commissioned as U.S. Attorney for the Eastern District of Pennsylvania, a position he retained for fourteen months. He experienced a setback, though, at the end of the decade when James Cooper, also a member of the Whig Party, bested him in a contest for a seat in the U.S. Senate. But political fortunes brightened considerably when Meredith was offered the post of U.S. Secretary of the Treasury by President Zachary Taylor.

Zachary Taylor, a hero of the Mexican War (1846–1848), selected William Meredith as Secretary of the Treasury. Meredith accepted and took office on March 8, 1849. The Cabinet was filled with lawyers and men with business experience rather than with strong connections in Congress (Hamilton, 167). The consensus seems to be that the Cabinet was mediocre, with little difference from its immediate predecessors. The assessments of Meredith vary most widely. Bauer (262) describes Meredith as "better than competent" and as "one of the strongest members of the Cabinet" (260). On the other hand, Nevins (231) claims that Meredith "proved quite incompetent as head of Treasury." He notes complaints from New York City merchants that correspondence was ignored, important matters were delegated to clerks, and ships were detained needlessly.

Taylor delegated the distribution of patronage in his administration to his Cabinet. Meredith and several other Cabinet members initially favored slow removal and replacement of incumbent (non-Whig) officeholders but eventually joined those advocating widespread removals. In the first year of the Taylor administration, about one third of the nation's 18,000 civil servants, most of whom were Democrats, either had quite or were replaced. Although the majority of the Cabinet were from slave states, the antislavery Whigs seemed to have had the President's ear, much to the disgust of Southern Whigs. It would hardly be the last time that a Southern President caused disappointment south of the Mason-Dixon line.

Meredith, in particular, seemed to grow close to Taylor, and the former's charming wife contributed to this. Thurlow Weed, a powerful Whig figure in New York and the archrival of Vice President Fillmore, also influenced Taylor. For example, in the early days of the administration, both Weed and Taylor visited the Treasury Secretary, and the President asked Meredith if "our friends are getting their share of the offices" (quoted in Dyer, 325). Also, Weed used his influence to convince Meredith to block the appointment of John Young, a former Governor whom Weed opposed. Interestingly, one of the Democratic officeholders who lost his job in Salem was Nathaniel Hawthorne. Webster wrote to Meredith that "it will be best to leave Mr. Hawthorne where he is" (quoted in Hamilton, 213–14); but this was not to be.

That Taylor's Cabinet lacked political experience at the national level was especially regrettable because the nation faced a major crisis. If Polk's administration reaped the benefit of adding a vast chunk of real estate to the southwestern United States, Taylor faced the thorny question of the status of slavery in the new western lands. Both the Democratic and Whig parties had split on this issue. The situation was especially complicated because Texas was involved in a border dispute with what is today New Mexico. The President proposed bringing both California and New Mexico into the Union as states. By avoiding territorial status, the people of the new states could decide the question of slavery for themselves. In early 1850, Henry Clay offered his famous Compromise: California was to be admitted to the Union as a "free state"; the remainder of the lands of the Southwest were to be formed into two territories, and Congress would not decide the status of slavery in this area. Texas would concede the boundary dispute with New Mexico in return for the U.S. government's accepting the debt that Texas had accumulated when winning its independence. The slave trade was to be abolished in the District of Columbia, but a more effective fugitive slave law would be passed. Unfortunately, Clay made the mistake of publicly criticizing the President, and it seemed that if Congress eventually approved a compromise, it was likely to be vetoed by the President. Meredith also seems to have had doubts about Clay's compromise efforts. At this point, the President, who had fallen ill near Meadville on his westward trip through Pennsylvania during the summer of 1849, died suddenly in Washington from typhoid fever.

On the President's summer 1849 tour through the Northeast, the question of the tariff was often raised. In Pittsburgh, for example, a delegation complained of inadequate protection for iron manufacturers under the existing tariff legislation. Taylor informed his audience that he and Treasury Secretary Meredith would bring the need for protection to the attention of Congress. Dramatic increases in tariffs were unlikely, however. Democrats outnumbered Whigs by 35 to 25 in the Senate and 112 to 109 in the House. Tariffs had been increased during Tyler's administration in 1842, only to be reduced during Polk's administration in 1846. Among the principles that Secretary Walker had articulated were that tariffs should be levied for protection, rather than revenue, and that tariffs should be levied on an ad valorem basis rather than as specific duties. For example, under the 1842 tariff, imported pig iron was subject to a duty of $10 per ton. Under the 1846 tariff, the 30 percent ad valorem duty amounted to only $4 in 1849 and $3.80 in 1850. Taussig (133) argued that the protective duties of 1842 encouraged inefficient production and slowed the conversion from charcoal to anthracite that began around 1840. The Walker Tariff of 1846, not surprisingly, was opposed in the Middle Atlantic and New England regions; it had generally strong support in the South and West.

An innovation in custom administration during Polk's administration was the creation of government warehouses where imported goods could be placed with duty unpaid for a period of time. Also, a second Independent Treasury was established. Government depositories were created in several leading commercial centers, thus divorcing the Treasury's fiscal operations from the banks. The Treasury was to issue its own notes, and only gold and silver coins, along with Treasury notes, would be accepted by the Treasury as payment. During the Mexican War, the Independent Treasury performed adequately; government securities sold above par, and inflationary pressure was reduced because Treasury deposits were not available to support (the potentially excessive) issue of bank notes.

Meredith's only Treasury report was that of December 1849. In it he made clear his case for raising needed revenues and protecting American manufacturing with higher tariff duties. At the outset, he showed a Treasury balance of $2.2 million for the fiscal year ending June 30, 1849. However, for the next two fiscal years, he anticipated deficits of $5.8 million and $10.5 million. He argued that the number of customs inspectors was inadequate for the effective carrying out of their duties and noted that of 110 collection districts, only for 56 of these did gross revenues offset expenses. At this point, Meredith turned to the public debt, which amounted to approximately $65 million. Approximately $49 million of this was long-term (ten- and twenty-year bonds paying 6 percent interest), issued between 1846 and 1848 to finance the Mexican War. Ways and means, discussed next, was perhaps the most interesting segment of his report. Comparing the increase in expenditure by both the Army and Navy from April 1846 to April 1849 with the three years immediately before this period, Meredith estimated the cost of the Mexican War at about $64 million. In addition, the United States was obligated to pay Mexico war-related reparations; in the fiscal year ending in June 30, 1849, over $7.5 million had been paid. In light of these financial developments, Meredith argued that it was necessary to raise revenue, and the most likely candidate was to raise the duties on imports.

Among the reasons for amending the tariff rate structure upward were these: First, Congress was under no constitutional obligation to levy duties at the minimum that guaranteed maximum revenue. Next he argued that producers in each industry were also consumers of the outputs of other industries. Therefore, prosperity given to one branch of industry (via protection) increased that of the rest. Thus, converting raw cotton, wool, and iron into manufactured goods would greatly increase the nation's wealth and power. An abundance of raw materials, including fuel and food, and an efficient workforce all would help make this goal achievable. An alleged capital shortage, the high cost of labor, wide price fluctuations in foreign markets, and "undue" foreign competition seemed to militate against its success. Meredith erased these doubts by arguing that capital requirements for large-scale production were not prohibitively high; and he also noted that the domestic availability of capital was likely to increase over time. The superior ability to acquire skills, the higher level of intelligence of the domestic workman, and his better living conditions and educational attainment all created greater efficiency that offset the relatively higher American wage rate. Also cited were instances in the New England textile factories where workers were involved in profit-sharing arrangements that provided employees an incentive to work harder than otherwise. Finally, Meredith argued that dramatic reversals of government policy toward business, such as the adoption of the 1846 tariff, discouraged investment. The guarantee of consistent protection to manufacturers would have the opposite effect.

Next, Meredith made specific policy proposals concerning the tariff. First, an increase in duties on imported goods sufficient to both permit the development of domestic manufacturers and provide an increase in government revenue was necessary. He noted that tariff revenue between the years 1845–1846 and 1848–1849 rose slightly for imported woolens, iron, and unmanufactured hemp but fell sharply for cottons, sugar, salt, hempen goods, and coal. Higher duties, he maintained, would lead to greater revenue. Next, the Secretary proposed a return to a system of specific duties rather than ad valorem tariff rates. One of the key reasons for this was the difficulty in determining the foreign market value of imported goods, which did not arise under specific rates. Further, ad valorem duties exacerbated fluctuations in prices of foreign imports. He argued that if the price overseas for a good fluctuated between $20 and $50—a range of $30, with a 30 percent ad valorem rate—the range for the imported good in the United States would vary from $26 to $65—a range of $39.

Although the most interesting discussion in Meredith's report involved his scheme to return to a protectionist tariff policy, he also was critical of the government warehouse scheme initiated by Secretary Walker; Meredith argued the expenses involved were not offset by revenues. He also criticized the return to the Independent Treasury and noted some areas where it produced "great inconvenience." First, when funds needed to be disbursed at places distant from where they are deposited, this could create great transactions costs for disbursing officers. This was especially the case in the South, where (bulky) silver coins accounted for much of those in circulation. In addition, the number of clerks authorized under the law recreating the Independent Treasury was inadequate for the tasks involved; in some cases, there was the question of whether depository sites were sufficiently secure to hold public funds. At the end of his report, Meredith noted the unprecedented boom in California and proposed that a branch mint be constructed at San Francisco and that lighthouses, buoys, and a marine hospital all be built there. Unfortunately for the Secretary, his cherished tariff reform was not in the cards. The Democrats had control of Congress, and for the rest of the decade, the direction of tariff duties was lower, not higher.

Easily the most unpleasant time in Meredith's career as Secretary of the Treasury involved his role in the Galphin Scandal. George Galphin had been owed debts by the Creek and Cherokee Indians of Georgia with whom he traded. In payment for these, the British crown promised to compensate him with revenues generated by the sale of lands surrendered to the British by the Indians. Before this payment could be made, however, the American Revolution broke out, and with it vanished any prospect of the claim being paid by Britain. After the Revolution, Congress took the responsibility for settling claims against the federal government. The Galphin heirs won a partial victory in 1848 when Congress passed an act that required Treasury Secretary Walker to pay the amount of the original debt; the question of whether accrued interest of nearly three quarters of a century should be paid was left to Meredith, Walker's successor. When Meredith became Secretary, Judge Joseph Bryan presented him with Millidge Galphin's interest claim. Meredith referred this to the Controller, and when advised against payment, the interest claim was brought before Attorney General Reverdy Johnson. Johnson recommended payment, and this accrued interest amounted to $191,000. When combined with Walker's payment of approximately $44,000, the total received by the Galphin heirs amounted to $235,000. The size of this payment, in itself, might have led the administration's harshest critics to complain of a Treasury "raid." Much worse was to come. Judge Joseph Bryan had been retained to assist Secretary of War Crawford. The latter, it turned out, had been the Galphins' attorney since 1832 and was to receive a payment of one half of any claim settlement with the government.

By spring 1850, the Whig administration was suddenly facing a barrage of questions—What did the President (and his Cabinet) know? and When did (t)he(y) know it? Once the scandal broke, Crawford called for a congressional investigation, which determined that neither Meredith nor Johnson knew of the War Secretary's personal stake in the Galphin claim until after the payment had been made. Crawford testified before the House Committee investigating the affair that he had told Taylor in May 1849 that he was involved in the claim and that the President had assured him that by taking the Cabinet post the Georgian had not forfeited his rights to serve as claimant for the Galphin family. At this point, however, the President probably did not realize the full extent to which his Secretary of War was to benefit. According to Crawford, he had a second discussion with the President in March 1850 in which the President apparently had a clearer perspective on the matter. However, the judgment of the President remained the same. It would be interesting to have the President's thoughts on this, and other key issues, but unfortunately relatively few of Taylor's private papers have survived. Walker, Polk's Treasury Secretary, testified on Meredith's behalf that given Attorney General Johnson's opinion, Walker, too, would have paid out the interest accrued on the claim. Nevertheless, on July 8, 1850, the House passed three resolutions. First, the Galphin claim against the United States was not a just one; second, the 1848 congressional act did require payment of the principal of the claim; but third, Meredith was not authorized to pay interest on the claim (Brandon, 138).

Just before his death, Taylor was planning to make a clean sweep of his Cabinet. According to Thurlow Weed, New York Governor Hamilton Fish would have replaced Meredith at Treasury (Nevins, 321). This shift was obviated when Taylor's sudden death elevated Vice President Millard Fillmore to the presidency. Thomas Corwin, after first declining the offer, eventually agreed to replace Meredith as Treasury Secretary, and Meredith left office on July 9, 1850. As a postscript, Congress enacted a law in 1853 that prohibited either members of Congress or federal employees from receiving payment for helping private parties in settling claims against the United States government.

After his experience in Washington, William Meredith returned to his practice in Philadelphia. The highest professional honor was bestowed on him in 1857 when he succeeded Joseph Ingersoll as Chancellor of the Bar Association of the former's native city. From 1861 to 1867, the former Treasury Secretary served as Attorney General of Pennsylvania. Sidney George Fisher reported that Meredith turned down the post several times on grounds of ill health; Fisher convinced him that his (Meredith's) experience in government and knowledge of constitutional law were indispensable to the state in a time of national crisis (Wainwright, 391–92). Interestingly, Fisher's diary also reveals that Meredith supported Seward, rather than Lincoln, for the 1860 presidential nomination (354). He (Meredith) thought Lincoln "honest but deficient in force, knowledge, and ability . . . unable to appreciate and grasp the case of the country or the true nature of the war" (quoted in Wainwright, 443).

In 1861 Meredith was appointed as a delegate to the ill-starred Peace Convention that assembled in Philadelphia. From 1863 to 1865 he was first President of the Union League; upon retirement he was awarded a gold medal for his efforts. His last great service to his state came a decade later when he presided over the State Constitutional Convention of 1873, which eventually readopted the Constitution of 1790. His health deteriorated, and he died Sunday morning, August 17, 1873.

BIBLIOGRAPHY

Appleton's Cyclopaedia of American Biography. New York: D. Appleton & Co., 1888.

Bauer, K. Jack. *Zachary Taylor: Soldier, Planter, Statesman of the Old Southwest.* Baton Rouge: Louisiana State University Press, 1985.

Biographical Encyclopedia of Pennsylvania. Philadelphia: Galaxy Publishing Co., 1874.

Brandon, William P. "The Galphin Claim." *Georgia Historical Quarterly* 15(June 1931): 113–41.

Clement, Priscilla F. "The Philadelphia Welfare Crisis of the 1820s." *Pennsylvania Magazine of History and Biography* 105(April 1981): 150–65.

Dewey, Davis R. *Financial History of the United States.* 3rd ed. New York: Longmans, Green, & Co., 1907.

Dictionary of American Biography. Vol. 12. New York: Scribner's Sons, 1933.

Dyer, Brainerd. *Zachary Taylor.* Baton Rouge: Louisiana State University Press, 1946.

Hamilton, Holman. *Zachary Taylor: Soldier in the White House.* Indianapolis and New York: Bobbs-Merrill Company, 1951.

Meredith, William M. "Letter from the Secretary of the Treasury transmitting his Annual Report on the State of the Finances." *Executive Documents,* December 1949.

Nevins, Allan. *Ordeal of the Union.* Vol. 1. New York: Charles Scribner's Sons, 1947.

Roberts, Robert N. *White House Ethics: The History of the Politics of Conflict of Interest Regulation.* Westport, CT: Greenwood Press, 1988.

Taussig, Frank W. *The Tariff History of the United States.* 7th ed. New York: G. P. Putnam's Sons, 1923.

Wainwright, Nicholas B. *A Philadelphia Perspective: The Diary of Sidney George Fisher Covering the Years 1834–1871.* Philadelphia: Historical Society of Pennsylvania, 1967.

Woodward, C. Vann, ed. *Responses of the Presidents to Charges of Misconduct.* New York: Delacorte Press, 1974.

JOHN M. GOLDEN

G. WILLIAM MILLER (March 9, 1925–   ). Having held the post of Federal Reserve Chairman since March 1978, G. William Miller resigned in order to serve as Secretary of the Treasury under President Jimmy Carter from August 7, 1979 to January 20, 1981.

The son of James Dick and Hazel Deane (Orrick) Miller, George William Miller was born on March 9, 1925, in Sapulpa, Oklahoma. In the following year the discovery of oil in the Texas Panhandle lured the Miller family to Borger, Texas. They opened a furniture store only to have it fail during the Great Depression. During these hard times, young Bill Miller worked odd jobs after school and on weekends to supplement the family's income. His father worked in a carbon-black plant.

After graduating from high school, Miller attended Amarillo Junior College for a year before entering the United States Coast Guard Academy in New London, Connecticut. At the academy he earned a B.S. degree in marine engineering. In 1945 he was ordered to the Pacific, serving four years as a line officer, mainly in Okinawa and Shanghai. While stationed in Shanghai, Miller met and married a Russian émigrée, the former Ariadna Rogojarsky. Leaving the Coast Guard in 1949, Miller enrolled in graduate school at the University of California,

Berkeley. Miller was an excellent law student. He earned his J.D. degree in 1952, graduating at the top of his class.

Faced with many job offers, Miller opted for prestige instead of high salary. His choice was Cravath, Swaine and Moore, a Wall Street law firm. While working for the firm, Miller helped Textron, Incorporated, win a proxy battle for control of the American Woolen Company. At this time, Textron was a small textile outfit looking to diversify its operations. Instrumental in the victory, Miller was offered a job by Textron Chairman and chief executive officer (CEO) Royal Little. Accepting the job, Miller went to work searching for new acquisitions. By 1957 Miller had been promoted to Vice President and Treasurer of Textron.

In 1960 Miller became Textron's President and Chief Operating Officer after Little stepped down and Rupert C. Thompson, Jr., stepped up as CEO. Textron continued to acquire new companies during this time but shifted priority to stabilization and internal growth. Besides introducing numerous administrative reforms during this period, Bill Miller began to serve and speak out in many civic and governmental organizations. These organizations included the National Alliance of Businessmen, President John Kennedy's Committee on Equal Employment Opportunities, and the National Council on the Humanities.

In January 1968 Miller succeeded Rupert Thompson as CEO of Textron, Incorporated. By this time, Textron was one of the largest conglomerates in the United States. Textron now had major operations in aerospace, consumer goods, industrial equipment, and metal products. At the end of Miller's first year as CEO, Textron had achieved a record $1.7 billion in sales. By the early 1970s when other manufacturing companies were suffering losses due to the recession, Textron was suffering only minor declines in profit. After Miller was named Chairman of the Board in 1974, Textron experienced a remarkable period of sales and net income growth. With the company doing extremely well, Miller took a leave of absence in 1977 to serve as Chairman of the United States Industrial Payroll Savings Plan. Miller also agreed to head the Department of Labor's Help through Industry Retraining and Employment (HIRE) program, when urged to do so by President Carter.

On December 28, 1977, President Carter named Miller to succeed Arthur Burns as Chairman of the Board of Governors of the Federal Reserve System. Even though Burns's term expired on January 31, 1978, it took until March 8, 1978, for Miller to clear confirmation and be sworn in. Questions concerning Miller's experience, integrity, and business ethics were raised during the confirmation hearings.

In complete contrast to the policies of Arthur Burns, a well-known inflation-fighter, Bill Miller believed that the twin ills of unemployment and inflation could be "tackled simultaneously." Miller also believed that the Federal Reserve had a responsibility to conduct monetary policy that was in harmony with the fiscal policies of the President—again, in complete contrast to his predecessor. As inflation continued to rise in late 1978 and early 1979, Miller cautiously curbed the growth in the money supply and tightened credit. These actions later proved to have had little impact on lowering inflation. Time after time during this period, Miller showed his reluctance in making any bold changes in the money supply, opting instead for actions such as small changes in the discount rate and proposals such as voluntary wage and price controls.

When President Carter finally decided it was time for some personnel changes, he fired Treasury Secretary Michael Blumenthal and replaced him with Bill Miller, who resigned his chairmanship of the Fed in order to take over at the Treasury. In Miller's place at the Fed, Carter appointed Paul A. Volcker. Bill Miller became the sixty-fifth Secretary of the Treasury August 7, 1979. In his new roll as official spokesperson of the economy, Miller was probably better suited compared to his position at the Federal Reserve, yet the same stubborn problems remained. Rising inflation, rising unemployment, and rising oil prices continued to plague him at the Treasury Department. Volcker's first move at the Fed was to raise the discount rate one half of a percent. Eventually, Volcker would be victorious at driving down inflation. The cost, like the Carter administration believed all along, was, in fact, a recession.

Miller's term expired in January 1981 when Donald Regan became Secretary of the Treasury under President Ronald Reagan. After the Treasury Department, Miller remained in Washington and became active in venture capitalism. He founded G. William Miller and Company, a venture capital firm that specializes in turning around corporations that are in declining industries.

In 1990 Bill Miller took over as Chairman and CEO of Federated Department Stores. His goal is to turn the firm around by eliminating the enormous debt it has racked up in defending itself from leveraged buyouts. Miller maintains board memberships with Repligen Corporation; Georgetown Industries, Incorporated; Kleinwort Benson Australian Income Fund, Incorporated; Ralph's Supermarkets, Incorporated; Gulf Canada Resources, Limited; and DeBartolo Realty Corporation.

BIBLIOGRAPHY

Current Biography. New York: H. W. Wilson, 1978.
Katz, Bernard S., ed. Biographical Dictionary of the Board of Governors of the Federal Reserve. Westport, CT: Greenwood Press, 1991.
"Miller's Worst Bind Yet." BusinessWeek, July 30, 1979, 23.
Peltz, Michael. "The Man Who Bailed Out Bloomie's." Institutional Investor (April 1993): 77–78.
Who's Who in America. Chicago: A. N. Marquis, 1994.

STEVEN T. PETTY

OGDEN L. MILLS (August 23, 1884–October 11, 1937). Ogden Livingston Mills was invited to join President Herbert Hoover's Cabinet as Secretary of the Treasury on February 13, 1932. He served in this position until March 4, 1933, replaced by President Franklin Roosevelt's appointee, William H. Woodin.

During Mill's short tenure as Secretary, the U.S. economy was in the depths of its severest depression of the twentieth century. While there were new efforts initiated under Mills's stewardship to invigorate the economy, his belief in the virtues of the balanced budget to ensure the integrity of the currency did little to hasten the economic turning point of the depression.

The son of Ogden and Ruth (Livingston) Mills, Ogden L. Mills was born to wealth and power in Newport, Rhode Island, on August 23, 1884. The source of the family fortune was Mills's grandfather, Darius Ogden Mills, a Forty-niner, who prospected for gold behind a storefront and counter. Gaining influence, income, and property in California, he returned to New York with the authority that accompanies personal fortunes. Darius Mills eventually returned to San Francisco, where he died on January 3, 1910, leaving an estate valued at $36 million.

While the Mills family home had been established in Staatsburg, New York, Secretary Mills spent most of his life in New York City and Washington, D.C. As a young man, Mills attended the Browning School in New York City, which was followed by four years at Harvard University, where he graduated in 1904. He then entered Harvard Law School, graduating in 1907.

In 1908 Mills began practicing law in New York. He also began his lifelong political involvement with the Republican Party. His strong attachment to the party's ideas of conservatism and individualism guided both his career and beliefs until his death.

Prior to his first political appointments, Mills sailed to Europe and married Margaret Stuyvesant Rutherford, daughter of W. K. Vanderbilt, at the Vanderbilt château in Deauville, France, on September 20, 1911. The marriage ended in divorce in 1919. Mills married again on September 2, 1924, to Mrs. Dorothy R. Fell. Both of Mills's marriages were childless.

Mills's political journey began with his appointment as a delegate to the Republican National Conventions at Chicago in 1912 and then again in 1916 and 1920. In 1912 he also ran, unsuccessfully, as a candidate for the 63rd Congress. His political ambitions were realized in 1914, as he was elected to the New York State Senate, where he served until resigning in 1917 to enlist in the U.S. Army.

During his service in the Senate, he earned a reputation as an authority on finance and taxation. He once explained his interest in these fields as they were too important to be ignored and that he would be filling a vacuum created by others who believed the field to be both too dry and too difficult.

Upon his enlistment into the Army, Mills asked Henry Stinson, later Secretary of State under Hoover, to intercede on his behalf to obtain an Army commission. Captain Mills served from January 1918 until March 1919, with most of his time spent in Europe.

Returning to his peacetime activities, Mills reasserted his political ambitions and was elected to the U.S. House of Representatives on the Republican ticket. He served in the 67th, 68th, and 69th Congresses representing the 17th New York Congressional District from March 4, 1921, until March 3, 1927. During his membership in the House, Mills served on the important Ways and Means

Committee, where he was able to further sharpen his skills in government finance. In fact, it is the membership in the House Committee that is to eventually bring him into Hoover's Cabinet.

In 1926 Mills faced a career question: He had the choice of running for reelection in the U.S. House of Representatives or resigning from the House to seek the governorship of the state of New York. He chose the statehouse.

Mills was indeed an imposing and attractive candidate. His years in the New York State Senate, his service record, and his experience in the U.S. House of Representatives all spoke well for his political and legislative experience. Standing five feet ten inches, an ex-amateur boxer, tanned from his time on the golf and tennis courts, his physical appearance added to his voter appeal. His wealth and family position undoubtedly supported his polished and vigorous charm, and a powerful voice brought home his outspoken opinions.

A weakness on the campaign trail was Mills's "lack of fire" and "down home" approach to his logical, but cool, stump speeches. He did not have that personal appeal for the man on the street. His world was one of money and privilege. Edward Ellis, in his book A Nation in Torment (197), tells us that in the midst of the depression Mrs. Mills reduced the number of household servants. In response, Ogden Mills is reported to have said, "Dorothy, there are only ten servants in the house! Never before in my life have we had fewer than fifteen." It has also been said of Mills that he lacked the spirit of conciliation that was so essential for political success. Nevertheless, the Mills supporters believed that his run for Governor was but a prelude to the presidency.

Unfortunately, Mills's opponent in the gubernatorial race was the very popular and politically astute Alfred E. Smith. Al Smith handily won the election, and with Smith's victory, Mills's political career appeared to be over. But this was only appearance, as the resolute Mills would not fade, and his role in the national public life was only about to begin.

In 1921 President Harding appointed Andrew Mellon as Secretary of the Treasury. With his taciturn demeanor and often dogmatic behavior, Mellon created a position that would represent to the public and the press the views and policies of his office. The post of the Undersecretary of the Treasury was a Mellon creation.

In early 1927 the Undersecretary position, recently vacated by Garrard B. Winston, was ready to be filled. Congressman Mills, a staunch Republican, considered an expert on taxation, well grounded in public finance, and just completing his last term in Congress, was the logical choice for Mellon's Undersecretary position. Mills fit in well, as Mellon needed his practical legislative experience on the House Ways and Means Committee to enable him to fit a tax program to the politics of Congress. Mills accepted and served in this position from March 4, 1927, until February 11, 1932, when he was selected by Hoover to replace Secretary Mellon, who became Ambassador to Great Britain.

Mills became Undersecretary of the Treasury under President Coolidge. With the presidential election of 1928 soon to take place, he threw his personality and influence completely into the support of Herbert Hoover.

In his campaign to become the Republican Party's nominee for President, Hoover never appointed a "manager." Nevertheless, a group of men, including Mills, came together and informally took over the preconvention campaign. Mills's support of Hoover resulted in a growing association between the two men, whose economic and financial views were in close harmony. In their growing affiliation, Hoover was to say that Mills was a man of uncanny economic sense and courage and with first-order administrative abilities.

When Hoover was elected President in 1929, he continued the appointment of Mellon as Secretary of the Treasury. Although Hoover did not agree with Mellon on a number of positions, his appointment was very much a concession to the conservative center of the Republican Party that revered Mellon and his conservative economic and financial policy views.

With the depression beginning in 1929, and its continuing into the 1930s, Mellon saw little reason for the government to intervene. In fact, Mellon viewed the process of the depression as but a weeding out of the weak and inefficient firms that had grown during the 1920s. To Mellon any intervention by government into the economy would have done more harm than good. It would have only interfered with the natural process of economic and business adjustment that was required as the depression ran its course. Hoover, however, believed that there was a role, however limited, that the government should play during the extreme economic conditions of the 1930s. Hoover had a number of allies (the New Patriots) to this thinking; one of them was his Undersecretary of the Treasury, Ogden Mills.

According to Hoover's memoirs, by the end of 1931, Secretary Mellon was urging him to have Ogden Mills take his place. Hoover did believe that Mills was more suited to the position, as he had a younger and more vigorous mind as well as a belief that government should take action to cushion the grave economic conditions that were mauling the economy. Hoover, however, did admit that Mills had one major fault, an aversion to discussing matters with those he called "dumb" or "boll weevils." Hoover accorded Mills the compliment that he had one of the finest intellects in the country and was a man of the highest integrity and devotion to the public interest.

There were a number of factors at work that suggested there should be changes in Treasury leadership. By 1931 the depression was in its third year, and the only hopeful outlook was based on the words rather than the deeds of the President and Treasury Secretary. Mellon was advancing in years and had already served at the Treasury longer than any other appointee. Hoover also felt that a less strenuous position for Mellon would serve both Mellon and the country best. One other factor was at work.

By the end of 1931 the Reconstruction Finance Corporation (RFC) was about to be put in place to aid the failing economy. Hoover was going to appoint Mellon as one of the directors of the corporation. Mellon, recognizing the heavy schedule of work involved with the RFC, demurred, and as the position of Ambassador to Great Britain was open, Mellon's ambition and Hoover's need were satisfied. Mills was appointed as a director to the RFC as well as Secretary of the Treasury and was sworn into office on February 13, 1932.

Mills took office at the lowest ebb of the depression, with both the gross national product and the level of industrial production reflecting the collapse of the U.S. economy. Strange as it may seem from today's perspective, to Ogden Mills those difficult times called for increases in federal taxation and decreases in the level of government expenditures. A time for belt tightening as the U.S. Treasury was running a deficit in its government accounts, outlays were running ahead of inflows, and to Mills this was an anathema.

Mills interpreted the continuing depression as but the psychology of fear gripping the financial, banking, and business communities. This fear, he believed, could be swept away by adhering to sound principles that would reaffirm and give confidence to the entire national credit structure, from banks to borrowers. He believed that once confidence in the credit and banking structure was reestablished, the economy would begin its recovery. Mills believed that the key to the reaffirmation of the nation's finances and credit was a balanced budget. Sound money was the cornerstone of the recovery, and this required the United States staying on the gold standard and maintaining a balanced budget. While perhaps sounding simplistic, Mills was but pronouncing the orthodoxy of the day.

At the time of the depression, there were few who would have used government spending to buoy national demand for output; there were few who would have argued for the government's function as a macromanager. It was gospel that the government should act on businesslike principles; it should spend only on those projects where the direct benefits equaled their cost. There was no comprehensive fiscal theory that said otherwise. Mills was a sound money man, a fiscal traditionalist.

The fiscally conservative position of the 1930s is not unlike that of today. A balanced budget assured an equitable allocation of resources; it assured that "crowding out" would not occur—that is, with borrowing, the government would get to the money markets first, increase interest rates, and preempt private investment from available funds. If the Federal Reserve was to purchase Treasury bonds, this would result in money creation, followed by inflation, and this was to be stubbornly avoided. Finally, continuing deficits would eventually destroy the credit of the federal government, and this would have dire consequences beyond an even greater depression.

In his book *America's Greatest Depression*, Lester Chandler quotes a 1932 radio speech by Mills in which he proposes a frailty of the credit system that appears extreme today but that surely had its informed adherents:

Our private credit structure is inextricably bound to the credit of the United States Government. Our currency rests predominately upon the credit of the United States. Impair that credit and every dollar you handle will be handled with suspicion. The foundation of our commercial credit system, the Federal Reserve Banks, and all other banks which depend upon them, is tied into and dependent upon the credit of the United States Government. Impair that credit today, and the day after thousands of development projects—they are still going on—will stop; thousands of businessmen dependent upon credit renewals will get refusals from their bankers; thousands of mortgages that would otherwise be renewed or extended will be foreclosed; merchants who would buy on credit will cancel orders. . . . Impair the credit of the United States Government and all that we have sought to accomplish in the course of the last few months is, to a large extent, nullified. (123–24)

To Mills the solutions to America's problems lay more in the realm of money and credit than it did in spending and taxation. While a fiscal conservative, Mills was still a relatively bold and imaginative executive willing to experiment with new mechanisms to restore faith and production to the business and factory community. Mills's hand is evident in Hoover's programs to directly establish financial institutions aimed at bringing relief to the beleaguered economy.

The institutions that were conceived to fight the effects and causes of the depression and yet stay within a conservative financial structure became operative in 1932. They were the Reconstruction Finance Corporation (RFC), the National Credit Corporation, and the Federal Home Loan Bank System. The most important of these was the RFC.

The RFC was created as a type of banking institution intended to finance sound medium- and small-size corporations that found themselves in financial difficulty. Eugene Meyer was Chairman, Charles C. Dawes was President, and Ogden Mills was appointed as one of the directors.

The RFC ran into public credibility problems almost immediately. While established to help the smaller bank and firm, the first RFC loan went to the Bank of America in California, one of the largest financial institutions in the United States. One of the next applications was from the Sweringen brothers who owned the most track mileage for any railroad system in the United States. They owed $1.5 million to the House of Morgan, who loaned the money to the brothers on the basis that they would obtain an RFC loan. After an impassioned argument by Mills, the RFC loaned the Sweringens $14.7 million.

The RFC was the right institution at the right time, but it was too timidly conceived and too slow to action to offset the powerful negative forces at work. The RFC was able to issue its own obligations, limited initially to only $500 million. The U.S. Treasury could purchase these obligations by borrowing the money from individuals, corporations, or banks. In this fashion the government began to finance industry and commerce, extending credit and assuming the risks of lending. The process, however, moved too slowly, and the capitalization was set too low. Although further authorization permitted the RFC to make loans to states and municipalities, Mills argued against any further increases for relief loans, which was requested by congressional Democrats. Mills argued that greater RFC financial commitments would only unbalance the budget, and even the Democrats respected the balanced budget.

The two other institutions, the National Credit Corporation and the Federal Home Loan Bank System, suffered the same weaknesses of the RFC: too small and too slow to have any significant impact.

Mills was more than a strong supporter of the "Glass-Steagall Act," which was passed under his urging in 1932. Succinctly, the new act, affecting the Federal Reserve System, permitted the use of U.S. securities as collateral for Federal Reserve notes. This significantly freed the use of gold as a backing of currency, and the act also reduced bank indebtedness to the Federal Reserve.

The freeing of the gold assured the United States remaining on the gold standard without any changes to gold content values, and the banks, now that their debts to the Fed were reduced, were in a better liquidity position than they had been. This act was vital to the Hoover administration.

Mills cheered the creation of the lending institutions such as the RFC and welcomed the Glass-Steagall Act. All of these were changes, in some fashion, to the financial system as they were money- or lending-oriented innovations, ways in which the Treasury could affect the expansion of central banking activity. However, when it came to expanding the fiscal role of the government, Mills was more than bashful; he was backward. But he was not alone in his silence.

In 1931 the government's budget was in deficit by over $2 billion. President Hoover and others called for tax increases and spending reductions. In response, Mills submitted his tax increase to Congress, who then amended and changed it out of recognition, but it ended up as the largest percentage tax increase in American peacetime history. This was accompanied by a spending reduction of some $40 million. All this took place with the urging of Democratic leaders of the House and Senate. Roosevelt in his campaign for President in 1932 castigated Hoover for his continuing deficits. While Mills's balanced budget fervor had a shared history, he, nevertheless, pursued a fiscal policy that was strongly deflationary.

As 1932 started to wane, and the election choice between Hoover and Roosevelt took center stage, Mills became the workhorse of the Republican campaign. Articulate, confident, and aristocratic in bearing, Mills served as Republican spokesperson to the eastern establishment. The energy given in support of Hoover most assuredly was spurred on by his loyalty to the Republican Party, as well as his disdain both for the "Socialist" platform of the Democratic Party and for his Harvard classmate, Franklin Roosevelt.

To the credit of Ogden Mills, upon the defeat of the Republicans, Mills gave his great capacity for work to the Democrats over the transition period. Mills worked with William Woodin to ensure that as steady a financial ship of state as possible would be given to Roosevelt as he took office.

After March 4, 1933, Ogden Mills retired from public life and sailed the Long Island Sound. It did not take long, however, for Mills to reignite his work ethic, and he began his career of popularizer of the conservative and Republican ethic, as well as severe critic of the Roosevelt administration. He authored *What of Tomorrow* in 1935, *Liberalism Fights On* in 1936, and *The Seventeen Million* in

1937, the year of his death. His books were politely received but were more polemic than analytical. A *New York Times* reviewer observed that his 1937 book would not rally the faithful.

At the time of his passing, Mills was a member of the Union, Knickerbocker, Racquet & Tennis, and Harvard Clubs. He was also a director of the Chase Manhattan Bank, the Herald Tribune, the Museum of Natural History, and the Metropolitan Museum of Art, among others. Ogden L. Mills died at his New York City home at 2 East 69th Street on October 11, 1937, of an apparent heart attack. He is buried in the St. James Churchyard, Staatsburg, New York.

BIBLIOGRAPHY

Chandler, Lester V. *America's Greatest Depression*. New York: Harper & Row, 1970.

Ellis, Edward R. *A Nation in Torment*. New York: Coward, McCann, Geoghegan, 1970.

Fausold, Martin. *The Presidency of Herbert C. Hoover*. Lawrence: University Press of Kansas, 1985.

Feis, Herbert. *1933, Characters in Crisis*. Boston: Little, Brown, 1966.

Hoover, Herbert. *The Memoirs of Herbert Hoover—The Cabinet and the Presidency*. New York: Macmillan Company, 1952.

———. *The Memoirs of Herbert Hoover—The Great Depression, 1929–41*. New York: Macmillan Company, 1952.

Mills, Ogden L. *What of Tomorrow*. New York: Macmillan, 1935.

———. *Liberalism Fights On*. New York: Macmillan, 1936.

———. *The Seventeen Million*. New York: Macmillan, 1937.

New York Times. February 5, 1932, 5; October 5, 1937, 1.

Sobel, Robert, ed. *Biographical Directory of the United States Executive Branch, 1774–1989*. Westport: Greenwood Press, 1990.

Taus, Esther R. *Central Banking Functions of the United States Treasury, 1789–1941*. New York: Columbia University Press, 1943.

BERNARD S. KATZ

HENRY MORGENTHAU, JR. (May 11, 1891–February 6, 1967). Henry Morgenthau served as Secretary of the Treasury from 1934 to 1945. During this twelve-year period, the United States suffered through the Great Depression and fought World War II. This turbulent period also produced important changes in economic policy, ranging from the New Deal to the Bretton Woods exchange rate system. As Secretary of the Treasury, Henry Morgenthau was deeply involved in these events and policy changes. His actions were instrumental in financing both the New Deal and the Allied war effort, and he also helped to pass the Bretton Woods Agreement that created a new international monetary system.

Morgenthau was a humanitarian who cared greatly about the plight of the poor and oppressed. His actions were directed at alleviating this plight, and he was willing to challenge conventional wisdom when it clashed with his liberal ideals. For example, Morgenthau recognized that temporary increases in federal spending were necessary to relieve suffering during the depression, even if these increases produced budget deficits that were unacceptable to orthodox economists of the day. He also rejected the isolationism that was widely popular prior to World War II and argued instead that aggression and political repression should be resisted rather than appeased. Morgenthau's willingness to act forcefully on his beliefs made him an important agent for change during a critical period in American history.

Henry Morgenthau II was born in New York City on May 11, 1891. Morgenthau was the third child and only son of his wealthy Jewish parents. His father, Henry Morgenthau I, got his start in law and real estate and went on to accumulate a substantial fortune. Having made his fortune, he turned to a career in public service and politics, eventually rising to the position of American Ambassador to Turkey during World War I. Morgenthau's mother, Josephine Sykes, was also involved in public service and supported both the arts and organizations such as the Henry Street Settlement House, which provided social services to poor Jewish immigrants. His parents' dedication to public service made a lasting impression on Morgenthau.

As a child and a young man, Morgenthau was never very successful in his studies. While obviously intelligent, he was unable to translate his intelligence into academic success, and there is some evidence that he may have had a learning disability. He began his schooling at Sach's Collegiate Institute and Phillips Exeter Academy and eventually went on to attend Cornell University. At Cornell, he studied architecture but dropped out after only three semesters.

Two events in 1911 had a great influence on Morgenthau's life. The first occurred shortly after he dropped out of Cornell. At his father's suggestion, Morgenthau began to serve at the Henry Street Settlement House. This service opened his eyes to the terrible poverty of many Jews, and Morgenthau later attributed his devotion to the less fortunate to his experience at Henry Street. The second event occurred after Morgenthau fell ill with typhus and was sent to a Texas ranch to convalesce. At the ranch, he was given his first exposure to agriculture, and this exposure led him to pursue a career in farming. Morgenthau's decision to become a farmer would ultimately lead to his appointment as Secretary of the Treasury.

Upon his return to New York, Morgenthau again enrolled at Cornell, this time to study agriculture. His second stay at Cornell was even shorter and less successful than his first, and he dropped out after only a few months. In 1913, Morgenthau, with his father's financial assistance, purchased a large farm in Dutchess County, New York. There he took up dairy farming and also planted an apple orchard. Morgenthau would immerse himself in farming for the next two decades.

In 1916, Morgenthau married Elinor Fatman, a childhood friend, and their marriage was to last until Elinor's death thirty-three years later. The two settled down on their farm and eventually had three children. It was at about this time that Morgenthau first met Franklin Roosevelt, who also owned property in Dutchess County. The two were to become fast friends in later years, and their friendship was a boon to both of them.

Morgenthau's first step into public life came in 1922, when he purchased (again with his father's assistance) the *American Agriculturist,* a weekly farm publication covering the New York region. Morgenthau used the *American Agriculturist* as a platform for his own ideas, and the paper was imbued with his honesty and integrity. Most of his ideas focused on rural reforms such as infrastructure improvements, lower rural taxes, and increased educational spending; he also espoused policies such as the reclamation of wastelands, reforestation, and conservation. All of these ideas proved very popular in rural communities, and they helped Morgenthau earn the support of these communities.

This popularity helped him gain his first public appointment in 1928, the same year in which Franklin Roosevelt was first elected Governor of New York. By this time, the friendship between Roosevelt and Morgenthau had grown so strong that Morgenthau was now one of Roosevelt's most trusted advisers. After his election, Roosevelt appointed Morgenthau Chairman of the Agriculture Advisory Commission, a commission that eventually made many recommendations designed to improve rural life. Almost without exception, these recommendations were enacted, and this helped Roosevelt gain the enthusiastic support of farmers throughout New York.

After Roosevelt was reelected Governor in 1930, he chose Morgenthau to head the Conservation Commission. This commission was responsible for overseeing public lands, and as its head, Morgenthau displayed great organizational and administrative abilities. Morgenthau, along with Harry Hopkins, also put together a package of progressive reforms that was a precursor to the New Deal policies of 1933. For example, Morgenthau and Hopkins assembled and helped enact a reforestation program that employed some 10,000 men during the early years of the depression. In this way, Morgenthau contributed directly to the humanitarian vision that inspired Roosevelt's New Deal.

Morgenthau played an important role in Roosevelt's 1932 presidential campaign by mustering rural support for Roosevelt. After Roosevelt's election, Morgenthau was appointed head of the Farm Credit Administration (FCA), which was responsible for administering the federal government's rural credit programs.

Morgenthau's new job was daunting. Farmers had suffered more than any other group during the early years of the depression, in part because they had never really shared in the prosperity of the 1920s. When the depression began in earnest, conditions deteriorated rapidly as farm prices plunged by over 50 percent. The drop in farm prices was matched by an even more precipitous decline in net farm income, which fell by nearly 70 percent during the same period. The drop in farm income made it difficult for many farmers to make debt payments, and the result was high loan delinquency and foreclosure rates. The failure of many farms also jeopardized rural banks.

Morgenthau undertook two sets of policies to address these problems. The first set of policies focused on expanding and reorganizing federal farm credit programs. Morgenthau oversaw reforms at the FCA that produced over a half million new loans involving some $1.3 billion in 1933 alone. The FCA also helped thousands of farmers refinance their debts at more favorable interest rates.

The second set of policies focused on increasing farm prices. Using funds from the FCA, Morgenthau began purchasing large quantities of crops whose prices were particularly depressed, Morgenthau continued making purchases for several months, but the purchases raised prices only temporarily because they failed to address the fundamental problem of excess supply. Morgenthau began to search for another way to increase farm prices and became convinced that the best option was an increase in the dollar price of gold. This increase would devalue the dollar relative to other currencies and allow U.S. farmers to increase their prices without suffering a loss of competitiveness in their export markets.

While Morgenthau supported an increase in the dollar price of gold, most economists and financial institutions in 1933 opposed such an increase. The dollar price of gold had been fixed at $20.67 per ounce since 1900, and the conventional view at the time was that an increase in this price would trigger substantial inflation. This view was contradicted by events outside the United States, particularly in Britain, where the pound had been decoupled from gold in 1931. The resulting depreciation of the pound had helped Britain and other countries in the "sterling area" gain competitiveness at the expense of the United States. The loss of U.S. competitiveness had produced deflationary pressure, particularly in agricultural markets.

Roosevelt was well aware of this and had decided very early after his election that the dollar price of gold had to be increased despite the reservations of his advisers. There is no evidence that Morgenthau had any influence on Roosevelt's decision, but once the decision was reached, Morgenthau enthusiastically supported it. The next step was finding a means for increasing the dollar price of gold, and Roosevelt decided that the best approach was for the federal government to purchase gold. This plan was put into effect in October 1933, against the will of the Undersecretary of the Treasury, Dean Acheson.

Acheson had effectively become the Acting Secretary since William Woodin, Roosevelt's original appointee, was seriously ill. Acheson's resistance to the gold purchase plan infuriated Roosevelt, and Acheson was forced to resign in early November. After Roosevelt had requested that Woodin step down, he asked Morgenthau to become the Acting Secretary of the Treasury. Somewhat stunned, Morgenthau accepted the second-highest position in the Cabinet and was confirmed shortly thereafter, taking office on January 1, 1934.

The gold purchase plan eventually drove the price of gold up to $35 per ounce in January 1934 but was not as successful as had been hoped. While both agricultural and industrial prices did rise, the increase was not as great as expected. Indeed, it is doubtful that Roosevelt ever believed that the plan would meet its expectations. Nonetheless, the increase in the dollar price of gold did stem deflationary pressure and did produce modest price increases. Perhaps as important, the plan demonstrated the willingness of New Dealers such as Roosevelt and Morgenthau to experiment rather than just stand by and do nothing.

The gold purchase plan ultimately produced the Gold Reserve Act of 1934, which fixed the dollar price of gold at $35 per ounce but effectively took the

United States off the gold standard. This is because the Gold Reserve Act eliminated the dollar's convertibility into gold and thereby handed control of monetary policy over to the Federal Reserve System. This was a critical policy change because it cleared the way for easier credit and lower interest rates, both of which were essential to economic recovery.

After officially entering office in 1934, Morgenthau was immediately immersed in financing Roosevelt's New Deal. The New Deal was a collection of programs designed to relieve the massive unemployment and poverty generated by the depression. These programs provided direct relief to the unemployed, but they also created government-sponsored public works projects and produced a massive expansion of federal lending in both urban and rural areas. Morgenthau had little direct say in the design of most of these programs because they were formulated while he was still head of the FCA. He was, however, a staunch advocate of the New Deal because he believed that the federal government was morally obligated to help the poor and unemployed. He also believed that the federal government was the only institution that could address the problems created by the depression.

As Secretary of the Treasury, he was responsible for financing New Deal programs such as the Federal Emergency Relief Administration, the Civil Works Administration, and the Public Works Administration, all of which provided jobs or other forms of relief to the unemployed. While Morgenthau fully supported these programs, he was disturbed by the large federal budget deficits that had to be incurred to finance them. Morgenthau understood that these budget deficits were necessary to relieve the suffering produced by the depression, but he never accepted the idea popularized by John Maynard Keynes at the time that deficit spending could be used to attain full employment. In Morgenthau's view, budget deficits were an essential means for providing humanitarian assistance and were to be incurred only until the immediate economic crisis had passed. Once recovery was under way, any deficits should be eliminated since they undermined the solvency of the federal government, reduced business confidence, and threatened private investment.

Thus, while Morgenthau accepted the need for budget deficits, he tried to limit these deficits to the minimum necessary to provide relief. He was no different from Roosevelt and many others in this belief, and Keynesian economists have argued since that the fiscal conservatism of Morgenthau and Roosevelt resulted in much smaller deficits than were necessary to stimulate recovery. In hindsight, this view is probably correct, but it should be remembered that Keynes's views on deficit spending were not widely known or accepted at the time. It is also important to understand the historical context of the New Deal. In 1929, total federal expenditures represented only 2.5 percent of the gross national product (GNP). By 1936, this figure had increased to 10.5 percent, an increase that shows how massive spending increases under the New Deal were. Combining these massive spending increases with the political and judicial resistance to the New Deal, it is arguable that much greater spending increases were not feasible.

As the economy began to recover in 1935, Morgenthau took steps to reduce the budget deficits he felt were increasingly unnecessary. He focused much of his effort on making the tax system more progressive, which he felt would reduce the burden on the poor and middle class by forcing the rich to pay "their fair share." Morgenthau and Roosevelt were successful in 1935 in increasing inheritance and gift taxes, in closing tax loopholes, and in raising marginal tax rates for the wealthy. They also won approval for a graduated corporate income tax and a tax on undistributed profits. The last tax was viewed as a way of stimulating recovery since it would encourage the distribution of profits in the form of dividends, which would raise consumption. One important tax increase passed in 1935 was not related to deficit reduction. This was the Social Security tax, which alone increased federal tax revenues by 25 percent.

Morgenthau also began to press Roosevelt in 1936 for spending cuts. Morgenthau felt that Roosevelt was vulnerable to Republican attacks against the budget deficit similar to those that Roosevelt had made against Hoover in 1932. Roosevelt agreed and cut spending. As the recovery progressed, Morgenthau began to believe that the entire deficit could be eliminated by 1938, and he pressed Roosevelt for even greater spending restraint. In the end, however, the combination of higher taxes and reduced spending triggered a deep recession in 1938. This recession caused Roosevelt to reverse his position on deficit spending, something Morgenthau was never able to do. Indeed, Morgenthau viewed the 1938 recession as a product of declining business confidence rather than contractionary fiscal policy.

The debate over deficit spending began to fade after 1938, mainly because of the threat of war in Europe. Since his appointment as Secretary, Morgenthau had observed with increasing alarm the aggressive behavior of both Germany and Japan. Morgenthau believed that this behavior would produce a global conflict unless the United States acted forcefully to contain aggression. He used his position to argue for financial assistance for China, France, and Britain, but his attempts were largely thwarted by the isolationist mood of many Americans, including Secretary of State Cordell Hull and others in Congress who sought to keep the United States out of any new war. Morgenthau believed that U.S. isolationism would only encourage further aggression and that such aggression would eventually drag the United States into a new war. Roosevelt agreed with Morgenthau, but congressional leaders were much more isolationist and took measures, such as the Neutrality Act of 1937, that greatly limited the assistance Morgenthau could provide to countries confronted with aggression.

As war became increasingly likely in 1939, Morgenthau was approached by Britain and France, who were seeking to purchase arms from the United States. Neither country had a military capability comparable to Germany's, and both were desperately trying to catch up. While Morgenthau wanted to help both countries rearm, he was confronted with several problems. First, Congress had passed several measures that forbid U.S. exports of weapons. While these measures were overturned by the Neutrality Act of 1939, this act required that all arms sales be paid for in full within ninety days. This restriction greatly hampered sales to Britain and France, who lacked the resources necessary to pay for full military mobilization.

Within these confines, Morgenthau sought to arrange whatever sales he could. But he faced a second problem, which was the inadequacy of U.S. military production at the time. This problem was further aggravated in 1940 when the United States began to mobilize its own military. The combination of limited U.S. productive capacity and growing U.S. demand squeezed arms sales to Britain and France, but it also pointed out to Morgenthau and others the inadequacy of U.S. military capability. As a result, plans were rapidly made to expand U.S. productive capacity. Without the arms sales arranged by Morgenthau, this capacity would not have grown nearly as quickly.

As the war in Europe accelerated in 1940, Britain faced an increasingly difficult situation. It was importing massive quantities of arms and other goods and paying for these imports by liquidating its financial assets at a dizzying pace. Morgenthau and Roosevelt both saw that Britain's financial assets would be completely liquidated by 1941, at which point its war effort would collapse. To prevent this, Roosevelt devised the Lend-Lease program, which allowed the United States to lend Britain whatever it needed, provided that Britain would repay the United States in kind after the war. Roosevelt gave Morgenthau the job of drafting a Lend-Lease bill and pushing it through Congress. Morgenthau's Lend-Lease bill clearly violated the spirit of the Neutrality Acts of 1937 and 1939, but because it did not involve the provision of financial credit, Morgenthau and other key Cabinet officials were able to sway Congress. The Lend-Lease program was critical to Britain's war effort, and there is little doubt that the British would have been defeated without it.

After the Japanese bombed Pearl Harbor in 1941 and America entered the war, Morgenthau was faced with the task of financing the massive expenditures needed to fuel the Allied war effort. All told, the war cost the U.S. Treasury some $300 billion, a figure that is still substantial fifty years later even without adjusting for inflation. Between 1942 and 1945, federal government outlays represented over 40 percent of U.S. GNP; in no other year have federal expenditures ever exceeded even 25 percent of GNP. Budget deficits during this period approached 25 percent of U.S. GNP, while the national debt rose by 350 percent to a level that exceeded U.S. GNP in 1945. No other Treasury Secretary has ever had to confront a more difficult task.

From the beginning, Morgenthau sought to raise revenues by relying equally on increased borrowing and higher taxes. Morgenthau also wanted to ensure that the burden imposed by greater borrowing and higher taxes reflected an individual's ability to pay and did not jeopardize the New Deal principles he still cherished. For this reason, he strongly supported a voluntary war bond program rather than compulsory saving, which was favored by virtually every public official other than Roosevelt.

In the eyes of Morgenthau and Roosevelt, the voluntary war bond program was critical because it did not burden anyone with compulsory saving. Both men also supported the war bond effort because war bond advertising could be used to raise American consciousness of the war. Morgenthau even believed that any compulsory savings program enacted by Congress would probably be accompanied by smaller tax increases. He argued that Congress would be much less likely to enact tax increases in the presence of compulsory saving because it would seek to offset the burden imposed by compulsory saving. Given the limited tax increases passed by Congress during the war (relative to those supported by the Treasury Department) even in the absence of a compulsory savings program, this view appears justified.

Morgenthau's war bond program was a great success and raised some $49 billion, nearly one sixth the cost of the war. Additional borrowing was accomplished through bond sales to corporations and financial institutions and through direct borrowing from private banks. All told, roughly 55 percent of the war's cost was financed through borrowing, somewhat more than Morgenthau would have liked. The reason for this was Congress's reluctance to enact the tax increases recommended by the Treasury Department and the Roosevelt administration.

Tax increases were problematic from the start. They were clearly necessary to finance the war and to control inflationary pressure, but there was widespread disagreement over what taxes should be increased. Morgenthau favored a spending tax that would be levied on expenditures for nonnecessities because such a tax was progressive and also anti-inflationary. He also sought to increase Social Security taxes and taxes that would limit wartime profiteering. Morgenthau strongly opposed any increase in sales taxes and any reduction in personal income tax exemptions because he viewed these changes as regressive.

Unfortunately for Morgenthau, Congress rejected most of his recommendations. Instead, Congress increased personal income taxes by 5 percent, reduced personal exemptions, and put taxes on a "pay as you go" basis. Morgenthau particularly despised the last measure since it forgave a substantial portion of the income taxes owed by the wealthy from the previous year. Congress did increase corporate income tax rates, but it failed to raise Social Security taxes or adopt a spending tax, and the end result was an increase in tax revenues that failed to come close to that supported by the Roosevelt administration. In 1943, for example, Morgenthau sent the House Ways and Means Committee a request for an increase in taxes of $10.5 billion for 1944; Congress later approved (over Roosevelt's veto) a tax package that raised taxes by only $2 billion.

In short, Morgenthau's attempts to finance the war through an equal increase in both taxes and borrowing failed. This was despite the success of his war bond drive, which was widely lauded and obviated any need for a compulsory savings program. He failed because his attempts to raise taxes were thwarted by a Congress motivated by political concerns. Morgenthau was even unhappy with the tax increases enacted by Congress because they were less equitable than he would have liked.

In July 1944, just after the Allied invasion of Normandy, Morgenthau convened a conference at Bretton Woods, New Hampshire, to discuss plans for a new international monetary system. The conference brought together all the Allied powers, but the plan produced by the conference was designed almost entirely by Harry Dexter White and John Maynard Keynes, two eminent monetary theorists. The plan created a new exchange rate system, the so-called Bretton Woods system, along with two new international agencies, the International Monetary Fund (IMF) and the Bank for Reconstruction and Development (now known as the World Bank). While Morgenthau had relatively little input into the plan, he provided the original impetus for it and played a pivotal role in shepherding the plan through Congress.

The seeds of the Bretton Woods system were sown in 1936, when the Tripartite Agreement was reached. This agreement represented a multilateral attempt to stabilize exchange rates through central bank cooperation and the establishment of stabilization funds. Morgenthau was a central figure in the negotiations that produced the Tripartite Agreement, and he believed that it was an important step to greater international security since the agreement bolstered the sagging French economy. He also believed that the uncoordinated and frequently self-serving exchange rate policies of the late 1920s and early 1930s had undermined international trade and economic growth. The Tripartite Agreement reflected Morgenthau's desire for multilateral economic cooperation and exchange rate stability, a desire that ultimately produced the Bretton Woods system.

The Tripartite Agreement was largely unsuccessful, but despite this, Morgenthau asked Harry Dexter White in 1941 to draft a plan for an international stabilization fund. White's plan, which was completed several months later, featured a fixed exchange rate system and two new agencies, the IMF and the World Bank. The role of the IMF in the new system was to lend official reserves to countries seeking to support the value of their currencies. The purpose of the World Bank was to accelerate global economic expansion by providing credit to war-torn and developing economies.

Morgenthau was greatly impressed with White's plan and immediately set about the task of negotiating an international agreement. The United States and Britain were the two most important powers in the negotiations, primarily because of U.S. economic power and the brilliance of Britain's chief negotiator, John Maynard Keynes. Both Keynes and White produced drafts of their individual plans in 1943, and negotiations between the two resulted in a joint draft in 1944. This draft was modified slightly at the Bretton Woods conference, where it received unanimous approval.

Morgenthau served as a facilitator for the Bretton Woods agreement by requesting the original plan and by bringing the negotiating parties together. Perhaps even more important, he was responsible for gaining congressional approval for the Bretton Woods Agreement. Roosevelt's attention at the time was focused on the war, and he granted Morgenthau a free hand in winning congressional approval. Morgenthau had already managed to defuse the agreement as an election year issue, and he skillfully steered the plan through the House of Representatives. While Morgenthau left office two weeks before the Senate vote, he was instrumental in gaining Senate approval. Morgenthau's role in the formation and passage of the new international monetary system represents one of his most lasting accomplishments.

On the morning of April 12, 1945, Franklin Roosevelt died, and later that day, Harry Truman was sworn in as President. The death of Roosevelt effectively ended Henry Morgenthau's twelve years as Secretary of the Treasury, although he did not resign for another three months—on July 22, 1945. Morgenthau resigned in part because he knew Truman intended to appoint a new Secretary of the Treasury and in part because he had been drained by his own experience as Secretary.

About ten years after he resigned his position, Morgenthau began working with John Blum on a detailed history of his years at the Treasury Department. Morgenthau died on February 6, 1967, shortly after he and Blum had completed this history. In summing up Morgenthau's career, Blum wrote:

He was a farmer, a reformer, a democrat, one of the children of American plenty whose spirits transcended the material advantages of their personal inheritances. With another man of wealth and independence and high purpose he tried, to the exhausting limits of his energy and determination, to make the world a better place in which all men could live a better life. In that, he felt, he had succeeded. More important, he knew he had tried without stint or let or compromise. (648)

BIBLIOGRAPHY
Badger, Anthony J. *The New Deal: The Depression Years, 1933–40*. New York: Hill and Wang, 1989.
Blum, John M. *Roosevelt and Morgenthau*. Boston: Houghton Mifflin Company, 1970.
Chandler, Lester V. *America's Greatest Depression*. New York: Harper and Row, 1970.
Dam, Kenneth W. *The Rules of the Game: Reform and Evolution in the International Monetary System*. Chicago: University of Chicago Press, 1982.
Davies, Walter E. *The New Deal: Interpretations*. New York: Macmillan Company, 1964.
Eichengreen, Barry. *Golden Fetters: The Gold Standard and the Great Depression*. New York: Oxford University Press, 1992.
Morgenthau III, Henry. *Mostly Morgenthaus: A Family History*. New York: Ticknor and Fields, 1991.
Schlesinger, Arthur M. *The Coming of the New Deal*. Cambridge: Riverside Press, 1958.
———. *The Politics of Upheaval*. Cambridge: Riverside Press, 1960.
Young, Roland. *Congressional Politics in the Second World War*. New York: Columbia University Press, 1956.

JAMES M. DEVAULT

LOT M. MORRILL (May 3, 1813–January 10, 1883). On June 21, 1876, in the last months of the floundering Grant administration, Lot Myrick Morrill, a leading Republican Senator of the day, was appointed Secretary of the Treasury by President Grant. Morrill's predecessor at the Treasury, Benjamin Helms Bristow, had just resigned and would go on to represent the reform wing of the

Republican Party in the presidential campaign of 1876. Bristow had served in the Treasury for two years and had spent his time trying to reform a department steeped in scandal. During these two years, Bristow's working relationship with President Grant became increasingly strained. Bristow was a loyal Republican who felt the corrupt Grant administration would bring the party down to defeat in the coming election. Grant viewed Bristow's efforts at reform with open suspicion, feeling he was a traitor to the administration he was supposed to serve.

When Bristow finally resigned, Grant needed a loyal Republican at the Treasury who would not be seen as undermining his administration. Senator Lot M. Morrill was viewed by Grant as the ideal replacement. As Senator, he had actively followed legislation concerning the financial questions of the day, and he agreed with views expressed by the Grant administration. Morrill assumed the Treasury post on July 7, 1876, and served just eight months. He resigned on March 8, 1877, days after Rutherford B. Hayes became President of the United States. Morrill was respected as a hardworking and faithful public servant, and when Hayes took over, he offered Morrill a choice of administrative posts. Morrill, who was not in good health, picked a post that would bring him back to his native Maine, Collector of Customs for the Portland Maine District.

Lot M. Morrill was born on May 3, 1813, in Belgrade, Maine, the son of Peaslee and Nancy (Macomber) Morrill. His parents had seven sons and seven daughters. He went to local schools and early on decided he wanted to become a lawyer. At sixteen he was teaching school himself, in order to earn money to go on to Waterville College (now Colby) for one year. He left after one year to start work in a law office. In 1839, he was admitted to the bar, and he then resettled to Augusta, Maine, the state capital. In 1845, he married Charlotte Holland Vance, and they raised four daughters.

Morrill was a Democrat and became Chairman of the Democratic State Committee in 1849, remaining in that post until 1856. He was elected to the Maine House of Representatives in 1854, and in 1856 to the state Senate, where he served as Presiding Officer. However, throughout these pre–Civil War years, he disagreed with the Democratic Party over its views on the slavery question. Because of this disagreement, he joined the Republican Party in 1856. Two years later in 1858, he was elected Governor of Maine as a Republican. He served as Governor until 1860, when the state legislature of Maine selected him to replace U.S. Senator Hannibal Hamlin, who had resigned to become Vice President under President Abraham Lincoln. Morrill was reelected in 1863 and served until 1869.

During his first year in the Senate, Lot served as a member of the Peace Convention, which met to peacefully resolve slavery issues. He endorsed the policy of confiscating the property of those who supported the Confederacy. He favored freeing the slaves and headed a movement in 1862 that led to the freeing of the slaves in the District of Columbia. In 1867 he was defeated by one vote in his reelection bid for the Senate and returned to law practice in Maine. In 1869 he was again selected by the Maine state legislature to fill a vacated U.S. Senate seat. He was reelected in 1871 and remained in the Senate until 1876, when Grant appointed him Secretary of the Treasury.

While Morrill was in the Senate, he had opposed the Inflation Bill of 1874, which would have increased the money supply during that depression year. This bill and the rationale behind it would be debated for years to come: Should the government influence the economy by manipulating the money supply, and if so, when should the supply be expanded or contracted? Morrill was a conservative on this issue, always inveighing against excessive money supply expansion.

Lot M. Morrill was not in the Treasury long enough to have any lasting effect on the department but was said to have run the operation efficiently. After his many years in Washington, he was glad to return home to Augusta, Maine, in 1877. He died there on January 10, 1883.

BIBLIOGRAPHY

Biographical Encyclopedia of Maine of the Nineteenth Century. Boston: Metropolitan Publishing and Engraving Co., 1885.

Hasseltine, William B. *Ulysses S. Grant, Politician.* New York: F. Ungar Publishing Co., 1957.

McFeely, William B. *Grant, a Biography.* New York: W. W. Norton & Co., 1981.

Moran, Philip, ed. *Ulysses S. Grant, 1882–1885.* Dobbs Ferry, NY: Oceana Publications, 1968.

Nevins, Allan. *Hamilton Fish: The Inner History of the Grant Administration.* New York: Dodd, Mead and Co., 1936.

Vexler, Robert I. *The Vice Presidents and Cabinet Members.* Vol. 1. Dobbs Ferry, NY: Oceana Publications, 1975.

JULIANNE CICARELLI

R

DONALD T. REGAN (December 21, 1918–   ). Donald T. Regan was born to William Francis Regan and Kathleen (Ahearn) Regan on December 21, 1918, in Cambridge, Massachusetts. The family was Irish to the bone and lived on the ground floor of a three-story wood frame house in South Boston. Donald's father was a policeman, fired during the police strike of 1919 by Governor Calvin Coolidge. The impression on Don lasted; he has always found it difficult to cross picket lines. The other significant family experiences that lingered were the tragic death of his brother Billy, at twelve, and the condition of his sister, a diabetic who was eventually blinded. The insulated neighborhood and its Catholic school instructors provided a strict education that kept Don, his brother, and friends from straying into the rough gangs. His father, an occasional boxer, presented his six-day-week check to his mother, who handled the family finances. As Don describes it, the father was the symbol of authority in the family, but his mother was its embodiment. Despite rough conditions, Don was taught manners, morality, and respectfulness and never appeared scruffy.

Regan aspired to be a lawyer and enrolled in Harvard shortly before World War II. He worked at various jobs in high school, including caddie, usher, and electrician's helper. His first taste of entrepreneurial activity came after he worked as a tour guide in Harvard Square. He bought the business after its owner graduated, and expanded it. He had money in the bank when he left school. It's no wonder that he remembers the jobs more than the classes. The abstract, he says, has never been an interest to him.

In September 1940, he entered law school on schedule but a month later found himself at Quantico in the Marine Corps officer training. Surprised to be assigned as a gunnery officer, he was initially posted to Iceland. Later he moved to the Pacific Theater, fighting five major campaigns from Guadalcanal to Okinawa. Like many of his generation, he never forgot or forgave the bitter battles of the South Pacific.

While training in the reserves, he met Ann Buchanan on a blind date, and the two dated every weekend. In between the posting from Reykjavik to San

Diego, the two were married on July 11, 1942. Following a brief honeymoon, he reported to duty and did not see her again for thirty-three months. He met his wife in San Francisco, at the Top of the Mark Hopkins Hotel, and when he returned to Washington, he met his daughter of two years, Donna Ann. There, the couple had three more children.

After the war, Regan stumbled into management training at Merrill Lynch (then Merrill Lynch, Pierce, Fenner and Beane) and gave up his dream of becoming a lawyer. His career advancement at Merrill was swift. Carefully groomed to the top, he spent his last ten years as Chairman and chief executive officer. Merrill, an extraordinarily successful brokerage house, was viewed as maverick under his leadership, more capitalist than cartelist. For example, Regan promoted eliminating the price fixing among brokers (the minimum commissions). This fit nicely with Merrill long-term growth and diversification strategy: Competitors with income derived from brokerage only would suffer. Walter Wriston, famous Chairman of Citicorp, was asked in 1980 what his dream bank might look like. He replied that it already existed—that "Don Regan runs it." Success at Merrill was based on the combination of his formidable capabilities, his earnestness, and his willingness to plunge in and speak his mind. Some of Ronald Reagan's closest allies perhaps came to despise those qualities once they were redirected.

In 1972, Regan's *A View from the Street* was published, analyzing Wall Street's problems in 1969 and 1970. In 1988, Regan authored *For the Record,* an account of his life. The book was a *New York Times* number-one best-seller, a plainspoken, harsh account of the presidency from up close. Reviewers were enthusiastic, describing its content as "devastating," "riveting," and "explosive." Such praises were not a response to accomplishments in the Treasury but to Regan's account of his own role in the Iran-Contra scandal. A quarter of the book is a stretched-out answer to the question, "What did the President know and when did he know it?" If history is indeed scandal, then forsake his tenure at Treasury for a greater indiscretion: Regan is the man who informed the American public how Nancy Reagan dictated the schedule of the President of the United States— and by implication, important world events—based on the detailed advice of her *astrologer.*

Don Regan never ran for election and, though a lifelong Republican, often contributed to Democratic candidates. He is not an ideological man and is suspicious of ideas. His free market advocacy was rooted more in his lifelong corporate and entrepreneurial experience. His core beliefs as presented are simple and sensible, free from the policy dogma that he observed in the Reagan administration. He feels more comfortable to stand alone, carefully delineating his differences with his associates. In light of the rancorous political debate that emerged during the Reagan years, it's no surprise that he would keep to a small island of belief. He joined himself to the supply-side movement because he believed in classical free market economics, especially the effects of incentives. He was a late comer to the specifically Reaganite policy agenda and never a full member of supply-side intellectual leadership, like Jack Kemp. It was Regan's show at Treasury, and he declined to hire one of the leading supply-siders to the number-two post.

The beliefs that motivated him in public life were uncomplicated. While Regan's successor James A. Baker III passed through the office as part of Grand Design, and Nicholas Brady later occupied the position as trusted confidant of Bush, Don Regan's tenure appears in contrast a sincere adventure in public service, lasting from January 22, 1981, to February 1, 1985. It was spirited at first and, by the end, in Ronald Reagan's second midterm as White House Chief of Staff, bitter. Of the three Secretaries under Reagan and Bush, Regan was the one required to adopt the most ideological policy stance. This was a timing issue: The first year of a presidency is typically the period of the highest political capital. In advocating the position that lowering taxes both reduced punitive effects *and* raised government revenue, he preached a heresy that Congress never bought. However, Regan was more than spokesman: The revenue projections were negotiable, but the principle of incentive effects was not. After the career of the volatile Office of Management and Budget (OMB) Director Stockman imploded due to indiscreet comments published in a 1981 interview, Regan emerged front and center as the administration's policy representative. Though uncomfortable with people like Stockman, whom he considered dogmatic, Regan nevertheless carried the day for a movement largely in synch with his own sympathies. As a skilled administrator, Regan brought a crucial set of talents to bear on Republican goals. There are few reasons to doubt that his personal goals dovetailed with the public spirit of the presidency.

Regan confesses that he had only met President Reagan briefly before being offered the Secretary position. He was surprised to discover that his marching orders were delivered through the public speeches of the President. As adviser to the President, he got surprisingly very little time alone with him. He soon found that the best way to get the President's ear was to use the same method that the President used so effectively with the public: use short, lively stories with strong policy implications. For example, when he informed the President that several of America's largest corporations did not pay a dime in taxes because of loopholes, the President saw the importance of tax fairness and the political implications of an administration oblivious to it. Regan's attention to this and other IRS tax administration issues did not sit well with the libertarian elements of the Republican coalition. IRS duty was a thankless task in an antitax environment. And one thing in which Regan agreed with Stockman was that the President ultimately lacked the will to make the hard domestic spending cuts. Regan was very much a devotee of the Ronald Reagan presidency through the end. The Regan book, with its magnifying glass on pettiness and skirmish, is at worst a parting blow to the practices of *presidency* (not to mention *First Ladyship*) and certainly not a repudiation of the leader whom he admires.

As administrator of the office, he was criticized for bringing his CEO style to Washington. The Washington "insider" attack on him, subsequently filtered into the media, suggested that he barreled through without political savvy. True, the "private sector Regan" often bumped up against the public sector: He once criticized the House Ways and Means Committee for only working three days a week on Ronald Reagan's tax cut proposals. As a former Chairman and CEO of one of the most successful companies of all time, we must give him the benefit of the doubt; one could argue that the job wasn't up to the man. While it is true that he was ill-suited for the sensitive Chief of Staff position, it is certainly less true of his Treasury term. He was clearly a gifted executive. He was known to blow up and claimed to run a leak-proof operation. George Will and other observers criticized his managerial arrogance, claiming, "He didn't know what he did not know." He was one of the first to suggest publicly that wealthy seniors not receive Social Security—*in an election year*. Perhaps, like Ross Perot, he was one part entrepreneur, one part prophet, and one part blunderer—a walking time bomb in Washington, D.C.

Peripheral agendas of the Regan Treasury included the promotion of Wall Street interests. For example, one of the arguments he offered in support of the Strategic Petroleum Reserve was that the volume of securities trading would increase. Also, the Swiss-owned Union Bank of Switzerland offered to sell U.S. government securities in a broader market outside the United States, but Regan "couldn't imagine it." Believing that the separation of commercial and investment banking would be obsolete in a few short years, Regan was as avid a supporter of deregulation as anybody in the administration. However, he fought for delay of easing of ceilings on interest rates paid by depositories, which had the effect of prolonging the drain on the source of funds to savings and loans, weakening them vis-à-vis growing competitors like Merrill Lynch.

Regan's role behind the scenes in the savings and loan crisis has never been fully documented. The signals that a deep problem was emerging on his watch were met by a wall of silence at Treasury. Investigators have asked why the clear signs of problems were ignored or never reached the top. There's no record in *For the Record*. The question put to Regan and other Reagan Cabinet members should be: "What should they have known, and when should they have known it?" Iran-Contra, a partisan battle, got all of the attention that the savings and loan *bipartisan* disaster deserved. The former head regulator of the industry suggests Treasury negligence, fostered by deep arrogance, and perhaps financial interests, at the top ranks. All three Treasury Secretaries under Reagan and Bush escaped with clean hands. Once again, we are reminded that Treasury is a deeply political office, not an economic one.

After Regan's confirmation, the substance of Reagan policy was considered well in hand. It was packaging, the pitch for the President's tax cut program that would guide Regan's course. But the big issue that emerged was, of course, deficits or, rather, deficit fetish. Regan's initiative was always to rationalizing debt, not eliminating it. His primary commitment was to revitalizing the economy, and budget issues were second. That is, spending cuts were important, but not as critical as phasing in the tax cuts to create opportunities. This put Regan at odds with others in the administration who preferred a complete budget package, inclusive of tax increases, if necessary. To the President and Regan, to give in to the House on the tax increases was to lose. The Regan posture and conviction was that Stockman of the OMB and Feldstein of the Council of Economic Advisers (CEA) were the bed wetters of the Reagan Revolution. In turn, they thought Regan was irresponsible and disingenuous (Stockman). The President's call to arms was simple enough: We have deficits because government spends too much, not because the public is taxed too little. Besides, it was whispered, deficits will constrain the addition of new spending programs by the Congress.

Don Regan did not believe that deficits are the cause of high interest rates. An elaborate Treasury report issued in 1984 substantiated Regan's side of this public and fractious policy debate. Regan expressed concern about the effects of budgets on capital markets but nevertheless focused on the tax and revenue side. In some ways, his position was political: "Deficits don't matter." In a less-charged political atmosphere, Regan conceded in a speech that deficits "constrict capital formation." As Economic Adviser, Martin Feldstein found that his own position was never accepted by the President, in whatever modified form it appeared. The center of gravity in the administration was Milton Friedman-esque, that taxation was always worse than the effects of deficits on capital markets. Despite that trade-off, none in the administration would disagree that in the long run, deficits must matter somehow. To the President and Regan, the whole public argument was disingenuous anyway: Liberals use the argument against the deficit to beat more money out of taxpayers, since more revenues justify greater spending. Despite the subtle arguments about causal links of budget deficits and interest rates, the writing was on the wall. From Don Regan's perspective, the only way to enhance revenues, after plenty of administrative toughening, tightening, and limiting, was the supply-side model.

Regan is candid about how the President's agenda was undermined from within by concessions to the Democrats in the tax negotiations. Such budget negotiations with Tip O'Neill's Democrats were a kind of domestic policy version of Mutual Assured Destruction, a particularly apt description in light of the flaring Irish tempers at the bargaining table. The Stockman-Feldstein-Darman-Baker faction was decidedly pragmatic, perhaps embarrassed by presidential stridency. To get along, they went along. Regan describes a set of secret meetings among congressional and administration staff to hammer out a deal along the lines of "cuts in $3 or $2 of spending for every $1 in tax increases." Once the administration agreed to tax increases, the trap was shut. Democrats took the deal, dispensed with the spending cuts, and voted only on the tax increases. According to Regan, such perfidy shocked unsophisticated White House negotiators. And Ronald Reagan could never understand the wiliness of O'Neill.

Treasury never claimed dominion over interest rate policy. Regan's dealings with the Volcker Fed were high-pitched initially, modulating only over time. He met with Volcker regularly and was openly critical of Fed policy, which was not unexpected. Fed sympathizers were a rare commodity in the 1981–1982 recession. Regan, like many, did not like the alleged erratic policy of the Fed. Nor did he like the tightness, thinking that the bumpy ride to zero tolerance could be a lot smoother. In 1982, he stepped up criticism. Regan's Treasury pressured the institutional arrangement by conducting a study of the Fed's independence. The stated reason was to achieve greater coordination, and perhaps accountability, but not to gain control. By mid-1984, Regan adopted a hands-off policy toward the Fed, while still professing the desire to take administrative control over many of its functions.

Don Regan must be given a great deal of credit for conceiving the first version of the Treasury Tax Reform Plan (T I) that eventually passed into law in 1986. Regan transformed himself from someone who had been more likely in past years to lobby for special breaks to a man beckoned to a historical calling. Regan took the President's public pronouncements very seriously and sensed that a radical tax plan would put him and his bruised ego at the center of things. The philosophical thrust of T I was that all income should be treated equally by the tax system, regardless of where it comes from, what form it takes, or what it's used for. Move the tax code toward neutrality and away from affecting private decisions. No more social and economic engineering. Even the investment tax credits promoted by Regan in 1981 offended this new, grander vision of the public good. After Regan and his staff worked under tight secrecy, purged of all political considerations, the plan was finally released, but as a *Regan* Treasury tax package to deflect criticism away from the President. The project was pronounced dead-on-arrival; even President Reagan had bowed to the rumors of doom by announcing that he wouldn't touch the home mortgage deduction. Nevertheless, the project gained considerable momentum, partly by the President's own force of character and partly by buying personal income tax reduction with a rise in the corporate tax. It was left to the Baker/Darman Treasury in Reagan's second administration to work through the plan's enormous political implications.

Ronald Reagan was one of the most successful Presidents in living memory. Donald Regan's infusion of Wall Street talent was a necessary element of the new Republican program. Despite its clumsy end, Donald Regan was the right man for the job as Treasury Secretary and deserves credit for selling Reagan's central plank over the objections of a belligerent Congress and the Republican wets. As Paul Craig Roberts remarks, Regan's forecasts were actually right. The 1981 tax reform act did what they said it would do: Marginal tax *rates* were cut, and revenue actually increased. And American labor productivity was restored by increasing the after-tax rate of return on U.S. investments. History should be kinder, gentler to him than were the press or Nancy Reagan. Until then, a clouded legacy looms from his public service as Chief of Staff—the job he swapped with incoming Treasury Secretary James Baker III—a task for which he was temperamentally unsuited.

Peggy Noonan, a witness to the Revolution, has the last word, saying that Regan's fall was savage and hurt him. She has observed that Regan wouldn't admit he was finished. He wrote his book, gave the speeches, and then went to the country club.

BIBLIOGRAPHY
Bartley, Robert. *The Seven Fat Years and How to Do It Again*. New York: Free Press, 1992.
Birnbaum, Jeffrey H., and Alan S. Murray. *Showdown at Gucci Gulch*. New York: Random House, 1987.
Birstein, Michael. "Gray" (Interview with Edwin Gray). *Regardie's* October 1988.
Friedman, Benjamin M. *Day of Reckoning: The Consequences of American Policy*. New York: Random House, 1988.
Kirkland, Richard I., Jr. "The Reaganites' Civil War Over Deficits." *Fortune*, October 17, 1983.
Noonan, Peggy. *What I Saw at the Revolution*. New York: Ivy Books, 1990.
Reagan, Nancy, with William Novak. *My Turn*. New York: Dell, 1989.
Regan, Donald. *A View from the Street*. New York: New American Library, 1972.
———. *For the Record: From Wall Street to Washington*. New York: St. Martin's Press, 1988.
Roberts, Paul Craig. *Business Week*, various columns, 1983–1986.
Stockman, David A. *The Triumph of Politics: How the Reagan Revolution Failed*. New York: Harper and Row, 1986.
Wall Street Journal Index. 1980–1992.

JEFF SCOTT

WILLIAM A. RICHARDSON (November 2, 1821–October 19, 1896). In March 1873 Grant began his second term as President of the United States. At the same time, George S. Boutwell, his Secretary of the Treasury, resigned to enter the Senate representing Massachusetts. As his replacement Boutwell suggested his friend and First Assistant at the Treasury, William A. Richardson, a probate judge from Massachusetts.

William Adams Richardson was born on November 2, 1821, in Tynsborough, Massachusetts, the son of Daniel and Mary (Adams) Richardson. He studied at the Pinkerton Academy in Derry and then went on to Lawrence Academy in Groton, Massachusetts. He graduated from Harvard in 1843, then entered Harvard Law School. He began his legal practice with his brother Daniel in Lowell, Massachusetts. He married Anna Maria Marston on October 29, 1848, and they had one daughter. Richardson was active in the Whig Party until its decline, and in 1855 he became a Republican. That same year he was made a probate judge in Middlesex County.

Upon Boutwell's recommendation, Richardson was named his Assistant at the Treasury in March 1869. During the four years Richardson served as First Assistant Treasurer to Boutwell, he continued to serve as a probate judge in Massachusetts. He was responsible for the Treasury's funding operations in London in 1871 and 1872. In 1872 he published *Practical Information Covering the Debt of the United States and National Banking Laws* (Vexler, 270).

Insiders in Washington considered Richardson an untrustworthy politician who based Treasury decisions on whether or not they would help the Republican Party win elections. Knowing that there would be opposition to his appointment, Richardson blatantly campaigned for the Treasury post. He went uninvited to the home of Hamilton Fish, Grant's Secretary of State, saying that he wished to make a personal plea for the job. Even Boutwell who recommended him feared that Richardson could not keep his own counsel (Nevins, 698). But Boutwell felt, and Grant concurred, that Richardson would do for a while, since he was familiar with the workings of the Treasury. Richardson was so anxious to get the post that he said he would serve in a temporary capacity, resigning after the current congressional term was over. He believed he deserved the Treasury post; he felt he was entitled to recognition and considerations for his services to the Republican Party and that after a short time in the post he could go on to a gainful job in the private sector. This, then, was the person Grant appointed to head the Treasury Department during what was to become one of the most severe economic crises of this country. Richardson was confirmed as Secretary of the Treasury on March 17, 1873.

Grant had started his first term in a time of prosperity and business expansion. By his second inaugural in 1873, just the opposite was true. By then the country was in the midst of its most severe crisis, a crisis that would leave the country in its deepest depression, lasting over six years (McFeely, 392–94). The crisis was triggered by the collapse on September 18, 1873, of the firm of Jay Cooke and Company, which had overextended itself trying to finance the Northern Pacific Railway. Banker Jay Cooke was known as the financier of the Civil War, and when his company went down, it caused panic both on Wall Street and in banks all over the country. Two days after Cooke and Company collapsed, the stock exchange suspended trading.

Wall Street and the financial community were in a state of hysteria. Grant and Richardson went to New York. For two days they consulted with New York bankers and others in the financial community. The advice given to Grant and Richardson was divided as to how to end this financial crisis. The more conservative-minded bankers said a return to a currency based on silver and gold would ensure a secure dollar with which to conduct foreign trade. Others said this advice would lead to a contraction of the money supply, hurting workers and small businessmen who needed capital for business expansion. As usual, Grant wavered. He told Richardson to reissue greenbacks (money not secured by previous metals), which had been held in reserve in the Treasury. These greenbacks, reissued to the tune of $26 million, helped Wall Street past its immediate crisis but did little to affect the deepening depression.

The national Treasury was nearly empty, and the national debt was increasing rapidly. Still, Grant and his Secretary of the Treasury wavered. They did little to help failing businesses, struggling farmers, and unemployed or underemployed workers. The Congress and the President argued back and forth about expanding the money supply and helping expand the economy or contracting the money supply to help protect the already successful. Grant finally came down on the side of sound money. With his ever-wavering battles over the economy, and without any clear position of his own, Grant angered people on both sides of the issue. Those who were angry at Grant could do little about the President; it was amazingly simple to get rid of Richardson, his Secretary of the Treasury. The way was the deeply rooted corruption in the Grant administration: corruption that was so open that it was being reported in the daily press. When the Democrats and Republican reformers in the House and Senate began investigating corruption in what came to be called the Sanborn Contracts, Richardson was quickly implicated.

John D. Sanborn was a Massachusetts politician who had friends in high office, friends in the Congress, and friends who reached all the way up to the presidency. Early in 1874, the House Ways and Means Committee began to investigate John Sanborn. They found out that Richardson, when he was Assistant Secretary of the Treasury, had conferred on Sanborn the right to collect delinquent internal revenue taxes from railroads, liquor distillers, and others who did not pay their taxes. In fact, Treasury officials were so corrupt that they virtually warned those with tax liabilities not to pay their taxes so that Sanborn might have more money to collect (Nevins, 708). Under this scheme, Sanborn collected over $500,000 in a time when the United States Treasury was nearly bankrupt. He turned some over to the government, paid off some others for "expenses," and enriched his own pockets. The whole affair looked like a conspiracy, overseen by Boutwell and Richardson, for defrauding the Treasury of the United States and enriching the powerful few.

If Richardson and his predecessor Boutwell were corrupt, they were not alone. There were plenty of others who were corrupt: in Grant's administration, in the Congress itself, and in all levels of both public and private life. Boutwell was now safely a U.S. Senator, some said with Sanborn's help, leaving Richardson vulnerable as Secretary of the Treasury, and it was his name that was on the Sanborn Contracts. With members of the Ways and Means Committee now saying out loud what may have been known in private and even condoned, it was now up to Grant to decide what to do about Richardson and the whole disgraceful affair, which reflected badly on the administration. The scandal was reported daily in the newspapers. After a three-month investigation, the committee members decided that Richardson deserved severe condemnation. Richardson and his Assistant Secretary resigned before they faced even more public shame. Grant was forced by the shame of the scandal to appoint a new Secretary of the Treasury, one Benjamin Bristow, who was known as a reformer.

When Richardson resigned on June 3, 1874, Grant appointed him to the Massachusetts Court of Appeals. In 1879, Richardson began teaching at Georgetown Law School. He stayed at the law school until 1894. He became Chief Justice of the Massachusetts Court of Appeals in 1885. William A. Richardson died on October 19, 1896, in Washington, D.C.

BIBLIOGRAPHY

Hackett, Frank W. A Sketch of the Life and Public Services of William Adams Richardson. Washington, D.C.: Press of H. L. McQueen, 1898.

Haworth, Paul L. The United States in Our Own Times 1865–1920. New York: Charles Scribner's Sons, 1920.

Hesseltine, William B. *Ulysses S. Grant, Politician*. New York: F. Ungar Publishing Co., 1957.
McFeely, William S. *Grant, a Biography*. New York: W. W. Norton and Co., 1981.
Nevins, Allan. *Hamilton Fish: The Inner History of the Grant Administration*. New York: Dodd, Mead & Co., 1936.
Vexler, Robert A. *The Vice Presidents and Cabinet Members*. Vol. 1. New York: Oceana Publishers, 1975.
Vinton, John A. *The Richardson Memorial*. Portland, ME: B. Thurston and Co., 1876.

JULIANNE CICARELLI

ROBERT E. RUBIN (August 29, 1938–   ). Robert Edward Rubin was nominated by President Bill Clinton to replace Secretary of the Treasury Lloyd Bentsen, who had resigned from his position on December 22, 1994. Rubin, a former investment banker, at the time of his nomination was associated with the Clinton presidency as head of the National Economic Council. Centered in the White House, the council's function has been to elevate economic issues to a higher level of integration with presidential environmental and foreign policies. On a more pragmatic basis, Rubin's function has been to forge consensus among the President's economic team and to communicate and put in place the President's economic policies.

While Rubin was born on August 29, 1938, in New York City, the son of Alexander and Sylvia (Seiderman) Rubin, the family soon moved to Miami Beach, Florida, where the senior Rubin set up a successful real estate law practice. After growing up in Miami Beach, Rubin attended Harvard College in Cambridge, Massachusetts, graduating summa cum laude, in economics, in 1960. Rubin then spent a year in England, where he studied at the London School of Economics. In 1961 he returned to the United States, went to New Haven, Connecticut, and attended Yale Law School, graduating in 1964. While at Yale, Rubin married Judith Leah Oxenberg on March 27, 1963. The couple has two sons, James Samuel and Philip Matthew.

After his 1964 graduation, Rubin went into practice with the New York City firm of Cleary, Gottlieb, Steen and Hamilton. However, after only two years, Rubin left law for the more volatile trading world of foreign currencies, stocks, bonds, and commodities, joining the firm of Goldman, Sachs in 1966. Rubin's twenty-six-year tenure at Goldman, Sachs was highly successful, as he worked his way up the organization to become one of its two Cochairmen before joining President Clinton in Washington (his 1992 earnings exceeded $26 million). Rubin's achievement at Goldman, Sachs has been attributed to his team approach to problem solving as much as to his intellect and business and political acumen, qualities that will again have to be proved as Secretary.

Rubin was very active in Democratic Party politics prior to his White House appointment. He had been one of the most important fund-raisers in New York City, providing contributions for Walter Mondale and Michael Dukakis and other candidates from across the country. He has served on advisory panels for

New York Governor Mario Cuomo and New York City Mayor David Dinkins. He chaired the host committee for the 1992 Democratic Convention in New York and was one of Clinton's economic policy advisers during his presidential campaign.

In addition to his Goldman, Sachs career, Rubin has been a member of a Security and Exchange Commission advisory committee on market oversight and a Director of the New York Stock Exchange. His time given to public and community efforts and his membership and directorship boards is both extensive and diverse, ranging from the American Ballet Theater Foundation to the Carnegie Corporation of New York to membership in the Harvard Club.

His participatory achievements at Goldman, Sachs have been repeated at the White House, as there appears to be none who ventured a negative word about the debut of this new, wealthy (his personal wealth is estimated at $100 million), and powerful personality. His success is due in part to his style as much as his consensus approach to problem solving. For one, he is a dedicated worker, frequently in his office from 7 A.M. to 9 P.M. He is said to be self-effacing, carrying his papers about in an accordion file while wearing rumpled suits, hardly a power dresser. He is also said to be an excellent listener and an intense "but gracious" questioner and has even passed up private time with the President if he had little to contribute. This is not to suggest that the new Secretary does not carry his own agenda. On the contrary.

Whereas the work of the Treasury was more political than fiscal for Bentsen, it is expected that the Secretary's desk will seat a more financial activist under Rubin. In his role in the National Economic Council, Rubin has used his position to center the debates about pro-business and pro–free trade issues that he favors. It can be anticipated that these same concerns will be carried over to the Cabinet position. It can also be expected that Secretary Rubin will add to his reputation as a deficit hawk, warning that any increase in the deficit will result in soaring interest rates, an anathema for a Wall Street trader.

Rubin's concern about deficits is exemplified in his role as presidential economic adviser. *The Economist*, December 10, 1994, relates the story that as candidate President Clinton promised to reduce the deficit and to invest $200 billion in education and training. After the election, Clinton's council, led by Rubin, argued for a focus on the former rather than the latter, and the falling deficit accompanied by the 1994 soaring economy attests to Rubin's success.

Rubin's pro-business orientation is also recorded in the same issue of *The Economist*. As a result of the Republican sweep of the 1994 midterm elections, President Clinton is again in the throes of a budget debate, having previously promised tax relief to the middle class. Labor Secretary Robert Reich suggested an attack on "corporate welfare"—subsidies and tax breaks—in order to ease the financial strain of the ordinary taxpayer. In quick order, it is reported, Rubin was on the phone to the media, distancing the administration from the views of the Labor Secretary.

Rubin's agenda is not limited to deficits and business, as he has indicated his concern with social and urban issues. In accepting his nomination in the White House Rose Garden, Rubin said that he hoped to use his Treasury post to seek solutions to the problems of the public education system, the inner cities, and "the ever-worsening income disparity" within the nation.

At the time of Rubin's nomination, his confirmation into the President's Cabinet was almost assured. Senate Majority Leader Bob Dole was quickly on record to state that Rubin was a man of honesty and integrity who "was most certainly qualified to be Secretary of the Treasury." On January 10, 1995, Dole's view of Rubin was shared by the Senate, as the former Wall Street executive was confirmed by a vote of ninety-nine to zero.

Secretary Rubin was placed quickly into the spotlight by both world events with the dramatic fall of the Mexican peso and the new Republican majority in Congress as they sought to implement a constitutional amendment for a balanced budget. A Mexican currency crisis began erupting at the start of 1995. The peso decline in value was an initial 30 percent as 1995 began. Rather than stabilizing at this new low level, the currency continued to lose value and appeared to have no bottom as it drifted to new lows almost daily. With Mexico as America's number-one export market, not only were U.S. jobs threatened by the peso's collapse, but world financial markets were also shaken. Mexico's imminent default on billions of dollars in bonds threatened both U.S. financial organizations as well as prompted a global financial withdrawal from many of the emerging markets that were promising economic growth to the lower-income nations. Rubin argued that Mexico played a unique role in the past half decade as a prototype developing country. "It is the linch pin, the model," and Rubin led the administration's program to rescue the peso, and the world's emerging markets, by providing U.S. dollar assurances for Mexico's debt.

Congress was both slow and hesitant to react to President Clinton's proposals of a $40 billion loan guarantee program to Mexico that would shore up the peso by providing dollar liquidity to Mexico's maturing short-term bonds. The program was backed by Mexican pledges by economic program reforms as well as U.S. access to Mexican oil revenues. Nevertheless, the program's speedy passage through the Republican Congress was in doubt. And if the story is correct, it was a late-evening sharing of a pizza that brought together Secretary Rubin, Chief of Staff Leon Panetta, and the President to act with greater resolve by issuing an extraordinary order to use $20 billion in Treasury funds under the President's control to keep Mexico from defaulting on its short-term bonds and to help bring order and confidence to nervous international financial markets. These U.S. funds were then augmented by an additional $18 billion by the International Monetary Fund.

All of this was rather firm and quick action by a newly confirmed, and also very concerned, Secretary of the Treasury. He had set the tone of his tenure with his twenty-hour workdays in shirtsleeves and loose-knotted tie.

In these first days of his new position, Secretary Rubin was also acting as the administration's point man in its attempt to blunt the new Republican majority's thrust for a balanced budget amendment to the Constitution of the United States. Congress, by its own admittance, has not been able to control national spending without continually increasing the national debt. To finally come to grips with a debt that was threatening the financial future of the nation, the Republicans offered a constitutional amendment that national yearly budgets, government revenues, and spending were to be in balance. The procedure for a constitutional amendment required passage by Congress and then acceptance by two thirds of the states—a long, drawn-out procedure that would have affected future administrations. Nevertheless, the Clinton administration was adamantly against the proposed amendment, and Secretary Rubin led the rebuttal.

While there were many reasons given for defeating the amendment by the members of Congress and the administration, Rubin's main argument was clear: The amendment would eliminate the government's use of discretionary contra-cyclical fiscal policy, a standard of modern macroeconomic management that has become the major tool to reduce the fluctuations and social costs of the business cycle. Rubin, aided by other administration spokespeople, presented the basic Keynesian arguments to all audiences. As the Republican proposal was as much a political statement as an economic one, the effect of Rubin's arguments is problematic; nevertheless, the proposal lost in the Senate by a single vote.

Rubin's first months in office have been extremely busy. He is reported to put in twenty-hour days. Representative Jim Leach, the Iowa Republican who heads the House Banking Committee, has remarked that Rubin has brought with him a manner that is competent and quiet, without being arrogant. He also stated that, almost overnight, he has become the preeminent cabinet member.

BIBLIOGRAPHY

Business Week. December 19, 1994, 32.
The Economist. December 10, 1994, 28.
New York Times. December 7, 1993, 12.
Wall Street Journal. December 7, 1994, A2.
Who's Who in America, 1996. 50th ed. Vol. 2: *Marquis Who's Who.* New Providence, NJ: Reed Reference Publishing Co., 1996.

BERNARD S. KATZ

RICHARD RUSH (August 29, 1780–July 30, 1859). Richard Rush was a prominent and respected man of his time. He served six U.S. Presidents in a number of different capacities, which included three different Cabinet posts: Attorney General, 1814–1817; Secretary of State, ad interim 1817; and Secretary of the Treasury, 1825–1829. Historians on both sides of the Atlantic have praised Rush's contributions to the new nation.

A public notice published at Rush's death expresses the depth of the American public's admiration for Rush:

He was a diplomatist and statesman, a jurist, a scholar, and a writer; and he was of first class in every one of these pursuits. The country will sincerely regret the death of one whose name carries the reader back to Jefferson's time, and who was associated with the generation of great men, all of whom have passed away, and whom he has gone to join, after a long, pure, and useful life, in a course of which he wronged no one; but bore himself as if conscious that he was responsible for the proper discharge of talents intrusted to him. His name will have a high place in American history, and will figure there with equal honor, whether the historian shall write of our politics or our literature. ("Richard Rush," 80–81)

Richard Rush was born in Philadelphia on August 29, 1780, second son and third child of Dr. Benjamin and Mrs. Julia (Stockton) Rush. Rush was raised in a cultured home. Benjamin Rush was a physician, educator, statesman, Revolutionary patriot, and one of the signers of the Declaration of Independence. Benjamin Rush greatly influenced his son.

Richard's early education was administered first by his father and then by private preparatory schools. In 1794, Rush, at the age of fourteen, entered the College of New Jersey (now called Princeton). He graduated the youngest in a class of thirty-three students in 1797. During his college years, he showed remarkable ability in the area of debate and oratorical exercises.

After college, Rush decided to pursue a career in law. He accepted a position in the office of William Lewis, Esq., one of the leaders of the Philadelphia Bar Association. He was admitted to the Philadelphia bar in December 1800. Rush's law practice was unspectacular, and prominence eluded him until 1808, when he defended Col. William Duane, editor of the publication *Aurora*, on the charge of libel against the Governor of Pennsylvania, Thomas McKean. Rush's successful defense of Duane vastly improved his reputation as a lawyer. Consequently, his law practice expanded rapidly.

In 1809, on his twenty-ninth birthday, Rush married Catherine E. Murray, daughter of Dr. James and Mrs. Sarah E. Murray of Piney Grove, Pennsylvania. They had ten children of which three died during childhood. In 1810, Rush was approached to run for Congress by the Republican Party of Pennsylvania, but he declined and became Solicitor of the Guardians of the Poor of Philadelphia. In January 1811, the Governor of Pennsylvania appointed Rush to the post of Attorney General.

As a Republican, Rush opposed the renewal of the First Bank of the United States' charter. The bank's request for the renewal of its charter by Congress was a controversial issue in 1811. Rush's stand against the bank attracted President James Madison's attention, and he was subsequently appointed to the position of Comptroller of the Treasury in November 1811. Rush's acceptance of this position distressed his father greatly. Dr. Rush died on April 19, 1813; he would never know that this position that he opposed was just the first step in his son's distinguished political career.

On February 10, 1814, President Madison appointed Rush to replace William Pinkney as Attorney General of the United States. During his tenure as Attorney General, Rush made his first important contribution to the new nation; he superintended the publication of *The Laws of the United States from 1789 to 1815* (1815), the first codification of the laws of the United States. Rush continued as Attorney General in the Monroe Cabinet until President Monroe appointed him as Secretary of State, ad interim, until the return of John Quincy Adams from England. During his secretaryship, Rush proved his diplomatic skills in negotiations with the British Minister to the United States, Charles Bagot. The outcome of the negotiations was the Rush-Bagot Convention of 1817. The Anglo-American diplomatic agreement was the first instance of reciprocal naval disarmament in the history of international relations. It established a limitation of naval armaments on the Great Lakes. Because he was so impressed with Rush's diplomatic skills, President Monroe appointed Rush to the post of Minister Plenipotentiary to the Court of St. James (England) to replace Adams.

Richard Rush served as America's Minister to London until 1825. His appointment to this position had a profound and positive influence on American-British relations that prior to Rush's appointment was one of great mistrust between the two nations. Although the signing of the Treaty of Ghent (1815) had ended the War of 1812, the issues that drove the two nations into war were for the most part left unsettled. Rush's predecessor, John Q. Adams, was bitter and hostile toward the British; he thoroughly mistrusted them. Rush, unlike Adams, moved with ease in British society and was anxious to establish good relations with England. Rush's attitude toward the English allowed him to develop a congenial relationship with Lord Castlereagh, the British Foreign Minister, and with Castlereagh's successor, George Canning. Rush's ability to develop a cordial relationship with the British Foreign Minister allowed him to resolve most of the issues left unsettled by the Treaty of Ghent.

In October 1818, Rush negotiated the Convention of 1818, which ended the border dispute between the United States and Canada. The agreement declared the forty-ninth parallel as the northern boundary of the Louisiana Territory between the Lake of the Woods and the Rockies and agreed to the joint control of the Oregon Territory for a ten-year period. The other important issues resolved through negotiations by Rush included (1) the dispute over American fishing rights in the Labrador and Newfoundland fisheries and (2) the disagreement concerning England's liability with regard to American monetary losses incurred from the British act of setting American slaves free during the War of 1812.

Andrew Jackson's invasion of Spanish Florida in 1818 and his decision to execute two British citizens created an international incident that provided the next test of Rush's diplomatic skills. The executions outraged the British public and press. Talk of war grew in the British press. Rush handled the incident with consummate skill. Rush, in his *Memoranda of a Residence at the Court of London*, recalls a conversation with the British Foreign Minister, who comments on the seriousness of the incident: "Lord Castlereagh said that he believed 'war might have been produced by holding up a finger' " (120).

The diplomatic preliminaries leading up to the Monroe Doctrine constituted Rush's final contribution to American foreign policy during his ministership.

Rush's conversations with the new British Foreign Minister, George Canning, and his subsequent dispatches (August–September 1823) to Adams and Monroe on those meetings, convinced Monroe to deliver the speech that was later to become known as the Monroe Doctrine.

Rush left his post as Minister to London in 1825 to accept a Cabinet post in the Adams administration as Secretary of the Treasury and began service on March 7. Rush's contributions to American foreign policy and American-British relations were impressive. Rush, however, added to this remarkable contribution by writing *Memoranda of a Residence at the Court of London,* published in 1833. This literary work represents the first detailed written account of American diplomacy.

Except for the first few months of the Adams administration, Rush held the post of Secretary of the Treasury until Jackson assumed the presidency in March 1829, stepping down on March 5. Rush had strong views concerning his responsibilities as Secretary of the Treasury. He believed it was his obligation to express his views on current economic issues concerning the United States and to provide economic policy recommendations to the President and Congress. Rush clearly stated his view in a letter to Nicholas Biddle, regarding his preparation of the 1828 *Annual Report of the Secretary of the Treasury:* "But if these reports are to consist of nothing but an account current of the receipts of the year, set off in ruled lines and columns, any copying clerk in the department might annually save the secretary the trouble of drawing them up" (McGrane, 55). In his reports to Congress, Rush addressed a number of important economic issues including industrial development, development of infrastructure, international trade, the money supply, and banking—currency issues.

Rush greatly admired Alexander Hamilton. Hamilton's influence on Rush is reflected in Rush's praise of Hamilton in the 1828 report by the Secretary: "Such were the counsels of a departed statesman, whose name peculiarly lives in the records of this Department; who was first placed at its head, directing its operations with a forecast so luminous as still to throw a guiding light over the path of his successors" (Rush, "1828," 445). Rush strongly supported Hamilton's "infant industry argument." Rush argued strongly for the protection of American manufacturers in his annual reports. Rush believed that growth in manufacturing was the key to the future prosperity of the nation "since an intimate connexion is believed to exist between the full encouragement and success of domestic manufactures, and the wealth, the power, and the happiness of the country" (Rush, "1825," 321). Rush quotes the famous French economist J. B. Say to add weight to his argument for protection: "[H]opeless, indeed, would be their situation, were France to adopt the system which recommends the purchase of manufactures from foreign countries, with the raw produce of domestic agriculture" (324). In order to protect American manufacturers, Rush specifically recommended raising import duties on all foreign wool and woolen goods, fine cotton goods, bar iron, and hemp.

Rush, however, favored the lowering of duties on imports he believed were staples of American life and that did not compete directly with domestic producers. He recommended the lowering of duties on cocoa, tea, coffee, and wines for the benefit of the American consumer. Rush used two economic concepts in defense of his recommendation. First, he believed that lowering the tariff on coffee, tea, and cocoa would increase consumption and therefore would increase the consumption of sugar, benefiting domestic sugar producers. Rush's argument obviously alluded to the economic concept of complementary goods (326). Second, he believed that lowering the tariff on tea could actually increase tariff revenue—an argument alluding to the economic concept of the price elasticity of demand and its relationship to total revenue.

Rush used Europe as an example in his argument that government protection of manufacturing from foreign competition would not interfere with foreign commerce:

Nor has this policy been found to interfere with an abundant foreign commerce in the wealthiest and most industrious nations. It has, on the contrary, carried its bounds still further; since every nation, by its habits and position, will always command superior facilities for excelling in certain branches of labor and art, which it therefore chiefly cherishes, leaving to other nations the opportunity of excelling in other branches, or of running the career of beneficial rivalry in the same; by which system the artificial production of the world are augmented and improved. (324)

Rush believed it was the duty of the federal government to nurture economic development. He clearly states his view in his 1825 annual report:

[T]o augment the number and variety of occupations for its inhabitants; to hold out every degree of labor, and to every modification of skill, its appropriate object and inducement, these rank amongst the highest ends of legislation. To organize the whole labor of a country; to entice into the widest ranges its mechanical and intellectual capacities, instead of suffering them to slumber; to call forth, wherever hidden, latent ingenuity, giving to effort activity, and to emulation ardor; to create employment for the greatest amount of numbers, by adapting it to the diversified faculties, propensities, and situations of men, so that every particle of ability, every shade of genius, may come into requisition, is, in other words, to lift up the condition of a country, to increase its fiscal energy, to multiply the means and sources of its opulence. (322)

Rush continually supported government participation in the building of highways and canals.

Rush argued against excessive government land sales, which he believed would disperse the country's population and thus hinder capital accumulation and reduce growth in the nation's manufacturing sector: "The Maxim is held to be a sound one, that the ratio of capital to population should, if possible, be kept on the increase. When this takes place, the demand and compensation for labor will be proportionable increased, and the condition of the most numerous classes of the community become improved. If the ratio of capital to population be diminished, a contrary state of things will be the result" (Rush, "1827," 405). Rush argues that excessive land sales may increase the nation's population; however, the diffusion of the nation's population will retard capital creation due to the subsistence nature of new settlements. Within this argument he states that increased manufacturing, which is not present in new settlements, will increase the country's capital stock and will therefore raise the productivity of labor. Rush was clearly concerned with the government's role in the macromanagement of the economy.

Rush tempered his strong views on the government's role by promoting the virtues of competition and free markets in the expanding domestic economy. Rush believed that adhering to this principle would greatly benefit the country.

During his term as Treasury Secretary, Rush strongly supported the Second Bank of the United States. He believed in a sound banking system and that a stable and growing money supply was essential for continued American economic growth. In 1828, Rush contacted the President of the Second Bank of the United States, Nicholas Biddle, asking for his comments on the value of the bank to the economy of the United States for his 1828 report to Congress. Rush's reports on the bank's activities were glowing and regarded the bank's services as indispensable with respect to the health and stability of the U.S. economy.

In the 1828 presidential election, Rush was Adams's running mate. They were soundly defeated by the Jackson ticket. After the election loss, Rush returned to his private law practice in Philadelphia. In January 1831, Rush wrote to Biddle and asked to be considered for the post of President of the Washington branch of the bank; however, Biddle was unable to grant Rush's request. Rush ran for the Senate in Pennsylvania's 1832 election and lost, ironically because of political forces loyal to the Second Bank of the United States in the Pennsylvania legislature. The senatorial election loss so embittered Rush that he joined the forces of President Jackson in opposition to the bank. In 1834, he publicly attacked the bank, calling for its abolishment. This reversal of support in the "Bank War" alienated many of Rush's old political friends, including his old personal friend John Quincy Adams.

The political reversal by Rush on the issue of the Second Bank, however, did bear fruit. President Jackson appointed Rush to the committee assigned to reconcile a boundary dispute between Michigan and Ohio in 1835. Although the dispute was left unsettled, the committee was able to prevent the outbreak of hostilities. In July 1836, President Jackson appointed Rush to act as the representative for the United States with regard to the James Smithson legacy dispute, which was pending in the English chancery court. Rush handled the long and arduous court proceedings with great skill and returned to the United States in August 1838 with the entire amount of the Smithson legacy, $508,318.46. The Smithson legacy provided the initial endowment for the Smithsonian Institute. Rush played an important role in the establishment and unique mission of the Smithsonian Institute. There was strong support in Washington for using the Smithson legacy to fund a university or a library. Rush argued that this use of the legacy would be contrary to Smithson's wishes because the United States was in fact the trustee of Smithson's legacy. Therefore, it was the moral obligation of the United States to follow the spirit of Smithson's will. Rush's view prevailed, but not without considerable delay and some difficulty. In 1846, Congress passed the necessary enactment. The first meeting of the Board of Regents took place on September 7, 1846, with Rush a member. Rush worked tirelessly for the institute and remained a member of the Board of Regents until his death.

In March 1847, President James Polk appointed Rush as U.S. Minister to France, where he served until 1849. During his stay in France, Rush was an eyewitness to the Revolution of 1848 that toppled the French monarchy. He handled the chaotic transfer of power with his usual tact and intelligence. Acting without instructions from the U.S. government, but after careful study, Rush was one of the first foreign ministers to recognize the new republic in 1848. He received subsequent praise in the U.S. press for his actions. In 1849, the Whig Party regained power under President Fillmore, who recalled Rush from his post in Paris.

Rush returned to the United States in 1851 and continued to take an interest in public affairs as a private citizen. He spent the latter years of his life either at Sydenham, his country home, or at his home in Philadelphia. Rush again turned his attention and talents to literary pursuits, writing *Washington in Domestic Life* (1857), which consisted of personal letters from Washington to his private secretary, Col. Tobias Lear, and personal recollections of his life in Washington. His next and last literary project was *Occasional Productions, Political, Diplomatic, and Miscellaneous, Including a Glance at the Court and Government of Louis Philippe, and the French Revolution of 1848*, published by his sons in 1860.

Rush's wife Catherine died at their country home on March 24, 1854, and was buried in his family vault at North Laurel Hill Cemetery. Richard Rush died on July 30, 1859, at his Philadelphia home and was laid to rest next to his beloved wife.

Rush was a man of intellect and integrity, who believed in his country and worked for the betterment of his countrymen. Rush's economic insight and ability to formulate policy recommendations as Secretary of the Treasury were quite remarkable for one whose formal training was in law. Richard Rush was a great American living in an era that resonates with the names of great Americans. His name and record, though less familiar, deserve similar honor.

BIBLIOGRAPHY

Adler, Cyrus. "The Relation of Richard Rush to the Smithsonian Institution." In *Smithsonian Miscellaneous Collections*. Vol. 52. Washington, D.C.: Smithsonian Press, 1910.

Catterall, R. C. *The Second Bank of the United States*. Chicago: Chicago University Press, 1903.

Ford, W. C. "John Quincy Adams and the Monroe Doctrine." *American Historical Review* 7, no. 4 (1902): 676–96.

McGrane, R. C. *The Correspondence of Nicholas Biddle Dealing with National Affairs 1807–1844*. Boston: Houghton Mifflin Publishing Co., 1919.

Parton, J. *Life of Andrew Jackson*. Vols. 1–3. New York: Mason Brothers, 1861.

"Richard Rush." In *National Cyclopedia of American Biography*. Vol. 5. Ann Arbor, MI: University Microfilms, 1967.

Rush, R. "Report on Finances. December, 1825." In *Reports of the Secretary of the Treasury of the United States*. Washington, D.C.: Duff Green Publisher, 1829.

———. "Report on Finances. December, 1826." In *Reports of the Secretary of the Treasury of the United States*. Washington, D.C.: Duff Green Publisher, 1829.

———. "Report on Finances. December, 1827." In *Reports of the Secretary of the Treasury of the United States*. Washington, D.C.: Duff Green Publisher, 1829.

———. "Report on Finances. December, 1828." In *Reports of the Secretary of the Treasury of the United States*. Washington, D.C.: Duff Green Publisher, 1829.

———. *Memoranda of a Residence at the Court of London*. Philadelphia: Key and Biddle, 1833.

———. *Occasional Productions, Political, Diplomatic, and Miscellaneous, Including a Glance at the Court and Government of Louis Philippe, and the French Revolution of 1848*. London: Published by his sons, 1860.

Webster, C. K. *The Foreign Policy of Castlereagh*. London: G. Bell and Sons, Ltd., 1925.

SCOTT W. FAUSTI

S

LESLIE M. SHAW (November 2, 1848–March 28, 1932). Leslie M. Shaw held the position of Treasury Secretary from 1902 to 1907. One of the most innovative government officials of his day, Shaw attempted to transform the Treasury from mere fiscal agent into the active, responsible guardian the U.S. financial sector required.

Leslie Mortimer Shaw was born on November 2, 1848, in Morristown, Vermont. He was raised in the farming household of Louise (Spaulding) and Boardman Ozias Shaw. In 1869, after teaching school in Vermont, Shaw moved to Iowa, receiving his M.S. degree from Cornell College in 1874. In 1876 Shaw completed a course at the Iowa College of Law, was admitted to the bar, and began to practice law in Denison, Iowa. Shaw married Alice Crenshaw on December 6 of the following year. The couple had one son and two daughters. Raised in the Methodist religion, Shaw was a prominent lay delegate to the general conferences of the Methodist Church in 1884, 1888, and 1892.

In 1897 Shaw entered the race for Governor of Iowa. He was widely regarded as a "dark horse" candidate. A dynamic orator, Shaw was elected over the Democratic candidate, Fred E. White, by a popular vote of 224, 728 to 194,843. A third, Prohibitionist candidate, S. P. Leland, received 8,292. Reelected in 1899, Shaw again defeated Fred E. White, by the slightly wider margin of 239,543 to 183,326. The third candidate, M. W. Atwood, another Prohibitionist, received 7,650 votes. Notable during his two-term tenure as Governor was the passage of legislation creating a State Board of Control, which regulated the thirteen existing state custodial institutions.

Seeing an opportunity to co-opt a potential rival for the 1904 presidential nomination, Theodore Roosevelt chose Shaw to head up the Treasury after a personality conflict led to the resignation of Lyman Gage. Shaw, Roosevelt's second choice after Massachusetts Governor Winthrop Murray Crane, had considerable support among Republicans in Iowa, the Dakotas, and Nebraska and with eastern financial interests as a result of his strong pro-gold stance at the 1896 St. Louis Convention. Shaw assumed his post on February 1, 1902.

Shaw's tenure as Secretary of the Treasury was distinguished by his innovative actions and the controversies to which they gave rise. By the turn of the century the tradition of responding to financial sector difficulties had long been an element in Treasury operations. Previous Secretaries, including Charles Fairfield (1887–1889), William Windom (1889–1891), and Shaw's immediate successor Lyman Gage (1897–1902), had used various devices to support the financial sector during times of crisis. These included the prepayment of interest on government instruments, the repurchase of government bonds, and manipulation of government deposit accounts. The prepayment of interest, for example, prior to the date of redemption, provided national banks under pressure with usable funds. While utilizing these means as the occasion demanded, Shaw was not satisfied with the traditional tools available to him.

The development of new Treasury operation procedures during Shaw's tenure stemmed in large part from his belief that the Treasury should not confine itself to reacting to financial difficulties only after the panic level had been reached but, rather, should work to alleviate potential problems by engaging in the day-to-day supervision of the financial sector. The Treasury, in Shaw's design, was to perform many of the functions undertaken by central banks in other market economies.

A number of devices were developed to meet this end. These included altering the security national depository banks were required to hold against government deposits, eliminating the cash reserve against government deposits, radically revising the use of internal revenue, and finally, using the government surplus to encourage the importation of gold.

The first break with tradition came with the manipulation of national bank collateral requirements. In the fall of 1902 when the cash reserve against deposits in New York banks fell below the mandatory 25 percent level (their lowest level since 1893), Shaw responded in traditional fashion by prepaying the interest due on government bonds and by the outright purchase of government instruments at a premium (a premium as high as 35.6 percent). In conjunction with these traditional responses, Shaw revised the Treasury's position regarding government deposit collateral.

Depository banks had, since the inception of the National Banking System in 1863, been required to secure government deposits with Treasury bonds on a dollar-for-dollar basis. Beginning in September 1902, Secretary Shaw took a number of steps to weaken this requirement. As an initial step, Shaw offered to accept, in addition to Treasury instruments, state and municipal bonds approved by the state of New York for investment by savings banks. A month later the Secretary broadened the category of acceptable collateral to include all undefaulted municipal bonds. In January 1903 the order was rescinded. Nongovernment securities were to be replaced by government instruments by July of that year. This action allowed national banks to acquire access to additional notes through customary channels. For those unfamiliar with that process, national banks could acquire notes by depositing Treasury bonds with the Comptroller of the Currency. The latter would then issue notes to the bank equaling 90 percent of the face or market value of the bonds, whichever was lower.

The timing of these actions reveals Shaw's intent. Recognizing that the principal shortcoming of the U.S. financial sector lay in its lack of flexibility, the Secretary was attempting to develop mechanisms to address the problem. Central banks utilize the discount window to perform this function. Unable to perform that operation on a consistent basis, Shaw resorted, in this instance, to the alternative of manipulating bank collateral requirements.

In 1903 Shaw took a second, more radical step, one, in fact, of questionable constitutional legitimacy. Since the start of the Republic, the power of the Secretary of the Treasury had been constrained by the constitutional provision (Article I, Section 9, paragraph 7) that "no money shall be drawn from the Treasury but in consequence of appropriations made by law." As a result, internal revenue was customarily allowed to accumulate in depository national banks, as it was paid in but never removed from the Treasury—even in times of crisis—to relieve pressure on the banking system. By the fall of 1903, it can be noted, government funds were flowing into national banks at the rate of $500,000 per day. Arguing that national banks that served as depositories for government funds were, in actuality, an "arm" of the Treasury, Shaw suggested that the movement of funds from the Treasury to these banks entailed, in effect, a simple shifting of monies from one part of the Treasury to another.

During the following two years, Shaw was faced by the traditional bane of the active Treasury Secretary: a budget deficit. Due in large part to Panama Canal–related expenditures, the mild deficits of 1905–1906 briefly, but effectively, curtailed Shaw's ability to intervene in the financial sector. With prosperity, a surplus returned to the Treasury in 1906. Innovation followed quickly in its wake.

In September 1906, relying on his new interpretation of the Constitution, Shaw made $26 million in Treasury revenue available to national banks. These funds, deposited largely in country and reserve city banks (only $3 million was provided directly to New York central reserve city banks), were to be withdrawn February 1, 1907.

In April 1907 Shaw announced his final new program: altering the gold import point for designated national banks. Under Shaw's plan, any depository national bank anticipating a shipment of gold could, with appropriate collateral, apply for an equal amount in cash from the Treasury. This operation encouraged the importation of gold by reducing import costs by the interest gained during transit. In offering this advantage to national banks, Shaw was attempting to place the United States on a par with other market economies, for example, France and Germany, whose central banks extended a similar opportunity to their own gold importers. Expectedly, nonnational banks argued that the practice provided the beneficiaries with an unfair advantage.

The gold import scheme, however, was to be short-lived. The initial expansion of gold imports caused by the Treasury offer contributed to a fall in domestic interest rates, which, in turn, through the customary capital account effects, led to an overall reduction in gold imports. The policy was brought to an abrupt end in October 1906.

The various devices developed by Shaw during his tenure as Secretary of the Treasury did not receive universal approval. Supporters and beneficiaries regarded them as innovative. Opponents wasted no time in labeling many of Shaw's actions as unconstitutional and politically motivated. His semilegal actions certainly had precedents. In October 1872 and August 1873, for example, Secretaries Boutwell and Richardson, respectively, allowed, over congressional edict, the reissue of retired greenbacks during the monetary stringencies of those years. While criticized, particularly at the conclusion of his term, for using the instruments at his disposal to meet political ends, history has vindicated many of Shaw's actions. Many of Shaw's actions were later validated by congressional legislation. The Aldrich Act of 1908, for example, left the decision making regarding the appropriate collateral to be used to cover government deposits to the discretion of the Treasury Secretary. This legislation, in addition, removed the ban on the depositing of custom receipts. Ultimately, the Federal Reserve Act of 1913 served to validate Shaw's actions. While his personal motivation may be debated, it is very clear that Shaw was attempting to pursue many of the objectives that would, at a later date, become the province of the central bank.

Shaw, the controversial, the innovative, a man clearly ahead of his time, served as Secretary of the Treasury until March 3, 1907. He was succeeded by George B. Cortelyou. After leaving the Treasury, Shaw headed up the Carnegie Trust Company of New York (1907–1908) before moving on to First Mortgage Guarantee and Trust Company of Philadelphia (1909–1913). In 1913, Shaw moved to Washington, D.C., to write and lecture. He died in the capital on March 28, 1932, and was buried in Oakland Cemetery, Denison, Iowa.

BIBLIOGRAPHY

Annual Report of the Secretary of the Treasury. Washington, D.C.: U.S. Government Printing Office, various years.
Johnson, R. *The Twentieth Century Biographical Directory of Notable Americans*. Boston: Biographical Society, 1904.
Lossing, Benson John, ed. *Harper's Encyclopedia of U.S. History*. New York: Harper and Bros., 1905.
Sobel, Robert, ed. *Biographical Directory of the United States Executive Branch, 1774–1977*. Westport, CT: Greenwood Press, 1977.

PAUL J. KUBIK

JOHN SHERMAN (May 10, 1823–October 22, 1900). John Sherman, Secretary of the Treasury under Rutherford B. Hayes, was born on May 10, 1823, in Lancaster, Ohio. He was a lawyer and an Ohio Whig-Republican who served in the Cabinets of two Presidents and succeeded a third in the Senate. Sherman led in planning the National Banking System; he was the nation's foremost expert of his time on finance.

Sherman's father, Charles Robert Sherman, grew up in Norwalk, Connecticut, married Mary Hoyt, and settled in Lancaster, Ohio, where he practiced law. He was selected by the Ohio legislature to serve on the state supreme court. He died suddenly in 1829, when John was six years of age. The death of Charles Sherman left his wife Mary with eleven children, including John, and inadequate means to care for them all. As a result, the children were gradually scattered to the homes of friends and family who helped raise them. In the spring of 1831, a cousin, also named John Sherman, took his eight-year-old namesake to his home in Mount Vernon, Ohio, where the boy spent four years with only occasional visits to his mother. He attended good schools and progressed quickly until the age of twelve, when he returned to Lancaster and enrolled in Homer's Academy.

Within a few years, Sherman was deemed advanced enough in his schooling to enter the sophomore year in college. He had developed a liking for mathematics and surveying. Instead of pursuing his education, however, he left at age fourteen to accept a position as junior rodman with the Corps of Engineers constructing the Ohio Canal system. He was glad for the opportunity to make his own way. In the spring of 1838, he was placed temporarily in charge of the work at Beverly, Ohio—a sixteen-year-old supervising grown men in the building of a dam. He later said that his heavy responsibilities gave him "a better education than he could possibly have secured elsewhere in the same time." The next year, he lost his position because he was a Whig, and the Democrats had won an election and gained control.

Sherman went to Manchester, Ohio, to study law under his uncle and work in his brother's office. Even before being admitted to the bar in 1844, at age twenty-one, he had been performing much of a lawyer's work. He went into partnership with his brother, Charles T. Sherman. His mother and two sisters soon moved to Manchester and made a home for him. He launched into business and invested wisely in real estate, laying the foundation for a prosperous future.

Sherman's inclination toward politics was manifested early; as a twenty-year-old, he was making stump speeches, about which his brother chided him: "I thought you were too decent for that." However, he was not to be deterred. At the end of 1846, he traveled to Washington, D.C., stayed several weeks, and met most of the major leaders of the time. A little over a year later, in the spring of 1848, he became a delegate to the Whig National Convention in Philadelphia, Pennsylvania. A friend joked about Sherman that his home district was so solidly Democratic that he could never hope to get into office unless he did so at that convention; thereupon he was made Secretary of the convention. He was a strong supporter of Zachary Taylor's presidential campaign. He was to be chosen as delegate again four years later, when the national convention was held in Baltimore, Maryland. He was President of the first Ohio Republican State Convention in 1855 and took part in efforts to organize the national Republican Party.

In August 1848, Sherman married Cecelia Stewart of Mansfield, Ohio. The couple would later adopt a daughter. In 1853, they moved to Cleveland, Ohio, where he opened a law office. Sherman had become prosperous, taking over a successful manufacturing venture in addition to his law practice.

Sherman was elected to the House of Representatives in the 34th through 37th Congresses, serving from March 4, 1855, to March 21, 1861, when he resigned to run for the Senate. He was a vocal opponent of slavery; slavery was at the center of a fierce battle in the territory of Kansas. His appointment to serve on a three-person Kansas investigating committee was said to be a turning point in his career. The committee spent two months in Kansas, survived threats and attacks from enemies of their work, conducted a thorough and well-documented inquiry, and returned with a comprehensive report. Because of the ill health of the committee's Chairman, responsibility for preparing the report fell to Sherman; the report was regarded as definitive and was never controverted. It aroused deep feelings on the slavery issue and turned out to be influential in the coming presidential campaign.

In the House of Representatives, Sherman was an unfailing advocate for economy in public expenditures, scrutinizing all appropriations bills and arguing against the practice of entering into a contract in advance of an appropriation. He was appointed Chairman of the Committee on Ways and Means. He secured the passage of the bill authorizing the issue of what soon became known as the Treasury notes of 1860.

In February 1861, Sherman first met Abraham Lincoln, who was then the President-elect and who quickly became a lifelong friend. On March 4 of that year, the same day Lincoln was sworn in as President, Sherman took the Ohio Senate seat vacated by Salmon P. Chase, who had resigned to take the position of Secretary of the Treasury in Lincoln's Cabinet.

When the Civil War broke out, Sherman offered his services to General Robert Patterson and served as his aide-de-camp without pay until Congress resumed in July. When the session closed, he returned to Ohio and recruited at his own expense two regiments of infantry, a squadron of cavalry, and a battery of artillery. This force, later known as Sherman's Brigade, served throughout the war. Sherman thought of resigning his Senate seat in order to serve in the war, but Lincoln and his Secretary of the Treasury convinced Sherman to return to the Senate, as his support and leadership were needed for key legislation.

In the Senate, Sherman continued as an overseer of public finances, working to support the armies and strengthen the public credit. In fact, "strengthening the public credit" is generally cited as being among Sherman's greatest contributions to the nation. He took a leading role in advocating for a bill to issue U.S. Treasury notes and make them legal tender. In the summer of 1862, at Secretary Chase's request, he took charge of the national banking bill.

After the war, when Sherman was reelected to the Senate, he became Chairman of the Senate Committee on Finance, taking the place of William Fessenden, who was appointed Secretary of the Treasury. However, when Fessenden returned to the Senate, Sherman voluntarily relinquished the position. He initiated the movement for the resumption of specie payments and was primarily responsible for the refunding act. One observer remarks that Sherman saw in cancellation of greenbacks the most direct route to specie resumption and declared that a beneficial fall in prices must mark resumption. Since the Midwest was inflationary, resumption would follow naturally if the government just met its financial obligations. The amount of greenbacks outstanding was not large enough to endanger the economy. He supported the Tariff of 1867 and sponsored several acts repealing revenue taxes and reducing them to a low rate on whiskey and tobacco.

In 1874, Sherman chaired a committee of nine that prepared legislation to set a date for resumption of specie payment at January 1, 1879. The Senate passed the bill; later, as Secretary of the Treasury, Sherman would assume responsibility for implementing it. In December 1874, he was elected to the Senate for the third time.

In the 1876 presidential campaign, Sherman, along with Garfield, brought forward Rutherford B. Hayes as a candidate for nomination to the presidency. Hayes emphasized three major planks in his platform: merit-based civil service rather than political patronage; pacification of the South; and "honest money"—payment of public indebtedness and, in particular, specie payments.

Hayes assumed the presidency on March 5, 1877, after a long and acrimonious dispute over the results of the election. Each side questioned the results being reported by the states and charged the other with fraudulent conduct; finally, the election was decided by a special commission consisting of five Senators, five Representatives, and five Judges of the Supreme Court. Immediately upon assuming office, Hayes appointed John Sherman to his Cabinet as Secretary of the Treasury—an office he filled from March 10, 1877, to March 3, 1881; this appointment was a natural, given Sherman's ability, financial expertise, party loyalty, and strong support during the campaign.

Sherman similarly warmed to his new position. It made use of his native skill in financial management, and it allowed him to retreat from the inflationist tendencies of his constituencies. He immediately set out to sell 4.5 percent bonds for refunding purposes and made a contract with bankers to sell $3 billion that were outstanding at the time he assumed office. Within three months, he had improved the country's credit standing, here and in international markets, to the point where he was able to sell 4 percent bonds at par and open the offering to the public, selling $25 million within thirty days.

A general business stagnation and severe economic distress had prevailed throughout the country since the Crash of 1873. In addition, the Hayes administration encountered its own financial difficulties. Congress adjourned without making the appropriation needed to support the Army. The Army served without pay for a period of several months, being called upon to settle railroad strikes and quell insurrections.

Hayes vetoed an act passed by both houses of Congress that would have directed the Secretary of the Treasury to buy $2 million in silver a month and coin it into dollars as fast as purchased. Hayes objected that the commercial value of the silver was 8 to 10 percent less than its nominal value and that repaying debts in devalued currency would be an act of bad faith. He said that the silver dollar should be made legal tender, for payment of existing debts, only at its market value, and the standard of value should not be changed without the consent of both parties to the contract.

In Congress where he served continuously from 1855 to 1877, Sherman had shown exceptional ability in managing financial details; he understood the money market thoroughly and was a good judge of people. Dewey saw that his record on financial questions was inconsistent, citing a change of opinion on the refunding measures. Sherman relied on building up a gold reserve through the sale of bonds for coin. He saw that he would get no help from Congress, because in 1877 the inflationists were in control of both houses of Congress. The monetary system was threatened by the free coinage of silver. In this environment, it was no wonder that Sherman would have trouble selling government bonds. European financiers, alarmed by the greenback and silver coinage turmoil, expected new problems in U.S. finances; amid this uncertainty, they returned a considerable block of bonds for redemption, and this competed with the new issue.

In spite of all these obstacles, Sherman persisted in the policy of gold accumulation. He reckoned that 40 percent of the notes outstanding was the smallest safe reserve of gold; on this basis, some $138 million in coin was necessary. Sherman showed firmness and tact in carrying through resumption of specie payments. The lack of specie was solved when the balance of trade turned strongly in America's favor in 1878. Commerce had come to the rescue of finance. A large balance of trade surplus led to a large influx of gold; also, resumption led to a fall in prices, which in turn was a powerful magnet for attracting gold back into the country.

In his annual message of December 1, 1879, President Hayes found occasion to congratulate the country upon the successful resumption of specie payments and upon "a very great revival of business." He announced the reduction in the interest on the public debt (refunded at lower rates). He strongly urged Congress to authorize the Secretary of the Treasury to suspend the silver coinage, as the cheaper coin, if forced into circulation, would eventually become the sole standard of value. He recommended the retirement of U.S. notes with the capacity of legal tender in private contracts. He was convinced that the issue of legal tender paper money based wholly upon the authority and credit of the government, except in extreme emergency, was inconsistent with sound financial principles.

Hayes initiated numerous reforms in federal government. He encouraged Sherman to appoint an investigating committee to examine the New York Custom House. Hayes used the findings of this committee to support his prohibition, in May 1877, of partisan control of revenue officers and of revenue officers' participation in conventions, caucuses, or election campaigns. Two revenue officers defied these orders, and Hayes promptly asked for their resignations, appointing two others to take their place. The Senate at first refused to confirm the new nominations but later acquiesced, after considering a letter from Secretary Sherman that thoroughly exposed the custom house scandals.

After serving as part of Rutherford Hayes's Cabinet for four years, Sherman returned to the Senate to fill the seat vacated when James Garfield was elected President in 1881. He stayed in the Senate for another sixteen years. His Republican colleagues honored him with the position of President pro tempore of the Senate between 1885 and 1887 and listened deferentially whenever the esteemed former Secretary spoke on matters of finance.

In 1897, President McKinley offered Sherman the highest post in the Cabinet, the Secretary of State. He served in that capacity only nominally, the duties being performed by the Assistant Secretary. The Assistant Secretary was named Secretary in 1898, when Sherman retired because of failing health. Three years later, on October 22, 1900, Sherman died in Washington, D.C.

Observers have noted the longevity of Sherman's career in public service: forty-three years, many in elective office. This was an astounding feat, considering that during those years Ohio four times elected a Democratic Governor and three times sent a Democrat to accompany Sherman in the Senate. The explanation, it was said, was Sherman's cautious and reserved demeanor, well adapted to Ohio's uncertainties. Economically, his personal inclination was to favor the conservative point of view of a creditor. But politically, he understood the radical "debtor" psychology that characterized his constituents during a time of economic ups and downs. He understood the thinking of midwesterners and shaped his influence on national legislation accordingly.

On several occasions during the last twenty years of his life, Sherman was a candidate before the Republican Convention for nomination for the presidency of the United States. In 1880, James Garfield made such a stirring speech on behalf of Sherman's nomination that the convention delegates were moved to nominate Garfield himself rather than Sherman. According to reports, Sherman's candidacy for the nomination was never greeted with great enthusiasm but was seen as expected in light of his great accomplishments. He was sometimes characterized by observers as cold and unpopular but able.

Still, his former colleagues offered gracious eulogies at the time of his death. President McKinley took the unusual action of preparing a Proclamation expressing the nation's bereavement and ordering the national flag displayed at half mast. He stated:

Whether in debate during the dark hours of our civil war, or as the director of the country's finance during the period of rehabilitation, or as a trusted counselor in framing the Nation's laws for over forty years, or as the exponent of its foreign policy, his courage was ever marked by devotion to the best interests of his beloved land, and by able and conscientious effort to uphold its dignity and honor. His countrymen will long revere his memory and see in him a type of the patriotism, the uprightness, and the zeal that go to molding and strengthening a nation. ("John Sherman Is Dead," 5)

BIBLIOGRAPHY

Dewey, Davis R. *Financial History of the United States*. New York: Augustus M. Kelley, Publishers, Reprints of Economic Classics, 1968.

"John Sherman Is Dead—Ex-Secretary of State Expired at Dawn Yesterday." *New York Times*, October 23, 1900, 5.

Malone, Dumas, ed. *Dictionary of American Biography*. Vol. 8. New York: Charles Scribner's Sons, 1932.

———. *Dictionary of American Biography*. Vol. 17. New York: Charles Scribner's Sons, 1932.

Morris, Dan, and Inez Morris. *Who Was Who in American Politics*. New York: Hawthorn Books, Inc., 1974.

The National Cyclopaedia of American Biography. Vol. 3. New York: James T. White & Company, 1893.

Wilson, James Grant, and John Fiske. *Appleton's Cyclopaedia of American Biography*. Vol. III: Grinnell-Lockwood, New York: D. Appleton and Company, 1887.

———. *Appleton's Cyclopaedia of American Biography*. Vol. 5. New York: D. Appleton and Company, 1888.

MARY PLATT VENCILL

GEORGE P. SHULTZ (December 13, 1920–   ). Richard Nixon's first-term appointees included three very different Secretaries of the Treasury. George Pratt Shultz was the last of the three, following the very colorful and political John Connally and the earlier David Kennedy, a lifelong banker.

Where Kennedy had been known as a "gradualist," and as a rather quiet, "thoughtful" person, Connally was perceived as neither. He was known as a politically savvy, powerful persuader who would go for the big dramatic move. There might be high risk involved, but Connally would go for broke, for was that not the path to a high return? He was not reluctant to use government for economic or political advantage. It was he who had championed the wage price freeze imposed by the Nixon administration in 1971.

Shultz, like Kennedy, was known as "thoughtful" and even "professorial," reflecting his chosen occupation. Like Kennedy, he was educated, trained, and experienced in economic affairs. Shultz was the first professional economist to serve as Secretary of the Treasury and was a firm believer in the efficacy of a free market economy and a restricted role for government. Like Connally, Shultz was politically experienced but was not, however, viewed as a politician.

Connally painted his way with broad strokes and bold colors during his year and a half as Treasury Secretary. The national and international economic waters were hazardous and uncertain in the wake of his program of wage and price controls and the unilateral American abandonment of the international monetary accords. When Connally left the administration to pursue more exciting interests, there was a need for someone with a thoughtful, long-term perspective to clean up the turbulent littered waters, to restore calm and order. Nixon had named George Shultz the first director of the newly created Office of Management and Budget (OMB). In 1972, Nixon needed him at the helm of the Treasury.

George Shultz, an only child, was born in Manhattan, New York, on December 13, 1920, to Birl and Margaret Shultz. His family moved to Englewood, New Jersey, when George was two or three years old. His was a childhood of close family ties, stability, and relative affluence.

George Shultz's mother, Margaret, was likewise an only child, born in Shoshone, Idaho, the daughter of a Presbyterian missionary. Her parents had moved to Shoshone, where her father had gone to establish a church. Both of her parents died when she was but four years of age. She moved to New York, where she was raised by her aunt and uncle. Her uncle, George Pratt, after whom George Pratt Shultz was named, was an Episcopalian minister.

George Shultz's father, Birl, was one of seven children raised as a Quaker on a farm in Indiana. He was awarded a scholarship, which together with part-time work made it possible for him to attend DePauw University. At DePauw he played varsity football and later passed on his competitive spirit to young George. From DePauw, Birl Shultz went to Columbia University in New York, earning a Ph.D. in history. Among his accomplishments was the coauthorship of a book with noted historian Charles H. Beard. During the early 1920s Birl Shultz went to work with the New York Stock Exchange, developing educational programs on the operation of the stock market and exchange and on investment. He was an educator but outside a school or university.

Young George attended the Ivy League Princeton University as an undergraduate. Here he majored in economics, his interest perhaps having been peaked by the gravity of the Great Depression. In addition, he undertook a minor in public and international affairs. Shultz's senior thesis was an examination of the impact of the then-controversial Tennessee Valley Authority (TVA) on agriculture. While conducting his on-site research, George lived with a "hillbilly" family, learning solid lessons on the difference between the data gathered by government sources and the reality observed by the farmers. It seems that the farmers would provide that set of information that they felt would improve their chances for getting fertilizer and other government benefits. This was an important lesson in the operation of the "real world" and in recognizing the potential errors and limitations of economic data.

In his senior year at Princeton, George had hoped to play first-string varsity football but was sidelined by a serious knee injury. As a result, he opted to assist in coaching freshman football. In his autobiography, Shultz credits this with being his first teaching position. George Shultz graduated from Princeton with honors in 1942.

It was during his senior year at Princeton that the Japanese attacked Pearl Harbor. Like many young men at the time, Shultz was eager to see action in the war. His initial attempt was to get to the European Theater by enlisting in the Royal Canadian Air Force. Failing the Canadian Air Force's eye test, George applied for admission to the Massachusetts Institute of Technology's (MIT's) economics Ph.D. program and was accepted with a specialty in industrial economics. But his doctoral work was to wait. George joined the Marines, starting boot camp at Quantico, Virginia, in August 1942, followed by artillery training at New River, North Carolina. He served in the Pacific and saw action in battles in the Pacific islands, including Samoa.

At the end of the war, Shultz returned to the United States and in the fall of 1945 was assigned fortuitously to the Boston Navy Yard. He was able to combine this assignment with the start of his Ph.D. work at MIT. At this time, the graduate economics program at MIT was very small scale. Shultz studied with future Nobel Prize–winning economist Paul Samuelson. There was but one other student in this class! Shultz studied statistics with Harold Freeman, this time the only student! Such an ideal student-faculty ratio with top scholars must have been a remarkable learning experience.

While serving in the Pacific, George Shultz met an Army nurse, Helena O'Brien (known to her friends as O'Bie), while on leave on Kauai. Two years later, in February 1946, they were married while on midterm break at MIT. Both George and O'Bie were able to take advantage of the GI bill to help pay for their further study after the war. The Shultzes raised five children, three girls and two boys.

After completing his Ph.D. in 1949, Shultz accepted the offer by his graduate department to remain at MIT as a professor. He took leave in 1955 and served for a year in Washington, D.C., as a senior staff economist on the President's Council of Economic Advisers. He viewed it as most fortunate to have served under the chairmanship of noted economist Arthur Burns, who was on leave from Columbia University. The many lengthy discussions he had with Burns were a good education in economics and government policymaking.

In his autobiography, Shultz reports that his father was proud of his son's public service, and he gave his son the following advice before his death later that year: "Whatever you do, do what you think is right for you. Somehow, the material side of life will take care of itself" (Shultz, 28). George Shultz states that "I have always followed that advice."

Shultz left his teaching position at MIT in 1957 to join the faculty of the Graduate School of Business at the University of Chicago as professor of industrial relations. In 1962 he was appointed Dean of the School of Business, one of the most prestigious schools of business in the country. It was in this post that he sharpened his considerable skills at mediation and persuasion. As recounted by Shultz, an academic Dean is faced with competing constituencies, including the administration, academic prima donnas, and alumni. "I had the responsibility for the health of the organization, but the only real authority came from my persuasive powers." Anyone who has served in a leadership role in academia, from department head on up, can identify with this problem of being held responsible, without being given the concomitant authority to act. As stated so simply and eloquently by Shultz, concerning his experience as dean, "I learned to exercise responsibility in a sea of uncertain authority" (28).

In 1968 Shultz took leave as Dean at the University of Chicago to study at the Center for Advanced Study in the Behavioral Sciences at Stanford University. Here fifty scholars assemble each year to pursue their own research interests. It is a place for quiet contemplation and research free of outside interruptions.

But the era of research and quiet contemplation was to be interrupted. On December 3, 1968, Shultz received a call from Arthur Burns, his friend and mentor from his days on the Council of Economic Advisers. Burns was calling at the request of President-elect Nixon. Later that day Shultz talked by phone with Nixon. The following week he was introduced to the nation as the next Secretary of Labor. Shultz was himself surprised at being picked by the President, whom he had never met. Yet those who knew Shultz were not surprised. He was after all a noted authority on labor relations, and he had extensive experience in mediation and arbitration. He was noted for his pragmatic approach as well as his scholarship. A close friend at the time was quoted in the *New York Times*, "George is a guy who's moderate and open-minded. George isn't an intellectual. He can operate in an intellectual environment, but he tends to think pragmatically" (Jones, 17).

As Secretary of Labor, Shultz advocated change in the way that federal manpower programs were administered and funded, favoring a move toward greater flexibility and local control. The dozen or so programs, administered by a number of agencies, would be funded by block grants to state and local governments. They, in turn, would decide how to best use these funds to meet their objectives. This legislation was consistent with Shultz's philosophy of economic decentralization. A close friend judged, "As an economist, he's a moderate. He accepts the necessity of government action in some areas, but he doesn't see government as a cure all." A fellow academic pronounced George Shultz as "somewhat more distrustful of big government than many liberals" (17).

Shultz's tenure as Secretary of Labor was far from the quiet, contemplative environs of Stanford University. These eighteen months were a period of major labor unrest. By virtue of his office, he was involved with a major strike of East and Gulf coast longshoremen, a three-month-long strike at General Electric, a postal workers strike in 1970, as well as bargaining sessions to avoid other strikes.

Shultz's approach to labor strife was instructive and reflective of his general reliance on market economics and free collective bargaining. Rather than imposing "solutions," Shultz felt that it was better to let the parties to the conflict settle their differences. In 1968, President Lyndon Johnson had intervened in the longshoremen's strike, invoking the eighty-day "cooling off" period under the Taft-Hartley Act, and the strike was declared to be a national emergency. When Shultz took office in January 1969, the eighty-day period had run its course and the strike was again under way. Shultz convinced the new President, Richard Nixon, to avoid taking action, saying in effect that there was no emergency, that no emergency would develop, and that the economy would withstand any disruptions that might occur. As argued by Shultz in *Turmoil and Triumph*: "If we avoided direct intervention here, we would deliver a forceful message signaling the administration's commitment to the free collective bargaining system. We would also teach labor and management an important lesson about allowing private economic processes to work" (30). There was pressure on President Nixon to intervene. However, he was persuaded by George Shultz. After six weeks the pressures on labor and management were such that they settled their differences, and the longshoremen returned to work.

Shultz's position or economic philosophy is consistent with and reflective of the approach taken by what is known as the "Chicago School" of economics. Here, the emphasis is placed on the ability of the free market to make economic decisions. The role of government is very limited, being restricted to those activities that are inherently the government's responsibility, such as national defense and the maintenance of the system of law, order, and courts. Government should clearly define the "rules of the game," acting in a predictable, consistent manner rather than placing reliance on individual agencies to assert their authority. The focus should not be on short-term crises and crisis management; but, rather, there should be a long-term perspective. For example, in the area of monetary policy, the Federal Reserve should follow a consistent policy of a constant money growth rate that can be counted upon by decision makers such as business firms and financial agents when they are making their plans and exercising their decisions.

The alternative "activist" policy of adjusting the money supply in response to changing rates of interest, inflation, and unemployment is to be avoided. Further, such activist policies, argue the "Chicago School" economists, will probably cause more harm than good. The debate is conveniently summarized by economists as "rules vs. authority." Do we place our emphasis and faith in clearly established and enunciated rules governing economic actions, or do we rely on government authorities to make the correct decisions in response to changing economic conditions? George Shultz was clearly a firm supporter of the "rules" approach. But, as we will see, he was not inflexible or dogmatic. For Shultz was also a realist and pragmatist, conditioned by years of academic, administrative, and government experience.

In the area of labor relations, a consistent prescription is advocated by the "Chicagoans." Primary reliance should be placed on the operation of the labor and product markets and the signals and pressures generated by the actions of many independent decision makers that may impact on the bargaining process. The decisions on wages, hours, and working conditions should be left to the province of collective bargaining to be conducted by the parties involved, namely, unions and management, free of government interference. In a 1970 speech before the National Press Club, Shultz reiterated his position: "Some people think the Government should determine wages and working conditions, but that would not work long in a free country, except in time of extreme peril. . . . [L]abor-management peace seldom makes a sexy story. . . . [O]n the whole, collective bargaining does work out settlements peacefully" (Smith, 36). Further, Shultz argued:

We cannot allow labor peace to become the overriding objective in our collective bargaining. Here we are trying to get the inflation out of our system, and get ourselves back on a path of strong and stable economic growth. We know that is a period of hard transition. And we know what happens if there are not some companies willing to take strong positions at the bargaining table.

Union leaders cannot take the position that their members should not be asking for high wage increases. That's got to come from management, and if there are no people who take that position, we will never be able to solve these problems. (36)

This is in contrast to the "activist" position, which places a greater emphasis on short-term disruption and short-term costs to society—other firms, workers, and consumers. The activist position is typified by the use of "jawboning," bringing pressure by government officials, to effect a solution to the labor dispute. At issue in this debate are the extent of short-term damage from a delay in settlement, whether jawboning or other forms of activism can speed the process of settlement, plus any longer-term damage that could result from direct interference in the bargaining process and the expectations that this might raise in future negotiations in the affected industry, as well as other industries.

This is a continuing policy debate within the economics profession. The 1960s were a period when economic activism, under the Kennedy and Johnson administrations, was at its peak. The Kennedy administration employed jawboning and administration pressure to effect "noninflationary" wages and prices in the steel industry. This philosophy was similarly reflective of the Johnson administration and continued to the declaration of a national emergency in the last months of the administration in the case of the longshoremen's strike.

President Nixon was well impressed with Shultz's counsel, speaking highly of his approach to labor relations but also seeking his advice on a broader range of issues. As Labor Secretary, Shultz sought to make the operation of manpower training projects and other antipoverty programs more efficient and responsive to local needs. Among his first efforts was the revitalization of the manpower training programs and related programs in the Office of Economic Opportunity and the transfer of state employment agencies whose functions he felt could be conducted more effectively at the state and local level rather than relying on federal administration. These efforts were opposed by those who favored an increased federal presence in antipoverty programs.

However, Shultz's efforts to employ more blacks in the construction industry won praise from these critics. Similar praise met his efforts to activate the Office of Federal Contract Compliance. Shultz was also Vice President of President Nixon's Committee on School Desegregation. Said a colleague of Shultz's style, "He just sits there, never moves and rarely says anything. But the things he does say are usually the things everybody ultimately agrees on" (Smith, 36).

In April 1969, George Shultz and other administration officials were charged in a lawsuit by the NAACP (National Association for the Advancement of

Colored People) with failing to enforce equal employment practices. It was Shultz, however, who announced in July of that year the controversial "Philadelphia Plan," an effort directed at increasing the employment of minorities in construction companies with federal contracts. It was a program of manpower, affirmative action, and union reform rolled into one. Under the Philadelphia Plan, these construction firms were to hire a given number of minority workers, and this could be done at below-union scale. The U.S. Solicitor General ruled that the plan violated the 1964 Civil Rights Act. Labor unions were opposed to the plan. There were demonstrations by construction workers across the country. Shultz held firm in his commitment to increasing minority opportunities and warned the unions to voluntarily comply with the plan, threatening to extend the program to eighteen other cities. These were tough words for the usually reserved Shultz. However, he demonstrated his uncompromising commitment to equal opportunity and minority rights. The federal court in Philadelphia upheld the plan's constitutionality. In 1970, Shultz announced the expansion of the Philadelphia Plan to the nation's capital.

Labor leaders were generally supportive of George Shultz. While not always agreeing with his policies and his initiative, he was viewed as a man of integrity. Speaking at the time, AFL-CIO (American Federation of Labor and Congress of Industrial Organizations) President George Meany viewed Shultz as "an honest and forthright gentleman who keeps his word"—a consistent theme running through George Shultz's career.

Men in power trade in different currencies. Some intimidate and bluster. Not George Shultz. Consistently, he has been known for his quiet, reasoned approach. The currency in which he has traded is integrity. His unquestioned integrity served him, and the administrations with which he has been associated, well. But there were other areas besides labor that needed his attention.

The Nixon administration set about reforming the process by which the federal budget was handled. Part of this reform effort created the OMB, superseding the Bureau of the Budget. On June 10, 1970, President Nixon named George Shultz, his former Secretary of Labor, as the first Director of the new executive unit. Shultz was succeeded at Labor by James D. Hodgson. Caspar W. Weinberger, the former Chair of the Federal Trade Commission (FTC), was named the Deputy Director of the OMB under Shultz. In his address, President Nixon praised Shultz, adding, "I think we have the man who can do something about reorganizing the executive branch of government" (*New York Times*, 8).

But President Nixon wanted Shultz to continue his efforts well beyond the scope of budgetary matters. Shultz's tenure in the administration was noted by his rapid rise into a small circle of confidants whom Mr. Nixon consulted on issues involving both domestic and foreign policy. He continued to represent the administration on issues related to labor. For example, in July 1971 Shultz invited labor and management negotiators to the White House to ask that wage increases be met with increases in productivity. In August 1971, he announced a program to limit the promotions of federal employees in order "to get control of wages in the federal government."

But the economy was providing the Nixon administration one of its greatest challenges. While the nation was emerging from the 1969–1970 recession, inflation was beginning to heat up. In early 1971, President Nixon replaced David Kennedy with John Connally as Secretary of the Treasury. There was surprise and disappointment in Nixon's choice, for what qualifications did Connally have for this position? As reported by James Reston, Connally himself admitted to knowing virtually nothing about high finance. But Nixon wanted someone with political savvy and powers of persuasion.

Not only was the economy in 1971 plagued with the domestic problem of stagflation (anemic production, relatively high unemployment, and inflation), but international economic conditions were showing increased difficulties. The dollar was in retreat, and the United States was faced with gold reserves bordering on depletion. The system of stable international exchange rates that had been in effect since the end of World War II was being threatened. With an overvalued dollar, the United States was finding itself priced out of international markets. By the spring of 1971, Germany and the Netherlands allowed their currencies to float and Austria and Switzerland revalued their currencies. Nixon ordered Connally to have a plan ready by August 6.

Connally's plan called for closing the gold window—that is, unilaterally the United States would refuse to exchange foreign dollar holdings for gold—and imposing a freeze on wages and prices. President Nixon called his economic team to a major policy meeting at Camp David on August 11. The Chicago School economists were opposed to key elements of the plan. George Shultz, head of the OMB, and Herb Stein favored closing the gold window but argued against a wage price freeze. Paul Volcker also favored closing the gold window but argued that the 10 percent surcharge on imports proposed by Connally was too protectionist. Nixon accepted the plan and announced the program on August 15 (Reston, 408).

The program had numerous shortcomings. While the response to the wage and price controls was generally favorable, the freeze had been implemented for but ninety days initially. As orthodox economists are well aware, a freeze can repress inflation, but unless other measures are taken such as a tighter monetary and fiscal policy, the underlying pressures will continue to exist. If the expectations of continued inflation are not abated, lifting a freeze will certainly result in an upward bulge in prices. What does one do after the ninety-day freeze expires?

The freeze was but one limitation with the Nixon/Connally New Economic Policy (NEP). The 10 percent import surcharge was an anti–free trade protectionist measure that would surely offend our trading partners. And while we unilaterally closed the gold window, ending the convertibility of dollars into gold at the formerly agreed-upon price of $35 per ounce, what system would now take its place? The old system was mortally wounded, but a new system was not yet born. There was major uncertainty concerning the international sector.

While Shultz was opposed to the freeze, he continued on at OMB and even agreed to serve on President Nixon's Cost of Living Council. Other "Chicago" economists left the administration. Hendryk S. Houthakker had left the Council of Economic Advisers (CEA) in July, and before year's end, Paul W. McCracken, the head of the CEA, followed. Shultz was also appointed by the President to the National Commission on Productivity, which had been created to once again make the United States competitive in foreign markets. In September, Shultz met with representatives of the West Coast shippers and longshoremen to try to settle their three-month-old strike. And he made numerous appearances before Congress to report on the NEP.

In December, the finance ministers of the ten leading trading nations met at the Smithsonian Institution in Washington. Treasury Secretary Connally negotiated agreements to realign currencies, raising the price of gold from $35 to $38 per ounce and dropping the 10 percent import surcharge that was so unpopular with our allies. While President Nixon heralded the "Smithsonian Agreement" as a monumental achievement, it was but a transitional stage. A more permanent system of international exchange needed to be put into place.

The predictable shortages emerged as a result of the controls, and the popularity of the program waned. The ninety-day freeze was followed by Phase II, viewed more like a thaw than a freeze. Prices and wages would continue to be monitored. John Connally became increasingly impatient with work at the Treasury after all the bold moves for which he was known had been made. It was time for someone to do the mopping up.

On May 16, 1972, Connally resigned as Secretary of the Treasury, effective June 12, and President Nixon nominated George Shultz as his successor. The change was not merely in style but in philosophy and substance as well. Connally was the consummate politician. He would press his positions forcefully and bully his adversaries. When Connally was head of the Treasury, he was also Nixon's "economic czar." While Connally met with the other administration economic policymakers, most important matters were decided in one-on-one meetings with the President. This fit Connally's imperial style, and at the time, it fit Nixon as well. With Shultz as head of the Treasury, effective June 12, the process became more collegial. Shultz was a consensus builder. He, too, was a powerful persuader, but his weapons were fact and reason.

Where Connally had been the originator of the NEP and a supporter of wage and price controls, Shultz had spoken out against these controls. He was, after all, the economist, aware of the limitations of such measures. Connally, primarily a politician, dealt perhaps in political economy. While Connally had championed the 10 percent import tax, this had been dropped by Connally as part of the Smithsonian Agreement. Connally had dismantled the Bretton Woods Accords of fixed exchange rates, but a new system had not been implemented. The Smithsonian Agreement did, however, result in the first devaluation of the U.S. dollar since the 1930s. Shultz, of course, favored moves toward freer trade and freely floating exchange rates, and an elimination of controls.

The differences in style and policy between Connally and Shultz are in large part due to the differences between economists and politicians, a difference Shultz recognized:

My training in economics has had a major influence on the way I think about public policy tasks, even when they have no particular relationship to economics. Economics deals with markets and how they work and seeks out the wide ramifications of policies across industries and over time. Economic policies are partially anticipated and continue to affect the economy long after they have been in place. Results occur, but with a lag. The key to a successful policy is often to get the right process going. While the economist is used to the concept of lags, the politician likes instant results. The tension comes because . . . "the economist's lag is the politician's nightmare." (Shultz, 30)

Where politicians become impatient, and frequently impatient with economists, the economist by training knows that results take time. As is well known by economists, the existence of lags seriously limits economic policy activism. George Shultz knew this, but he was also aware that existing policies could not— perhaps should not—be dismantled immediately.

Shultz presided over the phasing out of the remnants of the wage and price controls. It was not a smooth ride. With the lifting of most all controls in early 1973, inflation surged. Meat prices surged, and on March 29, President Nixon again imposed controls on meat prices. In an effort to reduce pressures on the cost side, Shultz urged labor to accept the 5.5 percent wage guidelines that were in effect in Phase II. But the direction taken was generally toward decontrol.

Following President Nixon's reelection, the White House Press Secretary announced that George Shultz "will be the focal point and the overall coordinator of the entire economic policy decision-making process, both domestically and internationally." He was made the head of the new Cabinet-level Council on Economic Policy. He was given an office in the White House, signaling his arrival in the inner circle of presidential advisers.

As important as Shultz's contributions were in establishing order on the domestic front, his contributions were greater in the international sphere. The dollar had been weakening and subject to speculative pressures. In February, following consultation with other officials, Shultz announced the devaluation of the dollar by 10 percent. In March, the heads of the major international monetary authorities met in Brussels and Paris to seek a more permanent resolution to the international exchange crisis. Shultz was viewed by his international colleagues as a welcome change from Connally's "strong arm" tactics. Although he rejected the European reform proposals, he conveyed a cooperative attitude. At the Paris meetings, the vestiges of the system of fixed international exchange rates came to an end.

What has emerged is a system where most all currencies are freely floating. In other words, the relative values of the international currencies are determined by the forces of supply and demand. If the demand for U.S. dollars falls, then the value of the dollar will fall relative to the other currencies. However, it is not a pure system. Members of the European Union have sought to keep their currencies within a close band of other European currencies. Japan and at times the United States have intervened to keep the yen from dramatically rising in value relative to the U.S. dollar. This is effected by the central banks buying dollars on the international exchange markets. Thus, while there are elements of a "dirty float," the international exchange system is predominately one of freely floating currencies. It is difficult for government buying and selling of currencies to alter the course of major movements in currency demand.

On March 6, 1973, Shultz was named head of the East-West Trade Policy Committee, flying to Moscow to discuss trade with Soviet officials. In June he signed a series of trade protocols with the Soviet Union. In the fall he represented the United States at the meeting of the General Agreement on Tariffs and Trade (GATT), now superseded by the World Trade Organization (WTO). In late September he was in Nairobi, Kenya, at the International Monetary Fund (IMF) meetings called to assess how well the reforms to the international exchange rate system were working. From there, Shultz flew back to Moscow and then to Belgrade, Yugoslavia.

With the OPEC (Organization of Petroleum Exporting Countries)-originated oil price increases as a backdrop, Shultz headed the U.S. delegation to the IMF meetings in January 1974, where he called for a cut in oil prices. He repeated this call for a rollback in oil prices at an international conference in Washington, D.C.

As economists are fond of saying, and as recognized by Shultz, the price of money is the most important price in an economy. He traveled widely to build a stable system for determining international exchange rates. In the process, Shultz earned the respect of international leaders. Several of his counterparts became heads of their nations:

When you work through such hard problems with others, you form bonds that hold. Among the close friends I made during this period were Helmut Schmidt, finance minister of West Germany, soon to become chancellor, Valery Giscard d'Estaing, minister of finance for France, soon to become its president, and Takeo Fukuda, finance minister of Japan, later to become its prime minister. (Shultz, 29)

On March 14, 1974, George P. Shultz announced his resignation as Secretary of the Treasury, effective May 8, 1974. Many in Washington considered Shultz to be almost as powerful as Secretary of State Henry Kissinger. He had become a member of the President's inner circle of advisers and had been given duties well beyond those ordinarily reserved for a Secretary of the Treasury. He had been in charge of the administration's overall economic policymaking, both foreign and domestic. Why did he resign at this time? It was for personal reasons. There is "a tendency to stay too long" in government service. In response to questions, he stated that the "Watergate" scandal was not a consideration in his leaving. With the current economic stabilization program about to expire and with new international monetary negotiations to begin in the spring, he felt "this would be a good time for an orderly transition" (Apple, 1).

Shultz was the last of the original members of the Nixon Cabinet. He had started as Secretary of Labor, gone on to become the first head of the Office of Management and Budget, and ended his career in Nixon's ill-fated second term as the Secretary of the Treasury. Throughout, he maintained his reputation as a man of quiet reserve and principle. He was a scholar who knew politics. The expert in labor relations became noted for his expertise in international relations as well. A *New York Times* review stated that "Mr. Shultz generally assumed a role that experts regarded as unique in the evolution of economic policy. In one short period, he briefed the press on such disparate subjects as unemployment compensation, trade legislation, devaluation, energy, the budget and minimum wage policy. This illustrated the breadth of his responsibility" (13). George Shultz was succeeded at the Treasury by William Simon.

George Shultz's career in public life had yet far to go. But after leaving Washington, he joined the Bechtel Corporation in San Francisco as an Executive Vice President and rose to the presidency of the Bechtel Group, Inc., the holding company for Bechtel's three major operating divisions. Bechtel is a large international engineering and construction firm and is one of the largest privately held firms in the world. With Bechtel, George Shultz traveled widely and gained major experience in the Middle East where Bechtel had major construction contracts.

According to *New York Times* reporter Thomas J. Lueck, Shultz was responsible for the reorganization of Bechtel's international operations into three separate divisions in 1980. While Shultz managed these divisions, Bechtel engaged in projects of monumental proportions, building entire cities in the Middle East. They were involved in gold and copper mining in New Guinea as well as one of the world's largest hydroelectric projects in Canada (6). In the United States, Bechtel had played a major role in such enormous projects as the Hoover Dam and the Alaska pipeline.

On June 25, 1982, President Reagan announced the resignation of Alexander Haig as Secretary of State and his chosen successor, George P. Shultz. His broad experience in the Nixon administration had served him well. This experience was complemented by the added international experience that he gained at Bechtel.

The reception to the announcement was generally favorable. Walter Heller, liberal economist and head of the Council of Economic Advisers under Presidents Kennedy and Johnson, observed that Shultz was not one of those who changes direction in the wind. With good balanced judgment he was the right kind of conservative.

The praise was equally high from conservative economist Alan Greenspan, who was Chair of the Council of Economic Advisers under President Ford and who at the present time chairs the Federal Reserve. Greenspan observed that Shultz was an exceptionally good organizer and manager of ideas.

Shultz stayed with the Reagan administration through the remainder of the first term and for the full second term. He saw through incredible crises in the Middle East, Africa, as well as the beginning of major changes in the Soviet Union that ultimately resulted in its collapse.

At the conclusion of his service as Secretary of State, he was given a bipartisan tribute by the Senate. President Reagan presented him with the Medal of Freedom, this nation's highest civilian honor. George Shultz returned to Stanford University in California. The call from Arthur Burns on behalf of President Nixon had interrupted his research at the University in 1968. It was two decades later, but it was again a return to academia. Today, George Pratt Shultz is Senior Scholar at the Hoover Institution of War, Revolution and Peace at Stanford University. He is truly a man of many worlds.

BIBLIOGRAPHY

Apple, R. W., Jr. "Shultz Leaving Treasury; Simon May Be Successor." *New York Times*, March 15, 1974, 1.

Ashman, Charles. *Connally: The Adventures of Big Bad John*. New York: William Morrow & Company, 1974.

Evans, Rowland, Jr., and Robert D. Novak. *Nixon in the White House: The Frustration of Power*. New York: Random House, 1971.

Genovese, Michael A. *The Nixon Presidency: Power and Politics in Turbulent Times*. Westport, CT: Greenwood Press, 1990.

Jones, David R. "Mild Labor Secretary: George Pratt Shultz." *New York Times*, March 1, 1969, 17.

Lueck, Thomas J. "Bechtel Loses Another Officer to Reagan's Cabinet." *New York Times*, June 26, 1982, 6.

New York Times, July 3, 1970, 8.

Reston, James, Jr. *The Lone Star: The Life of John Connally*. New York: Harper and Row, 1989.

Schoenebaum, Eleanora W., ed. "Shultz, George P(ratt)." *Political Profiles: The Nixon/Ford Years*. New York: Facts on File, Inc., 1979.

Shultz, George P. *Turmoil and Triumph: My Years as Secretary of State*. New York: Charles Scribner's Sons, 1993.

Shultz, George P., and Kenneth Dam. *Economic Policy beyond the Headlines*. New York: W. W. Norton, 1978.

Smith, Robert M. "Reflective Administrator: George Pratt Shultz." *New York Times*, June 11, 1970, 36.

Wicker, Tom. *One of Us: Richard Nixon and the American Dream*. New York: Random House, 1995.

JACK W. OSMAN

WILLIAM E. SIMON (November 27, 1927–   ). Of all the Secretaries of the Treasury in the post–World War II era, William Simon was perhaps the one with the weakest academic credentials. Simon first came to public prominence during the energy crisis of the early 1970s, where, as head of the Federal Energy

Office, he was often referred to as "energy czar," due to the enormous powers given to his office at the time. Ironically, the man given command and control of the nation's energy supplies is a staunch conservative, even more so than the two Presidents he served under. Simon's reputation rested in part on his ability to charm journalists and play to the media; his prognostications were frequently quoted in the papers, often under the rubric "Simon Says." Those who know him well also refer to Simon's temper, which earned him the name "William the Terrible," as well as his taste for creamed spinach. Simon had political ambitions beyond a Cabinet post, including the presidency, but these ambitions were never realized.

Simon was born on November 27, 1927, in Paterson, New Jersey. He was the son of a moderately well-off insurance broker. He grew up in Spring Lake, on the Jersey shore, and attended two private schools, Blair Academy and Newark Academy. Simon's mother died when he was eight, and he was raised, along with his brother and two sisters, by his father.

Simon's aversion to academics apparently began early. He has been described as "nothing special" academically while at the two academies. He was overweight during early adolescence but lost over forty pounds through a strict regimen that included swimming, a pastime he kept for life. He is best remembered from his school days as an excellent swimmer who was quite popular at school.

Simon graduated from Newark Academy in 1946 and joined the U.S. Army. He served for two years in Japan during the U.S. occupation and continued his swimming, serving on the Army team during the Pacific Olympics. In 1948, he entered Lafayette College, serving as a prelaw student specializing in economics. He was a C student at Lafayette who, according to the *New York Post* (January 12, 1974), "apparently liked partying and sports a bit more than studying." When his studies at Lafayette were completed in 1952, he abandoned his plans to go to law school, deciding instead to try his luck on Wall Street. Simon joined the United Services Company, trading in municipal bonds, where he served in this capacity for five years. In 1957, he joined Weeden and Company, where he eventually became Vice President. Simon left Weeden for Salomon Brothers at the beginning of 1964 and became a partner after nine months, in charge of federal bonds and securities.

Simon arrived at Salomon Brothers at an opportune time. The company was growing rapidly. At least one source (*New York Times*, December 17, 1972) described him as "a major force in directing the firm's expansion," though more recent sources have been somewhat less complimentary. There is no doubt, however, that Simon's reputation (not to mention his personal wealth) was enhanced considerably while at Salomon Brothers, and by the end of the 1960s, he was regarded as one of Wall Street's most talented bond traders. He was elected to be the first President of the Association of Primary Dealers in 1969. The following year, he became a member of Salomon Brothers' inner circle, the seventeen-man management committee. By this time, his salary was well in the seven figures.

In the late 1960s, Simon also became active in Republican politics. He was an enthusiastic supporter of Richard Nixon in both the 1968 and 1972 campaigns. Early in the Nixon administration's second term, Simon was briefly vetted for the position of Secretary for Housing and Urban Development, but nothing came of it.

Among those who noticed William Simon at this time was George Shultz, who was then Secretary of the Treasury. Shultz asked Simon to serve as his Deputy. Simon was somewhat reluctant but acceded and joined the Nixon administration at the end of 1972.

Simon managed the day-to-day affairs of the Treasury Department for Shultz and also chaired the administration's Interagency Oil Policy Committee, a post that was later to have a profound effect on his government career. Simon's job required coordinating government policy with over sixty agencies and consulting with major oil companies. At the time the consumption of oil in the United States was rising, as the demand for electricity, gasoline, and a variety of energy-intensive consumer goods increased rapidly. Total production of crude oil in the United States was leveling off. Many oil industry analysts were predicting some sort of energy crisis as early as 1970.

The crisis did indeed arrive in 1973 in the form of the Organization of Petroleum Exporting Countries (OPEC) oil embargo. The Nixon administration proposed forming a Federal Energy Office in July 1973. John Love, then Governor of Colorado, was appointed to head the agency. Love had a bare-bones staff and little access to the White House. Some analysts have argued that Love's lack of access was due to his weakness as an advocate in Washington; others have argued that the Nixon administration was too preoccupied with Watergate; still others believe that it was Love's continued proposals for gasoline rationing that led to his ineffectiveness.

Simon also demonstrated his ability to schmooze with the press. Shultz preferred to stay out of the limelight, but Simon seemed to relish this aspect of the job. Despite a relatively low rank in the Nixon administration, Simon soon became the regular subject of newspaper columns and feature stories. He continued to espouse his conservative philosophy.

On December 4, 1973, the Nixon administration announced that Simon would succeed Love as head of the Federal Energy Office. Many considered the task a thankless job that would lead Simon nowhere, but he made the best of things and held a press conference immediately, cautioning about energy use and concluding that the country then faced the choice between comfort and convenience, or jobs.

In his two books, Simon is very clear to lay out his conservative philosophy including a strong criticism of government regulation, but in his job as head of the Federal Energy Office (FEO), Simon did indeed tamper with market forces. He was faced with a potential political and economic crisis. Something had to be done—or so it seemed. The market solution, allowing prices to rise, was politically unpopular. The Nixon administration also argued that since the oil price hike was the result of a cartel, and not the free market, the price of crude oil should be much lower. During the early 1970s, the price of crude oil sky-rocketed from $3 to $4 a barrel to $15 to $16. Simon and others argued that prices were artificially low beforehand, partly due to government price controls on natural gas but that the true equilibrium price of oil, without any cartel control or regulation, would be about $7 to $8 a barrel. The federal government used this analysis to justify its own market intervention. Price controls were placed on gasoline, and Simon ordered an energy allocation program on December 12, 1973, that forced the oil companies to reduce their refining of gasoline by 5 percent and increase their production of heating oil and fuel for business. Two years later, in an interview with *Business Week* (February 3, 1975), Simon de-fended his policy as the least objectionable. Apparently, Simon thought that a government program that forced refiners to produce more heating oil, placing most of the burden of the energy crisis on motorists, was "the market route."

In many ways, the pundits were correct; Simon had been given a thankless job. Simon's moves seemed to aggravate everyone. The oil companies did not like being told how to allocate their resources. His agency was sued by Gulf Oil, and he was regularly lambasted by Congressmen on Capitol Hill who desperately needed a scapegoat for the long lines at gasoline stations. The American people saw the energy crisis as a conspiracy brought about by big oil companies. He even provoked the military by ordering that 1.5 million barrels of jet fuel be converted to civilian use (eventually half of this amount was converted). Despite the con-troversy, or perhaps because of it, Simon became a national figure. And as an assistant Treasury Secretary and the head of a formerly obscure agency, he became a national figure profiled by all the major news magazines. At one point he was dubbed the "energy czar," and the title stuck.

Simon continued to extol the virtues of the free market even as he moved toward stricter regulation of energy policy. He blamed inflation on excessive government regulation and castigated the federal government for destroying American freedoms. Simon regularly cited a Central Intelligence Agency (CIA) report that estimated that government regulations cost the United States over $130 billion a year. He was especially fond of criticizing the Interstate Commerce Commission, which often forced truckers to haul cargo one way and return with empty trucks.

Simon's criticism of government policies eventually became a concern to the Nixon administration, which was trying to argue that it was indeed cutting gov-ernment spending and excessive regulation. The clash finally occurred over en-ergy policy. In February 1974, Roy Ash, Nixon's Director of the Budget, described the energy crisis as short term, but Simon was quick to respond on television that Roy should "keep his cotton-pickin' hands off energy policy." That same month, Simon publicly contradicted the shah of Iran's statement that the United States was importing as much oil as before the embargo. Simon went on to characterize the statement as "irresponsible and reckless." The Nixon adminis-tration still considered the shah an ally and privately reprimanded Simon.

Simon worked tirelessly, rising early and arriving at his office before eight for what would often be thirteen- or fourteen-hour days. He pushed for the authority to control oil supplies even further but with little success. His biggest task at the FEO, however, was to convince the American people that the energy crisis was real and not just a conspiracy of giant oil companies to raise the price of gasoline to exorbitant levels. In an editorial a year later, the *Wall Street Journal* argued that Simon's chief success as head of the FEO had been to counter the myth that the energy crisis was a conspiracy of the oil companies.

Simon was certainly successful in advancing his own interests. He exhibited enormous charm with the press and was always available to answer reporters' questions. He was meticulous when it came to giving testimony on Capitol Hill, which earned him a solid reputation among Congressmen and Senators.

Simon was nominated to be Secretary of the Treasury by President Nixon on April 17, 1974. At the time, the Nixon administration was preoccupied with Watergate. The nomination was very low key. Instead of the typical Cabinet-level announcement made with a great deal of fanfare with the President shaking hands with the new nominee in front of TV cameras, the appointment was made by Nixon's number-two press spokesperson, Gerald Warren, when Simon was out of town.

It soon became clear that Simon's influence was not to be as great as Shultz's. He was not a trusted Nixon associate nor a trained economist. Instead, the Nixon administration made it clear that Shultz's role as head of the Committee on Economic Policy would be taken over by Nixon himself. Similarly, Shultz's role as Assistant to the President for Economic Policy would go unfilled. Warren went on to state that Simon would be a spokesperson for the Nixon administration on economic policy, but not chief spokesperson, unlike his predecessors (*Wall Street Journal*, April 18, 1974, 3). Simon's former post as head of the Federal Energy Office was filled by John Sawhill.

Simon's swearing-in ceremony, several weeks later, on May 8, 1974, was more glamorous, complete with a ceremony in the East Room of the White House. Nixon graciously introduced Simon and his wife, referring to Simon as a "man of austerity" who was strongly in favor of reduced government spending. Nixon quipped that he didn't know if Simon would approve of taxpayers' money being spent on refreshments for the party. Nixon then began to talk about inflation, which had crossed the double-digit mark and was now running at 10.8 percent. He vowed that Simon would deal with inflation through "productivity, and not through wage and price controls" (*Wall Street Journal*, May 9, 1974, 2). Many onlookers criticized Simon's appointment due to his lack of experience in foreign economic policy, in particular, international monetary policy. In the wake of the collapse of Bretton Woods, a Treasury Secretary with a firm knowledge of currency markets was needed, they argued.

Simon continued to be unpopular with many Nixon administration insiders. One unnamed source told the *Wall Street Journal* that Simon was much more likely to yield to popular sentiment (witness his actions as head of the FEO where, despite his promarket stance, he took a strongly regulatory approach). This insider stated that Shultz's former authority would likely be split among Roy Asch, Director of the Office of Management and Budget, Arthur Burns, head of the Federal Reserve, John Dunlop, Chief of the Council on the Cost of Living, and Henry Kissinger, the Secretary of State.

Despite his apparent lack of authority, Simon continued to speak out. Simon was particularly concerned with inflation. At a conference sponsored by the American Bankers Association, he embraced the views of Fed Chairman Arthur Burns that a stringent monetary and fiscal policy was necessary to reduce inflation. He attacked congressional demands for a tax cut, stating that it would only worsen inflation, and he urged policies designed to increase production of agricultural products, energy, and raw materials. One of Simon's pet ideas was the development of oil from shale, which he believed would do a great deal to relieve the U.S. dependence on foreign oil. Simon also blamed federal banking officials for allowing the Franklin National Bank to lapse into failure with little warning, calling for greater surveillance of the banks' foreign exchange operations. He also called for a lift of the ban on gold ownership that the United States had imposed on its citizens for forty years (*Wall Street Journal*, June 5, 1974).

President Nixon resigned in August of 1974, throwing the country into a state of shock. Vice President Gerald Ford became the only unelected President of the United States. Nixon's resignation provided an opportunity for Simon, who had never had much authority in the Nixon administration. It soon became clear, however, that Simon's role under the Ford administration would be only marginally more powerful than it had been under Nixon. The Ford administration soon announced that while Simon would be its "chief economic spokesman," William Seidman would be named as Economic Policy Coordinator. Some dubbed Simon's role as "Mr. Outsider," the public spokesman for Ford policy, while Seidman would be "Mr. Insider," the formulator of such policies. In addition, Alan Greenspan was named to be head of President Ford's Council of Economic Advisers.

By the fall of 1974, it was clear that the U.S. economy was headed into a recession, and members of the Ford administration scrambled to figure out how to respond. Both Greenspan and Seidman alluded to the possibilities of a tax cut in public statements but denied that a cut was policy. They were only willing to admit that tax cuts were not being taken off the table as a policy option. Simon made it clear to the press that he was strongly opposed to tax cuts and argued that the country would lose "a magnificent opportunity" to reduce inflationary pressures if a stimulative macropolicy were embarked upon. He argued that within six months the United States would see a sharp drop in the upward momentum of prices if the administration was willing to stay the course. Simon made it clear that he was particularly opposed to any increases in federal spending, preferring that an expansionary policy take the form of a tax cut, but he indicated that a tax cut was not being seriously considered by the administration (*Wall Street Journal*, December 4, 1974, 4).

On Capitol Hill, Republicans were calling for strong action to stimulate the economy and criticized the Democrats for their do-nothing policies. Meanwhile, the Ford administration, despite Simon's admonitions to the contrary, was indeed seriously considering a tax cut. In his State of the Union message at the beginning of 1975, President Ford proposed a $16 billion tax cut coupled with a 5 percent cap on increases in government spending. In an interview with *Business Week*, Simon defended himself against charges that the Ford administration had ignored his own suggestions. Simon claimed that, in fact, he had been one of the chief architects of the policy, as Chairman of the Economic Policy Board. He also denied any rumors that the Ford administration was considering asking for his resignation. Simon did let the magazine know that he was concerned about the mounting federal budget deficit, which was projected to reach $35 billion in 1975. He went on to state that the Federal Reserve would accommodate the Ford administration's new economic policy but argued for a more modest growth in the rate of the money supply. Some analysts had been calling for a 9 percent growth rate. Simon thought 5 to 6 percent was more sustainable.

Lekachman examined the economic policy of this period and declared that the Ford administration obviously preferred depression to inflation (35). At least this seemed to be the persistent theme of Secretary Simon. Worrying early in 1975 about deficits and inflation, Simon told the House Ways and Means Committee that we did not dare do too much about unemployment and recession. Simon warned that if the deficits caused money supply increases, it would result in inflation. On the other hand, no increase in the money supply would mean tight credit and high interest rates. No wonder that President Truman, seeking unambiguous advice in his administration, had called for a "one-armed economist." What, then, did Simon recommend to the committee? He said that the solution would be to resist the temptation to deal with it by short-term remedies, that is, by more deficits.

Lekachman concludes that fallacies often have long lives. In the 1974 to 1975 period, Treasury Secretary Simon, described by Lekachman as the "Ford administration's most vigorous exponent of economic error," repeatedly warned Congress that more stimulus to the economy would "crowd out" private borrowers, renew inflation, and lead to even worse recession. In Lekachman's words, "Minds unbefuddled by reading too many of Mr. Simon's statements might have concluded that when unemployment was running at 9 percent levels, eight or nine million people were looking for jobs, factories were operating at 70 percent of capacity, and inventories were stacked in warehouses, there were plenty of resources available to be put to work by money borrowed by both sectors of the economy—private and public" (256).

In the short run, the inflation rate did fall from 12.3 percent in 1974 to 4.9 percent in 1976 as the deficit rose from $6 billion to about $74 billion. Unemployment rose from 4.9 percent in 1973 to 5.6 percent in 1974, 8.5 percent in 1975, and back to 7.7 percent in 1976. Simon was eventually exonerated in his concerns of runaway inflation and larger and larger deficits. By the year 1979, deficits and money creation had lowered the unemployment rate to 5.8 percent.

But the deficit was $41 billion in 1979 and $84 billion in 1980; inflation peaked at 13.3 percent in 1979 and was still in double digits at 12.5 percent in 1980. By late 1979, exceedingly tight money policy was adopted to engineer a recession designed to "break inflationary expectations." This may have been the sort of stop-and-go policy Secretary Simon was fretting about.

At the time (1975), Congress was also debating a tax on imported oil, which it felt would eventually reduce the U.S. dependency on oil as well as a "windfall profits tax" that would tax the profits that oil companies had earned after the OPEC embargo. Simon was generally sympathetic to the idea of an oil import fee but felt that oil companies should be allowed to exclude windfall profits taxes by plowing back the money into investments that would reduce the U.S. dependence on foreign oil. He continued to oppose wage and price controls and stated that the Ford administration was with him on the point.

Simon's next major battle was over the potential bankruptcy of New York City, which was looming. By the fall of 1974, it became clear that New York City might not be able to meet its debt obligations despite some assistance from the state. Some Democratic Senators such as Hubert Humphrey were calling for a federal bailout of New York City. The Ford administration was quite adamant that it would oppose any bailout plan, and William Simon, a former New York bond trader, was the administration's chief spokesman on the issue. Ford did propose taking over some of New York City's welfare payments but refused any other assistance, proposing instead further tax increases and drastically reduced public spending. A bailout of New York City was not popular outside of the state, so the Ford administration could push its conservative credentials without risking its popularity.

Simon argued that a bailout of New York City would not lead to a devastating financial collapse and that financial markets were quite resilient; most of New York City's creditors were large banks that could withstand the loss. The Federal Reserve Board and other bank regulatory agencies were willing to bail out a few small banks that would be affected by a default. Simon called for a temporary increase in the state's sales tax coupled with a loan from the state to the city of the future increased revenues. He did propose that in the event of a bankruptcy, the bankruptcy law, which called for notification of 51 percent of creditors and entailed a long, time-consuming process, should be simplified. He also pointed out that financial markets had already discounted much of New York's financial turmoil and that a default would make things only "somewhat worse."

Toward the end of his term, Simon's stance became more statesmanlike, and he wrote several pieces for the *Wall Street Journal* including an op-ed piece that warned (prophetically) of the coming crisis in the Social Security system. Simon has continued preaching his free market gospel to this day, including the publication of two books, *A Time for Truth* (1978) and *A Time for Action* (1980).

Simon tried to return to Salomon Brothers after leaving Washington on January 20, 1977, but was offered a lower-ranking job than the Senior partnership he had when he left—an insult. For the next four years, Simon earned several million dollars from consulting, speech making, and serving on corporate boards. He was almost appointed to be the head of Kennecott Corporation. Simon was offered the job but hesitated too long and lost out to Thomas Barron, a Senior Vice President of Exxon.

Simon was briefly rumored to be Ronald Reagan's vice presidential running mate in 1980, but the rumors quickly died and George Bush got the job. Simon served as part of Reagan's "kitchen Cabinet," the group that provided Reagan with potential nominees for his administration. It was also rumored that Simon would get a Cabinet post in the Reagan administration, most likely at Defense or Treasury, but many of Reagan's top advisers thought that Simon was too abrasive and even too right wing for the Reagan administration. Simon received no appointment, which effectively became the end of his political career.

In the early 1980s, Simon became President of the U.S. Olympic Committee, where he was instrumental in changing the criteria for "amateur" athletics, which Americans had long thought worked to the disadvantage of the United States. During this time, Simon also became partners with Ray Chambers, a former accountant at Price Waterhouse, and formed the Wesray Company. Many companies were dirt cheap in the 1980s, and the political connections that Simon and Chambers had allowed them to obtain access to hundreds of millions of dollars in debt. Chambers's accounting skills allowed him to seek out inexpensive companies that could be purchased for less than their true business value. Simon's job was to use his political contacts to obtain cheap financing from Citicorp, GE Capital, and other top lenders. The result was a company worth several hundred million dollars, most of it leveraged by junk bonds. Among the acquisitions were a briefcase manufacturer, a musical instrument manufacturer, and a crude oil transportation company. The company won fame in the investment community when it bought Gibson Greetings from RCA in 1982. Their personal investment was less than $1 million, but a few years later, they sold the company at a $140 million profit.

Chambers was the financial brain behind the deals. Their strategy was simple: (1) Buy out a cheap company with good cash flows with as little as possible in the way of personal capital, (2) reward the new management with incentive contracts, and (3) structure the company so that if anything went wrong, Simon and Chambers would be insulated and the holder of the debt would be stuck with the losses. Their strategy was so successful that by the end of the 1980s Simon's net wealth was estimated at about $300 million, and he was on the Forbes list of the 400 richest Americans. He owned four estates, including one of sixty-four acres, and was fond of sailing his 125-foot yacht.

Simon left Wesray in the mid-1980s but continued to be involved in business affairs, this time less successfully. Without Chambers's attention for detail, Simon began buying firms that were not good investments, including a number of California savings and loans (S&Ls). Simon set up WSGP Partners with an old friend from the Treasury Department, Gerald Parsky. During the late 1980s, after reading James Clavell's *Noble House*, he spent much of his time in the Pacific sailing his yacht and scuba diving, ostensibly looking for deals for his new company.

Parsky did not prove to have the business skills that Chambers had, and this time the strategy did not work. It was far more difficult for the new partnership to raise money. WSGP attempted to raise money from some Saudi sheiks and from an Australian wheat magnate but had little luck. His new creditors, outfits like Drexel Burnham, were far more stringent in requiring equity participation from WSGP. Despite Simon's connections with the Treasury Department, many of their deals lost money. They were able to pick up many S&Ls at very low prices, but there was often a reason for these low prices, and many of the deals went sour. Simon's health was deteriorating as well. In 1989 he had triple bypass surgery for his ailing heart. Today, Simon leads a rather quiet life. Many of his financial affairs are conducted by two of his sons.

BIBLIOGRAPHY
Lekachman, Robert. *Economists at Bay: Why the Experts Will Never Solve Your Problems.* New York: McGraw-Hill, 1976.
New York Post. January 12, 1974.
New York Times. December 17, 1972.
Simon, William E. "The Energy Policy Calamity." *Wall Street Journal*, June 10, 1977.
———. *A Time for Truth.* New York: McGraw-Hill, 1978.
———. *A Time for Action.* New York: McGraw-Hill, 1980.
"William E(dward) Simon." In *Political Profiles: The Nixon/Ford Years*, edited by Eleanora W. Schoenebaum, 597–601. New York: Facts on File, Inc., 1979.
Sobel, Robert. *The Worldly Economists.* New York: Free Press, 1980.
"Tarnished Legend." *Barron's*, May 3, 1993.
Wall Street Journal. April 18, 1974, 3.
———. May 9, 1974, 2.
———. June 5, 1974.
———. December 4, 1974, 4.
Wall Street Journal Index.

PHIL KING

JOHN W. SNYDER (June 21, 1895–October 8, 1985). In Frank Capra's *State of the Union*, a film set against the backdrop of 1948 presidential politics, one character observes, "If you were from Missouri you'd have a job in Washington"—an obvious reference to the "cronyism" that political commentators constantly attributed to President Harry Truman. John Snyder spent much of his adult life in Missouri, and he did, indeed, get a job in Washington.

John Wesley Snyder led a rather unremarkable life until a call from President Truman in 1945 catapulted him into the limelight of national politics. Born in Jonesboro, Arkansas, on June 21, 1895, to Ellen (Hatcher) and Jerre Hartwell Snyder, a druggist and minor inventor, he was admitted to Vanderbilt University in 1914 to study electrical engineering. An unfortunate decline in family finances compelled his withdrawal after a single year; Snyder spent the succeeding two years assisting in his uncle's farm and timber businesses in northeast Arkansas.

Enlisting in the Army upon the entry of the United States into World War I, Snyder was commissioned as a second lieutenant. While serving in France in the 57th Field Artillery Brigade of the 32nd Artillery Division, Snyder formed a friendship with Harry S. Truman, which was to have dramatic consequences in later years.

Truman and Snyder were attending the same artillery school in France, in 1918 when they made each other's acquaintance. Although they went separate ways after mustering out of the regular army, both obtained commissions in the U.S. Army Field Artillery Reserve and renewed their friendship annually at Reserve Corps summer encampments, as both advanced to positions as reserve colonels commanding regiments in the same brigade.

After the war Snyder returned to Arkansas as a captain and recipient of the Croix de Guerre. He courted and subsequently married Evelyn Cook on January 5, 1920. Between 1919 and 1931 he worked in several small town banks in Arkansas and Missouri, rising to the position of cashier.

Shortly after the onset of the Great Depression, the bank that employed Snyder collapsed, and he was appointed its liquidator. During the next six years he served as a national bank receiver with the Office of the Comptroller of the Currency and facilitated the liquidation or restructuring of many disaster-ridden Missouri banks.

In 1937 Snyder became the Regional Manager of the Reconstruction Finance Corporation (RFC) in St. Louis, Missouri. He was subsequently promoted to the position of Special Assistant to the Board of Directors of the RFC and served in Washington, D.C., from 1940 to 1943. After U.S. entry into World War II he was appointed the Executive Vice President and Director of the Defense Plants Corporation, a subsidiary of the RFC created to finance the construction of factories devoted to military production. He left government service and returned to St. Louis in 1943 to accept an appointment as Vice President of the First National Bank of St. Louis. However, he maintained his connection with the government and served in several advisory positions during the succeeding years.

At the request of President Truman, Snyder returned to full-time government service in April 1945 to replace Fred M. Vinson as the Federal Loan Administrator. He was to succeed Vinson twice more during 1945–1946, first as the Director of the Office of War Mobilization and Reconversion (OWMR) and then as Secretary of the Treasury. It was also during this period that he emerged as the President's closest personal adviser.

As Director of OWMR Snyder steered a bill providing government-insured education to veterans through Congress; this provision subsequently became a prominent part of the GI Bill of Rights. He was also responsible for the conversion of the economy from a wartime to a peacetime footing as well as the early planning of a national housing program.

Despite these successes, Snyder was subjected to strong criticism for his performance at OWMR. Although reconversion occurred with relatively little unemployment, he was censured for releasing the brakes on the economy without due care. For example, the abrupt removal of all priorities on raw materials and building materials at the end of the war was deemed the cause of an explosion of "nonessential" construction that left the Veteran's Housing Program scrambling for supplies. Similarly, the decontrol of raw materials led to the failure of many small businesses that had emerged during the war. The abandonment of controls permitted copper, aluminum, and steel producers to resume sales to their large prewar buyers, leaving these small manufacturers unable to acquire raw materials and, thus, forcing them out of business (Davidson, 63).

His handling of the steel crisis was an even greater fiasco. In early 1946 steelworkers were on the picket lines demanding higher wages, while management was asking for higher product prices. Chester Bowles, Director of the Office of Price Administration (OPA), recommended holding firm and allowing only limited wage and price increases (Cochran, 204). However, Truman and Snyder bypassed the OPA and, without consulting industry representatives, announced wage increases of eighteen and a half cents per hour. When the owners balked, the government agreed to compensate them by allowing price increases of $5.30 per ton. This incident spelled the beginning of the end for the administration's attempts at wage and price controls. As Bowles concluded in a letter to Truman: "[T]he conviction is growing in the public mind and on Capitol Hill that the Government's stabilization policy is not what you have stated it to be, but is instead one of improvising on a day-to-day, case-by-case basis, as one crisis leads to another—in short that there is no policy at all" (Bernstein and Matusow, 65–66).

Upon Vinson's appointment to the Supreme Court, Snyder was nominated to succeed him as Secretary of the Treasury. His nomination was referred to the Senate Finance Committee on June 6, 1946; he was confirmed on June 11 and took office on June 25. His appointment to the Cabinet was greeted with derision—the press wrote of "cronyism," while others claimed he was clearly unfit for the job (Davidson; Allen and Shannon, 121).

Although politically a Democrat, Snyder was perceived as an ally of business interests. His dealings with union demands for wage increases both at OWMR and at the Treasury convinced many people that he was antilabor, and he was accused of antagonizing a key element of the New Deal constituency. He maintained a steady confidence that, given a chance, everything would work itself out and was thus doubtful about the success of extensive government activism. This conservative outlook made him the subject of persistent and sometimes bitter journalistic attacks.

Despite widespread skepticism, Snyder was much more successful in his handling of the Treasury than he had been at OWMR. During 1947 he argued in favor of retiring the national debt; he recommended that Truman oppose the reduction of taxes, advice the President followed in vetoing two such congressional attempts. He was genuinely proud to be the first Treasury Secretary since Andrew Mellon to reduce the national debt while balancing the budget.

Since he considered fiscal restraint the appropriate policy for achieving stability and growth, Snyder came into conflict with Secretary of State George C.
Marshall. Marshall favored generous aid to England and Europe to combat the
Soviet threat; Snyder was unenthusiastic due to his responsibility for financing
such aid. However, a visit to Europe in the fall of 1947 led to a modification of
his views, and Snyder came to endorse short-term humanitarian aid to Europe
while continuing to express opposition to the grander aspects of the Marshall
Plan.

Domestic inflation made it difficult for Snyder to acquiesce to such an expansive aid policy. Consumer prices increased at an annual rate of 30 percent between July and December 1946 and by 9.1 percent during 1947. Given Truman's
and Snyder's continued resistance to higher interest rates, fiscal policy was the
only anti-inflationary measure available. President Truman declared the control
of inflation his top priority for 1948 and proposed a policy consisting of continued
price and rent controls, budgeting for a fiscal surplus, and selective credit control
by the Federal Reserve.

Although successive Federal Reserve Board Chairmen Marriner Eccles and
Thomas McCabe favored higher interest rates and tighter reserve requirements,
Snyder disagreed because of his concern with maintaining a market for government bonds. Part of the disagreement between the Federal Reserve and the Treasury can be ascribed to differing visions of the goals of monetary policy. Eccles
and McCabe had been persuaded that economic stabilization was the dominant
goal of the Fed and considered the stability of securities markets a secondary goal
(Stein, 255). Snyder believed otherwise, and this dispute over the appropriate
policy continued until March 1951 when the domination of Fed policy by the
Treasury finally ended.

Meanwhile, various groups continued to call for tax reductions. Early in 1950
Snyder presented a tax program to Congress that called for the reduction of some
excise taxes, changes in corporate taxes, and the merger of estate and gift taxes
into a "transfer tax" with a higher rate. However, the onset of the Korean War
in June 1950 blighted any hopes for tax relief; attention quickly shifted to methods for increasing revenues to pay for the war. In July Congress passed tax increases totaling almost $5 billion, and in November, an "excess profits tax" was
instituted. Truman favored paying the entire cost of the war through tax increases, and Snyder was largely successful in achieving this, a fact borne out by
the relatively small budget deficit accruing in the first year of the Korean War.

Snyder continued to insist upon a low rate of interest on long-term government securities despite the Federal Reserve Board's repeated calls for a rate increase. Truman supported this position, arguing that maintaining the confidence
of the public in government securities was one way of presenting a united front
against communism (Stein, 272). Thus, the Federal Reserve Banks were forced
to purchase government bonds to support the market whenever necessary. The
resulting inflation was dealt with through taxation and through controls exercised
by the National Security Resources Board.

On December 15, 1950, Truman declared a national emergency, and during the first half of 1951, stringent economic controls were established. These consisted of higher taxes, tighter credit limitations, and price and wage controls. In January the Office of Price Stabilization froze the prices of most commodities and services, and the Wage Stabilization Board ordered that wages and other compensation be frozen. In February, Truman recommended a "pay-as-you-go" tax program to Congress. In March, after extensive discussions and disagreements with Truman and the Treasury's representatives, the Fed's Open Market Committee officially abandoned its support of the government securities market. It argued, "In inflationary times like these our buying of Government securities does not provide confidence. It undermines confidence. The inevitable result is more and more money and cheaper and cheaper dollars" (Stein, 274).

These policies were largely successful, and by June 1952, talk had turned to the prospect of decontrolling wages and prices. However, both the Treasury and Commerce Departments joined the Council of Economic Advisers in urging that controls be maintained until the threat of inflation was clearly past.

On the international scene, Snyder perceived his role as one of ensuring the expansion of multilateral trade and a greater convertibility of currencies, especially among countries receiving U.S. assistance. He participated in the financial rehabilitation program for the Philippines in 1946 and the interim assistance program for France, Italy, and Austria in 1947. He also supervised the U.S. aid programs to Turkey and Greece in 1948 and financial reconstruction in Germany in 1948 and Japan in 1948–1949.

Snyder was Joint Chairman of the Board of Governors of both the International Monetary Fund (IMF) and the International Bank for Reconstruction and Development (IBRD). He insisted upon the continued independent operation of the IMF despite pressures to dissolve or merge it with the IBRD. As Governor of the IMF he insisted that "the Fund would not lend automatically to its members. . . . [I]t would not even lend to any 'credit-worthy' member. . . . [Its] resources were to be used only toward the abolition of trade restrictions" (Heidenheimer, 12). He also served as a member of the NATO (North Atlantic Treaty Organization) Council, advising on the financial implications of this mutual defense program.

Overall, Snyder successfully reduced the federal debt by $5 billion during his term in office while running budget surpluses in 1947, 1948, 1949, and 1951. He introduced programs to increase the efficiency of the Treasury and guided legislation through Congress for the reorganization and simplification of government accounting practices.

After leaving his post as Secretary of the Treasury on January 20, 1953, Snyder served as President, Chairman of the Finance Committee, and Director of the Overland Corporation of Toledo, Ohio. He was an adviser to the U.S. Treasury from 1955 to 1976. He was a member of the American Legion, Omicron Delta Kappa, Alpha Tau Omega, the Masonic order (33rd Degree), and numerous other clubs and organizations. In spite of his failure to attain an earned degree, he was awarded a number of honorary degrees in recognition of his accomplishments in public life. Preceded in death by his wife in 1956, Snyder passed away on October 8, 1985, at his home in South Carolina. He was survived by a daughter, Edith Cook Snyder Horton.

BIBLIOGRAPHY
Allen, Robert S., and William V. Shannon. *The Truman Merry-Go-Round*. New York: Vanguard Press, 1950.
Bernstein, Barton J., and Allen J. Matusow, eds. *The Truman Administration: A Documentary History*. New York: Harper & Row, 1966.
Cochran, Bert. *Harry Truman and the Crisis Presidency*. New York: Funk and Wagnalls, 1973.
Davidson, Bill. "He Knew Him When." *Collier's*, December 7, 1946, 16ff.
Heidenheimer, A. J. "John Snyder's Hope Chest." *New Republic*, October 15, 1951, 12–13.
McCullough, David. *Truman*. New York: Simon and Schuster, 1992.
National Cyclopedia of American Biography. New York: James T. White & Co., 1967.
Snyder, John W. "The Treasury and Economic Policy." In *Economics and the Truman Administration*, edited by Francis Heller. Lawrence, KS: Regents Press, 1981.
Stein, Herbert. *The Fiscal Revolution in America*. Washington, D.C.: American Enterprise Institute Press, 1990.

VIBHA KAPURIA-FOREMAN

JOHN C. SPENCER (January 8, 1788–May 17, 1855). John Canfield Spencer served as Secretary of the Treasury from March 8, 1843, to May 2, 1844. Prior to his service in the Treasury Department he had been Secretary of War from October 12, 1841, to May 3, 1843.

John C. Spencer was born in Hudson, New York, the eldest son of Ambrose Spencer and Laura (Canfield) Spencer. Soon after John was born the Spencer family moved to Albany, where his father became a prominent and influential member of the community. John Spencer, therefore, grew up as part of a well-to-do family, one of the leaders in Albany and in the state of New York. He enrolled in and spent a year at college in Williamstown, Massachusetts. Then he transferred to Union College, Schenectady, New York, from which he graduated with high honors in 1806. After graduation Spencer served as private secretary to New York Governor Daniel Tompkins and studied law. He was admitted to the bar in 1809 and began practice in Canandaigua, Ontario County, New York.

As an attorney he was successful and was appointed to a number of public offices including that of Postmaster at Canandaigua and that of district attorney for the five western counties of New York. While in the latter office he was elected a member of the U.S. House of Representatives for the term 1817–1819.

As a member of the House, Spencer was appointed Chairman of a five-person committee to "inspect the books and examine the proceedings" of the Second Bank of the United States. Serving on the committee with Spencer was John Tyler, a House member from Virginia and a future President of the United States.

Spencer drafted the committee's report, which was critical of the bank's operations but not the principles on which the bank was based. It should be noted, however, that staunch bank supporters called the report "exceedingly weak and in places incomprehensible."

Spencer was nominated by the Governor DeWitt Clinton faction in New York for a seat in the U.S. Senate while still a member of the House. The state legislature, however, which in that period elected Senators, chose someone else. He then served in the state General Assembly and later in the state Senate. In 1827, Clinton named Spencer to a committee of three to revise the state statutes. This was accomplished by 1829, and the work has been praised by many jurists. He became a member of the Anti-Masonic Party and in 1829 served as the special prosecuting officer in a famous abduction case. His actions in the case caused someone to attempt to assassinate him, but he persisted in the investigation. Eventually, the case was dropped because of a lack of funds.

Spencer joined the Whig Party and became the Secretary of State for New York in 1839. He was serving in this position in September 1841 when President Tyler sought replacements for Cabinet members who had resigned because of the President's veto of two bank bills. Spencer became Secretary of War on October 12, 1841. Tyler's ability to attract competent people to Cabinet positions was questioned, but critics conceded he appointed able and intelligent people. Spencer remained in this position until Walter Forward resigned as Secretary of the Treasury. Tyler nominated Caleb Cushing of Pennsylvania for this position, but the Senate refused confirmation. Tyler then named Spencer, whom the Senate confirmed. Spencer took office March 8, 1843. The President chose James Madison Porter, a Democrat from Pennsylvania, to replace Spencer as Secretary of War, but the Senate refused to confirm this appointment.

Spencer served Tyler loyally in the Treasury Department, but contemporaries noted that their friendship was cooling. There were several reasons for this. The issues of the Civil War were coming to the fore, and Tyler showed a preference for Southerners in his Cabinet. The North versus South or slavery issue arose over the proposed annexation of Texas, which would add two slave state Senators to Congress. Spencer opposed the President on this issue and said he thought it would lead to war with Mexico. Spencer was uncomfortable with the patronage or "spoils" approach to the appointment of collectors of custom duties and other government employees. Tyler had criticized this system when President Jackson began to use it, but he now directed that this policy be applied. Tyler adopted this system because he had been dismissed from the Whig Party and wanted to develop an organization for the 1844 election.

A break between Tyler and Spencer did not occur quickly. In January 1844 Tyler nominated Spencer to fill a vacancy on the Supreme Court. This may be evidence of continued confidence in Spencer, or it may have been a move to kick him upstairs and thus remove him from the Cabinet, as some contemporaries suspected. In any case, the Senate refused to confirm the nomination, as it did for many of Tyler's appointees.

The immediate cause of Spencer's resignation occurred when Tyler asked him to deposit secret service funds with a confidential agent in New York for possible use in an expedition against Mexico. Spencer believed this was illegal and resigned on May 2, 1844.

Spencer may have had a personal reason for leaving the Cabinet. In 1842 Spencer's son Philip was an Acting Midshipman on the U.S. brig *Somers*. The captain of the brig, Alexander S. Mackenzie, found Philip Spencer guilty of attempted mutiny while in foreign waters and ordered him executed. Upon arrival in a domestic port, a naval court was convened, the case was investigated, and Captain Mackenzie was acquitted of wrongdoing. Spencer urged the President to set aside the verdict and order a new trial, but Tyler said "he could do nothing but approve the sentence." This may have given Spencer a lasting grievance.

After resigning, Spencer returned to private life and the practice of law. His last famous case was the successful defense in 1853 of Dr. Eliphalet Nott, the President of Union College, against a charge of misappropriating college funds.

Spencer died on May 17, 1855, in Albany, New York.

BIBLIOGRAPHY

Chitwood, Oliver Perry. *John Tyler, Champion of the Old South*. New York: D. Appleton Century Company, 1939.

Cleanes, Freeman. *Old Tippecanoe*. New York: Charles Scribner's Sons, 1939.

Sause, George G. *Money, Banking and Economic Activity*. Boston: D. C. Heath, 1966, chap. 8.

Seager, Robert, II. *And Tyler Too*. New York: McGraw-Hill, 1963.

Whitney, David C. *The American Presidents*. New York: Doubleday & Company, 1967.

Wise, Henry A. *Seven Decades of the Union*. Philadelphia: J. B. Lippincott & Co., 1871.

GEORGE G. SAUSE

T

ROGER B. TANEY (March 17, 1777–October 12, 1864). Better known as the distinguished fifth Chief Justice of the United States, Roger Brooke Taney served the administration of President Andrew Jackson as Attorney General, Acting Secretary of War, and Secretary of the Treasury, a distinguished career. In each of these positions, Taney proved to be an unwavering supporter of the Jacksonian presidency, particularly in Jackson's efforts to destroy the Second Bank of the United States. Serving as a recess appointee as Secretary of the Treasury, Taney implemented Jackson's plan to withdraw federal deposit funds from the bank and, thus, effectively destroy it.

Taney was born on March 17, 1777, on the family tobacco plantation in Calvert County, Maryland. Both his father Michael and his mother Monica (Brooke) were descendants of wealthy planter families. Roger was educated by a tutor, then in the local schools before attending Dickinson College in Carlisle, Pennsylvania, in 1792, at age fifteen. After graduation as class valedictorian in 1795, he read law in the office of Judge Jeremiah Chase, in Annapolis, Maryland, and was admitted to the Maryland bar in 1799.

Taney's political career began with his election to the Maryland legislature in 1799 as the representative of Calvert County. A member of the Federalist Party, he served but one year before being defeated in the anti-Federalist tide of the Jeffersonian presidential victory of 1800. One year after his defeat, Taney moved to Frederick, Maryland, as his political opponents were claiming that he had been laughed out of town for being an aristocrat.

In 1806 Taney married Anne P. C. Key, daughter of a well-to-do farmer, John Ross Key, and the sister of Francis Scott Key. They had six daughters, and a son who died in infancy. Despite continuing poor health, Taney established a profitable law practice and became a community leader in Frederick.

Overcoming his defeat in the election of 1800, Taney continued to be active, becoming prominent in Federalist state politics. In 1812 he split with the Federalist leadership over their lack of support of the federal government's conduct of the war with Great Britain. The faction supporting the war became known as the "Coodies"; as its leader, Taney was known as "King Coody." By 1816 the Coodies had gained enough influence that Taney was elected to a five-year term to the Maryland Senate by a lower house that was controlled by supporters of Taney.

In 1823 Taney moved to Annapolis to better position himself for professional and political opportunities. After his move, Taney received recognition as one of the more prominent lawyers in the state and built a very profitable law practice to support a growing family. As a lawyer, Taney was known as a master of the "technicalities of procedure."

With the collapse of the Federalist Party, Taney supported Andrew Jackson in the 1824 election. In 1827 Taney was elected Attorney General for Maryland, and when the National Democratic Party was organized to bring about Jackson's election in 1828, Taney was made Chairman of the Jackson Central Committee for his state. While Taney was not considered for a Cabinet position at the beginning of the Jackson administration, his strong advocacy of Jackson's spoils system of political appointments in Maryland drew the Jackson administration's attention.

When President Jackson reorganized his Cabinet in 1831 after the Eaton Affair, an apparent affront of Washington morality by the Secretary of War, Eaton, and his marriage to Peggy Timberlake, Taney accepted a recess appointment as Attorney General. He was confirmed by the Senate and took the oath of office on July 20. He also served for a short period of time as the Acting Secretary of War.

Taney brought to the Cabinet a respect and regard for the division of power between the federal and state governments and held this belief throughout his career. More important, perhaps, was that Taney's political philosophy closely matched that of President Jackson, and he was able to loyally, and enthusiastically, support Jackson's policies during Jackson's political life.

Taney also brought to the Cabinet an interest in banking and currency that had been developed during his legal and political career in Maryland. He was a Director of a branch of a state bank in Frederick from 1810 to 1815. In 1818 he successfully sponsored a bill to charter the Frederick County Bank, and served as a Director from 1818 to 1823. As a state Senator, he introduced legislation to prevent the circulation of bank notes at less than face value and to prevent the depreciation of the value of the notes of rural banks. It appears that in Taney's world legislative dictums were able to usurp economic laws.

His position on the subject of the Second Bank of the United States, an anathema to Jackson, appears to have changed from support in the 1810s to opposition a decade later. In 1816, he lobbied for the rechartering of the bank, and during the financial troubles of 1819, he again gave his support by voting against a bill to tax the notes of the bank's Baltimore branch. (This legislation did pass but was later struck down in the Supreme Court's important *McCulloch v. Maryland* decision.) During the 1820s Taney reversed his position on the bank. Successfully serving as an attorney in a suit brought against the bank for unethical practices, the disclosure of fraud and speculation by its officers caused him to reverse his attitude toward the bank.

When he entered the Cabinet, Taney informed Jackson that he believed that for the Second Bank to be rechartered there must be defined limits placed on its power. In 1832, when Congress passed legislation rechartering the bank prior to its 1936 charter expiration, Jackson vetoed the bill, and Taney was instrumental in writing the final draft of Jackson's now-famous veto message. The text combined a legal argument along with a sweeping political statement on the rights and duty of a President to veto legislation that he believed to be harmful to the nation, and not just unconstitutional, as had been the case of Jackson's predecessors.

The attempt at rechartering the Second Bank in 1832 further convinced Jackson that the bank was an institution that could not remain. Its head had to be severed; it had to be destroyed. He intended to accomplish this by placing government revenues in state banks and depriving the bank of its main source of deposits.

During the May 1833 Cabinet shakeup, Taney remained as Attorney General, although he appeared to be the strongest candidate to replace Louis McLane as Secretary of the Treasury. For a variety of political and personal reasons, Jackson selected William J. Duane of Pennsylvania as his new Treasury Secretary. Taney still remained on as one of Jackson's closest advisers on the issue of the bank. For example, when Jackson decided to move ahead with his plan to deposit federal funds in state banks and remove federal deposits from the bank, Taney wrote the final draft of the position paper that Jackson presented to his Cabinet as the rationale for his actions.

The withdrawal of government funds from the bank could only have been accomplished by the Secretary of the Treasury. Duane, the newly appointed Secretary of the Treasury, refused to carry out Jackson's orders to begin the state deposit process. Jackson removed him from office. With the Treasury's office again vacant, Jackson turned to his trusted and competent political ally, Roger Taney, for a recess appointment as Secretary of the Treasury, an office he held from September 23, 1833, to June 23, 1834.

Jackson once described Taney as a towering legal intellect. He has also been described as energetic, but taciturn, lacking a ready wit, but of balanced judgment. This scrawny, sharp-nosed, nearsighted, stooped, highly able individual walked the halls with a dour expression, continually enveloped in clouds of cigar smoke and displaying an unshakable loyalty toward Jackson.

With Taney ensconced as Secretary, the President rapidly moved to implement his program that would effectively end the power of the bank, through his scheme of deposit banking. On September 25, 1833, Taney issued an order that officially announced the government's policy to change its deposits regime from national to deposit banking beginning on October 1, 1833. Under this plan, Taney placed government deposits in selected state banks, commonly known as "pet banks," and withdrew funds from the Second Bank of the United States to meet ongoing government expenses. In this manner, the Second Bank would be depleted of U.S. government deposits in rapid order.

Taney began the deposit system with seven banks that had been selected prior to the new deposit plan's implementation, but this number quickly expanded to some twenty banks and by 1836 had reached thirty-three. Taney shepherded the pets safely through the Biddle Panic of the winter of 1834–1835. (In an attempt to restore the old system of deposits at the Second Bank, Biddle, the bank's President, began a process of calling in loans and contracting credit. This forced up short-term interest rates, which, in turn, brought commercial pressure on Jackson to restore the old system. However, credit was able to expand sufficiently under the new deposit banking system to deny Biddle his power play. More important was that this action proved the power of the Second Bank and validated Jackson's concerns about the institution. The action also lost Biddle any support he may have had among the business community.)

Taney's reputation, however, was slightly tarnished in his creation of pet banks. One of these new deposit banks was the Union Bank of Maryland. When it was disclosed that Taney owned stock as well as having been employed as an attorney by the bank, charges of conflict of interest were raised.

When Congress reconvened in December 1833, Taney issued a report to the Senate where he presented a justification for the removal of government funds from the Second Bank. On February 5, 1834, Taney's report was rejected by the Senate, and on March 28, Congress voted to censure Jackson for assuming "powers and authority not conferred by the constitution." Once again, Jackson turned to Taney to write a rebuttal. Known as the "Protest," this document takes the position that the custody of all public property, including public monies, is the responsibility of the executive branch of the government. The document further argued that it was the duty of the Secretary of the Treasury to transfer public funds whenever sufficient reason was demonstrated. Jackson, arguing in the position paper, went on to declare that he had determined that there was sufficient cause to remove the funds and that it was his duty to appoint a Secretary of the Treasury who shared the same views as he did. Jackson claimed that the President alone was a direct representative of the American people and that executive department Secretaries were subordinate to him.

As Taney was serving only as a recess appointment, Jackson had to submit his name for confirmation by the Senate before Congress ended its session on June 30, 1834. Due to the hostile political climate, Jackson delayed in submitting Taney's and other recess appointments' names until the conclusion of the congressional session. Finally, on June 23, Jackson submitted Taney for confirmation. The strong anti-Jackson mood in Congress was not to be denied. Rejected by Congress, Taney resigned immediately. Jackson then appointed McClinton Young, the chief clerk of the department, as Acting Secretary. Jackson again moved quickly to appoint Taney's successor and on June 29, 1834, submitted the name of Levi Woodbury, the then–Secretary of the Navy. Woodbury was confirmed unanimously, taking office on July 1, 1834.

After his resignation, Taney returned to his private law practice in Maryland. Jackson, meanwhile, waited for a change in the political climate as well as for an appropriate position to reward his supporter and adviser. The Democratic gains in the 1834 election provided Jackson sufficient supporters in the Senate to confer Jackson's appointees.

When Justice Gabriel Duvall of the U.S. Supreme Court resigned in 1835, Jackson nominated Taney for the position. However, it was not to be too easy to get Taney to the Court, as Daniel Webster spoke up against Taney, and the Senate decided to indefinitely postpone its decision, effectively rejecting Taney. However, with John Marshall's death on July 4, 1835, Jackson was given another opportunity to offer Taney's name to the Senate. This time, by a twenty-nine to fifteen vote, the Senate confirmed Taney's appointment.

Taney was a controversial appointment. The Whigs' opposition continued in their attacks on Taney, claiming that his political connections would prejudice his judicial decisions. Indeed, Taney maintained his ties with both the Maryland Democrats and the President. He continued to advise Jackson and was the major author of Jackson's farewell address.

Taney, who was also the first Roman Catholic to sit on the Court, had many political enemies, and his performance as Chief Justice of the Court did little to distill the vitriolic condemnation by his opponents.

Taney introduced several changes in the operation of the Court. One minor change was the wearing of trousers instead of knee breeches under the judicial robes. A major change was the way the Court issued opinions. Taney's Chief Justice predecessors had delivered most decisions in order to give the appearance of a unified Court. Taney changed that procedure by assigning the writing of many important decisions to associate judges—a practice that continues today.

Taney's tenure as Chief Justice of the U.S. Supreme Court was controversial, rivaling his time as Secretary of the Treasury. Taney was indeed a distinguished Justice, but his reputation as a jurist has been clouded by his reactionary opinion in the *Dred Scott* case of 1857. In attempting to issue a definitive ruling on the legality of slavery, Taney sought an argument that would save the nation from the sectional strife that was tearing it apart. In his decision, Taney asserted that the framers of the Constitution considered slaves so inferior that they possessed no legal rights and could have no standing in federal courts. His decision only inflamed the issue and brought Taney public condemnation.

Taney died in office on October 12, 1864. Unfortunately, his loyalty to Jackson, his part in ending the reign of the Second National Bank of the United States, and his refinement of American constitutional law are often overlooked due to his flawed attempt to resolve a major problem that rendered the American nation into warring halves.

BIBLIOGRAPHY

Bray, Hammond. *Banks and Politics in America*. Princeton, NJ: Princeton University Press, 1957.

Lewis, Walker. *Without Fear or Favor: A Biography of Chief Justice Roger Brooke Taney*. Boston: Houghton Mifflin, 1965.

Marshall, Lynn L. "The Authorship of Jackson's Bank Veto Message." *Mississippi Valley Historical Review* 50, no. 3 (1963): 466–77.

Remini, Roger V. *Andrew Jackson and the Course of American Democracy, 1833–1845*. New York: Harper and Row, 1984.

Tyler, Samuel. *Memoir of Roger Brooke Taney, LL.D., Chief Justice of the Supreme Court of the United States*. Baltimore: J. Murphy and Co., 1872.

RONALD ROBBINS and BERNARD S. KATZ

PHILIP F. THOMAS (September 12, 1810–October 2, 1890). Philip Francis Thomas served as James Buchanan's Treasury Secretary for one month during the precarious period immediately preceding the American Civil War, from December 12, 1860, to January 14, 1861. On November 6, 1860, Abraham Lincoln defeated Stephen Douglas and was elected the sixteenth President of the United States. For the next four months, until Lincoln's inauguration in early March 1861, lame-duck President Buchanan and his Cabinet struggled to hold the Southern states in the Union and keep the federal government financially solvent. Since his election in 1856, Buchanan, supported by his Cabinet, had maintained an uneasy truce between Northern and Southern interests by adopting a political position that has been interpreted by most historians as sympathetic to the Southern cause. The Buchanan administration supported strict enforcement of the fugitive slave laws and championed the faction that favored the extension of slavery into the territory of Kansas.

With the election of Lincoln, the truce was ended and the Southern leadership realized it had lost the uncritical support of the federal government. Led by South Carolina, several of the so-called cotton states began the formal process of withdrawing from the Union. As the conflict deepened, Buchanan's once-united Cabinet divided along regional lines. The first Southern Cabinet member to resign was Treasury Secretary Howell Cobb, one of Buchanan's best-loved and most trusted advisers. After breaking his ties to the administration in early December, Cobb returned to his native Georgia to lead the state out of the Union.

Buchanan turned to his Commissioner of Patents, Philip Francis Thomas, a career Democrat and former Governor of Maryland, to become his new Treasury Secretary. At the time, many observers questioned the wisdom of Thomas's appointment. The country needed a Treasury Secretary who could demonstrate strong fiscal leadership. He would first be required to restore order to the Treasury function. The federal Treasury was, for all practical purposes, empty in the early days of December 1860. The fiscal situation had deteriorated so badly that some members of Congress were unable to draw their salaries.

To obtain the funds necessary to cover the government's deficit and meet impending interest payments on the outstanding debt, the new Treasury Secretary would immediately have to borrow large sums in the New York City money market. The financing would be impossible unless he had the complete confidence of potential investors in government securities. Finally, the Secretary would have to be prepared to defend the Treasury's property and the right to collect customs revenue in the seceding states. These tasks represented a formidable challenge to the incoming Thomas. To what degree had Thomas's ability and previous experiences prepared him to meet this challenge?

Philip Francis Thomas was born on September 12, 1810, in Easton, Talbot County, Maryland. He was the son of Dr. Tristan and Maria (Francis) Thomas. Talbot County is located on Maryland's old Eastern Shore, and the Thomas family had been prominent in the area since 1666. Described as a high-spirited youth, Philip attended the Easton Academy and then Dickenson College in Carlisle, Pennsylvania—Buchanan's alma mater. After leaving Dickenson in 1830, he read law under William Haywood and was admitted to the Maryland bar in 1831. On February 5, 1835, he married Sarah Maria Kerr.

After admission to the bar, Thomas practiced law in Easton and took an immediate interest in Maryland politics. The young Thomas appeared to be an independent thinker and did not hesitate to take positions that challenged the Easton political establishment. Rebelling against his family's Federalist/Whig tradition, he became active in promoting Jacksonian Democracy. In 1836, when he was a delegate to the Maryland Constitutional Convention, he supported reapportionment, a highly controversial measure in Talbot County. Thomas was eager to hold elected office. In 1834, at age twenty-four, he ran for the state legislature but was defeated. He ran again in 1836 and 1837, also unsuccessfully. In spite of these early political failures, Thomas persisted and in 1838 was finally elected to the Maryland House of Delegates in a close election.

Later that year Thomas was elected to the 26th Congress of the United States, defeating James Alfred Pearce. He served in the House of Representatives from 1839 to 1841. After serving only one term in the House, he declined renomination for personal reasons.

Thomas returned to Maryland where he continued the practice of law and remained active in the service of the state. In 1841 he accepted a judgeship in the Land Office Court of the Eastern Shore of Maryland. He was twice more elected to the Maryland legislature, first in 1843 and again in 1845. He was elected Governor of Maryland in 1848 and served one three-year term. After leaving the governorship in 1851, Thomas served briefly as Maryland's first State Comptroller.

In 1852 the Democrats recaptured the presidency, and Franklin Pierce offered Thomas several positions in his administration. Thomas rejected the Navy portfolio as not sufficiently lucrative but was persuaded to accept a position as Collector of the Port of Baltimore. When James Buchanan was elected in 1856, he offered Thomas the governorship of the Utah Territory. The outbreak of the Mormon War, however, made the appointment unattractive, and Thomas declined the position. He retired to private life and the practice of law until February 1860 when Buchanan appointed him Commissioner of Patents, where he served under Interior Secretary Jacob Thompson. Thomas, by his own account, enjoyed his responsibilities in the Patent Office. One of the more interesting patent applications to come before Commissioner Thomas was Elias Howe's application for an extension of his sewing machine patent first granted in 1846. Contemporary accounts indicate the Patent Office was operated in a productive and efficient manner.

After serving as Patent Commissioner for less than a year, however, Thomas was tendered the Treasury Secretaryship in December 1860. Thomas, who had been happy as Commissioner of Patents, was reluctant to accept the position when it was offered, and Jacob Thompson, Secretary of the Interior from Mississippi, had to persuade him to become Treasury Secretary. Thomas recalled he would much rather have remained in the Patent Office. One can hardly blame him for his lack of enthusiasm regarding the appointment—in his own words, the Treasury was in sorry shape.

Although Thomas was well regarded in his home state of Maryland, he was not known nationally at the time of his appointment. When it became apparent that Cobb would resign, rumors about his replacement began to circulate. When word of Thomas's appointment finally reached the public, the announcement was greeted with a mixture of surprise and puzzlement. Even Thomas himself did not expect the appointment. Many observers questioned his qualifications, and few predicted success in the position. Two weak points were immediately identified—his lack of experience in finance and his potential Southern sympathies. Despite these drawbacks, his nomination was quickly confirmed by the Senate, and Thomas assumed office on December 12, 1860.

The political and economic challenges facing Cobb's replacement were formidable: Cobb had left his successor with an empty national Treasury, mounting financial obligations that included an immediate interest payment on the government debt, and a fragile financial market. The reluctant Thomas was being called upon to rescue a fiscal strategy gone astray. The *Annual Report of the Secretary of the Treasury* issued by Cobb in December 1860 indicated that the Treasury would have to raise an additional $10 million to cover the government deficit as well as to meet payments on the outstanding debt for the remainder of the fiscal year. Soon after the report was published, Cobb resigned.

As it was no longer possible for the government to float long-term debt, Congress authorized an additional $10 million of Treasury notes. The task of meeting these obligations and raising the necessary funds fell to the newly appointed Thomas. Thomas preferred what appeared to be the fiscally conservative route and advertised for only $5 million of the authorization, postponing the remainder until interest rates fell. At Buchanan's request, however, he subsequently advertised for the additional $5 million.

Buchanan tended to underplay the importance of the financial difficulties, believing instead that both the currency and the economy were basically sound and referring to the additional financing as small necessary loans. However, the "small loan" proved impossible to finance. The Treasury received bids for only $1,831,000 at acceptable rates. Although Robert Cisco, head of the New York Sub-Treasury, negotiated an agreement to raise the remainder through a consortium of New York City banks, the arrangement fell through reportedly because the bankers lacked confidence in Thomas's loyalty to the Union.

To what extent were the bankers' fears justified? Thomas's native Maryland technically was a slave state, and agitation for a state convention to consider the question of secession was widespread. Although Thomas supported the nullification doctrine and the right of a state to withdraw from the Union, he felt, at least initially, that this belief did not prevent him from conscientiously performing his duties as Secretary. He reasoned that as long as a person was acting as an agent of the Union, he must faithfully carry out his duties. Nonetheless, New York bankers remained suspicious of Thomas's intentions. Many investors refused to lend to the government while he was in charge of the Treasury and asked for his resignation. Thomas was clearly hurt by the lack of confidence in his honor.

Within a month of assuming office, Thomas resigned as Treasury Secretary. The reason given at the time and repeated by Buchanan in his history of the administration was that Thomas maintained a difference of opinion from the President and a majority of the Cabinet in regard to the measures that had been adopted against South Carolina and the purpose of the President to enforce the collection of customs at the port of Charleston. However, Thomas did later assert that the loan was the real reason (the direct cause) for his resignation.

Thomas's resignation had a strong, symbolic meaning to the nation. Thomas was considered the last of the secessionists in the Cabinet, and his resignation restored unity to the body and a large measure of confidence to the financial markets.

During the war, Thomas practiced law in Easton. Although Maryland elected to remain in the Union, Thomas's sympathies continued to lean toward the Confederate states, and his only son fought in the Confederate Army. Thomas's loyalty to the Southern cause, however, earned him the animosity of many Northerners. After being appointed Senator from Maryland in 1866, he was denied his seat on grounds of disloyalty because he had supplied his son with clothing and money during the war.

Despite this disappointment, Thomas persevered and was able to continue his political career in Maryland—initially as a member of the Maryland House of Delegates and subsequently in the United States Congress. He was elected to the Maryland legislature in 1866 and to the 44th Congress in 1874. After serving one term in the House of Representatives, he ran again, unsuccessfully, for the Senate. He continued to serve in the Maryland House of Delegates from 1878 to 1883 and resumed the practice of law in Easton.

Thomas's first wife died in 1870, and in May 1876 he remarried to Clintonia (Wright) May. Philip Francis Thomas died in Baltimore on October 2, 1890, at the age of eighty and is buried in Spring Hill Cemetery in Easton, Maryland. Thomas had thirteen children and was survived by three daughters.

BIBLIOGRAPHY

Auchampaugh, Philip Gerald. *James Buchanan and His Cabinet on the Eve of Secession*. Boston: J. S. Canner and Company, 1926.

Baker, Jean H. *The Politics of Continuity: Maryland Political Parties from 1858 to 1870*. Baltimore: Johns Hopkins University Press, 1973.

Buchanan, James. *Mr. Buchanan's Administration on the Eve of Rebellion*. New York: D. Appleton and Company, 1865.

Buchholz, Heinrich Ewald. *Governors of Maryland: From the Revolution to the Year 1908*. Baltimore: Williams & Wilkins Company, 1908.

Klein, Philip Shriver. *President James Buchanan: A Biography*. University Park: Pennsylvania State University Press, 1962.

Myers, Margaret G. *A Financial History of the United States*. New York: Columbia University Press, 1970.

Smith, Elbert B. *The Presidency of James Buchanan*. Lawrence: University Press of Kansas, 1975.

Studenski, Paul, and Herman E. Kroos. *Financial History of the United States*. New York: McGraw-Hill Book Company, 1963.

MARIE McCKINNEY

V

FREDERICK M. VINSON (January 22, 1890–September 8, 1953). Frederick Moore Vinson was born on January 22, 1890, in the Lawrence County Jail in Louisa, Kentucky, a fact he made frequent reference to during his service in all three branches of the federal government of the United States. The second son of Jim and Virginia Vinson, his avid interest in public service was inspired by his father. During Fred's childhood, Jim Vinson was successively elected the jailer and the town marshall of Louisa. Vinson's early years were marked by a familiarity with courtrooms, judges, and the law, as he regularly accompanied his father to the hearings of the circuit court (Hatcher, 288–91).

When Fred Vinson was five years old, his grandfather was murdered while transacting business in the nearby town of Catlettburg. Jim Vinson devoted the succeeding seven years in single-minded commitment to the apprehension, trial, and conviction of his father's murderers. Due to his father's frequent absences from his home, Fred Vinson spent much of this time under his mother's tutelage.

Virginia Vinson encouraged her son's interest in school and reading while "silently enduring his passion for baseball" (Hatcher, 298). In 1905, Fred enrolled in Kentucky Normal College. His tenure there was not pleasant. He was unpopular among his classmates and teachers and gained a reputation as an arrogant and overbearing student. After two years he transferred to Centre College; his academic record at Kentucky Normal was impressive enough for him to be admitted with senior status. Centre was a much more comfortable environment, and "Vin" became one of its most popular and successful students. This newly acquired ability to get along well with others stood him in good stead for the rest of his life; he later noted, "I never did fall out with anyone who didn't agree with me" ("The Great Persuader," 28). He graduated in 1909, winning a prestigious Alumni Prize for his accomplishments.

Thereafter, he matriculated at Centre Law School, earning a law degree in 1911. After a brief flirtation with professional baseball, Vinson returned to Louisa to begin private practice as a lawyer. Two years later he was appointed City Attorney. A short stint in the Army, spent mostly in Officer Training School, was followed by a few years' service as the commonwealth attorney for his district in Kentucky ("Available Vinson," 18).

Vinson was first elected to Congress in 1924 in a special election to fill a vacancy caused by the election of the incumbent as Governor ("Chief Justice Vinson," 1:2). He served a total of twelve terms in Congress, being regularly reelected with a single exception: In 1928 Vinson had supported Al Smith's campaign as Democratic presidential candidate and lost his seat in the Hoover landslide. Between 1924 and 1928 he served on the Appropriations Committee and distinguished himself by his demonstrated expertise in legal and tax matters.

Appointed to the House Ways and Means Committee in 1931, he served as the Chairman of its powerful tax subcommittee from 1933 to 1938. He ably shepherded New Deal legislation desired by Franklin D. Roosevelt, openly disagreeing with the President on only two occasions. In 1933 he opposed Roosevelt's Economy Bill on the grounds that it did an injustice to veterans. Similarly, in 1936 he favored the Veteran's Bonus Bill despite the President's opposition ("Available Vinson," 18). His most significant achievements on the Ways and Means Committee were the enactment of the undistributed profits tax of 1936 and the Revenue Act of 1938. The former was vigorously opposed by the business community, and its passage stands as testament to Vinson's political skills; the latter entailed a heated battle in the Senate and was an attempt to correct inequities in the tax system while increasing revenues.

Appointed an Associate Justice of the U.S. Court of Appeals in Washington, D.C., in 1938, Vinson moved swiftly through a succession of important posts during World War II. He acted as Chief Judge of the U.S. Emergency Court of Appeals beginning in 1942. This court provided judicial review of the decisions of the Office of Price Administration. He was responsible for holding the line on price and wage increases as the Director of Economic Stabilization in 1943. In the following year he became Vice Chairman of the U.S. delegation to the United Nations Monetary and Financial Conference at Bretton Woods, working tirelessly to wring agreement from the forty-four countries represented. He next headed the Federal Loan Administration and then became Director of War Mobilization and Reconversion. In July 1945, he was nominated and unanimously confirmed to be Secretary of the Treasury, a post he held from July 23, 1945, to June 23, 1946, before being appointed Chief Justice of the Supreme Court.

Secretary of the Treasury Vinson advised the President on domestic monetary and fiscal policies while engaging in the negotiations associated with the postwar loan to Britain and heading the National Advisory Council on International Monetary and Financial Problems.

A Southern Democrat, Vinson was conservative on economic matters; he favored balanced budgets and free enterprise. Although acknowledging the need for discretionary fiscal policy to combat inflation and ensure full employment, he was well aware of the dangers of excessive government intervention. "National economic policies must not be allowed to develop into regimentation of business, or labor, or agriculture, or of the people" ("Vinson as Treasurer," 12:1). Thus, he endorsed the Full Employment Bill in principle but argued that "such a bill should limit itself to providing the machinery to be followed to assist in arriving at national policy and full employment, rather than attempting to specify in advance measures to be used to meet future conditions" ("Man at the Head," 19). He preferred leaving such measures to the discretion of the President.

This same conservative perspective is revealed in Vinson's view of taxation. He argued that the tax system should avoid harm to the expansion of business investment and production. Thus, the Revenue Act of 1945, designed and championed by Vinson, reduced direct and indirect taxes. This act eliminated the "normal tax" (thus exempting 12 million taxpayers) and reduced the income surtax on individuals, decreased the corporate surtax, repealed the excess profits tax, and lowered many excise taxes (*U.S. Statutes at Large*, 566–97).

In promoting this tax reduction package, Vinson pointed to the mixture of inflationary and deflationary signals in the economy. Reduced federal expenditures, unemployment, and downgrading would depress the economy, while pent-up demand for capital and consumer goods and the government budget deficit would inflate it. Nevertheless, Vinson was optimistic. He argued that this tax measure was intended to provide the maximum aid and stimulus to reconversion and expansion compatible with the revenue needs of the government (Bernstein and Matusow, 51).

The final bill granted an estimated $700 million more in tax relief than Vinson had proposed and deeply disappointed Truman, who feared that it left the budget too unbalanced. "But as later events revealed, pessimistic forecasts of dwindling consumer demand proved grossly mistaken, and Vinson's policy was wiser than many economists would have judged in the early autumn of 1945" (Bernstein, 64).

In the succeeding months, Vinson preferred moral suasion to an interest rate increase for absorbing surplus consumer purchasing power. He pleaded for greater subscription to the Victory Loan as an anti-inflationary measure. He argued that continued low rates of interest would benefit businessmen, home buyers, and consumers and would permit a lower level of taxation. The Treasury was deeply concerned about the burden of public debt and did not endorse policies that would increase this burden. President Truman also opposed raising rates, remembering with disgust the decline in the price of the government bonds he held as a veteran of World War I.

Much to the dismay of the British government, Truman abruptly ended Lend-Lease operations with the Japanese surrender. The British sent a delegation to Washington headed by John Maynard Keynes and Lord Halifax to negotiate a loan. They wanted a $5 billion interest-free grant-in-aid or loan. The American delegation, led by Secretary Vinson and Assistant Secretary of State William L. Clayton, insisted the aid be a commercially viable arrangement and drove a hard bargain. "We loaded the British loan negotiations with all the conditions the traffic could bear," Clayton declared (Cochran, 192). The arrangement involved a $3.75 billion fifty-year loan at 2 percent interest with repayment to start after five years. The agreement provided for annual installment payments on principal and the waiver of interest payments in years when Britain was experiencing balance of payments difficulties. In addition, the loan agreement required that the British dismantle the Imperial Preference system and make the pound sterling freely convertible.

Vinson campaigned vigorously on behalf of the British loan. He argued that the alternative to the loan agreement would be continued restrictions on and discrimination in trade and currency transactions, the division of the world into rival blocs, and eventual economic warfare. On the other hand, ratification of the agreement would create greater production opportunities and enhanced income for American workers and was "not an expenditure but an investment. It is sound business for America" ("Vinson Campaigns," 13:4).

During his tenure as Treasury Secretary, Vinson chaired the National Advisory Council, a committee responsible for coordinating the government's credit policies. Whereas Vinson was concerned about the budgetary implications of foreign lending and Federal Reserve Board Chairman Mariner Eccles worried about its potential inflationary impact, Secretary of Commerce Henry A. Wallace argued in favor of liberal lending policies. The first report of the council reconciled these views by recommending that the bulk of the world's capital requirements be fulfilled by the International Bank for Reconstruction and Development. Since the International Bank would not be running smoothly until late 1946, the council urged Congress to authorize a maximum amount of $3.25 billion in loans for reconstruction by the Export Import Bank of the United States.

In May 1946, Vinson's name was mentioned in the press as the probable first President of the International Bank ("Vinson May Take World Bank Post," 1: 2). Instead, in the following month President Truman nominated him to be Chief Justice of the Supreme Court in the hope that he would use his skills to smooth over the wide and public disagreements among the justices ("Liberal Chief Justice," 71). He remained on the Court until his sudden death of a heart attack on September 8, 1953. He was survived by his widow Roberta Vinson and two sons, Fred M., Jr., and James Robert Vinson.

BIBLIOGRAPHY

"Available Vinson." Collier's, March 22, 1952, 18ff.

Bernstein, Barton J. "Charting a Course between Inflation and the Depression." Register of the Kentucky Historical Society 66 (1968): 53–64.

Bernstein, Barton J., and Allen J. Matusow, eds. The Truman Administration: A Documentary History. New York: Harper & Row, 1966.

"Chief Justice Vinson Dies of Heart Attack in Capital." New York Times, September 8, 1953, 1:2.

Cochran, Bert. Harry Truman and the Crisis Presidency. New York: Funk and Wagnalls, 1973.

"The Great Persuader." Newsweek, June 17, 1946, 28–29.

Hatcher, John Henry. "The Education of the Thirteenth United States Chief Justice: Frederick Moore Vinson." West Virginia History 39, no. 4 (1978): 285–323.

"Liberal Chief Justice." U.S. News, June 14, 1946, 70–73.

McCullough, David. *Truman*. New York: Simon and Schuster, 1992.
"The Man at the Head of the Treasury." *New York Times Magazine*, October 14, 1945, 18–19.
U.S. Statutes at Large. 79th Cong. 1st sess., 1945. Vol. 59, Part 1: *Public Laws*. Washington, D.C.: U.S. Government Printing Office, 1946.
"Vinson as Treasurer Faces Many New Tasks." *New York Times*, July 29, 1945, 12:1.
"Vinson Campaigns for British Loan." *New York Times*, January 10, 1946, 13:4.
"Vinson May Take World Bank Post." *New York Times*, May 28, 1946, 1:2.

VIBHA KAPURIA-FOREMAN

W

ROBERT J. WALKER (July 19, 1801–November 11, 1869). Robert J. Walker might be described as incongruent in that he did not fit the mold of what he appeared to be. Short (five foot two), slight (approximately 100 pounds), and sickly (some have described him as epileptic), Walker's lifestyle can be expressed as robust and profoundly diverse. Walker's occupations and avocations would eventually include lawyer, plantation owner, slaveholder, Senator, land speculator, railroad investor, Governor, bond salesman, and Secretary of the Treasury.

Robert John Walker was born on July 19, 1801, to Jonathan Hoge Walker and Lucretia (Duncan) Walker in Northumberland, Pennsylvania. After public and private schooling, he enrolled at the University of Pennsylvania and graduated at the top of his class in 1819. Walker studied law and was admitted to the bar in Pittsburgh in 1921. Early on, he displayed an affinity and aptitude for politics. Walker led the Allegheny County Republican delegation in supporting the candidacy of Andrew Jackson for President in 1824. In 1825, Robert Walker married Mary Bache, a great-granddaughter of Benjamin Franklin, who was to bear him eight children.

However, Walker selected to abandon his promising political and legal career in Pennsylvania in 1826 and join his brother in legal practice in Natchez, Mississippi. He soon caught the fever for land speculation that characterized the period of territorial expansion, investing heavily in western cropland. Consequently, his personal debts grew to several hundred thousand dollars. Although an ardent Jackson supporter, Walker did not become active in Mississippi politics until 1834, when he was selected by the Democrats to run for the U.S. Senate seat held by George Poindexter, a formidable opponent and a tenacious debater. Despite his diminutive stature and small, thin voice, Walker proved a vigorous campaigner and a worthy opponent in debate and carried the election.

Upon assuming office in February 1836, Walker quickly established himself as a champion of territorial expansion, state claims to newly acquired public lands, and squatters' rights to buy settled lands at a minimum price (preemption). Walker's appetite for territorial expansion was second to none. In essence, he characterized the concept of Manifest Destiny. Over his lifetime, Robert Walker would campaign for the acquisition of Texas, Cuba, Mexico, Alaska, and Nova Scotia.

In 1836, the Battle of San Jacinto effectively ended Texas' war for independence of Mexico. Citizens of the new Lone Star Republic sought annexation into the United States. Yet annexation was far from automatic because of the growing debate over the slavery issue. Due to its geographic positioning, it was assumed that Texas would be a slave state. Questions about the morality and legality of slavery were burgeoning in Congress like summer thunderheads.

President Tyler, who had succeeded William Henry Harrison in 1841, after the latter's death, sought the help of Senator Robert John Walker in pushing the Texas annexation issue through Congress. Walker, a Jacksonian, and thereby a proponent of minimalist government and westward expansion, was also a former slaveholder (it is reported that Walker freed his slaves in 1838). Tyler regarded Walker as being able to argue persuasively for annexation with both anti- and pro-slavery advocates. Indeed, though verbose and given to lengthy rather than short arguments, Walker was a skilled extemporaneous speaker as well as an artful negotiator. He enjoyed a deep reservoir of self-confidence, which facilitated his positive, cheery attitude in all matters of concern.

The fulcrum in Robert Walker's argument for annexation was a long letter to the *Washington Globe* entitled "Letter of Mr. Walker of Mississippi, Relative to the Annexation of Texas," published in 1844. Walker's treatise was essentially two-pronged: to allay the fears of Free-Soilers about the expansion of slavery and to raise public consciousness about the danger of growing British influence in an independent Texas.

In his letter to the *Globe*, Walker proposed that slavery was an issue that would eventually eliminate itself. Texas would provide a "safety valve" out of which the problems of slavery would be dissipated. Walker argued that slave-oriented agriculture tended to work land too intensively, leaching the soil's nutrients and continually requiring new lands to replace old, worn ground. Thus, Southern agriculture and slavery migrated west in search of new soils. Texas would provide a western terminus, where slaveholders, faced with the ultimate option of bankruptcy or freeing the slaves, would do the latter. The freed slaves, in turn, would choose to migrate south to Latin America where the climate, both meteorological and racial, was more benign. One of Walker's last functions in Congress was the crafting of a compromise piece of legislation that broke the logjam in the Senate and allowed for Texas' annexation into the Union.

In 1845, President Polk followed Tyler as President and was pressured by westerners to give Walker a key Cabinet post. Walker had acted as Democratic Campaign Chairman in helping Polk to defeat Martin Van Buren for the party's nomination. Appointed as Secretary of the Treasury, Robert Walker would prove a prodigious worker and a fountainhead of important legislation, holding office from March 8, 1845, to March 5, 1849. Under the Polk administration, the Cabinet served both as a sounding board and as a joint management team, in which each Cabinet Secretary could offer legislation in any bailiwick. James Polk and Robert Walker were kindred spirits in that both were westerners, expansionists, antiprotectionist in nature, and suspicious of large banking interests—particularly central banks.

Walker's most pressing assignment was to coordinate the financing of the Mexican War. In response to the annexation of Texas, Mexico had broken off diplomatic relations with the United States. When negotiations failed, war became inevitable. The U.S. victory was costly in terms of casualties, with nearly 13,000 Americans killed by action or disease, but it allowed for a huge acquisition of territory. The United States now stretched west to the Pacific and north to Canada. By all accounts, Walker handled the necessary Treasury war finance adroitly, acquiring the funds at relatively low interest rates. There was some question of cronyism, however, with federal acquisition funds parked too long in the accounts of favored financiers.

Walker's appetite for new territory exceeded James Polk's. He urged Polk to press for more Mexican territory than granted in the treaty of Guadelupe Hidalgo. He favored the acquisition of Cuba as well as the Yucatán. However, Walker was not one to ignore the less glamorous aspects of his job. He established a system for categorizing and warehousing imported goods that was to remain operative for some time. As one of his final acts as Secretary, he made public a study he had conducted of the relative efficiency of his warehousing system. Walker was instrumental in drawing up the bill that created the Department of the Interior in 1849, an addition that President Polk did not favor.

Walker's signature piece as Secretary of the Treasury was the passage of the Tariff Act of 1846, a bill that came to be known as the Walker Tariff. Walker and Polk were in concert in favoring a less restrictive, less protective (of favored industries) tariff. Polk's attitude toward the tariff was honed during fourteen years in Congress and the product of a Jeffersonian attitude that tariffs were injurious to labor and farmers and beneficial only to special interests. However, since tariffs provided the largest source of federal revenue, each tariff bill was a vital piece of legislation. The intent of the Tariff of 1846 was to lower rates while providing the minimum essential to fund government activity. Special interests, such as coal and iron industries, were no longer to receive special protection. In a contemporary perspective, with new sources of federal revenue, both Polk and Walker can be characterized as free traders and practitioners of laissez-faire economics.

The Walker Tariff was an ad valorem duty, imposed on broad categories of goods, rather than a system of good-specific excise taxes with a spectrum of rates. In formulating "his" tariff, Walker sought and gathered data from customs houses and importers, seeking to identify how responsive the flow of imports was to a particular level of tariff. If the reduction in imports of a good was greater than the relative price increase due to a higher tariff, then tariff revenue (and the U.S. government) would suffer. Walker's findings were accompanied by an extensive, detailed report to Congress. Therefore, more than any of its predecessor acts, the

Tariff of 1846 came to be regarded as a "scientific" tariff—a logical, economically inspired effort to maximize welfare while minimizing tax rates.

As originally drafted, the tariff proposed that goods be included in seven exclusive categories, each taxed at a different (ad valorem) rate. For instance, the first category included luxury items such as alcohol products, taxed at 75 percent of value. While the third category, raw materials, was taxed at 25 percent of value. While a tariff of 75 percent was certainly protective of the domestic spirits industry, it must again be noted that tariffs constituted, far and away, the largest source of federal operating revenues in 1846—as opposed to a percent or two today. The Walker Tariff was to remain law for eleven years, longer than any tariff measure during the nineteenth century.

A second, important item on Polk's domestic agenda was the Independent Treasury Bill, which became law almost concurrently with the tariff act. The issue of a Treasury divorced from the bank system (as well as its corollary, a central bank) had been a flash point during the Jackson and Van Buren administrations. The most recent efforts at an Independent Treasury had been repealed in 1841, with federal monies returned to state banks (characterized as "pet" banks, during the Jackson regime). Polk, Walker, and other neo-Jacksonians were of a mind in their preference for a hard money (specie-dominated) policy. Walker drafted the constitutional Treasury bill that cleared Congress with little difficulty.

Under the constitutional Treasury bill, government revenues would remain outside the bank system. The Treasury would sequester tax and other revenues in fireproof Treasury vaults, spending the monies as need be. Thus, the government would lend "soundness" to the money supply—whereas under a bank system, banks might use government monies as the base for speculative loans and an unwarranted expansion of the money supply.

Walker left Polk's Cabinet in 1849 but did not choose to reenter Mississippi politics. Rather, he selected to remain in Washington, D.C., while tending to his diverse business interests. Besides managing land speculations in Louisiana, Mississippi, and Wisconsin, Robert Walker found time to practice law before the Supreme Court, invest in a California mercury mine, and sell bonds of the Illinois Central Railroad in England.

Nonetheless, the magnet of politics did not release him. In 1853, Walker was offered, initially accepted, and eventually declined President Franklin Pierce's offer of the diplomatic mission in China. In 1856, James Buchanan, a fellow Cabinet member (Secretary of State) in the Polk administration, sought Walker's help in gaining the Democratic nomination for President. Upon attaining the presidency, Buchanan seriously considered Walker for his Secretary of State. However, Southern pro-slavery interests and Northern Democrats who viewed Walker's speculations and financier cronies rather dimly, successfully urged another choice on Buchanan.

However, Buchanan could not easily dismiss the needs that Walker's considerable skills might fulfill in his administration. In 1857, he offered Walker the governorship of Kansas Territory, a position filled by three different individuals during the Pierce years. The job would prove a thorn to any incumbent. Kansas was at the forefront of the growing slavery issue and the cynosure of media attention over whether it would be admitted to the Union as a slaveholding or a nonslaveholding state. Only a man supremely confident of his political acumen and one with larger political aspirations that might flourish under intense media scrutiny would consider accepting. Buchanan was relentless in importuning Walker to take the position. So it was with serious reservations (including those of his wife) that Robert Walker accepted the appointment as Governor of Kansas Territory in March 1857.

Walker's acceptance was subject to certain terms, to which President Buchanan agreed. Paramount among these conditions was that the administration fully support Walker in requiring the Kansas state constitution to be ratified by a fair vote of all the territorial residents. Prior to Walker's nomination, a territorial legislature had been elected in a fraudulent process where thousands of "Border Ruffians" crossed the Missouri border to vote. The legislature, in turn, enacted a slave code and set in motion the process for a state constitutional convention as a preamble to statehood. "Free-staters" refused to have anything to do with the legislative process and set up their own rump government in Topeka.

At the Lecompton constitutional convention, pro-slavery delegates drafted a constitution (which included the crux of Missouri's and Kentucky's slave codes) and did not include a provision for full document ratification by territorial residents. Walker knew that if the full document were presented to all voters, the great majority of whom were antislavery, the constitution would be defeated. Walker asked President Buchanan to support him in calling for full ratification as a condition for statehood.

Buchanan, however, had other concerns that seemed more pressing. Buchanan's support from Southern Democrats was eroding, as was their support for the Union, and he may have thought a compromise was in order to save the Union. Alternately, other biographers position Buchanan as a strict legalist. Therefore, since ratification of a state constitution was not mandated by U.S. law, he would not press for it. Regardless, Buchanan reneged on his covenant with Robert Walker in not supporting Walker's call for ratification of Kansas' constitution by all territorial residents. In 1858, Kansans would turn down the proposed state constitution, with its pro-slavery clauses, by a six-to-one margin.

Robert J. Walker, meanwhile, had no choice but to resign the governorship on December 15, 1857. Kansas would have its fifth Governor in four years. In a long, impassioned letter (he knew no other format) to Buchanan, Walker explained his feelings about the perpetrated electoral frauds in Kansas and the feelings of Kansans about the Lecompton constitution beyond the slavery issue. He noted that he could not remain as Governor while abandoning deeply held personal principles.

Following his resignation, Robert Walker returned to his law practice in Washington, D.C., and the management of his widespread investments. There was never any question that Walker, a transplanted Northerner, was an ardent Unionist. At the onset of the Civil War in 1861, he took to speaking at pro-Union rallies. In 1862, with F. P. Stanton, Walker became an owner of the *Continental Monthly*, a periodical that staunchly supported the Union cause. In 1863 and 1864, Walker acted as a revenue agent for the government, selling war bonds in Europe. Unsurprisingly, he was an extremely effective salesman and sold over $200 million in bonds. Walker was particularly welcome in England, where his record as Treasury Secretary and Governor stimulated bond sales. While in England, Walker also became a Union pamphleteer, tying the issue of slavery (an abomination to most British) to the rebellion and the likelihood of Confederate default on British loans.

Following the Civil War, Walker, acting in character, helped lobby the $7.2 million Alaska acquisition bill through Congress in 1867 and authored an article on the potential benefits of annexation to the United States for Nova Scotians. He maintained his Washington law practice, specializing in land claims law.

Long in ill health, Walker died in Washington on November 11, 1869. He was buried in Oak Hill Cemetery and was survived by five of his eight children.

BIBLIOGRAPHY

Bergeron, Paul H. *The Presidency of James K. Polk*. Lawrence: University of Kansas Press, 1987.

Dictionary of American Biography. New York: Charles Scribner's & Sons, 1936.

Merk, Frederick. *Fruits of Propaganda in the Tyler Administration*. Cambridge, MA: Harvard University Press, 1971.

Nevins, Allan. *Polk, the Diary of a President*. New York: Longmans, Green and Co., 1929.

———. *Ordeal of the Union*. Vol. 1. New York: Charles Scribner & Sons, 1947.

Sellers, Charles. *James K. Polk, Continentalist*. Princeton, NJ: Princeton University Press, 1966.

Stampp, Kenneth M. *America in 1857*. New York: Oxford University Press, 1990.

Vexler, Robert. *Vice Presidents and Cabinet Members*. Dobbs Ferry, NY: Oceana Publications, 1975.

JOHN A. SONDEY

WILLIAM WINDOM (May 10, 1827–January 29, 1891). William Windom, considered a favorite son of Minnesota, was actually born in Belmont County, Ohio, on May 10, 1827. He was the younger of two sons of Quaker pioneer settlers, Hezekiah and Mercy (Spencer) Windom. The family moved to Knox County, Ohio, in 1837 seeking more virgin territory. The Quaker philosophy instilled by his parents served as the foundation for Windom's political career and directed him throughout his life.

Windom received a formal education at Martinsburg Academy in Martinsburg, Ohio. He served as a tailor's apprentice in Frederickton, but to the dismay of his parents, Windom decided to study law. The family farm was mortgaged to cover much of the educational expense, with Windom working on the farm in the summer and teaching school at the academy in the winter. Studying with Judge R. C. Hurd of Mount Vernon, Ohio, he was admitted to the bar in 1850 at the age of twenty-three. Two years later in 1852 Windom was elected prosecuting attorney of Knox County on the Whig ticket.

Wanting a change, Windom moved to Winona, Minnesota, in 1855. He tried his hand at real estate and practiced with the law firm of Sargent, Wilson and Windom. He married Ellen P. Hatch of Warwick, Massachusetts, on August 20, 1856. The couple eventually had two daughters and a son.

Again entering politics as a Republican when Minnesota became a state in 1858, he served from March 4, 1859, until March 3, 1869, in the 36th through 40th Congresses.

Being appointed to the Committee on Public Lands gave Windom his first opportunity to debate in the House. In a speech given on March 14, 1860, concerning the Homestead Bill, Windom set the tone for his political career. In it he said: "A state is great, rich, and powerful not in proportion to the mass of wealth which it may accumulate in its treasury, but in proportion as the men who constitute it are prosperous, honest, brave, and happy. . . . [L]et every man who is willing to work have a homestead of his own" (Wright, 7, 10). Although Windom spoke eloquently, the Homestead Bill did not pass for another two years.

While serving in the House, Windom also served on the Committee of Thirty-three and also as the Chairman of the Committee on Indian Affairs for two terms. In 1865, while on the Committee on Indian Affairs, Windom chaired a special committee that conducted visits to the Indian tribes. He also headed another committee in 1867 conceived to investigate alleged misconduct of the Indian commissioner. Although Windom's attitude toward Indians was generally fair to those tribes he considered friendly, in 1862, following a Sioux outbreak in his own congressional district, Windom, along with other members of Congress, signed a memorial urging the President to have all the captured Indians hanged. Despite this harsh action, Windom did believe that aiding the Indians in becoming self-sufficient and less nomadic would be far less costly than war. "While I am not a defender of the Indian, still I believe there is not a civilized nation on the face of the earth which would treat the Indians as we have treated them" (Wright, 23, 27).

It was on the Indian issue in December 1868 that Windom and Garfield (who would later nominate Windom for Secretary of the Treasury) were on opposing sides. Garfield strongly supported transferring the Department of Indian Affairs from the Department of Interior to the War Department. Between 1866 and 1868, Indian outbreaks had been prevalent, causing difficulties with construction of the Pacific Railroad as well as tremendous suffering in the territory. The belief was that the corruption of Indian Bureau agents was largely responsible for these uprisings. Garfield argued that such a transfer would reduce the corruption and fraud present in the agents by turning authority over to the Army, which operated under a code of honor and military discipline. Windom argued that the cost of supervising Indian affairs would rise substantially.

Windom called it "a bill to massacre the Indians and deplete the Treasury" (Wright, 26). Garfield forced the measure through the House with a vote of 116 to 33, which angered Windom, who felt Garfield was meddling in Windom's committee's affairs. Although the Senate failed to pass the bill, Garfield attempted to get the measure passed by slipping the motion into Indian appropriations bills. "Garfield's persistence, sneered Windom, had made him the laughingstock of Congress" (Peskin, 298).

Windom made an unsuccessful bid for a Senate seat in 1865. However, he was appointed to the Senate on July 15, 1870, to fill a vacancy caused by the death of Daniel S. Norton. On January 22, 1871, O. P. Stearns was chosen to fill the remaining weeks, giving Windom the opportunity to be elected for a full six-year term from 1871 to 1877. He was reelected in 1877 but resigned on March 7, 1881, to accept the Cabinet position of Secretary of the Treasury under President Garfield.

While in the Senate, Windom served as Chairman of the Appropriations Committee (1876–1881) as well as the special Committee on Transportation Routes to the Seaboard. He was an advocate of federal railroad regulation, not as a hindrance to the railroad industry but as a way of guaranteeing the railroads a reasonable profit. In an 1874 report, Windom proposed a Bureau of Commerce. Thirteen years later, the Interstate Commerce Commission, with many similarities to Windom's bureau, was established.

As Chairman of the Committee on Transportation Routes to the Seaboard, Windom believed that agriculture represented a large portion of the country's wealth. As the country expanded westward, the problem of transporting crops to market at a reasonable cost to the farmer was exacerbated. Windom felt that it was the government's duty to establish commercial routes either on land or by waterway between the East and the West. One of the highlights of Windom's career occurred when he submitted a report to Congress advocating "competitive routes under governmental control, development of waterways, and the establishment of a bureau to collect and publish facts" (Malone, 383).

In 1881, Windom became Chairman of the Foreign Relations Committee. Windom was in favor of the United States building a canal across Nicaragua, although both the House and the Senate were deadlocked on the issue. When a French company proposed the Panama Canal, Windom, a strong nationalist, vowed on February 28, 1881, that "under no circumstances [should] a foreign government, or a company chartered by a foreign government, have control over an isthmian highway" (Malone, 383).

Windom was generally associated with sound money policies throughout his career. He had approved the plan to establish a National Banking System in 1863. He voted in 1873 to eliminate silver dollar coinage basically because it had not been in use for over forty years. This vote, along with an increased supply of both silver and gold, caused the price of silver to drop, resulting in loud protests from the silver-producing western states.

Five years later, Windom voted for the Bland-Allison Silver Purchase Act, which restored the silver dollar to full legal tender. Being a bimetallist, however, Windom disapproved of the devalued silver dollar that the Senate proposed to coin. Windom protested, "Any vote I shall give today will be at least with the hope that the silver dollar to be coined will be equal to the gold dollar" (Wright, 64).

At the Republican National Convention of 1880, Windom was nominated for the presidency. On the first ballot, he received the entire Minnesota delegation's ten votes. Ohio Senator James A. Garfield was not nominated until the second ballot, at which time he received only one vote. By the thirty-fifth ballot, Garfield's votes had increased to fifty, and on the thirty-sixth ballot, Garfield became the Republican "dark horse" nominee for President, winning out over the heavily favored Grant.

The selection of Garfield's Cabinet developed into a difficult task for the President-elect. Garfield set his sights on Windom for Secretary of the Treasury early on. This choice was approved by former Secretary John Sherman who characterized Windom as an honest man. However, James G. Blaine, the newly selected Secretary of State and a personal friend of Garfield, strongly opposed that decision. According to Blaine, "He's profoundly and absolutely ignorant of our finances except as Appropriation Bills teach—which is nothing and on the wrong side. Any darned . . . fool can spend money! [Windom] has the Presidential bee in his bonnet terribly, and would be looking to that all the time" (Peskin, 524). Blaine favored William B. Allison of Iowa and lobbied for him strongly. Although Garfield had misgivings about Allison, he eventually bowed to Blaine's pressure, and on the night before his inauguration on March 4, 1881, he offered Allison the position of Secretary of the Treasury. Allison accepted, and Garfield's Cabinet worries were over. However, the next morning, Allison emotionally declined the position due to his wife's poor health and the poor health of Iowa's political climate.

Garfield hurriedly offered the position to his first choice, William Windom, who Garfield called in for a conference that night after the Inaugural Ball. The two talked for about an hour. The next morning at ten, Windom agreed to take the position and took office on March 8, 1881.

Hardly had Windom begun his term when the first test of the new Secretary occurred. Windom came into office with a large Treasury surplus that reached over $100 million a year by the 1880s. About $200 million of 6 percent bonds were to fall due on July 1, 1881. Congress had not provided for the refunding of those bonds before closing session on March 4. Garfield looked for some way to refund the bonds without having to call a special session of Congress. Whether the credit for the original idea goes to Garfield or Windom, it was considered to be "one of the most brilliant operations in our financial history" (Hepburn, 239). The plan was to refund a portion of the mostly 6 percent bonds outright while allowing the rest to be continued at a rate of 3.5 percent. Of the original bonds, only a small portion was actually refunded from the Treasury. The majority of the bonds were reissued at the lower interest rate, saving the country an estimated $10.5 million in annual interest payments. The cost of the entire project amounted to less than $10,500.

According to Hepburn, "Few men could have so skillfully devised a plan calculated to satisfy the silver advocates, the Greenbackers, the gold men, and the inflationists, as well as those who favored contraction" (249). The *Wall Street Daily News* applauded the action. "Chase was the father of the legal tender, Sherman the master of resumption of specie payments, Windom the author and successful agent of a refunding scheme at which a minister with the resources of Europe at his command would have quailed" (Wright, 71).

On July 2, 1881, Windom and several other members of the Cabinet were waiting aboard a train at Pennsylvania Station to accompany the President on a trip to Williamstown. Two shots rang out as President Garfield was mortally wounded. During the first twenty-four hours after the shooting, Mrs. Windom and other wives of Cabinet members served as volunteer nurses for the dying President. Although mortally wounded, Garfield continued to conduct business from his bed in the White House for several weeks before he died. By September 10, Windom informed the President at his bedside that the funding operations had been completed successfully.

After only months in office, Windom resigned on November 13, shortly following the death of President Garfield. He returned to fill his unexpired term in the Senate, having been reelected October 26. He ran for the Senate again in 1883 but was unexpectedly defeated. One of several factors contributing to his loss was the opposition of Mark Hill Dunnell for congressional reappointment.

Greatly disturbed by the defeat, Windom spent a year vacationing in Europe. Upon his return to the States, he left Minnesota permanently and moved to New York City. For the next six years, Windom once again practiced law and managed his extensive holdings in real estate and railroad securities while also serving as President of the Atlantic and Pacific Railway Company.

Early in 1889, the newly elected President Benjamin Harrison was beginning the task of assembling his Cabinet. At the age of sixty-one, Windom was a conservative cross between the East and the West with years of experience in both branches of Congress as well as being former Secretary of the Treasury. Although Windom was not the first choice of the newly elected Harrison, he was considered a safe candidate. William Allison, the first choice of Garfield and now Harrison, declined the position offered by Harrison for much the same reasons that he declined the same position under Garfield. Although once again the runner-up for the office, William Windom again became Secretary of the Treasury on March 7, 1889.

His first annual report in December was consumed with the silver question, which was once again an issue. Although several options were explored, Windom authored a rather radical bill that was introduced by Senator Morrill in January 1890. The goal was to create an artificial demand for silver, thereby raising its price while halting silver coinage by asking the government to "purchase all silver bullion, foreign as well as domestic, at the market price and to pay for it with U.S. treasury notes" (Socolofsky, 57). These Treasury notes could be redeemed for either silver bullion or dollars or, with governmental approval, in gold.

Because Sherman later modified the bill, it became known as the Sherman Silver Purchase Act. This required the government to make monthly purchases of 4.5 million ounces of silver, essentially the entire domestic production of silver, and then to issue notes that would serve as legal tender based on those purchases. Windom, along with Sherman, considered this to be a safe bill and urged Harrison to sign it.

According to Windom, his "greatest service as Secretary of the Treasury in Harrison's cabinet was probably in freeing or adding to the currency in circulation, the sum of $98,000,000 and in preventing a dangerous silver inflation. According to all authorities a panic was narrowly averted at this time" (Wright, 72).

During Windom's political career, he also worked with such issues as improving the conditions and stopping the abuse of immigrants to America. He had also worked with improving the merchant marine; on January 29, 1891, Windom was guest of honor at the annual banquet of the New York Board of Trade and Commerce. The banquet was held at Delmonicos Restaurant in New York, and the title of his speech was to be "Our Country's Prosperity Dependent Upon Its Instruments of Commerce." In Windom's view, transportation and money were closely related. The speech was considered by some to be the "best effort of his life" and was enthusiastically received. In it he said, "As poison in the blood permeates arteries, veins, nerves, brain, and heart, and speedily brings paralysis or death, so does a debased or fluctuating currency permeate all the arteries of trade, paralyze all kinds of business, and brings disaster to all classes of people" (Barnes, 229). The last statement of the speech and his life was, "He that loveth silver shall not be satisfied with silver" (229).

As quickly as his speech ended, however, so did William Windom's life. As all those present looked on, "a change came over Mr. Windom's countenance and to the horror of all present, Mr. Windom's life flickered out right there and then, death being instant and painless" (Wright, 74). He was buried in Rock Creek Cemetery in Washington, D.C.

His Quaker foundation never left him in all his years of public service. He was characterized by his peers in office as a faithful, honorable, and sincere man who had never been involved in scandal and who possessed a spotless reputation.

Perhaps Mark Hanna, a nephew of Windom's, tells the reason for such respect: "You value highest your uncle's ability as a financier, but I want to tell you he was more than that—he was what very few men in public life have been—a servant of the Lord Jesus Christ—a consistent Christian" (Wright, 86). Windom was an excellent example of the fact that absolute honesty and politics do not have to be mutually exclusive and that the practice of high moral values need not hamper success.

BIBLIOGRAPHY

Barnes, James A. *John G. Carlisle, Financial Statesman.* New York: Dodd, Mead & Company, 1931.

Caldwell, Robert Granville. *James A. Garfield, Party Chieftain*. New York: Dodd, Mead & Company, 1931.

Hepburn, A. Barton. *A History of Currency in the United States*. New York: Macmillan Company, 1924.

Howe, George Frederick. *Chester A. Arthur, a Quarter-Century of Machine Politics*. New York: Frederick Ungar Publishing Co., 1957.

Johnson, Rossiter, ed. *The Twentieth Century Biographical Dictionary of Notable Americans*. Vol. 10. Detroit: Gale Research Company, 1968.

Lass, William E. *Minnesota: A Bicentennial History*. New York: W. W. Norton & Company Inc., 1977.

Malone, Dumas, ed. *Dictionary of American Biography*. Vol. 1. New York: Charles Scribner's Sons, 1936.

Peck, Harry Thurston. *Twenty Years of the Republic, 1885–1905*. New York: Dodd, Mead & Company, 1913.

Peskin, Allan. *Garfield*. Kent, OH: Kent State University Press, 1978.

Pletcher, David M. *The Awkward Years—American Foreign Relations under Garfield and Arthur*. Columbia: University of Missouri Press, 1961.

Sobel, Robert, ed. *Biographical Directory of the United States Executive Branch, 1774–1977*. Westport, CT: Greenwood Publishing Company, 1977.

Socolofsky, Homer E., and Allan B. Spetter. *The Presidency of Benjamin Harrison*. Lawrence: University Press of Kansas, 1987.

Wright, G. A. "Wm. Windom, 1827–1890." Master's thesis, University of Wisconsin (Minnesota Historical Society: Memorial Tributes to the Character and Public Services of Wm. Windom, Together with His Last Address), 1891.

PENNY KUGLER

OLIVER WOLCOTT, JR. (January 11, 1760–June 1, 1833). Oliver Wolcott, Jr., was a Revolutionary War hero, banker, farmer, and close friend and confidant of Alexander Hamilton. He was a Connecticut Federalist who later became a Democrat. Wolcott was born in Litchfield, Connecticut, on January 11, 1760, the son of General and Governor Oliver Wolcott and Laura (Collins) Wolcott.

He received a classic schooling, entering Litchfield Grammar School at age eleven, and finishing at age thirteen to enter Yale. At age seventeen, he participated as a militiaman in skirmishes with the British who attempted to capture the Continental stores at Danbury. After graduating from Yale in 1778, he returned to Litchfield to study law under Judge Tapping Reeve. In 1779 he briefly served as aide-de-camp to his father. Eventually, he was admitted to the Connecticut bar in 1781 and thereupon moved to Hartford to take a job as clerk in the financial offices of the State Department. His talents were quickly noticed, and he was appointed a member of the Central Board of Accountants in January 1782, a post he held until the office was abolished in May 1788.

Wolcott married Elizabeth Stoughton on June 1, 1785, and became the father of five sons and two daughters. He was an early member of the literary circle of John Trumbull and Joel Barlow and participated in the organization of the Hartford County bar in November 1783. In May 1784, Wolcott was commissioned, together with Oliver Ellsworth, to settle claims of Connecticut against the federal government. He was in charge of the state's Office of Comptroller of Public Accounts until September 1789, when the new national Constitution took effect. He was immediately appointed the first Auditor of the U.S. Treasury for the period 1789–1791 and then was promoted to Comptroller of the Treasury in the spring of 1791 after rejecting an offer to become President of the United States Bank.

On February 3, 1795, Oliver Wolcott succeeded Alexander Hamilton as Secretary of the Treasury, an office he continued to hold under President John Adams. He offered his resignation when Adams became President but was continued in office until November 8, 1800, when he peremptorily resigned, leaving office December 31, 1800.

Wolcott's appointment by Washington as Secretary of the Treasury occurred two days after Hamilton's resignation. Hamilton had viewed the Treasury Department, in the opinion of some, as his own private political club; he had made every effort to recruit men who had shown by their intelligence and personal loyalty capabilities as political lieutenants.

Wolcott had been Hamilton's understudy and was a thorough devotee of his financial views. Wolcott was justly regarded by the Republicans as the tool of his predecessor; from 1795 on, he was subjected to continued suspicion by those who were trying to ruin Hamilton's past reputation. In fact, both James McHenry and Wolcott were Hamilton protégés. Wolcott was the cleverer of the two, and he was Hamilton's chief lieutenant during the election of 1796 and throughout the years of the Adams administration.

George Washington was also favorably impressed by the "young man from Connecticut" and wrote on June 16, 1791, to Robert Morris that Wolcott's advancement from auditor to comptroller was made possible by his own merits.

Wolcott was by no means brilliant, but he was completely honest and certainly familiar with all the details of the Treasury Department. No one questioned his qualifications to replace Hamilton. Because he had always devoted all his energies to official duties, he had never had time left over to delve into the arena of active politics. It is likely that the inclination had never been developed. But this meant he brought no political strength, experience, or acumen into the President's Cabinet. On the other hand, he was saved from many attacks such as those Hamilton had been obliged to face, and this was an advantage to him, his party, and the country. Wolcott was widely perceived as a good bureaucrat, and a general feeling prevailed to let him run his affairs of office in peace.

Wolcott's administration of the Treasury Department was humdrum in comparison with that of his gifted predecessor. Hamilton had marked a new renaissance in finance. When he took office, chaos existed across the entire realm of public finance, but Wolcott inherited a management system and procedures that were pretty much refined and developed.

During his six-year tenure, Wolcott negotiated six loans totaling $2.8 million. Some of the appropriations needed were extraordinary—for example, the expenses of suppressing the Whiskey Insurrection of 1794 and the sum required to conclude the treaty of peace with Algiers in 1795. To raise the money, Wolcott went to the domestic capital market, an expedient that marked the beginning of a new era in our government finance. This was the creation of new bonds ("stocks") in the United States. No loan had been previously sold at home, solely to our own citizens. Between 1795 and 1798, alternative issues of 4 to 6 percent were marketed.

However, by 1798, the financial condition of the United States had become somewhat of an embarrassment. The threat of war with France raised the risk of government default. Foreign loans were precarious and improvident. The going rate of interest rose to a startling 8 percent, due to the uncertainty, speculation, and war buildup in the late 1790s.

War ships were commissioned, fortifications constructed, and troops enlisted. A Navy Department was created at that time, with the Republicans maintaining their objections. There had to be creative ways invented to pay for these extraordinary government expenses. The Committee of Ways and Means requested the Secretary of the Treasury to estimate the amount that would be required for these defense measures, and the probability of floating a new, permanent loan of $5 million in irredeemable stock, based on new revenues, with an efficient sinking fund. Wolcott succeeded in recommending the financing package, even if it involved temporary borrowing either from the Bank of the United States or from the Bank of New York.

When it came to floating government bonds in the domestic market to cover government budget deficits, Wolcott, however, was adamant in declaring that, to obtain money at reasonable interest rates, creditors must be assured that means would be provided for loan reimbursement.

To ensure success of deficit finance of the war buildup, and to guard against abuse of the system, Wolcott declared that it was of the utmost importance to establish adequate funds for the reimbursement, in a reasonable time, of any sum that might be borrowed. He wanted loans of definite maturity, and the provision of a sinking fund, such as the committee had suggested in their letter to him, he considered an indispensable element of the funding proposal.

Wolcott was worried: with increases in government war buildup expenditures and congressional neglect in provisions to pay for them, the credit rating of government was declining. He had already pointed out that the government was borrowing at the worst time, when credit markets were tight and the public's demand for money was high. Despite his efforts, Wolcott could not obtain domestic financing for the government debt at less than 8 percent. He issued stock at that rate, payable quarterly, and this stock was not redeemable for five years; after that time, whenever the government desired. At that time, 8 percent was an unheard of rate of interest. In January 1799, the loan was fully subscribed, but the rate paid caused a loud outcry from the Republicans. It continued to form the basis for much criticism and was one of the causes contributing to the downfall of the Federalists. However, because of an excess demand for money in that period, it is unlikely that methods could be found for the government to borrow these sums at a lower rate.

Adams attempted to take certain steps to prevent further concentration of powers in the hands of the Treasury Department. He complained to Wolcott that there seemed to be a tendency to make this department too independent of the executive. The greatest effort he made to oppose Wolcott's policy was an attempt to have the interest rate of the $5 million loan placed at 6 percent, rather than 8 percent, which Wolcott contended was necessary. Hamilton, in a letter to Wolcott, December 28, 1798, supported the 8 percent coupon rate.

This period continued to define a sharp divergence between the two parties, and Wolcott was in the middle of the dispute. Should the Federalist Party continue to increase defense spending and create an army and navy to resist foreign aggression, or were the Republicans correct that the highest priority of revenue was the repayment of the public debt?

There were considerable debates over the need and expenses of a large standing army for domestic purposes after the French fleet was destroyed on August 1, 1798, and there was no real danger of a French invasion. The federal budget for the period 1796–1800 reflects the cost burden of maintaining a large military establishment by an agrarian nation of only 4 million people. For the year 1798, the cost of maintaining the federal government had risen to almost $8 million. The cost of government had nearly doubled during the Adams administration. The cost of the proposed military and naval establishment for 1799 was $11.5 million.

In spite of political machinations surrounding him, Wolcott had a job to do. He regarded as a primary maxim of finance that it was better to borrow the required sum at par, at a higher coupon rate of interest, than for a lower coupon rate, but with the bond selling at a discount below par in order to provide a higher yield to maturity. Modern financial theory would inform us that there is absolutely no practical difference between the two approaches. In both cases, the financing cost, called "yield to maturity," is the same to the Treasury, and the government's credit rating does not suffer by its new issues selling below face value in the open market. In fact, the Treasury has more flexibility if it markets its coupon bonds with their ability to sell above or below par, depending on private market supply and demand conditions.

Wolcott held the office of Secretary during a large portion of Washington's second term of office, and almost the whole of Adams's. He was ready to retire, particularly since his relations with Adams were no longer amicable. He had been around longer than any other member of the President's Cabinet.

Wolcott suddenly resigned—some say in protest against the investigation of the suspicious arson at the Treasury that occurred under his watch. Others say it was occasioned by the open breach between Adams and the Hamilton wing of the Federalist Party. Wolcott's sympathies were wholly with his old chief. Nevertheless, he was appointed by President Adams as a judge of the U.S. Circuit Court, Second District, which included Vermont, New York, and Connecticut.

Wolcott served in this capacity until 1802 when the judiciary act under which he had been appointed was repealed.

After his service on the U.S. Circuit Court, Wolcott moved to New York City in 1802 and established himself in the mercantile business. He became President of the Merchants Bank in 1803 and later founded and acted as President of the Bank of North America from 1812 to 1814.

In 1815, he decided to take up the life of gentleman farmer and began the manufacture of textiles in partnership with his brother, Frederick, in "Wolcott-ville." He subsequently ran for Governor of Connecticut in 1816 but was defeated. In August 1818 he presided over the convention for constitutional revisions. In 1817 he again ran for Governor on the Democratic ticket; this time he was elected and on August 26, 1818, was a member of the convention that framed the new state constitution and was chosen to preside over that body. He was annually reelected to the governorship for ten years (1817–1827).

Honorary LL.D. degrees were conferred upon him by Brown, Princeton, and Yale. He died in New York City on June 1, 1833 at age seventy-three and was buried in Litchfield, Connecticut.

BIBLIOGRAPHY

Bolles, Albert S. *The Financial History of the United States from 1789 to 1860.* Vols. 1–3 (1894). New York: Augustus M. Kelley, 1969.

Dauer, Manning J. *The Adams Federalists.* Baltimore: Johns Hopkins University Press, 1968.

Hammond, Bray. *Banks and Politics in America from the Revolution to the Civil War.* Princeton, NJ: Princeton University Press, 1957.

Kurtz, Stephen G. *The Presidency of John Adams—The Collapse of Federalism, 1795–1800.* Philadelphia: University of Pennsylvania Press, 1957.

Malone, Dumas. *Dictionary of American Biography.* New York: Charles Scribner's Sons, 1932.

Morris, Dan, and Inez Morris. *Who Was Who in American Politics.* New York: Hawthorn Books, 1974.

Stevens, John Austin. *Albert Gallatin.* Boston: Houghton, Mifflin and Co., 1892.

C. DANIEL VENCILL

LEVI WOODBURY (December 22, 1789–September 4, 1851). A significant political figure at the state, regional, and national level for over four decades, Levi Woodbury served as Secretary of the Treasury during the last years of the Jackson administration and the length of the Martin Van Buren presidency.

Woodbury was born on December 22, 1789, in Francestown, New Hampshire. He was the second of twelve children and the first son of Peter and Mary Woodbury. Peter Woodbury was a farmer, businessman, and politician and a direct descendant of John Woodbury, one of the earliest Puritan settlers in New England, coming to North America in 1623.

Levi attended Atkinson Academy prior to entering Dartmouth College, where he graduated Phi Beta Kappa in 1809. Deciding on a legal and political career, Woodbury then studied law at Judge Tapping Reeve's legal school in Litchfield,

Connecticut. After one term, he elected to read law in the law offices of Samuel Dana in Boston and Judge Jermiah Smith in Exeter, New Hampshire. Woodbury was admitted to the New Hampshire bar in 1812 and opened a law practice in Francestown.

Woodbury's political career also began in 1812 when he delivered a stirring defense of the war with England to a meeting of Jeffersonian Republicans in Amherst, New Hampshire. His call to war so impressed the county Republicans that he was asked to draft a series of resolutions, the Hillsborough Resolves, supporting President Madison's policies and denouncing those who opposed the war.

The demise of the Federalist Party by the end of the war allowed Woodbury a rapid political rise. During the war years, he had become well known for his efforts in developing a strong Republican organization in the state as well as becoming an effective and popular speaker. After attaining some local positions, Woodbury became a state official in 1816 when William Plumer, the state Republican Governor, appointed him as Clerk of the New Hampshire Senate. Later that year Plumer again came to Woodbury and placed him on the Board of Trustees of Dartmouth University. Dartmouth College had recently become state chartered as a political solution to the academic, religious, and political controversy that had been waged on the once-sedate New Hampshire campus. The matter, however, was not laid to rest.

In 1817 the Governor again turned to young Woodbury, who was but twenty-seven at the time, and appointed him as a judge to the state superior court. Known as the "baby judge," Woodbury's rising star was still overshadowed by the state's Chief Justice, William Richardson.

As a member of the court hearing the argument brought by the old Dartmouth College's Board of Trustees against its chartering as a public state university, Woodbury resigned from the Dartmouth Board to avoid a conflict of interest problem. He then voted with the court to uphold the state's right to reorganize the college as a public institution. In 1819, however, Chief Justice John Marshall of the United States Supreme Court overturned the state court's ruling on the basis that a state legislature could not negate a colonial-era charter.

In 1819 Woodbury married Elizabeth Williams Clapp, daughter of Asa Clapp, a prominent Maine businessman and politician. Clapp was a leader of the New England Republicans group, and he used his wealth and position to further his son-in-law's rising political career. Woodbury and his wife settled in Portsmouth, New Hampshire, the center of the state's political and business leadership. The Woodburys eventually had five children, a son and four daughters.

In 1822 Woodbury won his first popular election, a one-year term as Governor. Running as a fusion candidate, with support from both Republicans and some Federalists, it resulted in a bitter interparty Republican struggle.

In his inaugural address, Governor Woodbury spoke to the need for social reform and argued that free education would eliminate poverty and help bring about national prosperity. He proposed that the state establish a public, but not free, university. He also advocated the establishment of adult education programs. The new Governor also attempted, but failed, to reconcile a split state Republican Party. This failure at reconciliation caused the loss of his short-lived governorship to David L. Morril in the 1823 election.

With his defeat, Woodbury returned to his legal practice in Portsmouth. Not to be denied, in 1825 Woodbury reentered the political fray as the representative from Portsmouth to the State House of Representatives and was immediately named as Speaker. Later that year he was selected by the legislature to fill a vacant U.S. Senate seat. His national political career had begun.

Woodbury went to Washington intent on representing the commercial interests of New England. His performance in that role was so adept that Thomas Hart Benson of Missouri dubbed him "the rock of New England Democracy." While in the Senate, he served on the Commerce, Navy, and Agriculture Committees. His time in Washington was put to good use as he was becoming an accomplished politician. Not only was he able to become allied with the conservative Republican camp of Martin Van Buren, he was also able to establish good relations with Southern leaders such as John C. Calhoun of South Carolina and John Randolph of Virginia. Woodbury's ability to span disparate regional interests was a strong asset throughout his entire political career.

Woodbury joined the opposition to John Quincy Adams over the issue of American participation in the Panama Conference of 1826. Those opposing Adams charged that participation would infringe upon American sovereignty. This Panama debate served as a catalyst for the organization of a party supporting Andrew Jackson's election as President in 1828. After aligning himself with the Jacksonians, Woodbury quickly became a leader of their efforts in the Senate.

Sectional disputes over tariff legislation were a major feature of American politics in the 1820s. The Tariff Act of 1828 was the first significant tariff legislation after the Jacksonians had become a major force in Congress. Although the tariff penalized New England manufacturers, forcing them to pay higher tariffs on raw materials, Woodbury voted with the Jacksonians. The Southerners, who depended upon manufactured imports, did not take long in declaring the imported duty as the "tariff of abomination," and the tariff debate was another schism in the rapidly splintering Republican Party.

Woodbury actively campaigned in New England for Jackson's election in 1928, and prior to the election, Woodbury and Isaac Hill, a bitter political foe, resolved their differences to unite in opposition against Adams. The Woodbury-Hill axis then dominated New Hampshire politics for over four decades.

Woodbury did not run for reelection to his Senate seat in 1831; rather, he accepted election to the New Hampshire Senate. However, upon returning to his home state he quickly returned to Washington to accept the Secretary of the Navy position in Jackson's Cabinet, as the President was forced to reorganize his advisers in the wake of political scandals.

Woodbury accepted this Cabinet position and rapidly became the mediator in disputes among the President's appointees. As Navy Secretary he took a very active role in reforming the Navy's rules of conduct and became the first Secretary to actually visit the naval yards.

During the national crises resulting from the passage of the Tariff Act of 1832, Woodbury, acting on Jackson's orders, replaced the Charlestown, South Carolina, naval forces with those more loyal to the Union and readied a flotilla in Norfolk, to be sent to Charlestown to ensure the execution of the duties of the custom authorities.

The battle between Jackson and the Second Bank of the United States (hereafter Bank) was raging while Woodbury was Secretary of the Navy. The Bank, chartered by Congress, functioned as fiscal agent for the federal government, dispersing and collecting revenues. It held about 50 percent of the U.S. specie reserves, and its bank notes circulated on par with gold throughout the nation. The government owned about one fifth of the Bank's stock.

President Jackson, however, was adamantly against the Bank. As many populist Presidents, he was against bigness and centralization of business and banks, believing they threatened republican government and liberty. In this instance, he also believed that the Bank served the interests of the privileged with little favor given to the average citizen.

The Bank's recharter was to come before Congress in 1836. President Jackson had indicated that while the Bank's business was not in the best interest of the nation, he would accept the recharter, provided that certain safeguards were introduced to provide more equitable benefits to all of the nation's citizens. However, those in favor of the Bank, rather than risk Jackson's efforts in 1836, believed they would be better off by bringing the recharter issue before Congress in 1832. They also believed that Jackson's wrath would be held in check, as 1832 was an election year and he would not want to alienate any part of his constituency. The Bank Recharter Act of 1832 was pushed through Congress against Jackson's wishes. Jackson reacted in his typical Jacksonian fashion—strongly. He vetoed the bill when it came across his desk and then used his veto message to punish both Congress and the Bank.

He admonished Congress, arguing that it did not have the right to delegate its powers by turning over legitimate government functions to the Bank. He went on to argue that the President represented all the American people and was under an obligation to veto that legislation that favored one group over another. This attempt by the Bank's supporters to bypass Jackson by their early recharter ploy angered the President to the point that he was now determined to destroy the Bank's remaining powers before its charter expired in 1836.

Jackson's plan was to deposit all new government funds in selected state banks while drawing down balances held at the Bank to meet government expenses. In this fashion the Bank would atrophy and eventually wither away. However, as only the Secretary of the Treasury has the statutory power to deposit and remove federal monies, Jackson needed a Secretary who would follow his lead. It took a number of attempts and setbacks for Jackson to eventually find his Secretary, Levi Woodbury.

Woodbury had openly criticized the political activities and loan policies of the Portsmouth, New Hampshire, branch of the Bank as early as 1829. It was also known that he favored the implementation of safeguards before the rechartering of the bank. Despite his beliefs on the Bank, Woodbury was his usual cautious self in Cabinet discussions on the issue. However, when Jackson first appointed William Duane, who was quickly followed by Attorney General Roger Taney to the Treasury position, Woodbury was required to publicly support the President and Secretary Taney. Woodbury was forced to actively assist Taney in establishing a series of state banks to accept federal deposits.

Woodbury's role would have ended there had not the Senate refused to confirm Taney's nomination as Secretary of the Treasury. With Taney's Senate rejection, Jackson appointed McClinton Young, the Chief Clerk of the Treasury Department, as Acting Secretary. Jackson then nominated Woodbury to the Treasury position. Woodbury was confirmed unanimously by the Senate on the same day as his nomination, June 27, 1834, and he took office on July 1. Levi Woodbury became Jackson's Secretary of the Treasury and would serve in that position through the Van Buren presidency.

Once in place as Secretary, Woodbury continued the policies ordered by Jackson and implemented by Taney. Woodbury also proved himself a capable administrator by developing policies and procedures for the operation of the new deposit system. Woodbury concentrated government deposits in New York banks, which was both a recognition of the increasing financial power of New York City and an acknowledgment of the political power of Vice President Martin Van Buren.

As Secretary of the Treasury, Woodbury adopted an increasingly hostile and strident anti-Bank position. In January 1835 he refused to accept the Bank's drafts in payment of debts owed the government. He censured the Bank for retaining the dividends from the French indemnity payments and took a harsh stance by disposing of the Bank stock owned by the government.

While more moderate than Jackson with respect to paper versus specie money, Woodbury was an opponent to any inflation of the currency. He instituted regulation of small notes by forbidding deposit banks to accept notes of $5. Woodbury also insisted on the security of public money by requiring the deposit banks to pledge security in specie whenever government funds exceeded one half of the bank's capital. This had the effect, however, of imposing a restraint on credit.

During this period, the country was growing rapidly, and the government's budget was in surplus, which Woodbury placed in a few favored Wall Street banks. However, this surplus was not finding its way back into the nation's money system, as restrictive New York State banking regulations defined the percentage of reserves that banks could loan out, resulting in rising amounts of the government's deposits lying idle. Woodbury, in his conservative money views, opposed using public money for reloaning and private gain, claiming that loaning of public money was never the intention of the public banking system. The nation was chafing under an unwieldy banking system that was unable to react to the nation's growing money needs. Politically, both Jackson and Woodbury were paying a price for their conservative money stances.

Democrats in Congress were calling for a more flexible monetary policy, and Woodbury's critics were arguing that the Secretary was too regulatory, too deflationary, and too selective. They also resented the almost monopoly position of the Wall Street deposit banks favored by Woodbury. These attitudes led to the passage of the Distribution-Deposit Act of 1836, which increased the number of deposit banks and also restricted the amount of federal deposits in any one bank to 75 percent of that bank's capital. This limitation brought about an extensive transfer of funds between banks that facilitated the flow of currency and exchange throughout the banking system.

Woodbury generally opposed the Deposit Act and implemented as little of it as possible. He continued to urge his favored banks to adhere to his conservative money views and to increase their specie holdings as backing for their paper notes. This policy predictably led to a shortage of specie for use by state banks, who unfortunately responded by issuing more i.e., paper money.

Alarmed by this increase in paper money and the western land speculation that was fed by growing bank credit, Jackson pressured Woodbury to issue the "Specie Circular" of 1836. Although he issued the Circular and had sympathy for its intent, Woodbury referred to it as that "most unfortunate deposit act of 1836" and defied Jackson by again taking little initiative in implementing the policy. The Circular required that payments for public lands be made only in gold and silver. It was believed the western land offices would deposit the specie receipts of the land sales, and the specie reserves of the western deposit banks would be built up, reducing the growing amount of bank notes, i.e., paper money.

Congress was not as enamored with the Circular idea as Jackson and, in fact, believed it harmful to the West's development; in 1837, Congress rescinded the Circular and continued the policy of easy access to government lands. Jackson, however, always true to his hard money beliefs, pocket vetoed the legislation.

By the end of Jackson's second term in 1837 the credit structure of the United States had become overextended and weak. Jackson's anti–big bank attitude and his bank deposit system had failed to produce a money-and-credit economy that could meet the needs of a westward-expanding nation. In fact, after eight years Jackson's ideal of a specie currency system was as illusory as it had been at the beginning of his administration.

When Martin Van Buren became President in 1937, he continued Woodbury's tenure as Secretary of the Treasury. Van Buren needed this industrious, balding, heavyset Cabinet member, described by Jackson as a "trained" politician, both cautious and wary, more for his experience than for his counsel.

Woodbury, during his entire political career, worked diligently at not committing himself and, more often than not, hedged his bets even when forced to choose between options. His offered solutions to problems were often offset by his own further arguments as he sought to cover all contingencies. But, as Jackson noted, and respected, Woodbury's opinions, when given, were his own, both honest and independent.

While Van Buren noted that Woodbury had presidential pretensions and required a watchful eye, he needed his efficiency and political contacts. Moreover, Woodbury would balance his Cabinet, representing the difficult New England element. Van Buren was also respectful of Woodbury's political machinations in the conservative Northeast if let loose. Lastly, the keen-minded Woodbury was both conventional and fiscally conservative, values that Van Buren also considered important for his Secretary of the Treasury.

The Panic of 1837, a major national financial collapse, began only two weeks after Van Buren occupied the presidential office. And for the rest of his administration, Van Buren was engaged in coping with the initial recession and the ensuing depression.

The panic began with a bankruptcy of one of the largest New York dealers in domestic bills. This set off a chain reaction of bankruptcies and suspensions, and the Treasury found itself in a situation where it could do little to help the economy. Developments in New York provided a good example of the Treasury's plight. Under a double drain of specie, both foreign and domestic, New York City banks were forced to suspend payments in gold and silver, and the federal government, caught in the midst of transferring its surplus millions to the states, was helpless. It was unlawful for the Treasury to deposit funds to non-specie-paying banks, and the Treasury could not remove deposits as it could not accept depreciated paper currency. The lack of a central bank, or its facsimile, caused havoc in the financial life of the nation. The Treasury's fiscal operations were so handicapped during this period that a new method of handling Treasury funds seemed needed.

The plight of the nation's financial system was not lost on Van Buren, and for the rest of his administration, he sought to provide the nation a central banking service without the establishment of an institution called a central bank. The plan that finally evolved was the Independent Treasury System. It was to be a series of banks, under Treasury control, that would hold public monies, make payments, and lay a foundation for the currency and banking system by performing several banking functions.

Introduced in 1837, Congress was cool to the proposal and did not act on the President's recommendation. Secretary Woodbury was indulgent. He was one of the few Secretaries whose experience recognized the connection between government finance, the banks, and the need to adjust Treasury operations to the needs of the money market. To this extent, in his *Annual Report* for 1937, he recommended changes to Van Buren's Treasury plan, making it less inflexible and more workable.

Despite Woodbury's recommendations, Congress continued to show little enthusiasm for the Independent Treasury System, and it wasn't passed until June 1839, to go into effect one year later, July 4, 1840. The act was short-lived, as

Van Buren lost the 1840 election, and the new Whig Congress repealed the act as soon as it could, on August 13, 1841.

One may argue that for a short period Secretary Woodbury was the nation's first central banker, as the specie receipts and disbursements of the Independent Treasury affected the reserves of the commercial banking system. While specie paid into the Treasury reduced bank reserves, specie disbursements by the Treasury rapidly replenished bank reserves, providing for an expansion of loans. The regulation of the monetary base of the banking system, a central bank function, was now carried out by the activities of the Independent Treasury, controlled, in turn, by the Secretary of the Treasury, Woodbury.

With Van Buren's 1840 election loss, Woodbury was freed from the tiring Treasury position. During his tenure as Secretary of the Treasury, his office became a focal point of the American banking system through both the deposit bank system and the Independent Treasury. Impetus for these changes and innovations came not through Woodbury but through the policies and attitudes of Andrew Jackson and Martin Van Buren.

After leaving the Treasury on March 3, 1841, Woodbury returned to the Senate, serving until he was appointed as an Associate Justice of the U.S. Supreme Court by President James Polk on September 20, 1845.

As a distinguished Justice, Woodbury continued to hold the balanced, middle-of-the-road positions that had been the hallmarks of his earlier offices. Woodbury continued to be a popular political figure throughout the country and was mentioned as a possible vice presidential candidate in 1844. In 1848 his conservative position on state's rights made him a contender for the presidential nomination. He lost the nomination to Lewis Cass of Michigan, who was defeated by Zachary Taylor.

Woodbury continued on the Supreme Court until his death in Portsmouth, New Hampshire, on September 4, 1851.

BIBLIOGRAPHY

Bray, Hammond. *Banks and Politics in America*. Princeton, NJ: Princeton University Press, 1957.

Capowski, Vincent J. "The Making of a Jacksonian Democracy: Levi Woodbury, 1789–1831." Ph.D. dissertation, Fordham University, 1966.

Cole, Donald B. *Jacksonian Democracy in New Hampshire, 1800–1851*. Cambridge, MA: Harvard University Press, 1970.

Niven, John. *Martin Van Buren*. New York: Oxford University Press, 1983.

Remini, Robert V. *Andrew Jackson and the Course of American Democracy, 1830–1845*. New York: Harper and Row, 1984.

Timberlake, Richard. *The Origins of Central Banking in the United States*. Cambridge, MA: Harvard University Press, 1978.

Woodbury, Levi. *Writings of Levi Woodbury, LL.D.* 3 vols. Boston: Little, Brown, 1852.

RONALD ROBBINS AND BERNARD S. KATZ

WILLIAM H. WOODIN (May 27, 1868–May 3, 1934). William Hartman Woodin, who was Franklin D. Roosevelt's first Secretary of the Treasury in 1933, was born on May 27, 1868, in Berwick, Pennsylvania, to Clemual Ricketts Woodin and Mary Louise (Dickerson) Woodin. The Woodins were an old iron-producing family going back to 1835. William was educated at Woodbridge School in New York City and was a member of the 1890 class of the School of Mines at Columbia University, even though he did not graduate. He married Annie Jessup of Montrose, Pennsylvania, on October 9, 1889; the marriage produced three daughters and one son.

Woodin worked in his father's business, Jackson and Woodin Manufacturing Company, until 1899. He was General Superintendent in 1892, Vice President in 1895, and President in 1899. He left shortly after becoming President to become District Manager of the American Car and Foundry Company. He became a Director in 1902 and President of that company in 1916.

Woodin served on many Boards of Directors, was Chairman of the Board of American Locomotive Company, and a Director of the Federal Reserve Bank of New York. A lifelong Republican, he met Franklin Roosevelt when they were fellow trustees of the Warm Springs Foundation. They became friends, and Woodin was soon one of FDR's inner circle of advisers, actively supporting him in the 1932 presidential election.

In addition to his business interests, Woodin was a published songwriter. He wrote compositions for the guitar, which he played, and wrote the "Franklin Delano Roosevelt Victory March," which was played at the inauguration. In June 1933, Syracuse University conferred an honorary Doctor of Music degree on him.

Woodin's tenure as Secretary of the Treasury was very short. After taking office on March 5, 1933, he was ill with a throat infection much of the time, missing several meetings; finally, in mid-November, he was granted a leave of absence to try and recuperate in Arizona. He never returned to the job, resigning in December, effective January 1, 1934.

The eight months that Woodin was actually in Washington were both momentous and controversial. Crucial questions of the time included closed banks, gold and currency hoarding, the issuance of greenbacks, the devaluation of the dollar, the abrogation of the gold clause in contracts, the removal of the Secretary of the Treasury from the Federal Reserve Board, the establishment of federal insurance or guarantees of bank deposits, and a special investigation of Woodin himself, concerning whether he received any special favors from J. P. Morgan.

A special Senate investigating committee discovered that Woodin's name appeared on a list of preferred customers of J. P. Morgan & Company back in February 1929, when he was President of the American Car and Foundry Company. As a preferred customer of Morgan, Woodin was allowed to buy 1,000 shares of Allegheny Corporation at $20 a share when the market price was between $31 and $35. Senators Borah of Idaho and Robinson of Indiana both called for his resignation, but FDR stood by him, and he was able to weather the storm.

When FDR was inaugurated on March 4, most of the nation's banks were either closed or operating under restrictions. On March 6, FDR declared a bank holiday; on March 9, he allowed Woodin to permit any bank to reopen, but no gold or gold certificates were to be paid out and no currency was to be issued for hoarding purposes. Member banks had to apply to get a license from Woodin's office, through their respective Federal Reserve Bank, while nonmember banks had to apply for reopening to their state bank authority. By March 15, about 5,077 member banks were open, holding about 90 percent of member bank deposits. By April 12, 7,392 nonmember banks had reopened, holding 79 percent of the deposits of those banks.

Even with many banks reopened, Woodin still lamented the lack of credit in the economy. He felt nonmember banks were hoarding currency in order to get their balance sheets in shape to be eligible for federal deposit insurance. He and FDR seemed to feel that "unleashed" money was just lying around idle in banks and that if banks would not voluntarily lend these funds, both men threatened to expand credit under the National Recovery Act, financed by Treasury advancing funds to the Reconstruction Finance Corporation (RFC). The RFC had been authorized to borrow an additional $4 billion from the Treasury, shortly after FDR's term had begun.

FDR and Woodin both strongly admonished gold hoarders. As a result of this fear, the Congress authorized the Federal Reserve to issue an emergency currency that had no gold backing. The regular Federal Reserve note had to have a 40 percent gold reserve; the special Federal Reserve Bank note could be issued against the Fed's holding of government bonds. It was issued on the old National Bank note form with the appropriate Federal Reserve Bank stamped as the issuer.

While not objecting to the emergency currency that saved on gold, neither FDR nor Woodin gave in to Senator Thomas and his "inflation amendment," which would have authorized the Treasury to issue $3 billion of greenbacks, similar to the Civil War fiat currency. Both men saw this as a "printing press" operation that would not be necessary with the RFC having more borrowing power and the Treasury being able to borrow funds at a very low interest rate.

Woodin seemed to agree with most, but not all, of FDR's gold policies. He did not object to forbidding banks to pay out gold, nor to requiring a license to export gold. He also did not publicly disagree with the very important June 5, 1933, law that rescinded the gold clause in all contracts, public or private. This law gave all currency whether it be National Bank notes, Federal Reserve notes, Federal Reserve Bank notes, or silver certificates, the same legal tender status as gold.

However, from various newspaper reports and editorial comments, it appeared that Woodin did not agree with FDR's scheme to lower the external value of the dollar by varying its gold content. FDR was influenced by the theories of Professor George F. Warren that an increase in the dollar price of gold would cause domestic prices to rise. FDR wanted to reinflate the economy, especially agricultural prices. The Reconstruction Finance Corporation was authorized to buy gold from U.S. mines and on world markets at a price set by the Secretary of the Treasury. By mid-July the dollar had dropped 30 percent against gold bloc currencies, but the Treasury was still selling gold at the old price of $20.67 to industrial users. But FDR's policy seemed to encourage speculators to become more bearish against the dollar. There was a great deal of uncertainty about what U.S. policy would be in this period, particularly about whether FDR would follow the dictates of the Thomas inflation amendment.

Woodin only admitted publicly that he did question the legality of FDR's gold purchase plan; he never came out against it. But there was strong opposition to it. Professor Walter Spahr wanted to remain on a gold standard. Banker James Warburg, the U.S. delegate to the London Economic Conference, resigned because of the gold purchases. Undersecretary of the Treasury Dean Acheson (later Truman's Secretary of State) resigned because of FDR's policy. Professor O. M. W. Sprague, an adviser to the Treasury, also resigned because he believed that a depreciating dollar would not restore prosperity. Sprague argued that the government was borrowing billions of dollars from the public on bad securities because these bonds could be paid off with a depreciated dollar. Woodin took Sprague to task for saying that any U.S. government bond could be a bad security—even though Woodin did agree that depreciation of the monetary unit alone would not cure the depression.

Woodin's major clash was with Senator Carter Glass over the emergency banking bill. The main disagreement occurred over whether the Secretary of the Treasury should be removed from the Federal Reserve Board. Glass believed this made the Federal Reserve a "footmat of the Treasury" because the Treasury floated its bonds through the Fed, and various member banks were forced to take an allotment of these bonds. Woodin won out on this point; the Secretary of the Treasury remained on the Federal Reserved Board until 1935, but Glass openly stated that the only reason the Secretary was not removed was because Woodin considered this a personal affront to himself.

Woodin also opposed the deposit insurance provision of the banking bill, but both Senator Glass and FDR also had serious reservations about that. It was Congressman Henry Steagall who was the strong advocate of 100 percent deposit insurance for all banks, whether members of the Federal Reserve System or not. Woodin did advocate that the RFC guarantee bank deposits temporarily while the emergency machinery was being put in place, but he and FDR did not want the deposit insurance fund in the banking bill. Others wanted the government to create a fund for deposit insurance from bank contributions, which they believed was not a misuse of government funds the way Woodin's plan for RFC guarantee of deposits would have been. Glass finally went along with deposit insurance if it covered only member banks and did not start for one year after passage of the law. Steagall later was able to get coverage for all banks.

Woodin did not oppose the other major provision of the 1933 Glass-Steagall Act, which separated commercial banking from investment banking.

One could conclude, as evidenced by the Treasury's annual report, that Woodin did not believe in compensatory fiscal policy, as Keynesians do. Even though there were emergency measures taken for financing public works, and support for farmers and credit for home owners, there was concern over imbalance of taxes and expenditures. FDR apparently believed as Woodin did during this period because he used the Economy Act of March 20, 1933, to cut all federal pay by 15 percent because the cost of living had gone down.

Woodin's annual report seemed apologetic for the increase in the national debt over 1932 even though the federal government had undertaken many new expenditures to relieve the depression. Woodin noted in his report that increases in tobacco and gasoline taxes, plus a new tax on the legalized 3.2 percent beer, would help bring in needed revenue. The report also pointed out that the Hawley-Smoot Tariff caused customs receipts for fiscal 1933 to fall to their lowest level since 1919, a drop of 23 percent from 1932.

Woodin's resignation was effective at the beginning of 1934. His health never recovered, and he died on May 3 that year. He was survived by his wife and four children.

BIBLIOGRAPHY

Annual Report of the Secretary of the Treasury, 1933. Washington, D.C.: U.S. Government Printing Office, 1934.

Dictionary of American Biography. New York: Scribner, 1928.

Literary Digest. May 9, 1933, 27.

———. June 24, 1933, 15.

New York Times. Various issues, 1933.

Yeager, Leland. *International Monetary Relations*. New York: Harper & Row, 1966.

DONALD R. WELLS

Index

Page numbers in **boldfaced** type refer to main entries.

107; public sector career of, 108–9; as Secretary, 109

Dillon, C. Douglas, **110–13**; background of, 110; on Fowler, 156; public sector career of, 111, 113; as Secretary, 111–13

Distribution-Deposit Act of 1836, 384

Dix, John A., **114–18**; background of, 114–15; political and military career of, 115–18; as Secretary, 114, 116–17

Douglas, Stephen, 62

Duane, William J., **118–23**; background of, 119; legal career of, 122–23; public sector career of, 119–22; as Secretary, 118–19, 239–40, 351

Dunlap, John, 337

Eaton, John, 215, 216

Eaton, Margaret, 215–16, 238, 350

Eccles, Marriner, xxiii, 178, 179, 344, 362

Economy Act of March 20, 1933, 390

Eisenhower, Dwight D., 3; Humphrey and, 207–10; support for Anderson by, 4

Eppes, John, 104

Ewing, Thomas, 23, **124–28**; background of, 124–25; legal career of, 127; public sector career of, 125, 127–28; as Secretary, 124–27, 147

Fair Trade in Financial Services Act, 19

Fairchild, Charles S., **129–34**; background of, 129; public sector career of, 129–30, 133; as Secretary, 129, 133, 160, 312

Farm Credit Administration (FCA), 281–83

Farm Credit System, 12

Federal Aid Road Act of 1916, 203

Federal Energy Office (FEO), 334, 336

Federal Farm Loan Act of 1916, 176, 203, 229

Federal Home Loan Bank System, 277, 278

Federal Open Market Committee (FOMC), 179

Federal Reserve Act, 161; 1935 amend-

ment, xviii; Glass and, 176; limitations of, 203, 228

Federal Reserve Bank (Fed): conflict between Treasury and, xx, xxii; establishment of, xviii

Federal Reserve Board: Glass and, 177; McAdoo and, 228

Federal Reserve System: Glass and, 176, 178–79; Houston and, 204; organization of, 203

Feldstein, Martin, 11

Fessenden, William P., **134–40**; background of, 134–35; legal career of, 135, 136; public sector career of, 135–40, 316; as Secretary, 138–39

Fillmore, Millard, 91

First Bank of the United States: failure to recharter, 125–26, 304; function of, 125

Fisk, James, 34

Folger, Charles J., **140–45**; background of, 140–41; illness and death of, 144; public sector career of, 141–42; as Secretary, 142–44, 235

Ford, Gerald, 85, 338

Forward, Walter, 22, **145–49**; background of, 145; private practice of, 148; public sector career of, 145–46; as Secretary, 146–48

Foster, Charles, **149–53**; background of, 149–50; business pursuits of, 151, 153; public sector career of, 150–52; as Secretary, 152–53

Fowler, Henry H., 14, 15, **153–58**; background of, 154; business pursuits of, 157; nomination as Secretary of, 153–54; public sector career of, 154–55; resignation of, 157; as Secretary, 155–58, 218

French Spoilage issue, 240

Fugitive Slave Act of 1793, 62–64, 137

Funding Act of 1790, 191–93

Gage, Lyman J., **159–63**; background of, 159; banking career of, 159–60, 162; public sector career of, 160; as Secretary, 159–62, 312

Gallatin, Albert, **163–74**; background of, 163–64; contributions of, 173–74; pub-

nally and, 78; death of, 85; election of 1960 and, 79; labor policy of, 323, 325
Jones, William, 51, 52

Kemp, Jack: on Baker, 8–9; Brady and, 42
Kendall, Amos, 121
Kennedy, David M., **218–25**; background of, 218–19; private and public sector career of, 219–20, 224–25; as Secretary, 77, 220–24
Kennedy, John F.: assassination of, 80; Dillon and, 111, 112; election of 1960 and, 79; Fowler and, 155, 156; labor policy of, 325; relationship with Barr, 15; tax cut and, 113
Kennedy, Robert, 81
King, Martin Luther, Jr., 81
Kissinger, Henry, 330, 337
Korean Conflict, Treasury-Fed relations during, xxii
Ku Klux Klan Act, 33

Lincoln, Abraham: Chase and, 63–64; emancipation of slaves and, 66–67; John Sherman and, 316; war preparations by, 137
Loan Act of 1847, 183
Lockheed loan, 82–83
Love, John, 334
Lueck, Thomas J., 331

MacVeagh, Franklin, **241–45**; background of, 241–42; public sector career of, 242; as Secretary, 242–45
Madison, James: Campbell and, 51–53; Crawford and, 95; Dallas and, 103, 104; writings of, 187
Manning, Daniel, 58, **245–50**; background of, 245–46; as Secretary, 234, 246–50
Marcosson, Isaac F., 56
Marshall, George C., 344
Martin, William McChesney, 3, 82, 158, 224
McAdoo, William Gibbs, xviii, **226–33**; background of, 226–27; private sector career of, 232–33; public sector career

of, 227, 231; as Secretary, 175, 176, 203, 227–31
McCabe, Thomas, 344
McCulloch, Hugh, 138, 142, **233–36**; background of, 233–34; public sector career of, 234; as Secretary, 234–36
McFarlane, Bud, 10
McGovern, George, 84, 85
McKinley, William, 160, 162, 319
McKinley Law of 1890, 181–82
McLane, Louis, 120–21, **236–41**; background of, 236–38; private sector career of, 240–41; public sector career of, 238; as Secretary, 238–39; as Secretary of State, 240
Mellon, Andrew W., **250–62**; as Ambassador, 259–60, 274, 276; background of, 250–52; investigations surrounding, 260; National Gallery of Art and, 261; private sector career of, 251–53, 260–61; as Secretary, 250, 253–62, 274, 275
Mellon Plan, 255–56
Meredith, William M., **262–70**; background of, 262–63; legal career of, 264, 269; public sector career of, 263–64; as Secretary, 264–69
Mexican War, 91, 93, 266, 267
Miller, G. William, **270–72**; background of, 270–71; as Fed chairman, 28–29, 271; private sector career of, 271, 272; as Secretary, 272
Mills, Ogden L., **272–79**; background of, 272–73; literary output of, 278–79; public sector career of, 273–75; as Secretary, 276–78; as Undersecretary, 258
Mills, Roger, 131, 132
Mint Act of 1792, 197
Missouri Compromise, 138
Mitchell, James, 3
Mongrel Tariff bill, 144, 235
Monroe, James: Crawford and, 96, 97; as Secretary of War, 53, 54
Monroe Doctrine, 305, 306
Morgan, J. P., 161
Morgenthau, Henry, Jr., **279–88**; background of, 280; public sector career of, 280–82, 288; as Secretary, 279, 283–88
Morrill, Anson, 138

About the Editors and Contributors

EARL W. ADAMS is Andrew Wells Robertson Professor and chair of the Economics Department at Allegheny College in Pennsylvania. His principal fields are fiscal and monetary economics, but he is particularly interested in innovative approaches to teaching introductory economics. His articles have appeared in *Applied Economics, Public Finance, Journal of Economics and Business* and other professional journals.

KRISTINE L. CHASE is professor of economics and former dean at St. Mary's College in Moraga, California, where she specializes in money, banking, and banking regulation. Her publications include "Comparative Advantage in the Home" in *Great Ideas for Teaching Economics,* and "National Banking: A Comparison of Policy Towards Nationwide Banking and Concentration of Power in Banking Markets in Canada and the U.S." in *Policy Studies Journal.* She is vice-president of Omicron Delta Epsilon, the national economics honor society.

JULIANNE CICARELLI is a journalist writing in the fields of women's studies, volunteer motivation, and economics. In addition to contributing biographies of Frederick A. Delano and Nancy H. Teeters to Bernard S. Katz, ed., *Biographical Dictionary of the Board of Governors of the Federal Reserve* (Greenwood, 1991), she is also the co-author, with James Cicarelli, of *Joan Robinson: A Bio-Bibliography* (Greenwood, 1996).

JAMES M. DEVAULT received his doctorate from the University of Wisconsin and is assistant professor of economics at Lafayette College in Pennsylvania, where his primary teaching fields are international trade and finance, macroeconomic theory, and environmental economics. His more recent publications include "The Welfare Effects of U.S. Antidumping Duties" in *Open Economies Review*; "The Efficacy of the U.S. Unfair Trade Laws" in *Weltwirtshaftliches Archiv*; and "Economics and the International Trade Commission" in the *Southern Economic Journal.*

SCOTT W. FAUSTI received his Ph.D. in economics from the University of
Illinois at Urbana-Champaign in October 1991. Currently, Dr. Fausti is an associate professor of economics at South Dakota State University, Brookings,
South Dakota. He has published a number of journal articles on agricultural
marketing issues and international trade issues. His current research provides
insight into the effects of uncertainty on factor markets.

JOHN M. GOLDEN is professor of economics at Allegheny College in Pennsylvania. Dr. Golden is an expert in several areas of economic history and teaches
both macroeconomics and microeconomics at the College. He has published
widely in the academic literature.

ROBERT STANLEY HERREN is associate professor of economics at North
Dakota State University. He has previously taught at the University of Mississippi
and at Vanderbilt University. His teaching and research interests lie in the areas
of macroeconomics and history of economic thought. His most recent
publications include several biographical essays and two articles in the *Journal of
Economics:* "A Retrospective Look at the Douglas Committee Report" and "Forgotten Presidents of the American Economic Association."

NAYYER HUSSAIN is associate professor of economics at Tougaloo College in
Tougaloo, Mississippi. His research and teaching interests lie in the fields of
history of economic thought and economic history. His recent publications include a review of the book, *Taking Sides—Clashing Views on Controversial Economic Issues,* edited by Thomas R. Swartz and Frank J. Bonello (1995).

VIBHA KAPURIA-FOREMAN is associate professor of economics at the Colorado College in Colorado Springs. She is a graduate of the University of Delhi,
India, and the University of Pittsburgh, Pennsylvania. She contributed an essay
on Roy A. Young to Bernard S. Katz, ed., *Biographical Dictionary of the Board of
Governors of the Federal Reserve* (Greenwood, 1991). She was coauthor of "An
Economic Historian's Economist: Remembering Simon Kuznets" in *The Economic Journal* (1995), and author of "Population Growth and Development Causality in Developing Countries" in *The Journal of Developing Areas.*

BERNARD S. KATZ is professor emeritus of economics, Lafayette College,
Easton, Pennsylvania, and is currently lecturer in economics at San Francisco
State University. Listed in numerous honorary directories, Filbert scholar in
China, Dr. Katz lectures and writes primarily in international economics. He is
author, editor, or co-editor of ten volumes including *Nobel Laureates in Economic
Sciences, The Economic Transformation of Eastern Europe* and *The Fountains of San
Francisco.*

PHIL KING is an associate professor of economics at San Francisco State University. He received his Ph.D. from Cornell University in 1987. Dr. King lectures and writes in the fields of development economics and international economics and edits *International Economics and International Economic Policy*. He is currently working on a project valuing California's beaches.

PAUL J. KUBIK is an assistant professor of economics at Arkansas State University. His research and teaching interests lie in the fields of economic history and economic development. He has published in both academic and nonacademic journals and has contributed biographies of David C. Wills and John R. Mitchell to Bernard S. Katz, ed., *Biographical Dictionary of the Board of Governors of the Federal Reserve* (Greenwood, 1991).

PENNY KUGLER is an instructor of economics at Central Missouri State University in Warrensburg. Mrs. Kugler writes predominantly in the field of economic education. She contributed to Bernard S. Katz, ed., *Biographical Dictionary of the Board of Governors of the Federal Reserve* (Greenwood, 1991), and her co-authored work, "Graphical Analysis and the Visually Impaired in Undergraduate Economics Course," is forthcoming in the *Journal of Economic Education*.

MARIE McKINNEY is associate professor of economics at Framingham State College in Massachusetts. Dr. McKinney has published in books and journals and lectures in the area of microeconomics. She contributed biographies of Lyle E. Gramley and G. William Miller to Bernard S. Katz, ed., *Biographical Dictionary of the Board of Governors of the Federal Reserve* (Greenwood, 1991).

JACK W. OSMAN is professor of economics at San Francisco State University. He received his Ph.D. from Rutgers and has published an introductory economics textbook as well as many journal articles and monographs. His fields of expertise include macroeconomics, public finance, financing public education, mathematical economics, and econometrics. He also teaches in the public administration masters program. His International expertise has taken him as guest scholar to Finland, Sweden, Norway, and Russia.

STEVEN T. PETTY is teaching associate of economics at Oklahoma State University in Stillwater. Mr. Petty has been teaching economics since 1987 and is currently completing his doctoral dissertation. His areas of interest are industrial organization and public sector theory.

ALFRED E. PIERCE is professor of economics at Lafayette College, Easton, Pennsylvania. His research and teaching interests are in the areas of macroeconomic theory and monetary economics. He is the author of numerous articles in the general area of economics.

RONALD ROBBINS is the head research librarian at Lafayette College in Pennsylvania. Mr. Robbins has published several biographies and is the editor of a volume on classical economic treatises. He wrote the biography of Edward H. Cunningham for Bernard S. Katz, ed., *Biographical Dictionary of the Board of Governors of the Federal Reserve* (Greenwood, 1991).

GEORGE G. SAUSE is professor emeritus of economics at Lafayette College in Pennsylvania where, in addition to money and banking, he taught courses in macroeconomics and public finance. He is the author of a book on money and banking and a number of articles on a variety of economic subjects.

JEFF SCOTT is a senior analyst with Wells Fargo Bank in California and a former economist with the Federal Home Loan Bank of San Francisco. Mr. Scott speaks and writes on the banking industry, modern finance, and ethics. His articles have been published in *Reason and Liberty* magazines, and he has completed a monograph on the "decade of greed," to be published by the Institute for Objectivist Studies in 1996.

JOHN A. SONDEY is associate professor of economics at South Dakota State University. His research interests include the human capital aspects of military service and rural revitalization incentives. His recent publications include "Enhanced Human Capital and the Military Experience," and a review of William B. Gould IV, *Agenda for Reform* (1993)—both in *Journal of Economics*.

NANCY M. THORNBORROW is the Lynn White, Jr., Professor of Economics at Mills College in Oakland, California. Her research and teaching interests lie in labor economics and macroeconomics. She has published numerous articles in academic journals and books and has contributed articles on John K. McKee and C. Canby Balderston to Bernard S. Katz, ed., *Biographical Dictionary of the Board of Governors of the Federal Reserve* (Greenwood, 1991).

C. DANIEL VENCILL received his Ph.D. from Stanford University as a Woodrow Wilson Fellow, taught at the University of California, Davis, and is professor of economics at San Francisco State University, where he teaches monetary theory and macroeconomics at the graduate level, as well as the economics of crime and labor economics. He is currently working on a book on corruption in transitioning economies. Dr. Vencill has an extensive list of publications, including an article on William McChesney Martin in Bernard S. Katz, ed., *Biographical Dictionary of the Board of Governors of the Federal Reserve* (Greenwood, 1991) and the biography of Kenneth Arrow in *Nobel Laureates in Economics Science*. He has also published in *Spectrum: The Journal of State Government* and the *Biographical Directory of the President's Council of Economic Advisers*. He has presented professional papers in Japan, Russia, The Netherlands, and London.

MARY PLATT VENCILL, a graduate of Stanford University and the University of California, Davis, is president of Berkeley Planning Associates, an employee-owned consulting firm. She specializes in field evaluations of government projects including employment, training, and drop-out prevention, as well as efforts to provide competitive employment for people with disabilities. She has many publications to her credit, including a nationally known evaluation of workplace accommodations for disabled workers in the private sector published by the U.S. Department of Labor.

DONALD R. WELLS is professor of economics at the University of Memphis. Dr. Wells teaches in the field of money and banking and has published articles on free banking, the history of Canadian banking, and various historical aspects of U.S. banking before the Federal Reserve. He also contributed to Bernard S. Katz, ed., *Biographical Dictionary of the Board of Governors of the Federal Reserve* (Greenwood, 1991).